To Don and Allison
for all of the 3PRIM8 memories

And to Katherine and Aaron
who help us create new ones

CURRENT WORLD POLITICAL REGIONS

ABBREVIATIONS

ALB.	ALBANIA
AUST.	AUSTRIA
BELG.	BELGIUM
BOS.	BOSNIA AND HERZEGOVINA
BULG.	BULGARIA
DEN.	DENMARK
DOM. REP.	DOMINICAN REPUBLIC
CRO.	CROATIA
CZECH.	CZECH REPUBLIC
EST.	ESTONIA
GER.	GERMANY
HUNG.	HUNGARY
LAT.	LATVIA
LITH.	LITHUANIA
LUX.	LUXEMBURG
MAC.	MACEDONIA
NETH.	NETHERLANDS
ROM.	ROMANIA
RUSS.	RUSSIA
SER.	SERBIA and MONTENEGRO
SLOVK.	SLOVAKIA
SLOVN.	SLOVENIA
SWITZ.	SWITZERLAND
U.A.E.	UNITED ARAB EMIRATES

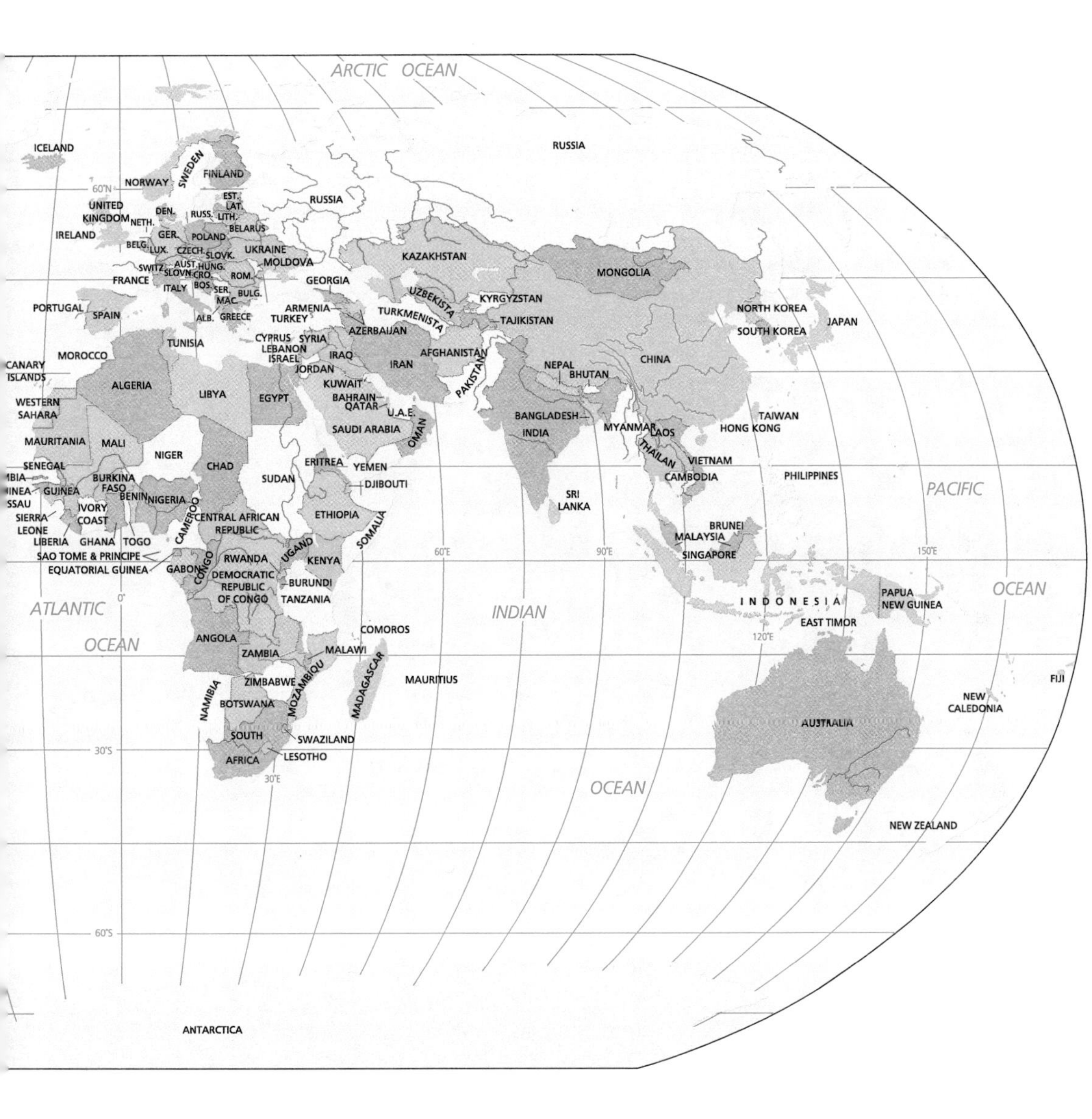
ARCTIC OCEAN
RUSSIA
ICELAND
SWEDEN
FINLAND
NORWAY
EST.
LAT.
LITH.
RUSS.
UNITED KINGDOM
DEN.
NETH.
IRELAND
BELARUS
BELG.
GER.
POLAND
UKRAINE
LUX.
CZECH.
SLOVK.
MOLDOVA
SWITZ.
AUST.
HUNG.
SLOVN.
CRO.
ROM.
FRANCE
ITALY
BOS.
SER.
BULG.
MAC.
ALB.
GREECE
PORTUGAL
SPAIN
KAZAKHSTAN
MONGOLIA
GEORGIA
UZBEKISTAN
KYRGYZSTAN
ARMENIA
TURKEY
TURKMENISTAN
TAJIKISTAN
AZERBAIJAN
NORTH KOREA
SOUTH KOREA
JAPAN
TUNISIA
CYPRUS
SYRIA
LEBANON
ISRAEL
IRAQ
AFGHANISTAN
MOROCCO
JORDAN
IRAN
PAKISTAN
NEPAL
BHUTAN
CHINA
CANARY ISLANDS
ALGERIA
LIBYA
EGYPT
KUWAIT
BAHRAIN
QATAR
U.A.E.
WESTERN SAHARA
SAUDI ARABIA
OMAN
BANGLADESH
INDIA
MYANMAR
LAOS
TAIWAN
HONG KONG
MAURITANIA
MALI
NIGER
CHAD
ERITREA
YEMEN
THAILAND
VIETNAM
SENEGAL
SUDAN
DJIBOUTI
CAMBODIA
PHILIPPINES
BURKINA FASO
GUINEA
BENIN
NIGERIA
SRI LANKA
PACIFIC
SIERRA LEONE
IVORY COAST
CENTRAL AFRICAN REPUBLIC
ETHIOPIA
CAMEROON
SOMALIA
BRUNEI
MALAYSIA
LIBERIA
GHANA
TOGO
UGANDA
SINGAPORE
SAO TOME & PRINCIPE
GABON
CONGO
RWANDA
KENYA
EQUATORIAL GUINEA
DEMOCRATIC REPUBLIC OF CONGO
BURUNDI
TANZANIA
INDONESIA
PAPUA NEW GUINEA
OCEAN
ATLANTIC
INDIAN
EAST TIMOR
COMOROS
OCEAN
ANGOLA
MALAWI
ZAMBIA
MADAGASCAR
MAURITIUS
FIJI
ZIMBABWE
MOZAMBIQUE
NAMIBIA
BOTSWANA
NEW CALEDONIA
AUSTRALIA
SOUTH AFRICA
SWAZILAND
LESOTHO
OCEAN
NEW ZEALAND
ANTARCTICA
60°N
0°
30°S
60°S
30°E
60°E
90°E
120°E
150°E

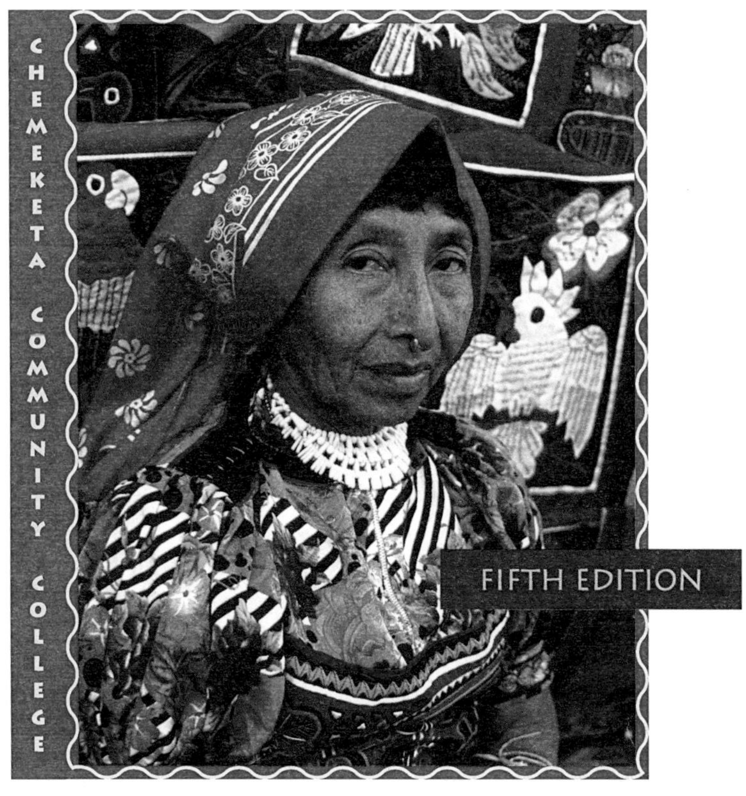

INTRODUCING

Cultural Anthropology

ROBERTA EDWARDS LENKEIT
Modesto Junior College

WITH ADDITIONAL MATERIALS

Boston Burr Ridge, IL Dubuque, IA New York San Francisco St. Louis
Bangkok Bogotá Caracas Lisbon London Madrid
Mexico City Milan New Delhi Seoul Singapore Sydney Taipei Toronto

The McGraw·Hill Companies

INTRODUCING CULTURAL ANTHROPOLOGY, Fifth Edition
With Additional Materials
Chemeketa Community College

This book is a McGraw-Hill Learning Solutions textbook and contains select material from:
Introducing Cultural Anthropology, Fifth Edition by Roberta Edwards Lenkeit. Copyright © 2012 by The McGraw-Hill Companies, Inc. Previous editions © 2009, 2007, and 2004.
Culture Sketches: Case Studies in Anthropology, Sixth Edition by Holly Peters-Golden. Copyright © 2012 by The McGraw-Hill Companies, Inc. Previous editions © 2009, 2006, and 2002.
Both reprinted with permission of the publisher. Many custom published texts are modified versions or adaptations of our best-selling textbooks. Some adaptations are printed in black and white to keep prices at a minimum, while others are in color.

1 2 3 4 5 6 7 8 9 0 QMF QMF 14 13 12

ISBN-13: 978-0-07-776082-3
ISBN-10: 0-07-776082-4

Learning Solutions Consultant: Michelle Payne
Learning Solutions Specialist: Kelly Casey
Production Editor: Kylie Weitz
Printer/Binder: Quad/Graphics

BRIEF CONTENTS

From Culture Sketches Case Studies in Anthropology, Sixth Edition
ISBN: 978-0-07-811702-2

CONTENTS

From Culture Sketches Case Studies in Anthropology, Sixth Edition
ISBN: 978-0-07-811702-2

ANTHROPOLOGY AROUND US BOXES

PREFACE

THE APPROACH OF THE TEXT

I believe that my primary task as a teacher is to excite students about the *possibilities* of anthropology and *to teach them the core perspectives, concepts, methods, and theories*. From its inception, I have had several objectives for the book. First, the text is designed to *introduce undergraduate students* to the field of cultural anthropology. Second, I want to show students that anthropology is *relevant* and *applicable* to their lives. Finally, the book is designed as a *shorter anchor text* so that ethnographies, topical books, and collections of readings can be part of the course's assigned readings while keeping costs down. Ethnographies give students in-depth insights into one culture and a holistic perspective on topics, plus the opportunity to apply the concepts introduced in the text.

I was motivated to write the text because years ago I was frustrated by encyclopedic texts, by texts that emphasized theory and were written in styles that were too formal, by shorter texts that lacked visual interest and targeted upper division students, and by texts that seemed to ignore the other fields of anthropology. I was encouraged by like-minded colleagues who belong to an informal group of anthropologists in California and teach introductory-level anthropology at both two- and four-year colleges. This informal group of anthropology educators has morphed over more than 30 years into a semiformal group, and we still meet annually to discuss developments in the field and pedagogy. We share what works in teaching and exciting introductory students about anthropology. I am pleased that my efforts in the previous four editions have been well received.

Cultural anthropology is diverse in subject matter and theoretical approaches to research and analysis. Data expands each year, and it is impossible to fit everything into a semester's lower division introductory course; it is my view that it is also pedagogically unsound. Less can be more. I have come to this conclusion based on more than three decades teaching introductory cultural anthropology courses. The holistic, comparative, scientific, and humanistic perspectives of the discipline are threads that are interlaced through each chapter. Additionally, the occasional relevant issue from archaeology and biological anthropology is woven into the text to emphasize the holistic view. As you might imagine, I applaud the recent resurgence and acknowledgement of the importance and uniqueness of the holistic perspective to our discipline. I have used an eclectic approach to theoretical issues throughout, and I've focused on those that are practical. When students have a firm understanding of a few paradigms, they have a foundation on which to examine others—and think critically about all.

Pedagogy is an important part of this text. I kept in mind the importance of *signposting* concepts as I wrote; these concepts are also *reinforced throughout* the text. To create a text *with unity*, I have used examples drawn from the same cultures in more than one chapter. Images are selected to illustrate specific points discussed in the text and to stimulate discussion. The Try This feature asks students to apply concepts they have learned or to make and test hypotheses about the topic at hand. Adopters of previous editions tell me that this feature is very useful for generating student involvement in both live and distance learning classes. A less formal writing style is part of the overall pedagogical design of the text. I write as though I am talking directly to students, while maintaining an appropriate scholarly tone. I am pleased that readers of previous editions applaud this style of writing.

HALLMARK FEATURES

Structure

- A manageable number of chapters, which can be covered in a semester, offer a brief introduction to the field. Organization by standard topics fits the teaching styles of most professors.
- The overall structure of this edition has stayed the same and reflects the author's pedagogical focus for students by clustering chapters into three sections: Part I addresses basic concepts and methods, Part II presents cross-cultural adaptive patterns, and Part III, the "So What" part of the text, looks at applying the anthropological perspective.
- An emphasis on how anthropology is relevant to students can be found in many examples and stories. This includes chapter-opening vignettes based on the author's experiences and aimed at drawing students into the chapter contents.

Pedagogy

- Learning objectives, chapter summaries, marginal running glossary, study questions, suggested readings at the end of chapters, and end glossary offer learning support.
- A strong visual appeal that underscores the chapter narratives with a wealth of concept illustrations and color photos. This provides pedagogical support for students.

- Reinforcement throughout the text of the holistic, scientific, humanistic, comparative approach of the discipline creates unity for student understanding of the anthropological approach.
- The appendix "How Do You Read an Ethnography?" guides students' reading and study of assigned supplemental ethnographies.
- Students are asked to think critically using the Try This activity prompts that are integrated throughout the text. These ask students to ponder, compare, analyze, hypothesize, and apply the concepts they have just read about. These are purposefully written at a variety of levels. A few are simple and don't require much analytical thought (for example, those labeled Ponder or Consider). Prompts such as Compare, Contrast, Analyze, Apply, and Hypothesize are intended to stimulate students' integrative thought processes by helping them apply concepts, perspectives, and methods. These prompts also provide focal points for in-class or on-line bulletin board discussions.
- A personal writing style that is lively and conversational as appropriate and more formal as needed to convey the principles of anthropology.

WHAT'S NEW TO THIS EDITION

- The text is **updated throughout**, including the latest research and areas of topical interest.
- Chapter 2 includes an **expanded** discussion of **Race as a Social Construct**.
- Chapter 12 includes **new** coverage of **Feminist Anthropology**.
- **Part III,** Applying the Anthropological Perspective, is **honed** and **expanded**. My goal for this part of the text is to acquaint the introductory student with how culture changes and how applied anthropology can illuminate and aid our understanding of and responses to problems—personal, local, and global. Additions to this section include:
    - Chapter 13 Culture Change and Globalization
        - **New sub-headings** better facilitate student reading in the section "Ethics Then and Now"
        - **New** material on ethics: ***Recent Issues: Human Terrain System Program***
        - **New** material: **Update on the Raikas and their camels**
        - **New** section heading **Tourism and Globalization**, includes **sharpened** material on approaches to tourism studies plus a **new** section titled **Tourism and Authenticity**
        - **Revised** section with **new** title **Globalization and the Media**

- Chapter 14 Applying Anthropology
  - **New** chapter **opening vignette**
  - **Rewritten** and **sharpened** section **What Is Applied Anthropology?** notes the domains of application in applied anthropology and methodological approaches
  - **New** section**: Agricultural Anthropology** with case studies
  - **New Medical Anthropology** coverage
  - **New** section **Evaluation Anthropology**
- Emphasis on pedagogy continues with **new** and **updated Try This** features in each chapter, reflecting the author's commitment to teaching.
- **Updated Anthropology Around Us boxes.** These boxes focus on current and timely issues that illustrate how the perspectives, topics, and concepts of anthropology are part of our everyday lives. Changes include
  - **Updates** to **data and issues in boxes throughout**
  - Substantial update of Chapter 5 box "Edible Insects"
  - Substantial update of Chapter 6 box "Vote with Your Fork"
  - Substantial update of Chapter 7 box "Outdated Traditions"

SUPPLEMENTS

As a full-service publisher of quality educational products, McGraw-Hill does much more than just sell textbooks. It creates and publishes an extensive array of print, video, and digital supplements for students and instructors. *Introducing Cultural Anthropology* boasts a comprehensive supplement package. Orders of new (versus used) textbooks help to defray the cost of developing such supplements, which is substantial. Please consult your local McGraw-Hill representative for more information on any of the supplements.

For the Student

The Student's Online Learning Center This free, Web-based student supplement features a large number of helpful tools, activities, links, and useful information at *www.mhhe.com/lenkeit5e*. Designed specifically to complement the individual chapters of the text, students access material by text chapter. Exciting activities and resources include

- Try This Internet exercises that offer chapter-related links to Web sites and activities for students to complete based on those sites

- Chapter objectives, outlines, and overviews that are designed to give students signposts for understanding and recognizing key chapter content
- Multiple choice and true/false questions that give students the opportunity to quiz themselves on chapter content
- Essay questions that allow students to explore key chapter concepts through their own writing
- A glossary that illustrates key terms
- An audio glossary that helps students with difficult-to-pronounce words through audio pronunciation help
- Vocabulary flashcards that allow students to test their mastery of key vocabulary terms
- General Web links that offer chapter-by-chapter links for further research
- Links to useful information on careers in anthropology

For the Instructor

The Instructor's Online Learning Center This password-protected site offers access to all of the student online materials plus important instructor support materials and downloadable supplements such as

- A complete Instructor's Manual offers helpful teaching tips along with chapter-by-chapter overviews, learning objectives, outlines, key terms, and suggested class activities.
- A computerized test bank offering numerous multiple choice, short answer, and essay questions in an easy-to-use program. McGraw-Hill's EZ Test is a flexible and easy-to-use electronic testing program. This program allows instructors to create tests from bookspecific items. It accommodates a wide range of question types, and instructors may add their own questions. Multiple versions of the test can be created, and any test can be exported for use with course management systems such as WebCT or BlackBoard. EZ Test Online is a new service that gives you a place to easily administer your EZ Test–created exams and quizzes online. The program is available for Windows and Macintosh environments.
- PowerPoint lecture slides give professors ready-made chapter-by-chapter presentation notes.
- Links to professional resources provide useful links to professional anthropological sites on the Internet.

ACKNOWLEDGMENTS

Special thanks to my husband, best friend, and fellow anthropologist, Don A. Lenkeit. He again provided in-house editing, research assistance, and all-round support, plus he made significant contributions to the text supplements. To my daughter and colleague, K. Allison Lenkeit Meezan, for her support, reviews, and inspiration, thank you. The resident felines Mr. Darwin and Mrs. Hobbes are, as before, appreciated for monitoring the printer and providing paperweight duty. To all of my students, thanks for your curiosity and enthusiasm; it made teaching an adventure each day.

To Debi Bolter, I appreciate as always your keen eye, thoughtful suggestions, and support. To Pam Ford of the CCCAT group, thank you for your support and input, particularly on the Try This prompts. To Todd Crane, my gratitude for steering me to the stimulating work being carried out in agricultural anthropology. My thanks to Andrea Cooper, Elisa Sobo, and Katharine Fernstorm for taking the time to contact me and offer perspectives that helped fine-tune this edition. I am also indebted to all of the members of the California Community College Anthropology Teachers group for the years of inspiration and stimulating meetings. As always, thanks to Jan Beatty, who sponsored this project in the first place and will always be a part of it. To Michael Park, my appreciation for all of your mentoring. To the reviewers of previous editions whose suggestions are reflected here still, I acknowledge and thank you again.

A special thanks to developmental editor Craig Leonard for shepherding this edition (including mentoring me on my first electronic revision) and for his extraordinary attention to details. Thanks to Brian Pecko, photo research manager, and my image find-it guru for all five editions. To Gina Boedeker, sponsoring editor of anthropology, sociology, and women's studies, it was great working with you again. To Debra Hash, senior sponsoring editor, I thank you for guiding the entire process. My appreciation to the McGraw-Hill production team that pulled everything together on this edition: editorial coordinator Jennifer Bartell, senior project manager Lisa Bruflodt, design coordinator Brenda Rolwes, and marketing manager Patrick Brown and everyone on the marketing team. And to Lachina senior project manager Bonnie Briggle, thanks for attending to the details.

I am grateful to the reviewers of this edition for all of their comments and helpful suggestions. They are:

Daniel Cring, University of Louisiana at Lafayette
Shepherd Jenks, Jr., Central New Mexico Community College
Thomas Colbert, Marshalltown Community College
Michele Safa, University of Memphis
Marie Wallace, Pima Community College
Kathleen Saunders, Western Washington University

Barbara Bonnekessen, New Mexico Tech
Juliana McDonald, University of Kentucky
Robin Hicks, Ball State University
Rita Sakitt, Suffolk County Community College
Sylvia Hart-Landsberg, Portland Community College

Thanks to professors and students who used previous editions and sent me their comments. Over the years such input has helped fine-tune text materials. I welcome your input or questions. I can be contacted at lenkeitr@mjc.edu.

NOTES TO STUDENTS

Anthropology often conjures up exotic visions of distant peoples, places, and customs. But this is only part of what cultural anthropology is about. It is about examining humanity from every angle and looking at how all aspects interrelate—what we call the holistic approach. It is about the common denominators of the human experience, as well as the differences. What constitutes the exotic is usually no more than those customs different from our own. I've written this text as a brief introduction to the core concepts in cultural anthropology. It is a summary of what we have learned from our quest to understand the adaptive patterns of human cultures.

My philosophy of teaching is that less can be more. If you can digest a concept and a solid example, I believe that you will remember it. Too many examples when you are first learning about a subject can muddy everything. If you engage with this text, you will have a strong foundation to do further work in anthropology. Even if you don't plan to go on in anthropology, the perspectives of anthropology will provide you with much that is useful. Cultural anthropology is applicable to many fields—health care, law enforcement, education, retail business, and any other field that requires working with people. Anthropology is inherently fascinating. We discover things about ourselves as we examine other cultures, and I hope that you will enjoy this process of discovery.

HOW TO USE THIS BOOK

You'll find many learning tools both within the text and at the text's Online Learning Center:

- Objectives at the beginning of each chapter state the aims of the chapter and are signposts to what you will learn. If you carefully read these and the chapter summary first, you will have an excellent framework to help you focus as you read. Additionally, chapter objectives, chapter outlines, and chapter overviews are available at the Student's Online Learning Center. This free Web-based supplement can be found at *www.mhhe.com/lenkeit5e*.
- Important anthropological concepts and terms are set in bold type throughout the text and are clearly explained. The running glossary placed in the margins helps you to focus on these important terms, and the Glossary at the back of the book provides an alphabetical list of all these terms along with their definitions. Go to the Online

Learning Center to test your mastery of key vocabulary by using the vocabulary flashcards. The audio glossary at this site helps you with difficult-to-pronounce words.

- Study questions appear at the end of each chapter so that you can test yourself on chapter content. Multiple choice and true/false questions posted at the Online Learning Center give you the opportunity to quiz yourself on chapter content and receive immediate feedback. Essay questions allow you to explore key chapter concepts through your own writing.
- The Try This prompts in the text were written to actively engage you with the material you've just read. Some of them are rather simple, and you can respond by just thinking about them. Others require you to be analytical and ask you to demonstrate your creativity and critical thinking skills. Recent research in the field of cognitive science reinforces that learning is tied to active involvement with a subject. Bottom line—if you engage with the Try This exercises, you will learn more about anthropology. Additionally, Try This Internet exercises at the Online Learning Center offer chapter-related links to Web sites and activities for you to complete based on these sites.
- Citations within the text are placed in parentheses and the full reference can be found in the References section. You'll also find suggested readings that will direct you to sources for further study. The Web site addresses I've provided were current at the time the book went to press.
- More activities and links are available at the Online Learning Center.

BASIC CONCEPTS AND METHODS IN ANTHROPOLOGY

THIS PART OF THE TEXT ADDRESSES THE CORE CONCEPTS AND METHODS OF CULTURAL ANTHROPOLOGY. Chapter 1 describes the various subfields of anthropology together with the uniqueness of the anthropological approach to the study of humans. Central to our field's perspective is the concept of culture, which is explored in Chapter 2 by considering various definitions and delineating the unique features of culture. A discussion of recent critiques of the culture concept is also included. In addition, the text examines the anthropological perspective on culture, ethnicity, and race in light of the data from biological anthropology. Next, given that anthropologists gather most of their primary data from field situations, the methods and challenges of ethnographic fieldwork are described in Chapter 3 using examples from my personal experiences. Finally, Chapter 4 turns to language, the symbolic system on which culture depends, and outlines the essential approaches of linguistic anthropology.

The chapters included in Part I are those that provide the foundation concepts and approaches of cultural anthropology. These are the platforms on which the remainder of the topics and chapters will build. The primary goal of the chapters in this part of the book is to provide you with the background for further analysis of cultural similarities and differences presented in Parts II and III. Practical applications of anthropology to your life will become evident as you follow the suggestions given in the Try This boxes in each chapter.

◀ Globalization touches traditional cultures worldwide, as seen in this image from Africa.

CHAPTER 1

Anthropology

What Are Its Subfields and Perspectives?

As we view ourselves through anthropological lenses, each day we can experience a world made more interesting and understandable. Today my morning began with some thoughts generated by archaeology, cultural anthropology, and biological anthropology. While sipping my first morning coffee, I glance at the kitchen floor. I make a mental note to sweep it because I spot a paper clip, two popcorn kernels, the top to a ballpoint pen, wisps of hair from the resident cat, and unidentifiable crumbs lying within three inches of the baseboard. The center of the floor is clean. I smile as I think about the implications of the *fringe effect.* This archaeological principle, which states that objects are more likely to accumulate next to walls than in traffic areas, helps to explain the distribution of artifacts in the archaeological record.

Issues and concepts of cultural anthropology flood my mind as I read a news headline and article about "honor killings." *The New York Times* (November 20, 2010) recounts a killing in Iraq—the couple's love blossomed via text messaging. The *San Francisco Chronicle* (January 23, 2008) recounts several recent honor killings in the United States and Canada and notes that, according to the United Nations Population Fund, approximately 5,000 women worldwide are murdered this way each year. The so-called honor killings occur where traditional Islamic values hold that women embody the family honor. If a woman is raped, dishonor befalls the family; and some believe that only in killing her can the family honor be regained. The United Nations Commission on Human Rights lists more than fifteen countries where such killings have been recorded. Women's rights activists are working to bring world attention to this problem and other violent acts against women, such as the much-publicized dowry deaths in India—brides killed because they did not bring a large-enough dowry into the marriage. Yet these acts reflect cultural values with long traditions in some cultures. Anthropology documents that our culture is powerful in shaping how we respond to such issues.

Another article (in my local paper) is about gangs in my city. The racial overtones of conflicts between gangs are central to the article. I sigh and contemplate whether biological anthropologists will ever be able to effectively communicate that the biological data do *not* support the validity of the notion of biological races. If the media would stick with the term *ethnic group* (a cultural grouping) rather than *racial group,* much scientific misunderstanding could be avoided. Ethnic identity is learned. No ethnic behaviors are inborn.

I'm running late. I quickly finish my breakfast (what I eat and when I eat are culturally learned behaviors), I shower and dress (ideals of personal cleanliness and styles of appropriate dress are also culturally learned behaviors), and I leave for my first class.

This recounting of the start of my day should have you thinking that anthropology is a broad field of study. It is, and this chapter introduces you to its subfields and their relationships.

The objectives of this chapter are to:

- Describe the goals of anthropology
- Introduce the scope and subfields of anthropology
- Delineate how anthropology is unique
- Explain how anthropology is a scientific discipline

◀ Travel offers the opportunity for each of us to glimpse other cultures and their customs, as is the case for this tourist talking with a Tuareg man in Algeria.

Cultural anthropologists study the diversity of cultural adaptations, including shelter. There are similarities and differences between the structure of housing on this street in Tunisia and on the street where you live.

WHAT ANTHROPOLOGISTS STUDY

OLC
mhhe • com / lenkeit5e

See chapter outline and chapter overview.

Anthropology provides a window to our past, a mirror for our present, and a lens through which we look to the future. Anthropologists research, observe, analyze, and apply what they learn toward an understanding of the many variations of the human condition. A grounding in past human adaptations, both biological and cultural, contributes to our understanding of adaptations today.

The goals for anthropological research include (1) describing, explaining, and analyzing human cultural similarities and differences, (2) describing and assessing the cultural development of our species as revealed in the archaeological record, (3) describing and analyzing the biological evolution of the human species as evidenced in the fossil record, and (4) describing and explaining human biological diversity today. In other words, anthropologists want to understand us: *Homo sapiens.* This is an enormous task.

THE SUBFIELDS OF ANTHROPOLOGY

anthropology
The science or study of *Homo sapiens* using a holistic approach.

The word ***anthropology*** comes from the Greek terms *anthropos*, meaning man, and *logia* or *logos*, meaning science or study of. In other words, anthropology literally means the science or study of man. *Man* in this context refers to the human species in its entirety. The scope of our study

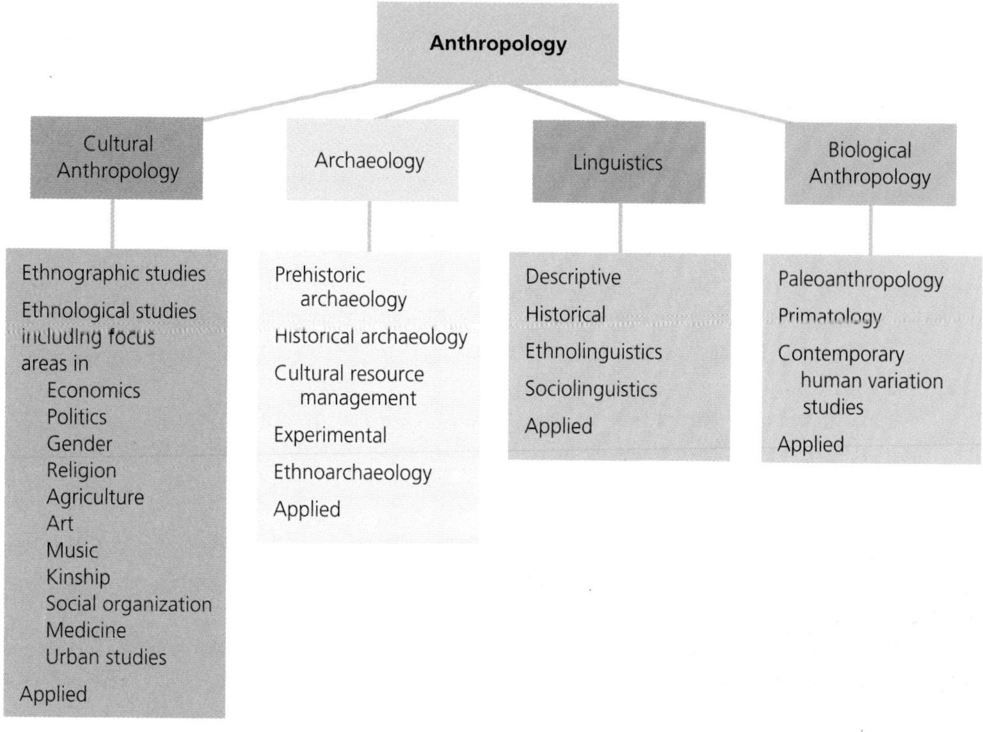

FIGURE 1.1 **The Four Fields of Anthropology**

of the human species includes all human groups, both cultural and biological, today and as they adapted and evolved in the past.

This text will follow the basic organization of the subfields of anthropology as recognized by the American Anthropological Association: cultural anthropology, archaeology, linguistics, and biological (also called physical) anthropology (Figure 1.1). Note that cultural anthropology, archaeology, and linguistics are all concerned with aspects of human culture. Many anthropologists add applied anthropology to this list as a fifth field of study, whereas others incorporate applied anthropology into each of anthropology's subfields.

Cultural Anthropology

Cultural anthropology is the description and comparison of the adaptations made by human groups to the diverse ecosystems of the earth. We call these adaptations *culture* (see Chapter 2 for an in-depth discussion of this concept). Traditional areas of focus within cultural anthropology include ethnographic and ethnological research.

cultural anthropology A subfield of anthropology that focuses on human sociocultural adaptations.

Ethnography is the descriptive study of one culture, subculture, or microculture based on fieldwork. The *field* situations can be quite diverse—in your own city or on the other side of the world; a whole community, a neighborhood, or a workplace. An ethnographer usually spends a minimum of one year in the field in order to record a complete yearly cycle of the culture. Most ethnographers realize, though, that one year is not nearly enough time to understand everything about a culture, so they commonly spend many years, off and on, with a particular culture or subculture, recording their way of life and how it changes. Other ethnographers focus on one aspect of the culture for a shorter period of time. For example, an anthropologist who is studying decision making within a large business corporation may spend a period of several months collecting data, reporting, and making recommendations. Often several anthropologists will study one culture together. Such ethnographic teams have been very successful because members can explore different questions and integrate their data into a more complete picture. These approaches are covered more fully in Chapter 3. Ethnographic works provide the specific data on which comparative ethnological studies are based.

Ethnology, the comparative study of cultures, presents analytical generalizations about human culture. The process leading to these generalizations involves explaining the similarities and differences in cultures. The subject of the comparison may be entire cultures or a particular aspect of culture such as gender, economics, violence, or shamanism. For example, a book titled *Tribal Economics* would be a comparative work that assesses how tribal cultures acquire food and other resources and how these resources are distributed. Such a work would be based on data about specific cultures that have been gathered in ethnographic fieldwork.

In its *Anthropology News* the American Anthropological Association publishes information from the four subfields, plus research interest groups (or sections) within the basic four subfields. To get an idea of the diverse interest areas in cultural anthropology, see Box 1.1.

ethnography
A written description of a culture based on data gathered from fieldwork.

ethnology
The comparative study of cultures with the aim of presenting analytical generalizations about human culture.

archaeology
The systematic study of the artifacts and ecofacts from past cultures as a means of reconstructing past lifeways.

Archaeology

Archaeology is the systematic study of the remains of previous cultures as a means of reconstructing the lifeways of people who lived in the past. To put it another way, archaeologists focus on culture, the culture of people we cannot interview or observe. We have only whatever remains in the sites they once occupied, which archaeologists use to study how these peoples adapted to their natural and sociocultural environments and how culture spread and changed through time. The goals of archaeological research are (1) to establish time lines for past cultures, (2) to describe

BOX 1.1

The following is a sample of the American Anthropological Association sections that relate to cultural anthropology:

- American Ethnological Society
- Anthropology and Environment Section
- Anthropology of Religion Section
- Association for Africanist Anthropology
- Association for Feminist Anthropology
- Association for Political and Legal Anthropology
- Council on Anthropology and Education
- Council for Museum Anthropology
- Council for the Anthropology of Food and Nutrition
- Culture and Agriculture Section
- National Association for the Practice of Anthropology
- Society for the Anthropology of Consciousness
- Society for the Anthropology of Work
- Society for Cultural Anthropology
- Society for Humanistic Anthropology
- Society for Medical Anthropology
- Society for Psychological Anthropology
- Society for Urban, National, Transnational/Global Anthropology
- Society for Visual Anthropology

Professionals doing research in these areas use ethnographic and ethnological methods in their studies.

past lifeways, and (3) to understand the process of adaptation and change in prehistory.

There are a number of areas of focus in archaeology. **Prehistoric archaeology** is the study of the remains of cultures that existed before the time of written records. Prehistoric archaeologists analyze the **artifacts** (objects made or altered by humans, such as spear points, baskets, or computers), **features** (nonportable evidence of technology such as roadways, building foundations, and fire hearths), and **ecofacts** (natural materials such as plant or animal remains—fossils, pollen, and soils) that are found in archaeological **sites** (locations where evidence of human activity is found). This is one of the fields of anthropology that has most captured the imagination of the public. The Indiana Jones movies make archaeology appear romantic and adventuresome. It is, but not in the way portrayed in the films. (Indy, by the way, wasn't really an anthropological archaeologist. He was a classical archaeologist. Classical archaeology is primarily

prehistoric archaeology
The analysis of the material remains of cultures that existed before the time of written records.

artifacts
Objects made by humans.

features
Nonportable evidence of technology at archaeological sites, such as roadways and fire hearths.

ecofacts
The remains of plants, animals, or naturally occurring nonorganic substances.

site
The location of archaeological remains such as artifacts and features.

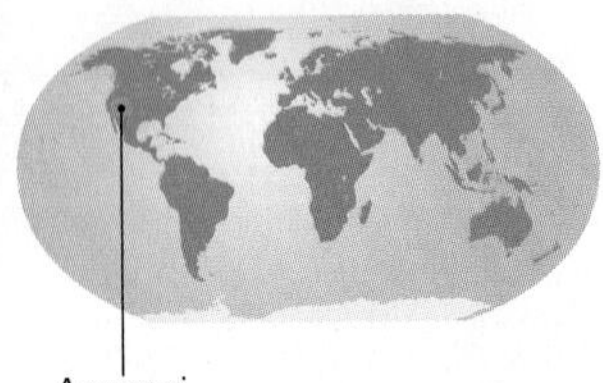

concerned with the art and architecture of the classical civilizations of the Mediterranean region. Such archaeologists are associated with university art history and classics departments.) Anthropological archaeologists work to reconstruct as much as possible about past cultures based on careful excavation, measurement, and recording of sites, and they do a great deal of scientific detective work to analyze their data before reporting on how ancient people lived. The romance and adventure of the actual excavation work, especially in remote regions, is more often, as Sir Mortimer Wheeler put it, "adventure remembered in tranquillity, devoid of the ills and anxieties, fleas, fevers, thirst, and toothache, which are liable to be the more insistent experience" (Wheeler 1956: 241).

OLC
mhhe • com / lenkeit5e
See Internet exercise.

Historical archaeology is the study of the remains of cultures and subcultures that have written records but about which little if anything was recorded. Historical archaeology, in other words, supplements historical evidence about the past. For example, the everyday lives of people were seldom recorded in colonial North America. Few if any written records exist to tell us about certain segments of past populations, such as the poor, disadvantaged, minorities, immigrants, and slaves. Information about how slaves lived on southern plantations in colonial America has been one focal point of research in this area. There are, of course, written records of what plantation owners paid for slaves and the number of slaves working on plantations, but there are few written accounts of how the slaves lived. Archaeological excavations of slave quarters have revealed details of their lives and their many valuable contributions to American colonial culture and economics. For example, it was African rice farming techniques brought to America by slaves and implemented by them that made many Carolina plantation owners wealthy. Thus historical archaeology is filling gaps in our knowledge of American history and correcting history that was once based primarily on documents written by the powerful and wealthy. The same careful methods of excavation and recording of data that are used in prehistoric digs are used in historical archaeology.

historical archaeology A subfield of archaeology that studies the remains of cultures that existed during the time of written records but about which little was recorded.

cultural resource management (CRM) The conservation and management of archaeological sites to protect them.

experimental archaeology An aspect of archaeology in which experiments are performed to learn how prehistoric artifacts and features were made and used.

ethnoarchaeology The study of contemporary societies' behaviors and uses of material objects in order to better understand how human behavior translates into the archaeological record.

Cultural resource management (CRM), is an important field for individuals with degrees in archaeology. CRM specialists work on threatened archaeological sites, produce environmental impact reports, and do salvage digs on sites that will be destroyed by contemporary building. **Experimental archaeology** plays a significant part in the analysis of prehistoric artifacts and technology. For example, researchers try to duplicate the prehistoric techniques of manufacturing stone tools and other artifacts to better understand and appreciate the technological knowledge of prehistoric peoples. **Ethnoarchaeology** also contributes to the analysis of artifacts and ecofacts by observing present-day societies' behaviors and uses of material objects. For example, studying how contemporary hunters and gatherers butcher and transport meat to their camps helps the archaeologist to interpret bones and their distribution in prehistoric sites.

These ancient Anasazi ruins in Colorado are features that help archaeologists to reconstruct the lifeways of early inhabitants of the American Southwest.

Applied archaeology is a focus area in archaeology that uses the methods of archaeology to study *contemporary* material culture with the aim of solving specific problems. Some CRM, experimental archaeology, and ethnoarchaeology fall in this category. The most widely known work in applied archaeology began at the University of Arizona in the 1970s under the direction of archaeologist William Rathje, who wanted to use archaeological methods to investigate patterns of household waste within the city of Tucson. This research is popularly called "garbology," or the study of garbage. Some archaeologists refer to it as **behavioral archaeology** because studies such as Rathje's look at the relationships between contemporary people's material culture and their behaviors. Just as the excavations of trash heaps (technically termed **middens,** or areas of discarded items) by prehistoric archaeologists reveal information about the diet and artifacts of past peoples, the trash of contemporary populations reveals information about societies today. These studies of what people discard can give us information that helps direct social programs and better understand waste disposal processes. In Rathje's

applied archaeology
The use of archaeological methods to study the material culture of contemporary societies. Data can be used to develop social programs.

behavioral archaeology
An area of applied archaeology that focuses on the relationships between material culture and people's behavior.

midden
Archaeological term to designate an area of discard; a trash heap.

Garbage Project, front-door interviewers found that 15 percent of respondents admitted to consuming beer. The trash discard data from this same area showed that over 80 percent of households consumed beer and 54 percent discarded over eight cans per week. Many other discrepancies were found between what householders told interviewers about their food and drink consumption and what they actually ate and drank. Data from the Garbage Project were so useful that this research expanded to include projects in other cities and an ongoing study of contemporary landfills.

Linguistics

Linguistics is the study of language. Anthropological linguists do not necessarily speak several languages (such a person is called a polyglot). Rather, linguists study language—how language is formed and how it works, the history and development of language, and its relationship to other aspects of culture. Linguistics became a part of anthropology for two reasons. First, language is the cornerstone of culture (more about culture in Chapter 2). Second, to do ethnographic fieldwork, anthropologists often had to begin by writing their own dictionaries and grammars of a native language. Today linguistics encompasses a number of research areas, including descriptive linguistics, historical linguistics, ethnolinguistics, and sociolinguistics.

Descriptive linguistics focuses on the mechanics of language. The linguist must first describe the sounds used in the language under study (called *phonology*). Sounds can be described according to the anatomical parts that are used to create them, such as the teeth, tongue, lips, voice, or lack of voice. Morphology and syntax, other aspects of describing a language, involve the identification of the smallest units of meaning in a language (morphemes) and the rules for combining words into sentences, what would popularly be called grammar (more about this in Chapter 4).

Historical linguistics works to reconstruct the history of languages, including their development and relationship to other languages. There are some limitations to historical linguistic research because not all contemporary languages have written forms, and many languages of past peoples did not have written records. Linguists can describe the comparative structure of contemporary related languages, however, and then use these comparisons to reconstruct some aspects of earlier forms of the root language.

Other categories of study in linguistic anthropology include ethnolinguistics and sociolinguistics. **Ethnolinguistics** is a specialized field that analyzes the relationship between a language and culture. It investigates questions such as Does your language create your reality? **Sociolinguistics**

linguistics
A subfield of anthropology that includes the study of the structure, history, and social aspects of human language.

descriptive linguistics
The part of anthropological linguistics that focuses on the mechanics of language.

historical linguistics
The study of the history of languages, including their development and relationship to other languages.

ethnolinguistics
A field of study in linguistics that analyzes the relationship between a language and culture.

sociolinguistics
A subfield of linguistics that analyzes the relationship between language and culture with a focus on how people speak in social contexts.

TRY THIS Compare

Select another of your introductory-level college courses—history, zoology, psychology, English, geography—and list three specific ways that the subject matter of anthropology is different from these disciplines and one way it is the same.

evaluates the relationship between language and culture with a focus on how people speak in social contexts such as in the workplace or at home (see Chapter 4 for details).

Biological Anthropology

Biological anthropology (also called **physical anthropology**) studies *Homo sapiens* as biological beings both in the present and in the past. Scientists working in this subfield seek to describe and explain the biological evolution of and variations in our species. To this end they also study the closely related primates (prosimians, monkeys, and apes) because their evolutionary history is similar to and related to ours. Three major areas of focus in biological anthropology include paleoanthropology, primatology, and contemporary human variation studies.

Paleoanthropology (the root word *paleo* means ancient) is the study of human biological evolution through an examination of the fossils of our ancient ancestors and relatives. Paleoanthropology relies heavily on comparative anatomy and evolutionary biology. For example, the researcher must know comparative details of the structure of leg bones between animals who walk on four legs (**quadrupeds**) and those who walk on two (**bipeds**) to determine whether an ancient femur (upper leg bone) belonged to an individual who walked bipedally. Some clues to bipedalism are found in the angle of the neck of the femur and in the distribution of weight, when standing, based on this angle.

The understanding and interpretation of the past requires an integration of information from many areas. Paleoanthropologists share information and interact with archaeologists as well as specialists from other fields such as geology and chemistry. For example, to understand the environment occupied by a fossil ancestor who lived fifty thousand years ago, the paleoanthropologist must collaborate with geologists who specialize in reconstructing paleoclimates and archaeologists who can reconstruct how this fossil ancestor made the stone tools found in the site.

Primatology is the study of our nearest animal relatives—the **primates.** This area of biological anthropology includes an investigation of the anatomy, physiology, genetics, and behaviors of apes, monkeys, and prosimians. We share many biological features with this group of animals, and data about their adaptations aid us in understanding ***Homo sapiens.***

biological anthropology
A subfield of anthropology that studies humans as a biological species. Also called physical anthropology.

physical anthropology
See *biological anthropology.*

paleoanthropology
The study of human biological evolution.

quadruped
An animal that walks on four limbs.

biped
An animal that walks on two legs.

primatology
The study of nonhuman primates.

primates
Animals in the order Primates; includes humans, apes, monkeys, and prosimians.

Homo sapiens
The taxonomic designation for humans.

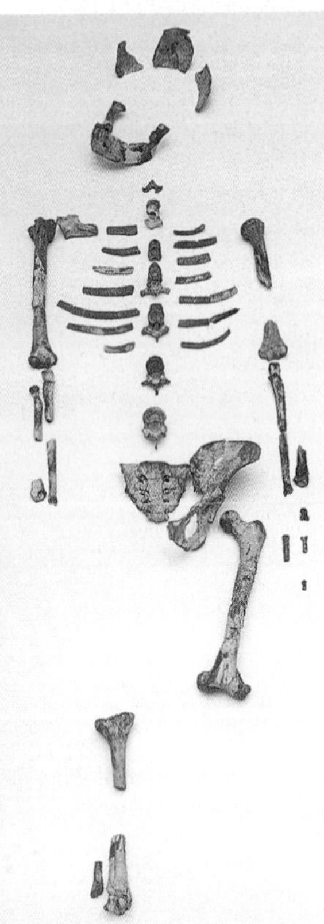

The Lucy fossils from the Hadar region of Ethiopia are examples of evidence that can be used by paleoanthropologists to reconstruct our early ancestors. Note the complete upper leg bone (femur). The angle of the head of the femur, plus the features of the pelvis, indicate that Lucy walked bipedally.

A common misunderstanding about primate research regards our relationship to chimpanzees. They are clearly our closest relative in the animal world, but they do not represent our ancestor. Rather, chimps and humans diverged from a common ancestor about five to seven million years ago, and since then each species has evolved separately.

Contemporary human variation studies, another area of research in biological anthropology, focus on living humans and how our anatomy and physiology vary. Genetics, including DNA research, contributes greatly to such studies, the long-range goal of which is to account for and offer explanations for the variation among humans, as well as to demonstrate our many similarities and shared biological adaptations. For example, if a difference in the frequency of a genetic disease is established for one particular population compared to others, research is undertaken to explain the frequency from an evolutionary viewpoint. Anthropologists working in this area often collaborate with geneticists and medical scientists.

Specialists known as **forensic anthropologists** apply their knowledge to legal issues. They are usually trained in biological anthropology, although they work closely with archaeologists who recover human remains. Forensic studies on human skeletal material can reveal such information as the sex of the individual, cause of death, diseases suffered, and nutritional deficiencies. This information can be useful in helping to identify human remains in natural disasters as well as to identify cause of death in homicide cases.

HOW ANTHROPOLOGY IS UNIQUE

Several key features of how anthropologists view *Homo sapiens* make our perspective unique: holism, fieldwork, the comparative method, and the perspective of cultural relativism. Other academic disciplines also use some of these features—biologists, for example, do fieldwork. Anthropology, however, is the only science that pulls all of these approaches together to study humanity.

Anthropology Is Holistic

Anthropology is a **holistic** science, which means that anthropologists view *Homo sapiens*, and the evolutionary ancestors of modern humans, in the broadest context possible—as both biological beings and cultural beings through a time span of approximately five million years (Figure 1.2). In other words, we study everything about people for as long as humans and their immediate humanlike precursors have existed as a species. We keep this broad, integrated perspective no matter what specific detail of human life we might be investigating. For example, a paleoanthropologist will

OLC
mhhe • com / lenkeit5e

See Internet exercise.

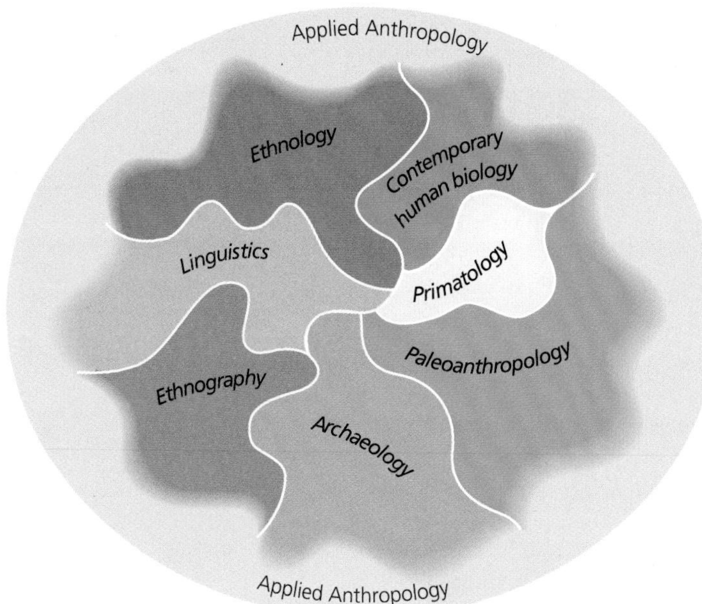

FIGURE 1.2
Anthropology is a holistic study of all cultural and biological aspects of the human species. Cultural anthropology includes ethnographic and ethnological studies as well as linguistics and archaeology. Biological anthropology includes paleoanthropology, primatology, and studies in contemporary human biology. Applied research encompasses all of anthropology.

consider the cultural adaptations (including tool use and possible social behavior) of the biological ancestors of modern humans. The broad time frame covered by anthropology is significant because anthropologists believe that any insights about contemporary human adaptations, either biological or cultural, should be made with an eye to past adaptations.

Anthropologists Do Fieldwork

Specialists in the various subfields of anthropology work to maintain their holistic vision. An extension of holism is to collect primary data in natural field settings. In the following paragraphs I discuss the types of data gathered in the field by the different kinds of anthropologists.

Cultural Anthropology in the Field. Cultural anthropologists gather their primary data in the field. Insights about peoples and their lifeways take on a whole new dimension when one experiences their culture firsthand. Anthropologists reason that to describe and explain the cultural adaptations and worldview of a tribe in Brazil, an urban gang in the United States, or cannery workers in Japan, one must participate in the culture. We believe that to really know another culture, subculture, or microculture one must commit to spending extensive time in that cultural environment. Ethnographic data, as noted earlier in this chapter, are the raw materials with which comparative analysis is done. Chapter 3 gives an in-depth discussion of the methods of ethnographic fieldwork.

contemporary human variation studies
The study of the biological variation in living humans.

forensic anthropologist
An applied biological anthropologist concerned with legal issues. Frequently focuses on the identification of skeletal material and the cause of death.

holistic
An integrated perspective that assumes interrelationships among the parts of a subject. Anthropology studies humans from a holistic perspective, including both biological and cultural aspects.

ANTHROPOLOGY AROUND US

Forensic Anthropology in the News

Forensics is a hot topic in the media. Forensic anthropologists identify the bones and teeth of missing persons, use skull comparisons to determine the sons of an Egyptian pharaoh, and run DNA analysis to determine if bones buried in a Spanish cathedral are those of Christopher Columbus. They determine the age and sex of skeletal remains and analyze impact wounds on bones to determine what implement made the wound. All of these topics of investigation have made headlines in recent years. The methods and data of forensic anthropologists are exhibited weekly on television dramas and in news articles, though these sources often do not distinguish between forensic anthropologists, forensic pathologists (medical doctors), odontologists (dentists), and police homicide investigators. The American Board of Forensic Anthropologists provides a rigorous program of certification in forensic anthropology that is similar to board certifications in medical specialty areas.

Forensic anthropology illustrates the holistic nature of anthropology. Human cultural behaviors in the way people use their bodies have an effect on bone development and the development of diseases such as osteoarthritis. A recent book, *Atlas of Occupational Markers on Human Remains* by Luigi Capasso, Kenneth A. R. Kennedy, and Cynthia A. Wilczak (Teramo, Italy: edigrafital SpA-S. Atto, 1999), describes nearly 150 conditions that reflect specific behaviors. Some of these conditions have nontechnical names such as Pipe Smoker's Teeth (mechanical marks on upper and lower incisor teeth caused by pipe smoking and regularly holding other hard objects in the teeth, such as a police officer's whistle) and Floorwalker's Foot (bony spurs and bursitis evidenced in several locations and caused by walking on hard pavement). The presence of such conditions helps forensic experts identify aspects of the lifestyle or work habits of the person whose skeleton is under investigation.

◎ Can you suggest the type of bone damage evidence that results from travel over rough terrain, such as on a snowmobile? Go to www.news.cornell.edu/releases/april99/occu_markers.hrs.html to find out if you are correct.

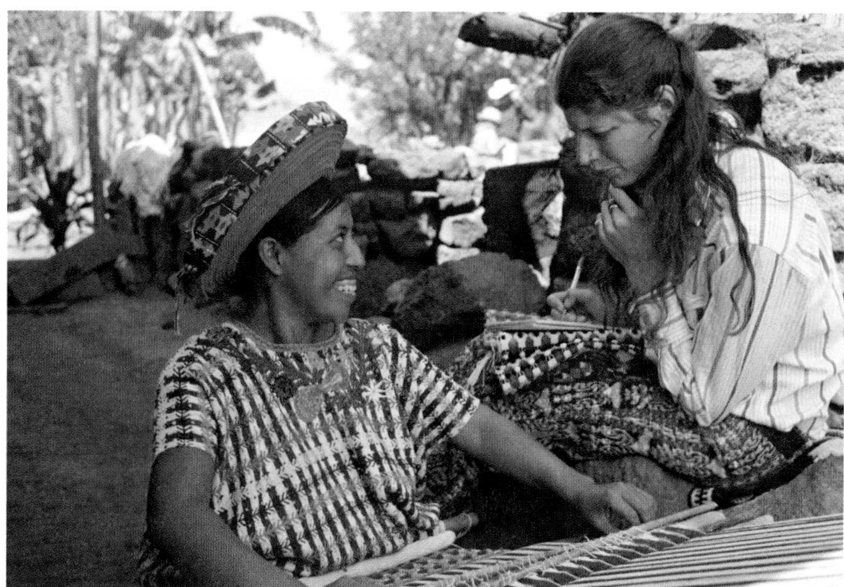

Anthropologists collect data primarily in field settings. Here Margaret Marlar Kieffer interviews a weaver in the village of Santiago Atitlan in Guatemala.

Archaeology in the Field. Archaeologists must dig and recover artifacts and ecofacts before they can begin the technical analysis of these materials in the lab. Fieldwork is the first step of data acquisition. Each archaeological site is mapped and recorded before digging begins. Excavation and measurement are done with care so that the exact location of each artifact, ecofact, and feature is recorded before any items are removed from the ground. Such detail is important for revealing patterns of artifact distribution. For example, the location of food preparation tools may always be inside of the house wall features for one prehistoric culture and outside of the walls for another.

Linguistics in the Field. Primary data are also gathered in the field for most aspects of linguistics. Descriptive linguistics depends on interactions with native speakers. Although this can take place in a laboratory setting, the majority of the initial work of describing the structure and other aspects of languages has been done in field settings. This fieldwork may be important to later understandings of how the language is used by individuals, and it may reveal features such as special language forms used when in the presence of elders.

Biological Anthropology in the Field. Paleoanthropologists who analyze and explain human evolution must have fossils to evaluate; to gather fossils they go into the field. The idea of human fossil hunters searching the barren, exposed early Pleistocene layers of Africa's Olduvai Gorge tickles

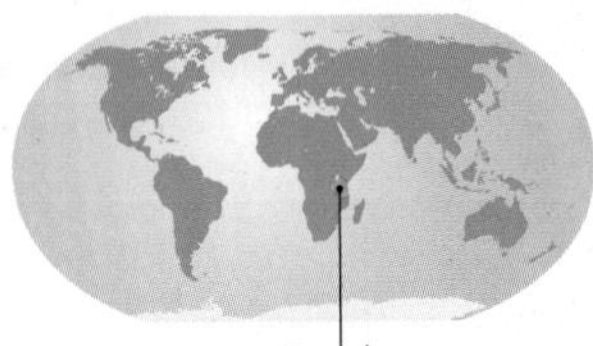

the soul of adventure in all of us. The field studies of primatologists Jane Goodall, who studies chimpanzees at the Gombe Preserve in Tanzania, and Dian Fossey, who observed gorillas in Rwanda, made world headlines and offered new perspectives on the behavior of these animals in their natural habitats. We now have decades of field studies focusing on the Gombe chimpanzees and another group of chimps on the Ivory Coast. The insights that we have gained about their behaviors are surprising and humbling. Observations of the Tai population of chimpanzees on the Ivory Coast of Africa, for example, show mother chimps *demonstrating* tool use to their offspring in the form of using rocks for cracking nuts.

The investigation of contemporary primate anatomy combines field observations with laboratory work. Research on chimpanzee locomotor anatomy involves describing the locomotor behavior of chimps in their natural habitat plus measuring, dissecting, and describing muscles and bones of deceased chimpanzees in the laboratory.

Biological anthropologists who study the variations in contemporary humans also gather data in the field—blood samples, specimens for DNA testing, morphological measurements—as they endeavor to explain human biological diversity. Of course, the follow-up analysis of much of these data is accomplished using computer and lab facilities.

Anthropologists Focus on the Comparative Method

Anthropologists gather and compare as much data as possible before making generalizations. We do not rely on data from just one study to make interpretative or analytical statements about the human condition. To examine the structure of human families, for example, a cultural anthropologist would look at data in the Human Relations Area Files that have been gathered from field studies in hundreds of different cultures. Features of family structure would be compared, and the similarities and differences would be described, numerically tabulated, and statistically analyzed. These data would be used to generate hypotheses to explain the variations noted, which in turn would necessitate formulating ways to test the hypotheses.

comparative method The methodological approach of comparing data. Anthropologists use the comparative method.

humanistic anthropology A label for research that focuses on individuals and their creative responses to cultural and historical forces.

The **comparative method** is also used in archaeology, linguistics, and biological anthropology. Paleoanthropologists use the comparative method when a new fossil skull is discovered. Comparative anatomical studies are carried out on many specimens before tentative assessments and interpretations are given. The interpretation is tentative because we continue to compare each new fossil as it is discovered; with more comparative data, the earlier interpretations may need adjustments. As you might imagine, the comparative approach makes for some lively discussions among anthropologists, because the data aren't always as clear as we would wish. The comparative method as described here is part of scientifically oriented anthropology. **Humanistic anthropology** focuses

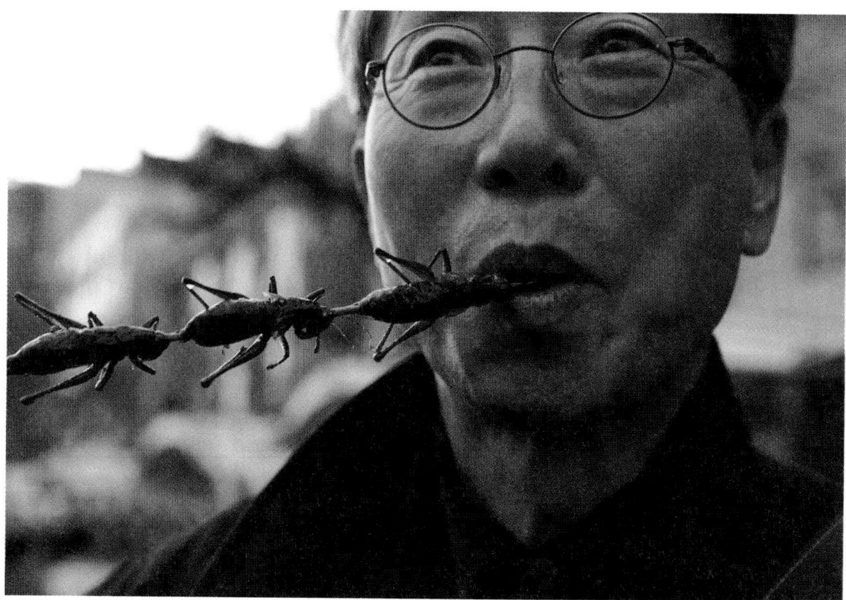

This man is about to enjoy a snack of insects. Members of cultures that do not eat protein-rich insects often react ethnocentrically when they see this behavior in others.

on the uniqueness of every individual and every culture and would not use the comparative method.

Anthropologists Use the Perspective of Cultural Relativism

One additional perspective of anthropology adds to its uniqueness. Anthropologists approach the study of other cultures using a perspective known as cultural relativism. **Cultural relativism** is the idea that any aspect of a culture must be viewed and evaluated within the context of that culture. The job of the anthropologist who is applying this perspective is to describe a cultural trait, custom, belief, activity, or any part of a culture and to show how it fits into the values and traditions of that cultural system. In other words, the anthropologist objectively describes a custom and then discusses how it is viewed within that culture. **Ethnocentrism,** the opposite of cultural relativism, makes value judgments when describing aspects of another culture. The value judgment is based on comparing elements of one's own culture with those of another culture; the other culture is "wrong," "weird," "strange," "unethical," or "backward." Any value-laden statement that uses one's own culture as the basis for the comparison reflects cultural ethnocentrism.

cultural relativism
The perspective that any aspect of a culture must be viewed and evaluated within the context of that culture.

ethnocentrism
Making value judgments based on one's own culture when describing aspects of another culture.

Consider this statement uttered by a non-Inuit: "The Inuit eat raw seal liver and they relish this traditional food." This statement is made from a relativistic perspective. It describes what the Inuit do and how they

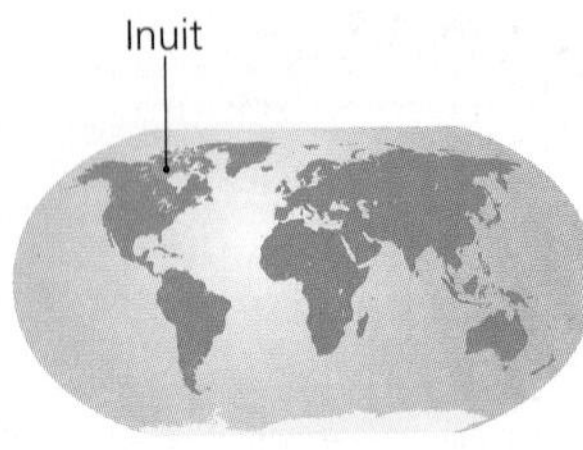

feel about it. Now, consider a person who is not an Inuit making this statement: "The Inuit have the repulsive custom of eating raw seal liver." This is an ethnocentric statement because the term *repulsive* evaluates the eating of raw liver from the cultural viewpoint of the speaker.

Ethnocentrism is a part of everyone and of every culture. We all judge other cultures' customs and behaviors based on our own customs and behaviors. Ethnocentrism is socially transmitted. One rarely speaks of it, and even your best friend will only rarely tell you that it is showing. Its symptoms can appear at any time, but they are most apparent when traveling in another country or watching a television program concerning other cultures. A trip to your local shopping center may also trigger ethnocentrism if you encounter people of other cultures and subcultures who dress, speak, and act differently than you do. It is important to recognize that cultural ethnocentrism is different from egocentrism, where one makes negative value judgments that are based on personal belief or behavior. Ethnocentrism is based on the culture of a social group.

Ethnocentrism can lead to conflict and misunderstanding. It can be considered to have adaptive value, however, because it may create social cohesion and help to hold a group together. The approach of cultural relativism, by contrast, can lead to an appreciation for, and understanding of, other cultures. In the previous example, a person with a relativistic approach to world cultures would acknowledge that raw seal liver is different from the food she eats. Further, she would acknowledge that if she grew up in a culture where parents and siblings all ate raw liver, she would probably enjoy eating it too.

TRY THIS
Consider

Could you eat raw liver for your next meal? Is it possible for anyone to set aside all of their ethnocentric attitudes?

Taking a perspective of cultural relativism does not mean that you should start eating raw meat. It means that you understand that behavioral differences, and the values behind them, are learned and are simply different. Such an approach can contribute to greater awareness, tolerance, and acceptance of people with different cultural backgrounds. Throughout the history of cultural anthropology as an academic discipline, the perspective of cultural relativism has guided research efforts. Figure 1.3 shows that a reliance on fieldwork, the comparative method, and a holistic perspective, together with cultural relativism, combine to make anthropology a unique academic discipline.

Should There Be Any Universal Values?

It seems reasonable to be relativistic about food preferences and modes of food consumption. But how can an American be culturally relativistic about practices such as female circumcision? Most Americans and peoples of many other cultures would say unequivocally that this practice is wrong, bad, evil. Why? If we are being completely candid, we would have to admit that it is wrong mainly because we don't do it. We would cite

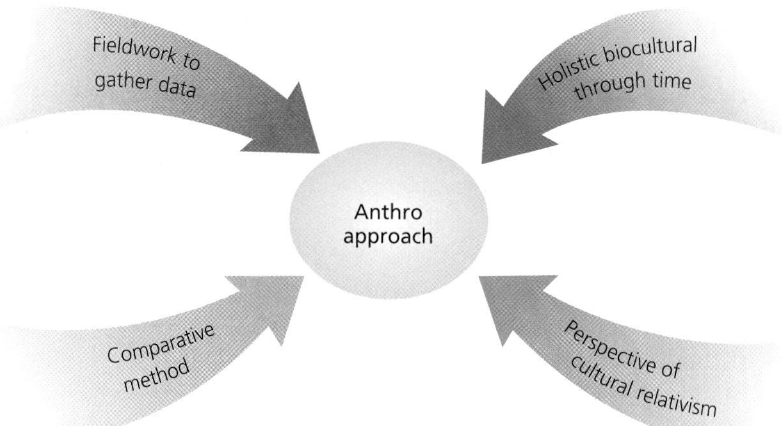

FIGURE 1.3
These four approaches, when used in concert with one another, give anthropology its unique perspective.

health, safety, and feminist issues and universal human rights to justify our objections to the practice. For the record, not all anthropologists agree about the degree to which we should apply cultural relativism or whether there is or should be a universal set of values for evaluating human rights.

Can there be universal human rights? What issues can be raised when trying to assert universal human rights? Who decides the bases for universal human rights?

THE SCIENTIFIC APPROACH IN ANTHROPOLOGY

To explain humanity, anthropologists apply a scientific approach. One of my favorite statements about science was made by Eugenie C. Scott of the National Center for Science Education. Scott states, "The goal of science is to explain how the natural world works. As humans are part of the natural world, they can be studied scientifically" (Scott 1996: 52). In his book *Reclaiming a Scientific Anthropology* (2008), Lawrence Kuznar recaps the history of anthropological science and delineates its current position, goals, and methodological principles. The goals include "knowing the empirical world, being able to explain and predict phenomena in the world, and generating progressively more accurate knowledge by proposing theories that can be scrutinized and refined through time" (Kuznar 2008: 15). Anthropologists strive to reach these goals by using the scientific method.

A key feature of the scientific method is the formulation of hypotheses to explain relationships among data. A hypothesis is an educated guess that explains a given phenomenon. Criteria used to judge the worth of a hypothesis include whether it is relevant, testable, and compatible with previous well-established hypotheses. Other important characteristics of a hypothesis include its power to explain or predict and its simplicity. A hypothesis, then, is not just a guess but a reasonable explanation that is formulated after a problem area is identified and background investigation

TRY THIS
Hypothesize

Formulate a hypothesis that could account for the different treatment of time in Brazilian culture as compared to North American culture. Offer two ways to test your hypothesis.

has been completed. Anthropologists use the scientific method when they include the formulation and testing of hypotheses with a careful definition of terms, quantification, and application of mathematical principles such as statistical methods. If data proves a hypothesis to be false, new hypotheses can be formulated; these in turn can be tested. This cumulative process leads to improved explanations.

You and I make hypotheses all the time. If students are fifteen minutes late to class, I might hypothesize that they ignored their alarm clock this morning and slept in. Or I might hypothesize that if the fog was thick in the rural areas this morning, then students might have had to drive more slowly, thus making them late to class. Both of these hypotheses are relevant, simple, and compatible with previous well-established hypotheses, and they explain the tardiness of the students. There are simple and obvious ways to test both of the hypotheses.

If I am late to class, you might make the same two hypotheses. These are two very probable and compatible reasons for lateness to class in our North American culture. If I were a visiting professor in a Brazilian university, I would need to formulate my hypotheses in ways that are relevant to Brazilian culture. Being fifteen minutes tardy in Brazil is culturally equal to being about one to two minutes late in North American culture and therefore is of no importance. No explanation for the lateness is needed. By using a scientific approach, one can decrease the likelihood of ethnocentric bias affecting the explanations given as one researches behavior in other cultures.

If the scientific method is used in trying to explain a phenomenon, then science is being done. Since anthropologists use the scientific method as they work to explain human biological evolution and variation and human cultural behavior, anthropology is a science. The social (or behavioral) sciences, where cultural anthropology is placed, have not been particularly effective in communicating that we use scientific methods.

There are a number of significant difficulties in consistently using the scientific method when investigating and explaining human cultural behavior. First, anthropologists are concerned with a very complex subject—human beings. No two humans have been raised in exactly the same way, nor have any two people had exactly the same life experiences. Second, anthropologists are often unable to isolate variables or perform experiments to test aspects of *Homo sapiens* in the same manner that other scientists carry out tests, in part because much of our research is based on observation in natural field settings where variables cannot be as easily controlled as they are in a laboratory setting. Another reason is that human behavioral researchers have ethical limitations, which does not mean that other sciences don't have ethical standards, but rather that additional standards are applied when we are dealing with human subjects. Finally, the explanations offered by anthropologists are often based on context. The context in which a behavior takes place must be considered. Therefore, an explanation may not have wide application. In ideal scientific explanations, place should not affect the veracity of the explanation.

For example, if we strive to explain why polyandry (marriage of one woman to two or more men at the same time) is practiced in a culture, we begin with a thorough, objective description of all aspects of the culture we are studying. A hypothesis is formulated that takes into account what we know about this particular culture and what we know about other cultures where polyandry is practiced (the comparative method discussed earlier in this chapter). Then the hypothesis is tested. If the hypothesis holds true for the tests and data from other cultures show the same consistent correlations we found in the original society, we may be able to make a generalization about why polyandry is practiced. The formulation of such generalizations is one of the goals of cultural anthropology.

TRY THIS
Explain

You are a member of a culture where the primary marriage practice is monogamy. Explain why we have only one spouse at a time.

The desire to maintain large landholdings was cited as a reason for the practice of polyandry by Tibetans living in northern Nepal in the 1987 study by Melvyn C. Goldstein. In this particular case, brothers share a wife, thus keeping the male-owned lands from being split up as property is passed from one generation to the next. Prior to Goldstein's work, one explanation for the practice of polyandry was that there was a shortage of women as a result of the practice of female infanticide. Goldstein's research revealed that there had never been institutionalized female infanticide in Tibet. Another early explanation for the practice of polyandry suggested that poor soil fertility and crop yields required brothers to share a wife in order to avoid starvation. Although ecological factors do play a role in the practice of polyandry in Tibet, Goldstein did not find polyandry to be a means of preventing starvation.

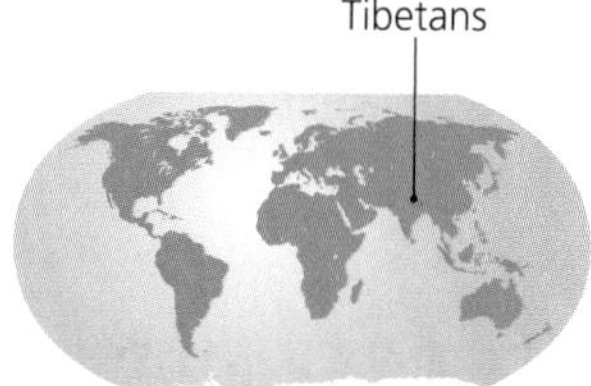

Of course, you might read this and think, Well, why not just *ask* members of the culture why they practice polyandry? Good question. Although every culture has members who are quite analytical and very helpful to the anthropologist, most people in a culture don't know why particular customs are followed.

POSTMODERNISM IN ANTHROPOLOGY

Postmodernists place the discipline of anthropology in the humanities rather than in the sciences. A humanistic view focuses on the uniqueness of each individual and on individual creativity within the confines of society and culture. This means that ethnographers must look to individual informants and record their voices and perspectives. It also means that the postmodern approach downplays the comparative method and quantitative analysis.

postmodernist
One who uses the paradigm of postmodernism.

postmodernism
A complex theoretical perspective that applies a humanistic approach to ethnography with a focus on individuals and their voices.

Postmodernism is considered a theoretical perspective with different meanings to different people (see Marcus and Fischer 1986; Fischer 1997;

Kuper 1999; and Kuznar 2008). Basically anthropologists with this theoretical perspective question the use of the scientific method in anthropology. They view culture as an abstraction. Further, they argue that it is impossible to be objective when studying other cultures. They focus on the premise that ethnographer objectivity is not possible because observers are always influenced by their own culture, gender, and social position, as well as by their feelings about what they observe. Therefore postmodernists claim that most theoretical constructs are not valid.

Although the postmodern movement is controversial, it has influenced anthropologists to be sensitive to issues such as power (as in when the ethnographer comes from a powerful culture and the native person being interviewed does not). It has also contributed to advocacy for a more vigorous representation of the native viewpoint. Many ethnographers, both those who use a scientific approach and those who use a postmodernist approach, now request that natives read and comment on their ethnographic data before they are published. A combination of methodological approaches and scrutiny of our theoretical orientations result in a better understanding of cultures.

SUMMARY

Anthropology is the study of humans throughout the world over approximately the last 5 million years. It is a holistic discipline, meaning that it views humans in the broadest possible context as both biological and cultural entities. This perspective is maintained regardless of the specific research undertaken. The four subfields of anthropology as recognized by the American Anthropological Association are cultural anthropology, archaeology, linguistics, and biological (or physical) anthropology. The holistic perspective, the use of the comparative method, fieldwork as a primary means of data acquisition, the perspective of cultural relativism, and avoidance of ethnocentrism make anthropology a unique discipline. Anthropologists seek to explain human cultural behavior using the scientific method. At the same time, anthropology includes a humanistic perspective.

Study Questions

OLC
mhhe • com / lenkeit5e
See Self Quiz.

1. What do anthropologists study? What are the four subfields of anthropology, and what do anthropologists working within each subfield study?
2. How is anthropology unique as a discipline?
3. Contrast the perspectives of ethnocentrism and cultural relativism.

4. Anthropologists use the scientific method to investigate and explain human cultural behavior. Why is it sometimes difficult to apply the scientific method in studies of other cultures?

Suggested Readings

See Web links.

Birx, James, ed. 2005. *Encyclopedia of Anthropology*. Thousand Oaks, Calif.: Sage. This multivolume reference is user-friendly and covers topics in all of the subfields of anthropology.

Endicott, K. M., and R. Welsch. 2008. *Taking Sides: Clashing Views on Controversial Issues in Anthropology*, 4th ed. Guilford, Conn.: McGraw-Hill/Dushkin. Opposing viewpoints regarding various issues in anthropology, including ethical dilemmas.

Feder, Kenneth L. 2011. *Frauds, Myths, and Mysteries: Science and Pseudoscience in Archaeology*, 7th ed. New York: McGraw-Hill. A must-read for anyone interested in archaeology. This book gives insight on how to approach and evaluate claims about prehistory that appear in the popular media.

Park, Michael Alan. 2010. *Biological Anthropology*, 6th ed. New York: McGraw-Hill. An excellent introduction to the field of biological anthropology.

Rathje, William, and Cullen Murphy. 2001. *Rubbish! The Archaeology of Garbage*. Tucson: University of Arizona Press. An entertaining and provocative book about Rathje's Garbage Project. Demonstrates the application of archaeological methods to contemporary issues.

Shubin, Neil. 2009. *Your Inner Fish: A Journey into the 3.5-Billion-Year History of the Human Body*. New York: Vintage Books. A very accessible overview of the full scope of human evolution. Written with verve and humor.

CHAPTER 2

Culture

What Makes Us Strangers When We Are Away from Home?

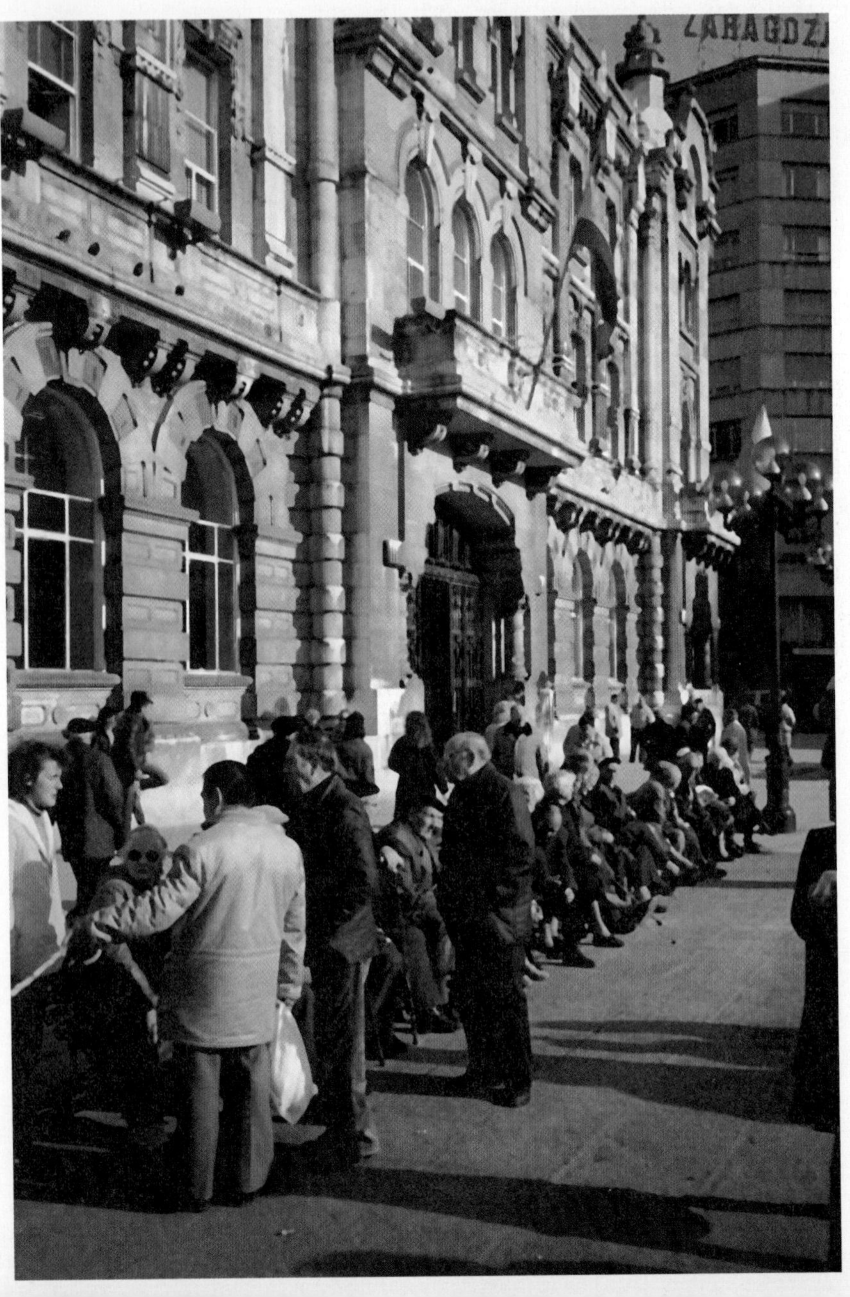

I had just cut a piece of chicken on the plate in front of me. I placed the knife on the upper right rim of the plate and transferred my fork from my left hand to my right hand and raised the tines of the fork bearing the chicken to my mouth. As I listened to a remark made by the man sitting on my right, I glanced down the length of the banquet table. There were twenty-five college professors, high-ranking government officials, and individuals representing various private organizations sitting at my table. I suddenly realized that I was the *only* person with a fork grasped in my right hand. Everyone else retained the fork in their left hand as they ate their meat, as is the Canadian custom. I *knew* that Canadians used table utensils in the European manner, but my behavior with utensils was learned in my culture of birth, American. I felt that everyone at the banquet table was looking at me and that I might as well be wearing a sign that said, "I Am an American." I quickly shifted my technique with the fork and pondered how cultural behaviors such as this were indeed what make us strangers when we are away from our own culture.

I spent two years living and teaching in Canada. The experience related above is an example of the many mistakes I made when trying to fit in with my surroundings. I knew that Canadian culture and its regional and ethnic variations were different from American culture and its many regional and ethnic variations. I tried very hard to view experiences through an anthropological lens, to note cultural similarities as well as differences. Yet I was and remained in most ways a stranger in this setting, because of my cultural upbringing.

Culture is an abstract concept. You can't touch it or see most of it, and much of it can't be measured. But it has molded each of us into who and what we are: the way we dress, what we eat for dinner *and how we eat it*, how we speak, what color we paint our houses, *and* what we think about these things. It makes us strangers when we are away from home because sights, smells, sounds, values, traditions, behaviors, objects, and the way other people think are not what we expect.

Culture is also what makes others view us as different from them. My Canadian friends remarked that they could always identify an American because we speak loudly. Understanding the role of culture in shaping us can provide an intellectual tool for better understanding who we are and why other individuals or groups of people are similar to or different from us. At the most fundamental level, anthropologists believe that if we examine other cultures we can come to better understand our own. As I tell my students, "How can you know Modesto [my city] if you only know Modesto?" This chapter explores the concept of culture.

The objectives of this chapter are to:

- Explain how anthropologists define culture
- Delineate important aspects of culture
- Discuss subcultures, ethnic groups, and race
- Describe culture in the subfields of anthropology
- Critique the concept of culture

OLC
mhhe • com / lenkeit5e

See chapter outline and chapter overview.

◀ The culture of Spain is reflected in this street scene from Santander, Cantabria, Spain.

Culture is what makes us strangers when we are away from home. Picture yourself in each of these settings and consider how different each is from your own cultural setting. Mealtime differs in the Arctic (*upper left*), in New Guinea (*right*), and in the Kalahari Desert of Africa (*bottom left*), where these people are preparing an ostrich egg omelet.

DEFINING CULTURE

culture
The sum total of the knowledge, ideas, behaviors, and material creations that are learned, shared, and transmitted primarily through the symbolic system of language. These components create a pattern that changes over time and serve as guides and standards of behavior for members of the society. The term *culture* is used in the abstract as well as to refer to a specific culture.

What exactly is **culture?** Abstract concepts such as culture are difficult to define. Other abstract concepts that are well known are love, justice, and equality. Not everyone, including experts in these areas, will agree on the precise definition of any of these concepts. Definitions are about using words to say what a word means. There are nuances of meaning between words, which is why it is difficult to obtain a consensus about the phrasing of a definition. This is particularly true of abstract concepts like love and culture. A writer's theoretical orientation or research focus may affect the words chosen to use in a definition. A poet uses different words than an attorney does when explaining what love is. The words an ecologically minded anthropologist uses to describe culture may differ from those chosen by an anthropological archaeologist. This does not mean that we are speaking of something different when we use the term *culture.* We just place different emphasis and use different words to explain the concept.

A sumo wrestling match in Japan. Not all Japanese people are fans of this sport, yet they would recognize it as a part of Japanese culture.

The culture concept is also a generalization. Even when speaking about a specific culture, we are making a generalization. No two Japanese people, for example, know or practice all aspects of Japanese culture. So when we speak of Japanese culture, we are citing a generalized version of the Japanese culture. A Japanese individual may think and act based on her traditional Japanese cultural roots sometimes and not at other times, even in similar situations. Ask anyone born and raised in England or Spain or Iran or the United States who visits Japan on a holiday, and they will indicate that the Japanese culture is different from their own culture.

Culture is a word that is used daily by many people all over the world. Most of these people do not mean precisely the same thing when they use the word. But as I read and listen to the usage of the word *culture*, I believe that most people know that it is an abstract idea. And I think that most people *get* the notion that this thing called culture makes people think and act in particular ways and that it is learned. Dissecting the idea of culture has been a hot topic in academic circles in the past, and it still is today.

Exactly what is culture? Does it really exist? How can we convey what it is? One way to examine what culture means to anthropologists is to look at definitions of culture and statements about culture. The sample definitions in Boxes 2.1, 2.2, and 2.3 are grouped by their focus on aspects of culture.

BOX 2.1 Definitions of Culture: Components

Culture . . . is that complex whole which includes knowledge, belief, art, law, morals, customs, and any other capabilities and habits acquired by man as a member of society. (E. B. Tylor 1958: 1; originally published in 1871)

Culture means the whole complex of traditional behavior which has been developed by the human race and is successively learned by each generation. (Mead 1937: 17; quoted in Kroeber and Kluckhohn 1952: 90)

Culture may be defined as the totality of mental and physical reactions and activities that characterize the behavior of the individuals composing a social group. (Boas 1938: 159; quoted in White and Dillingham 1973: 32)

Culture is . . . that complex whole which includes all the habits acquired by man as a member of society. (Benedict 1929: 806)

By culture we mean all those historically created designs for living, explicit and implicit, rational, irrational, and non-rational, which exist at any given time as potential guides for the behavior of men. (Kluckhohn and Kelly 1945: 97)

Components of Culture

The definitions in Box 2.1 are primarily lists of the various components of culture. Different words are used, but the definitions communicate essentially the same ideas. Culture consists of x, y, and z. In fact, if you were listening today to a group of anthropologists discussing culture, various specific components of culture would be mentioned. These components may be arranged in several categories (see Figure 2.1): (1) cognitive (processes of learning, knowing, and perceiving): ideas, knowledge, symbols, standards, values; (2) behavior (how we act or conduct ourselves): gestures, manners of eating, marriage ceremonies, dancing, social interactions; and (3) artifacts (human material creations): tools, pottery, clothing, architectural features, machines. In other words, within this group of definitions, culture consists of what people process cognitively and how the cognitive processes are reflected in human behaviors and in the artifacts, or objects, that humans create.

Cognitive Processes. What people think, how they think, what they believe, and what they value are a part of culture. Cognitive processes are not themselves directly observable, but they provide the framework of people's choices. All of the knowledge and perspective an individual acquires while growing up within a particular social group, including both formal and informal learning, is included in this component of culture. We cannot view the cognitive processes that create a value system within

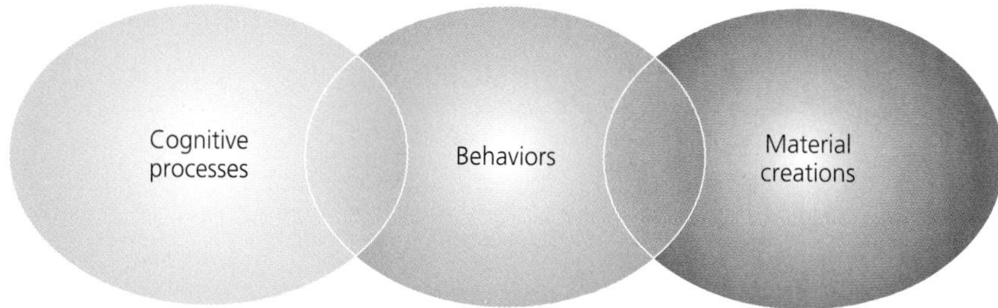

FIGURE 2.1 **Components of Culture** Early definitions of culture focused on its components.

an individual's mind, but we can view the *outcome* of those processes. If honesty is a value held by a culture (or subculture or microculture), we should be able to observe members of this culture carrying out behaviors that reflect this value.

Try to recount everything you have done today. Was it exciting? Or is most of your day made up of mundane tasks and behaviors? Focus on one specific behavior such as brushing your hair or teeth. Can you remember how you learned to do it? Did imitation play a role in your learning? Or did one person or many people teach you how to do it? Did trial and error play a role in your learning? Observe other family members doing this same behavior. Do they do it the same way you do?

Behaviors. Human behavior can be observed and described and includes all of the things we do—ways we use our bodies, all social interactions, and all creative expressions, such as playing a musical instrument or dancing. Cultural anthropologists spend much of their time in the field observing, describing, and recording behavior. Such descriptions include daily activities as well as ceremonial events that may occur only once a year or at periodic intervals. Descriptions of behavior in a natural setting include similar execution of behaviors as well as the many individual variations that occur. Ethnographers are trained to collect and record these data using a variety of techniques. The field methods ethnographers use are discussed in Chapter 3.

Material Creations. What people create, from artifacts to features, are products of human cultural activities. Ethnographers record and describe the artifacts and features of living cultural groups, whereas archaeologists describe artifacts and features made by peoples of past cultures. Artifacts and features provide a window into the minds and cultures of the people who make them. The examination of an 18,000-year-old cave painting, a contemporary artist's sculpture, an 11,000-year-old Clovis projectile point, the intricacies of a computer chip, and the latest engineered automobile design all tell us something about the individuals and cultures that produced them.

The objects we make reflect what and how we think. We can consider an artifact, whether a current or ancient one, as a fossilized idea (Deetz 1967). For example, a Yurok basket maker has an idea conceptualized in her brain of the basket she wants to make. She proceeds to make it, drawing on all of her knowledge and experience of where and how to gather raw materials plus the procedures for manufacturing the basket. Because her knowledge and experience have been shaped by her culture, the artifact she creates will reflect that culture. She will choose raw materials and process

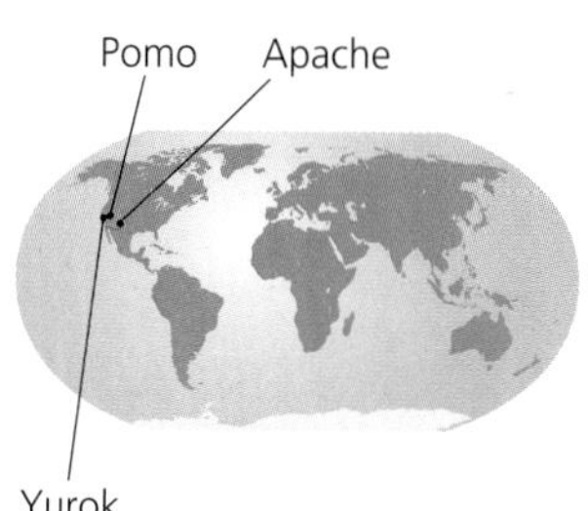

How many attribute differences can you identify between the Apache (Arizona and New Mexico) basket (*left*) and the Danakil (Ethiopia) basket (*right*)?

them according to the traditions of her people, perhaps with an occasional innovation. Such traditions dictate the attributes of the finished basket. An **attribute** is a discrete feature, such as the shape of the lip of the basket, a particular design element, or the location of that design element on the basket. Clusters of attributes combine to make an artifact. Hence the idea and the culture behind it are, in effect, producing a fossilized idea.

TRY THIS
Analyze

When do you give gifts to people? What is appropriate to give? How were you enculturated to this custom?

Cultural Processes

Each definition of culture in Box 2.2 includes something about the process of how culture is acquired, shared, and transmitted—in other words, how we learn it. These definitions began to appear in the 1930s and 1940s as anthropologists became increasingly interested in the *processes* of culture. Leslie White, an anthropologist who wrote extensively on this aspect of culture, pointed out that culture is learned, shared, and transmitted to future generations primarily by *symbolic systems*.

The most obvious symbolic system humans use is language—both spoken and written. It is primarily through language that we humans learn the cultural complexity that allows us to survive. Other ways of learning include observation and imitation of others, and trial and error.

White's definition also emphasizes that humans do not inherit culture genetically. This is what he meant by the phrase "extrasomatic context" in his definition. The word *soma* is derived from the Greek word that means pertaining to the body, and *extra* in this case means outside. So culture is

attribute
A discrete characteristic of an artifact. Attributes include shape, size, design elements and their placement, and techniques of manufacture.

BOX 2.2 Definitions of Culture: Cultural Processes

We define culture as that class of things and events dependent upon symboling, products of symboling, considered in an extrasomatic context. (White and Dillingham 1973: 29)

Culture consists of patterns, explicit and implicit, of and for behavior acquired and transmitted by symbols, constituting the distinctive achievement of human groups, including their embodiment in artifacts; [historically derived and selected] ideas and especially their attached values. (Kroeber and Kluckhohn 1952: 181)

The culture of any society consists of the sum total of the ideas, conditioned emotional responses, and patterns of habitual behavior which the members of that society have acquired through instruction or imitation and which they share to a greater or less degree. (Linton 1936: 288)

What is one behavior or value that is part of your culture? Do you personally behave in this way or live by this value? Can you think of a behavior or value that is part of your culture that you personally do not conform to?

outside of the physical body; it is not genetically inherited, though one could argue that it is dependent on having a physical body, including a complex brain. One is not born with a preference for eating peanut butter or a belief in a particular deity. You learn what foods to eat because they are the foods that are traditional and available in the environment of your culture. You learn about your god(s) from your parents and other adults in your social group. You are taught how many husbands or wives you should have at one time.

A recent student of mine was born in Korea, of Korean parents, and adopted as an infant by an American couple of European ancestry. She grew up speaking English and behaving and thinking as an American person, including all her gestures, facial expressions, prejudices, and values. Anthropologists use the term **enculturation** to describe the process of learning one's culture while growing up in it. To become enculturated is to become a member of your culture in all respects.

When an entire society consists of sixty individuals, about the size of many foraging band societies, most individuals do in fact share most values and exhibit most shared behaviors. This is because members of the culture interact with one another on a daily basis and thus reinforce values and behaviors. Individuals who deviate from the usual, shared way of doing things suffer ridicule and humiliation. Such sanctions are effective in returning the offender to the acceptable pattern of behavior. Small cultural groups such as this are called **homogeneous cultures** because most ideas, values, knowledge, behavior, and artifacts are shared by most individuals. In larger cultures, often referred to as **heterogeneous cultures,** there are fewer shared components. In a large, complex heterogeneous culture like the United States, shared components might be citizenship, liberty to pursue the American dream, and sharing the same governmental system.

enculturation
The process of learning one's culture while growing up in it.

homogeneous culture
Cultural group that shares most ideas, values, knowledge, behaviors, and artifacts. Typical of small cultural groups such as foragers.

heterogeneous culture
Cultural group that shares only a few components. Typical of large societies such as states, where there are many subcultures such as ethnic groups.

BOX 2.3 Definitions of Culture: Blueprints

Culture is best seen not as complexes of concrete behavior patterns—customs, usages, traditions, habit clusters—as has, by and large, been the case up to now, but as a set of control mechanisms—plans, recipes, rules, instructions (what computer engineers call "programs")—for the governing of behavior. (Geertz 1973: 44)

The culture concept . . . denotes an historically transmitted pattern of meanings embodied in symbols, a system of inherited conceptions expressed in symbolic forms by means of which men communicate, perpetuate, and develop their knowledge about and attitudes toward life. (Geertz 1973: 89)

A system of shared beliefs, values, customs, behaviors, and artifacts that the members of a society use to cope with one another and with their world and that are transmitted from generation to generation through learning. (Bates and Plog 1990: 466)

Culture: the ideals, values, and beliefs members of a society share to interpret experience and generate behavior and that are reflected by their behavior. (Haviland 1999: 36)

Blueprints

More recently, definitions of culture have focused on how it supplies a blueprint for behavior and the values that shape behavior (see Box 2.3). Culture supplies meanings, understandings, and ideas and is transmitted symbolically. Clifford Geertz, using a computer analogy, says that culture supplies *programs* for guiding people's behavior (1973). Ward Goodenough has written that "culture, then, consists of standards for deciding what is, standards for what can be, standards for deciding how one feels about it, standards for deciding what to do about it, and standards for deciding how to go about doing it" (Goodenough 1963: 258–59). Decades of ethnographic work have shown that there is enormous variation within any culture, and yet the blueprints, or programs, for behaviors are enculturated within a particular social group so that adult members share the same basic standards. Figure 2.2 shows how all the different definitions of culture work together to describe this complex concept.

Additional Features of Culture

Culture Is Shared. A social group shares *among* its members most of what constitutes its culture. This is a point that would stimulate lively discussion among a group of anthropologists. The notion of culture being shared is often a difficult property to articulate and is also an aspect of the

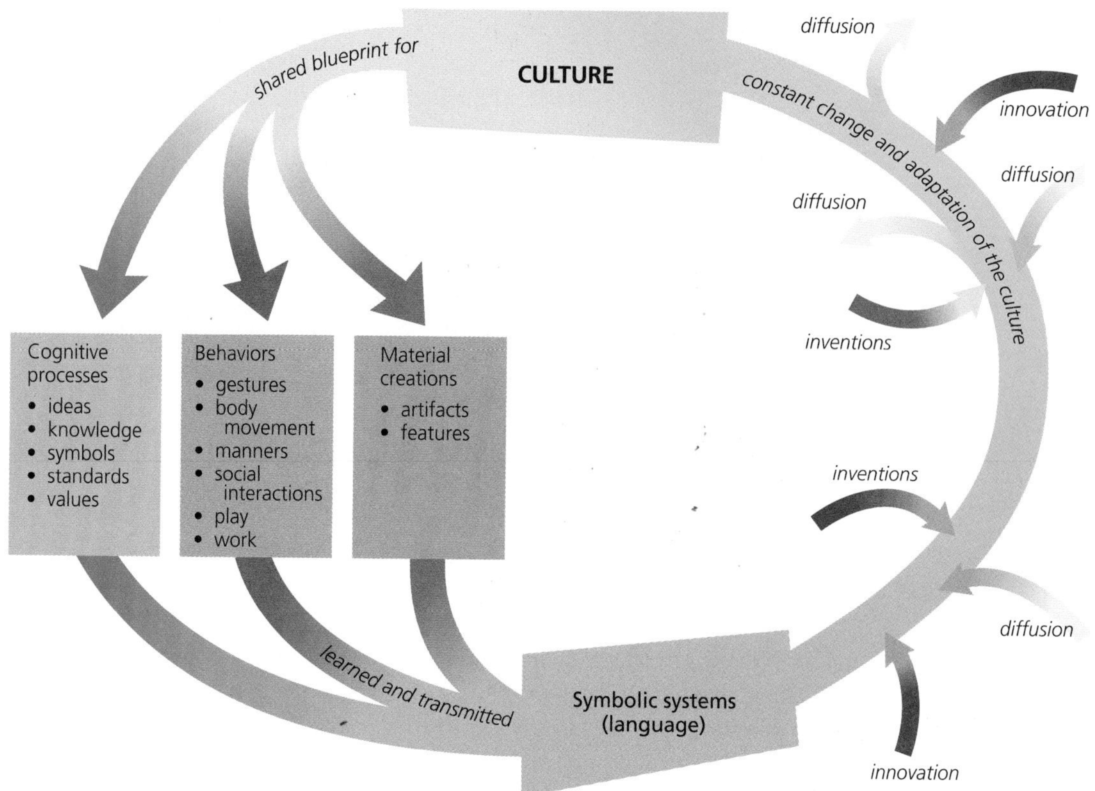

FIGURE 2.2 **The Culture Concept Today** The culture concept is viewed as a complex of cognitive processes, behaviors, and material creations that are learned, shared, and transmitted primarily through language. Culture is dynamic and adaptive.

concept that seems to give new students of anthropology some difficulty. How much of culture is shared? If 51 percent of the people share a behavior, is this enough for it to be considered a behavior of that culture? Should the requirement be that 65 percent of the people exhibit the behavior, or should it be 95 percent? And what if an individual exhibits the shared behavior or value on some occasions and not on others?

That the knowledge, behavior, value system, or other part of culture is shared by *most* individuals in the culture seems to be the standard applied by the majority of anthropologists. The shared nature of culture is implied in most definitions of culture, even when not directly stated. A member of a culture will recognize and be able to articulate a specific element of her culture *even if* that individual does not herself hold her culture's attitude or exhibit a specific behavior. For example, a North American man who has two wives (one in San Francisco and one in New York City) is not practicing the form of marriage dictated by law nor the religious standards

Examine this California house. What features does it share with houses in your North American neighborhood?

of Christianity. If this man were asked what the shared marriage form is in North American society, he would acknowledge that monogamy, one man married to one woman at any given time, is the American cultural custom.

Culture Is Cumulative, Dynamic, Adaptive, and Diverse. Anthropologists' observation that culture is cumulative is amply supported by the data of the archaeological and historical records. Discoveries—be they technological or ideological—are stored by language so that a culture builds through time. A culture adapts in response to its environment. The changing environment may be the result of alterations in the weather, such as a drought. Or it may be a change involving territorial infringement by a neighboring cultural group. To survive, the culture must respond by adapting to the change, accommodating it in some manner. Sometimes these changes are slow and go almost unnoticed; at other times the changes are quick and dramatic.

Culture is constantly changing. It changes internally through the fickleness of popular fads—the latest music, foods, slang, clothing fashions. It changes internally through **innovations** and **inventions**—new ideas and combinations of old ideas to create new things. Culture changes because of external influences through a process of **diffusion,** or the voluntary borrowing of items and ideas from other cultures. Most aspects of any contemporary culture have diffused from other cultures.

innovation
Something totally new.

invention
Something new that is created based on items or ideas that already exist.

diffusion
The borrowing and exchange of items or ideas between cultures.

Consider what you know about how adaptive and diverse culture is. People eat everything from fungus to flowers to fowl to fettuccine. Make your own list of foods based on what you have read and seen in films or

These Spanish children participate in a traditional village Saints' Day festival. Everyone in the village shares the knowledge of this festival even if they do not participate in it.

on the Internet. Inuit peoples of northern Canada learned to hunt seals through the ice and ate the raw meat, blubber, organs, and blood. Many Americans, especially those in California, have learned to eat the immature flower of the artichoke plant. Human cultures have adapted to a vast number of environmental conditions.

As noted previously, no culture or subculture is a tidy package in which everyone shares all knowledge, behaviors, or artifacts. Within a specific culture or subculture there is variation. During the time I lived in Spain, I became aware of the many differences among the various geographic regions of the country. Yet all who lived in those regions considered themselves Spaniards. My Guatemalan students from the cities consider themselves quite separate from rural Guatemalans. Rural farming communities in the United States are made up of people who share clusters of behaviors, values, knowledge, artifacts, and cognitive rules that govern their behaviors and values. These are different from the clusters of these features found in an inner city. Even within both the farm community and the inner city, there are many variations and many subcultural clusters along with the shared features.

TRY THIS
Analyze

Identify an aspect of present popular culture that diffused via media to North America from another world culture.

Culture Is Integrated. All of the parts of a culture are intermingled. This integrated nature of culture creates a pattern, and it is this pattern that an anthropologist endeavors to describe and explain. Cultural patterns typically reflect ecological and other adaptations that have occurred over time. Sea goddesses are worshipped by people who live near the sea, and the technology of such a society reflects knowledge of the sea and its resources. A society of desert dwellers has a different pattern of

The diffusion of technology such as the cell phone has been rapid around the world. Other aspects of culture may change much more slowly, such as this Maasai's herding traditions.

TRY THIS
Discuss

Discuss the value of honesty with a classmate. Identify three specific ways that Americans, who share the ideal cultural value of being honest, actually behave dishonestly.

integrated parts—economic systems, technological systems, ideological systems, kinship systems, political systems—each of which contributes to the cultural whole. This model has justifiably come under criticism. A culture isn't a tidy integrated whole. If it were, then it would be static. But cultures, in fact, are constantly changing. There are, however, clusters and patterns that at any given time uniquely identify a specific culture.

IDEAL CULTURE AND REAL CULTURE

ideal culture
What people believe they should do.

real culture
What people can be observed to do.

Anthropologists think in terms of **ideal culture** and **real culture.** Ideal culture consists of what people believe they *should do*, such as brushing their teeth after every meal or being honest, whereas real (or actual) culture is what people can be observed doing. In the case of brushing teeth, as you know, most of us are doing well if we brush twice a day. Here, there is a gap between ideal and real behavior. Brushing your teeth is also an example of an explicit cultural behavior, related to body hygiene, that

ANTHROPOLOGY AROUND US

Cute Protein

It is easy to identify ethnocentrism when it comes to food preferences. We consider what *we* eat to be correct food to eat. We base this not on nutritional evidence but on cultural custom. Most North Americans don't eat what a recent news article called *cute* protein—puppies, cats, and monkeys. We don't eat certain protein on moral grounds—horse, whale, and porpoise. In the 1998 General Election, California passed a state law forbidding the sale of horsemeat as food for humans. Three foreign-owned horse slaughter houses (two in Texas and one in Illinois) were effectively shut down by the United States Fifth Circuit Court of Appeals decision in January 2007. The decision upheld a Texas law banning the sale of horsemeat for human consumption. Canadian protesters are currently seeking to ban horsemeat for human consumption; many other countries are calling for bans on dog and cat meat.

Marvin Harris disagrees with the arguments explaining what we eat on its appearance or on moral issues. He notes that chicken, pigs, and cows are *efficient* sources of protein production compared to cats and dogs. This, in his view, is the reason to eliminate cats and dogs from our diet, not because they are cute pets (Harris 1998: 198).

◎ What do you think? Is the eating of certain animals and not others a practical or moral issue? Why?

can be directly observed. Honesty is a cultural value that can also be used to illustrate the dichotomy between the ideal and the actual. An objective anthropologist would find that Americans value honesty but do not always practice it. In a fieldwork situation, the anthropologist attempts to balance what people say with what they can be observed doing. So this distinction—ideal versus real—is very useful.

subculture
Smaller group within a large cultural complex. Behaviors, values, attitudes, and artifacts are shared by group members.

microculture
The smallest subgroup within a culture that shares specific cultural features such as values or behaviors.

SUBCULTURES AND ETHNIC GROUPS

Subcultures

Smaller groups within a larger cultural complex are called **subcultures.** These groups share behaviors, values, attitudes, and artifacts among their members. For example, college students constitute a subculture. The term **microculture** is sometimes used to denote even smaller groups in

TRY THIS
Analyze

You are enrolled in an anthropology class and are therefore a member of the student subculture. Quickly list the artifacts, values, and behaviors that you share with other members of this subculture and that, taken together, are not part of the larger North American culture.

which values, behaviors, attitudes, and artifacts are shared. International students on a college campus would constitute a microculture. The terms *subculture* and *microculture* are often imprecise and are sometimes used interchangeably. The only real agreement seems to be that these are units that share certain aspects and that they are part of a larger cultural group. Each individual within large heterogeneous cultures will belong to several subcultures and microcultures. The abstract idea of culture is often referred to as culture with a capital letter *C*. A specific culture, subculture, or microculture is referred to with a lowercase *c*.

Ethnic Groups

People who live in large heterogeneous cultures usually belong to several subcultures. Some of these subcultures share common languages or linguistic features not shared by all members of the larger culture. Members of subcultures may also share behaviors, beliefs, values, attitudes, and artifacts that are not shared by the rest of the population of the larger culture. One type of subculture is popularly called an ethnic group. **Ethnic groups** are subcultures that are characterized by members sharing a particular culture of origin, often one from another country. The language of the country of origin, rather than the official language of the adopted country, is often the primary language spoken in the homes of these subcultural groups. Ethnic group subcultures are often confused with race because popular perceptions are that an ethnic group consists of people of the same skin color and thus represents a biological group.

OLC
mhhe • com / lenkeit5e
See Internet exercises.

RACE

Humans have spent an extraordinary amount of energy, ink, and paper on the issues associated with human race. Exactly what is a human race? Do human races really exist, and, if so, how many races are there? Or is race, as one biological anthropologist puts it, "at best . . . just another four-letter word, empty of any biological significance" (Brace 2000b: 321)? A biological **race** is a segment of a species that is distinguishable from other segments based on a cluster of distinct biological traits. The view of the majority of biological anthropologists today is that human biological races do not exist and that this term should be abandoned. Yet the term *race* persists, and many people believe that races are real, definable biological entities. After all, people do look different, don't they? And aren't physical features determined by genetics? On one level, the answer to these questions is yes, but these two issues are typically oversimplified.

ethnic group
A type of subculture characterized by members sharing a culture of origin, often one originating in another country.

race
Biologically: a group within a species that shares a cluster of genetically determined traits. No such trait clusters occur among *Homo sapiens*. Culturally: a social construct based on differences interpreted through a cultural lens.

Anthropology is in a unique position to shed light on issues of race because of the holistic nature of the discipline. Recall the earlier statement that the culture concept is important in studies of biological anthropology because culture is the primary adaptive mechanism of our species. Conversely, biology has influence on human culture. Both biology and culture influence the physical appearance of human bodies; and the more sophisticated that science becomes, the more we understand the interrelationship.

OLC
mhhe • com / lenkeit5e
See Web links.

Prior to the compilation of an extensive database in comparative anatomy, physiology, and genetics, anthropologists tried to classify varieties of people. A race was viewed as a subspecies, and human races were based on physical features, geographic areas, and other criteria, even perceived personality traits. As data accumulated during the twentieth century, it became clear that there is only one species of *Homo sapiens* and no living subspecies. No group of humans has a *cluster* of genetic traits that separates it from other groups.

The scientific reality of human diversity is complex. To prepare the proper mind-set for considering this issue, think about the following two historical examples as analogous to the way that most people view race today. The history of science records a time when people believed that the world was flat because it *looked* flat when one stood and looked out at the horizon. And before Copernicus provided both the hypothesis and the data to prove that the earth revolved around the sun, people believed the opposite, that the sun rose in the east, moved overhead, set in the west, circled behind the earth, and rose again the next morning in the east. We can *see* the sun progress across the sky from dawn to dusk. It appears each morning on the horizon opposite the one where it set. Therefore, it must circle behind the earth during the night. Races, it is argued, must exist because groups of people look different from other groups. Or is it that we *perceive* differences, and are these perceptions enculturated and reinforced by our social group?

Human Biological Variation: Clines and Plasticity

Three features of the evolution of *Homo sapiens* point to humans belonging to one species with no biological subspecies or races. First, clinal variations in many traits have been documented. Biologists use the term **cline** to describe the variation of a particular trait along a geographic continuum. These are results of natural selection that fine-tuned and adapted human biological features to a variety of microenvironments. Second, the malleability of many traits has been demonstrated. The term **plasticity** is used in biological anthropology to describe biological traits being malleable, or pliable. Genes code for the potential of trait development, but the environment in which growth occurs affects the manifestation of this genetic potential. In other words, the traits show plasticity. Third, culture created circumstances that altered human evolution in many ways

cline
The variation of a biological trait along a geographic continuum. Human skin pigments show distribution along a cline from the equator north and south.

plasticity
The pliability or malleability of a biological feature. An individual's genetic growth potential is malleable depending on nutrition, maternal health, and exposure to sunlight.

over the course of human development: Clothing and fire replaced fur for warmth, and tools took the place of teeth in food procurement and defense. Because this is an introductory cultural anthropology text, the following discussion only touches on the vast body of data that relate to the topic of human variation and support the idea that biological races do not exist in our species.

Skin Color Clines. Human skin color is an example of a cline—it shows gradual change over large geographical areas. Most peoples do not have personal experiences that allow them to see the realities of world cline variations. North Americans, for example, had limited contact with diverse world populations until recently. A person with dark skin pigmentation was identified as African because North Americans had seen only West African peoples (the sources of the slave trade of the eighteenth and nineteenth centuries), whose skins were dark. But the African continent consisted, during aboriginal times as it does today, of tremendous diversity in skin pigmentation, ranging from people with lighter skin in the northeast to very dark skin in Central Africa and lighter pigmented skin again in the south. Most North Americans were simply ignorant of this variation as well as the existence of the very dark skinned peoples in India, New Guinea, western Australia, and Melanesia.

Skin color depends on the amount of **melanin** (a pigment) distributed in our skin. The amount of melanin depends on the rate at which it is synthesized in specialized cells located in the lowest level of our skin (Molnar 2002: 222–23). Complex processes are involved in the synthesis of this pigment. Melanin blocks the penetration of **UVB** light (B-range **ultraviolet radiation**) to the bottom layers of skin cells. UVB damage at the underlying cell layers leads to skin cancers on the surface of the skin. Skin with little melanin allows the penetration of UVB. Dark natural pigment or well-tanned skin blocks up to 95 percent of UVB (Brace 2000b: 297). Several hypotheses can explain how natural selection may have worked to produce variation in the rate of melanin synthesis. I'll discuss only two of these hypotheses but encourage you to read further on this entire subject. The suggested readings at the end of the chapter will give you a good place to begin.

melanin
A pigment in the outer layer of the skin. It is responsible for skin color and blocks UVB from damaging lower layers of the skin.

UVB
Ultraviolet radiation from the sun in the B wavelength.

ultraviolet radiation
A part of the electromagnetic energy from the sun that is not visible to the human eye.

The vitamin D hypothesis. The exposure of human skin to ultraviolet radiation from the sun is important for healthy bone development. The outer layers of skin synthesize vitamin D_3. Studies have demonstrated that vitamin D_3 formed by direct skin exposure to ultraviolet radiation is the most important form of the vitamin and that the dietary form of the vitamin (D_2) does not precisely duplicate it (Bogin 1988: 141). Vitamin D aids the intestines in the absorption of calcium and in other physiological reactions associated with healthy bone development (Bogin 1988; Brace 2000b). Vitamin D is essential to growth and development, but too much of this vitamin can be toxic (Molnar 2002: 234). Dark skin guards against too much ultraviolet radiation reaching the lower layers of the skin, thus protecting peoples near the equator from vitamin D toxicity by reducing the skin's synthesis of vitamin D, while at the same time producing enough of the vitamin for health. Near the equator then, natural selection favored individuals with dark skin; they lived longer and produced more children than individuals with pale skin.

The vitamin D hypothesis also explains the distribution of populations with less skin pigment. Peoples with the lightest skin pigments are found in northern and southern latitudes far away from the equator. In human evolutionary history, as populations moved farther away from equatorial zones, natural selection favored individuals with less skin melanin. They survived longer and produced more offspring than did individuals with more pigment because light skin is more efficient than darkly pigmented skin in synthesizing vitamin D. This ultimately resulted in some populations with almost no melanin, such as those in Norway and Finland.

Culture allowed humans to survive in latitudes to which they were not biologically adapted. People created clothing, built shelters, and made fires to keep warm. Clothing covered most of our skin surface, thus limiting the amount of ultraviolet radiation hitting the skin. In northern latitudes, individuals who had dark skin and who wore clothing were at risk of not getting enough vitamin D to ensure the healthy growth and development of the skeleton. Diets rich in fish oils, and the cultural practice of putting bundled up infants out in a sheltered spot in the sun (where faces were exposed to ultraviolet radiation), appear to be cultural adaptations that contributed to healthy bone development in these northern populations. Even though such populations did not know about the importance of vitamin D, people made some cause-and-effect connections between health and survival of infants who received such treatment. Such behaviors then became part of the folk traditions of these peoples.

The folate hypothesis. This hypothesis suggests that the evolution of dark skin in equatorial regions was related to the metabolite folate. **Folate** is essential for the production of healthy sperm and the development of the neural tube in embryos. UVB can destroy folate. Dark pigmentation, it is argued in this hypothesis, was selected for in individuals because it protects against the UVB destruction of folate. Thus individuals with more darkly pigmented skin produced healthy offspring (Jablonski and Chaplin 1999; Jablonski 2006).

Studies since the 1950s confirm that skin colors are adaptive, though we can't prove precisely which hypothesis is the correct explanation for this evolutionary adaptation. It may be that elements of each of these and other hypotheses are responsible for the distribution of human skin color. To further complicate matters, what seem to be anomalies exist in skin color distribution. The native peoples of Alaska and Canada, for example, don't seem to "fit" with the explanation of selection for lighter

folate
A metabolite essential for sperm and embryonic neural tube development that is destroyed by UVB.

skin as populations moved away from the equator. For help in explaining these apparent discrepancies, we can turn to the archaeological record and historical linguistics—the holistic approach again. Data from these anthropological subfields demonstrate that populations such as the native populations of Alaska moved *recently* to these latitudes—recent in terms of earth history, about twelve thousand years ago. They have not been in the extreme northern latitudes long enough for natural selection to show a decrease in pigmentation (Brace 2000b: 301). The ancestors of peoples in the Nordic countries of Finland and Norway, by comparison, have lived there for at least six hundred thousand years, and perhaps longer.

Stature and Plasticity. Biological plasticity means that traits determined by genes (in other words, coded by DNA) are influenced in the way they develop and grow. The degree to which a human grows to his or her full genetically coded height depends on factors such as nutrition during early years of life and the mother's health history. Poor nourishment or disease during the mother's growing years results in her having smaller stature, body size, and a smaller reproductive system. To state it another way, her body's ability to pass nutrients on to her fetus is compromised. A mother with this history gives birth to a baby of low birth weight, and data show that this child tends to grow slowly, reaching a shorter adult height than a well-nourished child of a healthy, well-nourished mother (Bogin 1998). Thus the child's adult height is not a direct reflection of his or her full genetic potential.

Developmental research comparing the skeletal growth of wild and captive chimps documents a slower pattern of growth in the wild populations with captive chimpanzees maturing as much as three years earlier. This suggests that nutrition affects the plasticity of skeletal development in our close primate relative as well (Zihlman, Bolter, and Boesch 2004; 2007; Bolter and Zihlman 2010).

Human growth rates are affected by exposure to light as well as nutrition. Research in Guatemala and Africa demonstrated that the growth rate of healthy children was more rapid during the months of the year when there was the most direct exposure to sunshine (i.e., with no clouds or haze blocking the sun) (Bogin 1988: 141).

People from populations with low socioeconomic resources and poor nutrition show height increases when they emigrate to more affluent countries, find work, and provide better lives for their children. Cultural assistance programs such as school breakfast and lunch programs, and prenatal care, plus the consumption of treated drinking water result in better health. Data on Mayan refugees from Guatemala, now living in Los Angeles, California, show an average height increase of 2.2 inches in one generation (Bogin 1998).

The demonstration of the adaptation and plasticity of human traits requires us to acknowledge that using any *biological traits* as a basis for classifying human groups is useless. Biological adaptation is a process that has been ongoing since the emergence of our first ancestors millions of years ago. It continues today. A comprehensive look at the DNA of modern humans shows that greater variation exists *within geographic areas and ethnic groups than between such groups.*

Race as a Social Construct

Culture, not biology, is the primary adaptive mechanism of humans, and it has been for a very long time. We were, and are, able to alter our environments and to create artifacts and behaviors that allow us to survive in new and different places. People moved about, married, had children, moved again, and their children did the same. This resulted in the reshuffling of genetic material and changes in material culture, behaviors, values, and beliefs through diffusion. Shifts in cultural identity and appearance occurred over and over again.

We compare others to ourselves. The process of distinguishing between us and them leads to classifying others into groups. These groups are based on differences we perceive or myths we have heard, and we label them "races" or "ethnic groups." Our perceptions are learned *social constructs* that are defined by a set of ever-changing cultural norms in our society. This is reflected in U.S. census categories by the addition or deletion of "racial" groups since the inception of the census in 1790. Census lists are constructed to address a variety of *social and political* issues such as access to medical services, bilingual education, and legislative redistricting. The current list of races for a person to check on the census form is based primarily on a person's country of origin (what is defined earlier in this chapter as an ethnic group), thus lumping together the numerous diverse ethnic groups found within any geopolitical entity. The government's continued use of the term "race" in the census contributes to the belief that biological clusters exist. They don't.

OLC
mhhe • com / lenkeit5e
See Internet exercises.

We create categories of people based on their behaviors, religion, values, dress, socioeconomic status, and geographical country of origin. These are not categories with a biological basis. They are culturally based classifications that should be recognized as social constructs..

CULTURE IN THE SUBFIELDS OF ANTHROPOLOGY

Since one of the hallmarks of anthropology is that it is holistic (see Chapter 1), this is an appropriate place to show how the subfields of anthropology use the culture concept. Even when anthropologists are carrying out specialized research, the culture concept helps us to retain the holistic perspective.

Cultural anthropologists study the various dimensions of culture by describing and analyzing living cultures, subcultures, and microcultures.

The dimensions of culture studied include, but are not limited to, language, family, kinship, gender, social organization, technology, economics, political structure, law, treatment of disease, play, myth, religion, body decorations, art, and music. Think about your own life and experiences. Every segment of your life has been influenced by the culture of your birth.

Archaeologists also study culture. The primary goals of archaeology are to reconstruct the lifeways of peoples of the past and to understand as much as possible about how their cultures interacted with the natural environment and other cultures. An understanding of the processes of living cultures is critical to archaeologists as they go about interpreting the human cultural past. Analogy with the present is a primary tool used by archaeologists to reconstruct how peoples lived in the prehistoric past. For example, an arrowhead from a prehistoric site is interpreted as an arrowhead in large part because living people use them in this way. Although most archaeologists point out that caution must be exercised when using analogous arguments, they also acknowledge that the use of cultural analogies is an important tool for reconstructing the past.

Linguistic anthropologists study the unique symbolic communicative process of *Homo sapiens*, language. Culture depends upon language. We share and transmit the components of culture by using language. Linguistic variations occur within cultures and subcultures and between people of different status and gender. Linguistic anthropologists investigate and describe these variations in language and language usage.

Biological anthropologists recognize that culture has been a primary adaptive mechanism for humans in the past. Flexibility in adapting behaviorally to an environment and the ability to transmit the skills learned to future generations was what made our ancestors successful. We can build shelters, make fires, and put on clothing in cold environments to which we are not biologically suited; we can transform deserts by importing water, and we can survive droughts by building dams and reservoirs.

Biological anthropologists must keep human cultural adaptation in mind as they study the fossil remains of our ancestors, genetic variation in contemporary human populations, and contemporary diseases. Human biology has been influenced by culture. Early in human evolution, natural selection favored people with large incisor teeth. Incisor teeth were used as tools, and the members of society that had big incisors survived longer and thus were able to reproduce more and pass along the genes for big teeth. The fossil record shows a reduction in incisors beginning around one hundred thousand years ago (Brace 1995: 215). This reduction corresponds with the appearance of many types of sharp-edged tools in the archaeological record. In terms of natural selection we would hypothesize that with a reduction in selective pressures for big incisors, more people with smaller incisors survived and thus reproduced as often as did individuals with big teeth. This led after a time to a population with smaller incisors than in the past.

CHALLENGES TO THE CULTURE CONCEPT

For some time now, a faction within cultural anthropology has been challenging the concept of culture. Advocates of this view believe that the concept is oversimplified and is too rigid. Moreover, they contend that it is a concept that does not reflect reality. These critics point out that culture is not homogeneous and uniformly shared, nor is it static and unchanging, nor is it a neatly packaged and integrated whole. It is my view that such criticisms are not new and that they focus on issues that most anthropologists have, in practice, acknowledged for decades. It has also been my experience that students recognize that all behaviors, thoughts, and material objects are not uniformly shared by everyone within a social group, that there is much variation, and that cultural change is continuous. I have reflected this position in my discussion of the concept.

Variations in culture—both through time and at a single point in time—cause complexity for those who try to describe the concept of culture. Christoph Brumann sifts through insights about the culture concept in his 1999 article "Writing for Culture," which appeared in the journal *Current Anthropology*. Several of his points need to be emphasized. First, culture is transmitted over time. This should be viewed as a complex process that is not exact. Many factors affect enculturation, and the transmission of a culture may be altered accordingly. Second, there are many variants within each culture, subculture, or microculture. An individual member of a culture may at any time make different choices from those made at another time. Third, the larger the group encompassed by the application of the term *culture*, the fewer the shared cluster of elements. These may be trivial things such as knowing of and consuming a particular soft drink or admiring and recognizing a particular musical artist (Brumann 1999).

Even with this complexity, Brumann argues that culture is a useful concept that we should keep, in part because "there is no denying that many ordinary people have grasped at least part of anthropology's message: culture is there, it is learned, it permeates all of everyday life, it is important, and it is far more responsible for differences among human groups than genes" (Brumann 1999: 12). To reiterate the theme of this chapter, your culture is what makes you a stranger when you are away from home. Everyone who has experienced living in another cultural environment will recognize that this is true. Finally, culture is a valid, if complex, concept.

SUMMARY

Culture is a concept that is used in each of the four fields of anthropology. Culture is an abstraction, a concept that refers to the sum total of the learned and shared knowledge, ideas, values, behaviors, and material items of a group of humans. It is learned largely through the symbolic system of language. A culture varies internally and is in a continual state of change. It is acquired through a process called enculturation and includes ideal and real elements. Ethnic groups and other subcultures make up the large complex heterogeneous cultures of much of the modern world. The members of a large heterogeneous culture share with one another fewer aspects of their culture than is the case in small homogeneous cultures, where everyone shares many more elements.

Ethnic groups and other subcultures are often confused with race. Biological anthropology demonstrates that our species cannot be divided into biological races because there is too much variation in traits. Additionally, culture influences human biology. Race is a social construct.

Study Questions

OLC
mhhe • com / lenkeit5e
See Self Quiz.

1. Explain the anthropological concept of culture. Support your discussion with examples from your own experiences.
2. Discuss how an understanding of the concept of culture can be useful when one is engaged in international business or travel. Cite specific examples from other assigned course readings.
3. "Your culture is what makes you a stranger when you are away from home." Discuss this statement with reference to an assigned reading or your own personal experience. Select two specific components of the culture concept and relate them to this statement and the other reading or your experience.
4. Why do anthropologists argue that race is a social construct and that there are no biological races in the human species?

Suggested Readings

OLC
mhhe • com / lenkeit5e
See Web links.

Brace, C. Loring. 2005. *"Race" Is a Four-Letter Word: The Genesis of the Concept*. New York: Oxford University Press. Exceptional historical overviews of the concept with emphasis on cultural and historical events of the past five hundred years that shape the scientific analysis of the concept.

Brumann, Cristoph. 1999. Writing for Culture. *Current Anthropology* 40 suppl. (February). A good overview of the history and current attitudes about the culture concept.

Fluehr-Lobban, Carolyn. 2006. *Race and Racism: An Introduction*. Lanhan, M.D.: Alta Mira. An excellent overview of the biological and social issues of race and racism and why American society doesn't discuss this issue openly.

Gould, Stephen J. 1996. *The Mismeasure of Man*. New York: Norton. A very accessible account of how nineteenth- and twentieth-century biological research on human variability was influenced by prevailing social attitudes.

Jablonski, Nina. 2006. *Skin: A Natural History*. Los Angeles: University of California Press. A readable account that incorporates the latest research on skin and its evolution.

CHAPTER 3

Fieldwork

How Are Data Gathered?

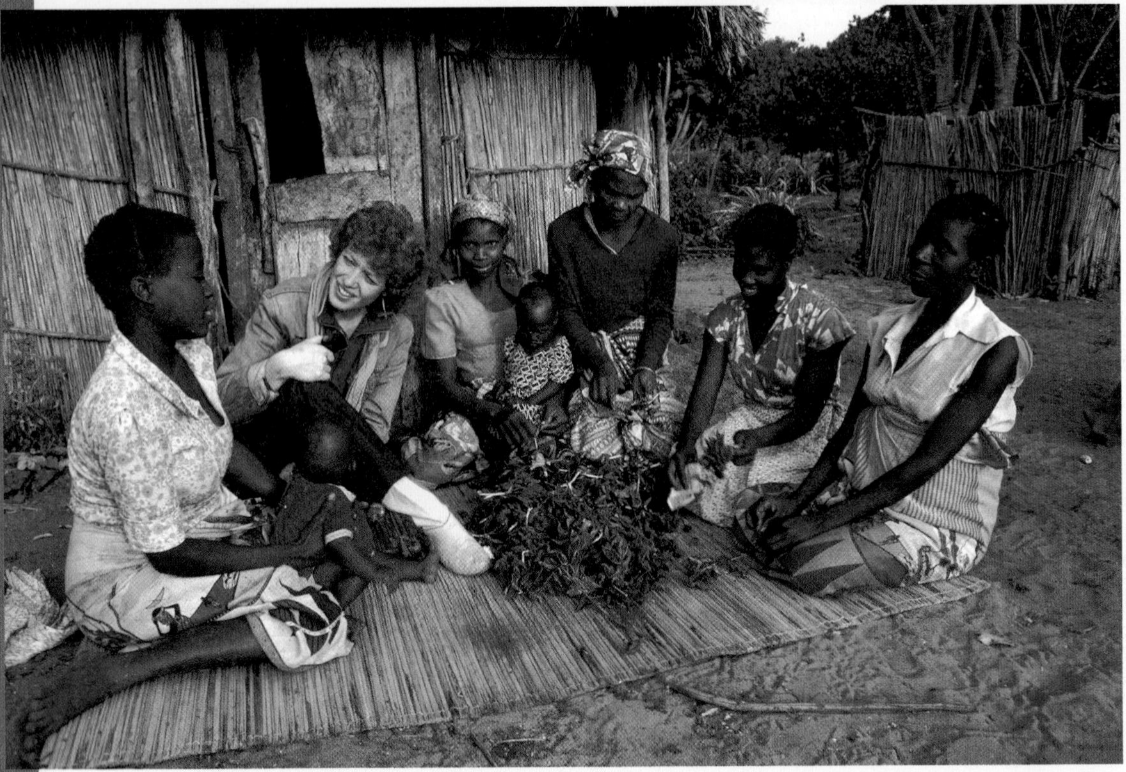

▲ Anthropologist Janine van Vugt, a worker with Oxfam-Novib, a Dutch NGO, talks to indigenous women while researching the impact of local development projects in Mozambique.

On our first evening in the small community in Spain, my family made our first contact with the locals by using string figures, a very old form of entertainment. One needs only a bit of string and a good story to tell, so it is a perfect game for travelers with limited luggage. At the end of a *paseo* (stroll) we sat on a bench in the plaza and did the string figures with our daughter, Karen, age nine. We have been enjoying the art of string figure making for many years, and our daughter always had string with her. Soon several community children joined us. They casually corrected our Spanish accents as we chatted and taught them several figures. The next evening these children brought friends. One young boy, Pablo, age nine, was accompanied by his grandfather. The grandfather taught us a figure he had learned as a boy. Soon more of the children were joining in our evening string figure sessions. Pablo is now a university student. He and his family became some of our best sources of information during our stay. They have also become special friends over the years. Karen and Pablo now correspond on the Internet, which shows how good global relationships may be built with a little string and cross-cultural openness and understanding.

Fieldwork. The very idea creates images of romantic adventure in exotic places. Reality is often another experience altogether. Homesickness and physical ills such as dysentery may be the more persistent experiences at first. Still, learning about another culture by participating in the society for extended periods of time yields a quality of information and perspective not available by other means. The difficulties and challenges encountered in the field usually dissipate with time as one acquires a working knowledge and understanding of the society's culture.

The society whose culture is under study may consist of workers on a shop floor assembly line in a North American manufacturing company, the people of a tribal village in Indonesia, or an urban neighborhood in Johannesburg, South Africa. In other words, anthropological fieldwork can involve the study of the microcultures or subcultures of contemporary urban societies as well as the cultures of traditional folk societies.

You will recall from Chapter 1 that the gathering of data in a natural, or "field," setting is also carried out by researchers in the other disciplines of anthropology. All anthropologists who gather their data in the field, whether they are sociocultural anthropologists, archaeologists, linguists, or biological anthropologists, usually participate in a cultural setting distinct from their own; each will encounter some of the same issues and difficulties associated with ethnographic data gathering, and all are schooled in the basics of its techniques (as a part of their holistic training in anthropology). A colleague who is a biological anthropologist emphasized this point as she recounted her fieldwork experiences in Bolivia. Her work involved gathering spit (saliva) for hormone studies of lactation. She found that time spent in establishing rapport with the local women and local trusted sources resulted in high levels of cooperation in the study.

Fieldwork is exciting and challenging. My family still talks about how much fun it was to share string figures that first evening in Spain. Of course, successful fieldwork involves much more than having fun. This chapter explores the processes and issues involved in doing ethnography.

The objectives of this chapter are to:

- Explain the background preparations for doing ethnographic fieldwork
- Describe the ethical standards that govern the fieldworker
- Describe the methods employed by fieldworkers and the problems associated with each method
- Discuss some of the challenges associated with fieldwork

PREPARING FOR THE FIELD

OLC
mhhe • com / lenkeit5e
See chapter outline and chapter overview.

The anthropologist setting off into a field situation carries a virtual tool box containing such basic methodological implements as cultural relativism, the culture concept, the holistic perspective, and the comparative method. The researcher will have honed these concepts and approaches while earning an undergraduate degree and completing two to four years of graduate work prior to undertaking major ethnographic research. During this time she will have studied, discussed, and debated these ideas along with the theories, data, and fieldwork of other anthropologists. She will also have thoroughly examined the ethical standards set by the discipline of anthropology.

Ethics

Anthropologists are very concerned with ethical issues associated with fieldwork. Researchers belong to many different cultures and subcultures and within each of these groups we have moral and ethical obligations. We also have ethical obligations to our communities and society at large as well as to the discipline of anthropology. Most of all we have responsibilities to the peoples whose lives we study. The American Anthropological Association (AAA) represents all subfields of the discipline and developed its code of ethics with the purpose of providing "guidelines for making ethical choices" to those doing fieldwork in anthropology: "Because anthropologists can find themselves in complex situations and subject to more than one code of ethics, the AAA Code of Ethics provides a framework, not an ironclad formula, for making decisions" (from the Code of Ethics of the AAA, approved February 2009).

OLC
mhhe • com / lenkeit5e
See Internet exercises and Web links.

The primary ethical responsibility for cultural anthropologists is toward the people with whom they work. The code of ethics requires that researchers must always be open about the purpose of their projects; they must never misrepresent themselves to their informants. They must fully inform everyone involved about the potential impact of their projects and do everything possible to ensure that no one is harmed physically or psychologically in any way. They must be open about the sources of funding and support for the project.

The full text of the code of ethics is available at the AAA Web site (www.aaanet.org). Also at this site are excerpts from the *Handbook on Ethical Issues in Anthropology*, special publication number 23 of the AAA, which contains sections on specific ethical cases and their solutions, such as "Robbers, Rogues, or Revolutionaries: Handling Armed Intimidation," "Hiding a Suspect," or "Witness to Murder." Ethical considerations have the highest priority among anthropologists and are a major part of our training. See Chapter 13, "Ethics Then and Now," for a discussion of ethics in directed-change programs, plus current issues.

Theoretical Models

Each anthropologist has likely found a particular theoretical platform from which to launch her or his field effort. A theoretical position serves as a framework to generate working hypotheses that will explain various aspects of the culture being studied—cognitive issues, behaviors, or material elements of culture. Remember that one of the most important foundations of the scientific method is its ability to correct itself. Over time, scientists fine-tune our understanding of humanity when more data are gathered and existing hypotheses are modified, accepted, or rejected.

I am partial to a theoretical perspective known as cultural ecology. This model has been popular since the 1970s and holds that cultural systems should be viewed as adaptive interactive systems between people and their environments (including both the natural environment and the environment provided by other societies). I also find a functionalist model useful. This theoretical model, made famous in the early 1900s by British social anthropologists Bronislaw Malinowski and A. R. Radcliffe-Brown, holds in part that a culture works, or functions, by virtue of all of its segments (economics, politics, kinship, etc.) working together. Further, a particular custom may be viewed as functioning to individually or collectively fulfill the needs of the members of a society (e.g., the need for food, shelter, social interaction, beliefs).

It should be obvious that these theoretical models are more complex than what I have presented here. Entire books and courses at the upper-division university level are devoted to the comprehension and assessment of theoretical models. Evaluating and debating the merits of such models can be stimulating for professional anthropologists as they strive for better ways to understand the human condition. Beginners in the field of anthropology are less well equipped with background data to undertake an in-depth critique of the various paradigms. What beginners should remember, though, is that models are devices for explaining and understanding; they are vehicles with which to formulate hypotheses. A great deal of testing is required before we can tentatively accept a model's explanation of human behavior. Later chapters will draw from several theoretical models, including those briefly mentioned here. In this way you can begin to see how theoretical models are used to explain data.

Contemplate the functions of the American Fourth of July holiday. Can you think of three ways that this celebration meets the needs of the members of our society individually and collectively?

Approaches to Ethnography

The early years of anthropology were marked by what are now termed classic ethnographies. These accounts were holistic, objective descriptions of a society's way of life that were typically carried out by a single fieldworker. Although these ethnographies contain much data, critics claim that they described cultures in somewhat idealized, romanticized terms. Societies were described with little, if any, reference to internal strife, culture change, or interaction of the group with other societies; women's voices and perspectives were often absent. Additionally, the roles or perspectives of the individual native members of the society were seldom included.

Today many ethnographers take an approach called **reflexive,** or **narrative, ethnography.** This broad category refers to accounts that include the personal perspectives and reactions of the fieldworker while immersed in the field situation. Data are often presented as if a dialogue were taking place between one or more native informants and the ethnographer; the ethnography thus resembles literary writing rather than scientific description. Such ethnographies typically do not include comparative data or the quantification of data. They reflect a humanistic and postmodernist view.

Still other ethnographers blend approaches, and also may work in teams. These ethnographers demonstrate commitment to the scientific method with emphasis on objective observation, comparative method, and quantification of data (review the discussion of the scientific approach in Chapter 1). At the same time, they include some reflexive elements, such as comments on their feelings while gathering data. Additionally, current ethnographers take a more collaborative approach that recognizes the active contributions of members of the study group and includes their voices and perspectives.

Research Proposals, Funding, and Budgets

Before undertaking field research, it is necessary to obtain funding for the project. Many public and private foundations are dedicated to the support of scientific research. Such institutions require detailed proposals to be submitted before they will grant financial support. The proposal process typically includes a statement of purpose, details of the methods that will be employed to gather data, proposed time parameters, potential applications for the results of the research, and a detailed budget. Often the funding requires that the study be published in an appropriate professional journal within a specific period of time after the research is completed. Many universities and corporations employ professional experts to help with the preparation of grant proposals, particularly the budget portions.

Budget preparation is often complex and can be a particularly thorny issue for the anthropologist who is going to another country, especially because fluctuating monetary exchange rates and different cultural expectations regarding money usage are not always predictable. What most Americans would consider bribes, for example, may be a normal part of certain transactions in other cultures. An additional consideration in budgeting is the financial responsibility one has at home, such as making mortgage payments, renewing insurance policies, and paying local, state, and federal taxes.

reflexive, or narrative, ethnography
An approach to fieldwork that focuses on the personal experiences and perspectives of the ethnographer, as well as the voices of the native members of a culture. Also called narrative ethnography.

ANTHROPOLOGY AROUND US

Ethnography in the Workplace

Native peoples of distant lands are only part of the anthropological agenda today. All around us ethnographers are quietly contributing to the solution of workplace issues. Today's native populations include workers, managers, and clients. In one project, reported in *U.S. News & World Report* (August 10, 1998), anthropologist Ken Erickson worked for months as a butcher learning to slice and cut meat in a slaughterhouse. He was investigating why there had been a wildcat strike. Managers thought the problems were due to language barriers. By being a participant observer and becoming a part of this microculture both during and after work, Erickson showed that the real issue was the attitude of managers. Managers treated the workers as though they were stupid, and the workers resented this. They wanted respect for their skills. This project resulted in new training programs.

In another case, anthropologist Julian Orr was hired by Xerox Corporation to solve a problem with its service repair program. Orr became a participant observer and was trained as a repairman. After several months he reported that the training program didn't teach workers an important part of service repair—showing clients how to fix minor problems themselves. Repair callbacks dropped dramatically when the new training in how to teach clients basic repairs was implemented (*Business Week*, September 30, 1991). Thousands of anthropologists now work for consulting firms and as full-time corporate, government, and NGO staff.

◎ What is one problem area on your campus or in your workplace that might be solved if someone actually got to know the job through doing the job?

ENTERING THE NATIVE COMMUNITY AND ADAPTING

Because every field situation is unique, there are few guidelines for how an ethnographer should enter another society. However, since the 1960s, anthropologists have been writing about various issues they have encountered while doing fieldwork, including initial contact with the subject culture. Common situations have emerged from such accounts. These accounts, plus networking with veteran ethnographers, serve to prepare the novice ethnographer for possible difficulties. There are two basic approaches for initial entry to the field environment: (1) have someone experienced in the society introduce you, and (2) enter by yourself. If you elect to have someone familiar with the community introduce you, there is a potential snag if the "natives" bear any animosity toward that person. Indeed, this has happened to ethnographers on numerous occasions, particularly when government officials are involved. What about the alternative of simply arriving by yourself? This is the approach that my husband and I took when we lived in northern Spain in a community with a population of fifteen hundred. It worked in our situation, in part because luck entered the picture in the form of our landlord.

There were no rental offices, no local papers with classified ads, and no apartment buildings in this village or the surrounding area. When we arrived, we simply looked for signs in windows that advertised rooms to rent. We found two such signs, but the rooms proved unsatisfactory for a family. We then began asking shopkeepers if they knew of any flats to rent. One particularly friendly man directed my husband to ask at a local bar for Javier, who might know someone with a flat to rent. Javier, the bar owner, indicated that he did know someone who might rent a part of his home, and he said he would be glad to make introductions when Enrique arrived. Enrique, to our relief, had a furnished flat to rent that served our needs and was within our budget. As the weeks passed, we found Enrique to be a veritable encyclopedia of knowledge—from local and national history to contemporary issues. He knew everyone and could always be counted on when we needed information. It was only months later that we discovered he had served on the governing body of the village for many years and was held in high esteem. Serendipitous luck for us!

Adapting Physically and Psychologically

The first month or two in a field setting is a time of adaptation. Issues of where and how to obtain food and shelter, adjustment to temperature and humidity, and staying healthy seem to take a disproportionately large amount of time when you are in a new setting. Mundane issues such as learning the schedule for the local bus and discovering the normal rhythms of your new environment take time—more time or less time depending on how different the setting is from what you are accustomed to.

After making the essential adaptations such as finding a steady source of food and acceptable shelter, many fieldworkers experience a "honeymoon" phase. Everything is new. You are *in the field* gathering data. The fieldworker recognizes that these moments are the realization of a goal

These are traditional homes in northern Spain. In the past, animals were kept on the ground floor, and the family lived above. Note the Roman castle ruins on the far hill.

pursued for several years. These first weeks are often very exciting. Once the initial honeymoon period is over, problems may surface.

There are dangers out there—viruses, vermin, bacteria, vicious dogs, wild pigs, poisonous critters and plants, drug-resistant malaria, accidents. Areas of political instability and volatility create additional fieldwork hazards. Ethnographers who are accustomed to life in industrialized countries with vaccines, up-to-date medical facilities, and 9-1-1 emergency response teams are often ill equipped to deal with such issues when working in remote areas. Many ethnographers describe the devastating impact illness and/or injuries had on their research and psychological well-being. Robert Dentan, who did his fieldwork with the Semai of Malaysia, reported that despite using a water filter and chlorine tablets and having typhoid and paratyphoid immunizations, he contracted amoebic dysentery, infectious hepatitis, and typhoid. He also noted that he worried about inadvertently grabbing the many plants with poisonous spines or bristles as he moved about the area. An earlier researcher to the area, P. D. R. Williams-Hunt, died from falling on a piece of razor-sharp split bamboo (Dentan 1970: 94–99). Nigel Barley, in his work in Africa's Cameroon, suffered from malaria, as did the daughter of Katherine Dettwyler who nearly died from a drug-resistant strain of the disease while with her mother in Mali.

Accounts of the physical and emotional trials fieldworkers undergo abound in the literature of fieldwork. Reading about them from the comfort of home or a library barely conveys the terror of actual experience. Dennis Werner tells of a scorpion sting that resulted in body numbness; violent, jerking muscle spasms; and a sense of suffocation while living among Brazil's Mekranoti Indians. A plane was called in by radio to evacuate him to a clinic 500 miles away (Werner 1990: 55–56). Napoleon Chagnon reported a similar experience while doing fieldwork among the Yąnomamö. "On the third day's march I began reacting violently to an insect bite, or a toxic plant, or a wild food that I had eaten. Large red welts appeared all over my body, I grew weak, nauseated, and developed diarrhea . . . my thirst became unquenchable, the itching and welts almost unbearable. . . . From time to time I had difficulty breathing, and was growing very alarmed about my condition" (Chagnon 1974: 174).

Lack of privacy often creates problems for Western ethnographers because we are enculturated to value it. Martha Ward reports in her work with the people of Pohnpei that key informants and others expressed pity for her solitude and brought female relatives to stay with her. "Privacy is a bad word in Pohnpeian; no one needs or wants an entire house to himself or herself. . . . I, however, craved privacy like a physical ache and lusted to be alone" (Ward 2005: 72). Napoleon Chagnon reports that "Privacy is one of our culture's most satisfying achievements, one you never think about until you suddenly have none" (Chagnon 1997: 16). Dealing with such issues contributes to culture shock.

The label **culture shock** is used to denote all of the resultant feelings and emotions people have when exposure to another society's culture makes them feel helpless, homesick, disoriented, angry, depressed, frustrated, or all of the above. (These are the most typical symptoms.) Actually, it is a large stew pot of emotions, and it is brought on because you are a stranger. You do not understand much of what is happening around you. You are embarrassed by your lack of ability to do things that any five-year-old member of this society can do. You are aware that you'll be in this setting for an extended period of time. As all of these feelings simmer, a voice inside cries, "What am I doing here? I'll never use the different verb tenses correctly or understand the significance of various forms of social address" or ". . . I just want to go home." It is not easy to admit to yourself that you are experiencing these things, let alone to admit it to others. As R. Lincoln Keiser recounted in his discussion of his fieldwork with the Vice Lords, a Chicago street gang, "On the streets of the ghetto I was functionally an infant, and like all infants, had to be taken care of. I did not understand the significance of most actions and many words. . . . When you are an infant in age, it is one thing to be helpless, but when you are twenty-nine years

culture shock
A label for the resultant feelings of homesickness, disorientation, helplessness, and frustration that occur after exposure to an unfamiliar culture.

old, it is quite something else. This feeling of helplessness was very difficult for me to handle. In the early part of my research it often made me feel so nervous and anxious that the events occurring around me seemed to merge in a blur of meaningless action" (Keiser 1979: 94–95). (Figure 3.1)

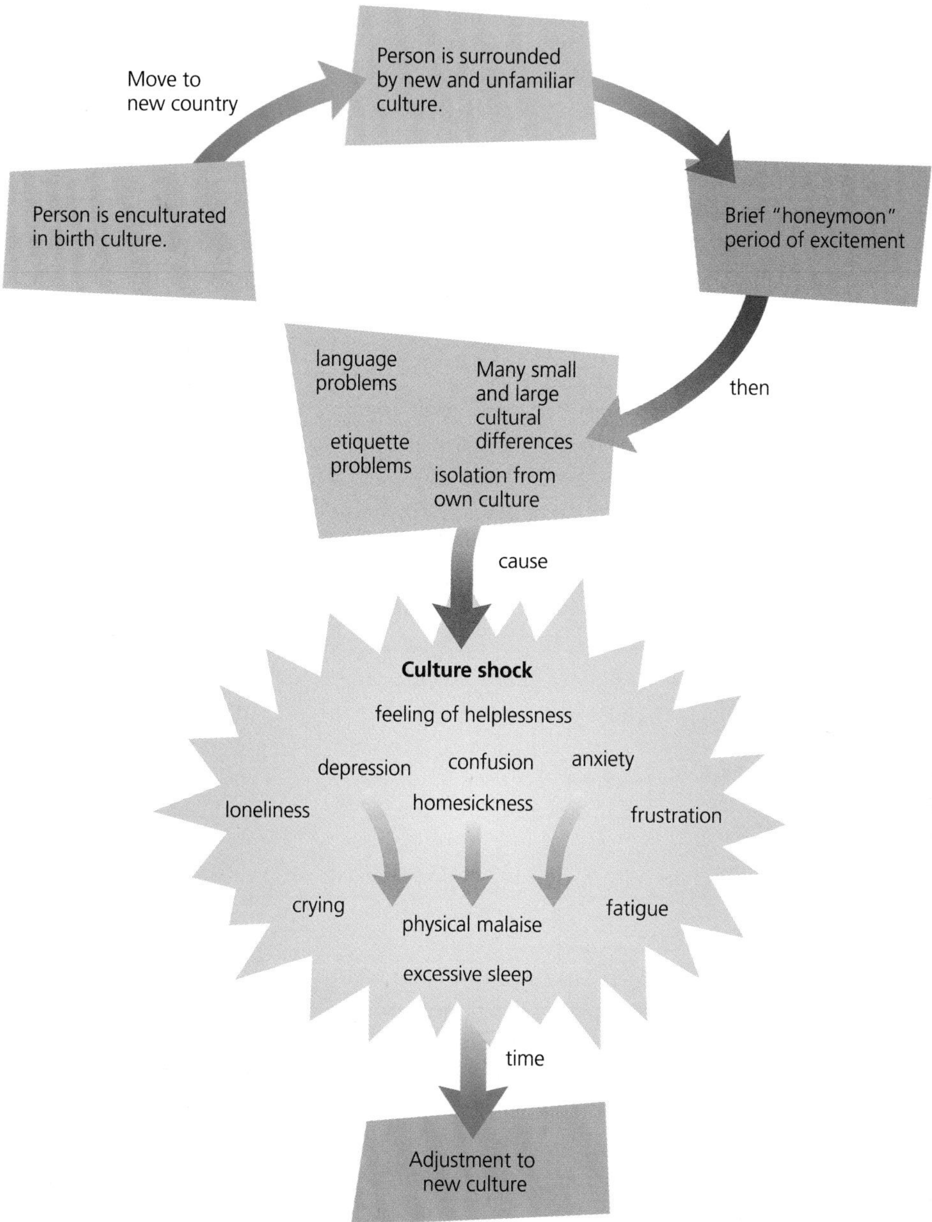

FIGURE 3.1 Culture shock is experienced when many small cultural differences overwhelm someone who is in a new cultural setting.

Virtually every ethnographer, whether working in a distant, exotic setting in another country or studying, for example, political processes in the capital city of his or her own country, has experienced culture shock to a greater or lesser degree. Many tourists have experienced culture shock even with fairly limited exposure to another cultural setting. Culture shock can happen at home too. I have had reentry students at my college confide in me that they experienced culture shock when they first returned to college. During the first two weeks they often felt disoriented and frustrated and wondered why they ever thought that they could return to school. They went home every day with a headache. But as they began to understand the academic culture and how to function within it, these symptoms subsided. It is the same way in long-term fieldwork situations.

Tourists often escape feelings of culture shock because they insulate themselves from a variety of experiences in other cultures. These are often the very situations that would give them a better understanding of what life is like in another society and culture. The choice of traveling with an organized group from one's own society, often composed of people from the same cultural or subcultural background, provides a highly choreographed experience. In such situations one has some exposure to the local culture—local cuisine, museums, architecture, dress, and plumbing. People speak a different language. There is usually a guide to handle major decisions like where to eat, sleep, or even shop for souvenirs. It is not unusual to have the guide be responsible for menu selections and room assignments. Airline, train, and bus connections are also handled by the guide, who is familiar with the local area. A protective or insulating group of fellow travelers usually keeps culture shock to a minimum.

TRY THIS
Identify

Identify symptoms of culture shock that you have experienced when joining in an activity of a subculture that is new to you.

Identify culture shock in an ethnographic account that you are reading as part of your class reading assignments. Note that the author often will not actually call the experience culture shock but instead will cite situations and feelings that illustrate the manifestations of culture shock.

My own symptoms of culture shock were brought on mostly because of difficulties with the language. It seemed that my several semesters of university-level Spanish courses and brief conversations with Spanish-speaking students had not prepared me to actually use the language. I was often corrected by Enrique for an incorrect usage of, for example, the subjunctive verb tense. At one level I knew that he was trying to be helpful, yet he never corrected my husband, who made many more mistakes than I did. I *knew* that this was a culture-specific gender issue (men did not correct other men, particularly in front of women), but it still created tremendous frustration at times during our first month in the community. Many other small issues contributed to culture shock. There was a lack of sufficient warm water for a shower. Our *cama de matrimonio* (double bed) did not adequately accommodate our tall frames. There were also time-consuming domestic chores, such as having to hang all of our wash on clotheslines outside our back window and then being on constant alert to quickly retrieve it when the frequent rain squalls began. We had to shop for meal preparation items each day because we had a very small refrigerator. Obtaining additional contact lens solution required an extended bus trip and consumed an entire day.

Energy is expensive in Spain, so most people dry their wash on lines that run outside of their windows.

Happily, culture shock passes as one begins to adjust to the new culture. I recall the first time I was able to make a little joke in Spanish to Enrique and was rewarded with a hardy laugh and his congratulations on the subtlety of my remark. And both my husband and I came to relish the daily trips to the bakery, the small market, and the fresh fish store where our preferences became known and we were always greeted with smiles. "*Señora, buenos días. Cuantos kilos de sardinas hoy?*" ("Good day! How many kilos of sardines today?") My family loved the small fresh sardines that were a local favorite.

Another experience that may confront an ethnographer is **life shock.** Life shock refers to a single sudden experience that is so unexpected that one does not have any time to deal with it psychologically. The result is that the person vomits, faints, or becomes hysterical. While in your own society, you function with an arsenal of psychological barriers that accumulated as you matured. We have become insulated to many unpleasant occurrences because we have seen actual events on the nightly news, on

life shock
A sudden unexpected experience that causes one to faint, become hysterical, or vomit. More likely to occur when immersed in an unfamiliar setting.

the streets where we live, or reenacted in the movies. It is possible to experience life shock in familiar surroundings, but it is more common when the subject is surrounded with the unfamiliar.

A former professor of mine described his experience of life shock while conducting his third field season in Southeast Asia. He was sitting just inside a thatched hut interviewing a woman he knew well about details of kinship organization. She was nursing her child. In an instant he smelled, heard, and saw that the baby had defecated in its mother's lap (babies wore no diapers); the mother continued talking about kinship, but gave a quick whistle, and a mongrel dog appeared and licked her lap and the baby's bottom clean. The fieldworker stumbled out the hut's door and vomited. While in the process, he reported that he actually thought "So this is life shock."

Establishing Rapport

Establishing **rapport** (a harmonious relationship) is an important ingredient for successful fieldwork. Techniques that have proven successful in accomplishing this include speaking the local language, respecting confidences, being generous with your time, and being forthright about your intentions and research. Most Americans have personally experienced being in a new school, new neighborhood, or new job. You have acquired some skills at meeting new people and trying to connect with them in a manner that will result in a positive working relationship. The same techniques generally work in other societies, although the ethnographer must carefully observe and ask for advice whenever possible.

Sometimes behaving in the manner of one's hosts will move relationships in the direction of good rapport, but one must proceed with caution. Napoleon Chagnon finally stumbled on this approach when first living among the Yąnomamö peoples of Venezuela. He had worked hard to cut a palm tree and make some boards to place on the bottom of his canoe in order to keep his gear dry. He discovered later that day that several Yąnomamö had made paddles for their own canoes by chopping up these new floor boards. Frustrated and angry he shouted at them, explained all of the work he had done to make the boards, and generally showed how he had suffered. As he tells the story, "Then, with exaggerated drama and finality, I withdrew my hunting knife as their grins disappeared and cut each one of their canoes loose and set it into the strong current of the Orinoco River where it was immediately swept up and carried downstream. I left without looking back and huffed over to the other side of the river to resume my work" (Chagnon 1997: 18). He was later told by the village headman, "with an approving chuckle" (Chagnon 1997: 18), that he had done the right thing. He goes on to discuss how his relationship

rapport
A harmonious relationship.

Ojibwa person making a string figure.

with the Yąnomamö improved whenever he stood up for himself and didn't let them bully him.

One technique for getting acquainted and initiating rapport that my family successfully used in Spain involved sharing **string figures,** as discussed in the vignette at the beginning of the chapter. We have used string figures in a number of different settings and in different countries, and they have always worked to create relaxed and enjoyable interactions. People also seem quite interested in the historical and cross-cultural perspectives about string figures and often ask where they can learn more. A short course of instruction on the topic is included in Appendix B (How Do You Make String Figures?), along with references and Web sites for you to visit and learn more. Enjoy!

TRY THIS
Analyze

Look in your assigned ethnographies and readings for examples of how anthropologists have established rapport. Authors seldom label activities that they employ to establish rapport as such, but now that you are alert to the importance of rapport in getting started in the field, you should be able to offer an analysis of how they achieved it based on the ethnographer's discussion. For example, Chagnon's act of cutting loose the Yąnomamö canoes helped to establish rapport.

string figures
A type of entertainment in which designs, or figures, are created by weaving string on the fingers. Patterns, tricks, and catches are performed and are often accompanied by stories.

GATHERING DATA

A comparison of the ethnographic literature reveals that there are a number of successful activities with which to begin gathering data. These activities are intermingled with adapting, getting settled, and gaining rapport.

Getting the lay of the land, both figuratively and literally, is basic. Making a detailed map of the area and doing a census are often the first activities employed to gather data because in most societies they are neutral and nonthreatening. This data may later be integrated with other data using Geographic Information Systems, a computerized data management system that is increasingly used in anthropological research. Spending time with people and talking with them, as well as offering to pitch in and help with chores, can give you time and opportunity to observe activities. Moreover, it gives the locals time to size you up and sort out their feelings about your presence. Of course, people will be curious about the ethnographer. The journal I kept of my time in northern Spain contains one such example. On the first day of our third week living in the area, I was paying for my daily purchase at the small local market, and the owner, a friendly man, questioned me as to how my husband and I were able to enjoy such a long holiday. I responded by telling him about our projects and how we came to this village and said that we would be there for several months. I was queried again in the bread store and later at the fish market. Locals were accustomed to visitors coming to the area for a week or ten days on holiday from the hot, central part of the country, but we had exceeded that time frame and they were interested to know why. That evening my landlord's wife, who owned the hair salon, told me that two of her clients that afternoon had recounted my conversation with the market owner!

Role of the Fieldworker

participant observer
The role of an anthropologist doing ethnographic fieldwork.

emic
An insider's view of a culture. This perspective in ethnography uses the categories and ideas that are relevant and meaningful to the culture under study.

etic
An outsider's view of a culture. This perspective in ethnography uses the categories of the anthropologist's culture to describe the culture under study.

participant observation
The process of an anthropologist doing ethnographic fieldwork.

The anthropologist in the field situation strives to achieve the role of **participant observer.** The ideal role is to participate in the society and learn about the culture and concurrently maintain the eye of an objective observer. One tries to see and experience the world as the native member of the culture does and record it. This insider's perspective is called the **emic** view. At the same time, the ethnographer aspires to present the analytical view of an objective observer. The outsider's view is labeled the **etic** view.

Participant observation has been at the heart of cultural anthropology since the early 1900s. Contemporary cultural anthropologists still rely on participant observation to give the uniquely anthropological perspective of a culture, subculture, or microculture. At the same time, we have incorporated sampling techniques developed by mathematicians and sociologists into our process of analysis, and these are used to gather data from large populations and to perform the statistical analysis of those data.

The ideal of participant observation is not without difficulty. The gender of the fieldworker, for example, may determine how he or she will be received in the field setting. One's gender may limit access to persons or events. Difficulties may arise for the participant observer that involve ethical issues. This is one reason the AAA has adopted a code of ethical

Ethnographers participate in the cultures they study. Here anthropologist Don Lenkeit helps his key informant with a load of firewood that is transported in a traditional horse cart with modern tires.

standards. Another potential problem involves objectivity. Something of the personality and cultural background of the individual ethnographer does show in ethnographic accounts. No matter how hard one tries, it is impossible to be totally removed and objective. Nevertheless, the unique view that ethnographers can gain by actually living and interacting on a daily basis with people is unparalleled in its potential. Although each culture and each ethnographer are unique, cultural patterns emerge from careful ethnographic studies. Restudies and comparisons can help us to fine-tune our hypotheses about the parameters of a particular society's culture and about the parameters of what it is to be human.

Recent ethnographic paradigms (postmodernism) and approaches (reflexive ethnography) acknowledge that it is a complex process. Some individuals would reject the idea that we can ever objectively describe another culture. They suggest that any description is abstract and incomplete at best, or that it contains the personal bias of the ethnographer at worst. Scientifically oriented ethnographers recognize these complexities and continue to do what science does—to as objectively as possible describe and offer explanations for human behavior. The self-correcting nature of science will continue.

TRY THIS
Analyze

Think of two reasons it might be necessary to select people to interview using a judgment sample. Do you think this form of bias is acceptable? Why or why not?

Sampling Methods

Historically, anthropologists have focused on small societies or small segments of larger societies, where during the course of their fieldwork they come in contact with and gather data from most of the inhabitants. When studying larger communities or societies, the anthropologist may become intimately involved as participant observer with a particular neighborhood and its people while gathering data from other segments of the population by employing sampling methods. A **random sample** aims at eliminating bias by giving everyone an equal chance of being interviewed or observed. This method in its most basic form involves placing each person's name on a slip of paper, placing the slips into a container, and then, without looking, reaching into the container, mixing the slips, and withdrawing a predetermined number. The names selected would constitute the sample; the sample's size would depend on the percentage of the population the researcher has decided to use as a database.

Households could be randomly selected by giving each house in the community a sequential number and then, using a mathematical table of random numbers, identifying the sample households from the compiled list. Random sampling can also be stratified (called a **stratified random sample**) by dividing the society's members into categories such as age, gender, wealth, and so on. A number of individuals are then selected from each category.

When the anthropologist selects informants based on her own evaluation of their knowledge, skills, or insights that may contribute to the depth or breadth of the study, the sample is called a **judgment sample.** The nature of participant observation is such that most ethnographers use data gathered from native members of the culture who have been selected using a judgment sample.

random sample
A sample method in which all members of a population have a statistically equal chance of being chosen.

stratified random sample
A random sample with divisions into categories such as age or socioeconomic level.

judgment sample
A sample that is chosen based on the judgment of the ethnographer.

informants
Native members of a society who give information about their culture to an ethnographer.

Problems with Sampling

The use of judgment sampling leaves anthropologists vulnerable to criticism because opinion and potential bias are involved. This is one reason that ethnographic research is said to be both a science and an art. Random sampling methods can also be criticized. Although in this case everyone has an equal chance of being selected in a random sample, such a sample may not yield the full range of knowledge, behaviors, and cultural values that are in fact part of the culture under study. This is particularly true if the sample size is small.

Use of Informants

Informants, members of the society under study who are interviewed about the various aspects of the culture, may be selected by random sample

Bronislaw Malinowski with some of his Trobriand informants. He was a participant observer among the Trobrianders for several years (1914–1918) and wrote several ethnographies about their society.

as noted above. Some prefer to use the terms *collaborator*, *teacher*, or *friend* rather than the term *informant*. Informants act as teachers and guides for anthropologists as they seek to understand various aspects of the culture of the society from the insider's perspective (emic view). Anthropologists select **key informants** using a judgment sample. A key informant is a member of the native culture who works closely with the fieldworker. Ethnographers are usually indebted to their key informants. Enrique, one of my key informants in the village in Spain, often anticipated my queries and wanted to make certain that I correctly represented his life, his community, and his country to all of my North American students. I was grateful for his sharp intellect, his political acumen in the community, and his friendship. Indeed, my daughter came to call Enrique and his wife, Teresa, *abuelo* and *abuela* (grandfather and grandmother), and she remembers fondly learning to prepare Spanish treats like *chocolate* (a hot chocolate made with whole milk that has special bar chocolate melted in it) and *churros* (a deep-fried pastry something like a doughnut) in Teresa's kitchen.

key informant
An ethnographic interview subject who has been selected by judgment sample; a knowledgeable native who plays a major role in teaching the ethnographer about the informant's culture.

Problems with using informants include the possibility of informants being untruthful or giving "ideal" rather than "actual" cultural information.

TRY THIS
Analyze

Review an assigned ethnographic reading and determine the interview methods used by the anthropologist. Can you make an educated guess about the method employed even if the ethnographer doesn't explicitly state the type of interviews given?

Such problems can usually be corrected with more time in the field, along with interviews and conversations with additional informants. Several ethnographers have had to discard months of data when inconsistencies and even coordinated group lying were uncovered by the fieldworker.

Interview Methods

Approaches to interviewing include **formal interviews** (also called **structured interviews**) and **informal interviews** (also called **unstructured interviews**). Formal interviews involve asking specific, scripted questions in the same sequence each time. Every interview is conducted in the same manner and, if possible, in the same setting. The attempt is made to eliminate as many distracting variables as possible. Any follow-up questions are also scripted. The goal of this approach is to solicit data that can be compared and validated.

Informal interviews are almost like a conversation—very open ended—and they are allowed to wander where the informant takes them. The ethnographer may ask something like "tell me about courtship customs" or "how does a person become a leader in your community?"

Formal Interviews. One advantage of formal interviews is the reduction of situational bias, because all respondents are asked the same questions in the same sequence and under the same conditions where possible. Another advantage is that comparable data are gathered. The ease of quantifying results is also an advantage. On the other hand, forcing the anthropologist to solicit responses that focus on the specific questions prepared by the fieldworker may be a disadvantage. The questions may not have centered on issues that are perceived to be important to the native. In short, the *wrong* questions may be asked and important questions may be missed. The time spent in this endeavor may inhibit or prevent the raising of additional issues that the interviewer deems important.

Informal Interviews. In an informal interview informants tell the ethnographer what is important to their culture. The interview can take place whenever an opportunity is present. Informants are more likely to reveal *actual* culture rather than *ideal* culture in a more relaxed setting. The primary disadvantage of informal interviewing is the difficulty encountered in quantifying information. In short, the fieldworker is less able to control the specific variables of the working hypotheses.

Problems with interviewing, whether formal or informal, often center on methods of recording the data. With informal interviews, the ethnographer may not be able to write down enough details of what the informant is saying, or an informant may carefully edit what he or she says if a tape recorder is being used or the ethnographer is observed writing down every

formal interviews
An ethnographic research method in which planned, scripted questions are asked of informants.

structured interviews
See *formal interviews.*

informal interviews
An ethnographic research method using open-ended questions that allow informants to talk about what they deem important.

unstructured interviews
See *informal interviews.*

word. This is where good rapport and honesty about your research is important in creating a comfortable interview situation.

One solution is to use only informal interviews during the initial part of data gathering and then, with the aid of key informants, to prepare a more formal set of interview questions or interview code sheets, which are forms with questions and common responses that can quickly be checked off during an interview.

Develop a set of questions, both formal and informal, and then interview an elder member of your culture. This can be an interesting and rewarding experience in its own right, but it will also give you some insight into the interview process and life history data.

Genealogical Method

When anthropologists began doing field ethnography, they often focused on small hunter-gatherer or horticultural societies. They found that everything revolved around kin relationships, and as a result much time was spent on gathering data about kinship relationships. The collection of such kinship information is called the **genealogical method.** Numerous patterns of such relationships emerged as this early field data began to be compared by ethnologists. Details of the types of categories that such data disclosed are delineated and discussed in Chapters 7 and 8.

Life Histories

Another method of gathering data in the field is to record **life histories** of individual members of the society. This involves extensive interviews and conversations with individual informants. Most ethnographers incorporate life histories with other data-gathering techniques because they are particularly useful in reconstructing something of events prior to the ethnographer's visit. The life history approach has also been the focus of research that resulted in the portrait of Nisa, a member of the African !Kung San peoples of the Kalahari Desert. *Nisa: The Life and Words of a !Kung Woman*, written by Marjorie Shostak in 1981, is a provocative look at the changes in San culture that Nisa experienced.

mhhe • com / lenkeit5e

See Internet exercises.

By comparing the life histories of a number of individuals within a culture, anthropologists find that patterns begin to emerge, which in turn provide a window to the changes that have affected a culture. This essential point reinforces the premise that culture is dynamic and continually in the process of change and adaptation. Of course, one must be cautious using information gained in a life history. Individuals often selectively remember events of the past and may even alter them in subtle ways.

genealogical method The ethnographic method of recording information about kinship relationships using symbols and diagrams.

life history The ethnographic method of gathering data based on extensive interviews with individuals about their memories of their culture from childhood through adulthood.

Photography

Visual anthropologist John Collier states that "the nonverbal language of photo realism is the language that is most understood interculturally and cross-culturally" (Collier 1967: 4). The still photographs that

Anthropologist Marjorie Shostak working with the San peoples in Botswana. Her work gives insights into women's roles in a foraging society.

TRY THIS
Ponder

Identify a travel or tourist experience you have undertaken with friends or family. Were there situations or places where the taking of photographs might have been inappropriate?

Assume that a group of foreign tourists has arrived in your community. Describe three places or situations where you would be uncomfortable having your photograph taken.

accompanied ethnography in the 1940s were soon accompanied by film, later by video records, and now by digital images. Photographs are a unique frozen image of an event or aspect of behavior and can be used as an analytical tool. In the investigation of proxemics (the space between people) or marriage ceremonies or the production of material culture, photographs have been especially important. The possibilities are endless. Some ethnographers take their own images and later ask informants about aspects of the image and what is happening in it. Others take film crews of photographic specialists to the field with them. The results give both anthropologists and the public unique insights into other cultures. Of course, there can be problems with taking photographs in the field situation. You may be viewed as a spy or be faulted for invading people's privacy. Consider, for example, how you might react if someone pulled out a video camera and recorded an argument you were having with your significant other. Sensitivity and ethical considerations must be maintained when using such techniques. During my stay in Spain, there were many times I would have liked to have recorded a particular image, but it was clearly inappropriate to do so.

ANALYZING DATA AND PREPARING A REPORT

The analysis of data begins in the field, but the majority of such work is done after the ethnographer returns from the field. Data are quantified and statistical analysis is completed. The development of computers has been a boon to comparative analysis of ethnographic field data. The quantitative data on food sources or data on residence patterns can be quickly assembled and analyzed.

The reporting of data gathered during ethnographic fieldwork may be in the form of an ethnographic monograph (a book about a single culture based on fieldwork). Articles based on fieldwork data are also

Anthropologist Richard Lee discusses the use of plants with several Ju/'hoansi foragers in the Kalahari Desert in Botswana. Lee's fieldwork and publications spanning many years gives us a definitive in-depth understanding of the foraging life.

reported in professional journals, such as *Current Anthropology* or *American Anthropologist.* Such articles are directed at research academicians and use a technical, formal style. Ethnographic data are also reported in the form of papers that are read at professional conferences. Short nontechnical articles are often written for publications such as *Natural History* (the magazine of the American Museum of Natural History) or *Smithsonian* (published by the Smithsonian Institution).

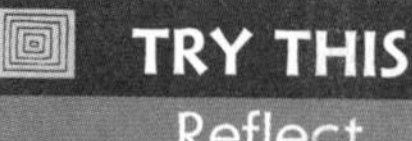

Does the availability of fieldwork data automatically open the people being studied to exploitation? Do subjects gain from being the focus of ethnographic fieldwork?

SUMMARY

Data gathered in a field setting are a hallmark of anthropological research and provide a unique perspective on other cultures. Ethnographers prepare for this experience by drafting a proposal and budget for the research and seeking funding. They draw on all of their background in anthropology when they enter the native community, whether it is a community in an urban setting, a business corporation, or a remote tribal village. The AAA Code of Ethics provides guidance to the ethnographer.

The adaptation phase of fieldwork includes arranging for shelter and food and coping with culture shock and sometimes life shock. The fieldworker must establish rapport with members of the culture while gathering initial data such as mapping and census taking. The active phase of fieldwork involves being a participant observer—literally observing behavior as objectively as possible and analyzing it (the etic view) while participating to the extent allowed by the local people. Random and judgment samples are used to select informants who will provide information about their culture. Key informants provide an insider's perspective (the emic view) and act as teachers and guides. Both formal and informal interview methods are used to gather information; each approach complements the other. Additional ethnographic methods commonly employed include the genealogical method, collecting life histories, and photography.

Study Questions

OLC
mhhe • com / lenkeit5e
See Self Quiz.

1. Discuss the field methods employed by anthropologists and the problems associated with each. Cite specific examples from ethnographic accounts that are part of your additional assigned reading.
2. Discuss both the importance and the limitations of participant observation in fieldwork.
3. Evaluate the use of formal and informal interviewing techniques, and suggest ways to determine the validity of the data gathered by each method.
4. Review your own work, school, and life experiences, and discuss a specific conflict situation in which the use of participant observation to gather data would have provided unique insights. Identify the sides in the conflict. Where did the "data" or information used by each side in the situation originate? How, specifically, might the data gathered by a trained anthropologist, who adheres to the anthropological code of ethics, help each side understand the other?
5. What are the primary ethical responsibilities of ethnographic fieldworkers?

Suggested Readings

OLC
mhhe • com / lenkeit5e
See Web links.

Barley, Nigel. 2000. *The Innocent Anthropologist: Notes from a Mud Hut.* Prospect Heights, Ill.: Waveland Press. This account of Barley's fieldwork in Cameroon leaves nothing out. Written in an engaging and wry style.

Bohannan, Paul, and Dirk Van der Elst. 1998. *Asking and Listening: Ethnography as Personal Adaptation.* Prospect Heights, Ill.: Waveland Press. A short, clearly written account of how anthropology developed the approach of ethnography and how it has changed from the 1880s to the present. Focuses on how everyone can use the ethnographic approach in their lives.

Hume, Lynne, and Jane Mulcock, eds. 2005. *Anthropologists in the Field: Cases in Participant Observation*. New York: Columbia University Press. A collection of essays addressing the many practical and ethical dilemmas encountered by fieldworkers in cultures near and far.

Orr, Julian. 1996. *Talking About Machines: An Ethnography of a Modern Job Review*. Ithaca, New York: ILR Press. This is a must-read for those interested in the application of ethnographic techniques. Orr describes his work for Xerox.

Spradley, James P. 1980. *Participant Observation*. New York: Holt, Rinehart and Winston. A step-by-step guide for conducting ethnographic research.

Language
Is This What Makes Us Human?

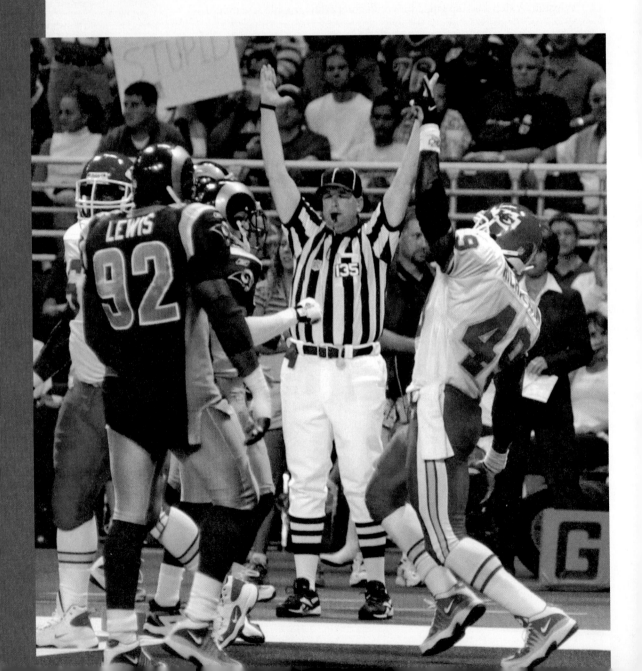

"*¿Cerveza?*" asked the woman behind the produce and meat counter at the small market. *Cerveza* means beer in Spanish. My husband repeated his request for "*un media kilo de cerezas, por favor*" [a half kilo of cherries, please]. This request was accompanied by exaggerated body language as he tilted his head, raised his eyebrows, and looked at the display of cherries in the box to his right. With a puzzled expression on her face that suddenly transformed into a smile, she said, "*¡Claro! ¿Queres cerezas, verdad?*" [Of course, you want cherries, correct?] "*Si, si,*" responded my spouse. The Castilian Spanish pronunciation was difficult for my husband. Learning a new language, one that has sounds that are not produced in one's native tongue, is difficult for most adults. The more different the sounds and the anatomy used to produce those sounds—teeth, tongue placement, and lips—the harder it seems to be. Children are more flexible. Our daughter speaks Spanish with barely a perceptible American English accent because she was immersed in Spanish as a child.

The study of language has a long history in anthropology, partly because of the preoccupation of early anthropologists with the study of aboriginal cultures. In order to conduct fieldwork in these cultures the ethnographers needed to speak the local language. These efforts led to studies of the structure of the language and to the writing of grammars and dictionaries. This work in turn led to investigations into differences in language usage within a culture, by age, class, and gender. Of course symbolic verbal communication may be combined with nonverbal symbolic communication. My husband often used this technique, as in the situation at the market. Because we were in a cultural setting where nonverbal cues were similar to those of our own culture, this strategy worked. Awareness of acceptable verbal and nonverbal symbols is important to avoid misunderstandings when one is in a different culture.

Symbolic communication is the foundation on which culture is built. Nearly all of what constitutes culture—cognitive processes, behaviors, and material creations—depends on some form of symbolizing. We use many forms of symbolic communication—spoken and written language, visual images, sounds, and fragrances—virtually anything that we can detect with our senses has been used as a symbol by humans. Our ability to symbolize is a unique human feature as far as we know right now. Language is our most important and most highly developed symbolic system. Some anthropologists have hypothesized that language actually shapes human perceptions.

The objectives of this chapter are to:

- Describe how anthropologists study language
- Discuss the relationship between language and culture
- Distinguish between human and nonhuman systems of communication
- Describe how nonverbal communication supplements verbal communication

◀ Gestures, uniforms, hats, and colors are part of a shared symbolic system understood by members of a culture. What is the individual with the upraised arms communicating?

An anthropologist shows native children in Kitari, Kenya, how to run a computer from a car battery. Record keeping and audio recordings are helpful tools in studying language in a field setting.

THE STUDY OF LANGUAGE

OLC
mhhe • com / lenkeit5e
See chapter outline and chapter overview.

OLC
mhhe • com / lenkeit5e
See Internet exercises.

Linguistics is the study of language. Language is a symbolic system consisting of sounds that are used to communicate thoughts and emotions. Linguists study language—how language is patterned and how it works, the history and development of language, and its relationship to other aspects of culture. To do ethnographic fieldwork, anthropologists have often had to begin by compiling their own dictionaries and grammars of the languages of the cultures they study because there are no formal language texts available similar to what we now associate with university-level language programs. Today, linguistics encompasses a number of research areas, including historical and descriptive linguistics. The relationship between language and culture is the focus of ethnolinguistics and sociolinguistics.

Descriptive Linguistics

The part of linguistics that focuses on the mechanics and patterning of language is called **descriptive linguistics.** To describe a language, a linguist must first describe the sounds used in the language under study.

descriptive linguistics The part of anthropological linguistics that focuses on the mechanics of language.

phonology The general study of the sounds used in human speech.

Phonology. The general study of the sounds used in speech is called **phonology;** phonetics includes the methods for describing the details of speech sounds. All of the sounds of human speech can be identified and described using the methods of phonetic analysis. Linguists use an internationally recognized system of symbols to represent the various sounds

TRY THIS Listen

This is a sample of the letter *a* in English, the dictionary symbols used to represent it, and key words for practicing the sound. Can you hear the differences in sounds? Much skill and practice are needed to accurately record the sounds used in a particular language.

Symbol in English Dictionary	Key Words
ă	fat, cat
ā	mate, ape
â	care, share
ä	car, are

of speech. Check out the key to pronunciation at the front of any dictionary for a sample of this symbolic system.

Regional dialects often result in different vowel phonemes being used for a word. In the United States, for example, the word *car* is pronounced differently in New Jersey than in Arizona.

Different languages use some of the same sounds and many that differ from the ones you use. Sounds can be described according to the anatomical parts that are used to create them, such as the vocal cords, tongue, teeth, and lips. For example, a labiodental fricative is a sound made using lips and teeth with friction created by passing the teeth over the lip. The English letters *v* and *f* are formed in this manner. Because we learn the sounds of our own language from birth, the sounds of other languages seem strange to us and are often difficult to copy. You have experienced different sounds, as well as the frustration of trying to create those sounds, if you have studied a second language. This is especially true if the language you are learning is quite different from your native language. George Lucas, writer and director of the *Star Wars* series of films, created distinctly different sounds and sound combinations as distinguishing features of the different galactic cultural groups represented in the films. Lucas acknowledges that he is a student of anthropology and that he uses insights gained from anthropological data when he creates his fantasy worlds.

Minimum units of sound are the building blocks of a language. English, for example, has forty-six minimum units of sound—many letters in the English alphabet have more than one pronunciation. The **phoneme** is the smallest unit of sound that will indicate a difference in meaning. Hence, in English, *p* (as in *pit*) is a phoneme. Another phoneme is *b* (as in *bit*). Each of these minimum units of sound when combined with the phonemes in the word *it* (which contains two phonemes) changes the meaning of the words—*pit* and *bit*. It is important to note that the *p* and *b* do not carry any meaning by themselves. Linguists use the International Phonetic Alphabet (IPA) of symbols to

phoneme
The smallest unit of sound in speech that will indicate a difference in meaning.

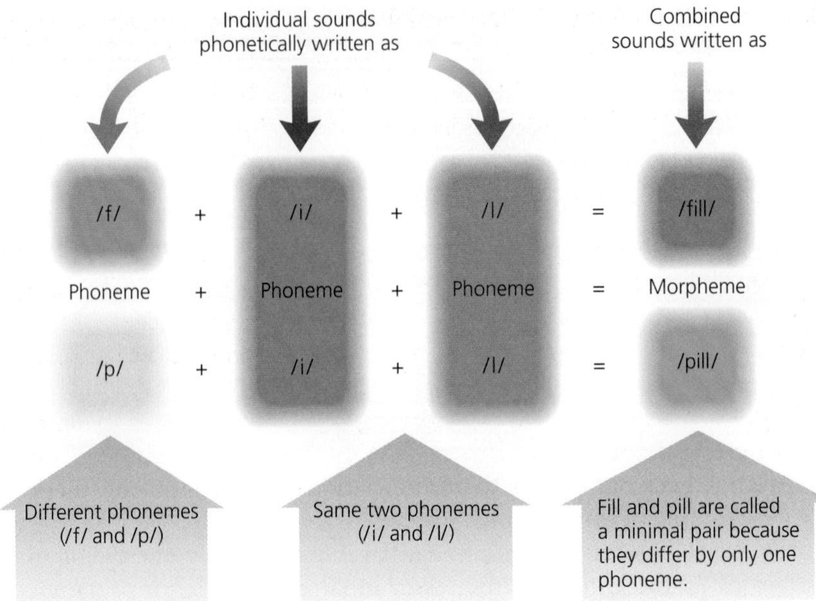

FIGURE 4.1
Phonemes combine to form morphemes.

denote all of the various sounds made in human speech. When IPA symbols are used to transcribe speech in a specific language, anyone familiar with the IPA will be able to correctly pronounce those words. (Figure 4.1)

TRY THIS
Compare

Can you think of any phonemes in the English language that can stand alone and carry meaning? What about in Spanish, German, Tagalog, or Mandarin? Ask your friends who speak other languages.

Morphology and Syntax. The other units of descriptive linguistics are morphology and syntax. The **morpheme** is the smallest combination of sounds that carry a meaning (e.g., *pit*). Each language has rules that govern how words are formed. In English, verbs must have a tense indicating when the action is occurring: past, present, or future. Often the tense is indicated by the addition of a morpheme to a root word—wash, wash*ed*, wash*ing*. The sentence *Dan wash Mary car* does not sound correct to a native English speaker, though it is in correct form for the sentence itself. That is to say, the subject, verb, and object are in the correct order. If the sentence is altered to read *Dan washed Mary's car*, it makes sense. English rules also dictate that the relationship between Mary and the car be included. Each language has such morphological rules about words that are often hard for nonnative speakers to learn. This is true because most languages have exceptions to their usual morphological rules.

morpheme
The smallest combination of sounds in human speech that carry a meaning.

syntax
The manner in which minimum units of meaning (morphemes) are combined.

Syntax is the manner in which minimum units of meaning (morphemes) are put together into phrases and sentences. In other words, syntax is what we English speakers would call grammar. Sentence structure in some languages will place verbs after nouns; in other languages the verb is placed first. Still others place the verb at the very end of a sentence. Differences in syntax present us with an interesting cross-cultural problem.

How do we explain these differences? Why have humans created so many ways to organize their grammars? And do these differences result in differences in our perceptions of the world around us? Linguists involved in the subfields of ethnolinguistics and sociolinguistics investigate these issues.

Historical Linguistics

Historical linguistics studies the relationships of languages to one another and reconstructs how languages change over time, though no general theory about the causes of change has been developed. One way to study language change takes the form of looking at how the phonology of a language changes over time. Shifts in vowel pronunciation, for example, have been studied. Linguists have established that all English long vowels underwent phonetic change during the fifteenth and sixteenth centuries that involved the raising of the tongue height toward the palate during pronunciation.

Social prestige seems to be a factor in which variations of pronunciation are adopted over time, as in the case of the word *meat* becoming pronounced like *meet.* Immediately after the vowel pronunciation shift noted above, the words *meet*, *meat*, and *mate* were pronounced differently. Then for a time *meat* and *mate* were both pronounced about like *mate* is pronounced today. Later *meat* changed to be pronounced like *meet*, the way the word is pronounced in standard language today (Weinreich et al. 1968: 95–188; Comrie 1997: 236).

Sophisticated statistical methods are now being used to quantify how words evolve over hundreds of years. One recent research group used this approach to analyze words from a comparative database of 200 basic vocabulary meanings in eighty-seven Indo-European languages. Data showed that words used less often, like *guts* and *dirty*, changed rapidly over thousands of years, while frequently used words such as *night*, *who*, and *two* evolved slowly (Bower 2007; Pagel et al. 2007).

Language and Culture

Ethnolinguistics is a specialized field that analyzes the relationship between a language and culture. It seems clear that culture influences language, certainly in the way that vocabulary is elaborated. There are many ethnographic examples of vocabularies that reflect adaptive features of a culture. I remember my fascination when first reading Evans-Pritchard's ethnography of the Nuer (1940), an East African pastoral society in the southern Sudan. I could scarcely believe that one could have so many words to describe a cow. There are hundreds of Nuer words used to describe cows—their color, color pattern combinations, and configurations of horns. Cattle are a central aspect of Nuer life. They provide food in the form of blood, milk, and occasionally meat. They are the primary currency

historical linguistics The study of the history of languages, including their development and relationship to other languages.

ethnolinguistics A field of study in linguistics that analyzes the relationship between a language and culture.

The Nuer of Sudan, Africa, use a rich vocabulary to describe their cattle. Young boys tend the cattle and often recite poems to their favorite animals.

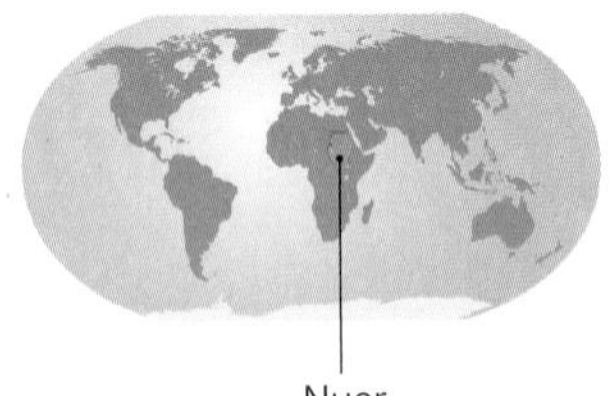

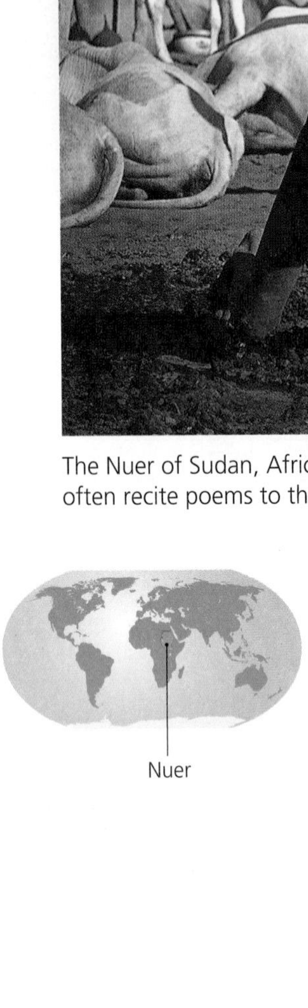

in bride price. Men can recite generations of genealogies of each of their cattle. Cattle serve as links with dead ancestors. Evans-Pritchard wrote that a knowledge of the rich vocabulary relating to cattle was central to working with and describing Nuer culture. I think of the Nuer each time I drive by cattle ranches and look at grazing cattle. My family has tried to delineate our own working vocabularies for describing cattle, and our vocabulary list is short indeed.

Even within microcultures the influence of culture on vocabulary is apparent. My daughter brought this to my attention when she was about three years old. We were standing with a neighbor in the back garden when suddenly my daughter said, "Look, Mom! There's a white-crowned sparrow together with the house finches at the bird feeder." My neighbor looked puzzled and said, "Do you mean one of those little brown birds?" My daughter's vocabulary for naming and classifying birds is a result of being in a family and social group that talks about birds a great deal.

The debate surrounding the influences of language on culture—or of culture on language—has been going on for decades. It is also a topic that has interested beginning students of anthropology because of its far-reaching implications. After studying the language of the Hopi and other cultures, Benjamin L. Whorf developed the idea that a language forces the native speaker of that language to perceive the world differently. Whorf worked closely with anthropologist and linguist Edward Sapir on issues relating to language and culture. Sapir focused more on culture influencing language: "Language is primarily a cultural or social product and must be understood as such" (Sapir 1964: 76). The **Sapir-Whorf hypothesis** states that language constructs our perception of reality. The English philosopher Ludwig Wittgenstein phrased the notion a bit differently when he suggested that the limits of language define the limits of one's world.

Early in the debate about the validity of this hypothesis, cultural vocabularies were often cited as examples of culture constructing realities. With this argument, the Nuer would "see" cattle differently from the way a North American (even a rancher) does because of the extensive vocabulary Nuer children acquired. Another argument put forth to support the hypothesis involves vocabularies to describe colors. Speakers of English usually name seven colors when viewing a rainbow—red, orange, yellow, green, blue, indigo, and violet. Shona speakers have only three names for the colors of the rainbow—orange, red, and purple are grouped under one word. Blue and green-blue are described by one term, and yellow and yellow-green colors are described with one word (Thompson 1975). Does this mean that Shona speakers see only three colors, or does it mean that they need or use only three terms in their daily life? Studies have clearly shown that all peoples can physiologically distinguish between small color variations. When two colors or two color hues are shown to individuals in various cultures and they are asked whether color A is the same as color B, everyone says that they are different. But when asked to name each color, they often will give one term for closely associated colors, as do the Shona speakers.

Data and testing have shown that the richness of vocabulary seems merely to give a more detailed map to one's world, not, as Sapir-Whorf suggest, a different reality. Typically, expanded and rich vocabularies correspond to items that are important to the culture.

Where the Sapir-Whorf hypothesis may have validity is in the area of verb usage and grammatical structure. Benjamin Whorf argued that the Hopi saw the world differently because they expressed verbs differently. Speakers of English have past, present, and future tenses, and thus they see the world as a linear sequence of events. Hopi, according to Whorf's analysis, have no past or future tense. Rather, they view things in one of two ways: things that are in existence *now*, and things that are in the process of *becoming*. Hence, according to Whorf, the past for the Hopi is viewed as events that accumulated in preparation for the present, rather than as a series of events that happened sequentially and are now over, which is how an English speaker would view the past. Whorf said that the things that

TRY THIS
Analyze

How is the vocabulary of a subculture or microculture to which you belong influenced by areas of importance for that subculture? Make a list of terms you use that describe something that is part of your microculture. Do friends who are not a part of the same subculture understand that vocabulary or the nuance of differences in attributes that the different symbols (words) represent?

Suggestion: Consider what specialized vocabulary is associated with a specific sport or job.

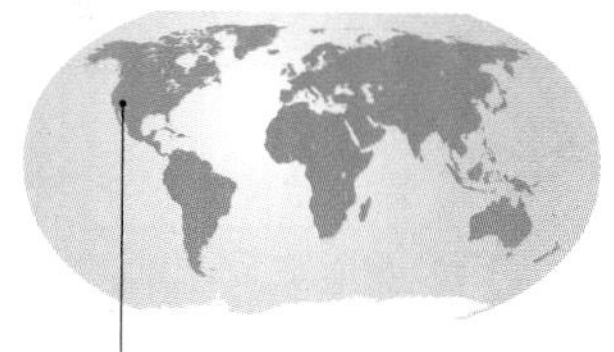

Sapir-Whorf hypothesis
A hypothesis about the relationship between language and culture that states that language constructs perceptions.

This North American Hopi may see the world differently than an English speaker due to the structure of his native Hopi language.

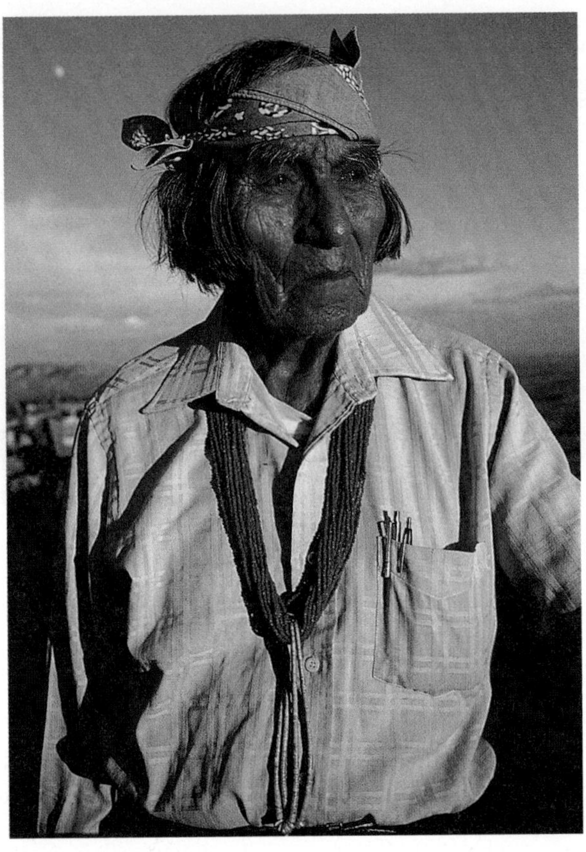

Hopi do now are part of preparing for things that will come. He believed that many of the activities of Hopi life were tied to these ideas of preparing, such as preparing the earth to plant and the many festivals and rituals associated with these preparations. According to Whorf, the Hopi perception of the world is different because of their language structure.

OLC
mhhe • com / lenkeit5e
See Internet exercises.

Others have contended that what Whorf saw was distorted. They argue that, because no one ever knows a second language and culture like a native, it is impossible to know exactly how people of another language and culture perceive the world.

The Pirahã (pronounced pee-da-HAN) of Brazil's Amazon rain forest present a recent and intriguing case in the debate over the Sapir-Whorf hypothesis and, moreover, the defining features of human language. Pirahã consciousness exists in the present. To them, only observable, immediate experience is real, according to linguist Daniel L. Everett (Everett et al. 2005; Stanlaw 2006). Everett reports that the Pirahã language lacks key features of most human language—no words for numbers, counting, or quantities such as *each*, *some*, *all*, or *most* and no vocabulary to describe colors.

In addition to words, the Pirahã communicate using whistles, singing, and humming. The Pirahã language has few verb tenses and no convincing evidence of the use of clauses or phrases in sentence construction. The use of clauses and phrases embedded within sentences is termed **recursion** by linguists and is considered a distinctive feature of human language. Everett also notes that two other features of language, productivity and displacement, are restricted by Pirahã culture (these features are discussed later in this chapter under the heading "Human Versus Nonhuman Systems of Communication"). A critic of Everett's work, psycholinguist Peter Gordon, spent several months in Brazil testing Pirahã counting abilities. In one task he asked participants to match numbers from one to ten with objects he showed them by lining up small AA batteries. He concluded that, like Australia's Warlpiri, they use counting words, *one*, *two*, and *many* but could not handle quantities over three (Gordon 2004; Bower 2005). Everett disputes Gordon's assertions about Pirahã counting words, saying he misinterpreted them (Bower 2005: 377; Colapinto 2007: 127). For example, Everett says that the word Gordon thought meant *one* actually refers to a small size or amount. He argues that it was only after spending the equivalent of seven years among the Pirahã that *he* grasped the subtleties embedded in their language. He further asserts that linguistic studies that rely on translators without the linguist himself gaining fluency and understanding the culture may lead to missing nuanced aspects of grammar.

Everett believes the Pirahã case supports the notion of culture shaping language (Sapir's focus). Noam Chomsky, a leader in linguistic theory, rejects the Sapir-Whorf hypothesis that language and culture influence each other and advocates the idea of universal grammar—that all humans are *genetically endowed* for language structure. Recursion, says Chomsky, is a cornerstone of this structure (Chomsky 1988; Hauser et al. 2002). A recent article by S. Kerby, M. Dowman, and T. L. Griffiths presents research on the evolution of language structure that underscores the

TRY THIS Analyze

The recursive feature of language allows clauses to be embedded in or added to sentences. Daniel Everett gives this example of recursion and the lack of it in the Pirahã language.

English speakers might say: *When I finish eating,* (clause) *I want to speak to you.*

The Pirahã have no way to say this. Instead they would use two simple sentences: *I finish eating. I speak to you* (Everett in Bower: 2005: 377). Analyze the following sentence and identify the clauses or phrases: The girl who was on the bike in the park rode home.

recursion
A feature of language that allows for the generation of variations in sentences by using embedded or added clauses and phrases.

important role of culture. They focus on interactions between three adaptive systems—biological evolution, experiential learning, and culture (Kerby et al. 2007). Many journal articles and Internet blogs weigh in on this issue and debate the veracity of Everett's claims. Yet Everett has strong credentials and worked on his Pirahã material for twenty-seven years before publishing his data and analysis. His research has certainly stirred up the anthropological community and may lead to a reevaluation of both theory and practice in linguistics.

The evaluation of the relationship between language and culture is the primary task of **sociolinguistics.** Issues considered in this area of focus include different language usage among socioeconomic classes and among various groups and in various social situations or contexts. We all subconsciously switch between the content and structure of the language we use in different situations. When talking to a grandparent, you don't speak in the same way you do when enjoying an evening out with peers or at a job interview. Much can be learned about social relationships and status by paying attention to the way people talk.

Language is a marker of social class and stratification. This was demonstrated by a study in England by Trudgill (1974), who showed how parallel patterns of speech are used by different classes. In this study, class membership was based on criteria such as occupation, father's occupation, education, and income. Higher-class speakers used standard forms of pronunciation whereas lower classes used nonstandard forms. For example, upper-class speakers used *ing* (written phonetically as /ng/) in words such as runn*ing*; by contrast, lower-class speakers used *n* (written /-n/ phonetically) to pronounce the word as runn*in* (Bonvillain 2000: 142). Other parallel patterns also clustered within class groupings.

Ethnicity also has an impact on language usage. In the United States the subsystem of English known as African American Vernacular English (AAVE) has been studied extensively in both its social and linguistic components. The origins of AAVE appear to come from two sources, although this is debated in linguistics. AAVE has features of phonology and morphology that seem to derive from white southerners (whose speech reflects their Scots-Irish ancestors). It also contains rules of syntax that derive from Creole. Like other languages AAVE has rich variations that adapt to situational contexts such as social factors (formal or informal situation), topics of conversation, and status relationships between individuals participating in the conversation. It is often used to show solidarity between a speaker and someone she or he is talking to. Many members of the African American community—working- and middle-class African American adults, African American students on college campuses, and rap and hip-hop artists—use AAVE to symbolize community membership, regardless of whether they were enculturated in the use of AAVE (Bonvillain 2000; Morgan 2001).

sociolinguistics
A subfield of linguistics that analyzes the relationship between language and culture with a focus on how people speak in social context.

The Complexity of Languages

Does your language have a word for the back of the knee or the place in the arm that is at the front of the elbow?

All human languages are complex. None is more difficult than another. It is our ethnocentrism—based on our own phonemes, morphemes, and syntax—that makes other languages seem more difficult or complex than ours. Of course, the more similar a language is to one's own, the easier it seems to be to learn. If one were to argue for one language being more complex than another, one would have to delineate criteria and then, depending on those criteria, measure the complexity of the languages in question. But what is the point of such an exercise?

All languages have different ways to categorize observable variations in the natural world. We, in a sense, create word maps of our world. Every language's mapping technique is different. The symbols used to denote locations on the map (phonemes and morphemes) vary, as do routes for getting from one place to another (syntax). These different maps will result in difficulties when translating from one language to another. If we compare the anatomical vocabulary of English with that of other languages, for example, some insight can be gained. Picture a human arm and add labels for its parts. For example, in English we have the words *arm*, *hand*, and *fingers*. The Arawak of South America distinguish between *daduna*, the upper arm and shoulder, and *dakabo*, the hand and lower arm. How would an Arawak who has learned English translate a speech in which the English word *hand* is used? She would likely use the term *dakabo* (Hickerson 1980: 107). Those of you who have learned another language know of many instances in which there is no English equivalent to the concept in Spanish, Chinese, Japanese, German, or French.

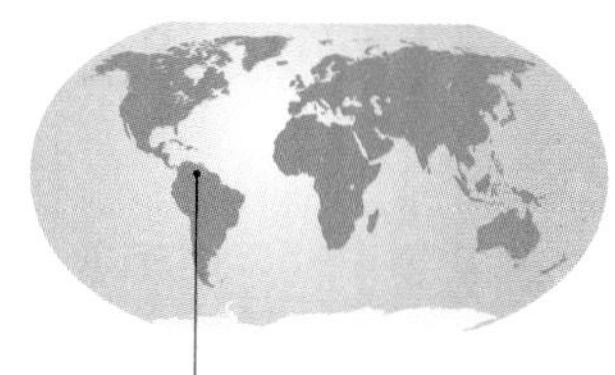

HUMAN VERSUS NONHUMAN SYSTEMS OF COMMUNICATION

How does human language differ from the communication system of other animals? Aspects of language that have been identified as being unique are production (including recursion) and displacement. As far as we are currently able to determine, these aspects of language are found only in human language.

Symbols can and do change. Humans produce new symbols as a need arises. The word *Internet* was created in 1985 to describe a new communication system using computer technology. Additionally, we adjust or reassign meaning to already existing symbols when need or whim dictates. The word *mouse* acquired a new meaning when used to describe a mechanical object with a wire attached that is used to move a cursor on a computer screen. Reassigned meanings are found in the sentence "Allison is surfing the Web." A generation ago these symbols referred exclusively

ANTHROPOLOGY AROUND US

Language and Gender

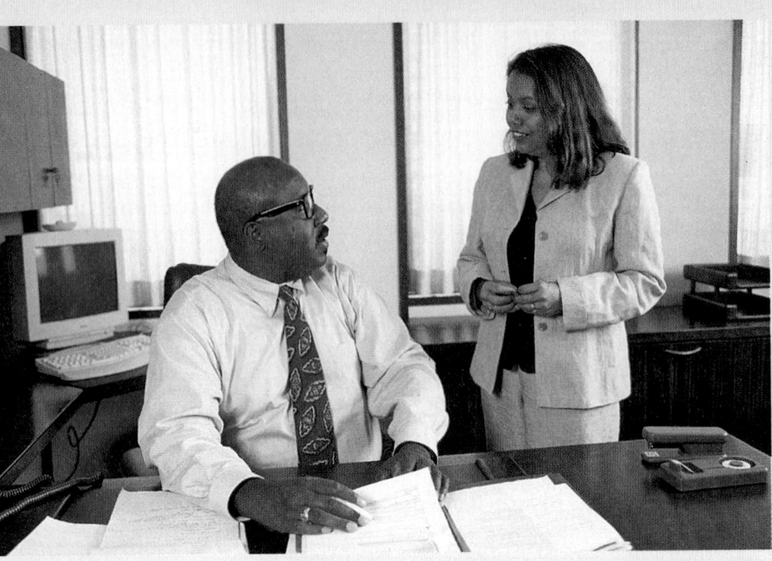

The ethnographic literature is resplendent with examples of gender differences in language usage. Closer to home each of us confronts such differences daily. Gender-neutral terms such as *chairperson* and *mail carrier* have replaced gender-specific terms *chairman* and *mailman* in most areas of North American life. Less obvious gender distinctions have been brought to our attention but are changing slowly, if at all.

Deborah Tannen tells us that men hear and speak a language of status and independence. Women, by contrast, hear and speak a language of intimacy and connections. She argues that we are enculturated this way. Boys learn their approach to language as they play sports, where the group is structured and status is earned and negotiated. Boys show off, boast, and compete to win. Girls play most often in pairs or small groups; intimacy is important in these settings; and peer pressure causes even bright, talented girls to be humble. Tannen also argues that boys learn to be direct with their speech whereas girls learn to be indirect. A female boss asks her secretary to *please* type a letter and to *do her a favor* and hold any calls while she is in a meeting. A male boss is usually more direct, simply telling the secretary to type the letter and hold the calls. These differences in approach are learned and gender specific. A man may view a woman boss who asks someone to please do something as a favor to her to be showing self-deprecation and weakness. A woman may view indirectness as a way to create rapport (Tannen 1990, 1994, 2005).

◎ Have you been in a boss-employer situation in which gender differences, as mentioned here, were obvious? Did you consider this to be gender-specific language behavior, or did you interpret it another way?

displacement
The ability of humans to communicate symbolically about distant time and place.

to riding ocean waves and to something spun by a spider. We humans also regularly produce new sentences with new messages and new ideas. These can be endlessly expanded using recursion—the embedding of clauses and phrases in sentences.

The creative flexibility of the human symbolic system enables communication about distant time and place—this is called **displacement.**

We can think about or discuss events in the past or the future, or events that are not within immediate proximity to our senses. Human communication is called an open system because it has both of these features: production (the creation, combination, or alteration of symbols) and displacement. Scientific studies of the communication systems of other animals show limited and unchanging numbers of vocal signals. Moreover, the call sounds that are used always communicate about objects and happenings within the immediate experience of the animal, such as finding food or encountering danger. Calls are specific and discrete and cannot be combined. Such communication systems are referred to as closed systems. The longitudinal research study of communication among the Gombe population of chimpanzees in Africa provides no evidence of new sounds being created nor any evidence of these animals being able to displace with vocalization. Young chimpanzees learn their behaviors from their social groups through imitation combined with trial and error. Young humans use these forms of learning as well, but the overwhelming amount of what we humans learn is acquired through the symbolic process of language.

Some other animal species, notably various primate species, have been taught human symbolic communication in laboratory settings. American Sign Language (ASL) has been taught to chimpanzees and gorillas, for example. These animals are able to learn some of the ASL symbols created by humans, and once they have learned them (and presumably the concept behind them), they have, in fact, both created and displaced using ASL. These animals, however, do not create or displace using the call systems of their species as far as science is currently able to determine. The chimpanzee Kanzi clearly uses symbols and has acquired a vocabulary of over 150 lexigrams. He and other apes were taught using geometric figure symbols called **lexigrams** rather than with ASL. They too can displace. Controversy exists, however, over whether Kanzi and the others make and use syntax. They do place symbols in order, but this is limited to compositions that equal those of human children of about two years of age (Foley 1997: 77).

Recall that Noam Chomsky contends that humans are born with innate attributes for acquiring language. He argues that the role of the culture that we grow up in is of secondary importance in language acquisition. The data from the various ape studies suggest that the chimps, with whom we share a recent biological past, may have some innate attributes for acquiring and using a symbolic system. Does this support Chomsky's view regarding human language?

Nonhuman primates also use some forms of nonverbal communication within their social groups—postures, gestures, facial expressions. Research on chimpanzees in the wild, for example, shows that there are traditions of nonverbal communication and these vary between populations. These communications are learned through direct observation and imitation; they

lexigrams
Geometric figure symbols used to teach apes symbolic communication.

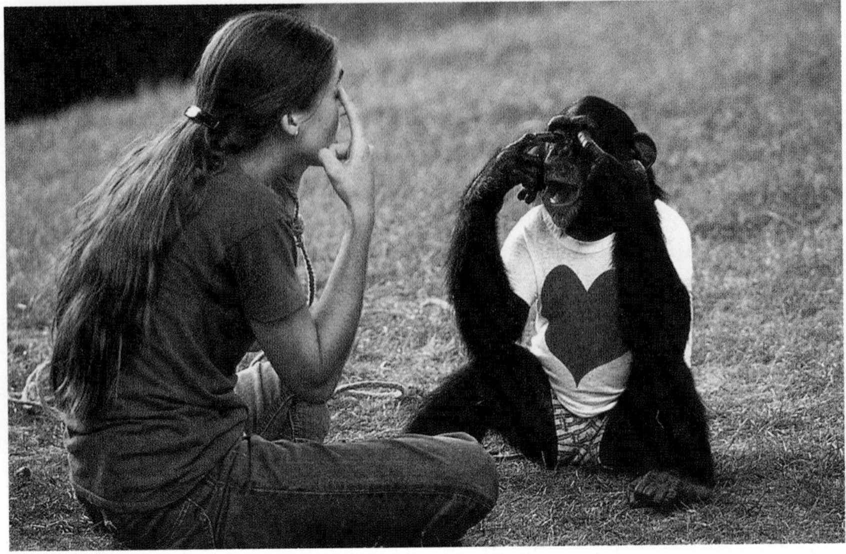

This primatologist is interacting with a chimpanzee using American Sign Language (ASL). Female chimps who have learned ASL have been observed using signs with their offspring.

are not genetically based (instinctual). Among human primates, nonverbal communications are important forms of symbolic communication that often combine with spoken language.

SILENT LANGUAGE AS PART OF SYMBOLIC COMMUNICATION

Emblazoned on the cover of *Newsweek* magazine on February 5, 1973, was a photograph of a U.S. serviceman smiling at the camera and holding up his right hand with his index and middle fingers extended and separated forming a V. His ring finger and pinkie were bent and held against his palm with his thumb, and the back of his hand faced toward the camera. The word *peace* was boldly printed just below the *Newsweek* logo. Many Americans probably didn't give this a second glance, assuming that the GI was flashing the gesture for peace. Some Europeans recognize this silent language symbol as an obscene gesture. It conveys the same message as the extended middle finger to an American. It is possible that this GI was making an obscene gesture to communicate his views at that point in history. Given a second, closer look at the photo, one notices that the serviceman's smile looks odd. It's not a broad, tooth-showing grin Americans would associate with great joy, but one of wry cynicism. What does this gesture mean today in your subculture?

silent language
All of a culture's nonverbal symbolic systems of communication, including kinesics and proxemics.

Nonverbal communication was labeled silent language by Edward T. Hall. **Silent language** refers to the myriad nonverbal ways that we

Rapper Jay-Z gives one of his often used gestures. Fans (members of a particular music subculture) share and understand the meaning of this and other gestures used in the rapper and hip-hop music world.

communicate within a culture. Such communication may take the form of (1) kinesics (the use of the body), (2) proxemics (the use of space), (3) cultural time (the use and treatment of time), (4) words, (5) silence, and (6) material culture. Silent language symbols are learned, as are all aspects of culture, through the enculturation process. Silent language can be one of the most difficult aspects of another culture to learn because it is not formally taught. It can be misinterpreted by people with different cultural or subcultural backgrounds. Lack of awareness of another culture's silent language can lead to embarrassment and misunderstandings. Because it easily generates frustration, it can feed one's ethnocentrism. Lack of awareness of silent language may even be dangerous, as in the case of inadvertently wearing a gang's colors or using a gesture that carries a confrontational message. Silent language is a powerful form of communication.

Kinesics

The opening paragraph of this section describes an example of kinesics. **Kinesics** is the study of the use of the body in communication. Specific kinesic studies analyze cultural gestures, facial expressions, and body positions. Common gestures such as the North American A-OK sign, made by placing the forefinger and thumb in a circle, can create misunderstandings outside of the United States. In some countries this gesture refers to a part of the anatomy and is used as a grave insult. In Japan it means money, and

kinesics
The use of the body to communicate—gestures, posture, and facial expression.

TRY THIS
Experiment

Stop giving any silent language cues during a conversation. Keep your face blank and head immobile. Continue the conversation, but do not use any kinesics. How long does it take for the person you are conversing with to ask, "What's wrong?" After you've tried this, use the opportunity to explain or discuss kinesics with your friend. Be certain to note that kinesics are different in other cultures.

in France it means that you think someone is a zero. In Malta and parts of Italy at one time it was a male homosexual gesture soliciting sex.

The familiar North American "come here" gesture of motioning with the palm held up, fingers folded into palm, and the index finger alternately extended and crooked toward the body can also be insulting when viewed through the lens of another culture. A student of mine from the Philippines recounted that an older relative of his, a recent immigrant to the United States, quit a job as a busboy in a restaurant because he constantly felt insulted when people would use this gesture toward him. In the Philippines this gesture is used to call animals, and the older relative felt that he was being treated like a dog. Because he was enculturated to interpret the gesture in a different way, even when the North American meaning was explained to him, the gesture made him very uncomfortable.

Remember that gestures are symbolic and the meaning assigned to them may change from time to time even within one culture. For this reason, I believe that it is more important to be alert to silent language issues rather than simply to memorize the meaning of gestures for various cultures.

We are all familiar with facial expressions, and most of us do a good job of reading them within our own culture. We've all had friends ask us if something is wrong when we thought that we were hiding our sadness or pain. Something about our facial expressions or the way we were holding our bodies communicated our true emotion. A student who was enculturated in Cambodia remarked that in his culture it was considered an insult and very bad manners to look at a teacher when she was talking to you. He was confused when he first entered an American classroom. He said that even after seven years in the American school system it was hard for him to look instructors in the eye when they spoke. In traditional American culture, people who don't look at you when you speak are considered inattentive and shifty, or even dishonest.

Body positions, such as arms tightly folded across the chest, also communicate. Actors are particularly good at studying and using body position as a means of communicating an attitude or emotion. The next time you watch a movie, try to articulate what it is about the body position and movement used by a particular actor that is communicating to you. The process of interpretation or reading of silent language cues happens almost instantly, and researchers are currently attempting to understand this complex process (Archer 1980).

Proxemics

proxemics
The study of the use of space in communication.

Another area of silent language is called **proxemics,** the study of how people of different cultures and subcultures perceive and use space.

Touch, spacing, and territorial distance between bodies are all aspects of proxemics.

According to Edward T. Hall (1959), the use of space within middle-class American culture is broken into four main distances in social relations and business: intimate, personal, social, and public. Those who have been enculturated into the middle-class American subculture understand these proxemic categories very well, though they were never formally taught about them. When sharing intimate information with a friend, middle-class Americans move in close, usually about six to eighteen inches. We lower the volume of our voices to a whisper or near whisper and share the bit of gossip or personal thought. As we grew up, we also learned about how far away to stand in ordinary conversation, and we learned to use the appropriate voice level. We become aware of these cultural spatial distances when someone violates them.

A visitor from a Latin American country, for example, often stands in our *intimate* space while using a voice level that we would use in personal or social distance. The middle-class American's reaction is to back away, trying to get comfortable with the distance. The Latin American visitor is suddenly uncomfortable and tries to move closer. The ethnocentric voice in the American's head is beginning to register: pushy, pushy Latin. The Latin's ethnocentric inner voice is beginning to say cold, standoffish North American. Unless one or both are culturally aware, unpleasant feelings will likely arise about the other person. If this happens to take place within the context of a business meeting, it does not bode well for the outcome of negotiations. It must be noted that this is an example only. Within Latin America, there are variations in the details of proxemics, just as there are proxemic variations within most societies.

At a state dinner in Korea, then-president Bill Clinton made a protocol flub involving spacial expectations. When Clinton stepped to the microphone for his after-dinner speech, he invited a translator to stand between himself and Korean president Kim Young Sam, who was seated. It is an insult in Korea for anyone to stand between two heads of state. The breach of protocol was reported by the world press.

Cultural Time

Time is another aspect of silent language. For the American business executive in an Arab country, frustrations about time can be particularly annoying. Five minutes in American time is about fifteen minutes in Arab time. To an American executive, a fifteen-minute wait in an outer office requires an apology. To an Arab, the equivalent cultural time would be forty-five minutes. The American feels that the Arab is rude indeed for being so late. The Arab feels right on time or even a bit early for the appointment and perceives that the American has been pushy and uptight. Looking anthropologically at the situation, we see that the Arab has only made the American wait the equivalent of about three minutes, U.S. time. The two simply operate on different value systems of expectation regarding time. We are enculturated to function with one particular concept of time. Awareness and understanding of different silent language systems is clearly important for international understanding in business and politics. The challenge is for us to acknowledge and learn to respect cultural differences at all levels.

Ritualized Phrases

TRY THIS
Consider

List four words or phrases you commonly use that carry meanings other than the literal, dictionary meanings and could cause problems for a newly arrived foreign student on your campus. Compare your list with that of another student.

Words and phrases may have meanings other than the formal, generally recognized ones. Symbolic meanings of common words are usually understood by members of a culture. This can, however, be quite confusing to members of other cultures. The phrase "see you later" caused many problems for foreign students at my college. In many cultures, customs of hospitality dictate that "see you later" means, literally, that the person expects to *see you later.* Foreign students report feelings of frustration when expecting to see a new friend stop by their apartments and the person never comes. Or the foreign student drops in on the new friend and is received with an uncomfortable coolness. Such experiences result in the new student viewing American students as unfriendly. Eventually they come to realize that "see you later" is merely a ritualized phrase of departure.

Silence

Silence is also a form of nonverbal communication. Its use is situationally dependent, and there is much variation in its use within a culture. In American culture, and most other cultures where this has been studied, status and social hierarchies are revealed in studies of silence. When two individuals of unequal social standing interact, high-ranking individuals talk more and low-status individuals are silent more (Bonvillain 2000: 44).

Material Culture

Artifacts and features are also part of silent language communication. Members of a particular culture share an understanding of the symbolic meaning of their material culture, and someone from another culture

Material objects and artifacts often communicate socioeconomic information to members of a society. Compare these two North American family residences.

does not. Artifacts such as clothing, jewelry, home furnishings, and make of vehicle can silently communicate about issues such as socioeconomic status, ethnic group membership, and job status. On our campus, wearing Wrangler jeans and a leather belt with a silver buckle communicates that this student is an aggie (agricultural major). Features such as backyard swimming pools or the number of household bathrooms also communicate socioeconomic status.

TRY THIS
Research

Ask an elder in your family to identify a material artifact from her youth that conveyed a person's socioeconomic status. Does this artifact symbolize the same status today?

SUMMARY

Language is a symbolic means of communication. Because it is the primary means by which humans acquire culture, its structure has been studied by anthropologists. The phonology, morphology, and syntax of language involves detailed analysis. Human language differs from the communication systems of other animals because we have *open* systems in which new symbols are produced and displacement is a feature. The call systems of other animals are *closed* systems of communication because the features of openness and displacement have not been demonstrated to be present. All human languages are equally complex.

The nonverbal symbolic communication systems of silent language are important aspects of culture—kinesics, proxemics, time, words, silence, and artifacts with alternate meanings. They are examples of cultural behaviors that we gain through enculturation and rarely think about, though they are powerful agents of communication. A lack of awareness of differences in silent language can lead to embarrassment and misunderstanding that can significantly undermine cross-cultural communication.

Study Questions

OLC
mhhe • com / lenkeit5e
See Self Quiz.

1. What are the types of studies that are undertaken by anthropological linguists?
2. What is silent language? Discuss how a knowledge of silent language is important if one is engaged in international travel or business. Cite examples from readings, the Internet, or print media to illustrate your discussion.
3. Describe three aspects of silent language that are discussed in one of your assigned ethnographies and cite specific examples.
4. Discuss how human language is different from the communication system of wild chimpanzees.

Suggested Readings

OLC
mhhe • com / lenkeit5e
See Web links.

Bonvillain, Nancy. 2007. *Language, Culture and Communication: The Meaning of the Messages*, 5th ed. Upper Saddle River, N.J.: Pearson. An introduction to the many meanings of language and how these meanings are used. Demonstrates the similarities and differences in human language.

Duranti, Alessandro, ed. 2009. *Linguistic Anthropology: A Reader*, 2nd ed. Malden, Mass.: Blackwell. A sophisticated mix of classic articles and new research in anthropological linguistics.

Foley, W. A. 1997. *Anthropological Linguistics: An Introduction.* Malden, Mass.: Blackwell. Wide-ranging coverage of anthropological linguistics. If you have only one book on the subject, this is the one to have.

Hall, Edward. 1940. *The Silent Language.* New York: Anchor Books. This remains one of the most readable and concise introductions to the cross-cultural impact of nonverbal symbolic systems.

Tannen, D. 2001. *You Just Don't Understand: Women and Men in Coversation.* New York: Quill. A popular treatment on gender differences in conversation styles.

PART

2

CROSS-CULTURAL ADAPTIVE PATTERNS

FOR AT LEAST 2 MILLION YEARS MEMBERS OF OUR GENUS (*HOMO*) HAVE HAD TO COPE WITH THE SAME BASIC ISSUES THAT ALL PEOPLE ON EARTH ENCOUNTER TODAY. We all have to eat. We require protection from natural elements. We must cope with other inhabitants of our territories—from viruses and varmints, flora and fauna, bacteria and beasts to family, friends, and foe. We have to manage interpersonal relationships, including group decision making and conflict. We need to express ourselves and consider issues such as why we are here, why things happen, and what happens after we die. These issues are interwoven, and each culture has evolved ways to address them. Many choices have been made along the way.

Part II of this text gives a summary of what we know, or believe we know, from over one hundred years of cultural anthropology. My goal is to present the results of widespread comparisons of ethnographic data—in other words, the results of ethnological analysis. I will organize this information within a loosely structured evolutionary-ecological framework. A uniform perspective is achieved when materials are organized in this manner, and it makes for a good starting point. Using this format also encourages critique and debate, and you'll find that there is quite a bit of this in the literature—and rightly so, because lively debate is what pushes science forward and ultimately leads to understanding.

The chapters in Part II are grouped together because they represent topics and issues common to people everywhere. Anthropologists have studied these topics for generations. The adaptive strategies discussed are diverse in detail, but many similar *patterns* emerge when ethnological analysis is employed. These patterns are emphasized in each chapter.

◀ Crickets are being harvested in China to supplement the local diet.

Subsistence Strategies and Resource Allocation I

What Challenges Face Foragers?

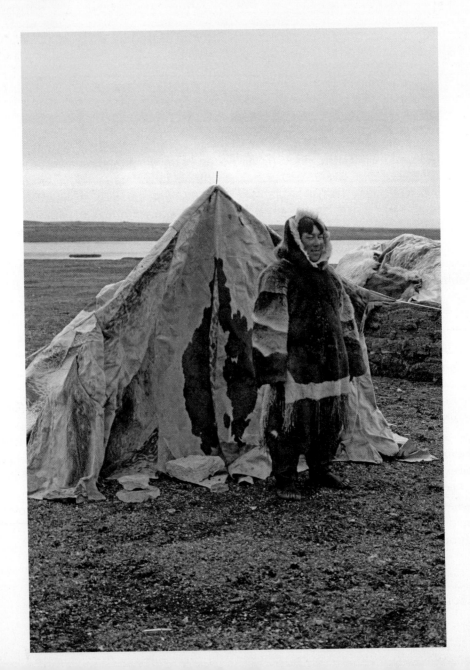

The meal was nearly complete. This was the first time that my daughter had a whole fried trout on her plate. I had decided that she was old enough at three years to learn to eat carefully and spit out the bones. She watched and copied her dad and me as we filleted one side of the fish and then removed the spine and most of the rib bones in one smooth movement. She ate with gusto but carefully. Finally, she asked if she could have more. Only the head and tail of her fish remained. I made eye contact with my husband and then remarked, "But you haven't finished your fish yet." She looked puzzled. "You haven't eaten the head yet. There are several small succulent bits of meat there. And you haven't eaten the eyes." I went on to remark that aboriginal Inuit children thought that the eyes were a special treat, except that they liked them raw. She asked how to eat them, and I told her to scoop one out with her spoon. She ate one, smiled, ate the other one, and then asked if she could have the fish eyes from the trout on my plate too. She is now thirty-five and still likes fish eyes.

What we consider acceptable to eat, what we consider nutritious, what we consider delicious, is learned. People make choices about what to eat, they acquire food in different ways, and they have various approaches to the distribution of foods and other resources. The details of these cultural adaptations differ, but patterns emerge when comparative analysis is carried out. In this chapter we apply a theoretical framework that uses both cultural evolution and ecology to explain the various human strategies for obtaining food and allocating resources.

The objectives of this chapter are to:

- Describe models of cultural evolution and cultural ecology
- Identify subsistence strategies within the framework of an evolutionary-ecological model
- Examine economic systems within the evolutionary-ecological model
- Examine the adaptive strategy of technology
- Identify the strategies common to foraging

◀ Foragers often occupy challenging environments. The land of the Inuit is harsh but their intimate knowledge of the Arctic ecosystem results in unique survival strategies. This Inuit summer camp shows how some contemporary Inuit are revitalizing their traditional lifeways.

AN EVOLUTIONARY-ECOLOGICAL PARADIGM

OLC
mhhe • com / lenkeit5e
See chapter outline and chapter overview.

We all have to eat. Because food is essential for survival, this is where we will begin our look at human adaptations and the data compiled by anthropologists. This chapter and the next are concerned with how human groups acquire and use their resources to obtain or produce food and how food and resources are distributed and consumed. To make the material more manageable for you, I have divided it into two chapters. The first focuses on models used for analysis and the adaptations of foraging societies. The second focuses on societies that produce their food. The data will be presented primarily within the framework of two theories—cultural evolution and cultural ecology. To state this another way, the framework around which the chapter is constructed is an eclectic one that draws mainly on these two theoretical approaches. When I was a beginning college student I found the study of theoretical models a nuisance. After a time, I realized that such models, with their hypotheses to explain vast amounts of data, are quite useful. To begin we will consider models and model building. This will give you an idea of the process that goes into developing a theoretical model.

Models assist one to approach material in an organized manner, and they provide a foundation for the comparison of cultural data. The evolutionary-ecological model used here provides an introductory perspective on the study of subsistence and economics.

The Evolutionary Model

Cultural evolution models delineate a sequence of culture change over time and the processes at work in this change. The first such models suggested that culture change moved in a direction from simple to complex. These were presented in the 1860s, having been stimulated by Charles Darwin's book *On the Origin of Species* (1859), which discussed the mechanism for biological evolution. These early attempts to explain cultural evolution were later labeled **unilineal evolution** because they laid out a sequence of cultural stages rather like rungs of a ladder. All cultures had mounted each rung, or were in the process of doing so, to reach the top rung of civilization (see Chapter 13 for a description of one such model by L. H. Morgan). By the early 1900s archaeological and ethnographic field data demonstrated that the early unilineal evolutionists were mistaken, and other theories developed to explain cultural similarities and differences.

cultural evolution
A model for the development of society that delineates a sequence of cultural change over time.

unilineal evolution
Early theoretical school that postulated that all cultures proceeded through a series of successive stages.

Cultural evolution became a hot topic again in the 1940s, 50s, and 60s. Models were again influenced by biological evolution, but anthropologists were careful to point out that while analogies could be made to biological evolution, cultural evolution was different. After all, societies did not reproduce genetically, and cultural adaptations were transmitted from one generation to the next using symbols. V. Gordon Child, Leslie White, Julian Steward, Elman R. Service, Marshall D. Sahlins, and others developed the most popular models. Each attempted to explain human cultural diversity, understand the varieties of human adaptations—ranging from small-scale societies based on foraging to large-scale industrialized societies based on intensive agriculture—and delineate patterns of human sociocultural development over time. I like aspects of many of the models. I like the idea of cultural evolution, perhaps because the holistic approach was emphasized in my education, and these models drew data from archaeology, biological anthropology, ethnography, and ethnology. Following is a quick summary of several of the later evolutionary models. Elements of these contribute to the evolutionary sequence presented as an organizing framework in this chapter, although I've drawn most heavily from Sahlins and Service.

V. Gordon Child, an archaeologist, viewed a series of major technological developments as responsible for cultural growth and believed that environmental factors stimulated adaptations as well as impeded cultures from growing. Leslie White outlined a model of cultural evolution that he called **neoevolution.** White proposed to assess a culture's level of evolutionary development by measuring its output of energy per person per year to procure and maintain people's basic needs, such as food and water. This idea, presented in his book *The Evolution of Culture* (1959b), was exciting to read about. But it became clear that it would be impossible to actually apply his mathematical formulas to real cultures because, for example, there were too many variables, such as differences in soil fertility, which resulted in different calorie contents for foods grown in different regions. Julian Steward rejected White's approach of trying to apply a formula to all cultures. Rather, Steward gathered both historical and archaeological data on a number of societies occupying a similar habitat and was able to document a similar *pattern* of how the cultures changed over time (how they evolved). Steward's model became known as the model of **multilinear evolution** because he hypothesized that the evolutionary pattern would differ for different habitats. For example, one pattern would be exhibited by groups living near the mouth of river-valley systems and a different evolutionary pattern by societies in a desert, tropical rain forest, or other habitat—hence, the name multilinear evolution.

Marshall D. Sahlins and Elman R. Service (1960) built their model as stages of general evolution. "General cultural evolution is the successive emergence of *new levels of all-round development*" (emphasis mine) (Sahlins and Service 1960: 28). They based their stages of cultural development on broad sociocultural adaptations. These adaptations were in the areas of social organization, including kinship types and political organization, and systems of distribution. Service focused on social organization in his

neoevolutionary model
A model of cultural evolution based on types of technology and food-procurement strategies, and the sociocultural adaptations that resulted from them.

multilinear evolution
An evolutionary model of culture emphasizing different development patterns for societies in different habitats.

writing (1962); Sahlins developed categories of economic redistribution (Sahlins 1968; 1972). They analyzed how new sociocultural adaptations resulted from changes that began with technology and food-getting strategies. They identified the stages of hunting-gathering bands, horticultural and pastoral tribes, agricultural chiefdoms, and finally state societies based on intensive agriculture. The next sections provide some of the evidence from archaeology and ethnography that contribute to this model.

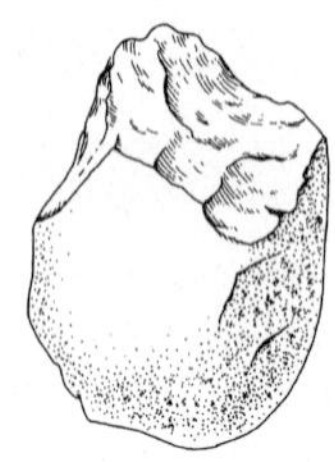

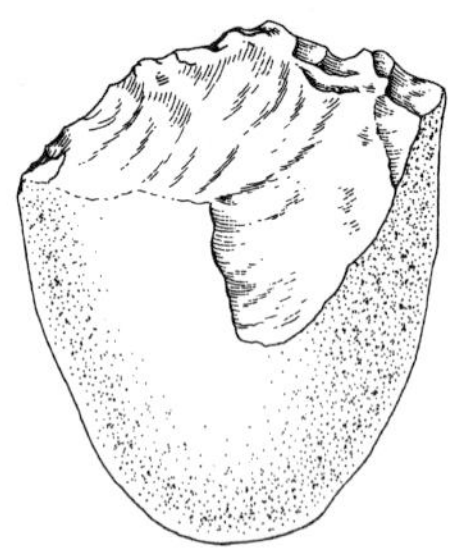

These Oldowan tools were made by striking several flakes off of the core rock. The flakes had sharp edges and were probably also used for cutting.

Building the Model: Archaeological Evidence. It is useful to dig into the archaeological record (okay, pun intended) for evidence to support an evolutionary model of human cultural adaptations. Humanity began several million years ago in Africa, when recognizable hominid (human-like) ancestors first emerged. They had cranial capacities about one-third the size of modern *Homo sapiens*', and they walked bipedally. At least three genuses and several species of early hominids have been found that exhibit these basic features, and there is lively discussion as to which were our direct ancestors. The evidence demonstrates that at least one of these species made stone cutting tools, known as **Oldowan tools** (after the site at Olduvai Gorge in Africa where they were first discovered). Oldowan tools date to about two million years ago and are found in numerous sites of comparable dates throughout southern and eastern Africa. Earlier tools, with a date of about 2.5 million years ago, have been identified at the site of Gona, Ethiopia, but as of yet widespread evidence of these tools has not been established. Fossil bones of various species of savanna animals have been found at the same sites as the Oldowan tools. Such bones appear to have been scavenged from the carcasses of animals after they were killed by large predators. Studies have been made of these fossil animal bones using scanning electron micrography, and numerous bones have marks that show specific characteristics that could have been made only by stone tools. Moreover, these cut markings often overlie the chew marks made by the teeth of the carnivores, indicating that the hominids scavenged from carnivore kills (Shipman 1984). This and other evidence point to a scavenging and foraging lifestyle for our early ancestors.

Oldowan tools
A very early African tool-making tradition associated with the first members of *Homo*.

Acheulean hand axes
Part of an African and European tool tradition associated with *Homo erectus* and *Homo ergaster*. The tradition also includes cleavers and some flake tools.

The Oldowan tools provide us with the first substantial material evidence of human culture. By a million years ago, our ancestors were making improved tools, including **Acheulean hand axes.** The hand ax attests to the increased technological abilities of its makers, including a consistent shape. Skills that were passed on to each new generation became incorporated into the knowledge base of the group. The archaeological record tells us that humans were foraging for a wide array of plant and animal foods for hundreds of thousands of years before they discovered how to domesticate plants and animals. The transition to fully sedentary lives based on the cultivation of plants was slow, and it took many more years before technological innovations and concentrations of population led to the development of agriculturally based city-states and finally nation-states. This prehistoric chronology provides the structure for an evolutionary model of cultural development. Of course, many aspects of human behavior and thought do not leave direct archaeological evidence, but the *sequence* of the appearance of the food-procurement strategies is clear.

It must be emphasized that the unfolding of cultural adaptations through time was not linear. Ideas diffused between groups, just as they do today. There were periods of quick change and other periods of gradual change. Viewed as a whole, we can see a sequence that supports a model of cultural evolution.

Tools such as this Acheulean hand ax were an improvement over the Oldowan tools. They are worked on both sides and have straighter, sharper edges.

Building the Model: Ethnographic Data. The next part in the development of the evolutionary-ecological model came from ethnography and ethnology. Data from societies with similar means of acquiring food were grouped together. In the case of hunter-gatherer-foragers the best-described societies (more than fifteen from five continents) were used as a database by Service (Service 1979). When compared, these cultures from diverse environments, but with similar food-procurement strategies, turned out to have other sociocultural adaptive strategies in common, such as the organization of kinship, type of leadership, or system of distribution. This became the basis of Service's and Sahlins' stages of cultural evolution. They hypothesized that over time, as new adaptations in food procurement developed, new adaptive sociocultural features also emerged.

The Ecological Model

The **ecological model** of cultural development grew out of extensive research in anthropology (and the biological sciences) during the 1970s and 1980s and continues today. This perspective views a culture as part of a larger global ecological system with each aspect of the system interacting with all the other parts. Julian Steward wrote that "**cultural ecology** is the study of the processes by which a society adapts to its environment. Its principal problem is to determine whether these adaptations initiate internal social transformations of evolutionary change" (Steward 1968: 337). The relationship of an organism to its habitat (where it lives) is its adaptation. Human adaptations are the processes used by groups of people to alter their relationship to a habitat over time (Cohen 1968: 3). Human adaptations are primarily cultural, not biological.

What circumstances must humans adapt to? Natural resources are finite in any environment, and each society develops within a specific physical environment that includes soils, elevation, water, minerals, wind, humidity, number of hours of sunlight, temperature (and seasonal variations), and the fauna and flora. Also, each society and its culture develops within a sociocultural environment that involves contact and interaction

ecological model
A model that views a culture as part of a larger global ecological system with each aspect of the system interacting with all of the other parts.

cultural ecology
The study of the processes by which a society adapts to its environment.

TRY THIS
Hypothesize

Jot down another possible hypothesis for adaptive strategies for foragers in desert environments. How might you test your hypothesis?

with other humans and their cultures. The dynamic, complex system that results is the focus of the ecological model.

Various specific models have been offered by ecologically oriented theorists as they examine what influences foraging behaviors. For example, paradigms known as **optimal-foraging models** have been developed, and these models aim at understanding how foragers optimize the gathering of food with the least expenditure of time, calories, or other factors. The choices available to the forager are considered, as are issues such as preparation time necessary to make the food edible. This model and others apply the scientific method and are useful for generating hypotheses for the study of past and present human adaptations.

For example, in researching the adaptive strategies of foragers living in a desert environment, one might make this hypothesis: If water sources are limited in a desert environment, then movements of foraging camps correspond to availability of water sources. Such a hypothesis can then be evaluated against the data available on foragers living in desert environments. The anthropologist might also consider how foragers in this particular environment optimize their gathering strategies.

The Evolutionary-Ecological Model

The bringing together of the models of cultural evolution and cultural ecology allow the anthropologist to take both a microview and a macroview of cultural processes. This is the **evolutionary-ecological model.** When ethnographic fieldwork focuses on the microadaptations (up close and in detail) of a particular society within its environment, the ethnographer is at the same time adding to our general knowledge of how human cultures adapt—the macroview. This macroview requires an alliance between ethnography, ethnology, and archaeology as data are compared between prehistoric and contemporary cultural adaptations. Such comparisons add to our understanding of both the past and the present.

optimal-foraging model
A model that aims at understanding how foragers optimize the gathering of food.

evolutionary-ecological model
A paradigm of human culture that combines both the neoevolutionary and ecological perspectives.

Economics and the Model

Economics is the study of how society acquires and uses resources to produce food and goods, how these are distributed and consumed, and what motivates people to produce, distribute, and consume. Economic anthropologists look at the natural resources and the technology used to acquire and process raw products and foods. They examine the units of production (individuals, households, private companies) and the division of labor and labor specialization (by gender and age), plus the means by which raw materials, food, goods, and services are distributed and how they are consumed. Attitudes, traditions, and motivations about work and the acquisition of material possessions are studied. To present a more holistic perspective, I have integrated these topics into the presentation of types of subsistence within the evolutionary-ecological model.

TECHNOLOGY AS AN ELEMENT IN PRODUCTION STRATEGIES

Stone tools represent a large portion of the artifacts recovered in archaeological excavations (because they do not decompose as natural fibers do). It follows that the study of a prehistoric culture's adaptations often begins with stone tool technology. Technology is also a starting point for examining the economic adaptations of contemporary cultures, because technology is used in obtaining, producing, and distributing food and goods.

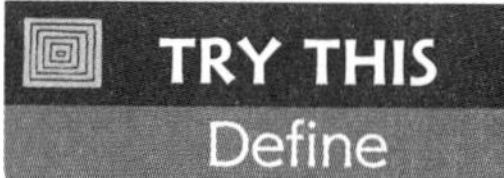

Quickly, define technology. What is it? Give two examples.

Anthropologists define **technology** as consisting of three components—knowledge, skills, and tools. These are used by humans when they manipulate and interact with their environment. Did your definition have all of these elements? Nearly all of my students over the years have focused on tools or machines when I asked them to define technology. Certainly this is one aspect of technology, but it is a narrow perspective. The knowledge that you carry around in your brain is a tool kit. This knowledge tool kit consists of a catalog of information that you have acquired, numerous manuals with procedures for problem solving, a list of social rules for successful collaboration with others, a checklist with procedures for evaluating risk, and a book of past successes and failures. Because environments have finite resources, the knowledge of how to use those resources to obtain food is critical. Many native California groups, for example, understood how to use fire to enhance their environments—technological knowledge. They burned brush and dry grass around oak trees to control pests and make acorn gathering easier. They also set controlled fires to increase grass and broad-leaf herbaceous plants. Seeds of these plants were important secondary food sources and were ground into flour with small portable mortars and pestles. When redbud plants are burned, they respond by sending up new shoots that are just the right dimensions needed for basket making. Many aspects of the analysis of technology relate to the optimal-foraging models mentioned previously.

TRY THIS
Ponder

Check through your knowledge tool kit and consider how you would decide whether to eat a bag of wild mushrooms that have been collected by a friend. Check your catalog of information, your manual for problem solving, your list of social rules, your checklist for evaluating risk, and your book of past successes and failures. Process all of this knowledge and decide.

The skills component of technology consists of the behaviors people have learned to use to manipulate their environment. The tools component of technology consists of all of the objects that are used to perform various tasks. Knowledge, of course, plays a role in deciding which skills to use. Tools are created through a combination of (1) knowledge of available raw materials, (2) knowledge and skills to obtain the raw materials, and (3) knowledge and skills to manipulate the raw materials to make the desired object. For example, you may know that obsidian (volcanic glass) rock when broken is sharp. To create a projectile point for the tip of an

technology
The knowledge, tools, and skills used by humans to manipulate their environments.

arrow, you must know where and how to obtain obsidian, you must have the understanding and skills to precisely control the breaking process to remove flakes, and you must know how to create a finished projectile point that can be attached to the shaft of the arrow.

The element of choice is a part of all cultural behavior, and a culture's technology reflects its choices. A society may know of numerous available protein sources but choose to use just a few of them. Why, for example, do North Americans include cows and not horses as part of their diet? Why do most people in Thailand include insects such as praying mantises as part of their diet, whereas North Americans ignore insects as a protein source? Choices were made generations ago by our ancestors, and each of us has been enculturated into a society where the acceptable choices are in place.

TRY THIS Analyze

Select a section from an assigned ethnography or other reading that focuses on a society's food-procurement strategies. Analyze the information available and sort the technological strategies into the categories of knowledge, skills, and tools. Naturally these are tightly intertwined aspects of technology, but new insights can be gained by trying to separate them.

This Inuit is wearing traditional goggles carved from ivory or bone. This technology reduces the harsh glare of the sun.

traditions
Cultural choices consistently made by a society and practiced generation to generation.

The skills used in obtaining and processing food may also reflect cultural choices. For example, someone who wants fish for dinner could use fly-fishing skills to catch fish or use a fish trap or distribute a poison in the water that will stun or kill the fish. This person might even make different choices on different occasions. Choices are also made when making a tool—which material to use in making the object, which manufacturing technique to use, which design elements to include. When particular choices are made consistently within a society, regardless of the reasons for those choices, we speak of them as **traditions.** For example, the choice to make a pot from red clay rather than gray clay may simply reflect a cultural choice (provided that several colors of clay are available and the clays' qualities are otherwise equal). Or, if the red clay produces a stronger, less-fragile finished pot, we could say that the choice is based on a functional assessment of this attribute that is valued by the users of such pots. Often we do not know why a choice was made. Ethnographers have learned that people may make a choice simply because it is tradition in their culture; no one living knows why that choice was made originally.

My preference in the study of technology is to observe and describe what the technology *does* for the people it serves—a functional and ecological approach. How does the technology function within the adaptive

ANTHROPOLOGY AROUND US

Edible Insects

Wet weather in the spring of 2010 brought lush vegetation growth in Australia's outback and the worst swarms of locusts in thirty years, resulting in crop devastation. Similar incidents occurred in the West Africa nation of Guinea-Bissau, where up to 150 locusts per square yard munched away at crops. Locusts eat nearly every plant in their path as they move, covering about a half mile per day.

People around the world capitalized on the ebb and flow of insect populations by routinely incorporating insects into their diets. Insects are nutritious. According to the Entomology Society of America, various insects—termites, locusts, houseflies, spiders, and ants, for example—contain more protein (24 to 64 percent protein) than do chicken, beef, pork, or lamb (17 to 23 percent protein). These insects are low in fat and many are rich in minerals such as iron and calcium. The mophane (*Imbrasia belina*)—the caterpillar of the emperor moth—is 56.8 percent protein. A Botswana woman can collect one 20-liter bucket of these in a day. Preparation is by gutting, boiling in salt water, and drying. They are sold in 40-kilogram bags (88 pounds) and are in demand commercially, including as restaurant fare. Collection of these and other insects may become important industries for the rural poor.

In the region that is now California and Nevada, native peoples consumed wasp larva, bees, ants, and Mormon crickets. In Mexico 1,700 insect species are eaten—grasshoppers are most popular (Raloff 2008: 18). Chinese peasants ate large quantities of insects, especially silkworm pupae, and the upper classes enjoyed cicadas and giant water beetles (Harris 1998: 156–61).

North Americans today eat insects in a variety of foods. The U.S. Food and Drug Administration allows thirty insect fragments per hundred grams of peanut butter; chocolate may contain sixty insect fragments per hundred grams, while tomato paste and pizza may contain up to thirty insect eggs or two maggots per hundred grams.

◎ It has been suggested that the commercial raising of insect pupae would supply a cheap and environmentally friendly form of protein. How would you market this idea globally?

strategies of the society? According to this perspective, technology's most important function is to aid the procurement of food and water and help to maintain body temperature. Technology also helps an individual or group maintain contact with other people through communication and travel. Finally, many tasks are made easier through technology. As you read the following pages, keep the definitions and functions of technology in mind.

FORAGING AS A SUBSISTENCE STRATEGY

TRY THIS
Analyze

Make a quick list of the ways that technology aids you in keeping cool or warm enough so that you don't die of hyperthermia or hypothermia. Which aspects of this technology fall into the categories of knowledge, skills, and tools?

Foraging is food procurement that involves collecting wild plant and animal foods and was the earliest adaptive strategy used by humans. The archaeological record shows that people were foragers for hundreds of thousands of years before the domestication of plants and animals. In the 1960s the label "hunting and gathering" was used to designate peoples who obtained food in this fashion, and the emphasis was placed on men being responsible for providing most of the group's food through hunting. Foods gathered by women were considered supplemental. This interpretation was both biased and oversimplified. In the following decades, ethnographers began to actually weigh and measure foods, evaluate the nutritional content of foods, and assess the contributions of both women and men to food procurement. The result was a much more complex picture of food procurement, and the term *foraging* better represents this human activity.

Media images of foraging peoples can be biased and result in misleading stereotypes. Early films of foraging societies like the Dobe Ju/'hoansi (pronounced "doebay zhutwasi" according to Lee 1993) and the Mbuti pygmies were and are often misleading. Dangerous situations, such as pygmies, armed only with spears, hunting elephants are used to create drama in a film sequence, whereas berry picking and mushroom gathering don't provide much excitement, drama, or danger. Film producers often aim for commercial success more than scholarly accuracy (which makes sense from a business standpoint), but such film footage led (and still leads) to stereotypes. One such stereotype is that native peoples who hunt and gather are primitive, simple, and backward. Another is that the natives are "noble savages"—idealized, romanticized peoples living in harmony with nature. Both perceptions are inaccurate. Be alert to question what you see in films.

In the mid–nineteenth century there were numerous foraging societies; today there are few—most are absorbed into societies that produce food through horticulture or agriculture. The groups highlighted in this chapter are written about in what is termed the *ethnographic present*. They are described as if they were still living the way they did when ethnographers first recorded their ways of life. Today many former foragers still supplement

foraging
A food-procurement strategy that involves collecting wild plant and animal foods.

Washo
Haida
Inuit
Yąnomamö
Dobe Ju/'hoansi
Nuer
Trobriand Islanders

NORTH AMERICA
EUROPE
ASIA
AFRICA
SOUTH AMERICA
AUSTRALIA

Ice cap
Tundra and alpine
Coniferous forest
Temperate and subtropical forest
Temperate grasslands (prairie)
Mediterranean mixed forest
Tropical rain forest
Grasslands (savanna)
Scrub and thorn forest
Steppe (shortgrass)
Desert shrub and waste
Unclassified highlands

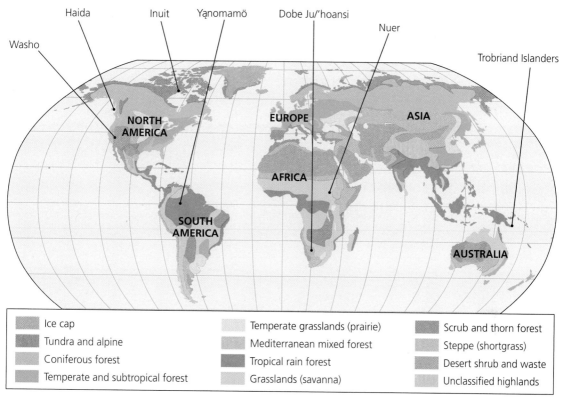

World ecoregions with locations of focus societies discussed in Chapters 5 and 6.

their diets with traditional food sources and retain other aspects of traditional life such as belief systems, rites of passage, and kin structure.

It is important to continually remind ourselves that all subsistence patterns change and adapt over time. Foragers are not like fossils representing preserved remnants of the past.

The Foraging Spectrum

Foraging represents a spectrum of food-getting activities. The sample tabulation in Table 5.1 gives a sense of the combination of enterprises that contribute to the diets of foragers. Foods gathered include berries, nuts, seeds, flowers, herbs, fungus, fruit, greens, eggs, shellfish, insects, and so forth. In one comparative study the percentage of gathered foods was as high as 80 percent of the total diet among foragers; hunting activities procured up to 60 percent of the food (the sources of this information did not uniformly distinguish between hunting for food that is eaten and food that is traded to nearby groups for horticultural produce) (Kelly 1995).

See Internet exercises.

TABLE 5.1 Diet Sources of a Sample of Foraging Cultures

Population Density (persons per 100 km²)	*Group*	*Gathering %*	*Hunting %*	*Fishing %*
0.02	Caribou Inuit, North America	10	50	40
62–96	Haida, North America	20	20	60
1.9	Plains Cree, North America	20	60	20
103	Maidu, North America	50	30	20
10–16	Dobe Ju/'hoansi, Africa	80	20	0
17	Mbuti, Africa	30	60	10
86	Andamese, Andaman Islands	40	20	40

Source: Based on data in Kelly 1995. Gathering includes plant materials, insects, small game, and sometimes shellfish. Fishing includes sea mammals and shellfish.

Features Associated with Foraging Lifeways

The general features associated with foraging lifeways that have been revealed by ethnological analysis are consistent, even though many details differ. These general features are sometimes called correlates to the foraging lifeway.

Production Based on Technological Mastery. Foragers have impressive technological mastery of their environment. It is not unusual to find foragers who are knowledgeable about more than a hundred edible plant species. They have the knowledge, skills, and tools to obtain these foods and prepare them for consumption. For example, the aboriginal Washo (also spelled Washoe) peoples of the Great Basin region of western North America drew upon a vast knowledge of food sources as they moved from the desert floor on the eastern side of the Sierra Nevada mountains and the foothills on the western slopes to the shores of Lake Tahoe at an elevation of 6,000–10,000 feet. Archaeological evidence indicates that ancestral Washo lived in this area for at least 6,000 years. They had to know about soils and microclimates as they searched for edible plants. Wild lettuces, for example, might be available in one spot, whereas conditions nearby might be such that the lettuce had not yet emerged. Chokecherries may ripen in one region weeks before they ripen in another.

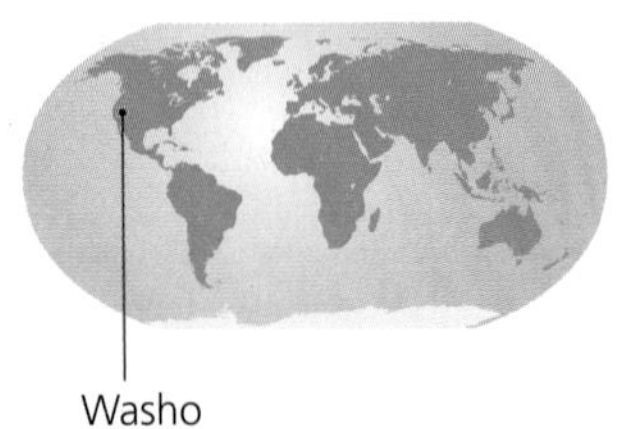
Washo

Hunters must know the habits and behaviors of the animals they hunt. Pronghorn antelope, known by the Washo and other Native Americans for their curiosity, could be lured within range of a bow. Mule deer required a

Ju/'hoansi hunters in the Kalahari Desert of Africa snare hares in underground burrows. One listens to activity on the end of his snare, while the other probes a burrow. These men can also identify animals by their dung and tracks.

different strategy. One strategy employed by Washo deer hunters was to stalk their prey while wearing a disguise—a stuffed deer head with body skin attached and draped over the hunter's shoulders. Experienced hunters were known to be able to move extremely close to herds of deer while wearing such disguises.

The Washo and other native populations of California relied on acorns as a primary food source. Acorns have high concentrations of tannic acid, are bitter to the taste, and are poisonous if consumed. Therefore, before they could be eaten, a laborious process had to be carried out. First, the acorns were gathered and shelled, which involved knowing the location of and ripening time for acorn-bearing oak trees. After shelling, the acorns were toasted and ground by hand using either a portable flat *mano* with a *metate* for grinding or a bedrock mortar and pestle. The resulting product had to be as fine as flour; otherwise it could not be properly leached of the tannic acid. I have ground acorns in this way and can attest that it takes quite a bit of time to grind the acorn meal to the

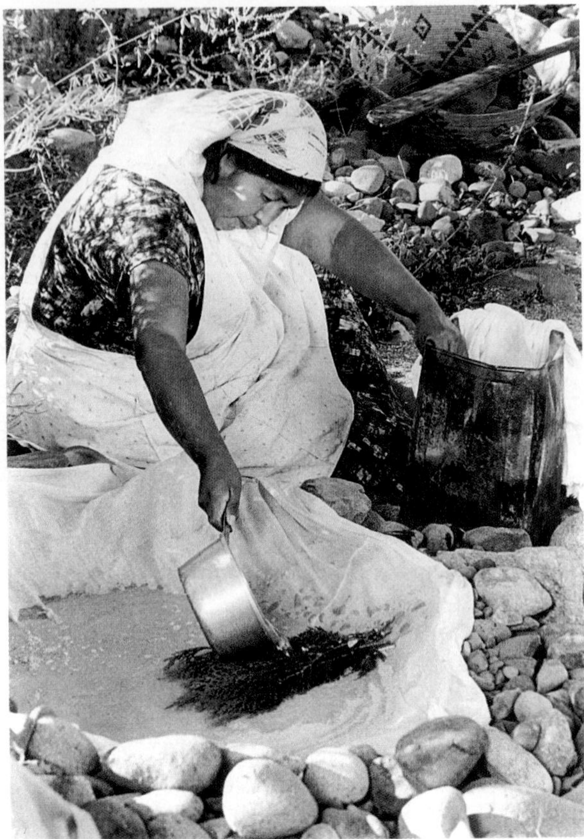

Acorn meal, once it is processed, provides more than 90 percent of the protein, fats, and carbohydrates found in wheat. This woman is leaching acorn flour in a cloth-lined sand pit (Carson Valley, Nevada, 1966).

TRY THIS
Compare

Compare the technology (knowledge, skills, and tools) involved in the preparation of acorn meal with the technology you personally must use to eat a bowl of oatmeal (or your favorite cereal). What technology must be used by others before you are able to purchase your oatmeal or cereal?

proper consistency. Moreover, pestles commonly weigh from two to five pounds, so one gets a real upper-body workout from the process. Finally, the acorn flour was placed in a sandy depression near a creek, and water was repeatedly poured over the flour to leach out the poisonous tannic acid. An alternative method involved placing the flour in a tightly woven basket and pouring water over the flour. Only then could this nutritious food be cooked and eaten.

Nomadic Lifestyle. Most foragers are nomadic. They must move with the availability of food and water. As an adaptive strategy, foraging must be fine-tuned to a particular environment. The frequency of movement is orchestrated to coincide with the availability of specific plants, animals, and water. The Washo were on the move from early spring, as soon as the Sierra snows began to melt, until the beginning of winter. Though they had many sources of food available to them, these were often widely dispersed, necessitating almost continual movement.

Foragers must also cope with risky situations. Unpredictable variation in weather or other ecological variables require flexible solutions, such as more frequent movement of camps when foods are scarce or maintaining camps by a year-round water hole during a drought. In the latter case, individuals would in essence be tethered to the water hole and would have to travel longer distances to forage.

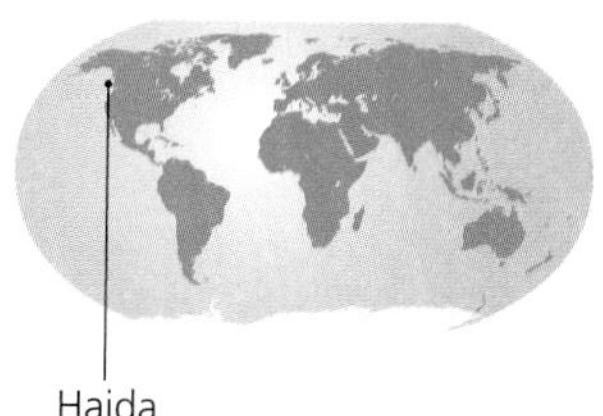

Interestingly, there are foraging societies that did not move, such as the Haida of the North Pacific coast. The abundant salmon, other fish species, shellfish, and deer in their territory assured the Haida, and other societies along the northwest coast, a plentiful food supply. This in turn allowed for a large population concentration. Groups such as the Haida make the creation of evolutionary models difficult, because such groups do not meet all the criteria of the model.

Biologists developed the concept of **carrying capacity**—the maximum population that a habitat can sustain, or carry. It is determined by the availability of food, water, and shelter and by the existence of predators and disease. The previous statement implies that the calculation of a region's carrying capacity is a simple matter. It is really quite complex because issues such as the nutritional quality of food—vitamins, minerals, and protein—are part of the equation, not merely how much food is available. Because foragers are not food producers, they must be regarded as just another species, and their population size is limited by the carrying capacity of their environment. Humans, of course, have culture as their primary adaptive mechanism and this can affect carrying capacity. A foraging group's accumulated knowledge of food resources, their ability to plan ahead and predict when a source will be available, and their ability to alter their behaviors accordingly may be factors in maximizing the carrying capacity potential for foragers in a particular region.

TRY THIS
Hypothesize

Why did some human groups stay on land with a very low carrying capacity? Write a hypothesis about the relationship between environments with low carrying capacities and human groups remaining for generations in such environments. How could you test or evaluate your hypothesis?

Organization of Groups. Foragers are organized into groups that anthropologists label **bands.** At the time of early contact and study by anthropologists (1900–1960), foragers commonly lived in groups based on two types of kinship. One type is a **family band,** which consists of a number of nuclear families (parents and their offspring) living within an area. These individual families come together to form a larger group when resources are abundant and split up again when resources are scarce or widely dispersed. This coming together and breaking apart characterizes many foraging societies. Sometimes, too, foragers move from one location to another simply to be nearer to a particular relative. In other words, choice of where to live and when to move may be motivated by issues other than resource availability. The Washo exemplify this pattern with wide dispersal of families and individuals during most of the year. Patterns of movement for the Washo were quite fluid, with each family or individual making independent decisions about when and where to go.

carrying capacity
The maximum population that a habitat can sustain.

bands
A type of society common in foraging groups and marked by egalitarian social structure and lack of specialization.

family band
A type of band organization consisting of nuclear family units that move independently within an area. Joins others when resources are plentiful; travels alone at other times.

The Kalahari Desert is rich in food sources if one knows where to look. This woman in Namibia, who can identify more than 100 edible plant species, shows the melons, berries, and starred tortoise that she has gathered.

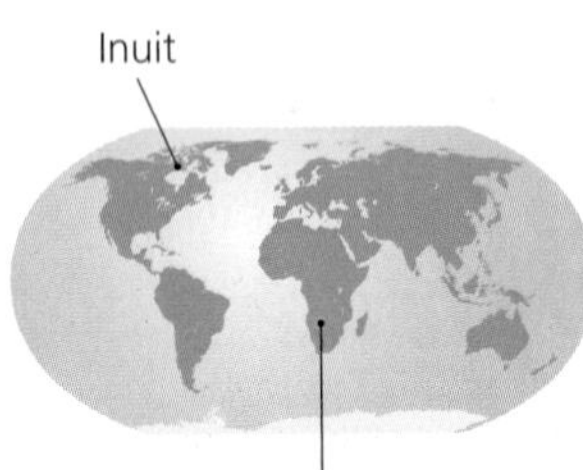

During the fall piñon nut harvests and early spring fish-spawning runs, numerous families came together. Winter camps, too, consisted of clusters of families. Another example of a family band is the Inuit peoples of the Arctic, where families came together to hunt seal through the winter ice. Several hunters waiting for a seal to surface at multiple breathing holes in the ice greatly increased the chance of a kill. During the summer, families dispersed to fish and forage. They came together periodically when cooperation was needed, as in hunting caribou or during fish migrations.

patrilocal band
A type of band consisting of related males and their wives and children who stay together and forage as a group.

The second type of foraging group is a **patrilocal band,** which numbers about fifty people and is made up of several nuclear families who are related through their male members—for example, a man and his wife, their three sons, and their wives and children. This is called residing in a patrilocal residence group (see Chapters 7 and 8 for details of kinship, and see Chapter 10 for a discussion of political structure). The goal or ideal in such foraging groups is patrilocal residence (that is, living near the husband's family), but people often live according to other arrangements at any given point in time. Among the Dobe Ju/'hoansi, for example, a girl is often married when quite young (eight or nine years old). In such cases, she and her husband typically live for years near her mother and father, moving to be with her husband's group only when she is older. Patrilocal bands live on land with more concentrated resources than the environments occupied by family bands. In other words, their environment's carrying capacity is greater and can support a larger group. In fact, fishing-based foragers usually have much higher population concentrations because of dependable and abundant food, as is true for the northwest coast societies, like the Haida, that depend on abundant salmon. Bands based on matrilocal residence (that is, living near the wife's family) are much less common and therefore are not listed as a *common* correlate to foraging.

Property and Ownership. Foragers have few material possessions. When everything one owns has to be carried from place to place on one's back, items are kept to a minimum. While the land and its resources are generally considered to belong to the whole group, particular resources may belong to a family and a tool might be personal property. For example, an Inuit woman's knife, or *ulu*, belongs to her, and among the Yurok of northern California, families owned acorn-bearing trees. Sharing, giving, receiving, and no one keeping track of what is given or received is the custom—a custom that is enculturated from infancy. Most access to tools occurs by sharing and borrowing rather than everyone having one of his or her own (living in close proximity facilitates sharing). Items given or received as personal gifts are often passed to the first person to admire them. Thus objects are constantly circulating within the group. Everyone always has something; everyone is equal. Many foraging societies have changed considerably since they began interacting more with contemporary industrialized societies. Some have borrowed ideas such as personal ownership.

TRY THIS
Hypothesize

Develop two hypotheses that might explain communal ownership of land and its resources among foragers. Offer two specific ways to test your hypotheses.

Distribution of Resources. Foraging societies are marked by the economic distribution system known as reciprocity. **Reciprocity** is the enculturated pattern in which people give and receive items of value in predictable ways. The giving of food, a tool, or an item of personal adornment are examples of such value items. The giving of one's time in the form of helping to build a hut or watching someone's child also illustrates something of value. This giving of items of value is part of the fabric of band societies.

Marshall D. Sahlins (1968) identified the following three categories of economic reciprocity: (1) **Generalized reciprocity** is when everyone gives of time, food, and artifacts and no one keeps track of what is given or received. It commonly occurs between kin who are perceived as being close, such as parents, siblings, and spouses. These are people whom one

reciprocity
A form of exchange that involves the mutual giving and receiving of food and other items between people who are socially equal.

generalized reciprocity
Institutionalized gift giving and exchange between close kin; accounts are not kept, and there is no expectation of immediate return.

TRY THIS
Analyze

Where is generalized reciprocity used in contemporary North American culture? Why? Where do we employ balanced reciprocity? Why? Is either form necessary for our survival? Why or why not?

interacts with regularly, and these individuals have an equal ability to give. (2) **Balanced reciprocity** involves the exchange of favors (such as helping with a task) or items while keeping mental records in the expectation that something of equal value will be returned within a reasonable period of time. This form of reciprocity usually takes place between those perceived as more distant relatives as well as those who are not related. Individuals participating in this form of reciprocity also have an equal ability to give. Both giver and receiver have equal access to items that are given; neither is significantly wealthier than the other. (3) **Negative reciprocity** occurs when one tries to get more than is given, often through haggling or even theft. Because it can create ill will, this giving typically takes place between unrelated individuals.

Among foragers, generalized reciprocity is dominant. It takes place, often on a daily basis, between persons who are close kin, which is everyone in the foraging band. Foragers are considered **egalitarian;** that is, members of the society have equal access to status, power, and wealth *within* the *same* category such as age or gender. For example, all male elders have equal access to status, power, and wealth. Everyone has an equal potential to give, and does. While thoughtful members of foraging bands have no doubt considered that it is in their own best interest to give goods and services, it is wrong to believe that members of such groups give only for selfish reasons. Enculturation results in this behavior being expected; most participants do not analyze it. Outsiders, such as anthropologists, are the ones to offer the analytical (or etic) view that this is how everyone survives.

Balanced reciprocity does not appear as a significant economic element within foraging societies. Rather, it surfaces when foragers interact with other societies. This is also the case with negative reciprocity—it is not usually undertaken with any person on whom you must depend or with whom you must maintain good relationships.

balanced reciprocity
Exchange and gift giving with the expectation of a return of equal value within a reasonable period of time.

negative reciprocity
An economic exchange aimed at receiving more than is given.

egalitarian
Refers to members of a society having equal access to status, power, and wealth within the same category, such as age or gender.

Nutritionally Balanced Diet. Foragers generally eat nutritionally balanced diets. The omnivorous nature of the diet of such peoples means that they use all possible food sources, though some choices are based on tradition. The foraging diet contains more variety than the diets of societies that produce their own foods and that specialize in two or three crops. The Washo used about 170 plant species and more than 30 animal species in their diet (Downs 1966; D'Azevedo 1986). Examine Table 5.2, and compare the diversity of the Washo diet to your own. For the Washo, none of these foods was in plentiful enough supply to support the population over an entire yearly cycle. However, at different times of the year specific foods were often plentiful. At Lake Tahoe, spawning runs of fish (trout in May and June, suckers in late June, and Lahoptan tui chub in July and August) provided large amounts of food. The various tributaries and

TABLE 5.2 Most Important Foods Used by the Washo Peoples of Western North America

Plants: 170 edible species, including		*Animals: More than 30 edible species, including*	
piñon nuts	Sierra plums	trout	ground squirrel
acorns	Sierra gooseberries	sucker fish	fox
chokecherries	manzanita berries	chub fish	badger
elderberries	watercress	rabbit	porcupine
serviceberries	wild rhubarb	mule deer	locusts
buckberries	mushrooms	pronghorn antelope	grasshoppers
currants	miner's lettuce	bighorn sheep	bee larvae
wild lettuce	bitterroot	quail	fly grubs
sunflower seeds	sego lilies	sage grouse	caterpillars
wild mustard seeds	wild onions	prairie chicken	lizard
pigweed seeds	tule and cattail	waterfowl	bird eggs

Source: Based on data from Downs 1966 and D'Azevedo 1986.

rivers emptying into Lake Tahoe and other lakes within the Washo territory provided fish throughout the year. Fish were taken with spears, nets, hooks and lines, traps, and weirs; ice fishing took place in winter. In the fall, harvests of piñon nuts could yield huge stores of rich nuts. A man and wife were said to be able to collect the equivalent of two gunny sacks full of nuts in a single day. Because of this diversity, foraging diets are generally more nutritious than the diets of food producers.

These piñon pinecones yield a harvest of nutrient rich nuts.

An adaptive advantage to the foraging lifestyle is that the groups have the ability to shift to alternative food resources if a specific resource is unavailable because of weather, pests, or disease. Of course, starvation is a real possibility for foragers if weather conditions alter the usual levels of plant productivity, which in turn affects animal populations in the environment. Ecosystems are also disrupted by outside influences such as war, imperialism, revolution, and even tourism.

Low Energy Budgets. Foragers exist on **low energy budgets.** They generally have more leisure time than peoples with other types of food-procurement strategies. A low energy budget means that people expend a minimum of energy to acquire the basic needs for survival. A single Ju/'hoansi woman walking to a mongongo nut tree and gathering the fallen nuts (rich in carbohydrates, protein, and fat) and cracking them to retrieve the meats inside, for example, has a lower yearly expenditure of calories than a woman growing a crop like corn or beans. Cultivating crops

low energy budget The expenditure of minimum energy to acquire the basic needs for survival.

requires digging and preparing the soil, sowing seed, watering, weeding, and finally harvesting the crop before the food can be eaten.

Economic Production Generalists. Foragers are generalists. Everyone knows just about everything associated with survival. Knowledge and skills are shared by all members of the group. No one specializes in just one activity to make a living. A woman knows how to hunt, though she may not do it often. A man knows how to cook and how to gather berries and nuts.

Kinship and Division of Labor. Foraging societies are kin based and have a flexible **division of labor.** All members of foraging groups are kin by blood or marriage or a fictive kin relationship. Fictive kin are people who are treated as though related by blood or marriage, such as a godparent. Each member knows her or his responsibilities and duties to each other member (see Chapter 8 for further discussion of the functions of kinship and Chapter 7 for consideration of other related issues). The division of labor, generally based on age and gender, may be flexible. Among the Washo, women generally gathered and prepared foods for drying and men hunted and fished. Ernestine Friedl (1978) and others have pointed out that the division of labor among foragers is usually more egalitarian than in agricultural and industrial societies. Friedl suggests that this is likely because both women and men contribute directly to the group's survival through food procurement.

Foraging Societies Today

Today there are few societies that live in the traditional foraging lifeways that were recorded from 1900 to 1960. It is fortunate that anthropologists were able to record the cultures of groups such as the Inuit, the Dobe Ju/'hoansi, the Mbuti, the Tiwi, and the Washo before the rapid changes that resulted from contact with industrialized societies. Of course, these societies also changed in the past. Few human groups were isolated and without contact with others, but contact was probably less frequent. Ethnographer Richard B. Lee noted that only one vehicle came to the Dobe area every four to six weeks during his 1963–64 fieldwork, whereas one every four to six hours was counted during 1986–87. Quick math will tell you that this is a change from about 12 per year in the early 1960s to between 1,400 and 2,200 in the late 1980s (Lee 1993: viii). During visits to Dobe in 1999–2001, Lee noted that road improvements reduced driving time into the area from 6–7 hours to only 2.5 hours, resulting in increased outside contact.

Health issues have emerged with dietary changes and more outside contact for the Dobe Ju/'hoansi. In 1964 they received 85 percent of their calories from foraging; in 1993 only about 30 percent of foods came from hunting and gathering, with the remainder consisting of meat and milk from domestic goats and cattle. Although they were once famous for having

division of labor
The manner of dividing work based on criteria such as age or gender.

low blood pressure and cholesterol, restudies in the late 1980s of the same groups showed higher cholesterol and blood pressures in all ages (Lee 2002: 170). The Ju/'hoansi are now reporting cases of HIV-positive individuals, although the incidence is quite low, between 3 and 6 percent HIV-positive compared to national averages for Namibia of 22.5 percent and Botswana of 38 percent (Lee and Susser 2003).

Today the Dobe are subsisting primarily as farm laborers, though some hunt and gather part time. A new borehole (well) at Dobe now supports eight hamlets with 150 residents. There is a new preschool and a soccer field. Students attend a primary school 20 kilometers away (Lee 2002: 182). The people are taking an active role in the development of the region, including involvement in ecocultural tourism. The traditional values of egalitarianism and reciprocity are still held, and Lee believes that "Their commitment to egalitarian politics and reciprocity gives them a tremendous source of strength and persistence" (Lee 2002: 198).

In 1998 the Ju/'hoansi were granted rights to 9,000 square kilometers of land (907,000 hectares) and a role in managing the natural resources within their territory. The territory occupied by the Ju/'hoansi of the Nyae Nyae area of Namibia and the Dobe region of Botswana is now called the Nyae Nyae Conservancy. The thirty-six villages dispersed throughout the conservancy represent approximately 2,000 Ju/'hoansi. The conservancy efforts opened or rehabilitated water sources for wildlife and, with the aid of various donors, reintroduced more than 1,000 animals, including species such as kudu, blue wildebeest, springbok, and eland. Some of these populations have since more than doubled. A hunting concession agreement with African Hunting Safaris resulted in an income of over a million Namibian dollars per year for the conservancy, making it fully self-financed (NACSO 2007; USAID 2007). Cash dividends are now being paid to members of the conservancy based on the revenues from both hunting concessions and handicrafts produced by Ju/'hoansi artisans. Several Living Museums are now operated in Namibia. Run by the Ju/'hoansi, these museums allow the preservation of their ancient culture while generating income from tourism. Still, most Ju/'hoansi live in poverty.

Today the Washo Tribe of Nevada and California is a federally recognized, self-governing tribe. They comprise four communities—one in California and three in Nevada. The Washo Hunting and Fishing Commission regulates hunting and fishing in the region and oversees wildlife and natural resource conservation. Washo participate in protection and restoration of endangered habitats. The Washo manage a resort at Lake Tahoe and hold an annual arts festival. Some Washo still supplement their modern diets with traditional wild foods such as piñon nuts.

Government officials, traders, tourists, medical personnel, and anthropologists all have an impact on indigenous peoples. Anthropologists are interested in understanding human adaptations; this includes understanding the processes of how cultures change and adapt through time. Ongoing studies, such as Lee's with the Dobe Ju/'hoansi, provide us with vital information about the processes of cultural change.

SUMMARY

We all have to eat. The subsistence strategies of foraging, horticulture, pastoralism, and agriculture represent the major types of human food-procurement adaptations arranged in order of their emergence in the archaeological record. By viewing cultures within an evolutionary-ecological model, we are able to compare cultures with similar subsistence strategies. Overall patterns become apparent when it is established that each subsistence strategy results in a similar sociocultural adaptation. Foragers are bands of nomadic, kin-based, egalitarian societies without the ownership of property except for a few personal possessions or a particular resource. Generalized reciprocity is the dominant system of distribution found among these generalists; everyone shares in the technology, and the division of labor is flexible.

Foragers were not static in the past nor are they today. There was a time when forager bands were viewed as societies that were somehow, like fossils, preserved remnants of past ways of life. Some of these societies are being absorbed by industrialized neighbors; others have continued many aspects of traditional lifeways while selectively adopting aspects of their neighbors' adaptations.

Study Questions

OLC
mhhe • com / lenkeit5e
See Self Quiz.

1. Describe foraging as a subsistence strategy, citing specific examples from the Washo and Dobe Ju/'hoansi.
2. Identify the adaptive features of technology and food procurement found in an ethnography assigned for class reading. How closely do these features match the general features of the adaptive strategy of foraging outlined in this chapter?
3. Discuss how the three components of technology aid you to keep warm during winter months so that you don't die of hypothermia.
4. Compare and contrast generalized and balanced reciprocity. Cite a specific example of each from your own experience and cite one from an ethnographic account.

Suggested Readings

OLC
mhhe • com / lenkeit5e
See Web links.

Harris, Marvin. 1998. *Good to Eat: Riddles of Food and Culture.* Prospect Heights, Ill.: Waveland Press. (Originally published 1985 as *The Sacred Cow and the Abominable Pig.*) Entertaining analysis of food preferences cross-culturally. Offers many insights into the dietary choices made by different cultures.

Knauft, Bruce. 2010. *The Gebusi: Lives Transformed in a Rainforest World*, 2nd ed. New York: McGraw-Hill. As the title suggests, this ethnography describes the transformation of Gebusi life from the author's 1980 work to his return in 1998. Personal stories vividly transport the reader to the field.

Lee, Richard B. 2002. *The Dobe Ju/'hoansi*, 3rd ed. Belmont, Calif.: Wadsworth. This book covers decades of Lee's fieldwork among the Ju/'hoansi (formerly called the !Kung Bushmen) and is an excellent example of an ecologically focused ethnography. Lee offers insight into the diversity of adaptations made by foragers.

Lee, Richard B., and Richard Daly, eds. 2005. *The Cambridge Encyclopedia of Hunters and Gatherers*. New York: Cambridge University Press. A definitive reference source covering the past, present, and future of indigenous hunters and gatherers.

Plattner, Stuart, ed. 1989. *Economic Anthropology*. Stanford, Calif.: Stanford University Press. An indispensable resource covering the economic features of societies ranging from foraging to industrial.

Subsistence Strategies and Resource Allocation II

How Did Food Production Transform Culture?

When an entrepreneur from Hawaii was visiting Tahiti many years ago, she was quite taken by the hand-woven palm fiber hats made and worn by the Tahitians. The hats were elaborate, and the finest ones were proudly worn to church by the native Tahitian women; everyday sun hats were not as detailed but still were unusual when compared to the simple straw hats worn for gardening or on the beach in Hawaii. She thought that the Tahitian hats would sell well in her Waikiki boutique as they were Polynesian native art. So she purchased some and took them home. Indeed they sold quickly, and she began to have requests for them. On a return trip to Tahiti she sought to arrange for someone to produce the hats for her and contacted several local weavers. She wanted many hats of one style and was frustrated to find that workers would readily accept employment but then would fail to show up to work after a day or two on the production line. Craftsmen would say that they were fed up (*fiu*). Making many hats of one design was boring. In fact working all day was not something that they wanted to do. Global economics and the spread of materialism had not yet seduced the native Tahitians. We heard many such stories about local attitudes toward work when in the Society Islands in early 1970.

Conversations with local Tahitians, French colonials, and missionaries revealed that outsiders often viewed the Tahitians as lazy. The more thoughtful among these, however, took a perspective of cultural relativism and pointed out that their culture was merely different in its attitude toward work. You could, they told us, contract with a local artisan to produce many hats, but they wouldn't be identical. Rather, the hats would show infinite variation in design. Moreover, the artisan would charge you less for varied hats than for identical hats. I carefully examined hats and other handmade items in the open market in Papeete and at roadside stands and small shops on the various islands, and rarely did I see any hats of the same design.

Attitudes toward work and what constitutes work vary widely from culture to culture, and today globalization is impacting attitudes about work. The North American work ethic was largely shaped in Europe during the Protestant Reformation by Martin Luther and John Calvin. Later, Benjamin Franklin fully secularized the importance of hard work in his *Poor Richard's Almanac* (1733–1758). American newspapers regularly run stories about those who achieve success by hard work. We applaud and revere those who toil and lift themselves out of poverty. Hard work is important; it pays off. Work dominates our lives. The first contact by Western cultures with others revealed a diversity of attitudes about work, production, distribution, and consumption. Anthropologists use these Western economic categories in ethnographic studies but acknowledge that they represent the view of others through our cultural lens.

The objectives of this chapter are to:

- Describe subsistence strategies and economics within an evolutionary-ecological model
- Examine sociocultural changes brought by food-producing subsistence strategies
- Identify strategies common to horticulture and pastoralism
- Identify the strategies common to agriculture and industrialism
- Describe issues associated with the globalization of agriculture

◀ Intensive rice terrace farming in China requires different technological skills than foraging.

THE EVOLUTIONARY-ECOLOGICAL MODEL CONTINUED

This chapter continues the discussion begun in Chapter 5. Here we consider how human groups acquire and use their resources to *produce* food and goods, how food and resources are distributed and consumed. Emphasis is on how subsistence strategies were changed by domestication and how socioeconomic adaptations occurred as a consequence. Again a holistic approach is maintained by interweaving discussion of subsistence strategies with economics, including production, division of labor and labor specialization, systems of distribution, and consumption. As with the discussion of foragers in the preceding chapter, sociocultural issues such as group organization and kinship are also touched on here because they too changed over time. Subsequent chapters cover kinship and political organization in more detail.

Some reminders: The evolutionary outline that is the framework of this presentation is the broad *sequential* one supported by archaeological and historical data; it does not mean that every culture progresses through exactly the same "stages" in development. It is important to emphasize that the boundaries between the following food-production strategies are not discrete. Horticulture, pastoralism, and intensive agriculture are points along a spectrum. There were many intermediate combinations of food-procurement adaptations. The evolutionary framework provides an organized way to introduce these topics. Every cultural group interacts in complex ways with its physical and social environment and has its own unique history of change over time. The theoretical perspective of cultural ecology also continues to be used.

HORTICULTURE AS A SUBSISTENCE STRATEGY

Horticulture is a food-procurement strategy that is based on a simple level of crop production. Seeds or cuttings are planted without benefit of cultivation or preparation of the soil; no fertilizers are used, and no irrigation is undertaken. The data of archaeology have contributed to knowledge of when and where horticulture first emerged as a food-procurement strategy. Our assessment of this emergence is aided by recent technologies for the gathering of data from the past. For example, accelerator mass spectrometry (AMS) in conjunction with carbon-14 dating has made it possible to date a single seed about the size of a sesame seed. Flotation techniques allow for the recovery of tiny specimens such as seeds, seed coats, and insect wings. These techniques, in conjunction with the electron microscope (which enables us to measure the thickness of seed coats—an important determinant of domestication), have revealed much about early plant domestication.

horticulture
A food-procurement strategy based on crop production without soil preparation, fertilizers, irrigation, or use of draft animals.

Early archaeologists hypothesized that plant domestication originated in a few widely dispersed geographic locations—rice in southeast Asia, millet in Africa, wheat in Asia Minor, corn in Mexico. From these points of origin the crops were thought to have diffused to other regions. Recent research, however, has revealed a much more complex and interesting process for this adaptation with many more centers of domestication and many more species of plants involved.

Bruce Smith has shown that *Chenopodium berlanderii* (a seed-bearing plant that yields tiny, highly nutritious seeds about the size of alfalfa seeds or poppy seeds) was domesticated east of the Mississippi River in North America about two thousand years before the arrival of *Zea mays* (corn), which diffused north from Mexico (Smith 1992). Further, Smith has demonstrated that other seed crops were domesticated in the same area and yielded nutrition-rich foods for prehistoric Native American populations as they learned to sow and harvest along the floodplains of river valleys. We should not be surprised to find that the shift from foraging ways of life to settled village life based on cultivating crops was a slow, gradual process rather than the revolution that was hypothesized earlier. It was most likely an adaptation to environmental and social stresses in particular habitats. Human culture is continually changing, some aspects slowly, others quickly, but even quick changes usually take close to a generation to be complete. Most horticulture developed in areas where there is sufficient rainfall to maintain crop growth or in floodplains where seasonal flooding provides moisture.

Features Associated with Horticultural Lifeways

The following are the common features of horticulturalists. Note that societies with horticulture as the primary food-procurement strategy are associated with societal types labeled tribes and chiefdoms. *Tribe* and *chiefdom* are terms describing political groupings (these are discussed in Chapter 10).

Production Based on Extensive Technology. Horticulturalists have extensive technology. The technology—knowledge, skills, and tools—used in simple cultivation is complex and requires understanding of plant cycles, seasonal weather conditions, soils, when and how to harvest, how to winnow hulls from seeds, how to store harvested crops, and how to select and store seeds for the next season's planting. Horticulturalists need the knowledge and skills to manipulate nature rather than focusing on understanding their natural surroundings as foragers do. This attests to the cumulative nature of culture. Knowledge builds through time as new discoveries are made and passed on to each generation.

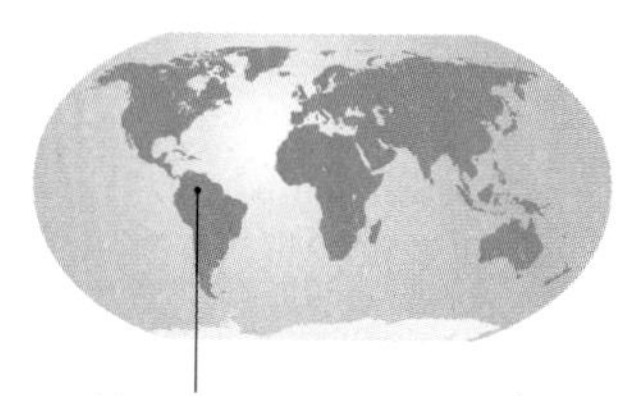

Yąnomamö

The Yąnomamö of Venezuela and Brazil cultivate gardens that provide 80 to 90 percent of their food; the remainder comes from hunting and some gathering of wild plants and insects such as grubs. Plantains provide 80 percent of the calories that the Yąnomamö consume, and most garden space is taken up by plantain trees. Each tree produces only one bunch of the banana-shaped fruit; then it is cut to the ground to make room for the young suckers that have been forming underground. Each sucker can grow into a new tree. Yąnomamö gardeners must keep track of these planting and harvesting cycles to ensure continuous crops. Other cultivated plants include peach palm trees, sweet manioc (a starchy root), a type of taro, sweet potatoes, and sometimes avocados, papaya, and hot peppers. Inedible crops include cotton and tobacco (Chagnon 1997).

Sedentary Lifestyle. Horticulturalists are sedentary. Unlike foragers, horticulturalists stay in one place for long periods of time—typically until the soil is exhausted. The most common type of horticulture is called **slash-and-burn** horticulture because ground cover is removed by cutting and burning. Large trees may be felled outright or girdled and allowed to die before they are burned. There are other local terms for this horticulture method (e.g., swidden), but the same process is used everywhere. You and I, as products of cultures with scientific technology, recognize that ashes contribute to the fertility of the soil, but slash-and-burn is primarily viewed by those who practice it as a means of clearing the land. When crop yield declines, new gardens are created by the same technique. Soils that have been exhausted in this way take many generations to recover sufficiently to support diverse plant life once more. At one time soil depletion was hypothesized as the only reason that horticulturalists moved. Today we know that declining soil fertility alone cannot account for village movements at least in the tropical forest of Amazonia. Napoleon Chagnon has reported that the Yąnomamö created new gardens adjacent to maturing ones because it was more convenient to do so, and he documented cases of villages staying in the same area for sixty to eighty years. One reason to stay in the same area is that cuttings of large plantain suckers (which will yield a new crop of plantains sooner than a small sucker) sometimes weigh ten pounds or more, so moves of a few hundred yards are much easier than long-distance moves. Chagnon also reports that unpleasant, thorny vegetation that grows in maturing gardens is both tedious and painful to remove, and snakes become a problem in old gardens. These are logical reasons to make what he calls micro movements (Chagnon 1997: 71–72).

slash-and-burn
The removal of plant materials by cutting and burning preparatory to planting.

Larger Groups and Kinship Structures. Horticulture results in larger populations and kinship systems with more segments than those encountered among foragers. This is due to the increase in carrying capacity that results from food production. Having large numbers of people (from several hundred to tens of thousands) requires organization if the society is to

This boy in Kenya is tending a rice field. The noise from banging on the can keeps the birds away.

work efficiently. Kinship ties and the responsibilities that accompany them are what weave the fabric of such societies. Kin groups based on descent and residence are a consistent correlate to horticulturally based societies. The various types of descent and residence groups are discussed in Chapters 7 and 8, and political aspects of tribes are discussed in Chapter 10.

Property and Ownership. Unlike foragers, horticulturalists own property. Property ownership is by kin groups, and these groups—lineages and clans, for example—work the land and reap the benefits of their labors. Common patterns among horticulturalists include small settlements of several related

TRY THIS
Compare

Compare the foods listed for the Trobrianders and the Yąnomamö with the foods of foragers listed in Tables 5.1 and 5.2 in the previous chapter. What differences do you see?

kin groups that are surrounded by gardens and fields. Land rights belong to a family or lineage or larger kin group. This is not ownership in terms of legal deeds to the land, as recognized in state societies. Rather, members of the society recognize traditional land rights, and such lands are passed from generation to generation. For example, in the Trobriand Islands archipelago (now part of Papua New Guinea and called the Kiriwina Islands), yams, taro, sweet potatoes, coconuts, bananas, greens, beans, squash, and breadfruit are grown in gardens owned by women and inherited through women. Horticulturalists also have more possessions than foragers. Extended living in one place, plus the need for tools to produce, harvest, store, and process the crops, results in more artifacts.

Poorer Nutrition. Horticulturalists have poorer overall nutrition than foragers. Vitamin and mineral intakes are reduced, or incomplete, because food is not as diverse. Both archaeological evidence from forensic analysis of the skeletons of prehistoric peoples and data from ethnography show that human nutrition and health declined with settled living and dietary reliance on one or a few grains. See Box 6.1 for an explanation of some of the negative consequences of diets based on the cultivation of domestic plants.

Higher Energy Budget. Horticulturalists have a higher energy budget than foragers. Many more calories are spent per person per week to procure basic survival needs. Clearing of land and planting of crops requires intense physical effort (horticulturalists do not use draft animals), but this is just the beginning of the planting cycle. Crops must be weeded, and birds and other animals must be deterred from eating the emerging seedlings. Harvest and preparation of foods for consumption as well as the maintenance of storage facilities must also be considered.

Economic Production Generalists. Horticulturalists, like foragers, are family-based generalists, not specialists. Each family must know how to carry out numerous tasks for survival; individuals do not support themselves singly by a specialized economic activity. Rather, all are involved in some aspect of tending the gardens.

Division of Labor. Horticulturalists have a well-defined division of labor. Men's work and women's work are clearly delineated and do not have the flexibility found among foragers. Some anthropologists have speculated that the more rigid division of labor that developed with horticultural economies may have been the beginning of important differences in the status of men and women. The issue of how rigid or flexible the division of labor is in societies with different systems of food procurement can be debated. This is one of the issues that is somewhat murky when viewed cross-culturally. For example, Annette Weiner reports that among the Trobriand

BOX 6.1 The Negative Consequences of Plant Domestication as Seen from Prehistoric and Historic Evidence

Feature	Negative Consequences	Evidence
Domestication of plants ca 10,000 B.P. Focus on intense cultivation of one or a few crops	Less diversity of diet Poorer nutrition	• Greek and Turkish skeletons Male Female Predomestication 5'9" 5'5" Postdomestication 5'3" 5'0" • Skeletons from Dixon Mounds (Illinois) after maize (corn) cultivation began, nearly 50% increase in dental enamel defects (indicates malnutrition), and 4 times more iron deficiency anemia
Increased carrying capacity of land	Increased potential for starvation (e.g., the Irish potato famine in the 1840s caused hundreds of thousands of deaths).	
Larger, denser population	Infections and contagious diseases increase due to:	• Airborne droplets from sneezing and coughing spread measles, colds, and flu • Absence of sanitation results in fecal contamination of water and food, spreading typhoid, cholera, diarrhea, parasites • Greater contact leads to higher rates of syphilis and scabies • Vectors: fleas and mosquitoes spread plague and malaria

Based on data from Campbell 1983 and Diamond 1987.

How do you participate in balanced reciprocity with neighbors and friends? Are these reciprocal exchanges necessary to your survival?

Islanders growing yams is primarily men's work. She notes, however, that husbands and wives work together in the strenuous labor of soil preparation. Men do most of the garden planting; women tend and weed growing crops (Weiner 1988).

Distribution of Goods. The systems of distribution found among horticulturalists are similar to those among foragers, but the emphasis is shifted. Generalized reciprocity still dominates within the nuclear family and extends to some other close kin, such as lineage members, but outside of these groups balanced reciprocity is the norm. Gifts of food, possessions, time, and energy are calculated, and the expectation is that items of equal value will be reciprocated within a reasonable period of time. Thus alliances and interdependencies are formed outside of one's own lineage, and clan and status or reputation may be enhanced by participating in reciprocal exchanges. The Yąnomamö give feasts for neighboring villages and give gifts to visitors who are expected to reciprocate when they host a feast. Everyone keeps mental track of what is given and received. Alliances are built through these exchanges.

In the case of the Trobriand exchange system known as the *kula*, first described by Bronislaw Malinowski, ornately made white arm shells and red shell necklaces are at the center of an elaborate and complex balanced reciprocal exchange system. These items move between trade partners on a group of islands that form a rough circular ring, so the exchange has been called the kula ring. Men labor to match the size and value of these two types of shells. An individual receives an arm shell from one trade partner during a visit to another island and is expected to reciprocate with a necklace of equal value at a later time when the trade partner visits his island. Necklaces move in a clockwise direction through the islands, whereas arm shells move counterclockwise. Trade of foods and other items takes place peripherally to the kula exchange, and early analysis suggested that such trade was really the important function of the exchange. However, according to Annette Weiner, who restudied the Trobriands in the 1980s, men's status is tied to the kula exchanges. As she states, "Trobriand men create their own individual fame by circulating these objects that accumulate the histories of their travels and the names of those who have possessed them" (Weiner 1988: 9).

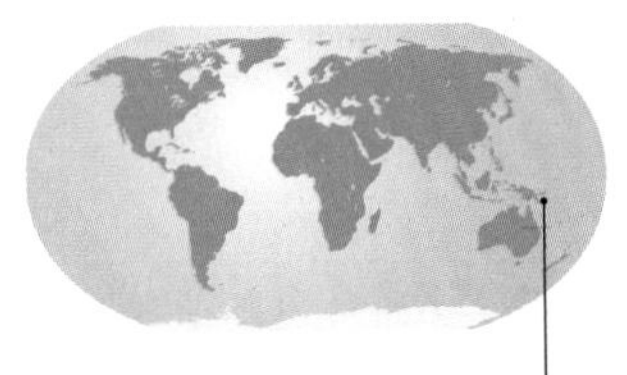

PASTORALISM AS A SUBSISTENCE STRATEGY

The archaeological evidence shows that humans began domesticating animals and plants at about the same time—around ten thousand years ago. Horticultural economies, with supplementation from domesticated animals, thrived for some time before lifeways emerged that focused on

Trobriand kula objects have histories that accompany them on the traditional trade routes.

herding. There were many different ecological conditions that fostered **pastoralism,** and many different animals have been the basis for a herding way of life—cattle, sheep, reindeer, goats, camels, horses, and llamas. Pastoralists learned to use many aspects of the animals they nurtured, maintaining the herds as a food bank reserve. Animals can eat natural plant materials that humans cannot consume directly, so animal husbandry may be viewed as an adaptive strategy that transforms energy sources into a form that humans can use. Milk, blood, hair, skin, bone, horn, antler, and hoof provide both sustenance and raw materials for making artifacts. Animals are rarely killed for food, usually only when associated with ceremonies (which may occur throughout the year, thus providing consistent, if small, amounts of meat protein).

As with other adaptive strategies of the evolutionary-ecological model, variation is found in the specifics of each pastoral society, whereas some general correlates emerge cross-culturally. Elman Service noted many general sociocultural similarities between horticulturalists and pastoralists, aside from their food-procurement strategies.

pastoralism
A food-producing strategy based on herding.

Features Associated with Pastoral Lifeways

The following are the common features of the pastoralist adaptation as described in various ethnographies.

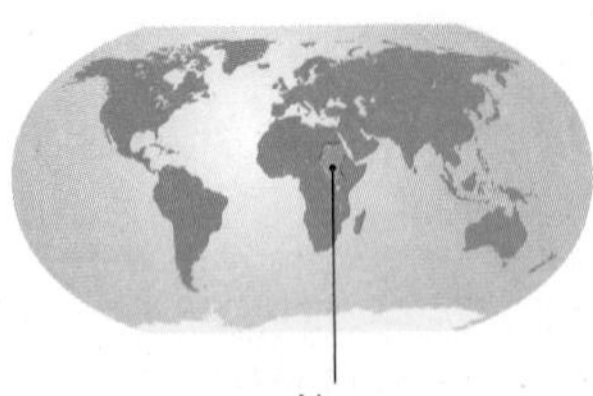

Production Based on Sophisticated Technology. Pastoralists have sophisticated technologies. Knowledge of their environment must be extensive to know where and when to move their herds to fresh pastures. They have knowledge and skills to successfully breed and maintain their animals. The Nuer of the southern Sudan in Africa are a society that focuses on animal husbandry in the form of cattle herding. They also raise gardens of millet, maize, and beans, but herding is the focus of their food production. The environment they live in is essentially flat land with marshes and grassy plains where few trees grow. Rivers flow through the region and flood vast areas during the wet season, requiring the Nuer to move their herds to higher grounds until the water recedes. The sandy soils of these slightly elevated areas allow the growing of millet, but because they lack pasture and water, movement back to the grassy plains is necessary. Clay soils in the flats and marshy areas hold water, which in turn supports grasses during the dry season.

Nomadic Lifestyle. Most pastoralists are nomadic. They must move frequently to fresh pastures. Ranching and dairy farming (which could be called sedentary pastoralism) are fairly recent occurrences in the history of human adaptations and are typically associated with industrialized societies. Two types of preindustrialized pastoral economies have been identified. **Nomadic pastoralism** is an adaptation that makes the most of available forage for the herd animals by frequent mobility. The entire group moves with their animals. **Transhumance** is a pastoral adaptation in which herds are moved seasonally such as up into mountains as spring and summer progress, or to rotating pasture areas. Only part of the group moves with the herds—men and boys, for example. Others stay in the home or village location. The Nuer, with their frequent moves because of the cycles of wet and dry, were labeled transhumant by E. E. Evans-Pritchard, who published accounts of their traditional life (Evans-Pritchard 1940).

nomadic pastoralism
A herding adaptation that makes the most of available forage for animals by frequent habitat moves.

transhumance
A variety of pastoralism in which herds are moved seasonally.

Large Populations. Pastoralism results in large populations and increases the carrying capacity of land that is relatively infertile. On land that can support only grass and scrub (and there is quite a bit of such land), pastoralism is an effective strategy that enables more people to live in an area than could live there by either foraging or horticulture. Pastoral people, who for obvious reasons are more widely dispersed across the landscape than horticultural groups, often consist of thousands of people. The Nuer numbered 200,000 when Evans-Pritchard worked among them in the 1940s.

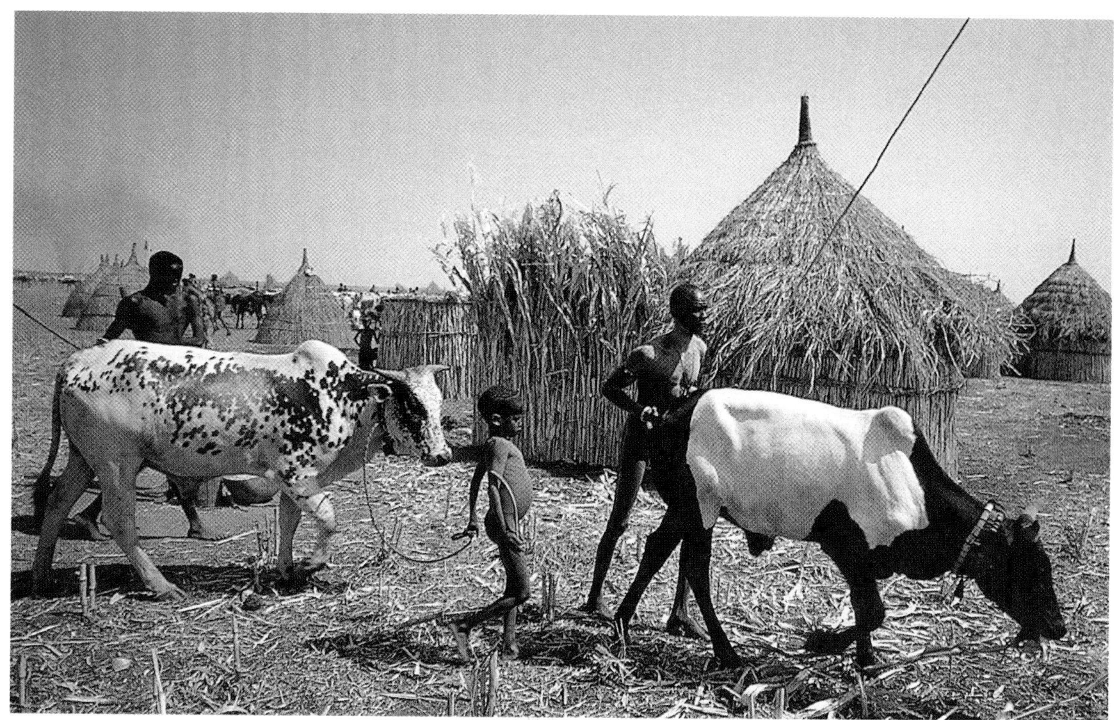

A Nuer man and child attend cattle.

Property Ownership. Pastoralists own property in the form of animals. The ownership of herd animals is at the core of the various groups who nurture and benefit from the animals. Because they are mobile, pastoralists have fewer material possessions than horticulturalists. There is much variation of detail regarding this feature of the pastoral lifeway because some pastoralists maintain semipermanent camps that they return to periodically and others use animals as beasts of burden to transport possessions.

Improved Nutrition. Pastoralists generally have better nutrition than horticulturalists, primarily because they have access to more complete protein in the form of milk, milk products, and blood. Pastoralists either maintain small kitchen gardens or trade with neighboring horticultural groups for grains and vegetables. The Nuer cattle supply milk, which is consumed fresh, sour, curdled, and as cheese. Blood let from veins in a cow's neck and collected in gourds is boiled and used as flavoring, or it is allowed to coagulate and is then roasted over hot coals before being eaten. The Nuer claim that bloodletting is done for cattle health. Blood is not a dietary staple although they admitted to Evans-Pritchard that roasted blood is delicious. The Nuer do not raise herds for slaughter.

Meat from cattle is eaten primarily at ceremonial occasions or if an animal dies. Evans-Pritchard notes "The Nuer are very fond of meat, and declare that on the death of a cow, 'The eyes and the heart are sad, but the teeth and the stomach are glad.' A man's stomach prays to God, independently of his mind, for such gifts" (Evans-Pritchard 1940: 26). Millet is eaten as porridge and made into beer. Some beans and maize are also grown. A few wild dates can be found in Nuer territory, but there is little else in the way of wild fruits or vegetables.

High Energy Budget. The energy budget of pastoralists is higher than that of foragers. Husbanding herd animals requires constant vigilance to ensure that the pasture is adequate, water is available, and animals are protected from various natural hazards. The weeding of gardens must be done several times during the growing season.

Kinship and Division of Labor. Pastoralists are kin-based groups in which the fabric of the society, as in the case of horticulturalists, is woven of various complex kinship ties and the responsibilities associated with them. Such large societies require organization if they are to function efficiently. Like large horticultural groups, societal organization and social interaction are based on kin descent and residence patterns. These large kin organizations are discussed in Chapters 7 and 8. Division of labor is by age and gender.

OLC
mhhe • com / lenkeit5e
See Internet exercises.

Distribution of Goods. The systems of distribution found among pastoralists involve generalized reciprocity between nuclear family and lineage members and balanced reciprocity with most others who are more distantly related. Balanced reciprocity through barter and trade took place with adjacent societies in the past. Today pastoralists exist on the periphery of societies based on market exchange, and they participate to some extent in these systems. The Nuer today number over one million, and there have been many changes, including those caused by decades of civil war and unrest in the Sudan, yet emphasis on cattle remains central to their cultural values.

Horticulturalists and Pastoralists Today

Culture is dynamic. Restudies of tribal peoples illustrate this concept. Contact with other tribal peoples, missionaries, traders, colonial governments, soldiers, and tourists, as well as warfare, led to acculturation and change for most tribal peoples. Two societies described in the previous sections, the Trobriand Islanders and the Nuer, experienced and are experiencing such changes. The Trobriand Islanders were first made famous by Malinowski's fieldwork that began in 1914. The Trobriands became

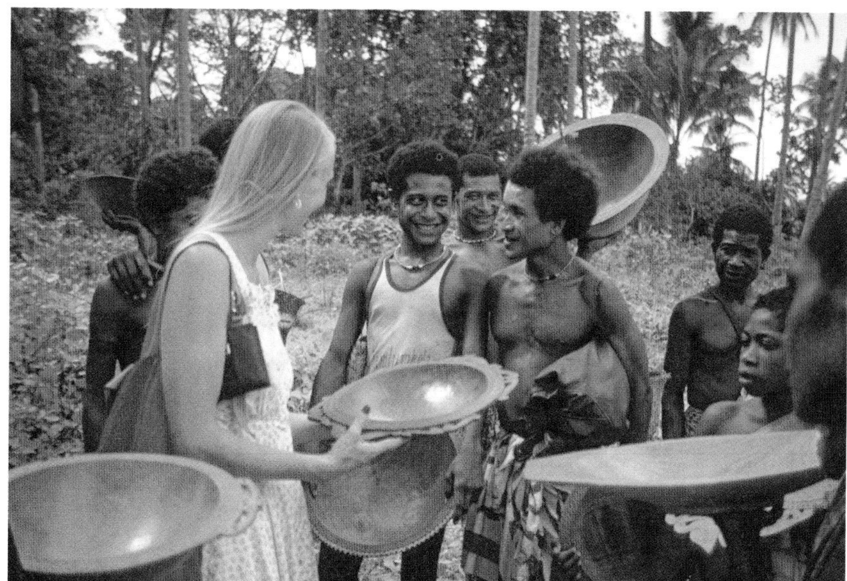

Today tourism is part of life in the Trobriand Islands (now called the Kiriwina Islands).

part of the nation-state of Papua New Guinea in 1975. Participation in a cash economy, due in large part to tourism, has detracted from traditional social activities (Peters-Golden 2002). Annette Weiner reported in 1988 that Trobrianders resist change and despite much contact and a period of active tourism, they maintained important traditional beliefs. She attributes this to the role of women. Women traditionally controlled their own wealth by manufacturing items of economic value such as banana leaf fiber skirts and banana leaf bundles. The major use of these items is in the payments—from thirty to several hundred bundles—made to mourners after death (Weiner 1988: 30–49). When an important chief died, she reports, even university-educated Trobrianders living in the urban capital attended the traditional distribution ceremony that was held (Weiner 1988: 31). Trobrianders are increasingly involved with a global economy including ecotourism.

The Nuer have experienced major upheavals since Evans-Pritchard recorded their way of life in the early 1930s. One civil war (1955–72) was fought to win autonomy for and unite the southern region. Then in the 1980s the national government proposed among other issues to divide the south into three regions (Hutchinson 1996: 3–4). Conflict escalated between north and south Sudan, with hundreds of thousands of southern Sudanese dying since the mid-1990s in war-provoked confrontations and from famine and disease. Thousands of Nuer were displaced from their homes and became refugees in camps in Ethiopia and Kenya.

Programs were designed to help find permanent homes for them. This resulted in nearly four thousand Nuer emigrating to the United States by 1996 (Holtzman 2000). Survivors and refugees are adapting. Some in the Sudan are trying to recapture the old ways of life. Life is challenging for Nuer refugees living in the United States. "They have had to learn how to negotiate a culture as centered on the automobile as their own culture is on cows" (Holtzman 2007: 135). Some are adapting well, have jobs, have earned or are earning college degrees and becoming citizens; others struggle. South Sudanese voted in January 2011 for independence from the north, bringing hope for future peace in the region. Some Nuer living in the United States say that they will return home if true peace is established.

AGRICULTURE AS A SUBSISTENCE STRATEGY

Agriculture is a subsistence-procurement strategy that is based on intensive, continuous use of land for the production of plant foods. One or more of these features is present: cultivation of soils, use of fertilizers, and irrigation. Soil cultivation is often elaborate and energy intensive. Draft animals or tractors are used to plow, to maintain cultivated land, and to harvest crops. Fertilizers are applied before planting and during plant growth, resulting in increased yields. Regular, planned irrigation ensures plant survival and optimum growth. As with the other systems of food production that have been discussed, there is a continuum of agricultural production. The range is from small single-family farm holdings to modern farming corporations. Small farms may use flood irrigation from a nearby river and have a single draft horse or ox. Large multifamily cooperative farms have complex irrigation systems and several draft animals or the use of a tractor that has been cooperatively purchased. Modern farms owned by corporations have thousands of acres in production and make extensive use of the resources and support of state-owned-and-operated irrigation systems and utilize energy from sources such as fossil fuels.

agriculture
A subsistence strategy based on intensive, continuous use of land for the production of plant foods. It typically includes one or more of the following: cultivation of soils, use of fertilizers, and irrigation.

The archaeological record is resplendent with data for the emergence of agriculture, because it often, though not always, coincides with the emergence of population centers, or cities. Emerging agricultural strategies tend to focus on production of one or a few crops, thus requiring networks of markets for acquiring other foodstuffs and necessities. Or, as in the case of chiefdoms, people acquire a variety of goods through redistribution. As noted earlier, any model contains categories and divisions that are somewhat arbitrary, and this is certainly the case with the distinctions between horticultural and agricultural adaptations. There is in reality a continuum from simple horticulture to intensive agricultural societies, with many permutations and combinations. Remember, as a starting point for comparative analysis, models, such as the evolutionary-ecological model, are useful.

Features Associated with Intensive Agricultural Lifeways

This discussion combines agriculture and intensive agriculture. The primary difference between these lies in the scale of production and the use of petroleum-based machinery. The following are correlates to the agricultural lifeway.

Production Based on More Levels of Technology. Agriculturalists have more levels of technology than horticulturalists, and they must have additional knowledge of plant cycles and soils. Technology at this level also includes detailed knowledge of plant-specific irrigation requirements. Irrigation systems are often quite creative and include water reservoirs and a variety of ways to deliver water to the crops (ditches, canals, and aqueducts). Farmers must know how to tame, train, and care for plow animals, or how to maintain and repair mechanical equipment. There are, quite simply, more different types of knowledge, skills, and tools. However, each individual's knowledge may not encompass all accumulated knowledge of the culture. We therefore need to take care that we do not consider agriculturally based societies as more advanced or better or smarter than societies with different food-procurement strategies. Agriculture, as with other human endeavors, emerged from cumulative, creative efforts of many people over many generations.

Sedentary Lifestyle. Agriculturalists are sedentary. The use of fertilizers to replace depleted soil nutrients means that farmers can remain on the same land for generations once it has been cleared, resulting in continuous residence and the construction of permanent structures—including storage facilities.

Stratified Societies. The carrying capacity of intensively cultivated lands increased dramatically. The well-known ancient Mexican city of Teotihuacán, for example, was in a region well suited for agricultural development, and by 2000 B.P. more than 60,000 people were living there (Feder 1996: 425). Clearly, concentrated numbers of people must have some form of societal organization. At one end of the agricultural continuum are **chiefdom** societies where the chief (this is most often a hereditary office) and his family have power and wealth that the other society members do not. This can be viewed as the beginning of **stratified societies**—societies with unequal access to resources within groups of the same gender and status. At the other end of the continuum are nation-states with many levels

chiefdom
A type of society with an office of chief, most commonly hereditary, social ranking, and redistributive economy.

stratified society
A society with unequal access to resources within groups of the same gender and status.

Rice terrace farming in Yuan Yang, Yunnan province, China, maximizes both land and water usage for food production.

of stratification. Between are states with fewer levels of stratification (see Chapter 10 for more detail on chiefdoms and stratified societies). Food producers, merchants, and various levels of government developed to organize the distribution of food and other materials.

Property Ownership. Agriculturalists own property. Ownership may be in the form of farmland, animals, a house, or a shop. They have material possessions that often extend beyond those that are necessary for mere survival. This is partly due to the sedentary nature of such societies where possessions can accumulate. Not all members of the society own the same amount of property, especially as stratification increases.

Poor-Quality Nutrition. Agriculturalists, like horticulturalists, often have poor overall nutrition, because food intake is not diverse. When one moves up the spectrum of agriculture into contemporary industrialized societies, the availability of diverse diets through the market increases, but whether people take advantage of this availability to maximize their nutritional

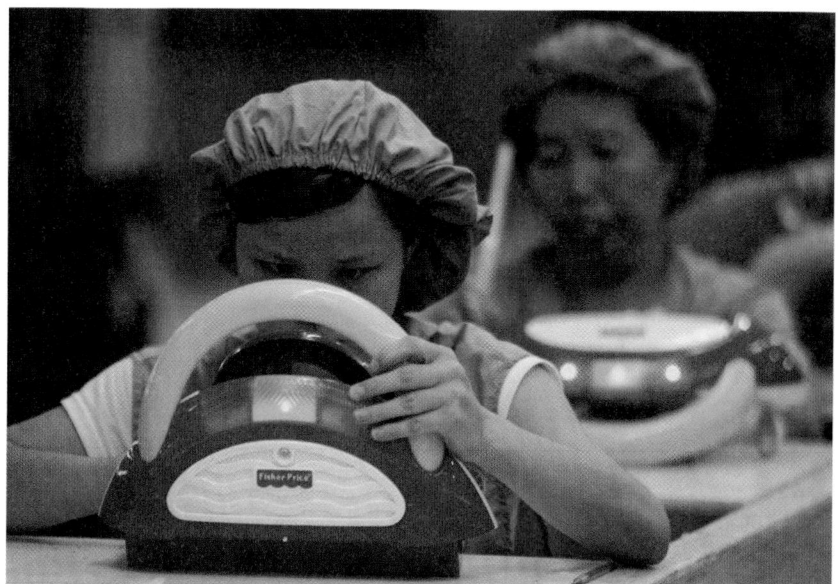

These toy factory workers in China manufacture products for export to world markets. In nation-states, many work at enterprises other than food production.

intake depends on many factors—income, education, and cultural ideas about acceptable food choices.

Lower Energy Budget. Agriculturalists have a lower energy budget than horticulturalists from an individual member's perspective. On average, fewer calories are spent per person per week in order to procure basic survival needs, because machines have taken over much labor-intensive work. For example, horse-drawn plows or tractors may have replaced hand tools used to till the soil. The overall energy consumption by the whole society, including that required to run machinery, may be high, but each individual is expending fewer calories to obtain food. The exceptions to this pattern are state societies with peripheral peasant cultures. The latter are farmers who produce food for their families rather than to sell for profit. The peasants have some dealings with the markets of the state society, but they are marginal.

Economic Production Specialists. Agriculture is based on economic specialization, and subsistence activities are no longer based solely on the efforts of the family. People make a living by specializing and selling their goods (foods, crafts, manufactured items, etc.), skills, or services in exchange for currency, which is then used to exchange for items that are not produced by the family, whereas among foragers, horticulturalists, and pastoralists, everything produced within the family was for exchange with other members through reciprocity.

Markets, such as this floating market near Bangkok, Thailand, are important in societies that have specialized the process of production.

TRY THIS
Consider

List four specific goods and four services that you have used in the past month that were provided by redistribution.

Division of Labor. There are many combinations and permutations to the division of labor among agricultural societies. Roles are determined by the specific traditions of individual cultures. In preindustrial societies, roles are most often assigned according to gender or age. Among industrialized societies the division of labor is more flexible.

Systems of Distribution. The systems of distribution in state-organized societies are redistribution and market exchange. **Redistribution** is a system of exchange in which material tribute or tax is paid to a central authority, which could be a chief, a large landowner if a sharecropping system is in place, or a central government if everyone owns property. The tribute gift or tax (which may be in the form of an actual portion of one's crop or a percentage of one's resources) is used to support the central authority, which could be an individual (such as a chief) or a governmental system. The surplus, beyond that used to maintain the authority itself, is redistributed to the population in the form of goods and services. In Polynesian chiefdoms, for example, surplus tribute that has been given to the chief is often redistributed as food and drink for ceremonial occasions.

redistribution
A system of exchange in which wealth is reallocated; found in chiefdom and state societies.

market exchange
The trading of goods and services through the use of currency.

Market exchange involves goods or services being traded or sold at a market. These are transactions in which supply and demand dictate the prices of the goods or services. Currency (we call this money) is often used in market exchange. The use of currency is more impersonal than face-to-face exchanges of reciprocity. Also, currency is portable—whether shells, beads, coins, or paper. You can easily carry it or save it, and it is permanent (i.e., it won't deteriorate). Currency is also divisible, and change can be readily made. This is not the case in direct barter exchanges, because one cannot easily divide a live pig if a transaction does not involve items of equal value. **Barter,** where goods and services are exchanged for other goods or services without the use of currency, was likely the first means of market exchange before the use of currency (Williams 1997).

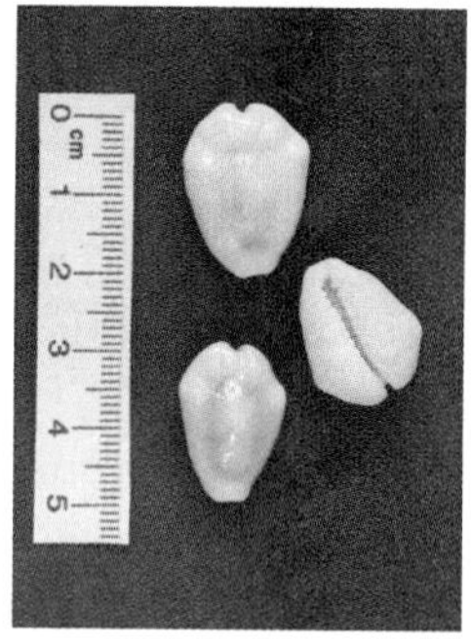

Cypraea moneta shells (money cowrie). These were used as currency in Africa and on many islands in the Pacific.

Markets vary in the types of currency used. Objects such as shells, furs, gold, or silver that are used as the medium of exchange are technically termed **commodity money.** The exchange item itself is of value. Paper currency is a medium of exchange that is backed by gold or silver. Nation-states introduced paper currency because it was easier to store and transport than gold or silver coins and could not be melted down. Paper money as a medium of exchange today is called **fiat money** (also called credit money)—paper money backed by the legal power of a nation-state and its claim of the economic value of the money. This money can be used to purchase goods and services; but, as in the United States today, it cannot be redeemed for gold and silver (Robbins 2005: 10).

Cowrie shells (primarily *Cypraea moneta*) have a rich history of use as currency in parts of Africa. In the interior of the continent the shells crossed many cultural areas and coexisted as currency with gold, silver, brass, salt bars, beads, and cloth (Saul 2004: 73). Cowrie shell money in Ghana provides an interesting case of both commodity and fiat monies coexisting today. The shells were used as a medium of exchange before the introduction by colonial governments of the West African pound and later the fiat currency known as the cedi (the name is believed to be derived from the Ghanaian word *sede*, for cowrie). Among the Dagaaba of northwestern Ghana they are still used for money alongside the cedi. Cowries are pierced and threaded on strings, or counted individually, and are used in a variety of transactions. The nonmonetary uses for cowries include use in religious rituals, for adornment and decoration, and as funeral displays and marriage transactions (Yiridoe 1995). Several analysts suggest that governmental instabilities in the past encourage the Dagaabe to save cowries, particularly if they do not have wage income.

TRY THIS
Research

Using your favorite search engine, research *Cypraea moneta*. Name societies on three different continents where this cowrie was used as currency.

Many agriculturally based societies function by a combination of redistribution and market exchange. Reciprocity is still in use but is focused primarily within a circle of family and friends and is no longer necessary for survival—everything can be purchased in the marketplace or received from governmental agencies. Both redistribution and market economies are associated with stratified cultures. See Chapter 10 for more information on stratification.

barter
Exchange of products that does not involve currency.

commodity money
Currency in the form of valued objects such as shells or gold.

fiat money
Paper currency backed by a nation-state's claim of its value.

ANTHROPOLOGY AROUND US

Vote with Your Fork?

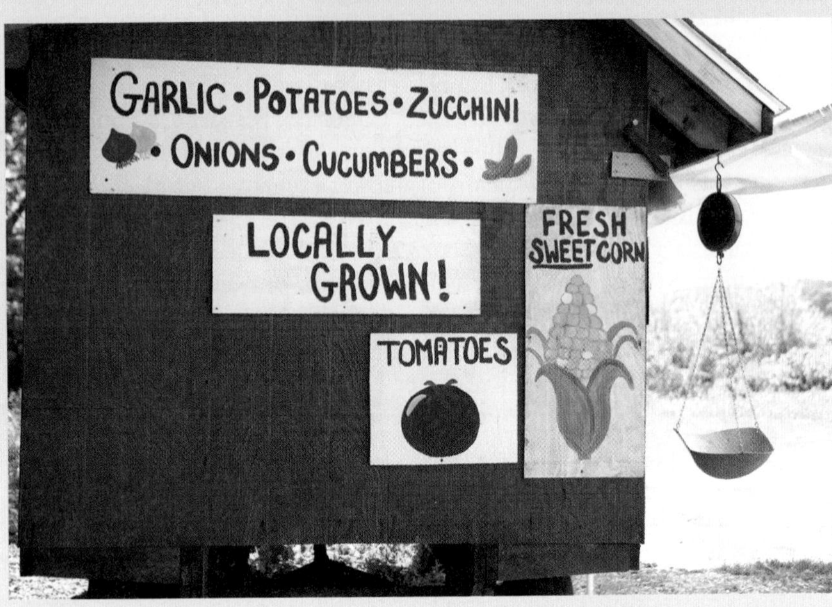

Farm commodities that grow quickly, give high yields, have a long shelf life, and characteristics that make them easier to harvest and transport to market are now the norm around the globe. Small farmers are displaced by large-scale corporate-owned farming operations, rural communities decline, and many people end up living in urban poverty, particularly in Africa and India. Fast-food chains are now ubiquitous worldwide. Slow Food is an international movement that promotes food and wine culture; it also advocates and defends traditional food-production methods based on organic techniques and plant biodiversity (Slow Food 2011). The opening of a McDonalds in Piazza Spagna in Rome in 1986 spurred Carlo Petrini to found Slow Food. He is passionate about promoting traditional regional foods and spending time enjoying the tastes of the foods we eat. This movement opposes foods that all taste the same—the standardized taste of supermarket and fast foods. Slow Food is active in protecting biodiversity and the environment, developing food education projects with schools and other community institutions, and organizing major food events that bring together food producers and consumers.

A recent (October 2010) international Slow Food convention, Salone del Gusto, held in Turin, Italy, had 200,000 visitors. Meeting at the same time were food and agriculture producers representing 150 nations who came to learn about building and sustaining local markets. The United Nations' Food and Agriculture Organization reports American specialty producers have taken note of how improved organic growing practices have increased production in various regions of the globe (Dilly 2005: 49).

The Locavore food movement shares many of the goals of Slow Food and challenges us to eat products grown, caught, and produced within a 100-mile radius of where we live. Locavore groups give the following reasons to eat locally: food freshness and taste, variety, better nutrition, soil stewardship (sustainable soil fertility), and energy conservation (decreased dependency on petroleum). These movements can have political and economic impact since they are in effect asking us to vote with our forks.

◎ What do you think? Are Slow Food and Locavore movements likely to gain momentum? What do you see as positive outcomes of these movements globally? Are such eating choices available to all socioeconomic groups?

AGRICULTURE AND GLOBALIZATION

Agricultural commodities are increasingly shipped worldwide, and the globalization of intensive Western agricultural methods is accelerating. Most of the foods on the dinner plates of people in North America and Europe travel an average of one thousand five hundred miles from farms to markets (Kingsolver 2007: 5). Intensive, large-scale, mechanized agricultural operations grow modern varieties of high-yield plants; confined animal farming operations, or CAFOs, also produce high yields of meat, poultry, and dairy products. Most of the foods in industrialized societies come from these sources and are the result of increased intensification of agriculture known as the production maximization model. An alternative model is that of sustainable agriculture.

A production maximization model of intensive agriculture strives to grow scientifically developed varieties with the aid of chemical fertilizers and pesticides. New technology to increase production is emphasized, with an outcome of higher yields that can bring farmers into the world market system. Centralized markets, it is argued, will maintain world food stability if there is production fluctuation due to regional environmental variables such as bad weather. The cultural value underlying this approach is that of maximum profit for all involved. Critics of this approach contend that it is equivalent to gambling long-term security for short-term gain (Cleveland 1993; Matson et al. 1997; Tilman et al. 2002).

A sustainable agriculture model takes a different prespective and has a foundation with different cultural values. As defined holistically, sustainable agriculture includes economic, environmental, and sociocultural stability (Cleveland and Soleri 2007). This approach emphasizes the maintenance of genetic diversity of crops by growing and maintaining folk varieties in addition to utilizing scientifically developed varieties. It calls for a flexible strategy that adapts to unique local conditions (Cleveland 1993). It includes experimentation, utilizes techniques from Western scientific agriculture, and incorporates folk knowledge, but without adopting the values of the production maximization approach. The cultural value of sustainable agriculture is long-term stability of food, soils, people, and communities.

On the plus side of the production maximization model: the price of food is less today than fifty years ago, when adjusted for inflation. Foods are shipped to world regions experiencing drought. Diet diversity is possible as never before—people in northern latitudes can eat leafy green vegetables, strawberries, and grapes while the ground outside of their door is covered in snow. Market exchange has moved beyond the boundaries of single or regional cultures, thus tying us together in an intricate web of production specialists, distributors, and consumers.

On the minus side: the genetic diversity of food plant and food animal species has significantly declined with increased agricultural intensification.

The Food and Agriculture Organization of the United Nations (FAO) estimates that 75 percent of the genetic diversity of agricultural crops has been lost since 1900 (Shand 1997: 21); in Europe 50 percent of domestic livestock breeds were lost during the same period (Shand 1997: 46). One outcome of this is that species selected for rapid growth and high yield, particularly when grown on thousand-acre monoculture farms and in CAFOs, are less hearty and more vulnerable to diseases. Growers must use antibiotics and other pharmaceuticals to maintain animal health. Soil and environmental degradation result from the many chemical fertilizer and pesticide applications to crops. It is also reported that cropland is eroding about 10 times faster than the topsoil is being replaced (Minderhout and Frantz 2009: 8).

On the plus side of sustainable agriculture: Maintenance of soil fertility with zero or minimal use of chemicals results in less pollution and soil erosion. Better nutrition results—advocates for sustainable agriculture note the alarming increases in obesity, diabetes, and heart disease that correlate with modern diets. Remember that correlation *does not*, in scientific terms, equal causation. Nonetheless, data suggest that nutritional issues underlie these conditions and that food-growing methods impact the nutritional values of foods. Folk varieties have undergone thousands of years of natural and human selection to thrive in particular econiches; but when humans intervene, the animals and plants are affected. For example, beef from cattle that are fed corn (not a natural food for herbivores) is fatter than beef from cattle raised wholly on grass; eggs from free-range grass-eating hens have less cholesterol and higher amounts of omega-3 fatty acids than eggs of CAFO-raised hens. An additional benefit of sustainable agriculture is revival of farming in non-industrialized cultures, where the market economy encourages wage-earning work over farming, even though jobs are few and low paying. Planting folk and scientific varieties together and using both folk and modern growing techniques helps traditional cultures maintain their local communities.

On the negative side: lower yields may mean less profit to producers and higher food costs to consumers. It is unclear whether sustainable agriculture can, in the long term with continued population growth, maintain yields equal to the production maximization model (Tilman et al. 2002). Cultural values are clearly a major issue in the choices made by societies between sustainable agriculture and agriculture based on production maximization alone. Anthropologists working on applied projects in agriculture keep a holistic view as they seek solutions to local problems. See Chapters 13 and 14 for discussions of case studies in applied anthropology.

SUMMARY

Food producers emerged after foragers in the history of human cultural development. This does not mean that they are more advanced. Rather, they adapted in new ways to environmental changes and challenges. While there is enormous diversity in the specific plants and animals that are raised for food, general patterns of sociocultural adaptations are apparent.

Horticulturalists and pastoralists are societies of both sedentary (horticulturalists) and nomadic (pastoralists) food producers; both are kin based, and property ownership, usually by a kin group, is at the core of the social complex. Agriculturally based societies are diverse in form—a continuum exists from those with the most basic features of agriculture carried out by extended families or villages to the intensive mechanized agriculture of industrialized societies. Agriculturalists own property individually, are stratified, have centralized authority, and are marked by systems of redistribution and market exchange, where currency is used.

Study Questions

1. Compare and contrast the foraging adaptation and the horticultural adaptation with respect to technology.
2. Identify the adaptive features of technology and food procurement found in an assigned ethnography. How closely do these features match the general features of one of the subsistence strategies outlined in this chapter?
3. Compare and contrast reciprocity, redistribution, and market exchange.
4. Compare and contrast the subsistence strategies and distribution systems of horticultural and agricultural societies.

See Self Quiz.

Suggested Readings

Evans-Pritchard, E. E. 1940. *The Nuer.* Oxford: Oxford University Press. The classic original ethnography on a tribal society.

Hutchinson, Sharon E. 1996. *Nuer Dilemmas.* Berkeley: University of California Press. A landmark and riveting account of the Nuer and what civil war and social unrest have done to these people.

Weiner, Annette B. 1988. *The Trobrianders of Papua New Guinea.* New York: Holt, Rinehart and Winston. Weiner revisited the Trobriand Islanders made famous by Bronislaw Malinowski in his 1922 book *Argonauts of the Western Pacific.* Weiner provides a perspective on women's roles and work in this horticultural society that were lacking in Malinowski's treatment, as well as a view of how this culture has changed.

See Web links.

Marriage, Family, and Residence

What Are the Possibilities?

The last loop and button have been sewn, all thirty-two are in place marching majestically down the back of the white satin gown. I have labored for hours over this dress, alternating between being pleased that our daughter asked me to make her wedding dress and wondering what possessed me to agree to do this. As I worked I contemplated the human institution of marriage and the traditions and customs surrounding it. The tradition of a white bridal dress, worn by brides of European ancestry and the Judeo-Christian religion, symbolizes purity. Among many Hindus the bride wears a traditional sari of red and white, often embroidered with gold, the red symbolizing fertility and abundance and the white, purity. Red is also the traditional color of the bridal dress worn in China, where this color is considered lucky. In past times, as now, there is much variation in bridal attire both between and within cultures. Some traditions are associated with belief systems whereas others are secular. Diffusion of traditions is also apparent in ceremonies today when elements of cultures and subcultures join.

Our daughter's marriage is not an arranged marriage. It has no formal financial exchanges associated with it such as bride price (or bridewealth), which is common in tribal pastoral societies, or dowry (a European tradition). My husband and I will not be washing the couple's feet with water and milk to signify purification (a Hindu custom). We won't be setting off firecrackers to frighten away evil spirits (a Chinese custom). Nor will the bride and groom jump over a broom signifying their entrance into marriage (a practice in some sub-Saharan African cultures). But there is a white dress with a train, a veil, a tiered cake, attendants, something old, something new, something borrowed, and something blue (all European American customs).

◀ Note that the scarves of the bride and groom are tied together. This joining of scarves symbolizes their eternal bond in this traditional Hindu wedding.

With her marriage, our daughter will acquire a whole new set of kinsmen—in-laws, we call them in North America. This will not only expand her family but also bring new obligations to her life. Duties that are different from those in other cultures, and yet ones that are alike. The recognition of these obligations, and the actions based on them, are of course the *ideal* cultural traditions associated with in-laws in North American society. Reflecting another North American ideal, my daughter and her husband will set up their own independent household.

Marriage and the purpose it serves for individuals and for societies have been of interest to anthropology since the 1860s. Merchant seamen's stories of the "strange" marriage customs they encountered in other lands caught the attention of early anthropologists. Models of cultural evolution, developed by men such as Scottish lawyer John McLennan, built on these stories and stimulated much debate in academic circles. When subsequent anthropologists began formal ethnographic studies, the starting point was often to focus on marriage, family, and kinship customs. The myriad forms of these cultural institutions speak again to the adaptive nature of human culture.

This chapter presents cross-cultural data on marriage, families, and the issue of where people reside after marriage.

The objectives of this chapter are to:

- Describe marriage rules found across cultures
- Describe marriage forms and their functions
- Examine mate choice and marriage finance
- Describe types of families and their functions
- Describe residence patterns and their functions

FIGURE 7.1
Symbols Used in Kinship Diagrams

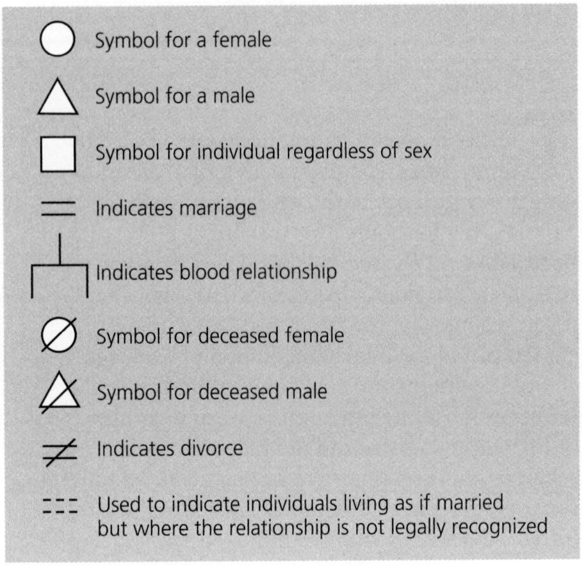

○	Symbol for a female
△	Symbol for a male
□	Symbol for individual regardless of sex
=	Indicates marriage
┌┴┐	Indicates blood relationship
∅	Symbol for deceased female
△ (crossed)	Symbol for deceased male
≠	Indicates divorce
- - -	Used to indicate individuals living as if married but where the relationship is not legally recognized

DIAGRAMMING KINSHIP

OLC
mhhe • com / lenkeit5e
See chapter outline and chapter overview.

Kinship diagrams are a shorthand method of representing and giving a clear visual picture of kin relationships. The symbols used in anthropological kin diagrams are shown in Figure 7.1. It is worthwhile to learn these symbols before you read about marriage, family, and residence in this chapter and about kinship and descent in Chapter 8 because (1) linguistic confusion can result when terms are translated from native languages to English, and (2) it is easier to trace and understand complex relationships with the use of these visual images.

A point of reference is always designated in a kin diagram by the designation *Ego.* When you interview someone, she or he is Ego in the diagram you draw. Knowing the person who is Ego is important because information about kin relationships, obligations, and terminology will be different when there is a change in the point of reference. Anthropologists also use a short method to *write* about kin relationships. There is no standardization to these abbreviations, but a simple approach is to use the first two letters of a kin term. For example, mother is written Mo, father is Fa, daughter is Da, sister is Si, and wife is Wi. If one is speaking about the blood kin relationship of one's mother's sister's daughter, it becomes MoSiDa. Other terms and their short form are husband, Hu; child, Ch; brother, Br; and son, So. Relationships by marriage (in-laws) are designated by the use of these terms as well. One way to write sister-in-law is BrWi. Other ways to designate a sister-in-law are HuBrWi (if Ego is a female) and WiBrWi (if Ego is a male).

Another method is to use the first letter of the kin relationship: mother (M), father (F), husband (H), wife (W), daughter (D), son (S), brother (B), and sister (Z). Because both son and sister begin with the same letter, Z is used for sister. According to this second shorthand method, mother's sister's daughter is MZD. When I was a beginning student I mixed up the Z and the S with this system, so I prefer to use the two-letter system.

Consider

You are Ego in the following diagrams. What terms would you use if you were telling me who each person was in relationship to you? Quickly copy these diagrams on a sheet of paper and write the terms that apply using one of the shorthand methods just discussed.

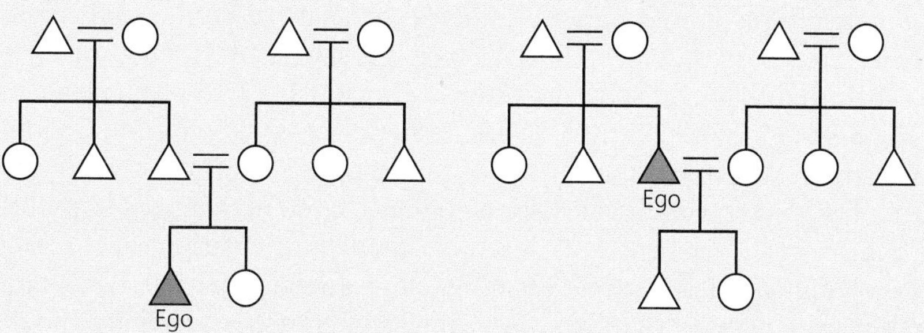

Now, look at the two diagrams. The designation of Ego is clearly important to the ethnographer gathering interview data because terms will change as Ego changes. This is an important point to remember when reading a complex kinship diagram.

MARRIAGE RULES

Exogamy and Endogamy

All cultures have rules about whom it is appropriate to marry. Some are formal rules that are part of the society's legal system; others are informal. Two marriage rules found in most cultures are the rules of exogamy and endogamy. A rule of **exogamy** specifies that a person must marry outside of a designated group of people. The most common group specified by exogamy is the **nuclear family** (i.e., a married couple and their children). Exogamous rules in nearly all cultures also include kin other than the nuclear family. The exception is found where a leader, such as a chief in ancient Hawaiian culture, was to marry his sister in order to retain a concentration of special powers in his offspring. Great variety exists across

exogamy
A cultural rule that dictates that one must marry outside of a designated group (e.g., outside of one's lineage, clan, or village).

nuclear family
A married couple and their children.

Jot down a hypothesis to explain why you cannot marry your brother, sister, mother, father, or MoBrCh (cousin). Now read on.

cultures concerning which kin are part of the forbidden group. In some cultures you cannot marry cousins. In other cultures you can marry certain cousins but not others. Sometimes a whole village is included in an exogamous rule. The members of a culture do not usually analyze the purpose or function of rules such as exogamy. We all have grown up with such rules in place. It is just the way things are. Anthropologists, however, are interested in trying to explain why such rules exist.

One hypothesis offered to explain exogamous rules is that they prevent incest, which in turn prevents deformities in offspring. This is the explanation given most often in North American culture for the exogamous rules that prohibit marriage to close relatives. (Is this the hypothesis you jotted down in the Try This exercise?) Did exogamous rules originate to prevent incestuous relations within a society? This explanation seems unlikely as a universal reason for the origin of these rules because anthropologists have studied cultures in which conception was not believed to be connected to sexual intercourse and yet taboos against incest existed. In such societies it was believed that clan spirits entered a woman's body to produce a child. The past tense is used in the previous sentence because today most peoples understand the biological realities of conception. Many non-Western cultures, however, made the biological connection, so perhaps the hypothesis about incest and unhealthy children is a correct explanation for the origin of exogamous rules in some cases. Modern genetics teaches that mating within a small group of individuals with a similar genetic background may increase the chances of recessive bad genes combining. The *probability* increases, which is not the same as a definite statement that a deformity *will* result if these genes combine.

Other hypotheses to explain the origin of exogamous rules include the suggestion that exogamous rules help to extend territory, create political alliances, or stimulate trade. Still others have suggested that exogamous rules came about to reduce conflict within families, where sexual liaisons with kin would cause jealousy. Each of these hypotheses has some data to support it. Perhaps societies developed exogamous rules for different reasons or combinations of reasons.

OLC
mhhe • com / lenkeit5e
See Internet exercises.

Endogamy, or endogamous rules, specify the groups *within* which a person should or must marry. A rule whereby a person is told to marry someone from the same religion is an endogamous rule. Other endogamous rules found in different world cultures include rules to marry within the same race or ethnic group, within the same socioeconomic stratum, or occasionally within the same descent group such as a clan (clans and other descent groups are discussed in Chapter 8). So, one function of endogamy is to maintain cultural identity. If you marry someone with the same background and status, there is less chance that customs will change or that conflict will occur between extended family over important values and beliefs.

endogamy
A cultural rule that dictates that one must marry within a designated group.

TRY THIS Analyze

How do North American parents try to ensure that their children marry the right person? Think carefully. We have informal means to encourage endogamy related to ethnic group origin, religion, and socioeconomic level, and these means are usually effective. What are they?

The Levirate and the Sororate

The levirate and the sororate are preferential marriage rules found in many cultures. Each specifies whom one should marry if one's spouse dies. Both rules serve the purpose of ensuring that everyone is economically protected in the case of a spouse's death. Such customs also ensure that the deceased person's children are raised by members of his or her group and that alliances remain between the families.

The **levirate** specifies that if a woman's husband dies, she should marry one of his brothers. Thus the levirate is often called brother-in-law marriage. The **sororate,** sister-in-law marriage, designates that a man should marry his wife's sister should his wife die. See Figure 7.2 for diagrams illustrating levirate and sororate marriage rules.

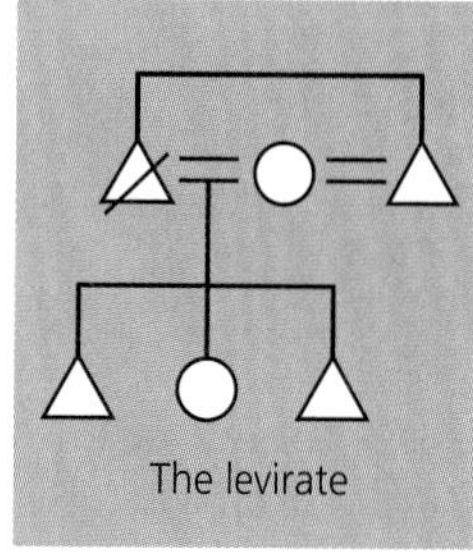

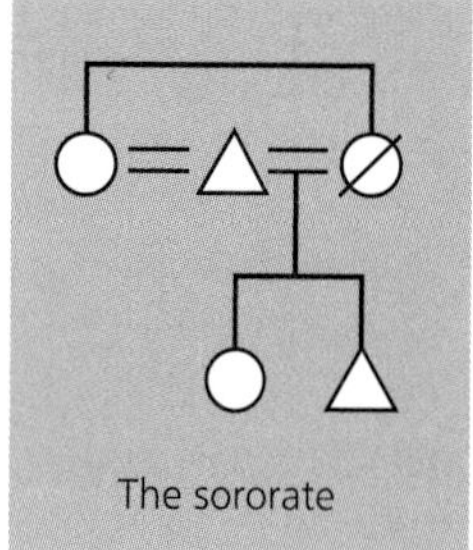

FIGURE 7.2
The Levirate and the Sororate

To anyone raised in contemporary North American cultures, levirate and sororate rules will likely generate ethnocentric reactions. We shudder at the thought of marriage to someone we don't love and may not even like. We have come to equate love with marriage. A bit of historical and cross-cultural research, however, reveals that throughout most of human history, in most places, marriages occurred for economic reasons. Romantic love was viewed as a poor basis for marriage and even as abnormal (Stephens 1963: 200–206). To be objective (and culturally relativistic) in considering the value of the levirate and the sororate, one must set aside the attitudes about romantic love that have been the basis of marriage in contemporary Western cultures only for the past century or so. Moreover, remember that we are examining *ideal* patterns of kinship within cultures—ethnographers have recorded data indicating that women do sometimes reject these rules even in societies where the custom is expected.

levirate
A marriage custom in which a widow marries her deceased husband's brother.

sororate
A marriage custom in which a widower marries a sister of his deceased wife.

Those who read the Bible will recognize the custom of the levirate from the Old Testament (Deuteronomy 25: 5–10). These verses state that the marriage of the deceased man's brother to his widow should take place if there are no sons, a requirement that is not present in all instances of the levirate. The first son then born to the woman would be considered the son of the deceased brother. George Murdock in his sample of 250 societies reported that 127 cultures (51 percent) practiced the levirate and 100 (40 percent) practiced the sororate (Murdock 1949: 29). Certainly the

ANTHROPOLOGY AROUND US

Outdated Traditions?

Why marry? A study at Rutgers University revealed that heterosexual men in today's North American society remain bachelors because it is easy to have sex outside of marriage, and they are fearful of the economic responsibilities of marriage, including having and rearing children. They want instead to find a soul mate—a woman who will hold the same view on most issues and make no demands on them (http://www.virginia.edu/marriageproject/). A 2010 Pew Research Center study showed about 39 percent of U.S. residents said that marriage was becoming obsolete (http://pewresearch.org/pubs/). Recent census data indicate that more people than ever are living together (and presumably having sex) without marriage. According to the 1980 U.S. Census there were 1,589,000 unmarried couple households; in 1990 there were 2,856,000 and in 2010, 7.5 million.

If you do marry, who pays for it? Long-standing American traditions include a wedding, reception, and honeymoon. Traditionally the bride's family was responsible for financing the wedding and reception party, while the groom's family financed the honeymoon. Wedding guests brought gifts aimed at helping the couple set up their new home. Engaged couples today increasingly make requests for cash to help pay for the wedding, a home mortgage, or honeymoon expenses. Etiquette experts call such requests crass and in poor taste. Advocates of the money-for-marriage movement claim that it is becoming a trend. One online wedding registry calls the honeymoon money registry a twenty-first-century tradition. Registry Web sites also point to customs in countries where the bride and groom are given money or even homes, although the latter usually come from family members.

◎ Ask your unmarried male friends what they think of the Rutgers study results. Are they searching for a soul mate? Do they plan to marry? What do you think? Is it tacky to ask for wedding cash? Or will money-for-marriage become a twenty-first-century replacement for other cultures' traditions of dowry and bridewealth?

widespread practice of these customs attests to their important functions in many cultures.

MARRIAGE FORMS AND FUNCTIONS

All societies studied by anthropologists have some form of marriage ceremony. Marriage is an event that marks an important change in both the **status** (a person's position in society) and **role** (the part a person plays in society) of individuals. In this case the change of status is from being single to being part of a couple with new responsibilities and rights. With marriage individuals take on new roles; now they are a wife or a husband and perhaps a stepparent in addition to their roles as daughter or son.

Anthropologists have noted the following features about marriage in most societies: (1) Marriage includes an exclusive sexual relationship between the partners (remember we are talking about the *ideal* here), (2) marriage usually involves some degree of economic interdependency—including property and labor, and (3) marriage legitimizes the couple's offspring in the eyes of the group, and child-rearing responsibilities are expected from the couple. There are exceptions to one or more of these features in at least some societies. For example, many cultures accept extramarital sex (most often for males), and in some cultures, such as the Nayar, these three features of marriage were absent in historic times. Because the Nayar presented an interesting case to ethnologists, I will briefly describe it to you to illustrate the variations that marriage can take.

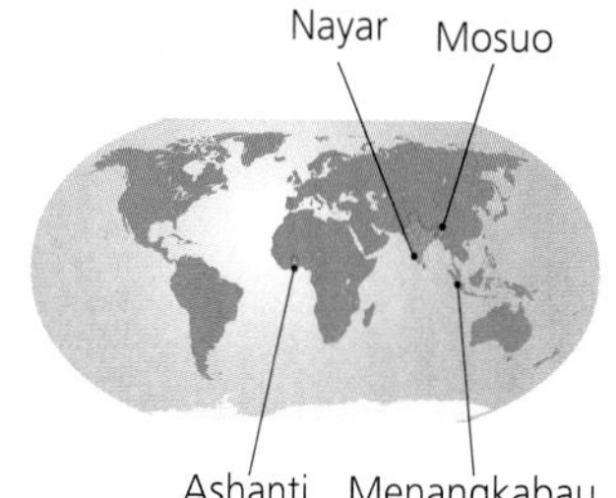

The Nayar are found in Malabar in southwest India. They are a society in which descent is traced through women. In the past the Nayar were a warrior caste, and men were full-time soldiers who spent most of their adult lives away from their homes either living in barracks or away at war. When they returned home, it was to the house where they were born, their mother's house. Young Nayar women were often household servants in Brahmin (upper caste) households and were often concubines to men of the household. Nayar marriage relationships were problematic to maintain under these circumstances, and an inventive system evolved.

Before puberty a Nayar woman was formally married to a man from a family with whom her family had a special relationship. The two were together for a few days, and then the marriage ended. The woman usually never saw this husband again, though she and her future children might mourn when this man died. After this marriage the woman was considered an adult and was free to take up to a dozen lovers. Each lover was part of a formal relationship approved by her family, and the man was required to give the woman gifts three times a year until the relationship ended. The "visiting husbands" as they were called, spent the night with a woman, leaving a shield or sword outside of her door so that other men

status
A person's position in society.

role
The culturally assigned behaviors and expectations for a person's social position.

with whom she had a similar relationship knew that another "husband" was visiting that night. The visiting husbands never resided with a woman, did not have any economic obligation to support her, and came and went as their military duties dictated. When a child was conceived, one of the visiting husbands established the child's legitimacy by claiming paternity and presenting gifts to the woman and to the midwife who delivered the child. He had no further economic responsibilities for this child, though he might take a social interest in it. The child lived with and was the economic responsibility of its mother's group. Although this custom is no longer practiced (it was outlawed by British colonial rule), it illustrates how cultures are flexible and develop many strategies to accommodate their survival. In this case men were away from home most of the time attending to their military duties. It made sense that the stable family unit centered on women. Men lived in their mother and sister's household when they were at home.

Quickly review what you believe to be the advantages of a monogamous marriage. Jot down these advantages, and keep them in mind as you read on.

The Nayar are not the only cultures whose customs do not align with the more common features of marriage described here. Space does not permit a discussion of additional examples, but you might want to research the Menangkabau of Malaysia, the Mosuo of China, and the Ashanti of Ghana, other societies that have developed creative solutions to complicated situations associated with marriage.

Monogamy

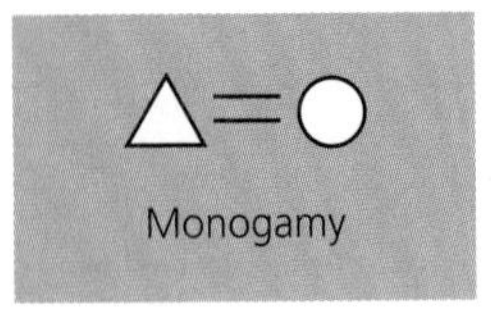

FIGURE 7.3
Monogamy

Monogamy, the form of marriage in which one woman is married to one man (Figure 7.3), is the most common form of marriage around the world. It is not, however, the most preferred; monogamy is the ideal and preferred form of marriage in only eighty-one cultures out of a sample of four hundred cultures (20 percent), according to a 1967 survey based on the Human Relations Area Files data (Textor 1967: 124). As a result of divorce or death, many individuals in monogamous societies will be in a series of monogamous marriages over the course of their lives (this is sometimes referred to as serial monogamy).

Polygamy

monogamy
A form of marriage in which one woman is married to one man.

polygamy
Multiple-spouse marriage.

polygyny
Marriage of one man to two or more women.

Polygamy refers to marriage in which there is more than one spouse (*poly* means *many*, and *gamy* means *marriage*). It is a word that the media use, but it is a poor choice because it does not indicate whether there are many husbands or many wives (Figure 7.4).

Polygyny. **Polygyny** is the specific case in which a man has more than one wife (an example diagram is shown in Figure 7.5). Cross-cultural research indicates that this is the preferred form of marriage in 314 cultures out of

400 (79 percent) (Textor 1967: 124). This research surveyed societies with populations numbering in the millions as well as those with populations of fewer than one hundred, so keep in mind that the percentage of cultures practicing a custom is not the same as the number of people worldwide who practice the custom. Furthermore, many societies have cultural rules that permit marrying multiple partners, which is what the society's members, both male and female, desire. Economic realities, however, often interfere with a man's ability to have multiple wives. As a result, most individuals participate in monogamous marriages.

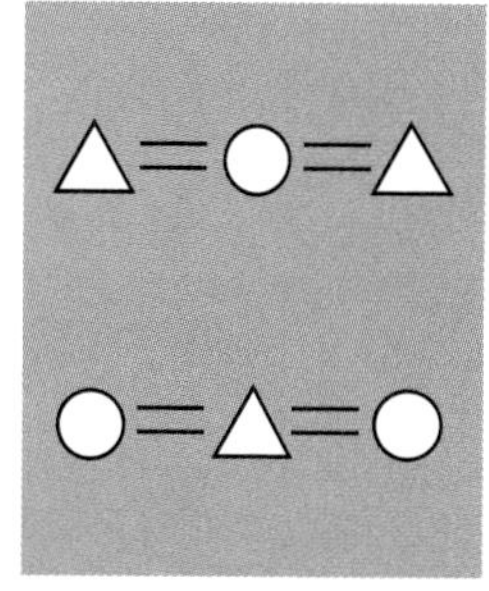

FIGURE 7.4
Polygamy Polygamy means multiple spouses and does not distinguish between these two marriage types.

The functions of polygyny include the opportunity for a man to gain status by having more than one wife and particularly by having many children. Polygyny is most common in preindustrial societies where horticulture or pastoralism is the basis of economic life. More wives means more workers. More wives means more children. More children also means more potential workers. Thus there is often an economic advantage to having more than one wife. Political status can also be gained by having more than one wife, as in the case of Melanesian Big Men, for whom fathering many children is also a way to gain prestige. Typically the wealthiest men are likely to have many wives because they can afford bridewealth payments. There is, of course, a negative side to polygyny. It can be expensive to maintain more than one household (if this is required within a particular culture), and jealousy (often over favoritism shown to one wife's children) can cause difficulties. Another drawback occurs when polygyny causes a shortage of wives for poor men.

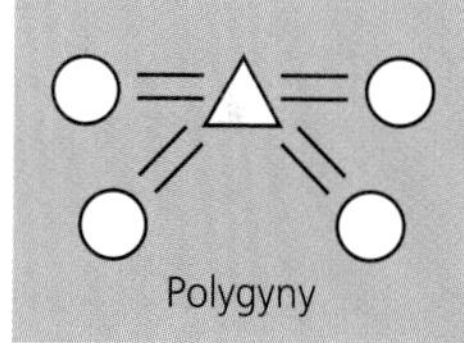

FIGURE 7.5
Polygyny

TRY THIS Analyze

If you are a woman, jot down two advantages of having co-wives. If you are a man, jot down two advantages of having more than one wife.

Compare and discuss your notes with a member of the opposite sex. Discuss your feelings about this form of marriage. Are you able to be culturally relativistic, or do your cultural ethnocentrisms creep in?

The original reasons societies became polygynous are unclear. Many hypotheses have been made, all having logic or data to support them, though few have been systematically examined. One exception is Melvin Ember's 1974 study that showed more women than men in societies that practiced polygyny—111 women for 100 men on average, compared to 94 women for 100 men in societies that were nonpolygynous (Pasternak, Ember, and Ember 1997: 90). This finding implies that an unbalanced sex ratio led to the adoption of polygyny. Other studies seem to contradict this one. A difficulty in gathering data on origin hypotheses for any social

A Muslim Rashaida Bedouin merchant and his three wives.

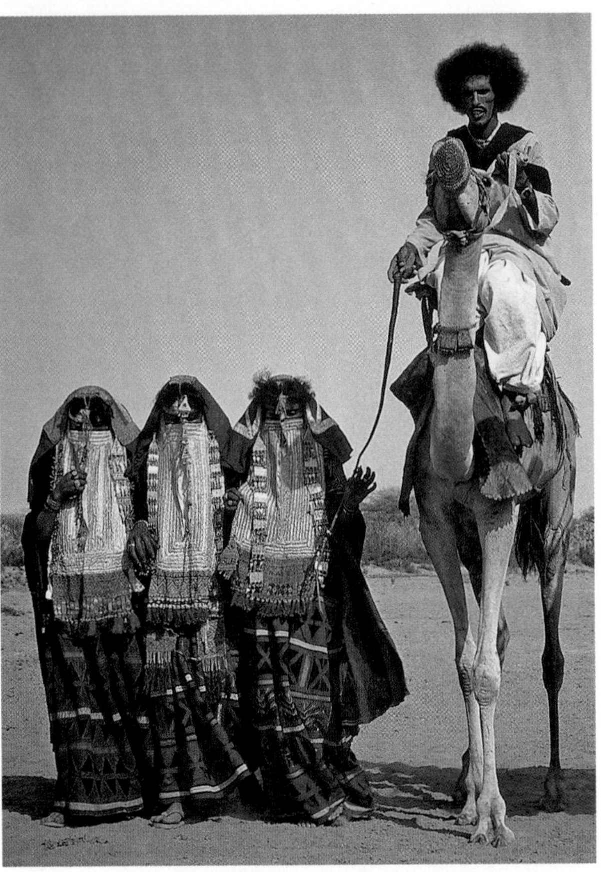

custom such as marriage form is that correlations shown in the data don't necessarily mean that causation is established.

TRY THIS Hypothesize

Try the intellectually stimulating exercise of seeing how many logical hypotheses you can devise to account for the high occurrence of, and preference among the world's cultures for, polygynous marriage. Pick the most promising hypothesis and devise several ways to collect data to test it.

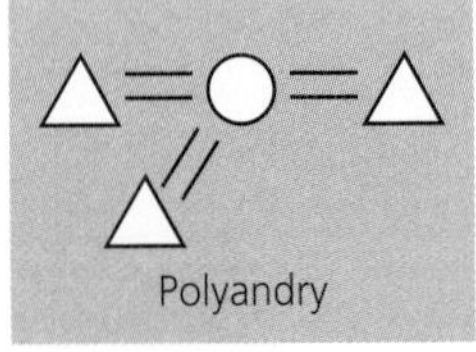

FIGURE 7.6
Polyandry

polyandry
Marriage of one woman to two or more men.

Polyandry. The form of marriage in which a woman has more than one husband is called **polyandry** (illustrated in Figure 7.6). Only three cultures out of a sample of four hundred (0.75 percent) practice this form of marriage (Textor 1967: 124). In the cultures that practice polyandry, there *may* be a shortage of women resulting from practices such as female infanticide. There

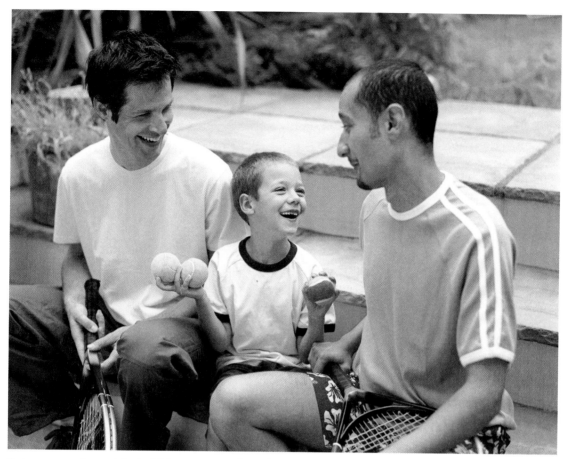

Same-sex couples and their children are part of North American family variation.

are conflicting reports on this issue (as noted in Chapter 1). A shortage of women may have been an issue, but it does not appear to have been the only, or even the major, cause. Rather, polyandry seems to be related to economics. Among Tibetans living in northern Nepal, when brothers share a wife, it is to keep large land holdings from being fragmented (Goldstein 1987).

Group Marriage. A group of individuals of both sexes married to each other is called group marriage. Although group marriage has surfaced in societies from time to time, such as the hippie communes of the 1960s, it is reported to be legal in only one society. This culture is the Kaingang in Brazil, where 8 percent of the population practiced this marriage form during historic times. The remainder of the population practiced monogamy (60 percent), polygyny (18 percent), or polyandry (14 percent). Obviously there are diverse ideas about marriage among the Kaingang (Murdock 1949: 24).

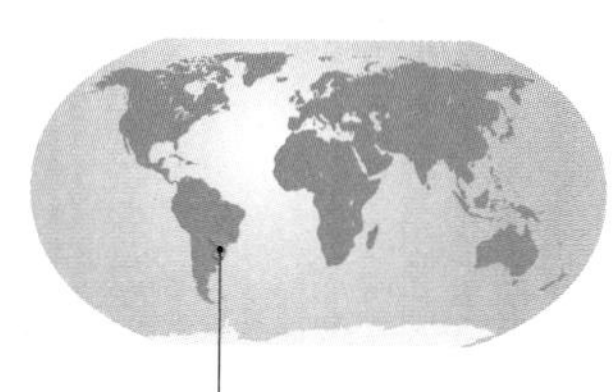

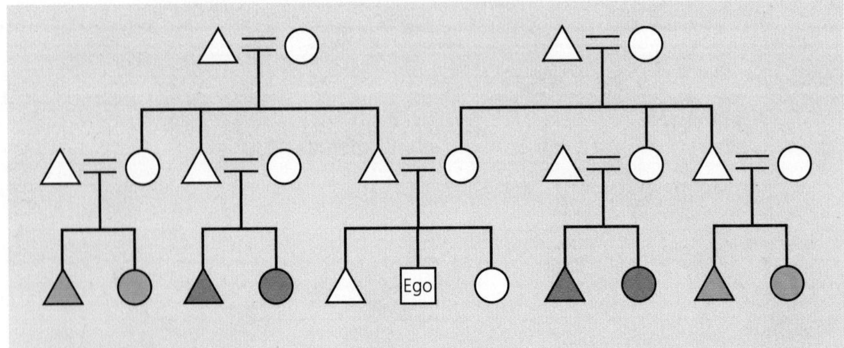

FIGURE 7.7
Cousins Ego's parallel cousins (MoSiCh and FaBrCh) are shown in red. Ego's cross-cousins (MoBrCh and FaSiCh) are shown in blue.

Same-Sex Marriage

Historical and cross-cultural data confirm that the institution of marriage, and its definition, is socially constructed and that the social construct may change over time. Data demonstrate that same-sex unions, including marriage, have been recognized in the histories of many cultures—Greek, Roman, and pre-Columbian Native American cultures, as well as various African cultures and numerous cultures in Asia and the Pacific (Eskridge 1993: 25). See Chapter 9 ("Gender") for a discussion of this marriage form among the Nandi of Africa.

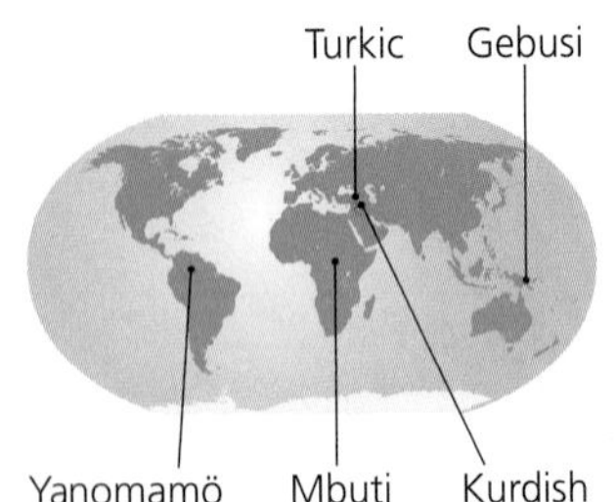

Sister Exchange Marriage

A type of marriage termed **sister exchange** is found in many cultures including the Mbuti pygmy, the Turkic, the Kurdish, the Gebusi, and the Yąnomamö. In speaking of a form of such exchange known as *berdel* in southeastern Turkey, anthropologist Serpil Altuntek has said "Berdel, cousin marriage, and similar arrangements are better viewed as part of a family's strategy to forge and maintain favorable political and economic alliances" (Ersen 2002: 75). Such alliances are part of the security network created by marriage ties.

While sister exchange may constitute a society's ideal marriage, other spouses are allowed as long as exogamous rules are obeyed. As anthropologist Bruce Knauft notes in his ethnography of the Gebusi, "the notion that Gebusi sister-exchange is 'preferential' means just that: sister-exchange is preferred 'if possible.' But if not, that's life. In actuality, just over half of all first Gebusi marriages (52 percent) were sister-exchanges" (Knauft 2010: 58).

Sister exchange typically involves the marriage of **cross-cousins** (MoBrCh or FaSiCh). Examine Figure 7.7. Although it may seem complicated to most North Americans to keep track of whether a cousin is a cross-cousin or **parallel-cousin** (MoSiCh or FaBrCh), the distinction isn't

sister exchange
A common type of marriage consisting of the marriage of cross-cousins. Men exchange their sisters as marriage partners.

cross-cousin
Ego's mother's brother's child and father's sister's child.

parallel-cousin
Ego's mother's sister's child and father's brother's child.

Newlyweds in southwest Turkey pose for a photograph. The two men from different villages have each married the other's sister. This custom, known as *berdel,* has economic and political advantages.

difficult for people who have been enculturated to use different terms for parallel-cousins and cross-cousins. Parallel-cousins are often called by the same word and treated the same as one's siblings. Cross-cousins are called by different terms and therefore are the only eligible marriage partners in one's own generation (providing lineage exogamy is practiced). The *sisters* who are exchanged represent all women in the category, not just a man's true sisters. Keep in mind that early ethnologists and ethnographers coined the terms *parallel-cousin* and *cross-cousin.* From an insider's view, members of a culture may, as Robin Fox (1983: 186) has suggested, view this *category* of people as possible marriage partners only because of generations of sister exchange marriage. In other words, they don't think about an eligible cross-cousin as a cross-cousin; they just exchange sisters.

TRY THIS Consider

How do you think about your relationship to your cousins? Do you think of them as your mother's brother's children, your mother's sister's children, your father's brother's or father's sister's children, or simply as your cousins? Does the etic view in this case truly represent the emic view?

MATE CHOICE AND MARRIAGE FINANCE

Mate Choice

TRY THIS
Analyze

How are web-based matchmaking sites similar to the custom and process involved in arranging a marriage? How are they different?

The ethnographic literature reflects three basic ways in which marriage partners are chosen: free choice of spouse, free choice with parental approval, and arranged marriage. In one small ethnographic sample, six societies allowed free choice of mates, six societies required the approval of parents or other kin, twelve societies showed a mix of free choice and arranged marriages, and sixteen had arranged marriages with occasional elopement (Stephens 1963: 198). To people enculturated to expect to choose their own marriage partner, data such as these can be puzzling, and thoughts of arranged marriages can trigger one's ethnocentric attitudes.

Arranged marriage was and is a common occurrence among humans. Many of the subcultures of India practice arranged marriages today, although financially independent young people of the urban middle class have more say in whom they marry. This custom extends to many people of Indian descent living abroad. When this topic is addressed in my classes, I nearly always have an Indian student who shares information about arranged marriages. Several students have brought in a copy of *India West*, a widely distributed North American Indian newspaper that contains matrimonial advertisements for those searching for suitable marriage partners. Indian students tell me that these ads are especially useful for Indian Americans with strong cultural ties to India and who wish to continue the practice of arranged marriages. The majority of the ads that I have read in this and other Indian publications begin with phrases such as "parents invite correspondence," "brother invites correspondence," or "uncle seeking . . . ." Desired traits sought in a mate and listed in these ads include "educated professional," "intelligent person," and "from a respectable family"; religion and caste are also often mentioned. These ads are aimed at initiating correspondence with potential mates. Though not limited to such societies, arranged marriage is quite common in societies in which large kin groups are important and households tend to be of the extended-family type. The entire kin group is important because of economic ties, and marriage finance is an important issue for everyone. My students tell me that large dowries are expected when marriages are arranged within the local Indian community (see the following discussion of marriage finance).

OLC
mhhe • com / lenkeit5e
See Internet exercises.

Where arranged marriage is the custom, families search and negotiate, often for years, for a mate for their offspring. Your family wants you to be secure economically and in a good marriage to someone from a stable family. They know you best and have your interests as well as their own in mind. Cultures that go through these laborious mate-selection processes must find traditional North American customs of mate selection flawed. Most North Americans marry strangers whom we meet at school, at work, in singles' bars, or while on a vacation. We know little about their families, and we seldom look at their bank accounts. Love, we say, will keep us together.

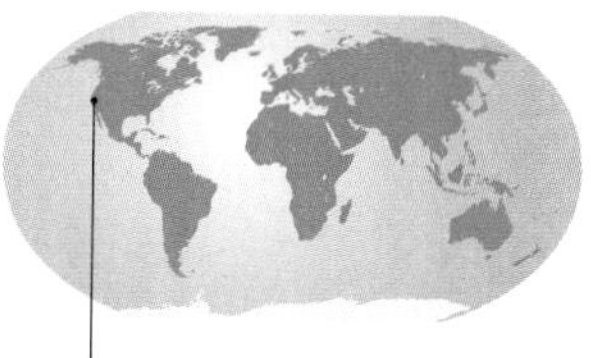

Marriage Finance

Important economic exchanges occur in many societies when marriage is proposed. To North Americans, **bridewealth** (gifts from the groom's family to the bride's family) and **dowry** (wealth brought with the bride when she marries) imply the treatment of women as objects. Although it is true that women have often been viewed historically and cross-culturally as property, the functions of marriage finance usually go beyond direct market exchange. The customary exchanges of property that take place during negotiations before marriage, at marriage, and after marriage cement relationships between families, lineages, and clans.

Bridewealth payments are often substantial. Today, among the Nuer of Africa, twenty-five to thirty head of cattle are given to the bride's family (with a value of US$100 to US$200 per head of cattle for a total of around US$5,000) (Hutchinson 1996: 263; Holtzman 2000: 105). For Nuer immigrants residing in the United States, cash payments are made instead of cattle. In one instance the payment was US$10,000 (Holtzman 2000: 105).

Arranging large bridewealth payments can be difficult. Everyone in a society is not of the same socioeconomic class or rank; thus everyone has different abilities to pay. And what if you are a fourth or fifth son in a family with no daughters? Will resources be available for you to make a bridewealth payment? Many societies developed variations on their ideal traditions to accommodate diverse socioeconomic circumstances. In past times the Yurok of the Lower Klamath River in northwestern California exhibited such a variation in their custom called **half-marriage.** In a full-marriage, a man paid bridewealth to the bride's family and took her to live with him in his house and community. Children of the union belonged to him and stayed with him if divorce occurred (unless the bridewealth was refunded). According to a 1909 census, three out of four marriages were of this form. Nearly one in four (23.4 percent) were of the half-marriage type, a statistic that remained consistent over five generations of Yurok marriage data (Waterman and Kroeber 1934: 1–5). A half-marriage involved a man making a reduced bridewealth payment, usually about half. The groom lived with the bride in her father's house, and children of the union belonged to the wife and her family. Men in such marriages were usually of low social rank and were poor. Other cultures made various arrangements for paying off a bridewealth debt. These often involved a man living with and working for the bride's family for an agreed-upon period of time and then bringing her back to his father's residence (see the discussion of matri-patrilocal residence later in the chapter).

TRY THIS
Hypothesize

Form a hypothesis regarding the relationship between the type of marriage finance within a society (bridewealth, dowry) and the divorce rate. How could you evaluate your hypothesis?

bridewealth
A form of marriage finance in which valuable gifts are given by the groom's kin to the bride's kin.

dowry
A form of marriage finance in which valuable gifts are given by the bride's kin to the groom's kin.

half-marriage
A custom among the Yurok of northwestern California and other patri-centered groups in which a man pays partial bridewealth and lives with the bride's family, and the couple's children belong to the wife and her family.

FAMILY

What exactly is a family? Early definitions of *family* refer to a social group that includes people with biological or marriage ties, reciprocal group economic obligations, shared child-rearing obligations, and common residence. These definitions were typically based on sociological studies of families in Western cultures, that is, families based on monogamous marriage. When ethnographic data from anthropology began to accumulate, it became apparent that a rigid definition of what constituted family did not apply across cultures.

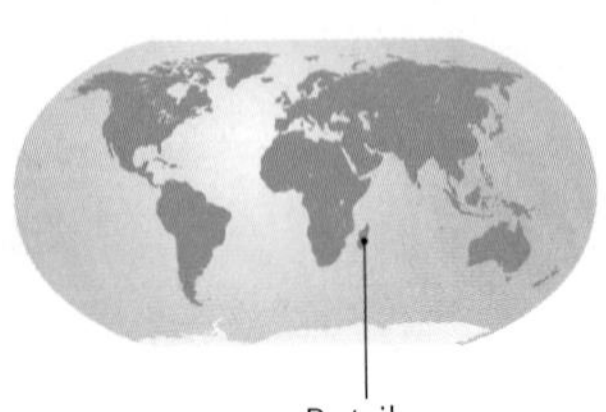

The criterion of common residence turned out to be a problem because in some cultures women and children live in one residence and men in another, yet both mother and father constitute an economic unit and share child-rearing responsibilities. Among the polygynous Betsileo of Madagascar, for example, a man and several of his wives live in different villages. A man resides most of the time with his senior wife and visits his other wives in other villages occasionally during the year. In still other cases, such as among the Maori of New Zealand and the Cook Islands, a child is often taken and reared by a grandmother in a distant household. I once had a conversation with a Maori woman while awaiting a plane at the small landing strip on the island of Aitutaki in the Cook Islands. She had an eight-month-old child with her, and she was on her way to another island to visit her daughter, the child's mother. Informants verified that this arrangement was a common occurrence and, in fact, that it was expected for grandmothers to claim the right to raise one or more of their grandchildren.

TRY THIS
Analyze

Based on the functions of family listed in the text, would the Betsileo man and his wives constitute a family? Defend your response.

The criterion of shared child-rearing obligations is not fully met in some cases. In some societies that practice descent through females, a child's mother and father may reside together but the father does not have primary economic or social responsibility for *his* children but rather for *his sister's* children because they belong to the same matrilineage. This matrilineal group has strong economic and ceremonial ties (see the discussion of matrilineages in Chapter 8).

Later studies of the family began to focus on the *functions* of family units. The functions listed most often include group responsibility for rearing children and the group acting as an economic corporation in which all members have reciprocal obligations to one another. Keep these functions in mind as you read about the following family forms.

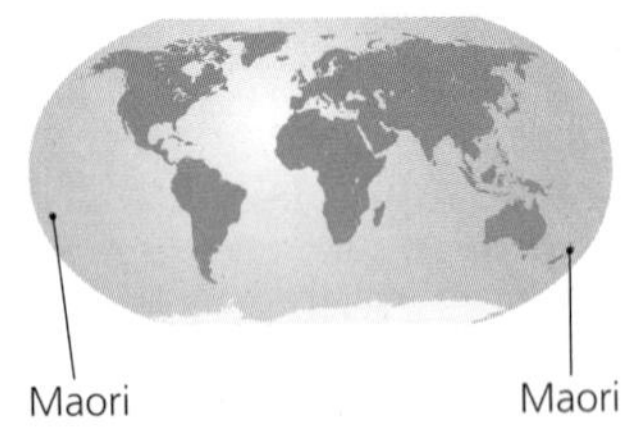

Traditional Family Forms

Family provides the most enduring relationships we have during our lifetime. A person is born (or adopted) into a kin group that we call *family*. In North America this consists of parents, brothers, sisters, grandparents, aunts and uncles, and cousins. These kin are what anthropologists call

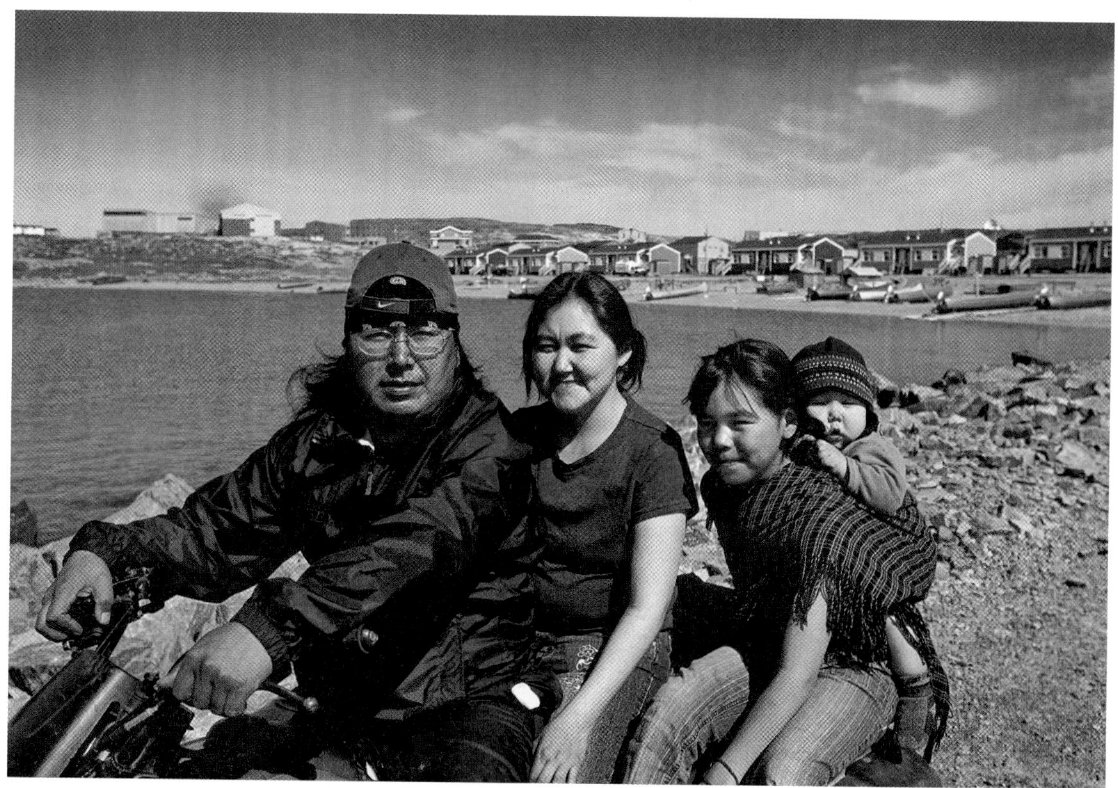

An Inuit nuclear family.

our **family of orientation.** This is the family in which you were a child, the family that orients, or enculturates, you. At the center of the family of orientation is the nuclear family. A nuclear family consists of a married couple and their children. It may be isolated and independent from other kin, or it may be part of a larger kin group. Because these members are related (or considered as if related) to one another by blood, they are referred to as **consanguineal relatives** or consanguines. The term *consanguine* derives from the Latin roots *con*, meaning with, and *sanguineus*, meaning blood.

Consanguinity can be a thorny issue when addressing kinship. Anthropologist Robin Fox noted, in his classic study of kinship systems, that "a consanguine is someone who is defined *by the society* as a consanguine, and 'blood' relationship in a genetic sense has not necessarily anything to do with it, although on the whole these tend to coincide in most societies of the world" (Fox 1983: 34). Today most humans are sophisticated about the role of egg and sperm in producing offspring. As noted in the earlier discussion of exogamy, not all peoples shared this understanding in the distant past, when various kinship groups were conceptualized. All peoples

family of orientation
A person's childhood family, where enculturation takes place.

consanguineal relatives
Kin related by blood.

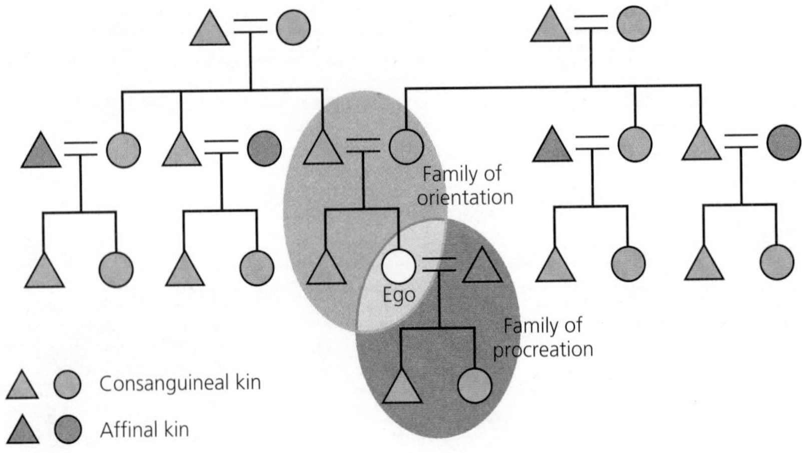

FIGURE 7.8
Diagram of a Kinship System

acknowledge a mother and her child, but there were cultures where the father was considered to be the mother's husband (and not the child's biological father). In such cultures, Ego's mother's husband was acknowledged by a term that designates this male as mother's husband and does not necessarily mean that the male is Ego's father (in the manner that modern peoples conceptualize the relationship). In some cultures, such as that of the Trobriand Islanders of Melanesia, a child is viewed as having been created wholly by the mother with the help of some of the mother's lineage spirits (Weiner 1988: 55). Modern Trobrianders have scientific understanding of the biology of inheritance yet maintain traditional kinship organization. North Americans would view mother, father, and child as constituting a nuclear family of blood relatives (consanguines), but the traditional view of Trobriand culture would be that the father is related only by marriage. This is why, as noted earlier, the use of diagrams with symbols is helpful in the study of these matters so that linguistic confusion is minimized.

Most people also belong to a **family of procreation** during their lifetime. By definition, a family of procreation is the family in which you become, or have the potential to become, a parent—you procreate. When you join a mate to form a family of procreation, you also acquire a whole set of nonblood kin, persons who are often called in-laws in North American society. Individuals who are related to you by marriage are called **affinal kin** (or affines).

family of procreation
A kin group consisting of an individual and the individual's spouse and children.

affinal kin
Kin related by marriage.

kinship system
The complexity of a culture's rules governing the relationships between affinal and consanguineal kin.

The complex system that results from people belonging to these two family types during their lives (a family of orientation and a family of procreation) and the role expectations for each person in these families is called a **kinship system.** In other words, a kinship system consists of the group made up of people who are considered consanguines and affines and the shared understanding as to how each should behave toward the other (Figure 7.8).

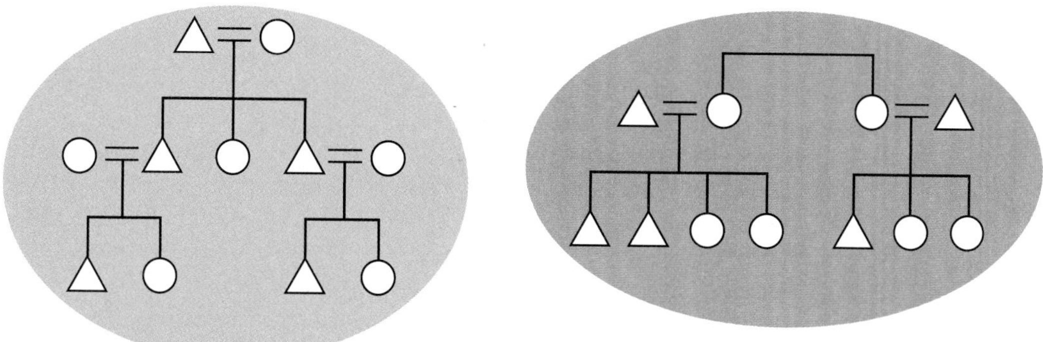

FIGURE 7.9 **Diagrams of Two Extended Families**

The term ***extended family*** is also used in anthropology. An extended family is defined as two or more nuclear families who are related in some way by blood and who live together in the same household, village, or territory. Descent relationships are the most common blood ties between members of extended families, and the eldest man or woman is the head of the family. About half of the world's societies view extended families as the ideal. Figure 7.9 shows that an extended family may or may not be generational. Historians often use the term *extended family* differently. They use it to mean whoever is living under the same roof—kin, hired help, and apprentice workers; so be certain that you have the anthropological definition in mind as you read the anthropological literature. Currently the term **household** is being used by many disciplines. A household is a group that resides together and acts as a corporate economic unit; it may consist of a family but it may also include, or fully consist of, nonkin. The use of this term for a living group that includes nonkin helps to avoid confusion with the usage of *extended family*.

TRY THIS
Hypothesize

Why do so many societies have extended family organization rather than independent nuclear family groups? Hypothesize a reason. How can you test your hypothesis?

Family Forms in Industrialized Societies

The industrialized world has been experiencing a revolution in family patterns in recent decades. Terms such as *expanded families* (families that include persons who are not kin), *blended families* (the result of divorce and remarriage), *matrifocal families* (in which the mother is dominant, with husband-father absent or present—typically the result of economic conditions such that the husband is unable to support the family [Pasternak, Ember, and Ember 1997: 246]), and *single-parent families* appear in local newspapers as well as international periodicals. The many variations in family types are not a new phenomenon. In the past, in Western industrialized societies, new families were often formed after death and

extended family
Two or more nuclear families that are related by blood and who reside in the same household, village, or territory (e.g., a man and wife, their sons, and their sons' wives and children).

household
A common residence-based economic unit.

TRY THIS
Consider

How many of your relatives (outside of your nuclear family) live within three miles of you? How often do you interact with these relatives: less than once a week, about once a week, or more than once a week?

remarriage; today, in the United States, an increasing divorce rate is the primary reason for varied family types. A cross-cultural perspective on the rate of divorce can offer insight. In one study of forty *preliterate* societies in North and South America, Africa, Asia, and Oceania, divorce was allowed in thirty-nine of the societies. Moreover, according to one analysis, the divorce rate in about 60 percent of preliterate societies was, at the time of the study, higher than in the United States (Murdock 1950, cited in Hutter 1981: 437).

Changes in family focus have often resulted from industrialization, which has been hypothesized as a causative factor in the decline of extended families and the rise in the numbers of socially isolated nuclear family units. This change occurs because people must move to where jobs can be found, and roles change as nuclear families have fewer local extended family support systems. We cannot, however, jump to hasty conclusions about the effect of industrialization on families. Many of these conditions and changes have occurred, but studies in West Africa and sub-Saharan Africa have found that the extended family system is in place and growing stronger since the removal of colonial governments (Hutter 1981: 111–35). However, data from contemporary studies of migration, such as that of the Nuer moving from Sudan to Minnesota, result in men or couples living apart from kin in independent nuclear families where they must resolve problems without the benefit of supportive kin (Holtzman 2000: 106). There is an extensive body of literature, from both anthropology and sociology, on the subject of family patterns associated with industrialized modern societies. The bottom line seems to be that human cultures continue to adapt.

RESIDENCE PATTERNS

Customs about where one lives after marriage are known as residence patterns. It is easy to identify residence patterns by noting the roots to each word. The inclusion of the word *local* (meaning *place*) in each type of residence is a flag that tells you that the word refers to residence.

The pattern regarding place of residence after marriage in which the newly married couple set up their own household away from both sets of parents is called **neolocal residence,** which is the residence custom most often practiced in North American culture. This is a popular residence pattern in industrialized societies, but it is the preferred residence pattern in only about 7 percent of all societies (Murdock 1949: 194). Whether in a contemporary urban culture or a foraging culture, neolocality is marked by economic independence and privacy for the newly married couple. The emergence of this residence pattern as societies became industrialized is one reflection of the adaptive nature of culture—people moved to be near

neolocal residence
A postmarriage residence rule that requires the bride and groom to set up an independent household away from both sets of parents.

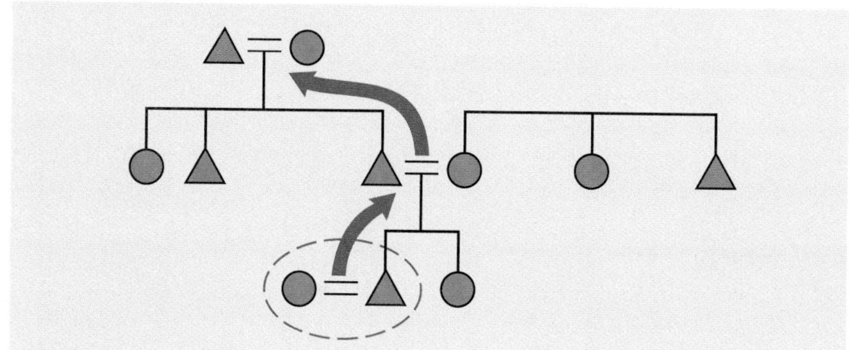

FIGURE 7.10
Patrilocal Residence
The newly married couple reside with or near the groom's father. The groom's father brought his bride to live with his father. This results in a patrilocal extended family.

their workplaces. This functioned well for one-income families. It seems less adaptive today for two-income families and single-parent families.

The residence pattern known as **patrilocal residence** (*pater* meaning *father*) refers to the custom in which the newly married couple go to live with the groom's father (Figure 7.10). The term **virilocal residence** (living with the husband's group) is also used to designate this form of residence and some anthropologists prefer this term. *Patrilocal residence* (the term used in this text) can mean living in the same house as the groom's father (the groom's mother is living there too, of course), on the father's property, or in the village of the father. Any pattern in which the new bride moves away from her family to live with or near the groom's father's group is considered patrilocal residence. This is overwhelmingly the most popular residence custom, with 58 percent of cultures practicing it (Murdock 1949: 194). One function of the bride moving away from her natal group is that it creates alliances between groups.

The patrilocal residence pattern is found most often in societies in which descent is traced through males and where property is passed through the male line. The predominant hypothesis to explain patrilocality is that it keeps men together where males work together for mutual profit. Another hypothesis to explain residence rules has emerged from an analysis of the cross-cultural data. A high correlation exists between the type of warfare practiced by a society and residence patterns. Societies with internal warfare, that is, where groups within the same society fight with one another (different villages or clans), usually practice patrilocal residence. It is argued that patrilocal residence keeps fathers, sons, and brothers together as a warring unit. It must be remembered, though, that correlation does not equal causation. Patrilocality and internal warfare may be a coincidence.

The Yąnomamö practice the custom of patrilocal residence. When a man marries, it is to a woman of a descent group different from his (such groups are exogamous among the Yąnomamö). Because two or three descent groups usually are represented in a village, marriage to a man who

patrilocal residence
A postmarriage residence rule that requires the bride and groom to live in or near the residence of the groom's father.

virilocal residence
The custom of living with the husband's relatives after marriage.

A large family based on polygynous marriage in Amman, Jordan. Patrilocal residence is practiced in this society. What type of descent would you expect them to practice? Why?

lives in the same village would merely mean that the woman would move to her husband's part of the village when she marries. A village consists of a series of living spaces under one roof, and families occupy a section of the village, or ***shabano*** (the native term for the village). Descent group members locate near each other. If a man marries a woman from a different *shabano*, a practice that is encouraged because it aids in alliance formation, the woman would move to her husband's village.

TRY THIS
Analyze

You are a person from a traditional culture that practices a strict postmarriage residence rule of patrilocality. How would you view the North American custom of neolocal residence? Why?

Matrilocal residence means that the newly married couple live with the bride's mother (*matri* meaning *mother*) (Figure 7.11). The term **uxorilocal** is also used for this residence form. Uxorilocal refers to living with the wife's group. The term *matrilocal* is used here.

This form of residence is found in 15 percent of cultures and is typically associated with societies in which descent is traced through women and property is passed from mother to daughter (Murdock 1949: 194). This residence pattern also has an economic function. Because the women-centered group owns the land or herds, it is logical that they would remain together and their husbands would move to live with them at marriage.

The Hopi, who farm and herd sheep, demonstrate matrilocal residence. A Hopi household consists of a woman, her daughters and their husbands and children, plus her unmarried sons (you no doubt recognize this as an extended family). Married sons usually live nearby and occasionally help out with farming. Her husband would also reside there if she is still married (divorce is an easy matter). Women have a great deal of influence among the Hopi; they control access to the land and own the harvest (Fox 1983; Keesing and Strathern 1998: 194).

shabano
A Yąnomamö village.

matrilocal residence
A postmarriage residence rule that requires the bride and groom to live in or near the residence of the bride's mother.

uxorilocal residence
The custom of living with the wife's relatives after marriage.

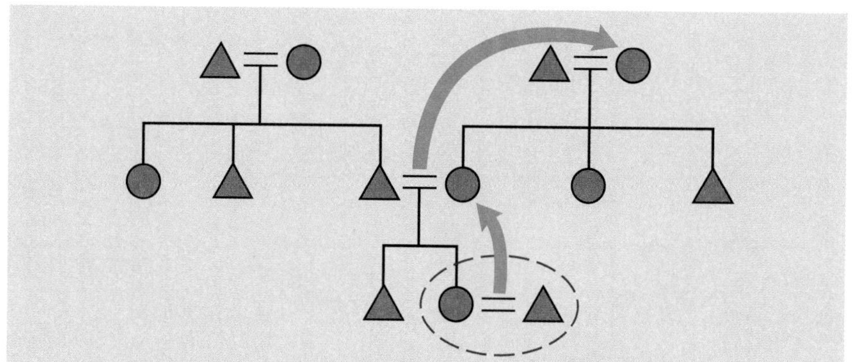

FIGURE 7.11
Matrilocal Residence
The newly married couple reside with or near the bride's mother, who in turn is living with or near her mother. This results in a matrilocal extended family.

A correlation also exists between type of warfare and this residence pattern. Matrilocal residence correlates with cultures in which warfare is external. Men leave to fight a different group and must travel away from home for periods of time. Recall the Nayar case discussed earlier in this chapter. Has the preceeding discussion helped you to respond to the Try This box on the previous page?

A woman and her children residing without co-residence of a husband is called **matrifocal residence.** This pattern is a result of economic conditions in which the husband leaves the residence because he is unable to support the family. In other words, matrifocal residence is a form of residence, but technically it is not a traditional pattern of residence in any society. Some anthropologists and sociologists place this as a form of family—the matrifocal family—rather than as a type of residence. Where would you place it?

Each residence pattern is associated with specific adaptations for the culture with which it is found. **Avunculocal residence** (representing 3 percent of the cultures in Murdock's sample) occurs when the newly married couple live with the groom's mother's brother (Murdock 1949: 194). This form of residence is often associated with sedentary, small-scale societies in which property is passed from generation to generation through females, and males help to manage the resources of their sisters. Examine Figure 7.12. Note that Ego's mother's brother is in the same descent group (known as a lineage and discussed further in Chapter 8) as Ego and thus shares the benefits of the same property. It would make economic sense, then, for Ego to live and work with his maternal uncle.

Choice is the rule with **bilocal residence** (also called **ambilocal residence**). A newly married couple live with or near *either* the groom's parents or the bride's parents. This residence type occurs in just over 7 percent of a sample of 250 cultures (Murdock 1949: 194). Which family the couple lives with or near is negotiated with everyone involved and is often related to economics. Such is the case when one family has all

matrifocal residence
A residence group consisting of a woman and her children residing without co-residence of a husband.

avunculocal residence
A postmarriage residence rule that requires the bride and groom to reside with or near the groom's mother's brother.

bilocal residence
The condition in which a newly married couple reside either with or near the groom's parents or the bride's parents.

ambilocal residence
See *bilocal residence.*

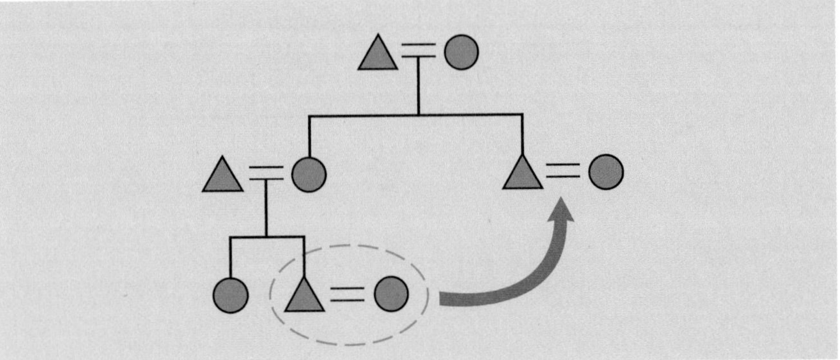

FIGURE 7.12 **Avunculocal Residence** The newly married couple reside with the groom's mother's brother. This is found in matrilineal societies.

daughters and negotiates to have one of the daughters and her husband live with them in order to have the husband's economic support.

Matri-patrilocal residence (a pattern named by Murdock [1949]) is really an interim residence form found primarily in societies in which bridewealth is paid. Similar to the case of the half-marriage of the Yurok discussed earlier, in matri-patrilocal residence the groom moves to live with the bride's family but this residence is temporary. In negotiating the marriage the groom agrees to live and work as an economic member of the bride's family until the agreed-upon period of time has passed, thus compensating for his inability to make the full bridewealth payment at the time of the wedding. Regular residence is patrilocal, which is the permanent residence once the bridewealth has been worked off. This then is a residence pattern that is an adaptive response to economic situations. Other patterns of residence exist but are practiced by few cultures and are not treated in this text. See the Suggested Readings at the end of this chapter for references that will lead you to more information.

matri-patrilocal residence
A temporary residence form in which the groom moves to live with the bride's family until bridewealth payments are complete and the couple take up permanent patrilocal residence.

SUMMARY

The rules and customs about mate selection and marriage differ widely around the world. Yet common patterns can be identified. There are both formal and informal rules regarding whom you can or should marry and whom you are forbidden to marry. Rules such as the levirate (brother-in-law marriage) and the sororate (sister-in-law marriage) provide security for a spouse and children should the other spouse die. Mate selection is either free choice or arranged. Marriage finance is often complex and includes bridewealth and dowry. There are several forms of marriage—one spouse (monogamy), multiple wives (polygyny), and multiple husbands (polyandry). Each form has its unique adaptive advantages. Families result from marriage (affinal) ties and blood (consanguineal) ties as these are constructed by individual cultures. Customs regarding residence after marriage are varied, and the functions of such residence patterns reflect issues that are important within each culture, such as economics and political alliance formation.

Study Questions

1. Discuss how the Nayar case illustrates the difficulties that anthropologists have in listing the common features of marriage found across cultures.
2. Describe the various forms of marriage found cross-culturally. Explain the advantages of each from a woman's viewpoint and from a man's viewpoint.
3. Discuss and evaluate the adaptive significance of exogamy and endogamy.
4. What are common features and functions of families around the world? Why is it difficult to define *family*?
5. What is an extended family? What is a household?
6. Describe traditional family forms. How have these forms changed in industrialized societies?
7. Compare and contrast the functions of neolocal, patrilocal, and matrilocal residence patterns.

OLC
mhhe • com / lenkeit5e
See Self Quiz.

Suggested Readings

Chagnon, Napoleon A. 1997. *Yąnomamö*, 5th ed. Fort Worth, Tex.: Harcourt Brace College Publishers. Chagnon discusses marriage and residence in the social organization chapter of this ethnography. Real situations illustrating ideal and actual behaviors are discussed and genealogies are diagrammed.

Fox, Robin. 1983. *Kinship and Marriage: An Anthropological Perspective.* Cambridge, England: Cambridge University Press (originally published in 1967). Fox offers one of the best introductory discussions of anthropological kinship analysis—widely used in most universities. Lots of detail but clearly written.

Knauft, Bruce. 2010. *The Gebusi: Lives Transformed in a Rainforest World*, 2nd ed. New York: McGraw-Hill.

Malinowski, Bronislaw. 1929. *The Sexual Life of Savages.* New York: Harcourt, Brace, Jovanovich. A classic account of courtship, marriage, love magic, and sexual norms among the Trobriand Islanders.

Pasternak, Burton, Carol R. Ember, and Melvin Ember. 1997. *Sex, Gender, and Kinship: A Cross-Cultural Perspective.* Upper Saddle River, N.J.: Pearson. A good read. Addresses many questions that may have occurred to you when you read this chapter.

Shostak, M. 2000. *Nisa, the Life and Words of a !Kung Woman.* Cambridge: Harvard University Press. A personal account of this Ju/'hoansi San woman's life with her feelings about marriage and family.

OLC
mhhe • com / lenkeit5e
See Web links.

CHAPTER 8

Kinship and Descent

Are These the Ties That Bind?

I am a mother-in-law. Given all of the stereotypes about mothers-in-law in North American culture, I wear this label with some trepidation, though I believe that my son-in-law and I have a harmonious relationship. I always remember how a Native American student who was in one of my classes in Canada told of his culture's solution to the mother-in-law issue. He avoided her. This was the tradition. If she came to visit and he was in the bedroom, he either stayed put behind a closed door or he exited through the bedroom window. Contemporary North American culture gives few guidelines as to proper behavior for a mother-in-law. The *ideal* seems to be a role of support and harmony. The *actual* relationship seems to miss this mark considerably if we are to believe all of the jokes told about mothers-in-law.

Mother-in-law avoidance taboos were reported for 137 societies in a sample of 250 groups (Murdock 1949). Avoidance of a man's wife's mother ranged from informal avoidance of situations in which a male Ego might encounter his wife's mother (twenty-six cultures, or 19 percent of the sample), to respect or reserved behavior in her presence (thirty-three cultures, or 24 percent), to true avoidance (seventy-eight cultures, or 57 percent) (Murdock 1949: 277). In the cultures that practice true avoidance, a man cannot be in the same room with his wife's mother. He must leave the immediate area if he sees her coming. Murdock lists thirty different categories of avoidance relationships for a male Ego, including wife's brother's wife, son's wife, and mother's sister's daughter. Mother-in-law avoidance and other avoidance taboos seem to correspond with incest taboos (Murdock 1949: 277). One explanation offered for such taboos is that some societies need an external support and reinforcement of incest taboos. The various avoidance taboos provide this reinforcement. This is an example of behavior being directed by rules within the kinship system.

A cross-cultural study of kinship provides insight into the flexibility of human adaptive strategies. Kin ties are often at the core of human culture, and anthropologists have learned that understanding them is often essential to a full understanding of a culture's economic system, political system, or religious structure.

If you are reading this book, you most likely live in an industrialized society. Many aspects of the lives of people in industrialized societies take place away from home and family. Friends and colleagues are usually not relatives. By contrast, nonindustrial societies revolve around kinship. As noted in Chapter 5, the archaeological record shows that societies based on subsistence strategies of foraging, horticulture, pastoralism, and early agriculture preceded large-scale societies. Thus we are able to gain glimpses of the possible roots of our own social organization by examining the kinship structure of societies today that have these subsistence strategies (always keeping in mind that present societies are not fossilized remnants of earlier ones). The following discussion is intended to provide you with the skills to read ethnographic accounts of the kinship organization of other cultures, including patterns of descent and terminological systems.

The objectives of this chapter are to:

- Describe and analyze the functions of kinship systems
- Describe and discuss the types of descent systems found around the world
- Explain the functions of associations based on descent
- Discuss the cross-cultural patterns of kinship terminology

◀ A grandfather and granddaughter in Papua New Guinea.

FUNCTIONS OF KINSHIP SYSTEMS

OLC
mhhe • com / lenkeit5e
See chapter outline and chapter overview.

Anthropologists have gathered detailed information about family and kinship from hundreds of different cultures. Although the specifics of the kinship systems differ, the goals of kinship are remarkably similar all over the world. Recall from Chapter 7 that a kinship system is the complexity that results from the affinal and consanguineal ties within a society and the traditions that govern how people in these relationships behave toward one another. Kinship systems achieve three major functions for their group members. As each function is discussed, think about how it applies to your culture's kinship system.

First, kinship systems function to organize people into groups. Families constitute one such group. Residence groups and descent groups are other types of organized kin groups within societies.

Second, kinship systems function to direct people's behavior. They do this because each of us is enculturated to know the **role** (the assigned behavioral expectations for a particular position within society and how it is acted out) for a particular kin classification. Role behaviors are reciprocal between *classes* of individuals within a kinship system. *Mother*, for example, is a class of people who are female parents (either by giving birth or by adoption). In North America, your role expectation when you interact with your mother is to show respect and love toward her. She, in turn, has a role to play in relation to you—to protect you, nurture you, provide for you while you are a child, and love you. The mother-in-law avoidance customs cited at the beginning of this chapter also illustrate how a kinship system's customs direct behavior.

Another aspect of the kinship function of directing behavior involves a person's **status** within the society. You are born into a kin group (or are adopted by the group) and automatically acquire the status of that group. Anthropologists call this **ascribed status.** Other forms of ascribed status include that conferred by virtue of gender, age, ethnic group, and subcultural affiliation. In most cultures, for example, an individual from a wealthy family is treated differently from a member of a poor family; elders have rights that children and young adults do not have. A person may also acquire status in a variety of other ways, for example, by developing skills as a midwife, hunter, gardener, mediator, and so forth. These forms of status are called **achieved status.** An individual's role in the society is how that person plays out or behaves in her or his position of ascribed and achieved status.

Third, kinship systems function to provide security for members of a kin group. The security can be economic—kin lend you money, share food, come to help you harvest crops. It can be security provided by support in the tasks of daily life—watching your baby while you run errands or helping you with household chores. The kin group also provides security

role
The culturally assigned behaviors and expectations for a person's social position.

status
A person's position in society.

ascribed status
The status a person is given at birth and over which that person has no control.

achieved status
A status position that is earned through an individual's skills, actions, and accomplishments.

and support during major life transitions—birth, marriage, divorce, death. The details of this security and the roles assigned to classes of kin often differ from one culture to the next. In small homogeneous societies, the kin group provides a person's only security. If a spouse dies, for example, specific relatives provide support for the remaining spouse and children. Social control issues, conflict resolution, and political decision making are other behaviors assigned to kin in such societies.

Kinship provides security in many of the same situations in complex heterogeneous societies. In such societies, however, governmental agencies, private agencies, and businesses have taken over the security functions of kinship in many situations. In North American culture, many people purchase life insurance policies so that their spouse and children will be financially cared for should they die. Or the state will take care of your children if you die without leaving any assets or designated guardians for them. Courts and professional mediators are designated to resolve conflicts in state societies.

Think of three specific ways your nuclear family provides you with security.

IDEAL VERSUS REAL PATTERNS OF KINSHIP

A word about ideal and real patterns of kinship, descent, and terminological systems must be made before we examine these systems. In Chapter 2 we discussed ideal and real (or actual) culture. When anthropologists describe a culture's kinship system, they are presenting the culture's ideal custom or the most common pattern. For example, monogamy is the ideal form of marriage in North American culture. In fact, most North Americans really *do* have only one spouse (at least only one at a time). This would be a case in which real and ideal cultural patterns are virtually the same. Nearly everyone, however, can recall a publicized case in which a man or woman had more than one spouse, though often the spouses did not know that their mate was married to someone else. There are also accounts of marriages in the United States in which men have several wives and each wife knows the other wives. Such cases, though rare, often receive a great deal of attention in the media because they are defined as illegal in all legal jurisdictions in the United States.

In the ethnographic literature, anthropologists most often discuss and present examples and analyses of ideal customs and behaviors. Real behaviors, and their variations, are also recorded in some but not all ethnographic accounts. Napoleon Chagnon's account of the Yąnomamö Indians of Venezuela and Brazil first presents the reader with a discussion of the ideal model of Yąnomamö society—exogamous patrilineages, bilateral cross-cousin marriage, and the classification of bilateral cross-cousins as wives (Chagnon 1997: 140). These terms will be explained shortly. Chagnon then diagrams and discusses a number of actual (real) marriages and kinship relationships that he encountered among the Yąnomamö, and quite a few do not match the ideal pattern.

Variations and exceptions to the ideal within a society nearly always occur. The *knowledge* of proper, accepted customs is usually shared by most members of a culture, even if all do not practice the custom or behave in the ideal manner. Human beings are complex, and human cultures are equally complex. Variations and exceptions to ideal behaviors add spice to the texture of social life everywhere if you consider that these are often the topics of gossip, song, sermon, and story. Careful ethnographic descriptions based on participant observation over a long period reveal these variations and exceptions. The ethnological analysis of data from hundreds of cultures has revealed the common *patterns* discussed in the following sections, but keep in mind the notions of ideal versus real culture.

DESCENT GROUPS

Descent groups are important in most kinship systems. A **descent group** consists of a group of people who share identity that is directly traced (or stipulated to come) from a common ancestor. As we established previously, all of our ancestors lived at one time in societies with economies based on foraging, horticulture, and pastoralism, and it was in these societies that ideas about descent began, although we will never know the details of how they originated. Most foraging cultures do not focus on descent groups; however, in societies with food-production strategies, where property is owned by corporate kin groups and populations are large and concentrated, the focus *is* on descent. These societies also exhibit the most variety and complexity in all aspects of kinship. We therefore think that ideas about descent likely began with food-producing societies. For these groups, property ownership led to the problem of how and to whom property would be left when one died.

Unilineal Descent Groups

Unilineal descent systems are often perplexing to individuals who have been raised in a society without such systems. Before reading about these kinship groups, you should set aside all thoughts of your own descent system and concentrate on the logic and functions of the unilineal systems presented. These systems reflect the ingenuity of humans in developing kin groups that made sense to them and that worked to each person's benefit.

As food-producing societies evolved, descent groups became something like modern business corporations, to use a contemporary analogy. Members of the corporate group act together and are governed by specific rights and duties. Because property ownership was an issue, large families

descent group
A group of people who share identity and come from a common ancestor.

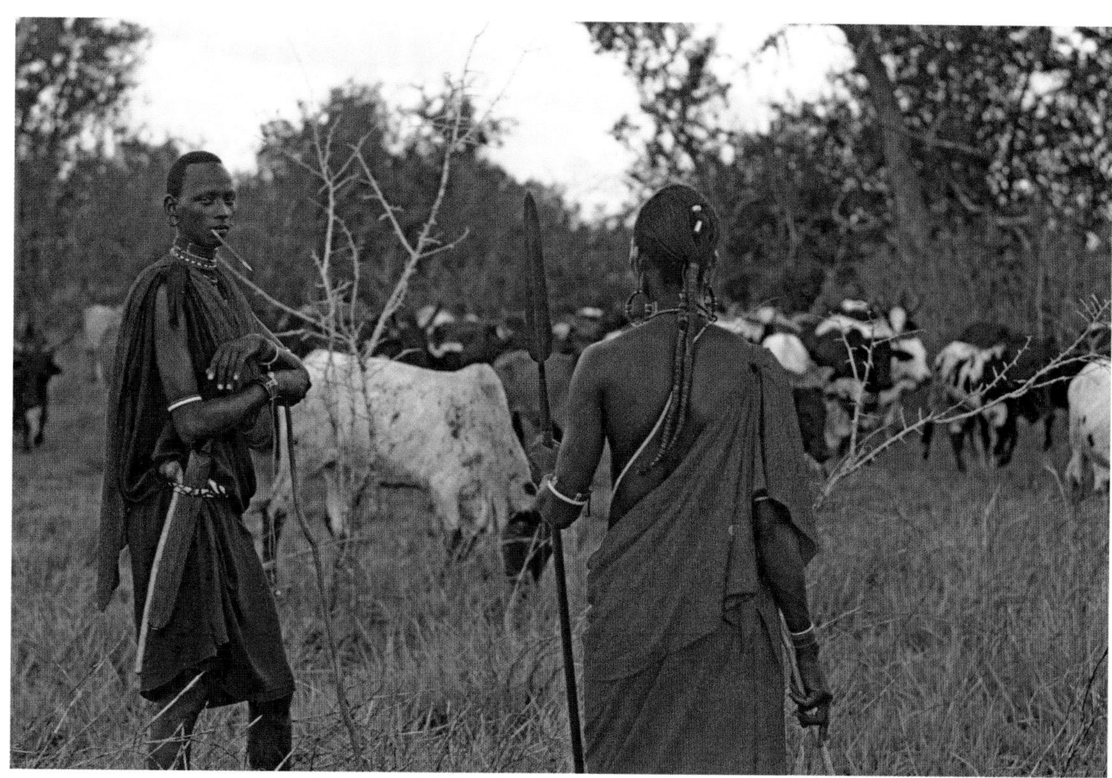

The cattle-herding Maasai of the Wakwafi tribe in Tanzania practice unilineal descent, specifically patrilineages. Members of these patrilineages own and herd their cattle together.

created descent groups to manage property. The most basic descent group is the **lineage.** Members of a lineage descent group can trace their ancestors back through several generations to a common ancestor. The lineage holds property in common (e.g., land, sheep, or cattle). All members benefit from this property, all contribute to its maintenance in some manner, and all view the other members of their lineage as their closest, most important relatives. Furthermore, authority and power in group decision making and cohesiveness are important functions of lineages. The lineage continues over time even as its members change through births and deaths. These features are what lead some researchers to point out that the lineage functions like a modern corporation.

Unilineal descent groups recognize consanguineal ties as being passed through only females or males. It is not that other blood relatives are unknown but rather that *by cultural definition* they belong to a descent group different from Ego's. For example, the father may be recognized as the male parent (a consanguineal relative) but may not be considered as a *lineal* relative. This underscores that unilineal descent groups are culturally defined groups.

lineage
A unilineal descent group that traces its consanguineal relatives back to a common ancestor.

FIGURE 8.1
Ego's Patrilineage

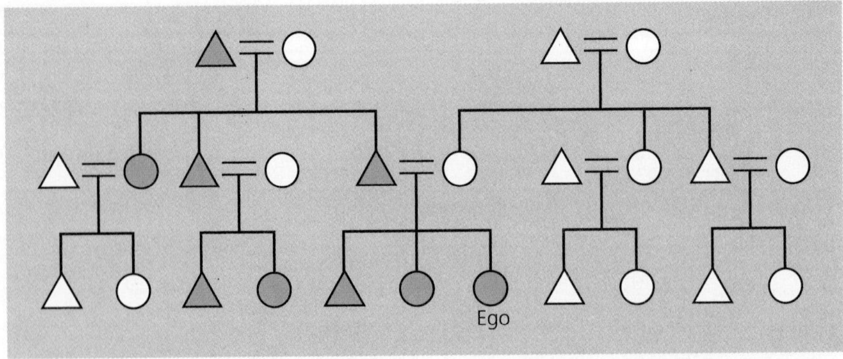

Patrilineal Descent. In a **patrilineage,** descent is passed through the male line. All members (both males and females) acquire their lineage from their father, but only males pass it on. This kin link through males is a link through what some anthropologists call **agnates** (a term in Roman law that is a synonym for members of a patrilineage) (Fox 1983: 45). Ego's agnates are all of the members of Ego's patrilineage (Figure 8.1). The term *agnates* is a specialized term, but it is used in ethnographic accounts such as that of the Yąnomamö, so it helps to be familiar with it.

A major function of patrilineal groups is to keep property for the males who own and manage it. This is the most common form of descent worldwide; 42 percent of societies (in a sample of 250 societies) practice it (Murdock 1949: 194). Lineages are permanent, often tight, cohesive groups. Lineage membership provides an individual with an ascribed status and group membership that is kept throughout his or her life. Even when an individual marries or changes residence, lineage membership is retained. Of course there are exceptions. Occasionally an individual is adopted by another lineage. This might happen if a man has all daughters and negotiates to adopt one of his daughter's husbands so that his line will continue.

The enculturated role behaviors and expectations for lineage members are that first responsibilities are always toward one's own lineage members. This does not mean that an individual does not care about the relatives acquired through marriage. It simply means that the culture is organized in such a manner that those affines are being looked after by the members of *their* lineage. Exceptions do occur and are typically related to political or economic practicalities. Among the patrilineal Yąnomamö, for example, a man's brothers-in-law are important political allies and are given priority consideration in many situations.

patrilineage
A unilineal descent group passed on through males and traced to a common male ancestor.

agnates
Members of a patrilineage.

matrilineage
A unilineal descent group with membership passed on through females and traced to a common female ancestor.

uterine descent group
See *matrilineage*.

Matrilineal Descent. A **matrilineage** (or **uterine descent group**) is characterized by descent that is traced through females. In matrilineal descent, representing 20 percent of cultures (from a sample of 250), both males

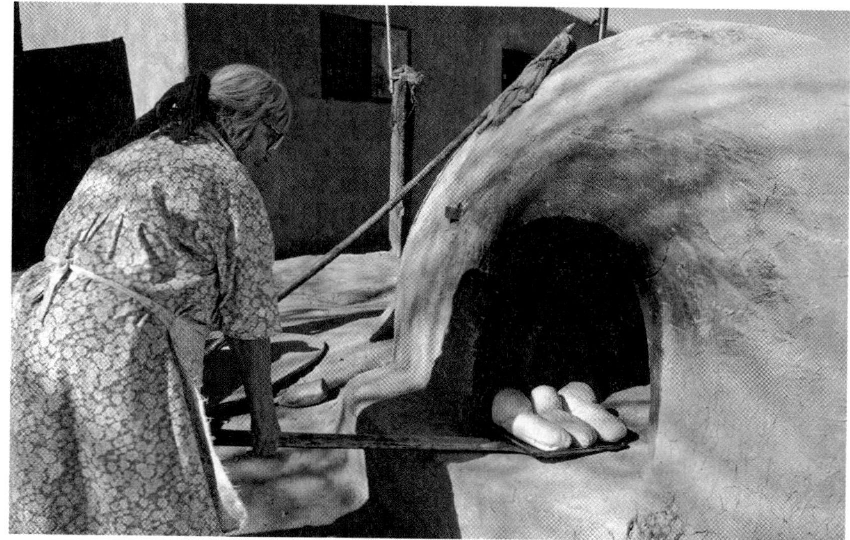

The Hopi people of the southwestern United States are matrilineal, with women having inheritance rights to property. This Hopi woman is baking in a traditional oven.

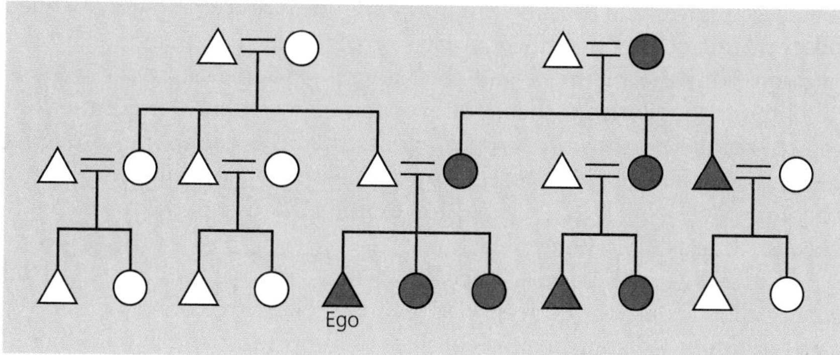

FIGURE 8.2
Ego's Matrilineage

and females acquire the lineage of their mother (Murdock 1949: 194). Only women can pass the lineage membership on to the next generation.

In matrilineal societies the women have inheritance rights to property, although within the corporate matrilineal group it is often their brothers (also members of the same matrilineage) who control it. The social organization of the Hopi of the southwestern United States is matrilineal, with the matrilineage acting as a corporate economic unit. Upon marriage a man joins the household of his wife and makes important economic contributions to farming and sheep herding but does not participate in the wife's lineage rituals. He still has ties to his mother and sisters through *his* lineage relationship and plays important roles in transmitting the ritual heritage of his matrilineage.

OLC
mhhe • com / lenkeit5e

See Internet exercises and Web links.

As you examine Figure 8.2, note that if the members of Ego's lineage were asked to name *their* lineage members, each would name exactly the same set of people. The same would hold true if you posed this same

FIGURE 8.3
Bilateral Descent

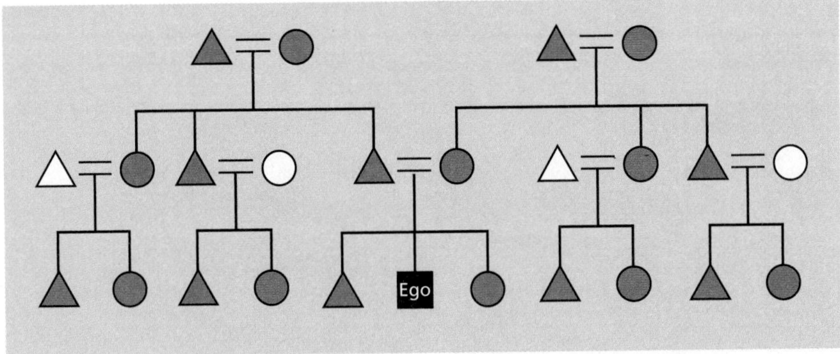

question to individual members of a patrilineage. The result is a closely knit permanent group.

Nonunilineal Descent Groups

OLC
mhhe • com / lenkeit5e
See Web links.

The best-known and most common nonunilineal descent system is called **bilateral descent.** An individual Ego recognizes all consanguineal relatives on both the mother's and the father's sides of the family. She or he inherits equally from them. This system is found in North American society among persons of European ancestry and is common in foraging societies. Such a bilateral descent group consists only of siblings and their consanguineal kin. Ego's cousin, for example, does not share the same ancestor line as Ego (Figure 8.3).

Within bilateral systems, every Ego belongs to what is called a **kindred** group, which consists of Ego's relatives and their degree of relationship to Ego (e.g., aunt, great uncle, first cousin). An interesting feature of a kindred group is that only siblings share exactly the same kindred and set of relatives (at least until they marry). Another way to describe a kindred is that it consists of Ego's nuclear family and consanguineal members of Ego's extended family. Study the diagram in Figure 8.4. Note that in Ego's kindred, Ego

bilateral descent
Descent that is traced equally through both mother and father.

kindred
A term associated with bilateral descent in which relatives calculate their degree of relationship to Ego. In a kindred, only siblings share the exact same set of relatives.

TRY THIS Consider

Imagine that you have a problem. You have a fence on your property that was knocked down in a recent storm, and you need help repairing it. In which descent system, unilineal (patrilineal or matrilineal) or nonunilineal (bilateral), would you expect to have the most relatives who would feel a real *obligation* to drop all of their weekend plans, cancel motel reservations and concert tickets, and come to your home to help with the fence repair? How many of your Facebook friends would feel an obligation to come and help?

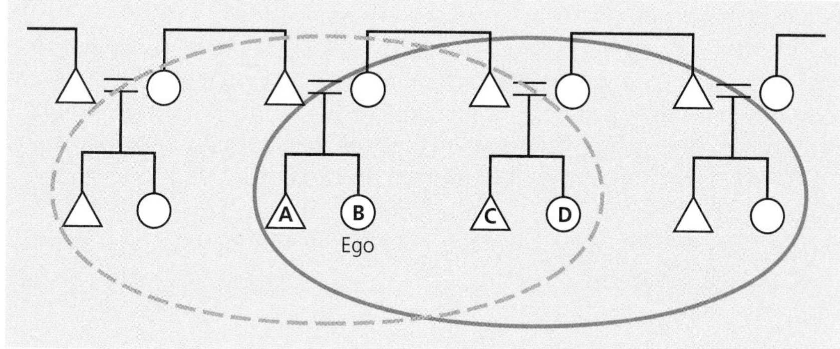

FIGURE 8.4
Kindred The kindred of siblings A and B are shown with the broken line. The kindred of siblings C and D are shown with the solid line. If you follow the kindreds back another generation, you'll see that A and B would have a different kindred from that of their mother and father.

A large North American kindred group. How many individuals can you name in your own kindred?

and Ego's brother have the same parents, grandparents, aunts, uncles, and cousins. Ego and her brother have the same consanguineal relatives and the same bilateral descent group, and they share the same kindred group. If you consider Ego's mother, her bilateral descent group includes Ego and Ego's brother and their children. However, Ego's mother will not name her husband (Ego's father) as part of her kindred because he and all of his consanguineal kin are related to Ego's mother affinally. In other words, kindred group members related to Ego do not share exactly the same set of biological ancestors unless they are siblings. What they have in common is Ego herself as a member of their kindred (Fox 1983: 164–74). Kindred groups are useful in societies in which people need occasional support and help. For example they might participate in rituals involving Ego such as a wedding or funeral. Within a kindred, focus is more often on one's nuclear family. Compare this with a matrilineage or patrilineage where Ego's focus is on the whole lineage.

Other Descent Groups

Other types of descent groups are less common than patrilineal, matrilineal, and bilateral descent. Each could be placed under unilineal descent types or nonunilineal descent types—there are arguments for each. For the sake of simplicity, they are classified here as other descent groups. After reading the description of each group, decide whether you would classify them as unilineal or nonunilineal systems.

Double Descent. **Double descent** is a system in which two separate lines of descent are recognized at the same time. In this system some property is passed down only through females, and other property is passed down only through males. An example of double descent would be a system in which land could be passed only from mother to daughter, whereas cattle could be passed only from father to son.

Ambilineal Descent. **Ambilineal descent** is a system in which everyone belongs to a unilineal descent group that is acquired through *either* the mother or the father. In other words, some members of the society trace their descent through their mothers, whereas other members of the same society determine their descent through their fathers. Discussions are held and traditional, economic, political, or other issues are considered before decisions are made about which system to follow.

double descent
A descent system with two separate lines of descent that are both recognized at the same time.

ambilineal descent
A unilineal descent system in which some members of the society acquire and pass on descent affiliation through females, whereas others do so through males.

Associations Based on Descent

Descent-based societies are effective. The threads created by marriages between lineages (recall that lineages are usually exogamous groups) combine with the strong ties of lineage membership itself to weave a cultural fabric of interdependent units. Common culture and language, plus the associations created by affinal and consanguineal ties, hold such groups together. There is no centralized leadership or governmental system. Leadership (discussed more fully in Chapter 10) remains within the immediate family and descent group.

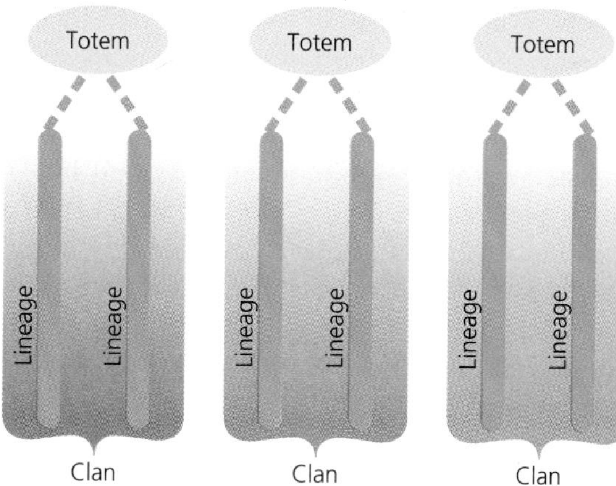

FIGURE 8.5
Second-Level Descent

Anthropologists have recorded additional types of kin-based organization in horticultural and pastoral societies with large populations. These are often called second-level descent groups because individuals first belong to a lineage. The second-level descent groups are clans, phratries, and moieties (Figure 8.5). These groups are unilineal, and membership in them is passed through either the female or the male line. In other words, you are assigned membership in a clan because your mother is a member (in a matrilineal society) or your father is a member (in a patrilineal society).

A **clan** is a group consisting of two or more lineages that share a common ancestor in the mythical past. A lineage, you will remember, is a descent group that can explicitly name ancestors back several generations. Clan members cannot name their ancestors all the way back to a common ancestor. In some societies, the ancestor of a clan is considered mythical or a symbol and is called its **totem.** Mythic ancestors often figure in a culture's origin myths. Clans may or may not be exogamous. When they are exogamous it forces members to seek spouses from other clans. The threads of marriage ties thus reach farther away from Ego, while at the same time Ego is bound closely by the clan association to members of other lineages (i.e., those in her or his own clan).

Additional levels of descent associations also occur in some societies, although these are rare. A **phratry** is a grouping formed by two or more clans when there are at least three or more such groupings (Schusky 1972: 75). It is also unilineal, but the original association is often vague or is based on some type of mutual relationship from past times in the culture's history. Phratries are also usually exogamous groups.

Finally, moieties are sometimes found in nonindustrial societies. A **moiety** association divides the society in half. Because a moiety is a unilineal association inherited through either women or men, it creates a common bond with many individuals. Moieties are usually exogamous too.

clan
A descent group consisting of two or more lineages that trace their origin to a mythical ancestor.

totem
Mythical ancestor or symbol of a clan.

phratry
A group of two or more clans that have a tie to one another, often based on a historical relationship; obligations and rights are expected between clans in this relationship.

moiety
An association that divides a society in half. Moiety affiliation is inherited unilineally and carries obligations to other members.

TRY THIS
Hypothesize

Suppose for a moment that you are an anthropologist. You have been reading about all of these unilineal, exogamous groups, here and in other assigned readings. Formulate a hypothesis that explains the purpose served by such associations. Share, compare, and discuss your hypothesis with a classmate. It might help you to study Figure 8.5 as you formulate your hypothesis.

Complete this hypothesis on another sheet of paper: If _______ exist within a society, then clans, phratries, and moieties serve to _______.

Now, determine two ways that you could test your hypothesis.

To recap, exogamous rules commonly apply to the nuclear family, lineage, clan, phratry, and moiety groups, thus forcing a complex network of marriage relations. Membership at each level of descent (lineage, clan, phratry, or moiety) carries specific obligations and expectations. Reflect on the functions of kinship listed at the beginning of this chapter. Imagine viewing the world through the lens of a person who is a member of a culture with this complex kinship structure.

Another rather common type of kin organization, **segmentary lineages,** found in some large food-producing societies seems to function in the same way as the clan and phratry. Instead of progressively larger groupings, however, the segmentary lineage system consists of smaller sublineage sets (Figure 8.6). Segmentary lineages are often found in large African tribes. The Nuer provide an example of this type of organization.

Nuer patrilineages consist of a large group of agnates who trace their descent to a common ancestor. Each major lineage is in turn segmented into minimal lineage segments. All property is owned and passed on through the males. All lineages are exogamous units. E. E. Evans-Pritchard (1940) noted that each Nuer could, when asked, readily name his ancestors back four to five generations. Lineages are usually three to five generations, and the major ones have ten to twelve generations. Evans-Pritchard graphically represents these lineages rather like a tree with thick branches that divide into smaller branches at the ends. The smaller, more recent lineage segments frequently further divide or recombine. Besides these actual traceable lineage relationships, termed *mar* (also spelled *maar*), the Nuer recognize another relationship termed *buth*. These *buth* relationships occur when there is believed to be a special relationship between two lineages but the actual links cannot be traced. The *buth* relationship would correspond to clans as discussed previously (Evans-Pritchard 1940: 192–200).

Voluntary Association Groups

Kinship groups are at the core of societies; they function to meet the needs of individuals and groups as discussed at the beginning of this chapter. Not all of an individual's needs may be met through various kin group associations, however. This is particularly true in large industrialized societies where kin group fragmentation often results from the mobility of individuals. An increase in voluntary association groups is one adaptation that is observed in such societies. Members of these groups fulfill some of the support roles once found only among family members, particularly in the realms of supporting one another in everyday activities and during life crisis situations. Examples of such associations in North America include formal groups such as the Boy Scouts of America, Rotary International, Elks, Jeep Owner's Club, AL-ANON, and the Canadian

segmentary lineage
A descent group consisting of sublineage sets.

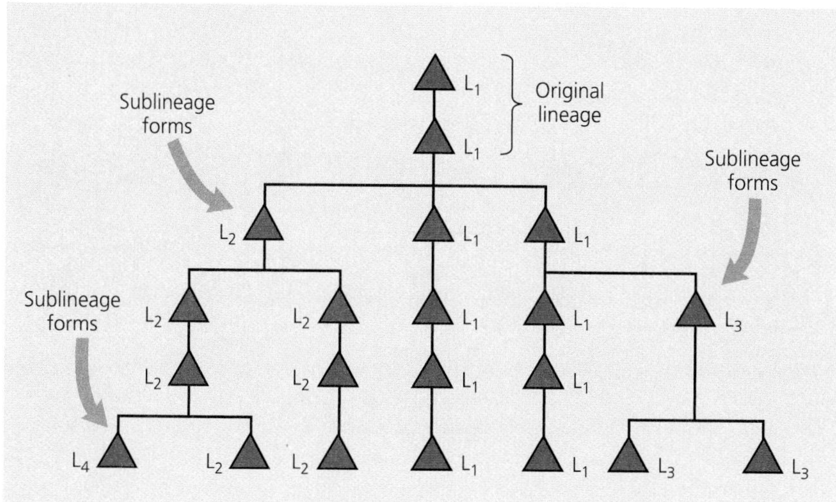

FIGURE 8.6
Segmentary Lineage
A lineage has segmented. Sublineages form when lineages get too large. Some members move and establish sublineages. They can still name lineage ancestors back four to five generations.

Kennel Club. Less formal groups also abound—quilters clubs, knitters clubs, book clubs, biking clubs, Web gamers, and even very informal groups such as the Friday morning coffee group or the pick-up basketball group that meets at the local park. Many voluntary association groups consist of local clubs that draw members from across a small geographic area, but the association may also create relationships across the larger society or even to individuals in other societies across the globe. Anthropologists use the term **sodality** for association groups that crosscut an entire society and whose membership is based on common interest rather than kinship or residence. Globalization has resulted in worldwide association groups, so perhaps we can speak of global sodalities. Among preindustrial societies, voluntary association groups are fewer in number. See Chapter 10 for further discussion of sodalities as integrative mechanisms in tribes.

TRY THIS
Consider

Name the voluntary association groups to which individual members of your nuclear family belong. What is one specific incident where one of these groups performed in a support role similar to what kin supply (or ideally are supposed to supply)?

PARALLEL-COUSINS AND CROSS-COUSINS REVISITED

To most North Americans of European descent, a cousin is a cousin is a cousin. This is because we use a type of kin terminological system in which all relatives in our own generation outside of our nuclear family are lumped and designated by a single term, *cousin*. So when we talk of a cousin who visited us yesterday, we are not giving much information about our relationship to this person. Is it our MoSiCh, our MoBrCh, our FaBrCh, or

sodality
A group that crosscuts a society and whose membership is based on common interest rather than kinship or residence.

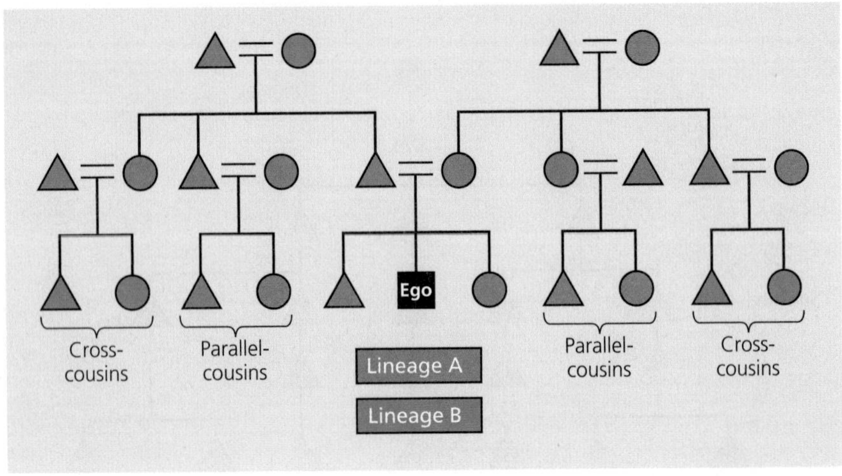

FIGURE 8.7 **Hypothetical Society with Only Two Patrilineages** The rule of lineage exogamy results in the marriages shown. All parallel-cousins will be of Ego's lineage, whereas cross-cousins will be possible marriage partners. This suggests that traditions of marrying certain cousins may have its roots in societies with two unilineal descent groups.

our FaSiCh? (See Figure 8.7.) The term doesn't even tell us if the cousin is female or male. Many cultures, most commonly those based on unilineal descent systems, recognize two types of cousins—**cross-cousins** and **parallel-cousins.** To appreciate the significance of these cousin types, you must set aside the knowledge that all cousins are equally related to you biologically. If one imagines a time when people may not have fully understood reproductive biology and genetics, the reasons some cousins are treated differently from others will be easier to comprehend. Traditional treatment of different types of cousins continues today, even when biological relationships are clearly understood. Why? In the emic view, the answer usually is, *tradition.*

As noted in Chapter 7, parallel-cousins are defined as the children of one's parent's sibling of the same sex, in other words, Ego's MoSiCh and Ego's FaBrCh. If you think of the word *parallel* and MoSi or FaBr, it may make more sense to you. These people's children are your parallel-cousins. Conversely, cross-cousins are the children of your parent's sibling of the opposite sex, or MoBrCh and FaSiCh. The cross can be remembered if you think of opposite sex of parent.

Knowing these distinctions between types of cousins is helpful in understanding some of the common terminological systems found in other cultures. Our own system does not make any distinction regarding cousins, but in some cultures, such as ones using the Iroquois terminological system, parallel-cousins are part of the incest taboo whereas cross-cousins are considered ideal marriage partners. One such system is called sister exchange marriage (discussed in Chapter 7), and it takes place between men who are cross-cousins. Each man arranges with a cross-cousin so that they marry each other's sisters. The Yąnomamö tribe of Venezuela and Brazil practice sister exchange, as do the Mbuti pygmy bands of Africa.

cross-cousin
Ego's mother's brother's child and father's sister's child.

parallel-cousin
Ego's mother's sister's child and father's brother's child.

Therefore, one could suggest that cousin designations, and the rules surrounding them, function to control mate selection.

TERMINOLOGICAL SYSTEMS

Terminology is an accompaniment to the kin structure. In foraging, horticultural, and pastoral societies, kinship is the primary manner in which people relate to one another. Furthermore, kin relations resulting from exogamous rules are central to the unity of the culture—they bind it together. It follows that kin roles and the obligations they carry are important. The complexity of terminological systems is relative. The system you have been enculturated to seems obvious and easy to you; other systems seem difficult and complex. A **kinship term** is a word that designates a culturally constructed social relationship between individuals who are related by blood or marriage (consanguines or affines). Kinship terminological systems are quite variable, but a comparative analysis shows that there are several basic terminological patterns. These patterns are most apparent in Ego's generation and Ego's parent's generation. These patterns have come to be called terminological systems. Several patterns that are repeatedly found in world cultures are Inuit (Eskimo), Iroquois, Hawaiian, Crow, Omaha, and Sudanese. Each system bears the name of the particular cultural group in which that terminological system was first recorded by ethnographers. These systems apparently developed independently in different parts of the world; that is, cultures in North America, South America, Africa, Asia, and Australia often independently developed the same *patterns* of terminology. Three of these terminological systems are discussed here: the Inuit, Iroquois, and Hawaiian.

Suppose you are being interviewed by an Amazonian anthropologist. She has just asked you the following question: Why do you use the same term for your MoBrCh, MoSiCh, FaBrCh, and FaSiCh? How would you respond? Ask someone else this question. Convey your seriousness in wanting a response.

The Inuit Terminology System

Terminological systems reflect recognized kin categories and often reflect values central to a culture. Cultures that use the Inuit, formerly Eskimo, terminology system (18 out of 250 societies, or 7 percent) focus on the nuclear family, in which each relative is given a separate term—Mo, Fa, Si, Br. Although this is not the most common terminological system, it is a good place to initiate an analysis of terminological systems because most North Americans use this one. Neolocal residence is often practiced in such cultures, thus making the nuclear family the central economic unit of the society (Murdock 1949: 249). Family band societies such as the Inuit (Eskimo) also typically exhibit this form of terminology. In these societies, kin outside of the nuclear family are lumped together terminologically. For example, MoBr and FaBr are both called by the same term (*uncle* in English), as are MoSi and FaSi (*aunt* in English). And all cousins are

kinship term
A word that designates a social relationship between individuals who are related by blood or marriage.

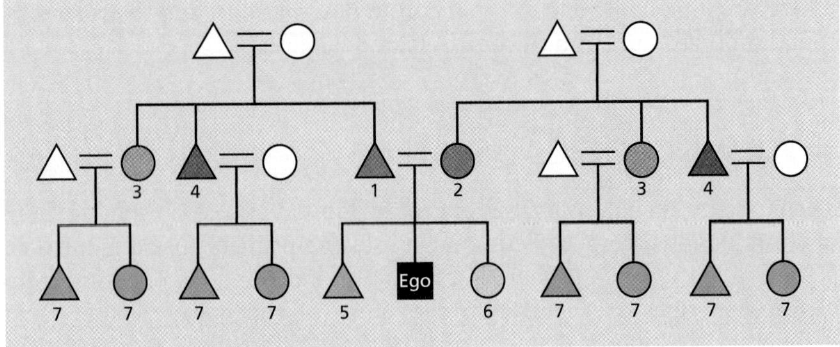

FIGURE 8.8
The Inuit Terminology System Each number in the diagram stands for a different term.

lumped with a single term (Figure 8.8). Of course, because each culture that exhibits the Inuit system speaks a different language, the words used are different. It is the *pattern* of usage that we are considering when we label a terminology as belonging to a particular system. Also, there are often cultures with variations on one of the basic terminological patterns that have been identified. For example, in Mexican culture the basic Inuit terminology system is used except that cousins are distinguished by sex (*primo* and *prima*). This variation is a reflection of the language (Spanish); that is, the male and female gender is built into all nouns. It does not appear that this distinction has any other significance. Such variations are minor, but they do point to the difficulty in precisely categorizing human cultures.

Now, toss aside your own cultural lens and through your imagination view the following systems. Pretend that you are looking through the cultural lens of a person who uses these terms. We are required to *really* think about the differences that our cultures have produced when we examine other terminological systems.

The Iroquois Terminology System

bifurcate
The distinction within kinship systems where father's side and mother's side of the family are labeled and treated differently, splitting mother's side of the family from father's side of the family.

fictive kin
Unrelated family friends who are addressed by kin terms.

The Iroquois system and its variations represent a common terminological pattern in the world cultures sample (33 societies of 250 sample, or 13 percent) (Murdock 1949: 249). Because it represents a common pattern of terminology that is quite different from the Inuit system, we'll consider it in more detail. Iroquois terminology is typically reported in cultures that practice unilineal descent and in which lineage affiliation is very important. In the Iroquois terminology pattern, members of Ego's nuclear family are each called by a separate term, but Ego's Fa and FaBr are called by the same term. Mo and MoSi are also called by the same term (Figure 8.9). Such a system is said to **bifurcate** (which means to separate into two categories). This means that Ego's mother's side of the family

ANTHROPOLOGY AROUND US

North American Kin Term Variations

What do you call your MoBr, FaBr, MoSi, or FaSi when speaking to them (using terms of address)? Studies show that many of us call these people aunt and uncle. We generally combine the kin term with the person's first name. Some of us drop the kin term when we are particularly fond of our aunt or uncle; others drop the kin terms when we don't like them and don't want to claim them as kin. Some Asian Americans use only the kin terms and do not include

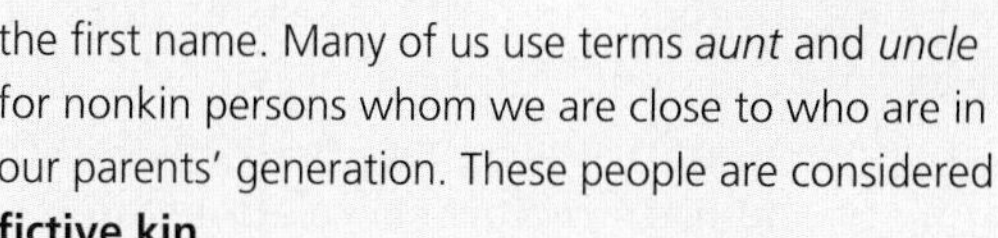

the first name. Many of us use terms *aunt* and *uncle* for nonkin persons whom we are close to who are in our parents' generation. These people are considered **fictive kin.**

Even though North American kinship terminology follows the Inuit type, we do make choices when *applying* formal kin terms as in the case of *aunt* and *uncle*. Formal kin terms dictate the type of behavior expected of the *class of individuals* who are in a particular kin position. The *actual* North American kin term usage reveals that the terms we use reflect attitudes we have toward individuals and the nature of our personal relationship with them. Schneider and Homans (1955) label these two aspects or functions of kin terms as their "classifying" aspect and their "role-designating" aspect. The tone, pitch, and decibel level in which the kin term is vocalized also communicates a great deal of culture-specific information to the listener.

A variety of alternate terms are used in the North American system. Mother (Ego's biological female parent) is often called *mama, mommy, mum, mom,* or *mother* when Ego is addressing her. To the listener the term indicates that this is the speaker's female parent (the classifying aspect). The variation of the term used communicates information to us about the role-designating aspect. The term used often changes as Ego grows older, though term usage may vary when certain social situations arise.

◎ What is the difference between the relationship and attitude of someone who addresses her parent as *mom* compared with *mother*? Does your use of a kin term variant reflect your attitude and feelings toward a kinsperson? Do the terms you use vary with the social situation? Do you have any fictive kin?

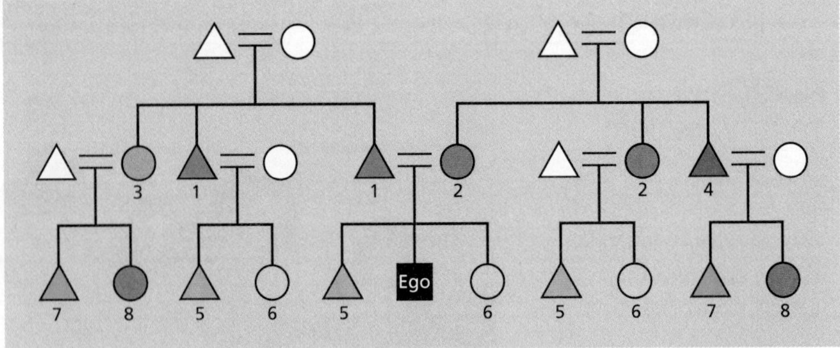

FIGURE 8.9
The Iroquois Terminology System
Each number in the diagram stands for a different term.

and Ego's father's side of the family are treated differently, and this difference is reflected in the kin terms used. At the same time, this pattern is called a bifurcate-merging pattern because *classes* of kin in the same generation—for example, Mo and MoSi (women in the generation above Ego *and* on Ego's mother's side of Ego's family)—are called by the same term. Naturally peoples who use such a pattern of terms don't analyze it in this way. They have been enculturated to the usage, and for them it is the proper way to name relatives.

The usage of the same word for mother and mother's sister does not mean Ego thinks that they are exactly the same. As noted previously, these women belong to a class or category of individuals that are defined in the culture. Ego understands that he or she has a reciprocal relationship with all women called by the mother term. This relationship involves mutual obligations and expectations (remember the goals or functions of a kinship system discussed earlier). There is still a special relationship between Ego and her or his actual biological mother, and often there is a linguistic designation for one's biological mother that is outside the kin terminology pattern.

OLC
mhhe • com / lenkeit5e
See Internet exercises.

It is evident from Figure 8.9 that this system has other interesting features. Cousins on each side of the family are distinguished by two sets of terms, one of which is the same as the terms for Ego's own siblings. Ego's parallel-cousins are the ones that Ego calls by the same terms used for Ego's own siblings. Cross-cousins are called by different terms. In some societies cross-cousins are Ego's ideal marriage partners. The Yąnomamö, for example, use the Iroquois terminology system, and cross-cousins are Ego's ideal marriage partners. For a male Ego the terms *suaboya* (FaSiDa and MoBrDa) and *soriwa* (FaSiSo and MoBrSo) are used for cross-cousins. These terms translate into English as *wife* and *brother-in-law*. The Yąnomamö terms represent *categories* of people, and for this male Ego, individuals in the *suaboya* category are possible mates. Each Yąnomamö knows the difference between his actual wife and other individuals in the category of *suaboya* (wife).

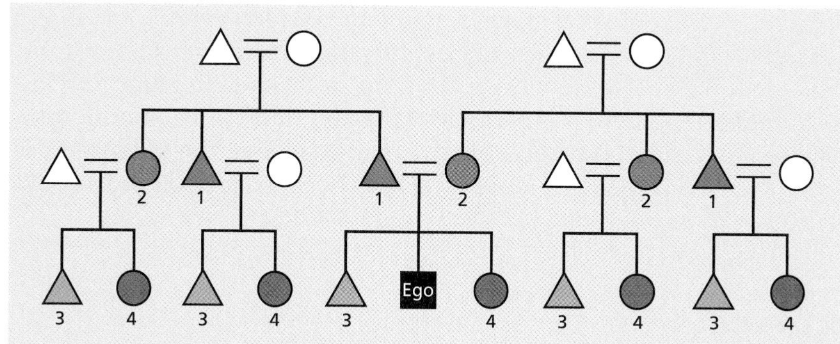

FIGURE 8.10
The Hawaiian Terminology System
Each number represents a different term.

The Hawaiian Terminology System

The Hawaiian terminology system (used in 45 out of 250 cultures, or 18 percent) and its variations are more widely used than the Inuit or Iroquois systems (Murdock 1949: 249). More than the others, this system, as Figure 8.10 illustrates, lumps relatives by generation and sex. Hawaiian terminology is typically associated with societies that do *not* have strong unilineal descent.

The Hawaiian system is often called a *generational* system. Everyone in Ego's generation is called by the same terms that Ego calls his or her siblings. Everyone in Ego's parents' generation is called by the same terms. For example, Mo, MoSi, and FaSi are called by the same term; and Fa, FaBr, and MoBr are called by the same term.

Other Systems

Other less common terminological systems are the Crow, Omaha, and Sudanese systems. And some cultures exhibit minor variations of each of the terminological systems described here. Because this is an introduction to the study of kinship, details of other systems are not included here. See the Suggested Readings list at the end of this chapter for readings with more information on terminology systems.

OLC
mhhe • com / lenkeit5e
See Web links.

Each of the terminological patterns described in this chapter represents unique human adaptations that ethnographers have recorded. Anthropologists have used a great deal of ink and paper writing hypotheses to explain the patterns. Explanations of terminological patterns often center on unilineal descent groups, economic considerations, and the identification of proper marriage partners. The bottom line is that we are unlikely to know for certain how these systems originated, because there are no fossils or records of the origins of these customs. Still, it is challenging to try to explain them based on all of the data that we can accumulate.

These terminological systems represent the ideal and the manner in which terminology is applied and used by most members of the culture. The reinforcement of the existing system, with its well-defined obligations and expectations, is in an individual's best interest. In cultures without social security, insurance, welfare, and litigation, the kin groups to which a person belongs are all that stand between that person and possible starvation or death from injury. Kin need each other.

SUMMARY

Anthropologists have gathered ethnographic data on hundreds of different cultures from every corner of the world. Although there is great diversity, numerous consistent patterns emerge that show how people organize themselves and culturally define whom they are related to and how—blood relatives (consanguines) and relatives by marriage (affines). The functions of kinship systems are common to a wide variety of cultures: People are organized into groups, behavioral expectations are dictated, and security is provided for group members. The North American system of bilateral descent groups known as kindreds is contrasted with unilineal descent groups known as patrilineages and matrilineages. Both types exhibit many of the same functions. The Inuit terminological pattern and the Iroquois terminological pattern illustrate how such systems dictate people's behavior toward their relatives.

Study Questions

OLC
mhhe • com / lenkeit5e
See Self Quiz.

1. Compare and contrast the functions of kinship in societies that have unilineal descent and those that have bilateral (or kindred) descent. Give specific examples from your assigned ethnography or other readings and from your own culture.
2. Describe the kinship structure within another culture (use an ethnographic source that is assigned reading for your class), and discuss how the goals and aims of kinship are illustrated in this ethnographic account.
3. Compare and contrast the Hawaiian and Iroquois terminological systems.

Suggested Readings

OLC
mhhe • com / lenkeit5e
See Web links.

Chagnon, Napoleon A. 1997. *Yąnomamö.* 5th ed. Fort Worth, Tex.: Harcourt Brace College Publishers. Chagnon discusses kinship in the social organization chapter of this ethnography. Real situations illustrating ideal and actual behaviors are discussed and geneaologies are diagrammed.

Evans-Pritchard, E. E. 1940. *The Nuer.* Oxford, England: Clarendon. This ethnography is still considered a classic in the study of kinship.

Fox, Robin. 1983. *Kinship and Marriage: An Anthropological Perspective.* Cambridge, England: Cambridge University Press (originally published in 1967). One of the best introductions to the details of anthropological kinship analysis. Lots of detail but clearly written.

Pasternak, Burton, Carol R. Ember, and Melvin Ember. 1997. *Sex, Gender, and Kinship: A Cross-Cultural Perspective.* Upper Saddle River, N.J.: Pearson. A good read. Addresses many questions that may have occurred to you when you read this chapter.

Stone, Linda, ed. 2001. *New Directions in Anthropological Kinship.* Lanham, MD: Rowman and Littlefield. A collection of essays detailing current anthropological research and approaches to kinship.

Gender and Sexuality

Nature or Nurture?

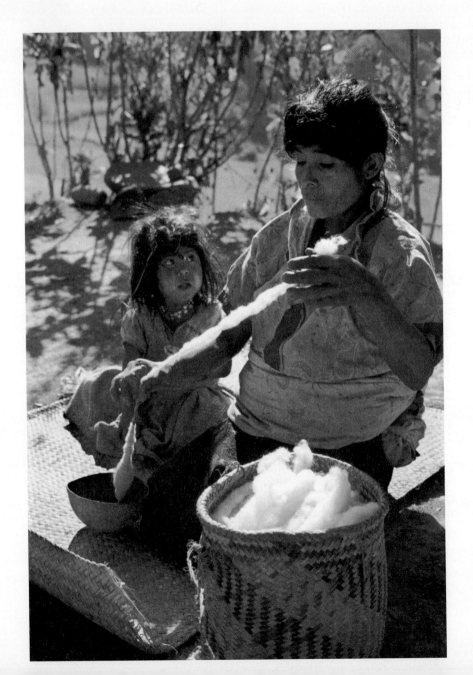

We were in a small bar on the island of Bora Bora in the Society Islands of Polynesia enjoying the music of local musicians. They entertained crowds at the bar nightly and usually drew both locals and tourists. The evening was well under way, and everyone seemed to be having a good time. Locals were asking tourists to dance, and many sang along with songs that were being played. Our attention was drawn to a nearby table where a group of local Tahitians began laughing heartily whenever a particular member of their group, a mature, rather stout, middle-aged woman, would get up to dance with one of the tourists. I recognized the woman as the person who was recommended to us as someone who did laundry for visitors as well as local residents. She was soft-spoken and friendly earlier in the day as we made the arrangements for our laundry. This evening she was attired the same way as other women her age, wore a flower in her hair, and smiled as she danced and chatted with the tourists. One male tourist in particular seemed to enjoy her company and kept asking her to dance. Each time he led her to the small dance floor, the other members of her party made a loud comment and they would break into song. I listened carefully but was unable to understand what was said. Finally, my husband bought a round of beers for the other table, and because we had talked to two of these men on other occasions and had established rapport with them, he asked them to share the source of their hilarity. The immediate response was that the tourist clearly did not know that he was dancing with a "he-she" (our informant said that this was an English translation for the Tahitian term; others have translated it as "half-man, half-woman"). They further remarked, matter-of-factly, that this person was one of the best dancers around.

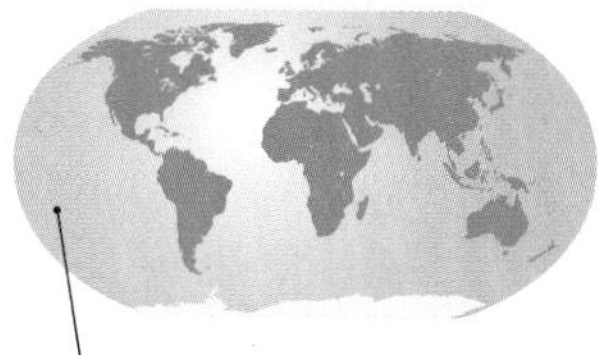

We knew of the third gender *(mahu)* in Tahiti and Hawaii (different names are used for these individuals in other places in Polynesia), but this was the first time we had met one. We asked for more details on the gender, gender role, and status of he-shes. We were answered politely, but our interest clearly perplexed the residents. This third gender was simply a part of their society, and no one thought it unusual in any way. Deborah Elliston (1999) has written that social acceptance of the gender variant role in Tahiti is legitimized by a longtime participation in the role behaviors. Recent accounts have noted that the *mahu*, as part of male gender diversity in Tahiti, participate in women's work and adopt feminine dress, speech, and silent language gestures. They also adopt feminine dance styles (Nanda 2000: 60).

To what extent does our culture shape our behavior as a man or woman (i.e., nurture), and what does biology contribute (i.e., nature)? How are gender roles defined in other cultures? This chapter explores these questions.

The objectives of this chapter are to:

- Distinguish between sex and gender cross-culturally
- Delineate factors affecting gender roles cross-culturally
- Give an overview of the variations in gender roles
- Explore human sexual behavior from a comparative perspective

◀ In all societies the enculturation of gender roles begins at an early age. This young Mixtec Indian girl in Oaxaca, Mexico, learns part of her gender role as she observes her mother spin cotton.

MARGARET MEAD AND EARLY GENDER STUDIES

OLC
mhhe • com / lenkeit5e
See chapter outline and chapter overview.

Western societies assume two gender roles: male and female. However, three or four genders are often accepted in other societies. Gender refers to the socially and culturally prescribed and perceived ways that males and females are expected to behave (in other words, their culturally assigned roles). Issues relating to gender are interwoven into all aspects of our existence from the moment of our birth.

Gender diversity and the debate over nature versus nurture have been issues of interest to anthropology from its inception as a discipline. Early investigations on gender were called culture and personality studies and later became known as part of **psychological anthropology**—the study of the relationship between culture and personality. Ethnographies written in the early years of anthropology included descriptions of the division of labor—the gender roles assigned to males and females. Margaret Mead, one of the first woman anthropologists, brought gender diversity issues to public attention with her 1935 (1963) book *Sex and Temperament in Three Primitive Societies*. In this work, Mead profiled three groups living in the same region of New Guinea—the Arapesh (occupying mountain terrain), the Mundugumor (a group inhabiting a riverbank econiche), and the Tchambuli (lakeside dwellers). She focused on what she called the temperament of men and women in these three cultures. When Mead began her work, many people believed that men and women were biologically programmed to behave in certain ways and exhibit certain temperaments. Women were genetically programmed to be dependent, nurturing, gentle, and passive. Men were programmed to be independent, tough, and aggressive. Mead found that the Arapesh women fit this stereotype, but the men did not. Men, like women, were maternal. According to Mead, "they see all life as an adventure in growing things, growing children, growing pigs, growing yams and taros and coconuts and sago, faithfully, carefully, observing all of the rules that make things grow" (Mead 1963: 32). Mundugumor of both sexes exhibited stereotypically male behaviors, with an emphasis on selfishness, aggressiveness, and a high level of sexuality. The enculturation process, according to Mead, involved behavioral conditioning that treated boys and girls alike: "little girls grow up as aggressive as little boys and with no expectation of docilely accepting their role in life" (Mead 1963: 201). The Tchambuli had distinct roles for males and females, but these role behaviors were the opposite of what they are in North American society. Tchambuli males were described as less responsible and more dependent, vain about their appearance, and constantly involved in gossiping. Women were independent, competent, businesslike, concerned with providing for their family, and sexually aggressive. With rich detail in her narrative descriptions, Mead painted intriguing pictures of these

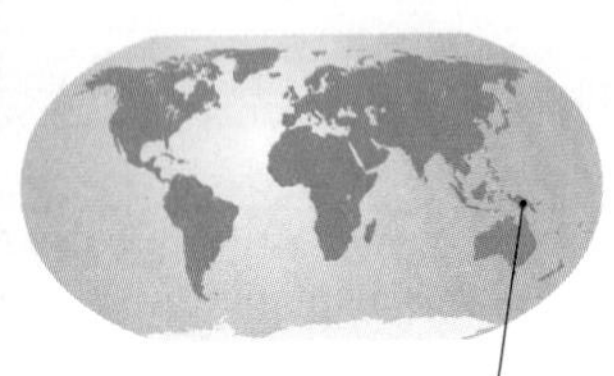

Arapesh
Mundugumor
Tchambuli

psychological anthropology
The study of the relationship between culture and personality.

Margaret Mead in New Guinea. Her 1972 autobiography *Blackberry Winter: My Early Years,* recounts her fieldwork experiences in New Guinea, Bali, and Samoa.

cultural groups where enculturation instilled some very different expectations and behaviors for men and women. Although some details of Mead's work have not held up to later scrutiny, her work made the important contribution of stimulating further research and study.

Feminist Anthropology. A theoretical approach focusing on women and their roles within the structure of society arose in the 1970s and called for a reanalysis of previous work—where women's roles were often downplayed or neglected. This approach looked at the social construction of gender and how gender is an important variable in the study of a culture—as much as issues such as class, power, and status. A varied and sometimes controversial approach, it has made anthropologists rethink their treatment of gender.

Today, while biologists, biological psychologists, and other scientists work to reveal the biological bases of behavior, anthropologists sort through the many forms of gender identity and gender roles that are found in world cultures. We are joined by researchers in other fields, notably psychology and sociology, who share our interest in exploring gender diversity.

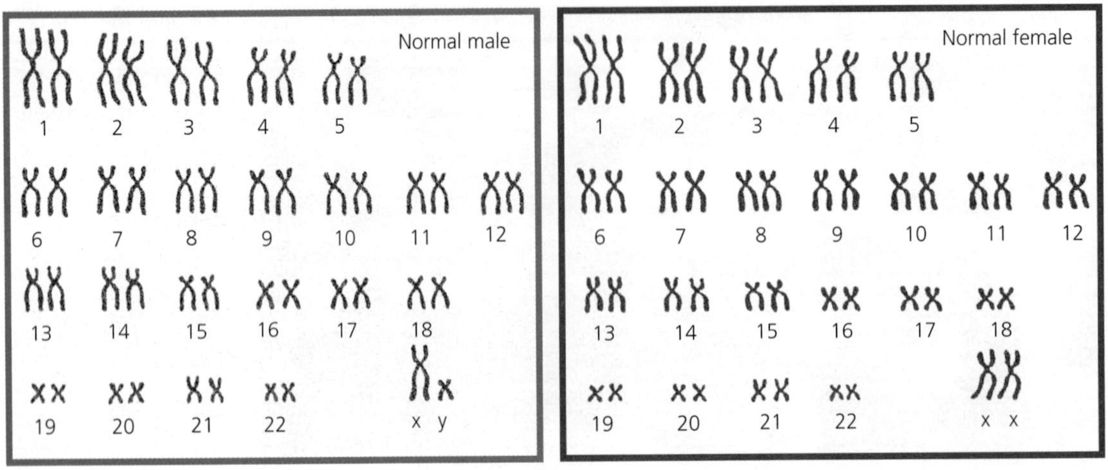

FIGURE 9.1
Notice that all of the pairs of these human chromosomes are similar in shape except the pair in the lower right. The normal male shows both a large X chromosome and a smaller Y chromosome. The normal female shows two X chromosomes.

SEX AND GENDER

Most people are assigned their biological sex at birth, based on the appearance of external genitalia. More technically, the term **sex** denotes whether an individual has two sex chromosomes that are alike in shape and size (the X chromosomes—XX, a female) or sex chromosomes that are not alike (an X chromosome and a Y chromosome—XY, a male) as shown in Figure 9.1. Sex, in other words, is a biological designation. This description is a simplification. There is, for example, a specific gene that has been identified on the Y chromosome—SRY (sex-determining region of the Y chromosome)—that controls biochemical reactions that result in the development of a male (anatomically and hormonally). However, nature is not quite as tidy as we might expect. Some individuals exhibit an extra sex chromosome—XXY, XXX, XYY—or a chromosome may be absent (X alone). Such chromosomal variations are not always easy to determine from the appearance of external genitalia. Few people have been genetically tested, so it is unclear how prevalent these variations are in the general population.

Biological anthropologists have extensive data regarding biological variation and sexual dimorphism among humans and other primate populations. **Sexual dimorphism** refers to the biological and behavioral differences between males and females (Figure 9.2). Many physical measurements are available for contemporary populations, and these show ranges of variation for males and females, with the distribution curves on most characteristics overlapping. Some features show more distinction than others for biological sex differences. The pelvis, for example, is the most diagnostic skeletal feature for determining the sex of an individual. A female pelvis has wider openings and wider angles than a male pelvis.

sex
The biological aspect of being female, male, or other, assigned at birth based on external genitalia.

sexual dimorphism
The biological and behavioral differences between males and females.

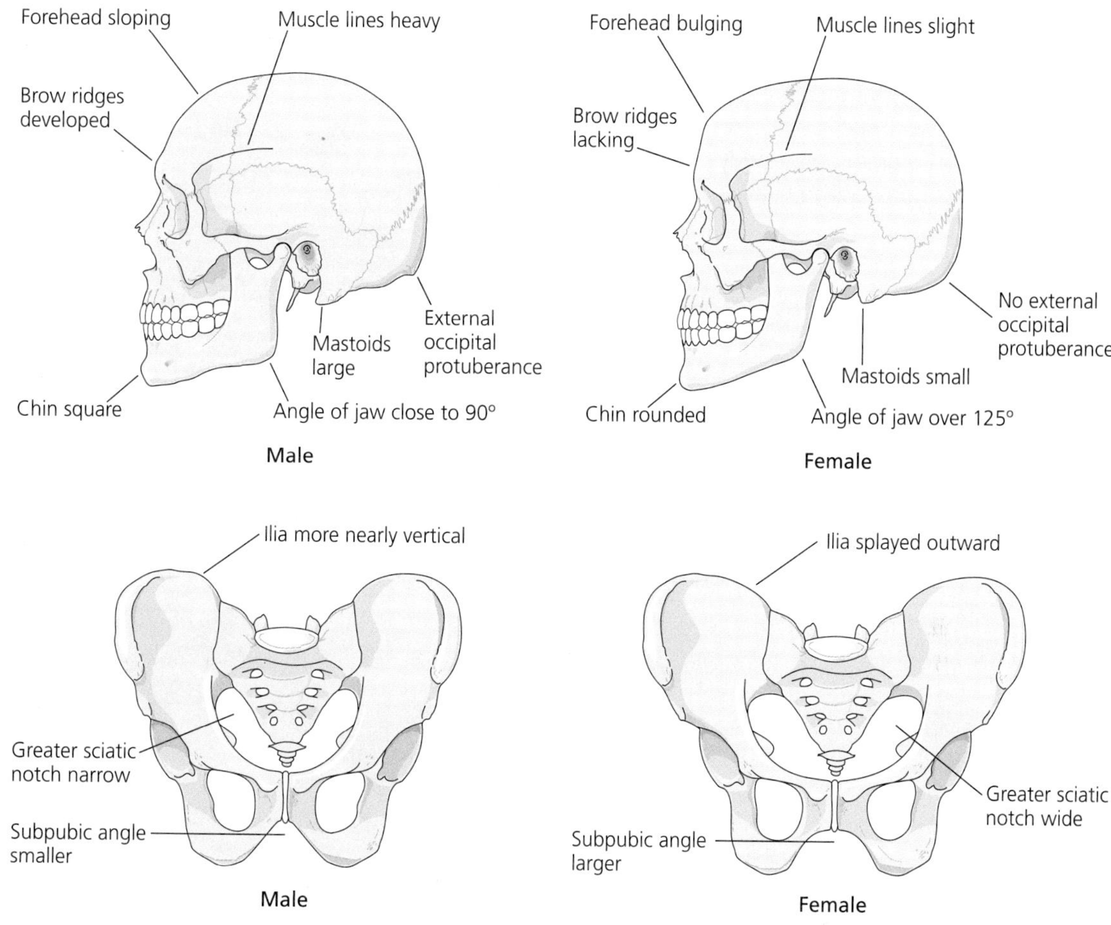

FIGURE 9.2
Sex differences in the skull and pelvis of humans.

If only the skull is present, there may be difficulties in identifying the subject's sex unless one is very familiar with the population that the skull comes from. For example, among one ancient archaeological population from eastern Oklahoma, all individuals were very gracile (slender, lacking in ruggedness) in the appearance of the skull. None of the individuals in this population was as robust in skull features as a typical female skull from a tribe of the northern plains. Therefore, it was initially difficult for archaeologists to differentiate females from males just by looking at the skulls. The point of this example is that skeletal dimorphism is present in our species, but there is overlap between measurements for males and females. Sexual dimorphism also exists among many of our primate relatives and in many other animals. The selective pressures that would produce greater sexual dimorphism in our own species have been reduced because humans have used cultural adaptations as their primary adaptive mechanism for more than a million years.

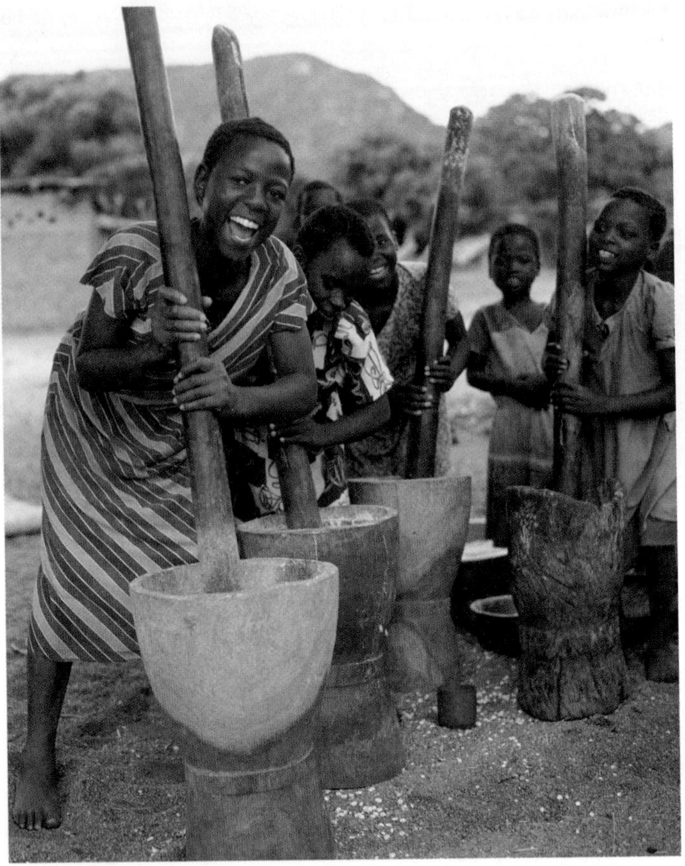

These young girls in Malawi are pounding corn into meal, a staple of the Malawian's diet. Many cultures assign strenuous work such as this to women, resulting in great upper-body strength; other cultures assign heavy work to men.

Only women can bear offspring, and only men can produce sperm. Biological mechanisms continue to maintain these differences in sexual characteristics. Yet, as more contemporary women work out and participate in sports, some of the previous diagnostic features that mark skeletal differences between males and females will become less useful to forensic specialists as they work to identify fragmentary skeletal remains. Rough places on bones at the points of muscle attachments indicate degree of muscle mass development. In human societies where men do most of the "heavy work," it is reflected on their bones. Such details have been used to identify and confirm the sex of skeletal remains, but these clues can be misleading if the gender role behaviors do not conform to the stereotype expectations. Among Native American societies where women pounded and ground acorns or corn, great upper-body muscle mass developed—mass that was reflected in the rough places on bones where muscles attach.

OLC
mhhe • com / lenkeit5e
See Internet exercises.

But what about dimorphic features of behavior in human populations today? It is clear that there are few jobs that cannot be performed equally well by both females and males. Both can do mathematics, drive tractors,

Today both women and men are often employed in jobs that are not traditional to their gender. It is only recently that women in North America have been employed as firefighters.

lay tile, cook, and change diapers. Cultural prescriptions of gender roles and behaviors are diverse and are becoming more diverse.

Gender role refers to the assigned role of an individual within a society. **Gender** encompasses the behavioral, psychological, and sociocultural aspects of being female or male. Most societies assign one of two gender roles, male or female, although the details of expected behaviors vary. These assignments are made at birth, usually though not always based on what external genitalia imply about the sex of the new baby. Babies designated as "girls" are immediately described using terms that the society assigns the female gender role, and "boys" are described using terms the society associates with male gender roles.

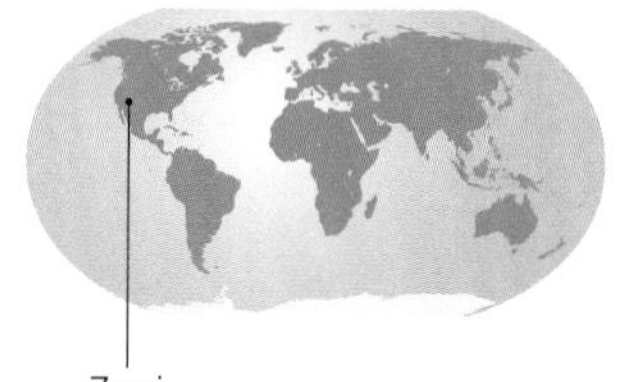

gender role
The task and behavior assigned by a culture to each sex.

gender
The sociocultural construct of masculine and feminine roles and the qualities assigned to these roles.

CULTURES WITH MORE THAN TWO GENDERS

The *mahu* gender discussed in the story at the beginning of this chapter is informally accepted in Polynesia. More formal third-gender roles have been assigned to individuals known as the *berdache* among the Zuni of the southwestern United States and to the *hijra* of northern India. The construct of variant genders is an example of the adaptability of human culture. As you read these examples, keep in mind that it is impossible to

A *berdache* of the Native American Crow tribe.

fully understand the cultural constructs about gender outside of a specific culture. Gender is interwoven into the total context of culture.

The Zuni are a matrilineal, matrilocal society that recognizes a gender role for individuals who are not men and not women. Zuni boys who like to play with girls, who participate in the domestic activities of girls, who experience strange illnesses, and who have unusual dreams are identified as gender variants, or two-spirits. These individuals often begin adopting women's dress and hairstyle during adolescence. These men-women often have marriagelike, long-term relationships with men and perform the roles of traditional women. This alternative gender was and is accepted as such by Zuni and other American Indian cultures.

Early anthropological literature used the term *berdache* to refer to these individuals; the word has a long and involved history of usage. American anthropologist Ruth Benedict and others worked among the Zuni and recorded data about this group of individuals who did not fit into a

This Indian *hijra* is an example of a third-gender-role person.

two-gender, male-female system. She and others used the term *berdache*, and it is still used in the literature. Today, gender researchers prefer to use more neutral reference terms such as *gender variant*. The term *two-spirit* is preferred by some, but it implies that the gender variants are made up of feminine and masculine. The gender variant of the *berdache* among the Zuni today is viewed as neither man nor woman; it is not viewed as merely part male and part female but is considered a separate gender that is a normative part of the culture.

The *hijras* of India offer another example of a third gender role that is integrated into the fabric of life. *Hijras* are a religious community of individuals who are culturally defined as neither man nor woman. These persons are born as males. They undergo voluntary ritual surgeries of emasculation (either in childhood or adulthood) that transform them into a third sex and gender category (Nanda 1999). The ritual surgery (which is potentially life-threatening) is performed by a "midwife" *hijra*, and both the penis and testicles are severed. Indian law prohibits this surgery, but it is secretly performed. Not all *hijras* undergo this surgery, though the

TRY THIS
Hypothesize

Make a list of ten gender roles for adult males and adult females in your culture. Describe expectations for each gender role that you have listed. Choose one of these and hypothesize how this gender role became normative in your culture. Delineate several ways that you could test the hypothesis.

cultural definition of *hijras* is that they are emasculated men. They dress, behave, and take occupations of women, including the taking of husbands. The major way that they are not men is that they do not sexually function as males during intercourse and reproduction. *Hijras* are distinct from males who seek same-sex partners and take the receptive role during sex. Anthropologist Serena Nanda has extensively researched the lives of *hijras*. She writes of their gender roles: "While hijras are 'man minus man,' they are also 'man plus woman'" (Nanda 2000: 30). *Hijras* take feminine names, dress in women's clothes, and imitate women in facial expressions, walk, hairstyles, and language. They view themselves as objects of men's sexual desires and have only male sex partners. At the same time, they are not like the traditional Indian female gender because they are aggressive in their sexual demeanor and use coarse speech. They are not women because they are unable to have children.

Hijras receive a call from their goddess, the Hindu Mother Goddess, to undergo the emasculation operation and change their gender by dressing in women's clothing and wearing their hair long. Males who become *hijras* are sexually impotent, and they themselves attribute this to a defective penis. *Hijras* are considered between sexes. They are neither men nor women as defined by Indian society, where marriage and reproduction are highly valued. The *hijras* renounce their families and sexual desires. To survive they depend on charity (alms) and earnings from performing rituals.

One of the *hijra*'s societal roles is to participate in a ritual performance on the occasion of the birth of a son to a family. The *hijra* blesses the child and provides entertainment for the assembled family and friends. During this ceremony the *hijra* inspects the baby's genitals, confirms its sex, and blesses it for having the ability to procreate and thus continue the family line (Nanda 1999; 2000). *Hijras* also perform at marriages. People have ambivalent attitudes toward *hijras* because they have chosen this different path in life and because they can bestow both blessings and curses. Often *hijras* perform as prostitutes. They also have long-term relationships with men whom they call their husbands. This sexual behavior is not approved of by all *hijras* as it runs counter to the role of *hijras* in Indian society. *Hijras* are supposed to lead a life of self-discipline and abstinence.

FACTORS AFFECTING GENDER ROLES

Many factors affect gender roles, and the issues surrounding gender are complex. This section highlights various facets of economic resources, kinship, and ideology as they relate to gender roles. There are excellent books that explore these topics in the detail they deserve and, most significantly, look at gender roles within the context of a whole society. It is not possible to include such complete coverage in a book of this nature, but I hope to interest you in further reading or possibly in taking an entire course in which this important topic is thoroughly explored.

Kinship

Kinship rules of descent and their associated residence patterns affect gender as it is perceived and constructed by a society. Recall from Chapters 7 and 8 that in patrilineal societies with patrilocal residence rules, men enjoy high status. Their gender owns the property and makes decisions for the group.

In traditional patrilineal (and patrilocal) Chinese society, gender roles are clearly defined. Males enjoy higher status than females, who serve only to produce sons. When a girl marries, she leaves her parents' household. She has no allies or friends among her in-laws. She becomes strong only in relationship to how many sons she bears. The gender bias is reflected even in personal names. Males acquire a variety of names over their lifetime, names that reflect deeds and accomplishments. Women do not. When a woman marries and moves to her husband's household, her name is not used. Rather, she becomes her husband's wife, a daughter-in-law, a sister-in-law.

Economic Resources

The example of "female husbands" among the Nandi of Africa can be used to illustrate how a number of African societies have integrated gender roles to accommodate special circumstances within the culture. The Nandi practice patrilineal descent; and wealth, primarily in the form of cattle and land, is inherited through the male line. The marriage of one woman to another woman, where one of the women takes the role of a husband, is a cultural adaptation that allows a woman without male heirs to transmit property. Men manage land and cattle. Women in the Nandi system of polygynous marriages are entitled to a share of the property owned by the house that they are part of. But traditionally that property could be transmitted only to male heirs.

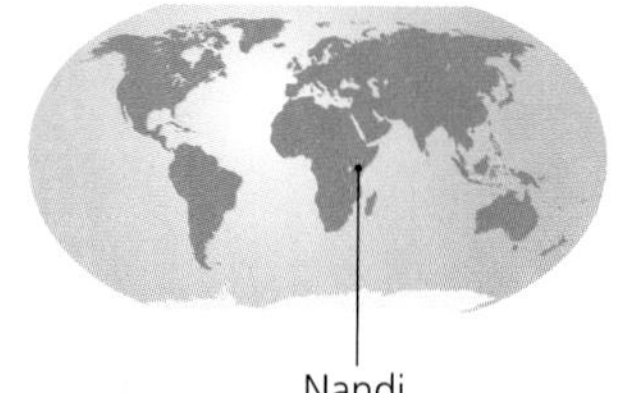

A woman who does not have a male heir has no one to whom she can leave property (her share of a household or other property that she has acquired). Several options are open to women in this situation. One option is to adopt a child, though this is difficult because few children are available for adoption. Another option is for the youngest daughter of a woman with no sons to stay at home rather than taking up the customary postmarriage residence pattern of patrilocality. This daughter's sons will inherit the house's property. The most common option for a woman without an heir is woman-to-woman marriage, in which the woman with no male heir becomes a husband to another woman. In a sample taken from one community of 286 Nandi households, just under 3 percent of the households were headed by female husbands (Oboler 1980: 69–88). Children born to this couple are considered heirs of the female husband. In other words, when the "wife" has a child, that child is considered to be the heir of the female husband.

Gender roles for female husbands are based on normative male behavioral expectations in the division of labor. The female husband should participate in cattle herding and cultivation along with her wife, as both sexes are involved in these activities. Female husbands often reinterpret these activities to be male work in order to affirm their status as males. Plowing, fencing, house frame building, thatching, digging of drainage ditches, and slaughtering are jobs reserved for men. Women cook, wash utensils, collect firewood, and carry water. Because female husbands are older, they do not often do heavy work, but informants told anthropologist Regina Smith Oboler (1980) that generally the division of labor is the same in female husband and wife relationships as it is for male husband and wife relationships. Female husbands and wives do not engage in a sexual relationship with one another. The female husband does not have sex with men or with other women either. The two occupy separate dwellings, which allows the wife in this relationship to maintain sexual relationships with other men.

The primary and most consistent factor that distinguishes a female husband from a woman and that makes her the same as a man is the legitimate right to transmit property to heirs. There are reported variations in other behaviors of the female husband among the Nandi, but there is conformity to male behavior in contexts associated with management of property. The Nandi have created a gender situation that is economically adaptive for a segment of their population—older women who are infertile or do not have male heirs. The gender of the female husband is culturally configured as a man. Variations on this type of woman-to-woman marriage are widespread in African societies.

Division of Labor. The division of labor as it relates to economic factors, such as systems of production and ownership of property, also reflects gender issues. Ernestine Friedl, a former president of the American Anthropological Association, has suggested that the control over scarce resources—determined by gender roles—is related to status and power in societies. Among foraging peoples such as the Washo and the Dobe Ju/'hoansi, gender roles are defined along traditional lines in which men hunt for food and women gather it. The distribution of meat through generalized reciprocity is important and creates obligations. Men control the process of dividing and giving meat, and through these activities they gain status and power. Even among foraging societies where it is documented that women provide, by their gathering activities, more than half

The division of labor is by gender among the Dugum Dani of New Guinea. This photograph shows men working cooperatively to scoop fertile silt from garden irrigation ditches. The silt is spread on garden beds before planting.

of the food in the diet, they do not have much power, nor do they have the same status as men. In these societies, the source of power is in the hands of males because they control the scarce commodity of meat protein. Such societies have defined females as the gatherers, though the strength and endurance that women have developed in walking and carrying the gathered foods (as well as small children) certainly would qualify them to be hunters.

In foraging groups such as the Inuit, where men provide the vast majority of the food through hunting of seals and caribou, women are subordinate to men. When women contribute more to the process of food procurement, as in the case of the Washo (where women work beside men in gathering and fishing), the society is more egalitarian. Friedl's hypothesis seems to fit the data—gender roles affect who controls valued resources, which in turn determines who has status and power.

In contemporary urban industrialized societies, household equality arises when women and men both bring income to the relationship (assuming their earnings are about equal). If one individual stays home and does not work and the other partner works to bring in the money that is then used to buy food and housing, the earning partner generally has the power within the home. Interestingly, research indicates that the division of labor *within* North American households differs along gender lines. The division of labor is most unequal in heterosexual relationships, it is fairly equal in gay male relationships, and it is most equal in lesbian relationships.

Ideology

TRY THIS
Surf the Web

Log on to your favorite search engine and see how many Hindu deities you can locate—in photos or in text descriptions—that have both male and female sexual features and gender features.

Ideologies prescribe a culture's values and serve many purposes (Chapter 11 discusses the many functions of belief systems). A culture's value system is founded in its belief system, which contributes in major ways to the enculturation of gender role expectations. Hinduism, for example, acknowledges many variants as well as the basic male and female oppositions. Ancient Hindu origin stories and ritual arts feature an array of variant mythical ancestors, including ones with androgynous (both male and female features and personalities) and hermaphroditic (again, having both male and female qualities) images such as male deities with breasts. India's *hijras* identify with the Hindu Mother Goddess, as Nanda writes:

> Popular Hindu mythology (and its hijra versions) abounds in images of the aggressive Mother Goddess as she devours, beheads, and castrates—-destructive acts that nevertheless contain the possibility of rebirth, as in the hijra emasculation ritual. This dual nature of the goddess provides the powerful symbolic and psychological context in which the hijras become culturally meaningful as an alternative sex/gender. (Nanda 2000: 32)

The ideology of the Yąnomamö tribe reinforces the relative positions of men and women. Men and women have separate origin myths. One origin myth holds that men came from Moon's blood (Figure 9.3). Moon was shot in the belly by an original human ancestor (the Yąnomamö are unclear as to where these came from, but they were part human, part spirit, and part animal, and they were distinct from living humans). Moon's blood fell to earth and changed into men. This is why men are fierce. There were no women, and the men wanted a woman to have sex with. One day the men were out collecting vines. One of the vines had a wabu fruit attached to it. The fruit was opened, and it had eyes on it. The man who saw it thought that it was what women looked like. One of the men tossed the wabu fruit onto the ground, where it changed into a woman and developed a long and hairy vagina. At first the men didn't notice her, but when they did, they were overcome with lust and took turns copulating with her. Eventually she had daughters, and as the daughters came out the men copulated with them, and that is how all of the Yąnomamö came to be (Chagnon 1997: 104–5).

The Yąnomamö believe that everyone has a *noreshi* in addition to a multifaceted soul. A *noreshi* is a person's animal counterpart. The animal lives

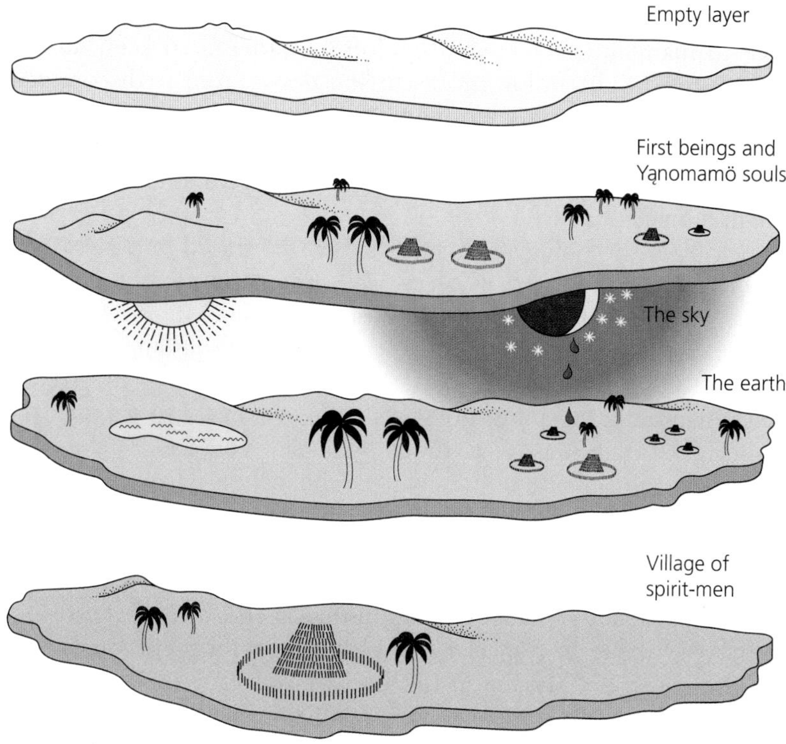

FIGURE 9.3
The Ya̧nomamö cosmos contains these four layers. One version of the origin story of the Ya̧nomamö tells of an ancestor shooting Moon in the belly, whereupon Moon's blood fell to earth and transformed into men.

in the forest but at the same time is a component of the person's psyche or body. Women inherit their *noreshi* from their mother, men from their father. Female *noreshi* are animals that are ground dwellers, like dogs and snakes; males have *noreshi* that are found in high places, such as hawks and monkeys. This creates a duality with men above women, and it is reflected in the division of labor. Women do all the menial tasks such as collecting firewood and fetching water, whereas men hunt, make war, and become shamans and headmen. The male above can also be seen in the traditional placement of hammocks—a woman's hammock is hung below her husband's.

PERSPECTIVES ON HUMAN SEXUAL BEHAVIOR

Sexuality refers to erotic desires and sexual practices. The term is also used to refer to sexual orientation. Sexuality is an interesting topic to consider from a comparative perspective. I had two goals in mind when I started to write this section: to emphasize the great diversity in attitudes toward sexuality and to describe some of the variations in accepted sexual behaviors from an emic viewpoint. Our attitudes toward sexuality are based on our cultural values, which in turn are based on ideology and tradition. These are the aspects of culture about which people are usually least able to maintain an attitude of cultural relativism so keep this in mind as you read. The following discussion draws from both contemporary reports and the earlier ethnographies. The ethnographic present (how a society did things at the time it was studied) is used for consistency. The amount of available data is not ideal, but it can give us a sense of the diversity in human sexuality.

TRY THIS
Analyze

Find a classmate with the same cultural background that you have. Discuss between yourselves and come up with a list of ways that the ideological foundations of your culture have influenced expectations of what constitutes the number of genders and acceptable gender role behaviors for your group.

Interest by anthropologists in sexuality can be traced in part to *The Sexual Life of Savages in North-Western Melanesia*, an important work on Trobriand society by Bronislaw Malinowski, published in 1929 (1987). Malinowski carried out ethnographic research in the Trobriands between 1914 and 1918. Until this study, most ethnographic research involved a few weeks or months, as anthropologists were in a hurry to gather data before aboriginal traditions were altered by outside contacts. Malinowski was interested in and critical of Freudian psychoanalysis. He was also critical of the then popular view of the origins of human institutions. Several theorists had explained the evolution of human institutions as originating in "savage" society, where promiscuous hordes of natives participated in unbridled sexual activity. Such explanations fed Western ethnocentrism.

Malinowski wrote in a special foreword to the third edition of *The Sexual Life of Savages:* "My aim in this book, however, was to show that from whichever side you approach it, the problem of sex, family, and kinship presents an organic unity which cannot be disrupted" (Malinowski 1987: lviii–lix). He had tried to focus attention on the holistic nature and integration of sexuality and adolescent sexual freedom with traditions of courtship, marriage, and family. He was disappointed that readers focused on "sensational details" of the "technicalities of love-making" (Malinowski 1987: lix). Herein lies the problem of presenting short examples of human sexuality in an introductory text. As I've pointed out before, context is important in studying any aspect of culture. So keep this in mind as you read the following brief overview.

TRY THIS
Recall

Recall how you learned about sexuality. How did you learn what was appropriate behavior and what was not? Do children in your culture experiment with sexuality? How do adults regulate children's sexual behavior?

Humans everywhere learn about what is sexually stimulating by watching, listening, and imitating those around them as they grow up. Some societies are permissive about sexuality and premarital sex. Sexuality is learned early in some societies, with adults either ignoring sexual experimentation or encouraging it. Among the Trobriand Islanders, Weiner reports that "By the time children are seven or eight years old, they begin playing erotic games with each other and imitating adult seductive attitudes. Four or five years later, they begin to pursue sexual partners in earnest. Young people change partners often, experimenting first with one person and then another" (Weiner 1988: 66).

Nisa, a Dobe Ju/'hoansi woman, was interviewed about her life by anthropologist Marjorie Shostak. The interview included the topic of sexuality, and Nisa described how children learn about sex. She notes that they lie in their parents' hut and hear everything that is happening with their parents when they make love. When they get a little older, they experiment. "At first, boys play that play with other boys—poking their genitals around one another's behinds—and girls play that play with little girls. Later, if a boy sees a little girl by herself, he takes her and 'has sex' with her. That's how little boys and little girls learn" (Shostak 1981: 114). Nisa also tells Shostak that adults don't necessarily approve of all of the experimentation, but they ignore it.

Other societies are restrictive regarding sexual experimentation and premarital sex. The East Bay people of the South Pacific are very concerned about sexual propriety. Children are discouraged by scolding and ridicule from touching their genitals in public. By age five, they are very conscious of lapses in modesty and have learned to avoid all physical contact with the opposite sex (Pasternak, Ember, and Ember 1997: 20).

SEXUAL ATTRACTION AND BEHAVIOR

There are no universal standards of sexual attractiveness. Early cross-cultural literature focused primarily on physical features of females (this was likely due to the Euro-American cultural preoccupation with women's bodies). The attractiveness of the male, if mentioned at all, was usually attributed to his skills and status rather than his physical attributes. The Chukchee, Maricopa, and Hidatsa reportedly like women with plump bodies, whereas the Dobuans and Maasai prefer women with a slim body build. Among the Siriono of Bolivia, corpulence is stimulating and desirable. Holmberg, who studied the Siriono, writes, "Besides being young, a desirable sex partner—especially a woman—should also be fat" (Holmberg 1946: 181; Ford and Beach 1951: 97).

Sex play varies considerably across cultures. Kissing, for example, includes sucking on the lips as well as deep kissing involving thrusting the tongue into the partner's mouth. This behavior is popular in contemporary Western societies, where motion pictures and television programs show this as the ideal for erotic sex play. Other societies include this form of kissing too, with the Kwakiutl, Trukese, and Trobrianders sucking the partner's lips and tongue. The Tinguian place their lips near the partner's face and suddenly inhale rather than kissing lip to lip. At the time of first contact with Europeans, some cultures did not kiss (the Chamorro, Balinese, Manus, Tinguian, Siriono, and Thonga). The Thonga remarked ethnocentrically when they first saw Europeans kissing, "Look at them—they eat each other's saliva and dirt" (Ford and Beach 1951: 58–59). The Mehinaku of the Amazon also consider kissing to be disgusting (Gregor 1985).

Identify several factors that have been responsible for changing sexual attitudes and behaviors among people in prestate societies and in modern state societies.

Genital stimulation is widespread among human groups. Manual stimulation of both female and male genitalia is common prior to intercourse.

Actors Minnie Driver and Matt Damon in the film *Good Will Hunting*. Kissing in this manner is considered disgusting in some cultures, particularly if it is done in public.

TRY THIS
Interview

Interview both a male and a female elder in your culture. Ask them to tell you how views of acceptable sexual behavior as portrayed on television have changed since they were teenagers.

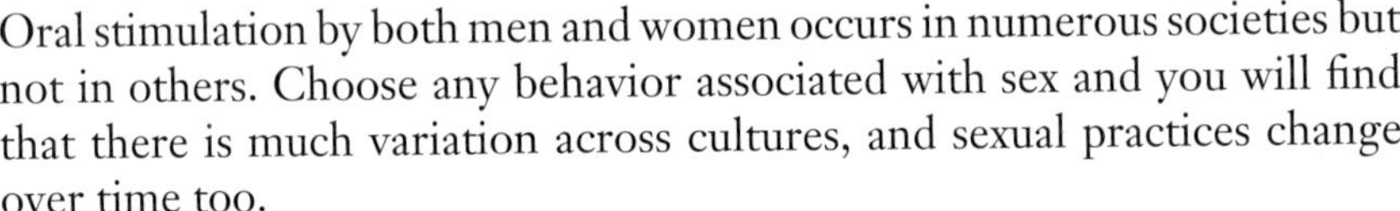

Oral stimulation by both men and women occurs in numerous societies but not in others. Choose any behavior associated with sex and you will find that there is much variation across cultures, and sexual practices change over time too.

SEXUAL PROHIBITIONS

Diversity also surrounds attitudes about sexual prohibitions. For many societies there are no prohibitions on sexual practices, except that in most groups sex is supposed to take place in private. Among the Mbuti pygmies, sex can take place during menstruation, pregnancy, and lactation. Other societies, such as the Onge of Little Andaman, do not have sex during menstruation—they believe that swelling of the arms and legs would occur if they did. The Chinese consider women to be polluting during menses and avoid intercourse at that time. Variations are found in attitudes about allowances and prohibitions of sex during pregnancy and after childbirth. It seems to come down to general attitudes toward sex. If the culture views sex positively, it is enjoyed frequently and with few prohibitions. Where people think of sex as dangerous, as among the Mae Enga of New Guinea, it occurs minimally and has many prohibitions. The Mae Enga view sex as dangerous, and men are afraid to have sex with women even in marriage. Men believe that they have vital fluids that are in their skin and that make them handsome and full of vigor, and the fluid is also in men's semen. Ejaculation, it is thought, depletes a man's vitality.

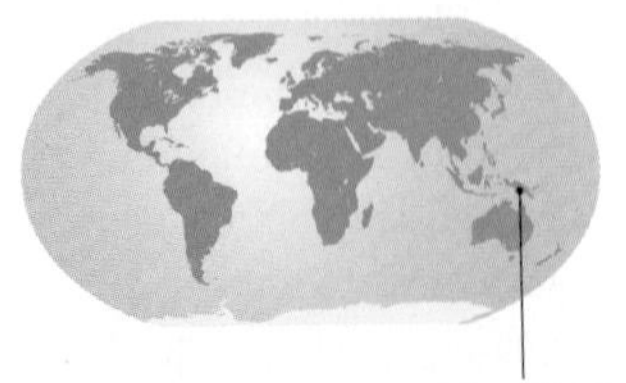

Extramarital sex is fairly common across cultures, and it is ignored by many as long as affairs are carried out with discretion. The Dobe Ju/'hoansi are an example of a society where tolerance of extramarital affairs exists: "In many Ju marriages the partners are strictly faithful to one another, while in a large minority there is evidence of extramarital affairs. . . . At one waterhole with about 50 married couples between the ages of 20 and 50, we recorded 16 couples in which one or another was having an affair. Both husbands and wives take lovers; there is no double standard among the Dobe Ju/'hoansi" (Lee 1993: 91).

OLC
mhhe • com / lenkeit5e
See Internet exercises.

SEXUAL ORIENTATION

Another dimension of sexuality is sexual orientation, the pattern of attraction, both sexual and emotional, that is based on the gender of one's partner. **Heterosexuality** refers to sexual attraction between men and women. **Homosexuality** is sexual orientation that involves same-sex attractions. These terms are used more broadly in contemporary European and American culture to mean a person's social identity, which is all-inclusive of self and personality. In Western cultures we speak meaningfully of gay, lesbian, and bisexual identities and communities. In other cultures, homosexual and heterosexual labels do not underscore an entire social identity or indicate community affiliation based on sexual orientation. In other words, the problem of taking Euro-American constructs and using them as categories to describe the behaviors and attitudes of other cultures could result in incorrect interpretations (at least from an emic perspective).

The cross-cultural incidence of homosexuality is difficult to estimate. The literature shows many societies that deny the occurrence of homosexuality; whether this is real or ideal behavior for these cultures is unclear. In other cases ethnographers do not mention the topic of sexuality; therefore, there are no useful comparative data. Perhaps not surprisingly some ethnographers have reported that they repeatedly asked about issues related to sexuality but received evasive answers. Ford and Beach (1951), in their comparative study of sexual behavior, had information on homosexuality from seventy-six societies. Homosexual activities were considered as normal and socially accepted for certain members of the group in 64 percent of these societies, whereas homosexual activities were reported to be absent, rare, or carried on only in secrecy in the remainder. Some societies in this latter group strongly disapproved of any homosexual behavior, whereas others claimed that it never occurred. Anyone who reads a newspaper is aware of the variety of opinions about same-sex sexual orientation in contemporary North American culture.

heterosexuality Sexual attraction between members of the opposite sex.

homosexuality Sexual attraction between members of the same sex.

Historical records indicate that ancient Greeks accepted same-sex relationships as natural. According to Greek cultural values, same-sex

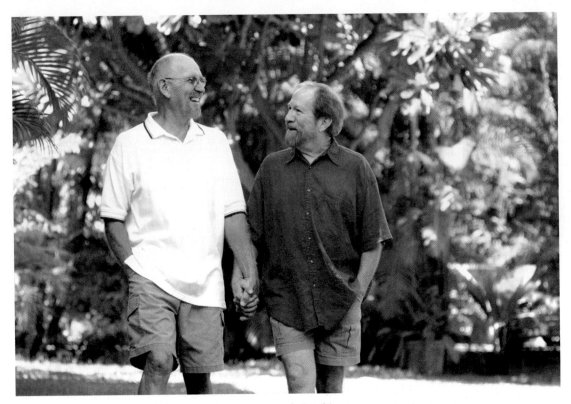

Once confined to secrecy in North America, same-sex relationships are now more open.

relationships between two males were considered to be the highest form of love. Sexuality was only one aspect of this relationship. It typically involved an older man and a youth whom the older man courted. The two had a close emotional relationship, and the older man was a mentor to the young man. This homosexual relationship coexisted with heterosexual marriages—marriage was viewed as necessary to produce children and continue the family.

The pattern of an older man with a younger man has been called transgenerational homosexuality. This form of homosexuality has been studied most thoroughly in New Guinea and Melanesia. Some 10 to 20 percent of New Guinea cultures have traditions that are similar to those of the Sambians, whose practices can be used to illustrate this point. The Sambian males go through a series of sexual encounters as they grow up. Young boys, seven or eight years old, begin sexual activities with older boys. Sambians believe that boys can grow to manhood only by ingesting

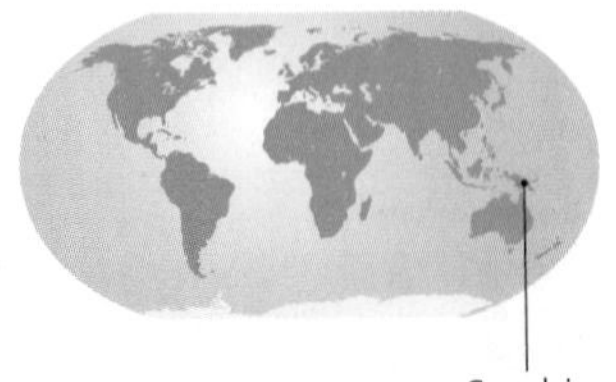

ANTHROPOLOGY AROUND US

Does Gender Affect Attitudes About Circumcision?

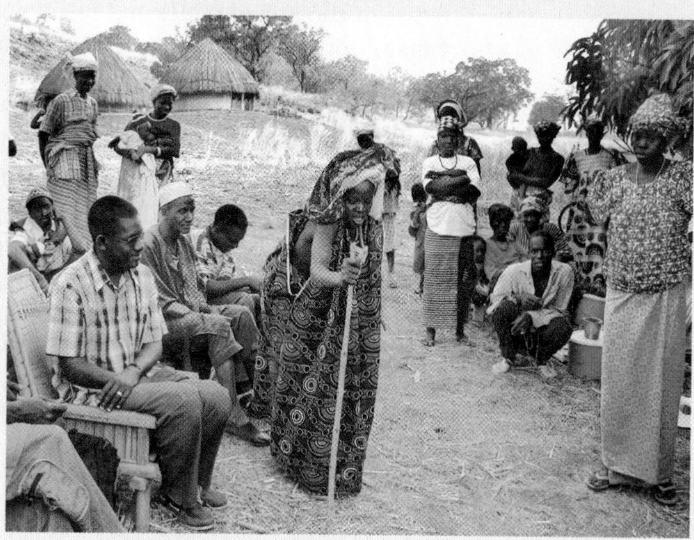

Female circumcision (and other forms of female genital cutting) and male circumcision are topics regularly covered in college human sexuality courses and often in anthropology courses. Female circumcision refers specifically to the removal of the clitoral prepuce (the foreskin covering the clitoris). Male circumcision involves the removal of the foreskin (the loose skin that covers the head of the penis). Various forms of these and other practices of genital cutting for both men and women are found throughout the world.

The outcry against female genital cutting in any form by the World Health Organization and various human rights groups is often reported in newspapers, women's magazines, and on television. These topics arouse strong reactions. Kirsten Bell, in a June 2005 article in the journal *Medical Anthropology Quarterly,* examined these practices anew after she consistently found her university students outraged at practices of female circumcision; they were even more outraged that Bell compared this practice to removal of the male foreskin. Her students argued that male circumcision was innocuous and even beneficial to one's health. Why, Bell wondered, did students have these attitudes? Bell's research and review of the historical and current literature on circumcision in Europe and North America led her to conclude that these attitudes are based on learned, culture-bound opinions regarding the differences between men and women. She demonstrates that "Medical and commonsense constructions of the human body are not divorced from cultural beliefs and values . . ." (Bell 2005: 140).

In cultures that practice it, female circumcision, like male circumcision, is considered an essential part of a child's socialization. Moreover, female circumcision ensures that daughters will be sought after as desired marriage partners. Yet most North Americans consider this operation to be mutilation and argue strongly against it. At the same time hundreds of baby boys are circumcised every day, and the claims that these operations are also a type of mutilation do not get much attention. Why? There are many activist and advocacy groups against circumcision for males.

◎ What do you think? The photo shows a village in Nagar, Senegal, where a play is being performed to raise awareness about the dangers of female genital mutilation. Do you think that such activities can change enculturated values?

semen—they say it is like mother's milk. During adolescence, boys engage in both homosexual and heterosexual relations. Betrothals are arranged between adolescent males and preadolescent girls. The betrothed couple engages in sexual activities. Meanwhile, these adolescent males provide semen to young boys so that they can develop into men. When the girls that they are betrothed to mature, the boys stop their involvement with other males and usually participate in heterosexual relationships from then on. Here, then, is a culture where all males participate in homosexual relationships during early phases of their lives and it is considered essential for the growth of boys into men (Herdt 1981; 1987).

Only a few accounts of transgenerational lesbianism are in the literature. In the Easter Islands, for example, middle-aged women are reported to seduce young women, but these relationships are not ritualized or participated in by all women (Greenberg 1988: 29). Ford and Beach (1951) found only seventeen societies in their sample of seventy-six with specific information on female homosexuality.

It should be apparent, even from this brief account, that homosexuality is viewed permissively and as part of nature in some cultures and is restricted and viewed as abhorrent behavior in others (and in some cultures there are mixed views). Attitudes depend on cultural constructs of sexuality.

SUMMARY

Gender, gender roles, and issues of human sexuality are of interest to people everywhere. Gender is the culturally assigned role given to individuals identified as male, female, or other. Gender roles are the prescribed ways that individuals identified as males, females, or others are expected to behave. Most societies recognize two genders, whereas some societies recognize a third and sometimes a fourth gender. Factors affecting gender roles include kinship, economics, and ideology.

Gender role expectations vary widely, as do issues associated with human sexuality. Sexuality—erotic desire, sexual practice, and sexual orientation—varies widely throughout human societies. Some are permissive, some restrictive. Premarital and extramarital sex are often approved and often disapproved. Sexual orientation and sexuality are best viewed and understood within the cultural context of which they are a part.

Study Questions

OLC
mhhe • com / lenkeit5e
See Self Quiz.

1. Define *sex* and *gender*. Then explain how a class reading or ethnography contributed to your understanding of gender as a cultural construct. Cite specific examples to support your discussion.
2. Discuss an example of a gender variant and the role taken by these individuals.

3. Compare the ideology of your culture to the ideology of the Yąnomamö with respect to gender.
4. How does studying Nandi female husbands, the *hijras*, *berdache*, or *mahu* contribute to the understanding of gender as a cultural construct?
5. What generalizations can be made about human sexuality across cultures?

Suggested Readings

Herdt, Gilbert. 1999. *Sambia Sexual Culture: Essays from the Field.* Chicago: University of Chicago Press. A collection of essays that cover the twenty years of fieldwork conducted in the Eastern Highlands Province of Papua New Guinea. Herdt's reflection of his time spent with the Sambia underscores how sexual behavior, gender politics, and ritual are integrated in a culture's worldview.

Nanda, Serena. 1999. *Neither Man Nor Woman*, 2nd ed. Belmont, Calif. Wadsworth. This is an excellent, short, focused introduction to the topic of gender diversity across cultures, and it has a good bibliography for further reading.

Pasternak, Burton, Carol R. Ember, and Melvin Ember. 1997. *Sex, Gender, and Kinship: A Cross-Cultural Perspective.* Upper Saddle River, N.J.: Pearson. This book is full of specific ethnographic examples and quotations to illustrate these topics, and major theoretical issues associated with each topic are covered.

Ward, Martha. 2009. *A World Full of Women*, 5th ed. Upper Saddle River, N.J.: Pearson. Gender issues are examined from societies around the world. Focus topics include love, finding partners, and work.

OLC
mhhe • com / lenkeit5e
See Web links.

Political Order, Disorder, and Social Control

Who Decides?

The shade of the large ironwood tree provided an ideal spot to sit and look out at the crystal-clear lagoon. I was chatting with a local Maori woman and asked about the pig that awakened everyone before dawn (again!) as it overturned garbage cans. She said that it shouldn't be a problem much longer as it was nearly fat enough to be given as a gift to the chief. My husband and daughter and I had been in the Cook Islands of Polynesia for a month as part of a sabbatical that included research on the culture of the Maori people. We had noticed pigs of varying sizes on many properties on the small island. They were nearly always tethered to a tree or a stake driven into the ground and often wallowed under a simple shelter of four posts and a tin roof. We surmised that these pigs were being raised as food for the resident family.

To my query about the many tethered pigs, the woman replied that most were being raised as gifts for the local paramount chief of the district, the Ariki. The Ariki granted favors such as giving a newly married couple a house and land. (Individuals did not own land; it was owned by the entire group and was under control of the chief.) It was exciting to learn of customs that until now I had only read about. To my further questions about the role of the Ariki and how he was chosen, my informant gave me a lecture on both the history of the paramount chief system and the genealogy of the local Ariki. She told of the hereditary system of selecting the chief, noting that the person always comes from one family and that although the chief is usually a man, since 1881 two women had been chosen to be chief by members of the family. Really warming to her topic, my informant proceeded to give me a history lesson on how the chief system was incorporated into the governing system with the arrival of Europeans before 1900. She emphasized that the information she was giving me was for the local district chief. She thought that the chiefs of the other districts were chosen in the same way, but she wasn't certain.

This Maori woman was telling me about how decisions were made in her community, and how, with the giving of fat pigs, people both showed appreciation to the Ariki and perhaps tried to influence his (or her) decisions. She was telling me about politics, the topic of this chapter.

The objectives of this chapter are to:

- Examine concepts used in the cross-cultural study of political systems
- Describe the cross-cultural forms of political organization
- Describe social stratification in societies
- Explore societal approaches to social control

◀ Voters in the Philippines choose their political leaders through election.

Britain's Queen Elizabeth delivers a speech to Parliament. Heads of state in many societies use speeches to wield their power. What type of power does the queen have?

POLITICS

OLC
mhhe • com / lenkeit5e

See chapter outline and chapter overview.

What exactly is politics? Defining what is meant by the word *politics* is a difficult problem because people tend to define it based on their own perspective—what their culture considers political. To people living in contemporary industrialized societies, politics comprises the process of selecting rulers who are empowered to make decisions for our **community** (an association of people who share a common identity, including geographic boundaries, common language, and culture). Political scientists seek to understand the structures and practices, including rules, that communities use and enforce. They study government and how it works. They examine power and authority, how these are distributed within the community, and how decisions are made.

community
An association of people who share a common identity, including geographic boundaries, common language, and culture.

Anthropologists study these same issues and concepts across cultures. Territorial groups and the activities that pertain to them are the focus of political organization studies by anthropologists. But it is not an easy task, because in non-Western cultures the political systems vary tremendously. What is considered political in one society may not be in another. Using the lens of our own culture to examine other cultures may cause us to miss what is there or to distort it by trying to make it fit into our preconceived categories. Still, we must try to observe objectively and analyze cultural phenomena such as politics with an attitude of cultural relativism. The concepts presented in this chapter provide a place to begin.

POWER AND AUTHORITY

Power is the ability to influence people or cause them to do things they would not do otherwise. Two basic types of power are common: coercive power and persuasive power. Coercive power involves the use of force, whereas persuasive power involves the use of argument, reciprocity, wealth, ideology, reputation, and other personal attributes. **Authority**, by contrast, is the exercise of legitimate power, *legitimate* meaning that the society or community has invested the rulers with the right to rule and that the people will be obedient to the rules. In other words, the members of the society have agreed to and accept the right of the rulers to rule, be they presidents, chiefs, or queens. In non-Western societies, particularly foraging, horticultural, and pastoral groups, power is present but authority often is not. A Yąnomamö headman, for example, wields his personal power by influencing the behavior of others, but he has no authority to force their compliance with his wishes. In societies with a chief, the chief has both power and authority. In state societies, authority and power are intertwined. The president of the United States, for example, has authority but must often use the powers of the office and personal persuasion to convince members of the U.S. Senate and House of Representatives to pass legislation that the president favors. Power is not equally distributed in any society, and it is not always easy to determine the sources of power.

Name one person in your college community who has authority. Identify what the authority is and where it comes from. Name one person in your college community who has power. Why does this person have power, and how does she or he use it? Discuss who, what, where, why, and how with a classmate.

FORMS OF POLITICAL ORGANIZATION AND LEADERSHIP

Several dimensions of political organization have been used to classify human societies. These dimensions are based on the criteria set out by Elman Service (1978) in the evolutionary-ecological model discussed in Chapter 5. Recall that, in my view, paradigms such as Service's provide a starting point to examine the various aspects of human culture. The dimensions of Service's scheme include (1) the type of authority within the system and the way it is focused within specific roles, (2) the degree to which political institutions are distinct within the structure of the society, and (3) the amount of political integration—the number of individuals and size of the territorial group that must be managed by the political structure.

Each of these dimensions may be viewed as features of political adaptations, or how people make decisions relating to their communities. Service delineated four basic types of political structure—the band, the tribe,

power
The ability to influence or cause people or groups to do certain things that they would not do otherwise.

authority
The exercise of legitimate power; the right to rule invested by members of the community in its leaders.

ANTHROPOLOGY AROUND US

Who Has the Power?

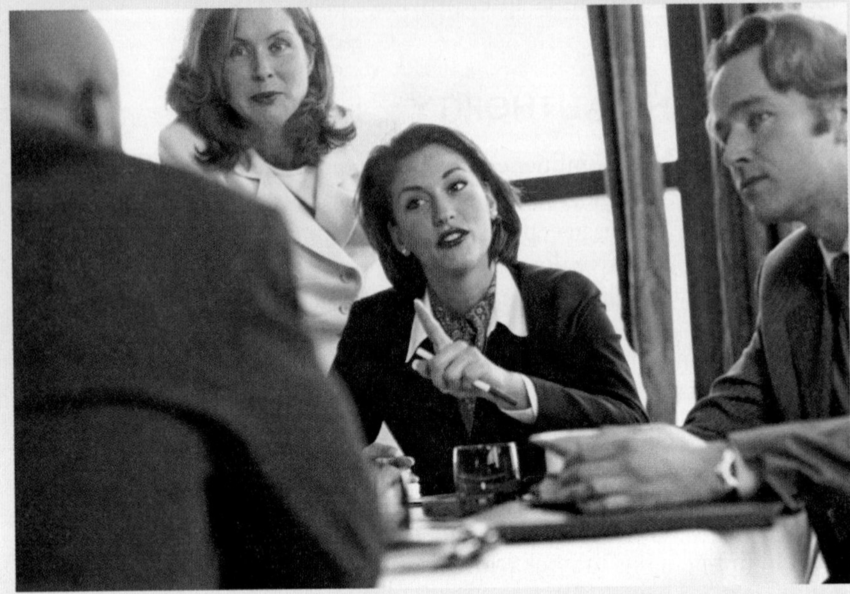

In the workplace, in our communities, and in the media *power* is generally misunderstood. Most people really mean *authority* when they speak of power, and they don't distinguish between persuasive and coercive power. When it is said that a CEO of an organization is a powerful woman, we tend to mean that she makes decisions and gets things done. Her decision making is a reflection of her authority—authority vested in her by the board of directors of the corporation. She is authorized to make decisions related to the corporation, and this authorization is explicitly delineated in her employment contract. She can also try to persuade people that the course of action that she thinks best is the course that they should follow. If they respect her and she has a good track record, they might be persuaded to support her plan. But she also has coercive power—in the form of sanctions. If an employee does not fall in line with the CEO's plan, she can block the employee's next raise or promotion. The bottom line is that she has the authority to make decisions, regardless of whether others support her.

Corporations and government agencies contain layers of employees with varying degrees of authority and power, as all who work in them understand. When something at the workplace goes wrong, or irregularities are uncovered, people often lose their job or go to jail. Who gets fired often depends on who has power. CEOs or managers may claim that they delegated authority to others and were not responsible. Every worker learns that he or she must understand and navigate the workplace minefield of who has the power and who has authority.

◎ What examples of a boss's use of authority and power have you experienced in the workplace? Is the authority you have over others clearly spelled out in your employment contract? Have you ever kept quiet about unethical or illegal behavior in your workplace for fear of a boss exercising his or her authority in a manner that would make your life difficult?

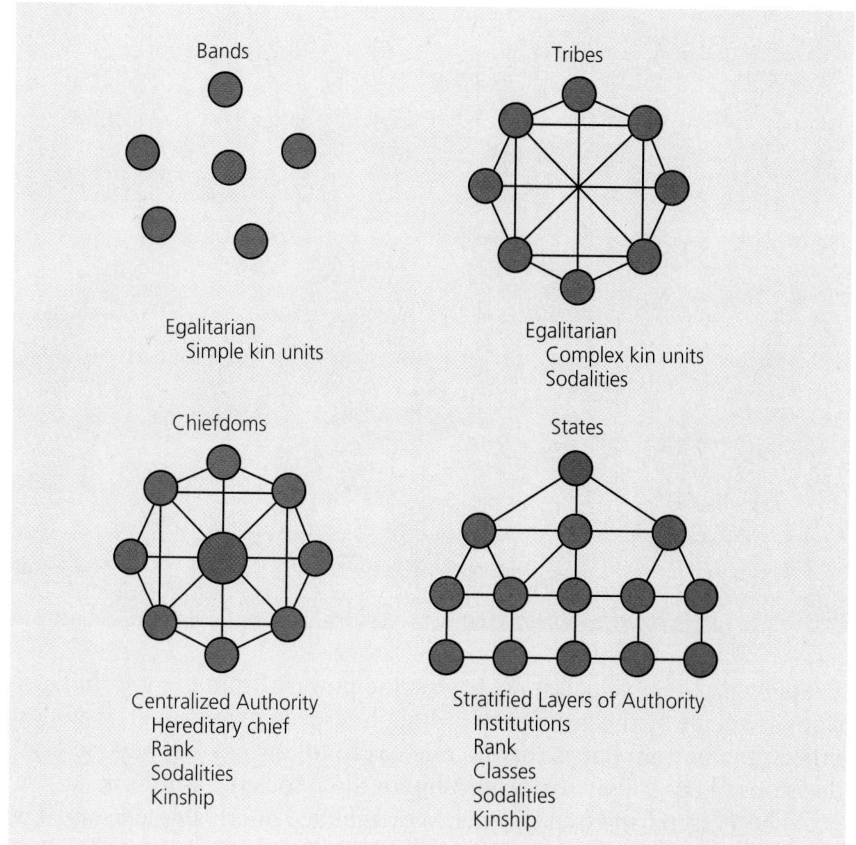

FIGURE 10.1
Organizational Bases of Societies

the chiefdom, and the state, which he described as levels of sociocultural integration, acknowledging the interrelationships of all parts of culture. The food-procurement patterns of societies, for example, influence the carrying capacity of land, which in turn influences the size of communities and necessitates types of integration and decision making for the adaptive success of the group. Keep in mind that societies are continually changing, and to give any example it is necessary to use the ethnographic present (the point in time when the culture was described). Today, the nonstate forms listed here have been incorporated in various ways into state systems. Still, by discussing them we can think about the array of human political adaptations (Figure 10.1).

Band Societies

Band societies are marked by an egalitarian social structure. In band societies there is no social stratification. Everyone within the same category such as age or gender has equal access to status mechanisms. There is no single authority; leadership is based on individual skills and earned respect.

band
A type of society common in foraging groups and marked by egalitarian social structure and lack of specialization.

The Ju/'hoansi of Botswana and Namibia, shown here at a camp among mongongo trees, follow informal leaders.

People with these valued traits have some power within the group. Decisions are made by the group, and although respected individuals may sway others, the bottom line is that no one has to follow or obey anyone else's decisions. Thus we say that leadership in these societies is informal.

The Washo band (see Chapter 5) exemplified informal leadership. The Washo turned for leadership to those who had special knowledge and skills as advisors, healers, midwives, warriors, and hunters. Their tenure in the leadership role was not predictable. A family leader was usually an older, respected, and trusted individual who knew people and had connections over a large area. Such an individual sometimes emerged as a spokesperson for a community of related families, though in aboriginal times this person had no real authority (as defined previously). Some groups of Washo, after extensive contact with settlers of European descent, recognized such leadership by group consensus for doing business with the settlers (D'Azevedo 1986: 488).

There is no separate, identifiable political institution within band societies. Political life is fully a part of social life. All aspects of social life are familistic in orientation, meaning that social, economic, and political activities are associated with kin. Everyone is related either consanguineally or affinally. Status is achieved through personal traits—an exceptional hunter, a knowledgeable midwife, a good storyteller—and the status disappears when the person dies.

Band organization is found among foraging societies. Group size varies from nuclear family units of several people to patrilocal groups of around fifty members. Each of these bands is a productive unit unto itself. The integration within bands occurs only as a result of kinship ties. A number of bands that share common language and culture are loosely integrated as a result of affinal ties created by exogamous marriages. Foraging bands are thought to represent the earliest form of societal organization.

Tribal Societies

The term **tribe** has a long and complex history both in anthropology and in general usage. One practice was to use the word as a catchall term for *primitive* people; that is, it was used as an ethnocentric term for *others*—meaning nonindustrialized, non-Western societies. Even some nineteenth- and early-twentieth-century anthropologists used it to mean *primitive*, a point of some embarrassment for contemporary anthropologists because we profess to acknowledge that all cultures are equally worthy of respect. Even today the term is often used in a pejorative manner to describe the political system of a non-state society.

Another usage of the term is as a stage in cultural evolution that came after bands and before chiefdoms. There have been variations over time within this usage, and debate continues today. Most views are tied to a particular paradigm, and differences of opinion about what constitutes a tribe are contingent on the veracity of the model. Because this text uses an evolutionary-ecological model to organize the discussion of systems of food procurement and resource allocation, the organization of political systems follows this approach for consistency.

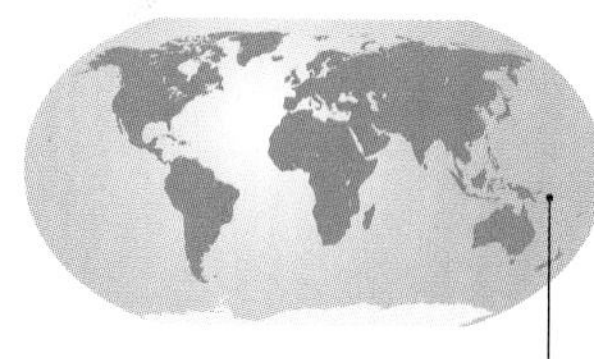

Tribal societies are similar to band societies in their forms of leadership, and they are egalitarian. Significantly, and in contrast with chiefdoms and states, tribes do not have a single leader with authority, and leaders generally do not have any form of coercive power to supplement an individual's achievements and personality traits. Instead, tribal leaders rely on their persuasive power. **Headmen** and **Big Men** exemplify leadership in such societies. To become a headman or Big Man, individuals persuade others to follow them. Being related to a headman or Big Man may give an individual status that aids his becoming a future headman. Among the Siuai of the Solomon Islands, leadership is acquired by becoming a *mumi*. Generosity and the use of wealth in giving feasts is the traditionally accepted way to gain prestige, status, and power—to become a *mumi*, a Big Man. Leadership depends on an individual's ability to organize friends, relatives, and neighbors to help give feasts, which are held to observe times of life crisis, to pay favors (balanced reciprocity), to solicit favors (asking for help to build a clubhouse, for example), and to honor a neighboring *mumi* (in fact, to test the neighbor's reciprocal power).

Giving feasts requires much preparation, and the aspiring *mumis* have to acquire wealth—much of it in the form of live pigs—so that they can demonstrate their generosity. Initially this preparation involves constructing

tribe
A type of society marked by egalitarian social structure, based on horticultural and pastoral economies, and integrated by various types of kinship organizations and sodalities.

headmen
Types of leaders found in tribal and chiefdom societies whose leadership is based on persuasive power. (See *Big Men.*)

Big Men
Alternate term for *headmen* common in Melanesian societies. (See *headmen.*)

Displays of generosity help Big Men, such as this one in Papua New Guinea, gain prestige.

OLC
mhhe • com / lenkeit5e
See Internet exercises.

pens for the pigs and then giving a feast for those who helped to build the pens. The aspiring *mumi* then must manipulate others to collect pigs—pigs that will be eaten and given away during feasts—by giving piglets to men who have been persuaded to help by raising the pigs. Or a reserve of pigs may be built by socially cultivating trade partners, friends, and kin. Alliances are formed as a result of the various activities of the aspiring *mumi*, and the clubhouses that the *mumis* eventually build serve as centers of social activities for their supporters. In the end, the man who has achieved *mumi* status through his generosity has acquired prestige and power in the community. Although his power to influence may be great, he still has no authority.

Political institutions are indistinct in tribes, just as they are in bands. Tribal societies are territorial groups who share a common language and culture and are based on food-procurement strategies of horticulture and pastoralism. These procurement strategies, you will recall from Chapter 6, result in much larger populations. Property ownership is in the hands of lineages and clans. The integration of large tribes, sometimes numbering hundreds of thousands of people, is still based primarily on kinship. Lineages and clans are the most common types of kin groupings in tribes,

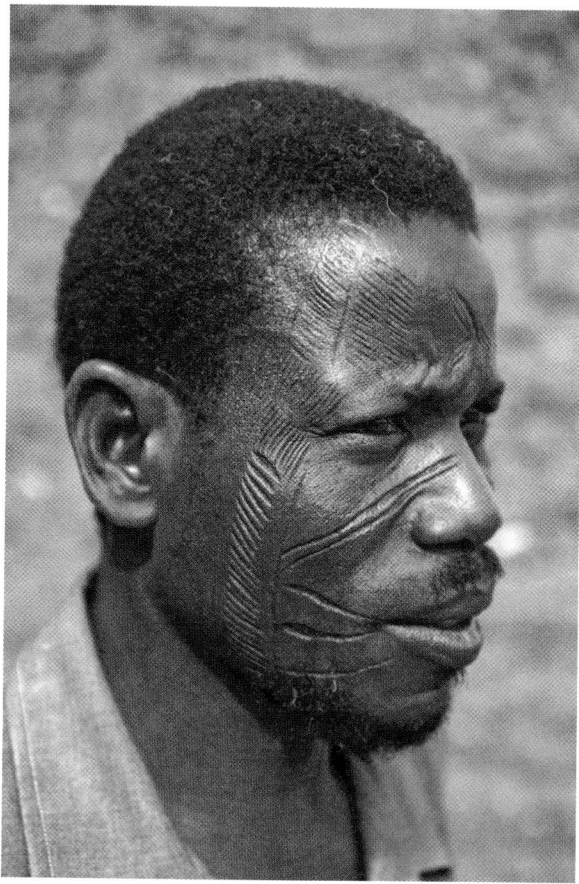

The face of this Bobo chief in Burkina Faso carries tribal scars. Such scars denote membership in age-set sodalities throughout much of sub-Saharan Africa.

and the complexity of relationships that result from exogamous marriages of these groups weaves the society together. In other words, the network of kin relationships is an integrative agent that holds the society together.

One other integrative agent in tribal societies—the **sodality**—is a group whose membership is based on common interest rather than on kinship affiliation or residence group; they may or may not be voluntary. Sodalities function to unite and integrate geographically dispersed local groups. They are also found in chiefdoms and state societies, where they serve similar functions. The most common sodalities within a tribe are the age-set groupings made up of males who were initiated into manhood at the same time. Age-set sodalities are often termed **pan-tribal sodalities,** and these may not be voluntary. These initiation groups are formed across the entire tribe when initiations are held every few years. Among the Nuer tribe of cattle herders in east Africa, male initiates between the ages of fourteen and sixteen are put through a series of rituals and ordeals, including cuts across their foreheads that result in scarification, which is an outward symbol of manhood. Because the initiations take place about every four years, the age-set system creates

sodality
A group that crosscuts a society and whose membership is based on common interest rather than kinship or residence.

pan-tribal sodality
An association group that crosscuts a tribe and unites tribal members, not always voluntary.

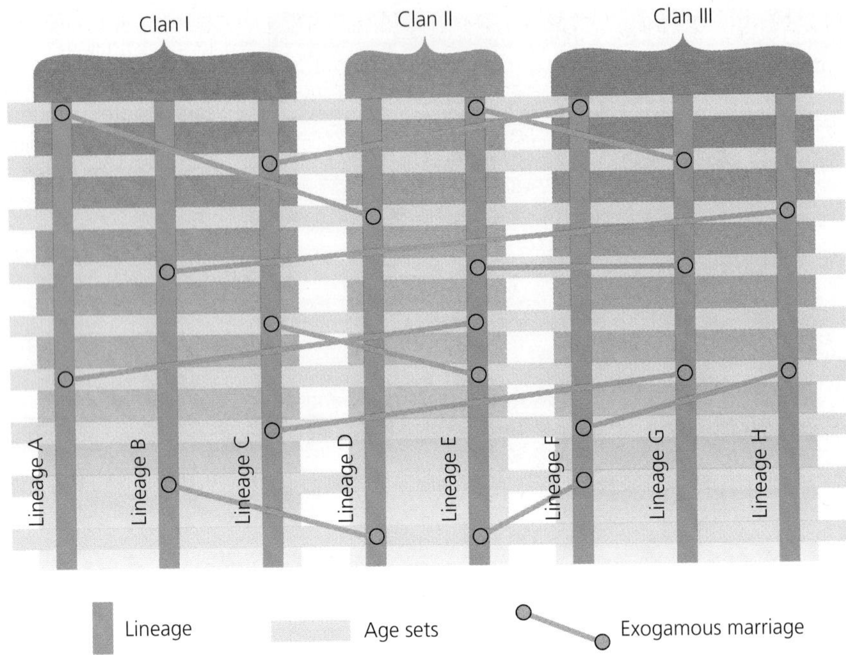

FIGURE 10.2
The integrative mechanisms in tribal societies are based primarily on lineage and clan affiliation. Exogamous marriage also integrates people. Finally, sodalities such as age sets unite people across the tribe.

groupings of males that crosscut the tribes' lineages. Boys who have been initiated together into these age sets have a lifelong comradeship (women take on the association group of their husbands). Additionally, men of an age set may act as a military unit during conflicts with neighboring tribes. Pan-tribal sodalities functioning in this manner were found in Africa and among Plains Indians in America up to the mid–nineteenth century. Not every tribal society has sodalities. For example, the Yąnomamö lack this integrative mechanism.

One can visualize a tribal society being rather like a cloth that is created by a series of many lineages (threads running in one direction) and clans that are woven together by exogamous marriage ties (threads that run in the other direction). The cloth is further made whole by wide swaths of groupings of different-colored threads that run across the entire cloth (representing age sets). Figure 10.2 illustrates this vision of societal integration. One additional tribal binding agent has been noted. The group's response to external conflict and to resource scarcity or abundance also works to bind tribes together (Braun and Plog 1984).

chiefdom
A type of society with a hereditary office of chief, most commonly hereditary, social ranking, and a redistributive economy.

Chiefdom Societies

Chiefdoms differ from tribes primarily in the office of chief, which is most commonly hereditary. This office bestows authority on the person who holds the office. Often the chief is believed to have a direct connection to the supernatural and is thus unique. Moreover, this supernatural connection provides the chief with a means to enforce judgments and punish individuals who break rules. The members of the society recognize and acknowledge the chief's authority. The leadership position of the chief gives the person holding the office not only authority but also prestige and status. By association, the chief's immediate family members also have prestige, status, power, and sometimes wealth. Because this ascribed status is not available to other members of the society, the chiefdom is not egalitarian. Rather, social ranking is present, consisting first of the chief and the chief's family members and second of the other members of the society.

The office of chief demands that tribute be paid to the chief, usually in the form of food surpluses and goods. Surplus tribute is redistributed to the community through communal feasts or a subsidy. Tribute serves as a way for individuals to show their support for the chief, and his redistribution of surplus functions to ensure that everyone has food. The reciprocity (both generalized and balanced) of bands and tribes can be found in personal exchanges within the chiefdom. The centralized office of chief and the redistributive system that arises from it serve to orchestrate economic production and encourage specialization. This specialization may take the form of different sections of the larger community specializing in the production of a particular type of food. The redistributive system will result in everyone receiving some of everything produced, so such specialization is in everyone's interest. Another way to specialize is for an entire group to work communally on food production, knowing that each will benefit and receive a portion of the foods produced.

Much variation occurs in chiefdom societies, as with other societal types. Yet the basic tenet of the office of chief and a redistributive economic system is always present. This system serves as the integrative mechanism for the society—it weaves the various groups together and makes them interdependent. Additional integration is provided by the complex of kin ties based on descent and marriage (exogamous lineages and clans are present in chiefdoms).

Do Internet gamers who play *StarCraft II*, *Call of Duty*, or *World of Warcraft* comprise a sodality? Make an argument that gamers today in fact create international sodalities that function in the same manner as sodalities in tribal societies.

State Societies

State societies are the most recent form of political organization to emerge in the history of humanity. **States** exhibit tremendous variety—there are democratic states, parliamentary states, authoritarian states, and communist states, to name a few. They all exhibit common features as well as differences. A state constitutes itself legally; that is, there are laws, and these laws are administered by the state. Specifically designated people are authorized and empowered to enforce the laws; in other words, policing is institutionalized. Ruling bureaucrats have varying degrees of authority and power, and political and economic classes stratify the society. Wealth is not equally distributed. There

state
A type of society characterized by a political structure with authority that is legally constituted.

is specialization at every level. Food producers carry out intensive agriculture that results in surplus crops, and these surpluses support the bureaucracy. The merchant class is part of an extensive market system of distribution, both within the state itself and with other state societies. Cities become common as states grow, and these cities eventually develop into vast urban centers.

Today we often speak of nation-states. Technically a *nation* is a group that has a symbolic identity, sharing some or all of the following: geographic location, culture, history, religion, and political structure. The term *state* designates a type of political structure. **Nation-state** refers to a group that shares both—a common cultural heritage and territory plus a legitimate (acknowledged by the people and willingly accepted) political structure. This is, of course, an ideal description.

RANK AND STRATIFICATION

A slightly different approach to classifying societies with regard to their organization originated with the work of anthropologist Morton Fried (1967). It is based on social structure and people's access to wealth, prestige, and power. This classification includes four types of societies: (1) egalitarian societies, (2) rank societies, (3) stratified societies, and (4) stratified state societies. The focus of such comparisons within these types is on equality and inequality. Because power is an aspect of the criteria for Fried's classification, it is included in this chapter. This classification does not precisely parallel Service's scheme (bands, tribes, chiefdoms, and states) because rank societies include both tribal and chiefdom groups. It does provide another lens for etic viewing of cultures.

Egalitarian Societies. In an **egalitarian society,** as noted earlier, everyone has equal access to wealth, prestige, and power within categories, usually based on age and gender. Foraging bands fit this category, where the economy is based on generalized reciprocity. The Washo, Dobe Ju/'hoansi, and Inuit, introduced in previous chapters, are considered egalitarian societies.

Rank Societies. In a **rank society** individuals gain prestige and wealth by the use of persuasive power. In other words, there are inequities in the society—the number of rank positions is limited so that not everyone, even those with the talent to achieve the status of the position, can do so. Rank may be associated with economics in the control of production, distribution, and consumption. It may be associated with the sociopolitical aspects of society such as authority to punish people who break rules. It may be ceremonial—inequity of access to ritual and the supernatural. Most tribal and chiefdom societies fit this category.

The Trobriand society profiled in Chapter 6 is ranked. Clans, villages, and individuals are ranked by prestige. Rank is seen primarily in

nation-state
A group that shares a common cultural heritage, territory, and legitimate political structure.

egalitarian society
A society in which individuals within the same category of age and gender have equal access to wealth, prestige, and power.

rank society
A society in which the individual's access to prestige and wealth is limited by the number of positions available. A society may be stratified by rank, such as in a chiefdom.

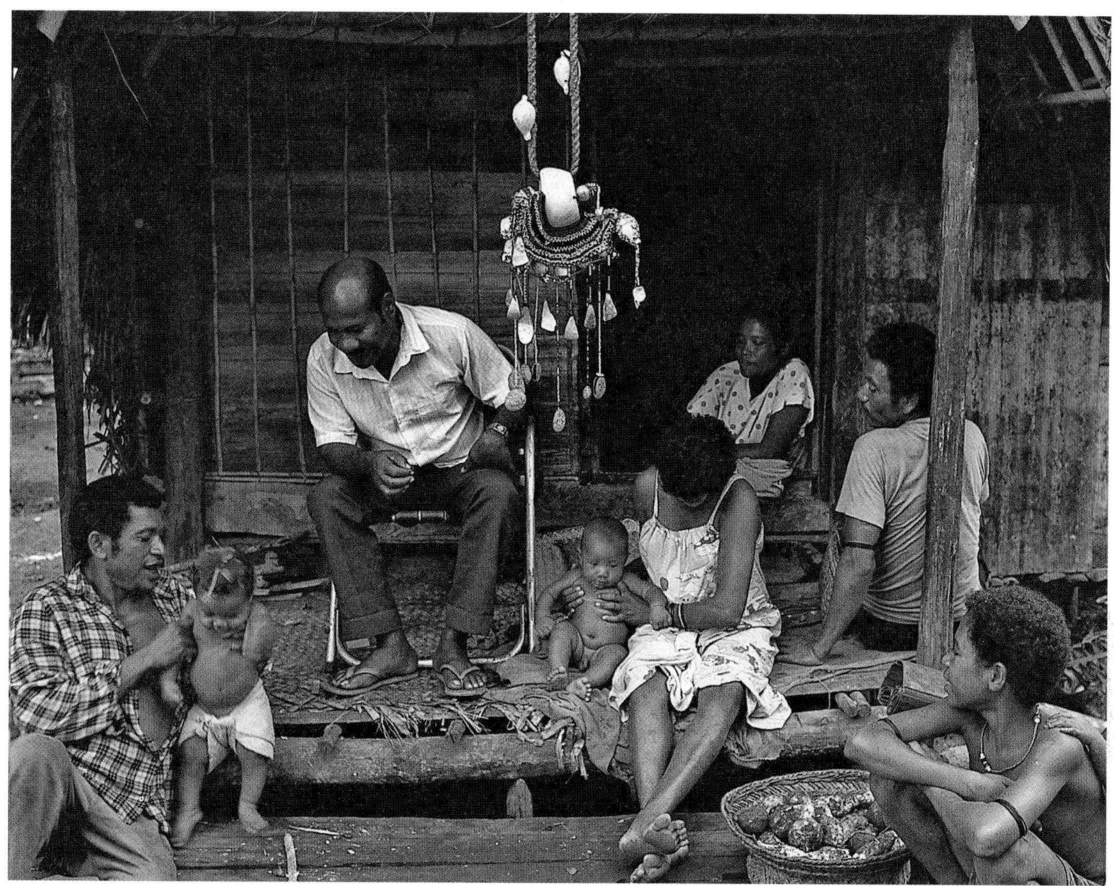

A Trobriand paramount chief visits the home of one of his two wives. Chiefs in some cultures practice polygyny as a right of their office. Note the Kula objects hanging in the foreground.

terms of etiquette. High-ranking individuals' heads must be higher than others, and these individuals have titles and the right to wear certain ornaments. High-ranking individuals, such as village headmen, are paid tribute in the form of garden produce at the time of harvest. A headman may gain wealth in this way, giving him more prestige. It is, however, not personal wealth—he redistributes it to pay for services he receives and to feed people at feasts and ceremonies. These social obligations outweigh the economic aspect of the headman's position (Malinowski 1922; Weiner 1988).

Hawaiian and other societies throughout Polynesia exhibit a range of ranks. The Hawaiians had three basic levels of rank, the high chief of an island (often called the paramount chief), a second-level chief who had less rank but who administered for the chief and was a distant relative of the paramount chief, and a third level of commoners who were most numerous. Other island societies such as the Maori of New Zealand and the Cook Islands had a rank system based on descent and segmentary lineages. One's rank depended on degree of nearness to the main line of descent (Sahlins 1958). Most chiefs in such societies enjoyed prestige and power but usually did not gain great wealth because they redistributed the majority of what they received from those of lower rank.

Stratified Societies. A **stratified society** is one in which individuals within the equivalent age and same sex status group do not have equal access to resources. In other words, these are societies based on inequity. Pure stratified societies were hypothesized as a level between rank societies and states, but these were likely unstable and quickly became state societies. While stratification is not theoretically limited to state societies, that is where it is exhibited today.

Stratified State Societies. A **stratified state society** consists of institutions in which coercive power and authority are determined in ways other than those of kin relationships, and social stratification is manifest in the institutions. The dimensions of **social stratification** include (1) economic status or wealth, (2) power status, (3) prestige or social status (recall that status is both ascribed and achieved; see Chapter 8 to review these concepts). Strata groups are known as classes, and inequities exist between classes with respect to these dimensions of stratification. A **class** is a group of people who have a similar relationship to the mechanisms of wealth, power, and social status. A ruling class, for example, is composed of people who have wealth and power. The access to resources by members of other classes within the same society—lower or underprivileged classes—is limited by the privileged ruling class, thus creating inequities.

Opinion about what constitutes a class is somewhat controversial. Some anthropologists say that for a class to exist it must be recognized from an emic viewpoint; that is, members of the class must themselves recognize this identity. Others note that from an etic view a class can exist whether members are conscious of it or not, if the outsider can identify the group based on the inequities that they have in common.

To anthropologists, states are by definition stratified into classes. They are not egalitarian, as are bands and tribes. Neither are chiefdoms stratified societies because the status system is based on whether one is a relative of the chief. In states, the strata consist of unrelated groups. So the type of *group* and its members collectively are the focus. To many sociologists, all societies are stratified, because the sociologists define stratification differently, with a focus on *individuals* and the inequalities that societies exhibit from one person to another. For example, an adult has advantages over a child, a man has advantages over a woman, a skilled worker has advantages over an unskilled worker.

Classes in some societies, such as Canada and Sweden, are mobile; that is, people can move from one class to another. This mobility in contemporary

stratified society
A society with unequal access to resources within the same gender and status group.

stratified state society
A society in which institutions are based on coercive power and authority. Inequality exists within social groupings.

social stratification
Ascribed and achieved differences between two classes within a society.

class
A group of people who have a similar relationship to wealth, power, and prestige.

societies is often the result of an increase in the availability of education. In other societies, such as Japan, mobility is more restricted. Caste-based societies are the most restricted. A **caste** is a ranked group with membership determined at birth. Because marriage is restricted to members of one's own caste, it is impossible for children to acquire another caste. India was once legally bound to a caste system. Today, it is possible for individuals to move up in the caste system economically, but religious and other traditions prevent marriage between members of different castes, so the caste hierarchy continues.

Class boundaries are based on traditions and customs, and each generation learns these traditions. The attitudes that each of us holds toward an upper or lower class are another example of how culture shapes us.

DISORDER AND SOCIAL CONTROL

Within every society, conflicts occur that lead to conditions of disorder. Conflicts arise when individuals or groups disagree with others, when people are murdered or injured, or when property is damaged or stolen. In other words, disorder occurs when people deviate from the accepted norms and rules of the society. **Social control,** an issue that must be addressed whatever the type of political organization—band, tribe, chiefdom, or state—refers to the way a society ensures that people behave themselves. Social control involves structures and mechanisms whose purpose is to ensure that people do not violate accepted forms of behavior. Both formal and informal means are used to address issues of **deviance** (violation of a society's ideal pattern of behavior). In prestate societies most conflicts took place between individuals or kin groups. As large state societies developed, beginning around six thousand years ago, economic and social stratification occurred, which included the development of an elite group of leaders who wielded power and authority. The lack of direct involvement in decision making by large segments of such societies resulted in new types of conflict, both internal and external.

OLC
mhhe • com / lenkeit5e
See Internet exercises.

Homicide is an example of a deviant behavior that occurs in every human society. The killing of another human being is a serious deviation from normative behavior that is highly disruptive. We can view the disruption caused to families and communities as we watch nightly television news broadcasts, and we are appalled by Federal Bureau of Investigation crime statistics that put the murder rate in the United States for the year 2009 at 5.0 persons per 100,000 population (FBI 2009).

Anthropologist Bruce M. Knauft (1987) has presented dramatic data on murder rates for prestate societies. Knauft's data are drawn from various ethnographic accounts, including his own work among the Gebusi of New Guinea. These data showed a homicide rate for the Dobe Ju/'hoansi of the Kalahari Desert for the year 1979 to be nearly three times that of the murder rate in the United States (Knauft 1987: 458). Knauft's genealogical

caste
A ranked group with membership determined at birth.

social control
A process involving a structure and mechanisms to ensure that people do not violate the society's accepted forms of behavior.

deviance
The violation of an ideal pattern of behavior within a society.

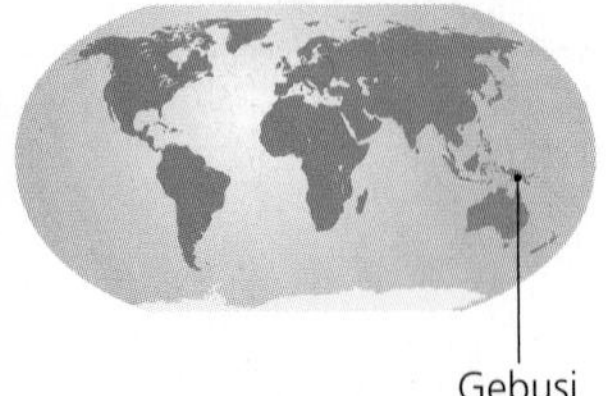

research on clans of the Gebusi of New Guinea revealed that between 1963 and 1982 by extrapolation the homicide rate was calculated to be equivalent to at least 419 per 100,000 per annum (Knauft 1987: 463). One must keep in mind that many prestate societies have small populations. Knauft therefore had to mathematically extrapolate the homicide numbers for each society in order to have comparative data. The FBI must do the same for towns and cities with varying population size. Knauft also notes that homicide reports in state societies rarely give totals from all sources. Rather, "Killings are tabulated separately (and in different types of reports) depending on whether they took place in warfare, nonlegitimate interpersonal aggression within the society or legitimate violence (e.g., killing in self defense, killing by officials in the line of duty, and legal executions)" (Knauft 1987: 463).

All disruptive behaviors must be dealt with by a society. In prestate societies with a lack of centralized authority, the means of social control are informal, whereas state societies focus on formal systems of social control.

Informal Means of Social Control

In societies such as bands and tribes, where there is no political entity with authority and there are no formal laws, informal sanctions must serve to provide control. The most common informal means of social control take place through the use of social pressures, including ridicule, gossip, and ostracism. These methods can be very effective in small-scale societies. When everyone with whom one interacts is making both direct and subtle negative comments about one's behavior and character, the pressure is difficult to ignore. Colin Turnbull's account of the treatment of Cephu, a member of a foraging Mbuti pygmy band, illustrates the effectiveness of group pressure to control behavior. The hunter Cephu had, in effect, stolen meat from the entire group by placing his hunting nets in front of the communal hunting net. Successful net hunting requires that everyone participate, and afterward the meat is shared by all. After stealing the meat, Cephu did not share it either. Back at camp the jeers began. Kenge said, "Cephu is an impotent old fool. No, he isn't, he is an impotent old animal—we have treated him like a man for long enough, now we should treat him like an animal. Animal!" (Turnbull 1987: 104). Youths ignored traditional rules of deference to elders and did not relinquish the chairs that they occupied as Cephu approached the communal fire. When he pointedly stood by a chair that was occupied by a younger man, he was told that "Animals lie on the ground" (Turnbull 1987: 105). After more name calling and oratory in which Cephu's behavior was blamed for the bad hunt and the bad camp, Turnbull records that Cephu was humiliated and defeated. "He apologized profusely, reiterated that he really did not know he had set up his net in front of the others, and said that in any case he would hand over all the meat" (Turnbull 1987: 107).

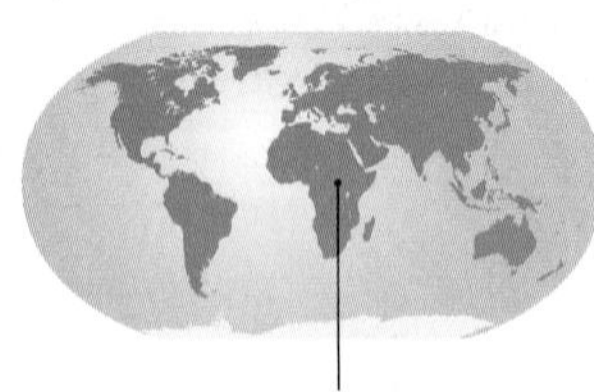

Among these Mbuti pygmies and other small-scale societies informal means of social control are effective.

Ridicule and ostracism, or the threat of ostracism, and gossip can be effective in small groups in any society—as most of us will recall from our childhood and early school experiences. However, the larger the society, the easier it is for individuals to withdraw from any uncomfortable situation and join other groups, thereby limiting the effectiveness of these informal means of social control.

Formal Means of Social Control

Law refers to cultural rules that are formulated by societies and backed up by sanctions. Formal means of social control involve consistent systems of sanctions that are applied when rules are violated. Some political anthropologists take the position that law should be defined more strictly. They would argue that law exists only when there is a codified system that involves judges and courts. Others take the broader view outlined here. Formal means of social control range from systematic sanctions found in prestate societies, such as the formal song duels used as a means of conflict resolution among the Inuit or the moot of many African societies. A moot is like an informal court where disputes are settled. Among the Kpelle of Liberia, there is an official formal court system, but disputes are

law
The cultural rules formulated by a society and backed up by sanctions.

State societies have formal systems of social control. Can you identify where this image was taken?

often settled in moots. Most disputes that are aired in the moot are those between kin and neighbors. There is a great deal of variation on when, where, and how the moot is held, but its function is to get the issues out in the open, air differences, and reach a consensual agreement. The process is therapeutic. Often small fines are levied against the guilty party, some restitution is awarded the wronged party, and a public apology is made.

Inuit song duels are essentially contests in which derisive, biting, witty songs are composed secretly by two individuals who are involved in a dispute. The dispute could be over adultery, sorcery, or theft. If informal means have not solved the issue, and gossip and insults are escalating rather than solving the issue, a song duel is performed in front of the entire community. These duels are ritualized with strict procedures; for example, the songs have to be in verse form. The opponents present their songs in turn. The songs bring the conflict into the open. Aggression is vented, and the entire group who hears the song acts as arbiter in the conflict. It is reported that the songs often deal with the whole personalities of the opponents rather than focusing on the specific grudge. After the performances, the audience decides who has presented the best song.

Not the merits of the dispute, but rather the construction of the song and performance are the deciding factor. Once the group has passed judgment, the issue is considered resolved. Song duels have not always ended the dispute; sometimes the disagreement has continued and led to fistfights, with the winner of the fistfight being declared the winner and the matter settled.

Law and adjudication in state societies are founded on penal systems with specific written rules and consequences for violation of these rules. Laws of this sort are often founded in religious value systems, such as the commandment "Thou shalt not steal." Because we have been enculturated with such laws, we feel that they are morally right and we avoid breaking them for that reason rather than because we fear legal punishment. It should be apparent from this example that law and social control are intertwined with other aspects of a society. In other words, the holistic approach must be applied if one is to fully understand and appreciate issues such as social control in any society.

EXTERNAL RELATIONS: CONFLICT, WAR, AND PEACE

When conflict arises between groups and the result is aggressive behavior and killing, it is usually called war. War is one form of conflict resolution that has been used by humans throughout history, and it occurred in prehistorical times as well. Societies often seek peace, but it seems elusive.

Anthropologists have written a great deal about warfare. This is a complex topic that is beyond the scope of this introductory book. Even definitions of what constitutes warfare differ from one account to another. Generally, there seems to be agreement that war involves conflict between groups of people, and it involves the use of weapons and organized force. Finally, it involves the killing of the enemy. Internal warfare occurs when the warring takes place between groups within the same tribe or nation-state, and external warfare takes place between distinct states (in a territorial and political context). Anthropologist Les Sponsel, who has written extensively on issues of war, peace, and nonviolence has stated:

> Although there may be some utility and even validity in a simple, broad definition of warfare, it does not seem to be very meaningful to group together under the same category called "warfare" the Yanomami, Cheyenne, Kwakiutl, Iroquois, Dani, Mae Enga, Maori, Ilongot, Nuer, Zulu, and other societies when the types, frequency, and intensity of their aggression are so extremely different. Neither would it seem to advance understanding to lump together Yanomami raids, Indian-White wars in colonial America, the American Civil War, the Vietnam War, the Gulf War, and wars in Somalia, former Yugoslavia, Afghanistan, and so on. (Sponsel 1998: 107)

The Dugum Dani of New Guinea wage war.

SUMMARY

The issues of who makes decisions for a society and how order is maintained are of concern to all people. Some fundamental differences between state societies and prestate societies such as bands, tribes, and chiefdoms are as follows: Leadership in bands and tribes is informal and is based on personal qualities of the leaders. Such individuals may have the power to persuade, but they do not have authority or coersive power to make people comply with their wishes. In chiefdoms, authority is vested in the office of chief, and in state societies authority is vested in the leaders. Authority is the exercise of legitimate power—power that has been agreed upon and accepted by the members of the society. Inequities in access to wealth, power, and prestige result in rank and stratified societies. Societies have developed both informal and formal means of dealing with conflicts and the disorder that results from conflict. Informal means of social control include ridicule and ostracism. Formal means of social control include formalized laws and sanctions. Methods for judicial settlement of such laws range from the formal song duels of the Inuits to the formal court system of the United States.

Study Questions

1. Distinguish between power and authority.
2. Compare and contrast the features of the leadership of bands, tribes, chiefdoms, and state societies.
3. Compare and contrast rank-based societies and stratified state societies.
4. Discuss the dimensions of social stratification and how these dimensions define state society.
5. What means are used in various societies to maintain social control? Cite examples to support your generalizations.

OLC
mhhe • com / lenkeit5e
See Self Quiz.

Suggested Readings

Chagnon, Napoleon. 1997. *Yąnomamö*, 5th ed. Fort Worth, Tex.: Harcourt Brace. Chagnon's work among the Yąnomamö spans more than thirty years. It is one of the best ethnographies covering the politics of conflict within and between tribal groups.

Fried, Morton. 1967. *The Evolution of Political Society*. New York: Random House. Detailed explanation of the essential features of Fried's model of egalitarian, rank, and stratified societies.

Heider, Karl G. 1997. *Grand Valley Dani: Peaceful Warriors*, 3rd ed. Fort Worth, Tex.: Holt, Rinehart, and Winston. Until recently the Dani participated in ritualized warfare with neighboring groups who speak the same language and share the same culture. Heider's ethnography is readable and a useful adjunct for exploring topics introduced in this chapter.

Keesing, Roger M. 1983. *Èlota's Story: The Life and Times of a Solomon Island Big Man*. New York: Holt, Rinehart and Winston. This is an interesting account of politics among the Kwaio, a Melanesian society in the Solomon Islands, South Pacific. It is essentially a life history account and includes the etic descriptions of Kwaio culture by Keesing but also many of Èlota's own comments.

Kurtz, Donald V. 2001. *Political Anthropology: Power and Paradigms*. Boulder, CO: Westview Press. Theoretical discussions of how anthropologists analyze political phenomena.

Maybury-Lewis, David. 2002. *Indigenous Peoples, Ethnic Groups, and the State*, 2nd ed. Upper Saddle River, NJ: Pearson. A timely book that uses case studies to examine the history, politics, and conflict of interethnic situations, particularly between states and ethnic minorities.

OLC
mhhe • com / lenkeit5e
See Web links.

Belief Systems

How Do We Explain the Unexplainable?

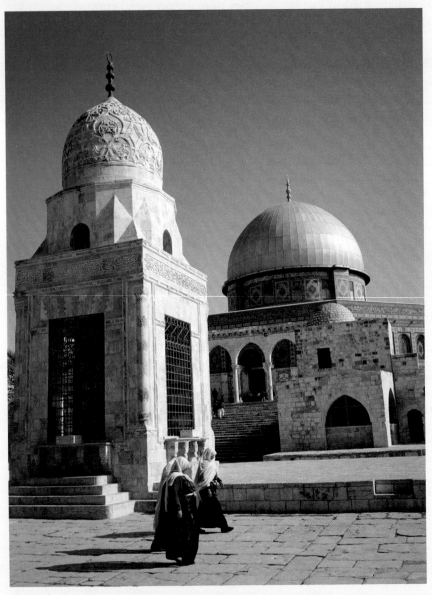

▲ The Islamic mosque of al-Aqsa in Jerusalem is the third holiest site in Islam.

We sat on benches in the small white wooden clapboard church on the island of Raiatea in French Polynesia, as the voices rose and fell in what to me were hauntingly beautiful hymns. The words were in Tahitian and I didn't understand them, but the rhythms reminded me of a lively Southern Baptist choir. The older women parishioners of this Christian Mission church were dressed in mumu style dresses of brightly colored print fabrics. Each wore a hat of finely woven palm fibers. All of the hats were different but had a similar style, and each hat held a band of small cowry shells around the crown.

Rituals associated with this church service were similar to the church services of my childhood, yet they were different. Feelings of euphoria permeated the gathering, and these mixed with the fragrance of the plumeria blossoms that grew outside the open windows on either side of the church. I was reminded of how belief systems can and do diffuse from one culture to another and how local belief systems often accommodate new ideas. I was also reminded that religious beliefs and the rituals associated with them differ widely around the world, but the adherence to a pattern of moral guidelines is essentially the same. And sitting in that church many thousands of miles from my own community reminded me of the long tradition in anthropology of studying religion and belief systems.

One of the earliest anthropology books, *Primitive Culture*, by E. B. Tylor, published in England in 1871, addressed the issue of belief systems in various world cultures. Supernatural beliefs and practices are found among all human groups and serve important roles by integrating the social, economic, and political components of a culture. Supernatural beliefs and practices also help regulate and shape the choices a culture makes about its social, economic, and political institutions. In other words, the values generated by and based on belief systems are at the core of cultural decision making.

Unfortunately, many of the examples cited by Tylor in 1871 were used to feed ethnocentric views of peoples in other parts of the world. Supernatural beliefs present, from the emic view, logical explanations of events that are an integral part of the culture. A quotation from an Islamic religious text, the Kasidah of Haji Abdu E-Yezdi, is a favorite of mine for underscoring our own group-centered attitudes regarding the topic of the supernatural and belief systems.

> All faith is False, all Faith is true:
> Truth is the shattered mirror strown
> In myriad bits; while each believes
> his little bit the whole to own. (Burton: 1991)

My experiences that day in the little church on Raiatea brought these words to mind. I was using an outsider's (etic) view when I evaluated the behaviors I saw, and this is what scientifically oriented anthropologists often do. This view is reflected in this chapter.

The objectives of this chapter are to:

- Define the supernatural world as it is viewed cross-culturally
- Discuss why people develop belief systems
- Describe the functions of supernatural belief systems and practices
- Describe the common types of beliefs found in most cultures, including supernatural beings and forces
- Describe supernatural practices and types of practitioners

BOX 11.1 Definitions of Religion

Religion is the belief in Spiritual Beings. (Tylor 1958: 424)

Religion [is] . . . a set of beliefs and patterned behaviors concerned with supernatural beings and forces. (Ferraro 1998a: 284)

[Religion is] a set of beliefs and practices pertaining to supernatural beings or forces. (Lehmann, Myers, and Moro 2005: 491)

[Religion is] an institution consisting of culturally postulated superhuman beings. (Spiro 1966: 96)

[Religion] is . . . all that is not natural, that which is regarded as extraordinary, not of the ordinary world, mysterious or unexplainable in ordinary terms. (Norbeck 1961: 11)

A religion is a system of symbols which acts to establish powerful, pervasive, and long lasting moods and motivations in men by formulating conceptions of a general order or existence and clothing these conceptions with such an aura of factuality that the moods and motivations seem uniquely realistic. (Geertz 1973: 90)

Religion [is] . . . that instituted process of interaction among the members of that society—and between them and the universe at large as they conceive it to be constituted—which provides them with meaning, coherence, direction, unity, easement and whatever degree of control that they perceive as possible. (Klass 1995: 38)

DEFINITIONS OF THE SUPERNATURAL

OLC
mhhe • com / lenkeit5e
See chapter outline and chapter overview.

Why use the term *supernaturalism* rather than the term *religion*? The moment you read the word *religion*, myriad symbols and ideas seep into your mind, each evoking thoughts and associations based on what *you* have been enculturated to believe. These images set the stage for ethnocentric reactions to other belief systems. The term *supernaturalism* is more neutral. It suggests that there are natural things in the universe and supernatural things, beyond or outside of the natural—most, but not all, cultures draw this distinction. There are things and events that can be explained, tested, and demonstrated, and there are things and events that cannot. Those that cannot be explained, tested, or demonstrated must be taken on faith. Hence, we may label them supernatural things and events. The selection of several anthropologists' definitions of religion listed in Box 11.1 all acknowledge or imply the dichotomy that is drawn in belief systems between what is natural and what is beyond the natural. These definitions also address other aspects of belief that will be examined later in the chapter.

What is considered natural to members of one culture may be in the realm of the supernatural in another culture. A thunderstorm may be explained as the result of high- and low-pressure zones in the atmosphere, or as the hurling of boulders by an angry god. Abdominal pain and diarrhea may be explained as having been caused by eating bacteria-tainted food or as the result of a magical spell cast by an enemy. This is a difficult issue to dissect because one might argue that it is ethnocentric to label an event or belief by others as being supernatural while labeling one's own culture's belief natural. Nonetheless, the present discussion embraces this dichotomy and defines a **supernatural belief** as any belief that transcends the observable, natural world. Several of the definitions in Box 11.1 (Norbeck, Geertz, and Klass) also include some of the functions served by belief systems. Because the functions of supernatural beliefs are central to any comparative discussion of this topic, they are addressed before the various types of beliefs are introduced.

WHY PEOPLE DEVELOP BELIEF SYSTEMS

Belief systems and practices explain the unexplainable. This is their overarching function—they give us explanations of what happens, why things happen, why we are on the earth, where we came from, and what happens after we die. Although they provide answers to these questions for individuals, supernatural practices and beliefs also serve the social group as a whole, and these functions have been labeled the *social* and *psychological* functions of supernaturalism. These are useful broad categories for the analysis of the functions of beliefs. The social functions take an etic view of how a society interacts as a whole and with its external social environment. The psychological functions take an outsider's look at what the belief system provides for individuals as they struggle with answers to the questions posed above.

I prefer to focus on specific functions based on an expanded version of what the early student of human behavior Emil Durkheim cited as the functions of religion in his book *The Elementary Forms of the Religious Life* (Durkheim 1961). Durkheim directed his analysis at Western religious practices, but his approach clearly may be applied to all supernatural belief systems, and I like his categories because they are specific (refer to Table 11.1 for a comparison of these two approaches).

Cohesion and Support

The cohesive and supportive functions of supernaturalism apply to both individuals and groups. People come together for ceremonies and rituals. Individuals are provided with social, economic, and political support from other group members during trying times. Each individual feels connected

supernatural belief
A belief that transcends the observable, natural world.

TABLE 11.1 Universal Functions of Supernatural Belief Systems

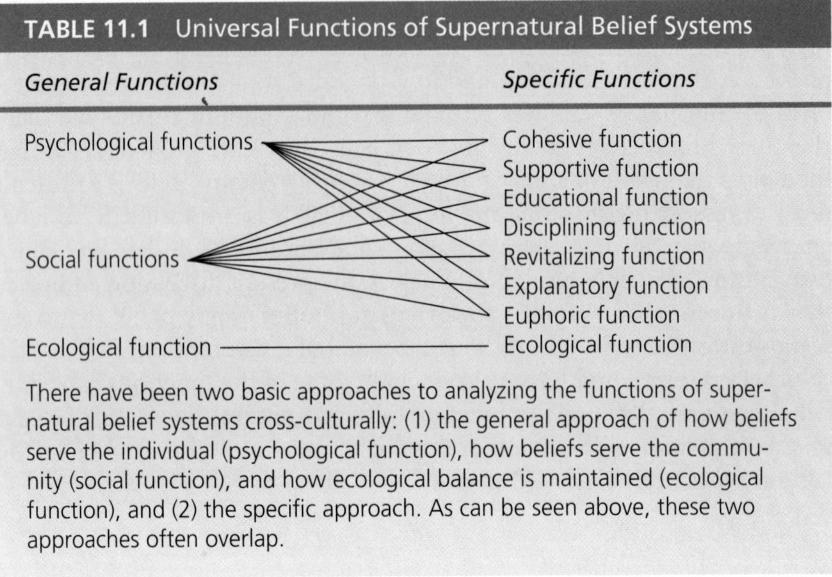

There have been two basic approaches to analyzing the functions of supernatural belief systems cross-culturally: (1) the general approach of how beliefs serve the individual (psychological function), how beliefs serve the community (social function), and how ecological balance is maintained (ecological function), and (2) the specific approach. As can be seen above, these two approaches often overlap.

to the group, bound together by common beliefs and actions. Specific symbols—such as a cross or a specific animal form—make it possible to quickly recognize fellow members of a belief system.

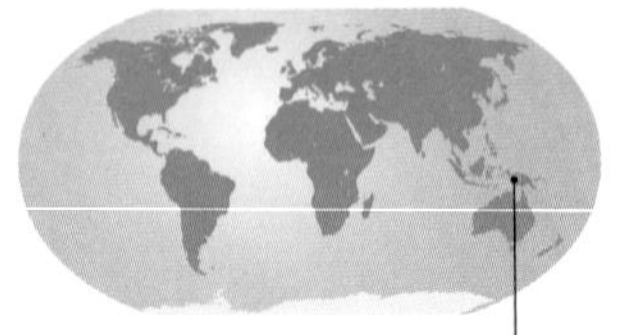

Dani

Among the Dani of New Guinea, deceased members are cremated. The Dani believe that the soul is released in the smoke of the funeral fire. If a loved one dies, others offer support by their actions and words during this ceremony. Comfort is found in this ritual, and it is supportive for the entire group because all of the participants are in effect saying that this is the right ritual to send the soul to the next place. Moreover, because it is obvious that all humans will die, the activities you perform for others will also be performed for you when you die. The ritual of the funeral supports and solidifies the values of the culture. Such rituals are the glue that holds the system together, providing a cohesive and mutually supportive base for individual members of the group. These two functions are obviously both psychological functions (serving the individual) and social functions (serving the group).

Education and Discipline

The educational and disciplining functions of supernaturalism are often interwoven. The Ten Commandments of the Judeo-Christian religions serve as an example. Children are taught group history about the origin of these governing rules and how their deity gave the commandments to Moses, an important early ancestor. At the same time, the commandments

Muslims pray together before a soccer game in Saudi Arabia. Prayer serves both a cohesive and a supportive function for participants.

serve to discipline because there are consequences for breaking them. Often-repeated origin stories, rules of behavior, and admonitions against committing transgressions become the growing child's foundations of ethical codes of behavior that shape the choices that are considered right and wrong. During the enculturation process, young children are told accounts of how specific individuals' lives changed because they did, or did not, follow the appropriate rules established by deities. Again, the more general functional categories of psychological and social functions apply to each of these more specific functions.

TRY THIS
Compare

Talk to a classmate who has a belief system different from yours, and identify and compare how your respective belief systems meet the cohesive and disciplining functions of supernaturalism.

Revitalization and Euphoria

The revitalizing function of supernaturalism involves regular and repetitious rituals and practices that result in a renewal and revitalization of the belief system, which serves to motivate and lift the mood of the individual participants as well as the entire group. When you observe the *molimo* ceremony of the Mbuti pygmies of the Congo region of Africa, the revitalizing function is clear. This ceremony serves to reawaken the forest in which the pygmies live. The forest, they say, is like their mother and father, and it must care for them. When the hunt has been going badly, someone will suggest that perhaps the forest is sleeping and that they should have a *molimo* to awaken the forest. Colin Turnbull quotes his informant and friend Moke as saying, "So when something big goes wrong, like illness or bad hunting or death, it must be because the forest is sleeping and not

In the Cook Islands one encounters family burial plots situated in front of the family home. What would be the function of this custom?

looking after its children. So what do we do? We wake it up. We wake it up by singing to it, and we do this because we want it to awaken happy" (Turnbull 1987: 92). Turnbull's description of the ceremony itself, and the elevated mood of the participants afterward, clearly demonstrates the revitalizing function. During one *molimo*, as participants sang around the fire, the *molimo* trumpet could be heard moving through the forest imitating the sounds of leopards, elephants, and buffalo. (*Molimo* trumpets were originally made of wood, but while Turnbull was with the Mbuti, they were using a trumpet fashioned from a metal drainpipe.) Turnbull writes, "it was a mysterious thing . . . alive and awe-inspiring and wonderfully beautiful; something that made the eyes of young and old alike light up with pleasure as they heard it sing" (Turnbull 1987: 89).

The euphoric function of supernaturalism is that believers experience a sense of well-being when they participate in the supernatural rituals. Individual and group anxiety is relieved, and a profound sense of joy and happiness occurs because the appropriate actions have been taken. Individuals

A Pentecostal church service in Los Angeles, California. An etic description of this scene by an American anthropologist would state that these people are experiencing euphoria.

who have experienced this euphoria describe it in terms such as elation, ecstasy, bliss, and rapture. Observe participants at a Christian tent revival meeting and you will see examples of this euphoria. You will also witness it during ritual trance in Bali and *hekura* chanting among the Yąnomamö.

Ecology

The ecological function of supernaturalism was not discussed by Durkheim, but it is clearly one of the functions of many belief systems. The ecological function involves any belief or ritual that contributes to the maintenance of the society's environment or resource management. For example, the Hindu religious system of India prohibits killing or eating cattle. Although cattle are a good source of protein-rich meat, they are also sources of fertilizer and fuel (dung), and they provide power for pulling plows. Anthropologist Marvin Harris has argued that the taboo against killing cattle makes sense in the long term as an ecological adaptation (Harris 1966).

Explanation

The explanatory function of supernatural beliefs serves both the individual and the group. Encoded within the belief system and its symbols, in texts and stories, revealed through prayer, trance, and divination are explanations that are culturally sanctioned and approved. Reasons for life. Reasons

Common functions of rituals can be identified even when specific details of belief systems differ. Buddhist monks in Thailand (right) and Hasidic Jews in Israel (below) pray.

for death. Reasons for good times. Reasons for bad times. It is comforting to have explanations for questions, large and small. Humans everywhere desire to understand why bad things happen, especially when they happen to good people—members of the culture who play by all of the rules. Answers given to the why questions include "It is the will of Allah," "It is Karma," "It is God's will." These are explanations that are acceptable to those with faith. We may not understand the reason for a specific unfortunate event, but we feel better because the belief system provides an answer.

Select two functions of supernaturalism from the text discussion, and identify specific examples of how they apply to your own belief system. Identify a specific example of how the same two functions apply to an article or ethnography you are reading as a class assignment.

TYPES OF BELIEFS

Each culture includes a variety of beliefs that are interwoven in the fabric of that culture. The details of belief systems are rich and varied. Over a century of anthropological study has revealed that common categories of belief are found in most cultures. The two categories of **supernatural beings** and **supernatural forces** are the most obvious. Native members of a culture do not themselves separate or categorize their beliefs in this way. It is, however, a useful dichotomy for a cross-cultural study of supernaturalism.

Supernatural Beings

Belief in invisible beings who exhibit form, personality, attitudes, and powers is found in all cultures. These beings are able to do things that humans cannot do. Humans can and do petition many of these beings, particularly gods and goddesses, to assist with life's difficulties. The beings may or may not respond to such petitions. Many supernatural beings are concerned with humans, but for reasons that are not revealed to us, they may not do what we ask. Their existence is taken on faith; it cannot be proven using scientific methods. A wide spectrum of such beings exists with great variation in the powers they wield. Some of the types of beings found in many different cultures include the following, though this is by no means a complete listing.

OLC
mhhe • com / lenkeit5e
See Internet exercises.

Gods and Goddesses. A wide array of gods (male gender beings) and goddesses (female gender beings) are to be found in most cultures. **Polytheistic** systems consist of belief in many of these beings, who are often of nearly equal powers, whereas **monotheistic** systems focus on one all-powerful god or goddess. Even within a monotheistic system, careful scrutiny will usually reveal more than one supernatural being that exhibits the features of a god or goddess. Gods and goddesses are often ancestral in nature. They are the source of human beings, or they have spent time living among humans. They are typically concerned with what humans do and often have given humans rules for behavior. They have many powers or few. Often, as in the

supernatural beings
Invisible beings that exhibit form, personality, attitudes, and powers.

supernatural forces
Unseen powers that are not personified and may be manipulated to achieve good or evil.

polytheistic
A belief system consisting of many supernatural beings of approximately equal power.

monotheistic
A belief system that focuses on one all-powerful supernatural being.

belief system of the ancient Greeks, the supernatural beings are placed in a hierarchy with specific tasks or responsibilities associated with each being.

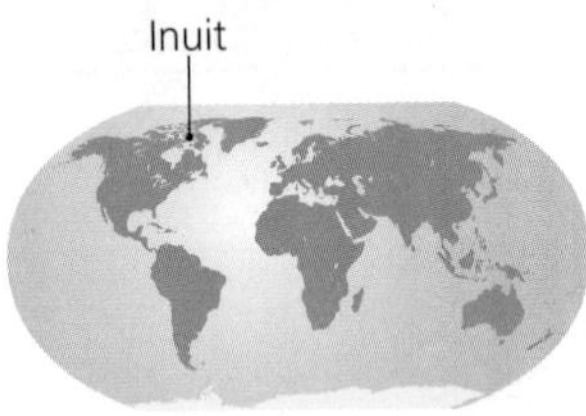

Sedna is a goddess of the Inuit, and her story was one of the ethnographic recordings made by anthropologist Franz Boas in the 1880s. Sedna was responsible for sending marine animals such as seals to be captured by the Inuit (seal meat was a primary food source for these aboriginal people). Sedna's story begins when, a long time ago, she left her father to live with a seabird that promised her that she would have plenty of food and that she would always be warm. Sedna soon discovered that the seabird had misrepresented his situation. Sedna's father came to rescue her and killed the seabird. A terrible storm caught the father and Sedna as they traveled by boat back to her home. Fearing that the seabirds wanted Sedna back, the father threw her into the ocean. Sedna clung to the boat, and the frantic and frightened father cut off her fingers. These became seals and other sea creatures. Believing Sedna to have drowned, the seabirds left and the storm abated. Sedna did not drown but survived to once again live with her father. Angry at her father for his behavior in the boat, Sedna directed her dogs to attack him and eat his hands and feet while he slept. Soon the father, the dogs, and Sedna were sent to the ocean bottom to live. From the depths, Sedna came to reign over the creatures of the sea. She makes decisions about whether to send creatures for the Inuit to kill (Boas 1964).

There have been numerous variations on the story of Sedna. In each variation, however, the main elements remain—Sedna is ancestral, she has power that ordinary Inuit do not have, and what happened to her explains why she is not always generous to humans. Much of Inuit seal hunting ritual involves appeasing Sedna so that she will continue to send seals to the Inuit. For example, before butchering a seal the Inuit offer it a ritual drink of water. Origin myths are present in most religions and often, as in Sedna's story, there are variations.

TRY THIS Analyze

Find a religion that is unfamiliar to you in the yellow pages of your local telephone book. Log on to an Internet search engine such as Google or Yahoo or Excite and search for information about this religion. Discover whether there are any gods or goddesses in this belief system that are ancestral to humans in some manner. What function (or functions) does the belief in the ancestral nature of beings have for a society?

Demons. The word *demon* is used to denote a negative, evil being. Most systems that have gods or goddesses also have one or more demons. Demons may try to steal the souls of people and force them to commit evil, antisocial acts. They are powerful and can change form, and they often do so to trick and lure humans. They provide a culturally appropriate explanation for people's inappropriate behavior. Demons are responsible for bad events that befall humans. In the Christian belief system, the devil is a demon who tempts humans to stray from the right path and commit sins.

Souls. The soul is considered the supernatural component of humans and sometimes other animals. This component is believed by most peoples to be what gives life and makes us what we are. The soul's existence is taken on faith, and the teachings of many of the world's belief systems describe how the gods and goddesses give humans their souls. There are many debates, even among theologians, as to when souls arrive in the physical body—at the moment of conception, when the fetal heart begins to beat, or at the moment of birth. Some cultures believe that the soul arrives at a designated point after birth. Elaborate parties and celebrations are held at that time, and a name is bestowed upon the child. It has been noted that societies that believe in late soul arrival are often societies with high infant mortality rates.

There are also many variations of beliefs regarding what happens to the soul at death. Among the Yąnomamö Indians of Brazil and Venezuela, the central part of the soul escapes the body at death and goes to a layer that exists, according to Yąnomamö cosmology, above the earth. We can see the underside of this layer (the sky) from earth. Arriving there, this part of the soul travels down a path until it reaches a fork in the trail, where a spirit inquires whether the soul has been generous or stingy. Stingy souls are sent on a path to the place of fire, and generous souls go on another path, to a place of tranquility (Chagnon 1997: 112). The Yąnomamö soul concepts are elaborate. Another portion of the soul is released at cremation and continues to live on earth and wander in the jungle.

The Berawan of Borneo believe that at death a person's soul undergoes a transformation into a spirit that will pass to a place where only the dead reside. Because there is a period of time before a person's body completely disappears (putrefies) and only bones remain, the soul must also slowly change. Until the body is nothing but bones, the soul will linger and be responsible for causing illness among the living (Metcalf 1978: 6–12).

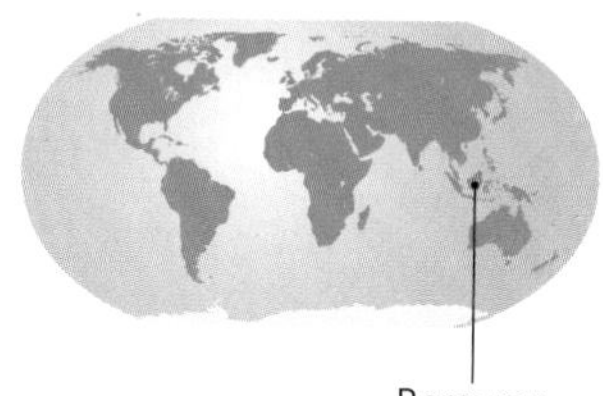

Ghosts. After the death of the physical body, souls are believed by many societies to transform into ghosts. Many societies, though not all, use the term *ghost* in place of the term *soul* after death. Ghosts are often viewed as beings with the potential to cause harm to the living. Anthropologists have suggested that this is one of the reasons for funeral rituals—a sendoff for the soul, now a ghost, to the next place before it can cause trouble among the living. Drawing on the functions of supernaturalism outlined previously, we could suggest that belief in ghosts serves as an explanation for bad things that happen, just as the Berawan attribute difficulties for the living to the lingering, transforming souls of the dead.

TRY THIS
Analyze

Make a list of supernatural beings that are believed in by a subculture (or portion of the subculture, such as children) with which you are familiar. Identify the subculture that holds these beliefs. What powers do these beings have? Consider how someone from a different subculture might view these beings and beliefs.

Tricksters. Most societies have one or more beings that fit this category. Tricksters are beings that play tricks or practical jokes on people. They typically mean no real harm and are more bothersome than anything. The trickster known as Coyote (or Old Man Coyote, or Old Man) lived among Native American cultures from the Pacific to the Great Plains. This trickster being was believed responsible for wickedness such as seducing women or being deceptive so that he could win races. He is also sometimes virtuous and often stupid. One story tells of Coyote diving into water to retrieve food that he sees there. The food he sees in the water is actually a reflection of the food he is carrying. Coyote also served as a negative role model, to show how a person should not behave in life.

Witches. In a historical and cross-cultural analysis, witches are supernatural beings. As such, these beings have power to affect the lives of humans, often in negative ways, but a supernatural being in human form never admits to being a witch, even when condemned to death. At the present time, Hollywood films and the current interest in neopagan Wiccan groups has muddied the understanding of witches. An individual who practices supernatural arts of magic and spells is not a witch in the historical and cross-cultural meaning of the term. The understanding of what constitutes a witch is a good example of how language and culture change over time. For more on the anthropological, historical, cross-cultural perspective, see Lucy Mair's book listed under Suggested Readings at the end of the chapter.

Supernatural Forces

Supernatural forces are typically neutral and surround us the way air does. These forces cannot be seen or felt, but their powers may be harnessed to accomplish good or evil ends. Individuals can learn to manipulate these forces directly by studying and learning from those who have gone before. Amateurs can and do manipulate these forces, but most believe that an individual with training or a special intuitive knack for such manipulations will achieve better results. Supernatural beings may also manipulate the supernatural forces.

mana
An impersonal supernatural force that flows in and out of people and objects.

Mana. **Mana** is a supernatural force that is part of cultures throughout Polynesia. Other cultures also believe in a similar force but call it by different terms. Mana is everywhere, though it is often concentrated in objects, or people, or even a part of a person. It may be harnessed by practitioners; it may flow into or out of objects and people. Some people are born with it, just as some objects naturally contain it. Mana may be drawn into objects, such as a pebble, by a practitioner who has the skills to manipulate it. Mana is a neutral but very powerful force. As such, it is

A member of the Iban tribe of Malaysia carries a mana object. Possession of such an object brings the owner the power of supernatural forces.

TRY THIS
Discuss

Describe what Americans call *luck*. Compare and contrast its features to those of mana.

potentially dangerous, and care must be taken with its use. If one obtains an object containing mana, it is believed to enhance one's behavior or opportunities; placing an object containing mana in one's garden, for example, is believed to ensure a good crop.

Magic. Magic is not actually a supernatural force. Rather, **magic** refers to the techniques used to manipulate various supernatural forces and sometimes supernatural beings. Individuals may use magical recipes or formulas, or they may call upon someone with special knowledge of these formulas to perform them. A **shaman** is such a person—a part-time practitioner who, by training or inheritance, has special powers to deal with the unseen universe. The following section on supernatural practitioners has more details on shamans.

magic
The techniques used to manipulate supernatural forces and beings.

shaman
A part-time practitioner of the supernatural who has special powers to mediate between the supernatural world and the community.

Magic shares some features with science. Specifically, magical formulas have been acquired by trial and error. For example, over time various practitioners may have given different herbal teas to people complaining of a

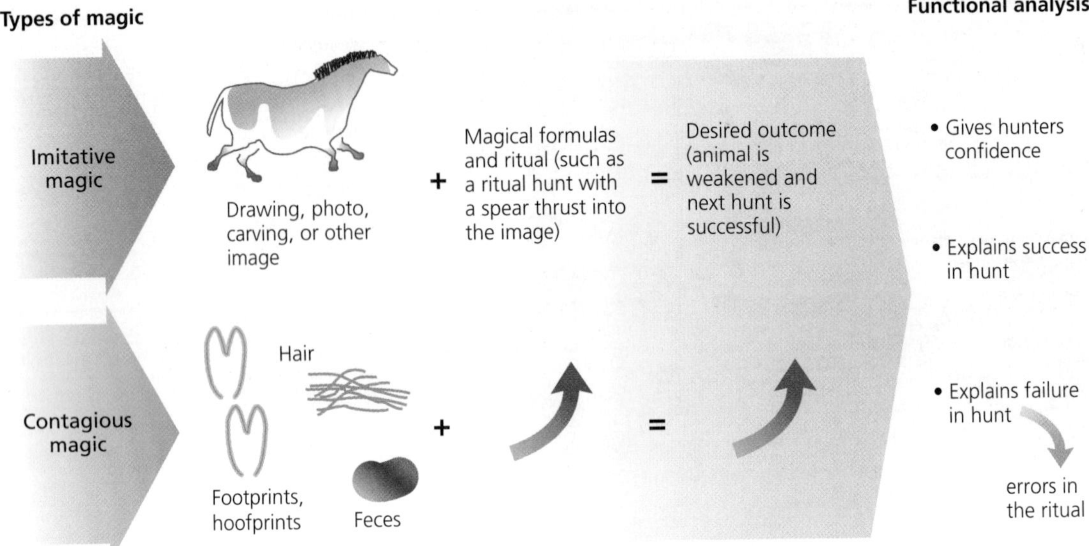

FIGURE 11.1 How imitative and contagious magic work.

headache. The herbs that relieved the most headaches were retained in the arsenal of magical curing formulas, and others were discarded. With much trial and error, a practitioner, over time, came to use certain herbs consistently to cure headaches. So, in essence, a hypothesis was formulated—this herb may relieve headache pain. It was tested—many people were given the herb for the complaint of a headache. The hypothesis was evaluated—most people given this herb reported a reduction in headache pain. Of course, shamans did not use formal, modern scientific methodology with control groups and blind tests, and they did not know the details of physiology and chemistry that modern scientists know. Their approach, in its broad terms, however, was what we would call scientific in that they were attempting to explain and control their environment and the events that affected them.

TRY THIS
Analyze

A person owns a scarf once worn by a rock star and carries it with him at all times for good luck. Is this an example of imitative magic or contagious magic? Why?

Anthropologist Sir James Frazer published a popular study and analysis of magic in 1911 and introduced the concepts of imitative magic and contagious magic to the reading public. He formulated two laws that are the governing principles of magic—the Law of Similarity and the Law of Contact. The Law of Similarity, or what is now called **imitative magic,** states that *like produces like*. The idea is that a drawing of a person, animal, or event (an imitative image or representation) can connect with an unseen world through the supernatural to influence what happens to that person or animal. A drawing of a deer with an arrow piercing its body would thus influence the outcome of a hunting expedition (Figure 11.1). The Law of

imitative magic
A type of magic based on the notion that working magic on an image of an animal or person will cause the same effect on the actual animal or person.

Contact, or **contagious magic,** operates under the same law but has as its premise that something that has contact with a person or animal contains some of the essence of that person or animal. Hair, a footprint, nail clippings, an article of clothing, excrement—all are used as part of formulas to affect the being that has had contact with the material. Voodoo practitioners often employ imitative and contagious magic. A little doll created to look like an enemy, dressed with a scrap of fabric torn from the enemy's clothing, can be used in a magical ceremony to cause injury or illness to the person. The practitioner who sticks pins in the doll would cause pain to the person. Typically someone lets the victim know that such a ceremony is in progress, or the person *believes* that magic is being worked against him. From an unbeliever's view the pain is caused by the psychophysiological processes associated with believing in the efficacy of magic.

Magic is effective. It works—if you do it correctly and believe it works. And this is one of its major appeals. In terms of the functions of belief systems, magic explains things. A relative's illness can be blamed on someone working evil magic. If the illness is cured by the magical practitioner, it is because the correct formula was used. If the ill person worsens or dies, it is attributed to one of several reasons: the diagnosis was in error and thus the wrong formula was used in the cure, or the curing formula was done incorrectly or incompletely, or another individual was using more powerful magic. Shamans often involve many people and steps in a curing ceremony. A skeptic might say that this is done so that there are many avenues of blame if the cure fails—someone gathered the wrong herbs from the wrong place, or someone did not observe the behavioral taboos called for by the practitioner (e.g., abstinence from sexual activity during a specified period).

TRY THIS
Compare

Compare the explanation given here for the failure of a magical cure with the explanation given by modern doctors when an attempt at a cure fails.

Supernatural Practices and Practitioners

Living in a community, whether large or small, brings universal dilemmas that must be addressed by the members of that group:

Why did someone become ill, and who or what was responsible?
What caused our loss at the World Cup match?
Why were we unsuccessful hunting?
Why are the crops failing?
When will it rain (or stop raining)?

Anthropologists refer to the individuals who address such concerns for a community as the supernatural specialists. They are specialists because they have special abilities to diagnose these kinds of problems and are able to provide culturally acceptable explanations and solutions for them. Individuals who act as intermediaries between the supernatural world and the natural world are found in every culture. These supernatural practitioners are called by many terms—witch doctor, medicine man, medicine woman,

contagious magic
A type of magic based on the idea that something that has contact with a person or animal contains some essence of that being and that magic performed on the item will have the same effect as if performed on the being.

A Dobe Ju/'hoansi shaman trances to contact supernatural forces and beings that will help him diagnose the other man's illness.

rabbi, pastor, prophet, sorcerer, parson, monk—and classifying them is difficult. To anthropologists there are two major classes of practitioners: shamans and priests. Nearly all practitioners of supernaturalism fall into these two categories and exhibit the general features of one or the other.

Shaman. The most common form of specialist is a shaman, who specializes in dealing with supernatural beings and forces. Shamans serve their communities in many capacities, often acting as healer, counselor, and mediator. Shamans are part-time practitioners. They aid their society by using their special skills, but they do not make a living from these activities. They live day to day like everyone else in the society except when called upon to interface with the supernatural.

The use of the term *shaman* is quite tangled in today's society, much like the term *tribe* that was discussed in Chapter 10. It is often broadly applied to *anyone* who deals with the supernatural, including New Age practitioners who focus on treating their own individual needs through drumming, dancing, and trancing. Alice Kehoe (2000) takes issue with such current broad uses of the term. She points out that among the Tungus-speaking cultures of Central Siberia where the term originated, the term *shaman* refers specifically to those who mediate with the supernatural on behalf of their *community*. Mari Womack (2001) argues that language changes over time, and most anthropologists use the word *shaman* to describe a specific behavior complex (discussed in the following paragraphs).

A shaman is culturally perceived as being supernaturally chosen for the role. The spirits have selected this individual to act as an intermediary between two worlds—the natural (or known) world and the supernatural (unknown or beyond the known) world. Shamanistic individuals are often identified because they have survived some extraordinary event such as being struck by lightning or escaping a dangerous situation that would have likely resulted in death or severe injury to most people. Some individuals become shamans because of what we might call their unstable personalities, to use a modern label. Or it may be that they have a culturally ambivalent sexuality or are either gay or lesbian. These events or conditions are an indication to the group that there is something unique and special about the person. It should be remembered that humans have often lived in communities with small populations. In such communities, someone who does not conform to the narrowly defined social and cultural expectations of behavior stands out readily. A person's differences can be channeled into a positive role within the community by labeling that person as *chosen* by the supernatural. An older shaman may apprentice such an individual. In this manner the knowledge and the appropriate techniques and strategies are transmitted to the next generation. An additional feature of many shamans is that they have a particular specialty in dealing with the supernatural. This might be a special relationship with a specific supernatural being or force. When that shaman dies, the connection is broken.

A shaman makes contact with the spirit world in a variety of ways. The Yąnomamö use mind-altering drugs to contact spirits, whereas Chuckee shamans interpret their dreams as an indication of contact with the spiritual universe. Prolonged and physically demanding dancing or listening to rhythmic music (often drumming) is used by the Dobe Ju/'hoansi to trance and contact spirits. Specific spiritual beings may then enter the shaman's body and speak to the community through him or her. Spirits will, in this way, provide an explanation of why something has happened. The appropriate course of action (or treatment) will then be explicated.

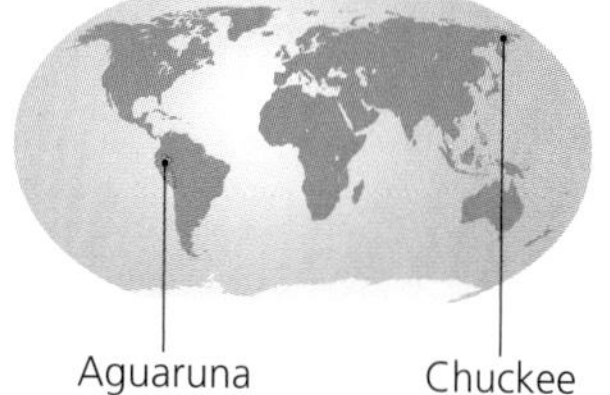

Shamans use a variety of techniques. A deep knowledge of the medicinal qualities of the local flora is used to cure common problems such as fevers or digestive ailments. Psychosomatic techniques are also used, and these are often very persuasive. Sucking a foreign object out of an afflicted person's body is a technique used by the Yąnomamö. The *object* is often a small piece of bone or stone or even an internal organ from a small animal that has been kept hidden from the patient. When the shaman spits out this object, it provides evidence of the cause of the person's problem. Alternatively the shaman may pull a contaminating spirit from a patient into his or her own body. The conflicting spirits—the shaman's and the contaminating spirit—will then engage in a vigorous struggle. This struggle often demonstrates through very dramatic body movements and gestures that the shaman's spirit is superior, and the contaminating spirit is subdued or cast out.

The shaman has most often been viewed as a key player ministering to the physical and mental well-being of a community, and anthropologists have always considered that role to be of utmost importance. The shaman can create and enforce a set of behavioral standards that will serve to create and maintain social order (remember the disciplining function of supernatural belief systems discussed earlier). However, as Michael Forbes Brown has shown, the shaman can also have a malevolent or dark side that is used to explain misfortune for a community; that is, the shaman is made the scapegoat (Brown 1989). Among the Aguaruna of northeastern Peru, illness and misfortune are believed to be attributable to the spirit darts that are sent by shamans from other communities. When someone in a community falls ill or dies, the shaman is able to identify the person responsible and thus set the stage for a victim's family to achieve reprisal and revenge.

Priests. The term **priest** is used by anthropologists to describe a special type of supernatural practitioner. Priests are often called by other terms—chaplain, pastor, or monk, for example. All of these practitioners have the same basic character and function, whatever they are called. Priests are supernatural specialists who hold a well-established place in societies that have centralized authority. Typically priests are part of organized agricultural societies. Agricultural societies, you will recall from Chapter 10, are stratified societies with central leadership and authority. Priests are specialized, full-time practitioners who are supported economically by the groups they serve. They perform regular calendrical rites and rituals that are fixed and serve the entire community. That is, the rituals follow a prescribed pattern and are always performed the same way. A priest learns rituals, protocols, and doctrines from other priests and typically performs rituals in a place of worship such as a temple, shrine, or sanctuary. Unlike the shaman, who is born with special qualities or has a special connection with the supernatural, the priest must *learn* how to be an intermediary to the supernatural world. The key difference between shamans and priests, then, is that priests undergo structured, formal training. Priests are part of a large bureaucracy, and there are often hierarchies of priests within their belief system such as that of the Catholic Church with the pope, cardinals, bishops, and priests.

priest
A full-time supernatural practitioner who is part of a bureaucracy.

Among societies with chiefs or kings (centralized political authorities), these officeholders may also have priestly functions. They may perform rituals associated with planting and harvest or attempting to control the weather. In other words, they serve as the political authority and at the same time are the primary supernatural authority. In other chiefdom and state societies the political and religious organizations and roles are separate.

RITUAL

Ritual is behavior that is formalized, is regularly repeated, and has symbolic content. It connects the natural and supernatural realms for individuals and for groups. Most anthropologists use the term as an analytical tool and primarily in association with religion. However, not all participants of formal, regularly repeated behaviors that include symbolic content "believe" in the supernatural. Some observers have suggested that behaviors associated with the supernatural should be called sacred rituals and others should be called secular rituals. Ceremonies such as Christmas, birthday parties, new year celebrations, homecoming, and anniversaries incorporate rituals. For some cultures (and some individuals) the rituals associated with such events encompass the supernatural; for others they do not.

Ritual occurs in two major categories of ceremonies across cultures: **rites of passage** and **rites of intensification.** A critical difference between the two categories is that rites of passage focus on the *individual* and rites of intensification focus on the *group*. These rituals reinforce group solidarity—the cohesive and supportive functions discussed earlier—for both the individual and the society.

TRY THIS
Analyze

Identify three rites of passage in your culture or subculture that are identified and defined culturally rather than biologically. Remember to use criteria such as change in status or role.

Rites of Passage. Rites of passage mark culturally defined biological and social phases that humans pass through in their lives—birth through puberty, adulthood, and death. None of us can avoid these phases as we move through what can be referred to as the *arc of life*. Ceremonial rituals are created to mark movement from one socially defined role (behavior) and status (social position) to another. Remember that as an individual moves from one biological or social stage to the next, that person's social role and status within a group change. For these reasons, rituals associated with rites of passage, although they focus on the individual, also involve the group. The group may be an entire culture, or a smaller unit within the culture such as the family, a religious group, a sorority, or business associates. Group involvement in such rites is necessary because the group members must be able to change the way they interact with the individual in the future.

All cultures, for example, have different role and status expectations for individuals who are viewed as *children* and those who are viewed as *adults*. Likewise, when a person dies, the group is obligated to alter its relationship with the deceased. Everyone in the group is affected by the change. Involvement in the activities and ceremonies of others, either as a participant or an observer, prepares you for your own movement through the arc of life phases.

ritual
Behavior that is formalized, is regularly repeated, and has symbolic content.

rites of passage
Rituals associated with the social movement of an individual from one culturally defined role and status to another during the passage from birth to death.

rites of intensification
Rituals, often seasonal, that reinforce group solidarity, cultural values, and group social and political status relationships.

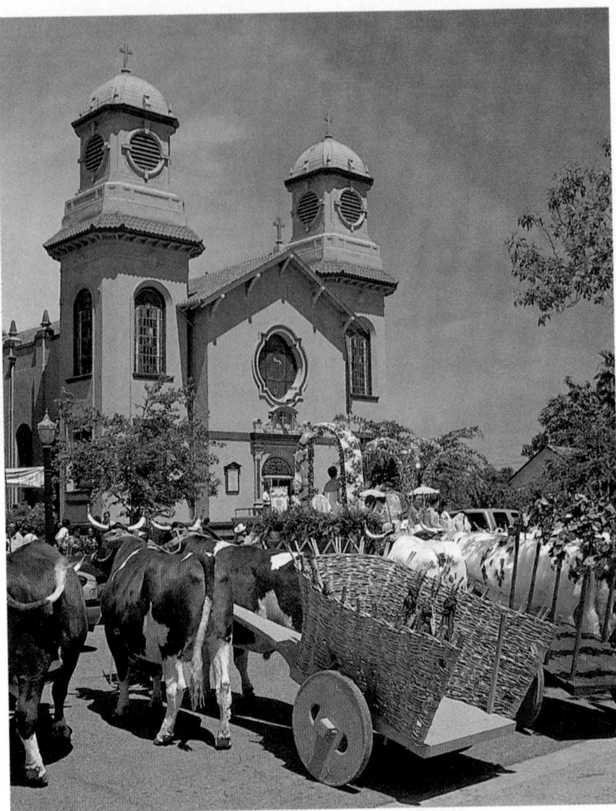
The ritual of blessing the cows is a traditional part of the *festa* celebration held by Portuguese Americans in Modesto, California. This celebration is a rite of intensification for this group.

TRY THIS
Hypothesize

The rituals associated with rites of passage in small-scale societies are often clearly defined. Some transitions in the arc of life among industrialized urban peoples lack such definition. Cite an example of a poorly defined status or role change in your culture (where specific cultural rituals are absent). Now write a hypothesis that might account for this lack of definition or associated ritual.

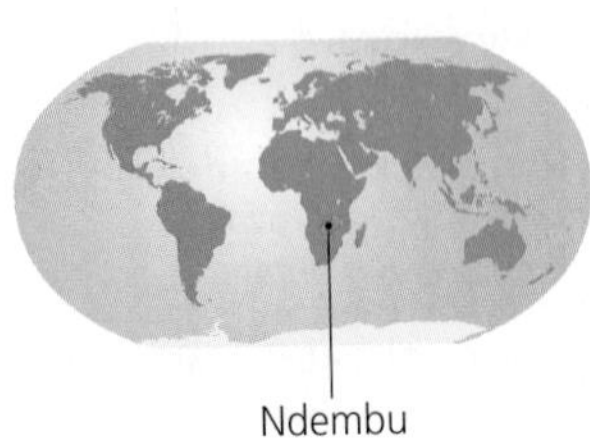

It is often easier to view these rituals by breaking them into three more or less distinct phases: separation, transition, and reincorporation. During the *separation* phase the individual is usually removed or separated from her or his present group. The *transition* phase is marked by a change of some sort happening to the person—circumcision, for example, in a puberty rite, or loss of virginity on the wedding night as part of the wedding ritual. *Reincorporation* occurs when the ceremonies reintegrate the person into the society as a member of a new group. For example, in the initiation rites of passage that occur among the Ndembu of East Africa, the initiate is often secluded and is considered ritually polluted (separation phase). During this period of seclusion the individual is stripped of clothing and possessions and is shown secret objects and given sacred knowledge; he also undergoes circumcision rites (transition phase). Finally, the initiate is reintroduced to society as an adult (reincorporation). Some analysts further subdivide the phases of rites of passage to show that they are not always clearly separated. Rather, the phases often blend from one to another. I have shortened the Ndembu rites considerably for purposes of illustration, and I've omitted discussing the rich symbolism associated with their rituals.

ANTHROPOLOGY AROUND US

Thanksgiving as a Rite of Intensification

Thanksgiving, the national holiday of giving thanks, is held in November in the United States and in October in Canada. Millions of people are caught up in preparations for this event. Families make travel plans to gather in one place; everyone discusses the menu; and family members buy and prepare special foods. It is the biggest travel holiday of the year. Federal and state offices close, and many businesses show their solidarity by also closing and giving employees the day off from work. Differences and disagreements within families are put aside for the day. These ritual preparations show our unanimity as families and as a nation.

Cultural values are reinforced when we give thanks to the deities of our subculture's belief systems. Some acknowledge their good fortune by saying a ritual blessing at the feast table or going to their place of worship for a special religious service. Some reinforce the value of helping those less fortunate than themselves by spending the day feeding the poor and homeless—people who have less to be thankful for.

The foods that are placed on the tables across the nation reflect and reinforce our many ethnic cultural heritages—turkey, ham, roast beef, lamb, enchiladas, kippered herring, curry, borsch, potatoes, rice, pasta, tortillas, sweet potato pie, pumpkin pie, lemon meringue pie, flan.

Status relationships within the family are reinforced when respect is paid to elders who prepare special dishes and regale the assembled family with tales of past gatherings and events. Seat placement at the feast table(s) is important, and it reflects and reinforces the social status of each family member (many adults remember when they were first allowed to leave the children's table and sit with the adults).

We prepare for a change in behavior as we shift into the winter season of celebrations—Hanukkah, Christmas, New Year's. Many are distressed by the appearance of decorations and songs that celebrate these holidays *before* Thanksgiving. Yet the day after the Thanksgiving ritual is historically the busiest gift shopping day of the year.

◎ What rituals can you identify that are part of your family's Thanksgiving celebration? What acts of solidarity and reinforcement of cultural values are associated with the rite of intensification known as the Fourth of July?

Rites of Intensification. Several features of rites of intensification are recognized. They involve rituals that reinforce (1) group solidarity, (2) values of the culture, subculture, or microculture, and (3) social and political status relationships within the group.

Paul Kutsche (1998) has also suggested that these rituals, which are often seasonal, prepare the group for a pronounced change in their environment such as the end of the harvest season or the arrival of migratory fish or birds.

The Day of the Dead celebration in Mexico (*Día de los Muertos*) may be analyzed as a rite of intensification. It is celebrated during two Catholic holy days—November 1, All Saints' Day, and November 2, All Souls' Day. Symbolism is incorporated into the rituals of the celebration, particularly in the form of skeletal caricatures in such media as masks, effigies, and candy. The celebration is a blending of traditional Aztec beliefs and practices that honored the dead with rituals introduced by Spanish priests in the sixteenth century.

The Day of the Dead celebration illustrates the major features of rites of intensification, plus those features delineated by Kutsche. Mexican people travel great distances to return to their natal villages for this celebration that honors and remembers deceased relatives (reinforcement of solidarity). Many families create altars (*ofrendas*) in the home to honor the dead. Special foods that were favorites of the deceased are prepared for the home altar and are taken to the cemetery (more solidarity). At the cemetery a Catholic priest holds a mass (reinforcement of cultural values). The presence of the Catholic priest also affirms the status and role of the church in explaining events such as what happens at and after death (status affirmation). The timing of the celebration in the fall prepares people for the seasonal environmental changes ahead.

REVITALIZATION MOVEMENTS

OLC
mhhe • com / lenkeit5e
See Internet exercises.

Throughout human history there have been organized **revitalization movements,** which have been identified by various terms: nativistic movements, revitalization movements, or millenarian movements. Examples of these include the Ghost Dance religion (1869 and 1889) in North America, the Mau Mau religion (1950s) in Kenya, and Vailala Madness (1920s) in Papua New Guinea. More recently such groups as the Branch Davidians (1990s) have exhibited features common to revitalization movements.

revitalization movement
An organized movement, which occurs during times of change, that involves perceived loss of traditional cultural values. A prophet or charismatic leader predicts a revitalized society if a program is followed.

Considerable literature has analyzed these movements, and classifications and theories about them abound. Regardless of the details and differences, various common features and themes are found. One frequent theme is that they often arise during times of a perceived crisis, such as a loss of traditional cultural values, or during a time of economic distress or increased awareness of inequalities within the social structure. A charismatic leader will articulate the specific concerns for the group—often after having received a

Men from the Island of Tanna in Vanuatu participate in a revitalization movement. By mimicking the behavior of Western soldiers (using bamboo poles as rifles) they believe that they can attract a messiah who will bring them material goods.

special communication with a god or having had a personal encounter with the supernatural. Such a leader is often called a **prophet.**

The leader, or prophet, will outline a set of behavioral changes or a program that will return the group to a better, revitalized state. These changes often require the members to be physically or emotionally isolated from the rest of society. Members will often change their residence, manner of dress, diet, or even their name. Each of these acts underscores the attempt to leave the present set of cultural traditions and values and return to a former set of traditions and values. Both recent and historic fundamentalist movements in all major religions exhibit features of revitalization movements.

The classic example of such a movement is the Ghost Dance (also called the Spirit Dance) religion that spread among Native American cultures of North America. This movement actually arose twice—first in 1869 and again in 1889—from the same tribal source, the Paiute near Walker Lake, Nevada. A Paiute prophet claimed that revelations had been made to him during a trance. In the trance state he visited the spirit land of the dead and was told that if certain rituals were followed there would be universal peace between Native Americans and the Euro-Americans. Many people believed that the prophet was a messiah sent by God. The message was modified as it spread among different Native American groups. Some groups believed that the Euro-Americans would disappear and their dead ancestors would return. The Plains Indian cultures that adopted this movement held the belief that there would be a return of the vast bison herds of the past. This movement spread through many of the tribal groups that had been impoverished and marginalized by more than

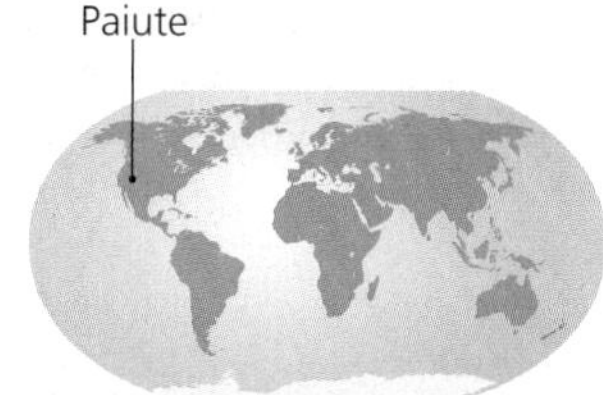

prophet
A person, usually charismatic, who has had direct communication with a god. Often receives a message that articulates a plan of action for the group.

A group of Arapaho participates in a Ghost Dance in the year 1893.

two hundred years of contact with the new Americans from Europe. When the promised changes did not occur after several years, the intense participation in the rituals declined and the movement largely died out. Alice Kehoe (1989) has suggested that the American Indian Movement of the 1970s could be viewed as a continuation of the Ghost Dance movement.

If we analyze such movements based on the previously discussed functions of religion, their popularity can be understood. The rituals and beliefs offer participants a cohesive and supportive group of like-minded, frustrated, and often unhappy people. Their cultural traditions are revitalized, and there is an opportunity to reinforce the group's history. Explanations are given for why conditions are as they are, and euphoria is achieved with the promise of deliverance from the current social and economic circumstances.

SUMMARY

Humans throughout the world distinguish between the natural and supernatural. Belief in the supernatural world, both supernatural beings and supernatural forces, provide answers to many of the questions of life—why we are here and why events happen. Belief systems function to support, educate, discipline, and explain for both individuals and groups. Supernatural practitioners such as shamans and priests serve both individuals and communities in their dealings with the supernatural. Rituals such as rites of passage focus our attention on biological and cultural transitions, whereas rites of intensification reinforce cultural values and promote group solidarity. When economic turmoil and rapid cultural changes occur, human groups often create revitalization movements, which can solidify group cohesion and offer the promise of positive change. From the perspective of participants, a revitalization movement usually means a return to older values. Such movements tend to dissipate when the change is not forthcoming.

Study Questions

1. Describe the functions of supernatural beliefs cross-culturally, and cite a specific example of each from your other assigned readings for this course.
2. Define ritual and describe in detail a common ritual that is practiced by you or members of your subculture.
3. Compare and contrast the general features of a belief system employing supernatural beings with one employing supernatural forces.
4. Describe the features of revitalization movements. Recount an example of such a movement and point out how it exhibits the features common to such movements.

OLC
mhhe • com / lenkeit5e
See Self Quiz.

Suggested Readings

Bowie, Fiona. 2006. *The Anthropology of Religion: An Introduction*, 2nd ed. Malden, Mass.: Blackwell. Readable introduction to the topic with excellent coverage of historical and contemporary scholarly analyses and an extensive bibliography.

Kehoe, Alice B. 2006. *The Ghost Dance: Ethnohistory and Revitalization*, 2nd ed. New York: Holt, Rinehart and Winston. The definitive treatment of this topic. Addresses history of the movement including the events surrounding the 1890 massacre at Wounded Knee Creek, South Dakota.

Mair, Lucy. 1969. *Witchcraft*. New York: McGraw-Hill. This is an excellent short cross-cultural and historical review of witchcraft.

Moro, Pamela A., and James Meyers. 2010. *Magic, Witchcraft, and Religion*, 8th ed. New York: McGraw-Hill. This collection of readings on supernatural topics serves as a good introduction to the topic. Extensive bibliographies are offered under topic headings that present a potpourri of interesting readings for more depth on any one topic.

OLC
mhhe • com / lenkeit5e
See Web links.

Expressions

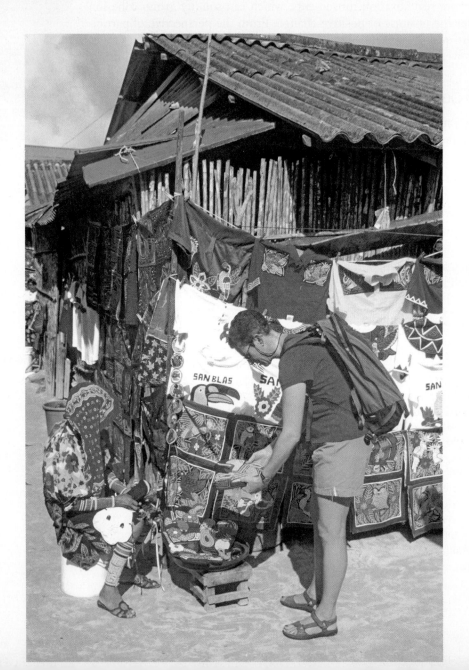

Is This Art?

Wet colors!!! The entire ceiling in the hall of bison looked as though it had just been painted. I had read, of course, about how fresh the paintings looked but was not prepared for this. None of the other caves that I have seen have paintings with this appearance. The colors are so vibrant. It has something to do with the particular type of seepage pattern of this cave, with the ceiling having a very slight incline to one side along which the seeping groundwater moves.

The above passage is my journal entry describing my first of three visits to the cave of Altamira in northern Spain, where artists painted wonderful images of animals fourteen thousand years ago. I have had the privilege of visiting more than a dozen of the caves in France and Spain where Upper Paleolithic artists expressed themselves, often in vivid color, on the cave walls and ceilings. To many artists and anthropologists today, these Upper Paleolithic caves represent the beginnings of human artistic expressions. Of course, there were likely many forms of expression that preceded these paintings, but they have not been preserved in the archaeological record.

Human artistic expression and its enculturation are multifaceted. At a family camp last summer, my two-year-old grandson was featured in his age group's talent show. I began to see this performance through my anthropological lens as his counselor called out, "Hey Robert, show me how ya get down." He replied, "No way." She then said, "Come on Robert, show me how ya get down." He replied, "Okay." Then the entire group repeatedly chanted "D, O, W, N, that's the way ya get down." Everyone danced to the chant, lifting their feet, kicking, waving their arms, and rocking body and head side to side. [Note: the meaning of "to get down" has changed through time, an example of the dynamic aspect of language. In this case "get down" meant to dance or party. Were the counselors aware, I wondered, of its sexual meaning as used in my generation?]

All chanting and dancing has the same basic function—uniting members of a group. It certainly had this effect on these children. This analysis is, of course, an etic view of the behavior. When I asked my grandkids what getting down did for them, both replied that it was fun—an emic view. While we seldom stop to think of the origin of expressive arts, their functions, or how we are enculturated to them, it is an interesting exercise.

The categories of expression that are surveyed in this chapter represent only a small sample of human expressive forms—prehistoric cave art, wood carving, textile art, body art, and music. I hope that these will pique your interest in finding out more about the cross-cultural nature of an expressive form of interest to you.

The objectives of this chapter are to:

- Delineate the parameters of human expression
- Describe the earliest known human expressive images from the Upper Paleolithic period
- Present a sample of aboriginal and contemporary expressive forms—carver's art, textile art, body art, and music
- Explore the functions of these human expressions

◀ A Cuna (or Kuna) marketplace in San Blas, Panama, displays creative *mola* art for sale to tourists.

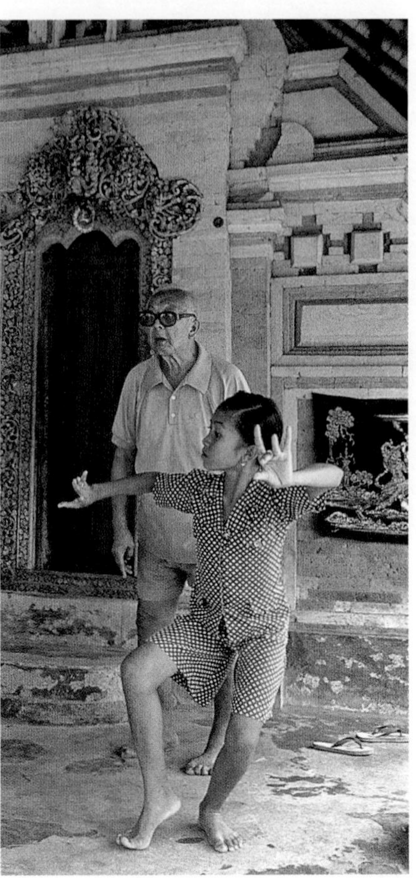

Apprenticeship is an important element in learning many forms of expressive arts. Young pupils learn the fine points of arm positions at the Joffrey Ballet School in New York City, and a master teacher instructs a dancer in Bali, Indonesia.

FORMS OF HUMAN EXPRESSION

OLC
mhhe • com / lenkeit5e
See chapter outline and chapter overview.

Forms of human expression are often the first aspects of another culture that we encounter. Our senses have come to recognize and feel comfortable with the sights and sounds that have surrounded us during our enculturation. The familiar becomes our yardstick in assessing the aesthetic quality of expressions. Since its inception, anthropology has brought the diversity of human expression to our attention. Human expressions—images, decorative arts, music, dance, storytelling, and the myriad other forms they may take—are cultural universals. Some forms of expression are found in all known human cultures. Many who study expressive arts cross-culturally and through time have concluded that they are fundamental to the completeness of human life.

Those of us who were raised in a society where creative artists exist as specialists who earn a living (or try to) by practicing their art tend to view and experience art, dance, and music in discrete categories of time and place. Art in contemporary North American culture is often peripheral to other aspects of life. We visit galleries and museums to view art, and it is placed in our homes to decorate our living space. In many other societies the arts are often more wholly integrated into everyday life and institutions. Some of this perception may be that we see with fresh eyes when viewing others' ways of life. If we pause and look around us, we can see many forms of expressive arts near home.

Expressive arts may be examined in several ways. One method takes the close-up approach of technical analysis, dissecting the content of decorative pigments or the structure of musical scales. Another looks at the functions of the expressive arts within the context of the culture that creates them. Both of these methods give an outsider's (etic) analytical view, which is emphasized here. Another approach is to try to understand or appreciate how expressive arts are experienced and viewed by those who create them (an emic view). Keep this approach in mind, and draw on your own experiences to represent this perspective.

TRY THIS
Define

Define *art* and make a quick list of features that you associate with art.

EXPRESSIVE BEGINNINGS: ART IN THE UPPER PALEOLITHIC PERIOD

The beginnings of human artistic expression are unknown. By the Upper Paleolithic, the archaeological period that dates from about 40,000 to 12,000 B.P. (before present), anatomically modern people in the Franco-Cantabrian region of Europe (France and northern Spain) began to produce what has been called parietal art (from the French *art parietal*) and mobile art (French *art mobilier*). **Parietal art** refers to all art executed on permanent features: walls, ceilings, and floors of rock shelters and caves. The term also applies to art on large blocks of limestone in or near inhabited rock shelters. **Mobile art,** as its name implies, is not fixed to any place and can be moved or carried about.

Franco-Cantabrian region

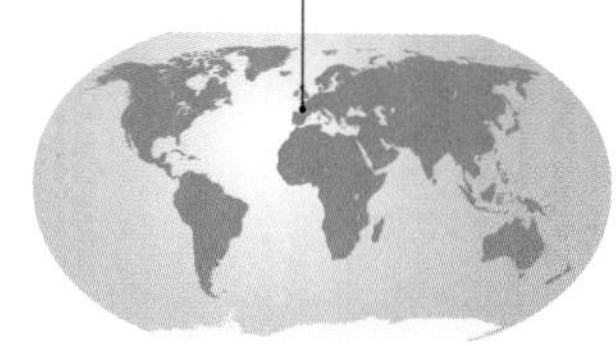

This discussion considers the images from the Upper Paleolithic as art—that is, things created for aesthetic purposes. Long-standing debates about the definitions of art (Conkey et al. 1997: 2) are not considered here. Parietal art is difficult to date, but recent developments in accelerator mass spectrometry have allowed the dating of paint samples. The paint pigment used in these caves can be dated in this way because some of it was made from compounds that included carbon-based material such as charcoal. In a recent analysis of thirty-four samples from six different cave sites, dates range from 12,180 ± 125 B.P. to 32,410 ± 720 B.P. (Davidson 1997: 149). Dates for isolated pieces of mobile art are between 26,000 B.P. and 32,000 B.P. (Davidson 1997).

parietal art
Art executed on permanent features such as cave walls, rock shelters, and large blocks of rock.

mobile art
Art forms that are not fixed to any place and can be moved or carried.

The Upper Paleolithic period French cavern Grotte Chauvet is filled with images of lions, rhinoceroses, horses, and bears. Other Upper Paleolithic French caves display images of different animals, such as bison and deer. Anthropologists do not have an explanation for this different emphasis in subject matter.

TRY THIS
Analyze

Defend the following statement: "Cave art represents a biased view of human expression during the Upper Paleolithic." What data would you need to back up this statement?

The well-preserved parietal art forms are firmly established in the Upper Paleolithic. Therefore, it is logical to presume that earlier forms existed but have not been discovered or have not survived in the archaeological record. The Upper Paleolithic cave art that has survived was sealed in limestone caves when the cave entrances collapsed. As recently as the early 1990s, a spectacular new cave, Grotte Chauvet, was discovered in France. The art at Grotte Chauvet was recently redated to 36,000 B.P., making it some of the earliest parietal art. Of the several caves discovered early in the twentieth century, most have suffered great damage due to the intrusion of bacteria, algae, and high levels of carbon dioxide created by human visitors. Most of these caves have been closed, or visits have been severely restricted, to preserve the paintings.

One of the most intriguing aspects of Upper Paleolithic cave art is the range of styles represented. Realism and naturalism are dominant, but abstraction, exaggeration, fantasy, portraiture, caricature, and elaborate decoration are found. Although many animals look slack and immobile, others appear in realistic and lively postures, such as the swimming stags of Lascaux Cave in France or the feline engravings from La Marche, also in France, that look as though they are in the middle of a roar. Bison predominate in the paintings at the cave of Altamira near the coast in northern Spain. The most spectacular frescoes in this cave are on the ceiling of one gallery, where twenty-five figures—crouching or lying bison in the

OLC
mhhe • com / lenkeit5e
See Internet exercises.

The deer on the ceiling of Altamira cave in northern Spain illustrates the use of distortion by Upper Paleolithic artists.

core group surrounded by standing bison and a red deer—are found covering an area of about 45 feet in length. These figures range from 4.5 feet to 6 feet in length. This ceiling has been hailed as the Sistine Chapel of prehistoric art and is viewed by some as coming close to an arranged composition (Conkey 1981: 24).

The bison at Altamira are very natural in appearance and attest to the competence of the artists in the use of what is labeled *tone*. Tone includes three properties—color, intensity, and value (the lightness or darkness). Other analytical aspects used in describing art may also be applied to the animals at Altamira. The use of line (which defines shape and form) and mass (the solidity of shapes) is apparent here. The bison were first outlined with a fine black line, and then color (reds, browns, and black) was applied. A washing or scraping technique was used to create shadings of the colors. Features such as eyes, nostrils, horns, and hooves were emphasized by incising the limestone surface. The effect was to model the bison's body with the use of light and shade. Also, natural rocky protuberances and bulges on the ceiling surface were incorporated into thighs, rumps, backs, and heads of the animals, making them even more realistic. There is harmony and balance to the paintings as well.

At the back of the Altamira gallery, on the ceiling behind the crouching bison, is a painting of a red deer. This doe was painted in the most subtle shadings of brown, taupe, and pale chamois. Amid the intense colors of the bison, it is an interesting contrast. There is another interesting aspect to the deer. She is in perfect proportion when viewed from the entrance to the gallery, but if one views her from directly below this section of the ceiling, her head is too small and her rump seems huge. This use of exaggeration of proportion was used by sixteenth-century artist Michelangelo in his statue of David (1501–1504 A.D.). The head and upper torso are out of proportion to the lower body if the statue is viewed from directly in front of it, but when viewed from below, with the statue on a pedestal, the head appears proportional to the lower body. This planned use of exaggeration by Upper Paleolithic artists is also found in other caves.

Author James Michener's comment when he first viewed the ceiling at Altamira focuses on the feature of this cave that most inspires those who view it:

> The thing that surprised me most, as I recall this amazing room, was the series of bulls constructed around rocky protuberances which jutted down from the ceiling. Mostly these extrusions are elliptical, but some are circular; they project eight or ten inches or perhaps even a foot, forming kinds of rocky hummocks standing forth from the rock pasture lands. On these humps the ancient artists, using a trickery not surpassed by Salvador Dalí, drew sleeping animals, wonderfully curled, with their feet tucked under them and their heads resting on their forelegs . . . the bulls look as if at any moment they might rise from their slumber. (Michener 1968: 616–17)

Each time I think about the art of these ancient ancestors I remember my first experience at Altamira, and I ponder their lives of fourteen thousand years ago. We know that these peoples were technologically sophisticated, as attested to by the thousands of artifacts and ecofacts that have been recovered by archaeologists. The artists sought various minerals, particularly ochre and ferrous and manganese oxide, which give gradations of color from light yellow through red, brown, black, violet, vermilion, orange, and gray. Technical analysis of prehistoric paint chips proves that these people mixed compounds to create just the right color of paint. The colors were sometimes mixed on stone palettes, which have been found with samples of colors spread in much the same way a modern artist would do (Marshack 1997: 100). They made brushes of juniper twigs, and they would even blow pigments through hollow bird bones to create the first airbrush painting. This latter technique achieved hazy outlines of a contour or space such as appears in the manes of horses at Lascaux. They built scaffolds inside of the cave of Lascaux in order to raise the artists to the part of the cave wall with the most desirable surface, and they lit the caves with stone lamps that held tallow and twisted juniper wicks.

TRY THIS
Consider

How would the experience of viewing art on the wall of a cave be different for people during the Upper Paleolithic compared to your viewing it today as a tourist or explorer?

We know what these people looked like and what they wore. More than four hundred drawings of humans have been found, although this achievement is dwarfed by the thousands of animal paintings and carvings of species such as bison, horses, ibex, red deer, roe deer, mammoth, elephants, lions, and bears. We know from the mobile art that they had a

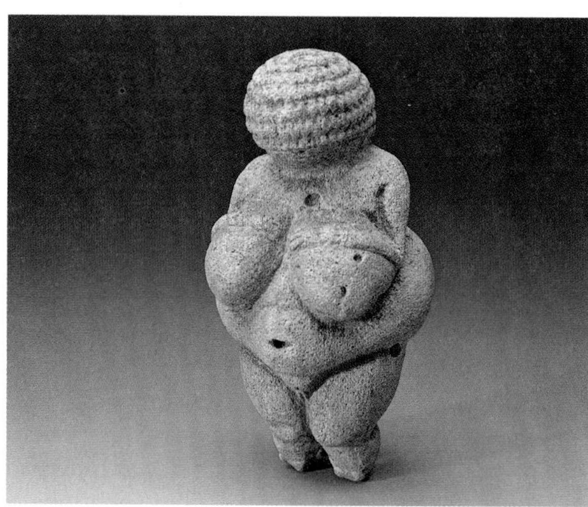

Small female images carved of ivory, bone, horn, and stone are examples of Upper Paleolithic mobile art. Such images may have served various purposes—as goddess symbols, magical amulets to ensure a safe pregnancy, fertility magic, or simply representations of female forms. This figure, called the Venus of Willendorf, is 4.5 inches high.

rich decorative tradition in the form of jewelry and carvings on utilitarian items. Despite knowing all of this, we do not know why they made these expressive forms. The same may be said of much of both indigenous folk art and contemporary art. We may analyze it according to content, form, type, and other comparative categories, but it is difficult to accurately know why people express themselves through art.

WHY DO ARTISTS CREATE ART?

Many reasons are offered for why people create art. Four hypotheses are offered here—art created for its own sake, art for use in imitative magic, art as a backdrop for ceremonies, and art as symbolism. The following discussion considers how these four hypotheses fit the case of Upper Paleolithic cave art.

Art for Art's Sake

The idea of creating art for its own sake is based on the argument that Paleolithic humans liked beautiful things and that the luxurious Upper Paleolithic environment provided the leisure time to develop art. Critics of this hypothesis argue that if Paleolithic humans liked art for aesthetic reasons, they would not have painted deep in caves that were difficult to get to. Others suggest that paintings are found in dark recesses simply because they first filled up wall spaces in the sheltered areas near cave mouths and progressively moved farther back in the caves. Unfortunately there is no real supportive evidence for this argument—some paintings are associated with living sites near cave entrances, but in some caves the paintings and engravings are found only deep within inaccessible areas of the cave. Studies have looked for correlations between location of art and a number of variables, but none has proven particularly successful. Contemporary artists often say that they create art simply because they enjoy the creative process.

Imitative Magic

One of the earlier hypotheses given for why prehistoric people created cave art was that the art was used for magic. The magic hypothesis is still popular today. In essence this hypothesis states that drawings represent attempts by prehistoric humans to control their world through the use of imitative magic. There are numerous ethnographic examples of imitative magic from around the world in which drawings are used in ceremonies, as with pygmy hunters drawing a picture of an antelope in the sand and shooting it prior to embarking on the hunt (Frobenius and Fox 1937: 22–23). This in itself, however, does not prove that the Upper Paleolithic drawings represent magical practices. In addition, quantifiable data to support this hypothesis are lacking. The number of animals that appear wounded or marked with projectiles in the European Upper Paleolithic caves is only 10 to 15 percent (Leroi-Gourhan 1967: 34; Hadingham 1979: 207).

Art as a Backdrop for Ceremonies

Ceremonies, such as rites of passage, have been suggested as possible reasons for the creation of cave art. Most proponents of this hypothesis cite as evidence the fact that rock paintings and engravings play important parts in the initiation ceremonies (rites of passage) of contemporary groups in both Australia and Africa. In these areas the engravings and paintings are used to instruct, explain, and teach.

Further, it has been suggested that if caves were used for ceremonies they would have been considered as sacred places by the cultural groups who lived in the area. Although this may be true, ethnographic parallels are lacking. Among the Australian aborigines, for example, anyone is free to admire the representations painted on the walls (Ucko and Rosenfeld 1971: 251). Among the Tiwi of Australia, children are expected to be present at all ceremonies, and they play by carrying out mock ceremonies in which adult behavior is mimicked (Goodale and Koss 1966: 198).

Some data support the argument for caves being used for ceremonies during the Upper Paleolithic. At the French cave of Tuc D'Adoubert, six rows of heel prints begin deep in the cave and fan out toward the entrance. At all known sites with footprints, both adults' and children's prints are present. For example, at Niaux Cave between one-third and one-half of the more than five hundred prints are considered to be those of children (Pfeiffer 1982: 177–79). This, it has been suggested, might indicate that children were brought to the caves for initiation ceremonies.

Art as Symbol

A number of researchers have suggested that prehistoric art such as that found in the Upper Paleolithic caves of Europe represents an early form of symbolism (Leroi-Gourhan 1967; Ucko and Rosenfeld 1967; Otten 1971; Marshack 1997). Symbols in the form of art are suggested as a means of the transmission of information. Some scholars who have argued for this interpretation have been quite ambitious in counting and mapping cave art figures. Researcher Leroi-Gourhan, for example, spent years visiting 66 out of 110 art caves and rock shelters in the Franco-Cantabrian region. He claimed to have identified pairings of animals in the art, such as horses with bison, and concluded that these were symbols representing males and females. His works have been heavily criticized on the basis of his statistical and other methodologies. Nonetheless, the idea of art as symbol is popular both in the interpretation of prehistoric art and in understanding contemporary art.

As noted earlier, one of the goals of archaeology is to establish chronological sequences (see Chapter 1 for review). Currently there is much interest in looking at prehistoric expressive material culture (art forms) within properly established chronological sequences (Morales 1997). This has not been accomplished in the past. Once we are able to sort out more precisely *when* particular cave images were made, we will be better able to integrate these peoples' expressive traditions with other cultural adaptations and variations at specific times and places, as well as view the process of artistic changes through time. In other words, when we can place the images within their proper temporal, cultural, and ecological contexts, we should be able to make more valid hypotheses about the reasons for the creation of prehistoric images. In the meantime these cave art images, at the very least, provide us with a window through which we can appreciate our rich and complex cultural ancestors.

DECORATIVE ARTS

In cultures around the globe there are an abundance of decorative art forms, which include decorative utilitarian objects, objects of adornment (such as jewelry), body art (tattoos, scarification, and body piercing), and sculpture. This section examines a sample of such decorative art, and discusses the functions of decorative arts in the cultures that create it.

Carving

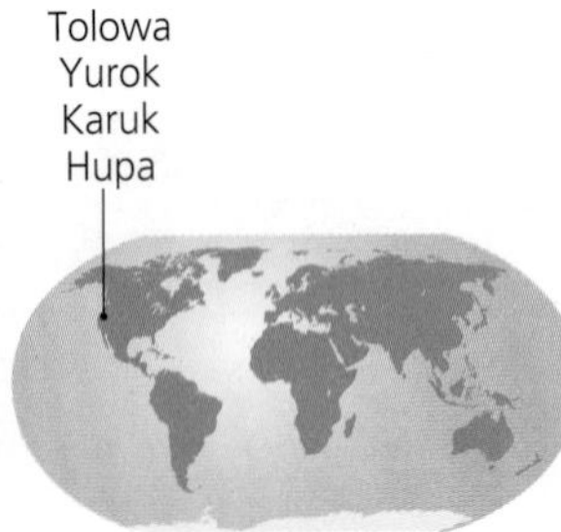

The wood, bone, and antler carving traditions of the native peoples of northwestern California illustrate expressive art that is an integral part of life. The purpose of this decorative art in these cultures is well known from ethnographic research. For the Yurok, the Karuk, the Hupa, and the Tolowa peoples of the Klamath River drainage region, the carving of wood, bone, and antler transcended the aesthetic function of adding beauty and pleasure to their world. Everyday use and display of the highly valued carvings also served an important social function by validating a person's inherited rank (Jacknis 1995). Emphasis on accumulated wealth and inherited social status was not unique to this group of Native Americans but rather was part of a long cultural tradition among the many coastal populations stretching from northern California to southern Alaska.

Members of the Yurok, Karuk, Hupa, and Tolowa cultures used a variety of objects to reinforce their social position. Valued items included large obsidian blades (up to 30 inches in length), white deerskins, and acorn woodpecker scalps. Decorated everyday household items, such as elaborately carved acorn cooking paddles and elk horn serving spoons, were also valued. Such possessions reinforced an individual's social status. The items could be purchased using strings of dentalium shell money, which was stored in intricate purses made from elk horn.

Artisans, almost always men, carved the acorn mush paddles and elk horn spoons with intricate geometric designs. Men of high social rank purchased and collected the elk horn spoons to serve their guests on ceremonial occasions. Low-ranking or poor individuals possessed far fewer elk horn spoons or used plain, undecorated spoons and acorn mush paddles.

Like any other element in a people's culture, art is continually changing. Too often anthropologists have inadvertently conveyed to the public the idea that the early cultures of North America changed little before their contact with Europeans. In fact, ideas and technologies were constantly being borrowed from peoples with whom they came in contact—other cultures within trade networks, for example. The early cultures of North America also borrowed from the nineteenth-century Anglo-Europeans who moved into their territories. This can be seen among the Yurok, Karuk, Hupa, and Tolowa carvers, who used European iron cutting tools to supplement and replace their own stone tools. The artistic tradition continues to evolve today as tribal carvers use modern band saws, gouges, chisels, files, and knives to complete their carvings.

Today carvers are also expanding the scope of their art by studying at contemporary art institutes and universities. The artists are borrowing indigenous designs from a century ago and combining them with new innovations to create an evolving tradition. The creations of present-day carvers are not confined to traditional places within the cultures of the

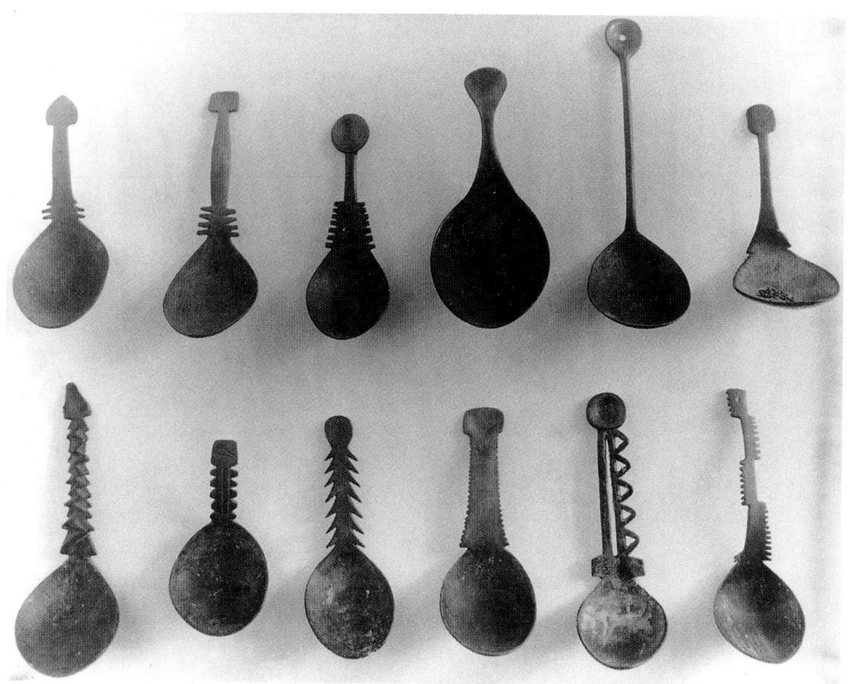

The carvers' art can be appreciated in the designs of these spoons carved from elk horn by the tribes of northwestern California.

A woman cooks acorn mush using a carved mush paddle.

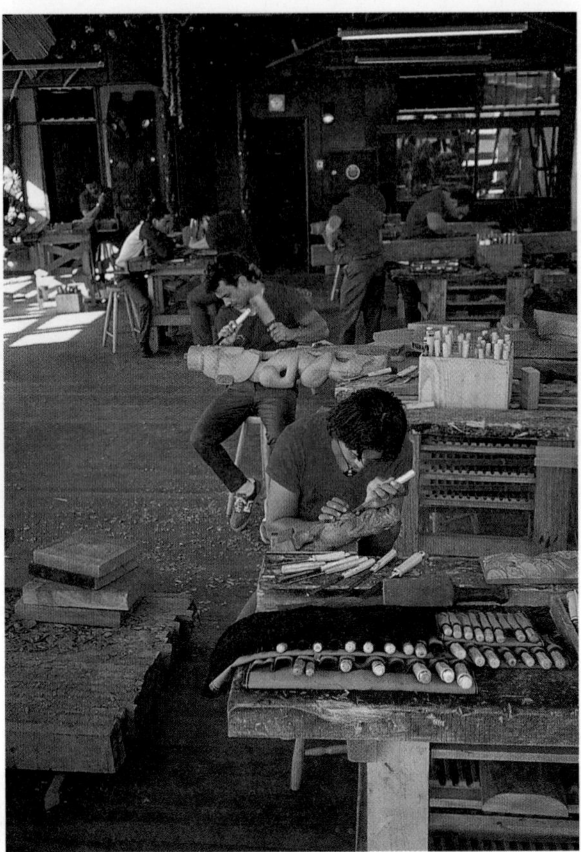

These contemporary Maori carvers in New Zealand apprentice at an art co-operative.

Klamath River drainage; they have found a new appreciative audience in the larger art world. The bold geometric designs of the wooden acorn mush paddles, elk horn serving spoons, and purses reflect a continuous link between the past and the future (Jacknis 1995).

Textiles

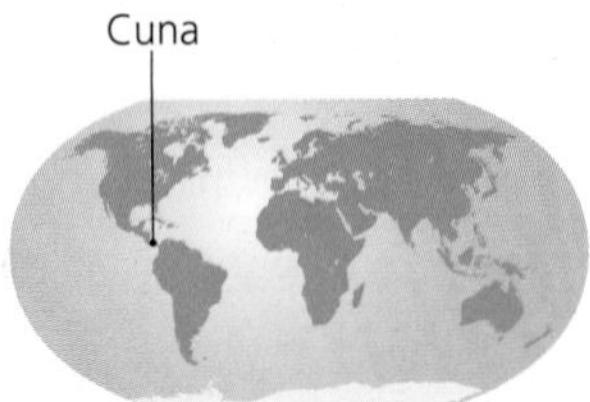

The Cuna (also spelled Kuna) of the island archipelago of San Blas, Panama, have a rich and varied expressive art in the form of *molas* (the Cuna word for a woman's blouse). These blouses are made of cotton, and the design is short-sleeved and boxy, something like a T-shirt in outline. Intricate patterns of geometric designs, stylized plants, animals, and humans are sewn on the front or back panels (or both) of the *molas*. The designs are a form of appliqué that involves from two to several layers of different colored cloth. The layers of cloth are basted together, and the design elements are formed by cutting through a top layer of cloth and

This *mola* once decorated the front of a Cuna woman's blouse. Note the layers of colored cloth that are exposed to reveal the design.

folding under the raw edges of the cut. Cut edges are then sewn down with hidden stitches. In this manner the color of the lower layer is exposed and the design is revealed. The traditional background color is black or a dark blue-black with designs in bright red, blue, yellow, orange, and green. Other colors are used but these are the most popular. Care is taken by the artists to create balance and harmony in their designs.

The origin of the *mola* appliqué technique is not known, but it developed after the introduction of manufactured cotton cloth, scissors, and metal sewing needles around 1900 (Salvador 1976: 171). The designs are believed to have evolved from traditional forms of body painting. The subject matter of the *mola* pictorial designs is taken primarily from the natural environment, but subjects include a girl's puberty celebration, recreational activities, religious themes drawn from missionaries, and political themes. Panamanian political candidates come to the islands to campaign, for example, and Cuna women create *molas* based on political party designs or even portraits of the candidates. *Mola* panels are often cut out of the *mola* blouse after a woman has gotten tired of it and sold to become a collectible art form in the United States and elsewhere. Cuna women take pride in the quality of their work and in showing it off. According to Mari Lyn Salvador (1976) *turista molas* are sometimes made and sold, but these are done quickly, the quality suffers (i.e., stitches are too large, colors are wrong, and design elements are not properly balanced), and the women who make them are criticized. A co-op was formed to create *molas* for sale, and it has a quality-control board.

TRY THIS
Consider

Is folk art produced for tourist souvenirs *authentic* art of indigenous peoples?

Throughout the world, traditional cultures are producing their art for outsiders, which can make good economic sense. Today Cuna women may choose to wear either contemporary Panamanian-style dress or the traditional *mola* and skirt. The *molas* that many of them make are still a functional art allowing aesthetic expression and storytelling; they are also considered a commercial fine art because "they adhere to culturally embedded aesthetic and formal standards" (Graburn 1976: 6). In contrast, souvenir-produced art, produced solely to make money, is considered to lack quality and does not reflect traditional aesthetics or standards of the culture.

Body Art

The use of the human body as a canvas for artistic expression has a long and rich history in world cultures. Permanent forms of such expression include body decoration, modification, and mutilation. The most common body arts include tattooing, piercing, scarification, branding, and creative dentistry. Temporary forms of body art include hairstyles, nail color, body painting, and temporary tattooing (such as the skin decorating called *mehndi* that uses a temporary dye derived from the leaves of the henna plant). Tattooing conventions and the publication of tattoo magazines in the 1970s and 1980s marked the modern body art revolution. People who did not consider body art forms a legitimate means of expression were exposed to it and began to embrace it. Major world museums now include photographic exhibits of contemporary body art in its various forms.

TRY THIS
Discuss

Who owns indigenous artistic designs such as *moko* facial tattoos? Should a person who is not a Maori be allowed to be tattooed with a *moko* motif?

Ethnographic literature describes various functions of body art, from symbols of initiation, status, familial clan or other group membership to decorative expressions of individual personality to enhancement of sexual attractiveness. Among the New Zealand Maori for example, the facial tattoo known as *moko* communicated extensive personal information, including clan membership, social rank, and personal history. This information was conveyed according to the location and the type of design. The *moko* application style was unique. The lines of the design were carved deep into the skin with an adz-like blade and dyes were applied. Spaces between the dyed lines became raised so the designs had texture as well as color. This combination of body art texture and color may have originated with the culture's elaborate wood-carving traditions. Traditional *moko* tattoos

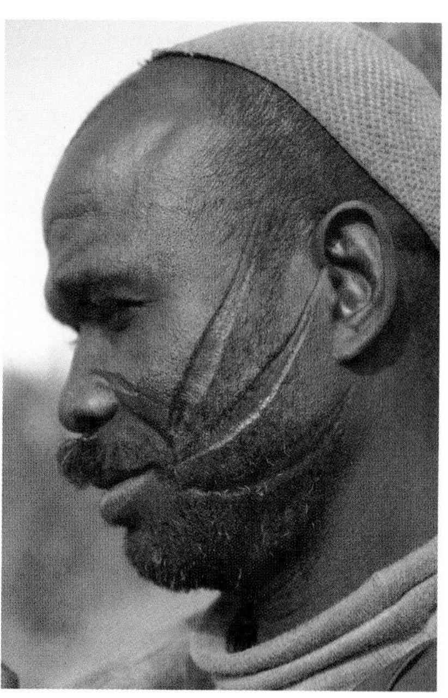

This New Zealand Maori wears a traditional full-face tattoo, and this Bobo man in Burkina Faso exhibits scarification. Many forms of body art have long histories across cultures.

are gaining in popularity as younger Maori assert their cultural identity. Elements of *moko* are now appearing in body art designs worldwide.

In most cultures, tattooing involves piercing of skin in various designs and the introduction of pigments—as with the tattoos of the yakuza gangsters in Japan whose tattoos signify group membership. Perhaps this was the purpose of some of the more than fifty tattoos on the 5,300-year-old Iceman found frozen in a glacier in the Alps between Austria and Italy. Or perhaps the parallel stripes around his wrist, the series of lines on his lower back and ankle, and the cross behind his knee marked his rank or status, were decorative, or served as protective symbols. Certainly body art may serve similar purposes today. Other ancient evidence of body decoration includes clay images with facial tattooing found in Osaka, Japan, that date to 2,500 years ago and tattoos on Egyptian mummies of 4,000 years ago.

Scarification is practiced among peoples such as the Nuer and Mbuti of Africa. Scarification is painful and is often included as part of ritual rites of passage. It may be for decoration or signify clan membership or symbolism. The practice of foot binding in China, prohibited since 1911, exemplifies body mutilation that was once considered beautiful and sexually stimulating. Mayan peoples in Guatemala, southeast Mexico, and Belize included, in addition to tattooing, scarification, and piercing, the molding of babies' heads to create what was considered an attractive sloping forehead starting at the bridge of the nose. Cultural ideals of what is beautiful vary and also change. Compare the practices mentioned here with current trends in molding healthy bodies with the use of silicon implants.

TRY THIS
Consider

Why do you or a friend have a tattoo or a piercing? Why do some mothers pierce their young female infants' ears? Why do many women modify the shape of their feet and body by wearing high-heeled shoes?

ANTHROPOLOGY AROUND US

Storytelling Festivals

The art of storytelling is enjoying a rebirth. All over North America and the world, modern peoples are discovering that there is drama, poetry, wisdom, and just plain fun in tales told. There are now many annual storytelling festivals that include workshops as well as performances.

Long before the written word, storytelling was a key device used by peoples to convey their history, values, etiquette, and religion, and to entertain. Theodora Kroeber in her book *The Inland Whale,* a classic collection of stories of the tribes of California, concludes that such stories with their patterns and structures represent the roots of later written literature.

Storytellers perform as they retell a tale. They use voice, gestures, facial expressions such as widening or rolling of the eyes, and body language to emphasize or embellish the narrative. A good storyteller draws the listener into the story as it unfolds. Johnny Moses, a Tulalip Native American from Vancouver Island, British Columbia, Canada, exemplifies the master storyteller. In his story about how the daily cycle of night and day came to be, for example, he weaves imagery, colors, and humor into a story that also teaches about values and the world around us. In this story, Ant Lady is in a contest with Bear Man. Ant Lady wants day-night cycles to continue; Bear Man wants a year of night so that he can sleep. Her steady, calm persistence during the contest helped her prevail over the large, fierce, and arrogant bear. That is why we have night and day. The storyteller's art joins with other forms of human expression to create a mosaic of that which makes us human.

◎ Recall a story told to you as a child. Did you realize as a child that the story embodied cultural values? Do you recognize as an adult that the story had a message?

MUSICAL ARTS

Expressive Beginnings

The oldest musical instruments from archaeological sites are flutes and flute fragments. Flutes constructed of mammoth ivory and vulture bone found in Hohle Fels cave in Germany date to between 35,000 and 40,000 years old. The early agricultural site of Jiahu in the Henan Province in Zhengzhou, China, has yielded six complete flutes made from the ulnae of cranes. There are another thirty fragmentary flutes from this site as well. Radiocarbon dating has established that the flutes are 9,000 years old. The best-preserved flute has been played and the sounds analyzed. This flute and the other five complete ones have seven main holes. Further testing of replicas of each of these bird-bone flutes is aimed at comparisons of the musical scale produced by these flutes and the current Chinese six-tone scale and seven-tone scale (Zhang et al. 1999: 366–68).

Ethnomusicology

The study of the music of a contemporary society within the context of that society is called **ethnomusicology.** Some anthropologists study musical sound structures, the people who make the music, and the cultural context in which the music is played. There are also specialists from the field of music who study world music within the context of its making. Both are considered ethnomusicologists. Ethnomusicologists have both the perspectives and interests of the social sciences and the humanities.

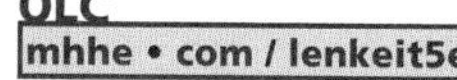

See Internet exercises.

Music, as it is created by humans, is different from natural musical sounds such as birdsong. One difference is that human music involves tonality—fixed scale systems. In Western music the tonal scale involves seven basic tones. In non-Western cultures, five-tone scales are common, and seven-tone scales are sometimes used. The seven-tone scale uses tonal intervals different from the European seven-tone system. Arabic music has smaller intervals between tones, resulting in scales with seventeen steps, and there are many other tonal variations. When you have been enculturated to hear one set of tones, other systems sound strange or out of tune, and it is often difficult to pick out melodies (sounds that are produced in a sequence).

Rhythm (a steady succession of beats) and harmony (sounds produced at the same time) are other aspects of music that vary widely from culture to culture and even within the same culture. In Western music a waltz has one kind of rhythm, a tango another. Some modern pop music has a number of different rhythms that shift. In other cultures, two musical rhythms may be carried on at the same time. These are some of the more technical aspects of musical analysis. When, where, and why people play and listen to music is also of interest to ethnomusicologists.

ethnomusicology The study of the music of a contemporary society within the context of that society.

Our music helps to define who we are, whether we are composers, performers, or listeners. It contains history and social commentary and elicits emotional responses from joy to sadness. Music is integrated into our systems of worship, and it is used as a rallying point for political activities.

Folk music was once the only music. A family—or a group of families—got together and with or without the accompaniment of handcrafted instruments joined in and sang. It was a bonding time, a time for the enculturation of values, a time to socialize, and a time to have fun. Singing also accompanied work and play and ritual. Colin Turnbull, for example, emphasized how central singing was to the Mbuti of the Ituri Forest. They sang songs during the honey harvest, during the joyous monthlong *elima* (female puberty rite), and while celebrating a successful elephant hunt. It was when they sang the simple refrain "The forest is good" (Turnbull 1987: 84) during a *molimo* that Turnbull began to understand—singing was essential to the pygmies and their relationship with the forest.

There are, of course, many other forms of human expression—verbal arts such as the telling of stories and legends, poetry, and dance—and there are subcategories within each of these. I encourage you to choose a category of expression that you participate in and investigate it on the Internet. The more you know about other peoples, the more you will come to celebrate not only human diversity but also the important commonalities among cultures.

SUMMARY

Human expressive arts are ancient. They date archaeologically to the Upper Paleolithic period, beginning around 32,000 years ago with carving, sculpting, and painting. It is likely that they date to much earlier times, but so far we have not recovered direct evidence of them. Many hypotheses have been put forward to explain why people create art. These explanations suggest that the arts serve as expressive outlets for individuals, as symbols, as a means of identity and solidarity for groups, as educational tools, and as a means of connecting with the supernatural.

Study Questions

OLC
mhhe • com / lenkeit5e
See Self Quiz.

1. Describe three features of Upper Paleolithic cave paintings that are also found in contemporary paintings.
2. Discuss two hypotheses that explain the purpose of prehistoric cave art, such as that at the Spanish cave of Altamira. What evidence is there that these are valid explanations for prehistoric art? Are they valid explanations for contemporary art?
3. Using either the example of wood carvings of northwestern California native peoples or the Cuna Indians of Panama, describe how expressive art is integrated into the everyday lives of a society. Compare and contrast this with art in your own life.

4. Describe past and present use of the human body as a canvas for expression.
5. What do ethnomusicologists study?

Suggested Readings

OLC
mhhe • com / lenkeit5e
See Web links.

Anderson, Richard L. 2004. *Calliope's Sisters: A Comparative Study of Philosophies of Art.* Upper Saddle River, N. J.: Pearson. Anderson focuses on the arts in ten societies, noting cultural similarities and differences in how they view their artistic traditions.

Conkey, Margaret W., Olga Soffer, Deborah Stratmann, and Nina Jablonski, eds. 1997. *Beyond Art: Pleistocene Image and Symbol.* Memoirs of the California Academy of Sciences, number 23. San Francisco: California Academy of Sciences. This is an excellent collection of papers that cover a range of topics about prehistoric art. Particularly impressive are the four articles that discuss the analytical methods, from dating to technologies of image making, and articles in section 4 that explore the interpretive process, including a consideration of context as an important part of interpretation. This selection also provides an excellent bibliographic source for additional reading.

Layton, Robert. 1991. *The Anthropology of Art*, 2nd ed. Cambridge, England: Cambridge University Press. Considered to be an outstanding introduction to non-Western art forms, this book addresses the difficult problem of what constitutes art across the diversity of artistic expressions found cross-culturally. Layton makes continual reference to an understanding of the cultural context in grappling with this dilemma.

Miller, Jean-Chris. 2004. *The Body Art Book: A Complete, Illustrated Guide to Tattoos, Piercings, and Other Body Modifications.* New York: Berkley Books. This little book combines a good historical overview of the major types of body art with lots of detail about contemporary designs.

Rosenberg, Donna. 1997. *Folklore, Myths, and Legends: A World Perspective.* New York: McGraw-Hill. Covering all parts of the world, the 120 verbal stories introduce a novice to the historical and cultural context of stories about heroes, fools, tricksters, parents, children, and animals. Her introduction offers an essential conceptual framework for an academic analysis of myths, legends, and folktales.

APPLYING THE ANTHROPOLOGICAL PERSPECTIVE

PART 3

THE UNIQUE PERSPECTIVE OF ANTHROPOLOGY HAS BEEN USED TO FOCUS ON HOW CULTURE CHANGES. Archaeological and ethnographic data, together with outcome analyses of programs of directed change, contribute to our understanding of the *processes* of change. We have learned, for example, that the human factor of cultural values and traditions may undermine the success of change programs.

Much of anthropology involves academic research, but we are also applying our findings to situations outside of academia. The anthropological perspective is relevant and useful in our everyday lives—I hope that you have seen this as you've analyzed, hypothesized, compared, and pondered in the various Try This boxes. The following chapters offer a glimpse of specific ways that anthropology can be applied, and how it can aid our understanding of the processes of culture change both locally and globally.

Chapter 13 offers what we understand of the processes of culture change and globalization and how this understanding can be used in our communities, jobs, and lives. Chapter 14 offers glimpses of the specific ways that anthropology can be applied by summarizing case studies in which anthropology made a difference. The chapters are grouped together because this is the "So What?" part of the book. You have read about anthropological perspectives, methods, and theories, plus cross-cultural data in many categories in Part I and Part II. Part III is about how all of the foregoing can be *used* to make a difference in our lives.

◀ All aspects of culture are dynamic. The Chinese city of Chongqing illustrates the blending of old and new.

Culture Change and Globalization

What Have We Learned?

▲ Culture change is evident in this Chinese village in Sichuan Province, where fifty herder families installed wind generators or solar-power generators.

The warmth of the sand beneath our toes, the sounds of waves lapping the beach, and the companionship of old friends lulled us into reminiscences. We had been away nearly four years, though we had kept in touch by mail and the occasional phone call. The beach was the same. As one looked north toward the small harbor one saw the same three fishing boats moored at the quay. The rocky cliffs to the west still held the monument to Christopher Columbus (local legend claimed that this coast was Columbus's first sighting of land upon his return from his explorations of the New World). To the east the high cliffs were as inspiring as they were when we regularly hiked along them.

The view to the south was a different matter. I stood and turned my back to the waves and faced a skyline that I barely recognized. There were several new high-rise apartment buildings. Two tall cranes were in constant motion lifting prefabricated wall sections up to the third floor of another condominium complex under construction. According to our friends, their quiet little village had been "discovered," and a real estate boom was on. This, of course, meant a boost to the local economy. But the negative side of this was that most of the building was for holiday residences whose owners spent only the month of July or August in the village. The year-around residents still numbered less than 2,000. During the summer 10,000–12,000 people converged on the area, bringing around-the-clock partying and trash along with their *pesetas* to spend. Our old landlord expressed concern and dismay that so much of the change was haphazard and unplanned, spurred by outside interests and money. A thoughtful man, he looked beyond the improved economic climate and worried about the long-term effects on the traditional culture of locals. Similar issues face people all over the globe. My local newspaper has carried headlines about parallel issues for the past year. The lack of foresight has resulted in major problems with infrastructures such as parks, sewers, schools, and roads to accommodate the traffic brought by the significant numbers of new residents to the area.

Cultures are constantly changing. Some change is accidental; some is by choice; and some is forced on people, as during colonial rule, war, or occupation by postwar victors. The pace of culture change seems to be accelerating everywhere, as it is in the Spanish village where I conducted fieldwork, and as it is in my hometown. In my community, as in the community in Spain, it is the lack of planning and short-sightedness regarding possible consequences of changes that are causing problems. The anthropological view of the processes of culture change can help us keep a perspective on what is happening around us and can be used to assist in planning programs for change, both near and far. This chapter addresses some of these issues.

The objectives of this chapter are to:

- Describe how culture changes and methods for studying change
- Consider lessons learned from directed-change programs
- Discuss issues of globalization
- Examine issues of culture change in urban settings

HOW CULTURES CHANGE

Data from studies in archaeology and cultural anthropology point to two primary sources for culture change: internal sources and external sources. Ideas and material culture items are recycled every so often within a culture (fluctuations), and new ideas or combinations of already existing ones (innovations and inventions) are generated within a culture and add to it. The areas of such changes range from technology to ideology.

Diffusion is responsible for most change and is a primary example of an external source of change. Many agents act to bring about diffusion (borrowing) between cultures—contact on territorial borders, during trade missions, during colonialism, during war and imperialism, and from contact on the Internet. In the distant past all diffusion occurred as a result of people's movements. Whenever people come into contact with one another, there is the possibility that one group will borrow an idea from the other group and incorporate it into their own customs, traditions, behaviors, technologies, and ideologies.

The process of diffusion that is termed **acculturation** involves the incorporation of knowledge, ideas, behaviors, and material creations from a different culture as a consequence of prolonged contact with that culture. The term is used primarily to refer to what happens to individuals or groups who immigrate to a society that is not part of their birth culture, but it can also refer to a native culture group changing due to occupation of their region by a dominant culture. Such individuals are enculturated with the culture of their birth; they become acculturated to their adopted culture (or the dominant occupying culture) over time.

We have evidence of the process of diffusion in the earliest written records and continuing throughout historical times. There is also much archaeological evidence of the diffusion of material culture in prehistoric times. Today, with the advent of global electronic communication, the process of diffusion and acculturation has accelerated.

HOW CHANGE IS STUDIED

There are numerous approaches to studying culture change. Each has its advantages and drawbacks. A combination of these approaches may give us the best view. A careful scrutiny of the *archaeological record* can reveal patterns and trends of culture change. For example, the diffusion of methods for raising domestic plants has been documented archaeologically. Research and analysis of *historical records* provide documents about change over time in such public aspects of culture as politics and economics. But other aspects of culture, such as the lives of everyday people, or women, may not be represented.

acculturation
The incorporation of knowledge, ideas, behaviors, and material creations from a different culture as a consequence of prolonged contact with that culture.

The ethnographic approach of taking *life histories* enables us to learn about culture change by talking to elder members of a culture and asking them to recount aspects of their lives. This information may be, in the absence of written documents or archaeological evidence, the only available way to gain some idea of how a culture has shifted and readjusted through time. Of course, selective memories may render some of this information suspect.

Documentation of change can come from *ethnographic restudies*, although restudy does not tell us what happened during the time between the studies, nor does it point to the processes of change. Finally, **impact studies** use ethnographic methods to look at a situation during and/or after a program of planned cultural restructuring has been implemented. Such studies often lead to an understanding of how change occurs, particularly with ongoing research. Such analytical approaches suggest impediments or stimulants to culture change, particularly if patterns emerge when studies are compared.

TRY THIS
Critique

Point out how and why the data acquired through historical records and life histories may not be accurate.

CULTURE CHANGE: A BRIEF HISTORICAL OVERVIEW

The discipline of anthropology began in the 1860s when European colonialism and imperialism was well under way. Theoretical perspectives at the time reflected an emphasis on social evolution, influenced by Charles Darwin's theory of biological evolution written in 1859. The **unilineal** (single line) **evolutionist's** perspective of early anthropologists, such as E. B. Tylor, who wrote his classic *Primitive Culture* in 1871, and Lewis Henry Morgan in his *Ancient Society* (1877), emphasized that every culture proceeded through a series of successive stages. Morgan stated that "The latest investigations respecting the early condition of the human race are tending to the conclusion that mankind commenced their career at the bottom of the scale and worked their way up from savagery to civilization through the slow accumulations of experimental knowledge" (Morgan 1963: 3, originally published 1877). No stages were skipped. Morgan's cultural evolutionary stages of savagery, barbarism, and civilization focused on cultural differences in food-procurement strategies and the technology that accompanied these at each stage. He proposed that all cultural groups progressed, or evolved, through these stages, and he gave specific criteria for each stage, such as cultures in the stage of savagery procuring food through foraging, hunting, and gathering and using tools such as the bow and arrow. Barbarism included the innovation of pottery, the domestication of animals and cereal plants, and in the later part of this stage, the smelting of iron ore. Civilization was marked by the invention of the alphabet. *Ancient Society* also included detailed discussions on kinship

impact studies
Ethnographic study of a situation to document effects of change. May take place during and/or after a program of cultural restructuring.

unilineal evolution
Early theoretical school that postulated that all cultures proceeded through a series of successive stages.

and political organization of societies and how these altered as subsistence strategies changed. Note that at the top of this sequence, and that of others proposed by the unilineal evolutionists, were the culture groups of the researchers themselves, which were considered "civilized." This means, of course, that an ethnocentric perspective guided the analysis.

These early models attempted to explain the quickly accumulating data regarding the many differences and some of the similarities between cultures. Unfortunately much of the data was incomplete, and field methods were inconsistent; indeed much of the information used in early evolutionary models came from letters, memoirs, and accounts of European and American missionaries, the military, explorers, and merchant seamen. Remember that the development of anthropological methods was just beginning. From our perspective today, we understand the early paradigms to be somewhat simplistic and incomplete. I like to consider, however, that Morgan and others of his time were making bold attempts to understand the world's cultures and how they developed over time. Additionally, Morgan, at least, had spent years working among the Iroquois (first as an attorney representing them in a legal dispute over land and later doing fieldwork) so he had some firsthand knowledge. Alas, we know today that such evolutionary models and the data generated were used by governments, bureaucracies, and individuals to fuel colonialism. From the indigenous peoples' view, this anthropological model was used to suppress and exploit. And we are more than a bit embarrassed that early anthropological data contributed to this.

diffusionism
Early theoretical school that explained the origin and spread of artifacts and ideas through borrowing between cultures.

historicalism
Theoretical school, established by Franz Boas, who hypothesized that each culture had its own particular history that could be documented through repeated ethnographies. Comparisons of many such histories could uncover underlying principles of culture change. Also termed historical particularism; American historicalism.

heliocentric diffusionism
Diffusionist school that pointed to ancient Egypt as the center of cultural innovations and inventions that spread around the world.

Responses to the models of the unilineal evolutionists came from two theoretical schools that rejected the evolutionary perspective: **diffusionism** and **historicalism** (also labeled **historical particularism,** or **American historicism**). The diffusionists focused on explaining the origin of artifacts and ideas and how cultures developed through time. They saw the mechanism as diffusion, the notion of the borrowing between cultures as they came in contact with one another. One diffusionist group known as the **heliocentric diffusionists** thought that historical and archaeological evidence pointed to ancient Egypt as the center of cultural innovations and inventions, and those innovations and inventions spread from the Egyptian cultural center to other cultures, eventually reaching around the world. These diffusionists viewed Mayan temples as evidence of diffusion from the great pyramids of Egypt. With hindsight we can say that this hypothesis failed to account for the complexity of intercultural contact and diffusion and ignored the possibility of independent innovation or invention by geographically distant cultures. Nonetheless, this was an attempt to explain how cultures changed over time. Today we acknowledge the diffusionist contribution because the borrowing between cultures is an important aspect of how cultures change as evidenced in archaeological and historical data.

Historicalism began in the early 1900s with Franz Boas (1858–1942), an important early figure in American anthropology. Boas began the first anthropology department in the United States at Columbia University and taught most of the first-generation anthropologists in this country. Among his noteworthy students were A. L. Kroeber, Robert Lowie, Margaret Mead, Ruth Benedict, and Edward Sapir, all considered foremothers and forefathers of today's anthropology. Boas received his university degree in physics, but redirected his life's work to anthropology. He brought scientific rigor and methodology to bear on his new profession of anthropology. He insisted that data should be gathered in the field through participant observation and the detailed recording of a specific culture's features—customs, practices, rituals, tools, clothing. He dismissed earlier stage models of cultural evolution primarily because they lacked sufficient field data to support their claims about how cultures evolved. He argued that each culture had its own particular history of change and that these were researchable through repeated and fact-laden ethnographic studies. He further suggested that if such repeated ethnographies were done over extended periods of time, with many cultures, we might then compile ethnological data to uncover underlying principles of cultural change.

Meanwhile, archaeologists were busy accumulating different kinds of evidence of change through time via the material record. Unfortunately, those early researchers were hampered by a dearth of accurate dating methods and thus could not always determine whether widely separated geographical regions and sites were older, more recent, or contemporary with one another. This lack of time frame made investigations of cultural evolution elusive.

The radiocarbon revolution in the 1940s provided a time framework for archaeological sites and made possible investigations of culture change in prehistory. Similarly, in biological anthropology, with discoveries in genetics, there was a shift from describing human variation and fossils to explaining why and how change had occurred. Cultural anthropology followed suit, moving away from data gathering and description as an end in itself, and shifted to a greater focus on *cultural process*. You will recall that Chapter 2 discusses how this shift was embraced by anthropology as the discipline fine-tuned definitions of culture to include the processes of acquiring culture.

At the end of World War II, European countries focused their economic and social resources on rebuilding their war-devastated cities. The United States became involved in rebuilding efforts and sought to help peoples around the world. Many were surprised at the high failure rate of programs to assist change. Anthropologists conducted impact studies and gathered data to document the successes and failures. We began to understand both barriers and stimulants to change and to appreciate fully the holistic nature of culture and how its parts are integrated (Figure 13.1).

An important contributor to our understanding of the process of diffusion and acculturation was George Foster. He presented his analysis of what stimulated the modification of cultural behavior patterns and what

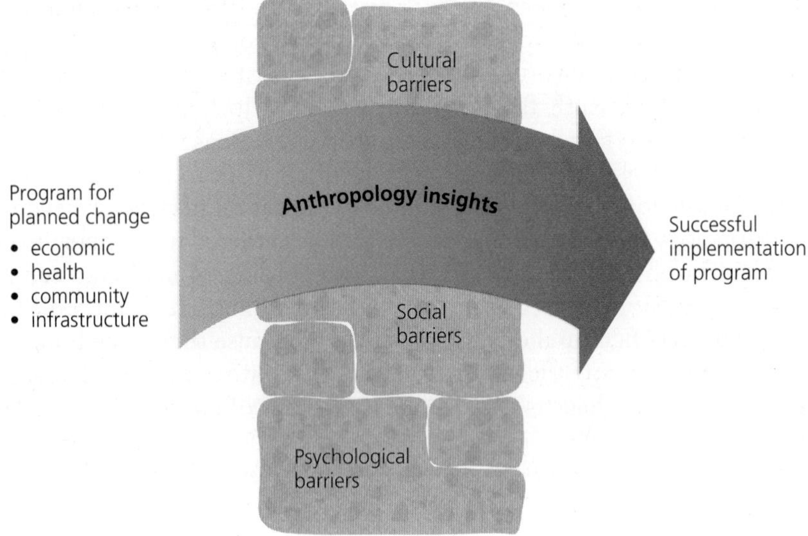

FIGURE 13.1
The insights of anthropology can aid the success of planned change or development programs.

forces prevented change in his seminal book *Traditional Cultures and the Impact of Technological Change* (1962). His analysis and the contributions of many others ultimately led to the specialty of applied anthropology.

Ethics Then and Now

But wait. Are attempts to effect change compatible with our discipline's ethical position? Historically, anthropologists' roles in directed-change programs and counterinsurgency activities caused numerous controversies. These issues are serious ones for all social scientists and strike at the core of how our data are used. Of course, hindsight often gives us a clearer view on the sociopolitical and economic climate during an incident.

Colonialism to World War II. The roots of anthropology developed during the age of colonialism. Some argue that anthropology was nurtured at that time to help solve problems for colonial administrators—today viewed by many as an unethical use of data. In the early 1900s, for example, anthropologists trained British colonial administrators in Africa, including colonial administrators of the Sudanese civil service (Farris 1973; Feuchtwang 1973; McFate 2005: 28). During World War I and World War II, numerous anthropologists worked closely with the American government. Margaret Mead, Gregory Bateson, Ruth Benedict, and others contributed to the war effort after the 1941 attack on Pearl Harbor. They worked for the Office of Strategic Services (OSS), the Office of War Information, and Army and Navy Intelligence. They aided these organizations in understanding the "national character" and cultures of enemy peoples. At this time such work was regarded as professionally appropriate.

1960s to 1990s. Project Camelot in the early 1960s engendered much debate and is often viewed as the beginning of the modern era for anthropological ethics. It was sponsored by the U.S. Army and the U.S. Department of Defense; it was designed by the Special Operations Research Office (SORO) at American University in Washington, D.C., and involved substantial funding. Project researchers were to be social scientists, including sociologists and anthropologists. The project's research design focus was to understand the factors within nations that contribute to unrest and revolution. The project goal was to provide comparative information plus recommendations to governments on how to respond to such situations. This information would help the American military predict the need for possible future military assistance to governments. In a broad sense the project involved how to bring about culture change. Preliminary background work was begun in Chile, although it was not a specific target country for the research in Latin America. Word of the project leaked to the liberal news media in Chile and their coverage provoked outrage in both Chile and the United States. Media commentary noted that Project Camelot's intent was to spy and interfere in other countries, including ones like Chile where the United States had good relationships. Investigations by the Chilean and American governments resulted in the Army canceling the project (Horowitz 1967: 3–67). Anthropologists and other social scientists were mixed in their reactions. Some contended that social scientists *should* be consulted by policymakers in government and that much useful comparative data would have been gained from the project. Others argued, on ethical grounds, that social science *should not* conduct research for a government's clandestine activities and that secret research was, in effect, spying. An additional central concern for anthropologists was stated by Nisbet: "For American social scientists at work in the field abroad, especially in those political areas where national patriotisms tend normally to be on trigger, Camelot was dynamite that might easily spell disaster for future foreign-area research everywhere" (Nisbet 1967: 314–15).

When yet another controversy arose over allegations of anthropologists engaged in counterinsurgency activities in Thailand during the Vietnam War, the American Anthropological Association (AAA) took action and adopted the Principles of Professional Responsibility (PPR) in 1971. This document emphasized that researchers should work independently from restrictions placed by governments and censure secret, covert activities. During the 1980s and 1990s, increasing numbers of anthropologists were employed outside of academia, which prompted revisions of the PPR. Applied anthropologists were concerned that they might be labeled unethical if they worked on any government-sponsored projects. The 1986 revised language of the PPR focused on responsibility to informants and employers and sponsors plus an emphasis on full, open access to research data.

OLC
mhhe • com / lenkeit5e
See Web links.

Recent Issues: Human Terrain System Program. A recent ongoing debate on ethics focuses on the Human Terrain System (HTS) program launched by the Department of Defense in 2007. A Human Terrain Team (HTT) consists of five persons, including anthropologists and other social and behavioral scientists. Research is carried out on local populations in regions of U.S. military deployment with the immediate goal of aiding the military in its understanding of the local sociocultural environment. Long-term goals include the desire to gain greater knowledge of local cultures and their relationships to larger geopolitical environments. HTTs work today in Iraq and Afghanistan.

To many anthropologists, the goals of the HTS program are much like the goals of the earlier project Camelot, and similar issues surround it. In 2008, the AAA Executive Board asked for a review of the HTS program by its Commission on the Engagement of Anthropology with the U.S. Security and Intelligence Communities (CEAUSSIC). The commission report (October 2009) was critical of the Army's HTS program, citing that anthropologists in a combat zone would find difficulty following the AAA ethical guidelines to avoid harm; additionally, such work would undermine the trust that anthropologists need in order to work in other world locations. Yet there are anthropologists who support HTS research and anthropologists who work as HTS team members. Anthropologist Montgomery McFate, who is employed by the U.S. Navy, writes:

> "Regardless of whether anthropologists decide to enter the national-security arena, cultural information will inevitably be used as the basis of military operations and public policy. And, if anthropologists refuse to contribute, how reliable will that information be? The result of using incomplete 'bad' anthropology is, invariably, failed operations and failed policy." (McFate 2005: 37)

The language of the current AAA Code of Ethics (adopted February 2009) focuses on openness and transparency in all research (in effect prohibiting secret research), but there is continued concern over the recruitment of anthropologists to work with national security agencies, the CIA, and the military. Might such work turn ethnographers into spies? How do we maintain ethical integrity and exhibit patriotism? One view is expressed by David Price: "As anthropologists we *should* brief government agencies, but we need to do so with complete transparency in ways that serve those we study" (Price 2007: 6–7).

Recent calls for revisions to the ethical code focus on strengthening it and whether or not to codify sanctions for unethical actions. While it would seem obvious that there ought to be sanctions for breaking an ethical code, the AAA cannot *legally* impose sanctions. Adherence to this ethical code, as with ethical codes of other social and behavioral science associations, is still up to the individual. Much debate and soul searching about ethics and our role—what it was, what it is, and what it should be—continues to engage AAA members.

So, *are* attempts to effect change compatible with the anthropologists' Principles of Professional Responsibility and Code of Ethics? Today, quite a spectrum of anthropological opinion exists on the entire issue of activism. Some believe that as scientists they should stay objectively neutral and not become involved in any planned and directed manipulation of a culture. At the other extreme are what some label **action anthropologists,** who believe that they have a moral obligation to take the side of indigenous populations whenever such peoples' rights to self-determination are violated. Still others take a middle ground with efforts to educate all sides in any issue. Whether one believes that anthropologists should be advocates or even agents of culture change, working with private groups or government agencies, our discipline was and is at the forefront of understanding change processes from within.

LESSONS LEARNED FROM DIRECTED-CHANGE PROGRAMS

Before turning to a consideration of anthropology's role in the study of global change today, I believe that a review of the highlights of George Foster's work will give important insights. Foster found that many change programs were initiated at the request of members of a culture or subculture. Yet aid and development change programs in agriculture, health care, and economics regularly failed and often made everyone uncomfortable. Foster documented the patterns of barriers and stimulants to the modification of people's customs, ideas, and behaviors. The barriers that emerged from his compilation of global development studies centered on cultural issues, plus some social and psychological issues. Technological and economic issues were not, he found, significant barriers to change, though both were often stimulants. Current globalization impact studies verify Foster's analysis regarding many of these barriers and stimulants. The following provides a quick sketch of Foster's work with specific examples analyzed. The issues he identified are directly relevant to issues of globalization today as discussed later in the chapter.

Cultural Barriers to Change

Different cultural values and attitudes are the most important barriers to change because they are difficult to overcome. These include

fatalistic outlooks (*Everyone dies; what will be will be.*)
tradition (*This is the way my father and his father tilled the land.*)
ethnocentrism (*We know more about mother earth than any college-educated city dweller; our way is best.*)

action anthropologist One who believes that he or she has a moral obligation to take the side of indigenous populations whenever such peoples' rights to self-determination are violated.

This squat toilet is in the international airport in Amman, Jordan. People from "sit toilet" cultures often find it difficult to change to living in houses with squat toilets, or using them while traveling.

TRY THIS
Evaluate

It is estimated that helmets worn by car occupants could cut traffic fatalities by 25 percent. Would you wear a helmet? Which of Foster's barriers to change would impede helmet wearing? Which would stimulate it? How were similar barriers overcome regarding kids' bicycle and ski helmets?

relative values (*I know motorcycle helmets save lives, but I like to feel the wind in my hair; I acknowledge the benefits, but I prefer my way.*)

norms of modesty (*I just could never have a male doctor examine me; I'd die of embarrassment.*)

The structure of cultures can themselves create barriers to change. First, there may be logical incompatibilities in the structure of cultures. An agricultural pest-control program, for example, might advocate the use of insecticides. The Buddhist belief system prohibits killing any life form, and therefore a program that introduced chemically based pest management to a society that practiced Buddhism would be incompatible with Buddhist cultural values. The belief system would be a barrier to the proposed pest-management program, and the program would likely fail.

Second, there may be unforeseen aspects of the culture's structure that could create barriers to change. These occur simply because the change is not compatible with the structure of the culture. Foster cites the case in the lowlands of Bolivia, where a new maize was introduced with the intention of improving people's diet. It had many advantages over the indigenous crop—higher yield, better nutrition, and rapid maturation. It also turned out to be difficult to grind and process for consumption. Nonetheless, it was very popular—but not for the reasons it was introduced. Rather, its popularity was due to the fact that it made an excellent commercial alcohol that sold well and at high prices (Foster 1962: 85).

The patterned ways people use their bodies can also create barriers to change. Many people of the world cultivate the soil by standing and bending at the waist, whereas others squat or rest on their knees. If an agricultural aid program to a country with these traditional body positions includes typical North American long-handled tools, the aid program may fail. Such aid is rejected because using the long-handled tools, and having to stand up straight to do so, results in back and shoulder pain.

TRY THIS
Explore

To experience just how your culture dictates the way you use your body, try sitting for a half hour on the floor with your legs stretched straight out in front of you (Inuit style), or try squatting balanced on your toes (Vietnamese style) for the same length of time.

Social and Psychological Barriers to Change

Group dynamics within a culture may be a source of barriers to change. Women who enjoy the dynamics of small-group interaction while cooking may be frustrated and unhappy if the North American architect of a new housing project in a developing country places the stove in a corner, facing a wall, away from the center of social activities (a common configuration in modern apartments in North America). Such cross-cultural errors have been made more than once and have derailed many projects. The reader has undoubtedly sensed the cultural ethnocentrism emanating from the architect in the preceding example. This is not to say that such errors are planned, but rather they result from a genuine lack of cross-cultural awareness and sensitivity in most instances.

Perceptions and miscommunication can provide barriers to change too. Of course the social and psychological barriers are extensions of cultural barriers, because both types of social groups and perceptions are learned and transmitted by individual members of cultures. The early days of the contraceptive pill illustrates these problems. There were many tales of errors in both perceptive differences and miscommunication regarding pill usage in Europe, North America, Africa, and elsewhere. Clients did not always understand the nature of an oral contraceptive and sometimes inserted the contraceptive pills into their vaginas or took them only when they had sex. Such mistakes usually were traceable to failure of health care workers to clarify the use of the pills. After all, until this time all contraceptive techniques directly involved the genitalia or consisted of herbal potions that induced abortion.

TRY THIS
Hypothesize

Read the community or metro section of your local paper, or read letters to the editor. Identify a controversial topic in your community regarding a proposed change (this might have to do with issues such as recycling, urban growth, the outlawing of leaf blowers—any local issue). Write a hypothesis about why the planned change is meeting opposition. Phrase your hypothesis in terms of one or more of the barriers discussed here. How might you test your hypothesis?

Stimulants to Change

Desire for economic gain is perhaps the biggest stimulant for change. Individuals themselves may identify a part of their lives that they want to change, especially if they perceive a positive economic outcome. Information and aid from the World Health Organization has been sought by people who want to plan the size of their family. Such people have themselves recognized that there are positive economic advantages to family planning. If an agricultural program demonstrates that different agricultural practices will lead to higher yields per acre, and thus to more crops

TRY THIS Analyze

Suppose that health care workers from another technologically advanced society have come to your community. They tell you that they have overwhelming scientific evidence that sitting on the typical North American toilet is bad for your circulation and is an unnatural position for a bowel movement. Squatting with legs bent and weight on flat feet (as is the tradition in a good number of world cultures) is how you should take care of bodily elimination. (A raised toilet would have to be replaced with just a hole in the bathroom floor.)

Discuss which of the three categories of cultural barriers discussed in the text might play a role in the rejection by you and your friends of this attempt at culture change.

OLC
mhhe • com / lenkeit5e
See Internet exercises.

to sell, traditional practices of cultivation will generally give way to new innovations. When planned change is directed at issues such as health, economic advantages may not be as obvious to the recipients. Motivators such as desire for prestige, pride in nationalism, or intracommunity competition may stimulate the target population to try the new approach or product or idea. All of these stimulants or motivators have been used by both insiders and outsiders—for reasons of altruism, politics, business, or religion—to bring about changes that are seen as desirable.

HUMAN PROBLEMS IN CHANGE

First, I am going to relate a very early study in technological change that involves the introduction of hybrid corn to farmers in New Mexico. I've selected this classic case because it is a direct example of the human cultural element that can impede a program of planned change—even one in which the people involved want the change. If you consider it closely, you will see many parallels to attempts by the government, the health care community, and educators to introduce change in your own culture. Next, I'll summarize a more recent case involving camel herders and economic change. Keep Foster's barriers to change in mind as you read these accounts, and see if you can anticipate the problems that affect the process of change. Finally, I'll relate an example of the negative consequences of development.

A Case Study of Hybrid Corn

Background. A community of Spanish American farmers in the southwestern United States grew a native variety of corn known as Indian corn.

Seed was saved each year from the harvest for planting the next year's crop. Yield of the corn was 25 bushels per acre. Soils were fertile, and fertility was maintained by the addition of some manure each year. Abundant water for irrigation of small fields came from the nearby river. The corn was used primarily to make tortillas, a diet staple for the people. Corn, in the past, had been ground by hand using a *mano* (handheld grinding stone) on stone mortars called *metates*. Currently the grinding was done commercially at a local mill. Surplus corn, as well as corn stalks, was fed to animals (Apodaca 1952).

Introduction of the Hybrid Seed. The local U.S. Department of Agriculture farm extension advisor, who spoke Spanish in the same way as the local farmers, had worked in the area for several years. He was familiar with all of the local farming practices and had good rapport with the farmers. He felt that the introduction of a hybrid variety of disease-resistant high-yield (about 100 bushels per acre) corn would benefit the farmers. He discussed this proposal with local leaders of the village, who acknowledged that the traditional seed strain was weak. A meeting was held, and everyone in the village was invited. At the meeting a movie about the hybrid corn was shown, and community leaders themselves discussed its advantages. A demonstration plot of corn was grown near the village so that farmers could see for themselves the increased yield from the hybrid variety compared to the local Indian corn (Apodaca 1952: 35–37).

The Result. At first the program seemed to be going well. Of the eighty-four growers in the village, forty planted a small amount of the hybrid corn and doubled their production of corn compared to the preceding year. The next planting season sixty farmers grew the new hybrid. The extension agent felt that the newly introduced hybrid corn was a success. Again the harvest yield was high. But the following year only thirty farmers planted the hybrid variety. By the next year the number of farmers planting the new hybrid had dropped to three (and these were farmers the extension agent considered to be progressive). Everyone else was again growing the traditional Indian corn, and there had been no diffusion of the hybrid variety to any surrounding villages (Apodaca 1952).

None of the farmers reported any problems with growing the new hybrid corn. They were pleased with the higher yields. There was a market for the surplus. There had been no difficulty in obtaining the seed to plant. Farmers even indicated that the Indian corn was clearly a weaker variety. Yet they had gone back to growing it. Why?

TRY THIS
Analyze

You are an anthropologist who has been hired to look at the hybrid corn case and offer suggestions for future programs of planned change. From the anthropological view, make a list of what the extension advisor did correctly to introduce the new corn in this cultural setting. Then, make a list of additional steps that should have been taken to increase the likelihood of success in this case.

Culture change often involves the blending of old and new. A camel cart with rubber tires transports goods past parked trucks in the city of Ahmedabad, Gujarat, India.

Unanticipated Barriers. The farmers' wives did not like the new corn. They had complained from the first harvest. The new hybrid did not have the proper texture, and it made poor tortillas that did not hang together well. They did not like the color of the tortillas that were produced from the hybrid corn flour, and they did not like the taste. Farmers continued to grow the new corn anyway for the first two years because it resulted in high yields and could be fed to animals. But their wives were very unhappy and in the end persuaded the farmers to return to the old Indian corn. In other words, in the terms laid out by George Foster, cultural values and attitudes, particularly tradition and relative values, had been barriers to the change.

A Case Study of Economic Change Among Pastoralists

Background. The Raikas, of the state of Rajasthan in India, are pastoral camel herders. They belong to a Hindu caste whose members breed live-stock and are well known as expert camel breeders, though they also keep cattle, sheep, and goats. Their expertise includes knowledge of selective breeding. They keep track of pedigrees of their animals, and they sell only male animals. Their traditional knowledge of diseases and the treatment of them is extensive. For example, the Raikas developed a technique for vaccinating camels against camel pox by taking skin from an infected camel, mixing it with water, and rubbing the solution into a small cut in the nose of the animal they wanted to protect from the pox.

Raikas live in permanent houses near villages where women, children, and elderly live year-round. Men travel up to one hundred miles herding their camels to pasture. Human population has dramatically increased in the region, and traditional open grazing land is decreasing as cultivated land increases. Historically, local maharajahs kept camel herds, maintained by the Raikas, in order to have a supply of camels for their warriors. Today there is a strong market for camels as draft animals, primarily for pulling carts.

Traditional Values Among the Raikas. Raikas believe that the Hindu god Lord Shiva created them from his own skin and sweat to care for camels. They follow a strict taboo against killing and eating camels. Fresh camel's milk is consumed, but in their belief system there is a prohibition against making yogurt and cheese from the milk. They also do not believe that milk should be sold.

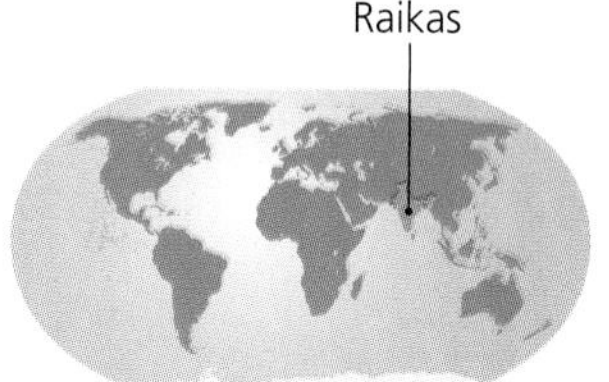

The Problem. Grazing land is diminishing, and underfed female camels mature later, are less fertile, and often abort. Because the birth interval for well-fed, healthy camels is a calf every two years, a reduction in fertility is a serious issue. Camel herds that numbered 10,000 animals fifty years ago were down to 1,000 in 1995 (Kohler-Rollefson 1995).

Possible Solutions. The slaughtering and selling of animals that are old or unproductive would be advantageous to the Raikas, and there is a market for camel meat. Other possible solutions include the selling of fresh camel's milk and the use of excess milk to make milk products that keep longer than fresh milk, such as cheese and yogurt.

Processes of Change. Just when the future of the Raikas seemed most bleak, because of the many cultural barriers to change, word came of successful camel's milk sales among a caste closely related to the Raikas. Twenty years earlier, these camel herders had begun to sell milk to tea stall owners (milk being considered an essential ingredient of tea in India). Camel's milk was found to keep longer and was cheaper than cow or buffalo milk. Sales had expanded over the years, and the supply was currently short of the demand. Raikas began to hear about the success of the other caste, and some Raika began looking to change their attitude about selling milk. The economic demand for camel's milk could save the herds. In this case, diffusion played a big role in bringing about change. It helped the Raikas see that traditional values could change to accommodate circumstances.

Update on the Raikas and Their Camels. Camel breeding is now supported by an Indian NGO that works to develop market strategies for milk, meat, leather, and wool, and also seeks to improve camel health. World attention to green technologies may renew interest in camel breeding, as camels are ecologically advantageous—camel grazing does not devastate the land the way goats, sheep, and cattle do because they disperse rather than herd while grazing, don't eat entire plants and have feet that plod softly on soils, and camel cart transportation doesn't pollute or require fossil fuels (Köhler-Rollefson 2005: 11–12). Camels' milk is being sold to tea stalls and private households. More camels are now sold for slaughter, and camel dung is increasingly recognized as an important fertilizer—considered by farmers to be better than cow dung (Köhler-Rollefson 2005: 11–12).

As in the case of the Raika, culture change may occur when economic survival is at stake. We have learned more about the processes of change in the years since Foster's analysis, but keep in mind the barriers to change that he identified, because those issues continue to impact culture change situations at home and abroad.

A Case Study of Development with a Negative Outcome

Many development projects aimed at culture change have negative impact on tribal and peasant peoples. The replacement of traditional diets, which evolved to provide protein and variety in vitamin and mineral intake, with diets high in calories, low in protein, and based on one or two food sources, causes malnutrition. Tribal peoples seeking employment in urban centers experience decreased health due to poor sanitation and increase in infectious diseases caused by crowding. Additionally, development places strain on ecosystems. New technologies, lower mortality rates, and increased consumption leads to environmental imbalance. Tribal peoples with lifeways once in balance with their environment experience resource depletion, species extinction, erosion, and other negative changes. Development proponents paint pictures of economic growth and improved living conditions as people move from subsistence economies to cash economies, but this dream is seldom realized by the majority of people. Instead wealth increases for a few and poverty results for many (Bodley 2008).

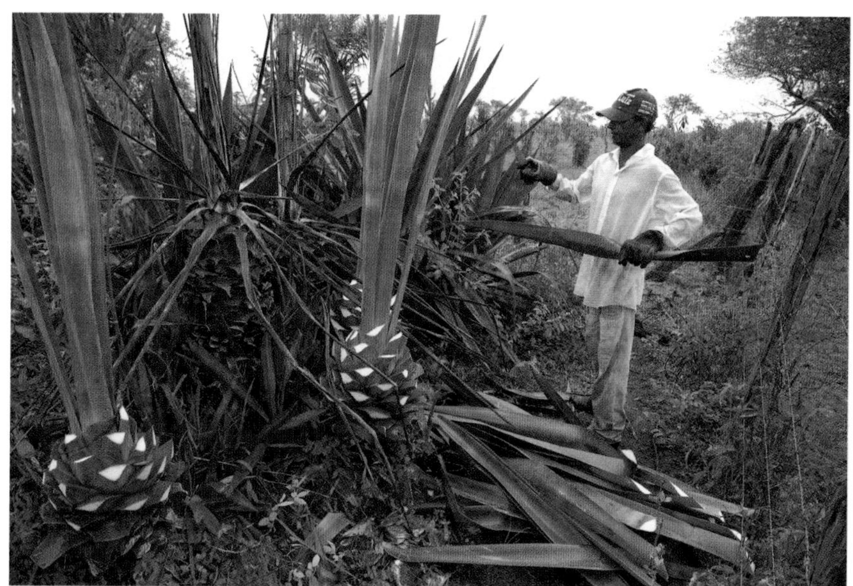

The introduction of sisal farming in Brazil was shown to have negative consequences for subsistence farmers in research by Daniel Gross. Fibers in the leaves of the sisal plant are used to make twine and rope.

Daniel Gross provides an example of the negative consequences to change in his classic study of the introduction of sisal production to Vila Nova, a small Brazilian community of five hundred subsistence farmers.

Background. Vila Nova is located in Brazil's *sertão*, an interior region plagued by cyclical drought. Small- and medium-sized landholders subsisted on what they grew—manioc, beans, and corn. Some meat and milk were also part of the diet. During drought years only a few of the larger landholders stayed in the area. Others migrated to the coast to labor on sugar plantations under harsh slavelike conditions. When a local farmer heard of the high prices and demand for sisal on the world market, everyone started growing it while they dreamed of profits to buy new homes, vehicles, and clothes. From 1951 to 1968 half of the land around Vila Nova was converted to growing sisal (Gross 2002: 257). Most small landowners soon began to work for low wages in the large landowners' sisal fields and processing operations; they needed cash to buy food since they no longer raised enough subsistence crops. Imported food was expensive.

Outcome. A few people with large sisal plantations became quite affluent. Others in a newly emerged economic class—shopkeepers and owners of sisal processing machines—also did well. Wage workers and small landowners experienced a decline in their way of life, and nutrition declined. These were the majority of people in Vila Nova.

Nutritional Decline Documented. Anthropologist Daniel Gross, who lived in the village for two years to study the impact of sisal crops, noticed changes in the economic and social structure plus ecological changes. He focused on quantifying the influence of sisal on diet and nutrition. He collected data on household cash and energy budgets. He studied families and measured and documented their inflow and outflow of energy in calories. He concluded that the working adults maintained their weight at the expense of calorie intake by their children. Of course, they were unaware this was happening; they simply consumed more based on their bodies' demands from the hard labor they were doing, and they had limited cash to purchase food. He found significant differences in the average body weight of two groups—the sisal workers as one group and the shopkeepers and machine owners as the other group; nutrition (as measured by body weight) declined in the worker group and improved in the shopkeeper/machine owner group. Children in sisal worker families were smaller than properly nourished children; the longer they experienced calorie deprivation, the more stunted their growth (Gross 2002: 258–60). Gross's conclusions agreed with similar data from many other studies in the developing world—development schemes often bring improvement to the lives of few and decline and poverty to the lives of many. A holistic ecological approach is needed in all development planning. In Vila Nova the stimulant for change was desire for economic gain. But lack of any regional planning or understanding of the area's ecological situation and social structure had serious negative effects on most of the population.

ANTHROPOLOGY AND GLOBALIZATION

Imperialism, colonialism, hegemony, and globalization are buzz terms among cultural anthropologists, and one or more of them appear in many current titles and articles. Looking back over the past two centuries, and particularly since the inception of anthropology as a discipline (1860s), we recognize that much of the change that has occurred in indigenous cultures (often called traditional or undeveloped, or Second or Third World cultures) was brought about due to actions on the part of First World nation-states in Europe and North America. Nation-states on these continents dominated territories and peoples economically, politically, socially, and culturally for extended periods of time as they exploited the natural resources of their territories. The term **imperialism** was used to describe influence and authority of one nation over another, often associated with the exploitation of natural and human resources. The proliferation of Coca-Cola, Shell Oil Corporation, Sony Corporation, and

imperialism
Influence and authority of one nation over another, often associated with exploitation of natural and human resources. See *colonialism; hegemony.*

McDonald's around the globe is an example of economic and cultural imperialism. **Colonialism** describes influence and dominance of one nation over another for the purpose of exploiting raw resources. Additionally the dominant nation-state establishes a physical presence in a territory and places a colonial government there—for example, the European governments in many parts of the African continent. The terms are often used as synonyms. We recognize that imperialist and colonial contact with the West is responsible for a great deal of what is currently termed hegemony. In the analysis of contemporary cultural change, this term appears to be replacing the terms *imperialism* and *colonialism*. **Hegemony** may be defined as the ideological domination by one cultural group over another through institutions, bureaucracy, education, and sometimes force. The term's use ranges from the analysis of the activities of nation-states in international relations to the analysis of class structure within a culture. The term is enjoying new popularity today among writers and scholars, but it has a long history of use beginning with the ancient Greeks. An example of hegemony is China's dominance over much of East Asia for long periods. I hope that this serves to alert you to some of the vocabulary you will encounter. Writers often assume that the reader understands the meaning of such widely used terms. Unfortunately, authors themselves sometimes attach slightly different meanings to their usages, so watch for this in your readings.

Anthropologists have joined many other disciplines in studying the culture change resulting from hegemony that began with imperialism and colonialism. It continues today with what are termed globalization studies. Since the 1980s, anthropologists have been increasingly interested in the dynamics of **globalization** and its impact on world cultures. Other disciplines—economics, sociology, geography, political science, health, communications, and others—also study globalization.

What exactly is globalization? The term is defined in a number of ways, each with a slightly different nuance, depending on the discipline involved; the vast literature on globalization makes a concise definition difficult. The term as most commonly used in anthropological writings refers to the rapid spread of economic, social, and cultural systems across continents. Issues of both time and space are relevant in the study of globalization. Time refers to the speed with which change occurs, and space refers to the spread of change between cultures and across traditional geographical and political boundaries.

In anthropology, cultural processes and their effects on individuals are the focus of most of our studies of global change. Jonathan Xavier Inda and Renato Rosaldo note that anthropologists interpret various approaches to aspects of globalization through "the prism of the cultural" (Inda and Rosaldo 2002: 9). I like this analogy. A prism breaks

colonialism
Influence and dominance of one nation over another for the purpose of exploiting raw resources. The dominant nation-state establishes a physical presence and a colonial government. See *imperialism; hegemony.*

hegemony
The ideological domination by one cultural group over another through institutions, bureaucracy, education, and sometimes force. See *imperialism; colonialism.*

globalization
In anthropology, the rapid spread of economic, social, and cultural systems across continents.

Evidence of globalization is seen in the many American fast food outlets found throughout the world. This McDonald's is located in China.

light into its component parts, and anthropology sees globalization's effect on culture as having many facets—among them economic, political, and social—that are reflected at the same time. The following sections will offer a sample of several types of anthropological research on global change.

Tourism and Globalization

Capitalism is rapidly diffusing to even the most isolated regions of the earth and is responsible for much acculturation. Most research on this phenomenon draws heavily from economic theory, but we focus on the effects on individuals and their culture. The study of global tourism offers one focal point for such research.

Tourism is big business, unquestionably the largest global industry. The diffusion of a desire for possessions (materialism) has contributed to the development of the tourist trade. Indigenous peoples have discovered

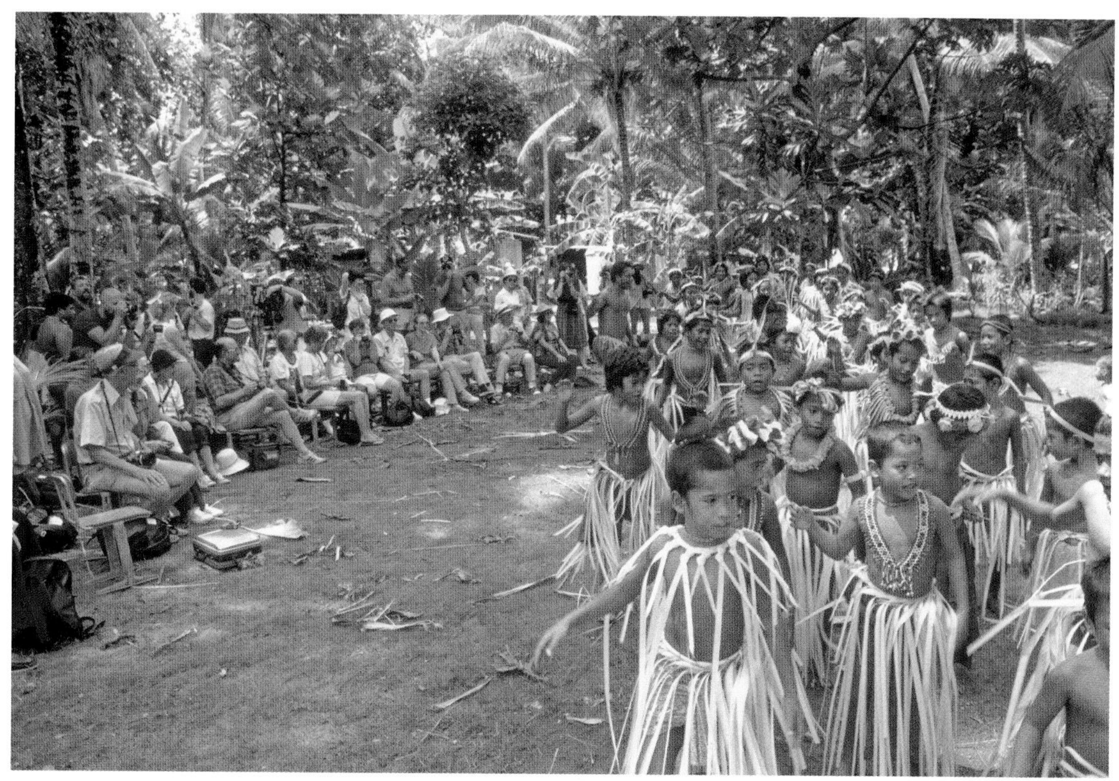

Tourists watch native dancers on Pulap Island, Federal States of Micronesia. Tourists and their money are important to many countries' economies today.

that wealthy people will pay to experience authentic "native" culture. So they produce it. It is part of the globalization of capitalism.

There are two main approaches to anthropological tourism research—academic and applied. Scholarly investigations of tourism and tourists include descriptions and typologies of tourism (historical, cultural, ethnic, ecotourism, recreational) and types of tourists (individual, adventurer, group). Other academic approaches look at issues associated with topics such as tourism authenticity, heritage, and tradition. In early tourism studies, researchers often focused on tourism's negative effects on traditional indigenous communities. Tourist money creates a new hegemony that some term "neocolonialism" (Douglass and Lacy 2005).

Applied researchers hold the view that both negative and positive outcomes of tourism are possible and that anthropologists "can contribute to neutralizing the negative aspects of tourism development projects without losing their wariness over the potential for harm that unrestrained tourism can cause, especially in smaller communities" (Wallace 2005: 10). Some argue that carefully conceived tourism projects may help to preserve aspects of indigenous culture. Applied anthropologists may work as advisors and consultants to the tourist industry, as well as researchers and even mediators. Of course ethical issues are of concern with applied work.

Ecotourism. Amazon ecotourism was studied by Palma Ingles, who, as an addition to her research, joined various tour companies as a tour guide. This gave her a unique view of both tourist and indigenous villager. Ingles became curious about the authenticity of dances that were performed for tourists and wondered if the dancers found it demeaning to sell their culture in this way. She discovered that the villagers had a positive view of tourism. They used the tour visits to sell locally made crafts directly to the tourists, and they could keep some of their traditions alive by staging the dances. Additionally, the money from tourism helped to preserve the ecology of the region because it increased household income and reduced the ecologically damaging aspects of slash-and-burn agriculture (Ingles 2005: 222–23).

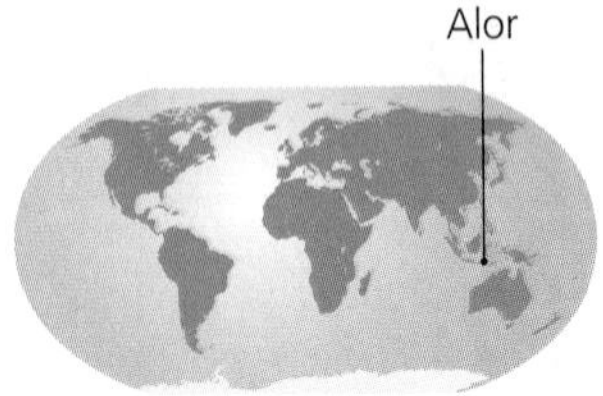

Tourism and Authenticity. What do tourists want from their experiences? Do they travel to learn about the lives and customs of others or are they seeking entertainment? It is suggested that there is a "Disney factor" at work in tourist encounters (Wilson 1991; Igoe 2011). I believe that what most people seek when they travel is a really good "E ticket ride" (the original ticket for the best rides at Disneyland). Rides in a Disney park allow one to "travel" to a locale with exotic flora and fauna and native village scenes. These settings look idyllic; they are fantasies. We don't see areas of environmental devastation from logging, mining, or dam building, nor do we see indigenous peoples exhibiting the malnutrition that typically follows resource exploitation and development in these aboriginal landscapes. So we don't have to think about these issues (Igoe 2011). Other venues, such as the popular heritage parks found globally, also shield visitors from negative realities suffered in the past. Tour agencies, governments, and aboriginal peoples worldwide recognize the economic value of presenting clients and visitors with E ticket rides.

Tourism among the Maasai of Tanzania and Kenya offers an illustration of carefully staged cultural experiences. One can participate in a tour that includes staying in a safari camp where the Maasai visit (dressed as traditional warriors carrying spears), present dances, interact with the tourists, and offer crafts for sale. Visits to "authentic" Maasai villages are part of the safari. These villages are carefully staged. Traditional dances performed during the safari, as well as at tourist hotels and auditoriums, most often reflect recent choreography and eclectic costumes. Most Maasai can no longer live the traditional pastoralist way of life due to loss of traditional lands; globalization efforts to make them consumer-oriented wage earners have not generally been successful (Bruner 2001; Igoe 2004; 2011), but some can make a living working the tourist trade.

So what do tourists think about such encounters? One tourism researcher, Edward Bruner, recounts a conversation he had with a group of tourists in Indonesia. After a dance performance, he pointed out to the visiting tourists that the dance was a creation choreographed specifically for the tourist trade and was not an indigenous traditional dance. They acknowledged and appreciated his efforts to expose the lack of authenticity, but they enjoyed the performance and all they wanted was a good show (Bruner 2005: 16). Authenticity implies that there is a *real* original culture. But no culture was or is frozen in time, and desire for economic gain motivates people to change traditional ways of making a living. Tourist industry work is just work.

A strong desire for economic gain motivates people to change traditional ways of making a living, from tourism in the Amazon jungle or on an Indonesian island, to global locations where cheap labor entices business from countries like the United States to build factories. The Coca-Cola and Nike corporations, for example, have gained attention for their factories in Third World countries, and this wage-based employment is often desired by those who participate. Our outsider's ethnocentrism regarding the "poor" working conditions, "injustices," "exploitation" of women and children, and the disruption of traditional cultures often do not represent the economic position of those indigenous peoples who want to provide for their families. On the other hand, such situations can be viewed as examples of hegemony resulting from economic globalization.

Globalization and the Media

Advancements in communication and media stimulate the globalization process. Analysis of their rapid diffusion, however, tells us that values may not diffuse with the same rapidity. I offer a topically narrow example to illustrate. Eric Michaels studied the Warlpiri Aborigines of Australia and looked at the impact of Hollywood videotapes on the people. During his three years of fieldwork, Michaels documented that the Warlpiri quickly adopted various components of electronic media. Videotapes were introduced to the aboriginal camps in the 1980s and satellite television a bit later. Both have been readily integrated into Aboriginal life. Four-wheel-drive vehicles and rifles are the only other rapidly accepted contemporary Western technologies. Aborigines are enthusiastic about Hollywood shows but view them through their own cultural lens. Kinship relationships between characters interest the Warlpiri, and they speculate about family relationships if the story doesn't have that information. They also look for supernatural reasons to explain events such as an individual's death. Both kin ties and supernatural explanations are important issues within Warlpiri culture (Michaels 1990; 2002).

Similar studies worldwide indicate that electronic media are readily embraced but that the message or values represented may not be crossing cultural borders. Films coming from the United States carry one worldview; films produced in India, China, and Mexico carry other culture-specific values. Media produced in other countries provide peoples with "alternatives that permit them to fashion modern forms of existing in the world without being weighted down by the ideological baggage of western cultural imperialism" (Inda and Rosaldo 2002: 309). Media can contribute to diffusion, but Foster's barriers to change also apply to this arena.

URBAN SETTINGS AND CHANGE

The anthropological study of urban lifeways is an integral part of anthropology today, and many of these studies involve the identification of patterns of change and adaptation. Urban places have their own social institutions that set them apart from small-scale societies. One feature of cities is that they are heterogeneous places with many segments that are quite distinct from the features of homogeneous foraging or horticultural societies. Moreover, the cross-cultural comparative studies of such places have revealed that there are differences in cities. In other words, the notion that a city is a city is a city is simply not true. There are many different types of cities, and they can be classified by their segments, focus of activities, geography, and so forth. Anthropologist Richard Fox has distinguished such city types as administrative cities, industrial cities, colonial cities, mercantile cities, and city-states (Fox 1977).

OLC
mhhe • com / lenkeit5e
See Internet exercises.

Numerous approaches have been taken toward developing an understanding of urban settings, and each has asked different questions. One approach is referred to as urbanism studies. A holistic conceptualization is the focus of this approach. The city is viewed as an integral part of a larger society (often referred to as a folk-urban continuum), and its place and influence are investigated. A second approach is that of studies of urban poverty. Urban poverty studies focus on ghetto populations, the homeless, urban alcoholic nomads, and Native American urban populations, to name a few. A third approach, known as **urbanization studies,** looks at the adaptations made by rural peoples as they move to cities. Much anthropological work in urbanization has centered on Latin America and Africa.

urbanization studies Studies of the adaptations made by rural peoples as they move to cities.

An example of the information that has come from urbanization studies is the change it has brought to what we know about family and kin in

ANTHROPOLOGY AROUND US

Mother's Milk

Data from both biological and cultural anthropology present us with information about breast-feeding. The contributions from primatologists, medical anthropologists, nutritional anthropologists, ethnographers, and ethnologists combine to support the view that mother's milk is best for infants and that family, friends, doctors, employers, business, and government should be joining in an all-out effort to support nursing mothers.

The biological facts are clear—breast milk is for most babies the ideal source of nutrition. Besides being food, breast milk is also, as reported by the University of Pennsylvania Health System (Hoke 1997), a bioactive compound containing important antibodies, hormones, and growth factors that defend against infection and aid the infant's immune system to fully develop. Numerous studies of thousands of infants show significantly less infant mortality among breast-fed infants. Also, children who were breast-fed had significantly fewer middle ear infections (otitis media). The protection offered by breast-feeding continues as long as the child is breast-fed. A recent study estimates that if 90 percent of U.S. women breast-fed exclusively for six months, more than 900 infant deaths could be prevented and billions of dollars per year saved in health care costs (Bartick and Reinhold 2010).

Ethnographic data tell us that across cultures, prior to the widespread use of infant formulas, children were nursed two to four years. Katherine Dettwyler has compared data on nonhuman primate growth, age at weaning, and other life history variables and concludes, "If humans weaned their offspring according to the primate pattern, without regard to beliefs and customs, most children would be weaned somewhere between 2.5 and 7 years of age" (Dettwyler 1995: 66).

The most recent U.S. data (2006) places rates for infants who were ever breast-fed as increasing from 60 percent for those born in 1993–1994, to 77 percent for those born in 2005–2006. However, less than 50 percent are still breast-feeding at six months (CDC 2008).

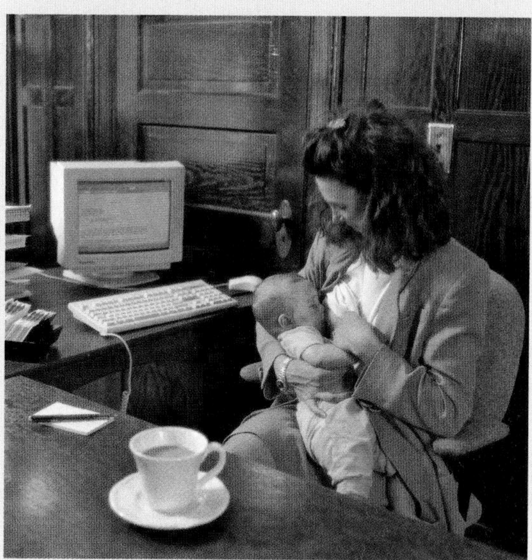

With all of the data to support the positive value of breast-feeding, why don't more American mothers breast-feed and why don't they do it for more than a few months? In the United States today the cultural context of breast-feeding includes the focus on female breasts as sexual objects (a view found to be amusing and perplexing from the perspective of many other cultures) and the attitude that breast-feeding should be limited to very young infants and should not occur in public.

◎ What other cultural views do Americans hold toward breast-feeding? Are you aware of any ethnic group differences in attitudes toward breast-feeding? Which of Foster's cultural barriers to change can you identify with respect to having more American women breast-feed and do it longer? How might these barriers be overcome?

urban settings. Before fieldwork-based urbanization studies were undertaken, the literature focused on the breakdown in social relations within extended families when a move was made to an urban center. It was thought that the transplanted rural family became a self-contained urban nuclear family, a family that was isolated from other kin. The importance of reciprocal economic, social, and emotional relationships were said to diminish. In the past, this was the prevailing thought on the subject. Ethnographic data from more recent urbanization studies do not support this view. Susan Emley Keefe's work among urban Mexican Americans and Anglo-Americans in southern California demonstrates this finding. Keefe found that these two groups differed only in the *proximity* of kin. For Mexican Americans, kin were found to be geographically local, whereas for Anglo-Americans, kin were more dispersed. In both groups, extended family continue to be important to them as they live, work, and adapt to the urban environment (Keefe 1996).

TRY THIS
Consider

How many times a week do you communicate with kin? Describe the forms of technology you use.

A combination of these approaches is obviously useful. And, of course, many other social scientists, such as sociologists and social psychologists, study urban populations. These researchers use data-gathering methodologies that focus on the use of surveys and standardized interview schedules and statistical analyses. These methodologies have been honed by sociologists and are useful for the study of large populations. Still, ethnographic interview techniques in which long-term contact takes place between an informant and the anthropologist provide texture and dimension to urban studies that simply are not present in a statistical survey approach. Each urban studies methodology complements the whole.

SUMMARY

Diffusion and acculturation are responsible for most culture change. Anthropologists use a number of approaches to study culture change, including scrutiny of the archaeological record, analysis of historical records, life histories, ethnographic restudies, and impact studies. Theories about how cultures develop and change began with the schools of unilineal evolutionism, diffusionism, and historicalism. Comparative studies of change programs after World War II led to the work of George Foster and his analysis of cultural barriers to change, such as traditional values and attitudes. Ethical issues arose when anthropologists participated in government-initiated change projects. Negative outcomes of development projects have been documented. Hegemony, the ideological domination by one cultural group over another, and the dynamics of globalization are current focal points for the anthropological study of change in world cultures. Finally, anthropology contributes to the study of change and adaptation in urban studies.

Study Questions

1. Present an argument to support the thesis that cultural barriers to change are the most important barriers. Support your argument with specific examples from the case studies presented here and in other course assignments.
2. Discuss the ethical debate within anthropology over the HTS program.
3. Discuss with examples what anthropologists have discovered about tourism and authenticity.

OLC
mhhe • com / lenkeit5e
See Self Quiz.

Suggested Readings

Bodley, John H. 2008. *Victims of Progress*, 5th ed. New York: Alta Mira Press. Looks at the impact of Western institutions and industrialization on small-scale societies.

Holtzman, Jon D. 2007. *Nuer Journeys: Nuer Lives.* 2nd ed. Boston: Allyn and Bacon. Chronicles the changes in traditional Nuer society as refugees adapt to life in Minnesota.

Igoe, Jim. 2004. *Conservation and Globalization*. Belmont, CA: Wadsworth. Gives a perspective on Western versus indigenous views on conservation.

OLC
mhhe • com / lenkeit5e
See Web links.

Applying Anthropology

How Does It Make a Difference?

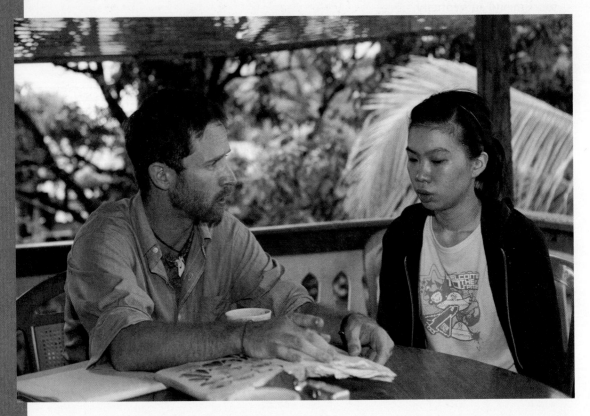

▲ As part of Operation Wallacea, a North American and British NGO, anthropologists worked with a multi-disciplinary team and local fishing families to develop sustainable management strategies for the Kaledupa Island reef fisheries in Sulawesi, Indonesia. A project worker confers with an Indonesian researcher.

Once upon a time, a monkey and a fish were caught up in a great flood. The monkey, agile and experienced, had the good fortune to scramble up a tree to safety. As he looked down into the raging waters, he saw a fish struggling against the swift current. Filled with a humanitarian desire to help his less fortunate fellow, he reached down and scooped the fish from the water. To the monkey's surprise, the fish was not very grateful for this aid. (Foster 1962:1)

I recall this fable from my first course in applied anthropology and the impact it had on me. The fable requires serious consideration by anyone undertaking to direct, plan, or participate in a program to bring about culture change. I suspect most of us have been in the monkey's shoes at some time, and quite a few of us have been in the position of the fish. Applied anthropologists help clients avoid the pitfalls of the monkey. We are trained not only to understand the monkey's view but also to seek and listen to the fish's perspective—our discipline's signature holistic approach again—and to work to devise successful programs that benefit the population being served and at the same time satisfy our client.

It can be difficult for those evaluating or developing programs to see their project objectively. The monkey in the fable was trying to do good from its perspective. Many programs of directed change are unsuccessful both because of monkey-like perspectives and/or because programs often employ only experts in a particular field (e.g., engineers, legislators, doctors, administrators). Most experts have a narrow point of view and fail to consider mitigating cultural factors.

Anthropologists who are trained to include a broad viewpoint as well as the voice and perspective of the focus community can and do make the difference between project success and failure. It is my hope that with the perspectives you gain from this chapter, plus what you have learned previously, you will apply anthropology to your everyday life and work.

The objectives of this chapter are to:

- Describe the field of applied anthropology and its methods
- Describe how the anthropological approach is used in business and in medicine
- Explain how anthropological knowledge is used in agriculture and in development programs

WHAT IS APPLIED ANTHROPOLOGY?

OLC
mhhe • com / lenkeit5e
See chapter outline and chapter overview.

The perspectives and methodologies of anthropology are used at many levels. I have placed this chapter at the end of the text not because applied anthropology is an afterthought but rather because I see it as the culmination of acquiring the basic tools of anthropology. **Applied anthropology** is the use of the various perspectives, methods, theories, and data of anthropology to identify, evaluate, and offer solutions to human problems. Applied anthropologists (also called practicing anthropologists) seldom refer to themselves as anthropologists; rather, they call themselves consultants. This is because most members of the general public do not understand the scope of anthropology—they think of anthropologists only as those people who dig up pottery and fossils and work at a university or a museum.

OLC
mhhe • com / lenkeit5e
See Internet exercise.

What do applied anthropologists do? Their jobs primarily include: (1) Research and data collection for use in policy development and programs. Such jobs are with businesses, corporations, and government at all levels—local, state, and federal. Additionally, research and policy development jobs are found in education, public health, nutrition, and natural resource management. (2) Data analysis, assessment of needs, project evaluation, or project impact. This work is done locally and globally for companies, government agencies, and NGOs.

Additional roles for practicing anthropologists may include action and advocacy in support of underrepresented groups, planning and development of intervention programs that are sensitive to local cultural issues, and action research involving long-term participation at a local level working with communities to develop programs that both empower and benefit them. The practicing anthropologist most often works as a team member with other social scientists and experts in specialty fields. The anthropological consultant approach is unique because efforts focus on bringing the voices of all participants into discussions and making the entire community active participants in research.

OLC
mhhe • com / lenkeit5e
See Web links.

Methodologies used in applied anthropology focus on anthropology's signature approach of ethnographic field methods, including an emphasis on participant observation. Both formal and informal interviews are used, plus a variety of sampling procedures and quantitative analytical techniques, such as statistics. Use of the comparative method and viewing settings in holistic terms, with the overarching concepts of culture with a capital *C* and culture with a lowercase *c*, are central to problem solving. And the practicing anthropologist is ever mindful of maintaining a perspective of cultural relativism while identifying ethnocentric attitudes—and their impact on projects—on the part of both the client and the target community. Ethical codes govern applied research. Both the Society for Applied Anthropology (SfAA) and the National Association for the Practice of Anthropology (NAPA) have ethical codes that provide guidelines for clarifying issues such as responsibilities to clients and to research subjects.

applied anthropology The branch of anthropology that focuses on the application of anthropological methods and approaches to the solution of problems, as distinct from academic anthropology.

Evaluation Anthropology

This is one of the core practices in applied anthropology today and is applicable in all types of programs—business, development programs, medicine, agriculture, all areas where anthropological methods can be applied, which is just about everywhere. An important element in evaluation consulting is to work within the target group and discover the how and why of a project's success or failure, as illustrated in the following case (Crain and Tashima 2005: 47).

The firm of LTG Associates, Inc., conducted an evaluation of a street outreach HIV/AIDS program and provided assistance to improve its effectiveness. Cathleen Crain worked on the street for several days with an outreach worker, an African American woman. This woman's work focused on prevention; she was considered a model for programs throughout the city, reaching large numbers of women and getting them tested and in counseling (Crain and Tashima 2005: 44–45). Crain's role was a participant observer, and she accompanied the worker carrying "bleach and teach" kits, HIV prevention literature, and condoms. She observed and noted the street environment and whom the outreach worker approached or didn't approach. Over several days Crain noted that Anglo and African American women were approached, but others, such as an Asian American woman and a Native American woman who stood on street corners (and appeared to the anthropologist to be prostitutes), were not approached. When these women were pointed out to the outreach worker, and she was asked what they were doing, she at first said that she didn't know. When the anthropologist asked if they were hooking (soliciting), the worker said that this was likely. In later discussions with the outreach worker, Crain discovered that the worker held stereotypes—only Anglo and African Americans were prostitutes. The other ethnic group women soliciting didn't fit her stereotype, so they weren't approached. Similar stereotyping was found in other outreach workers (Crain and Tashima 2005: 44).

The approach used in this case is more time consuming and thus more expensive than in-clinic questionnaires and interviews. By being with the outreach worker in the community setting, however, the anthropologist could place her observations in a large cultural context. Crain chatted with the worker and came to understand her vision for preventative outreach; at the same time, she spotted a pattern of stereotyping that this worker and others had overlooked. This discovery led to improved training for this and other programs.

ANTHROPOLOGY IN BUSINESS

The world of business has borrowed and embraced the idea of culture. Business management books now use phrases like *corporate culture*, *organizational*

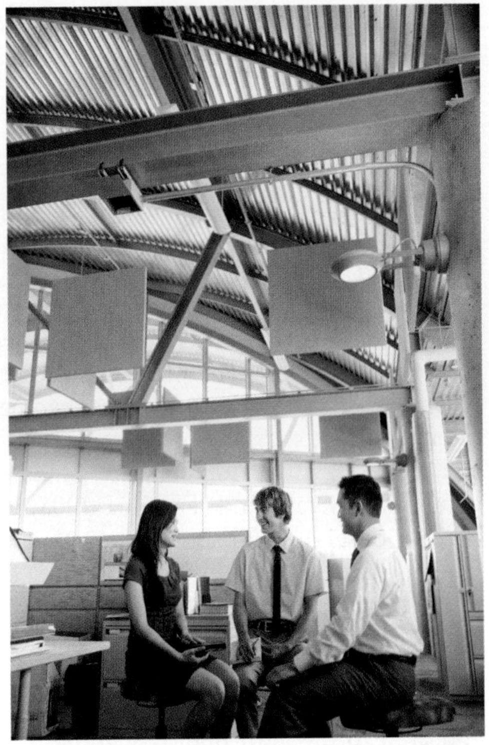

Ethnographic techniques used by one research team working for an office furniture manufacturer led to a design of office space focused on worker needs. Here a quick business conference takes place in meeting space provided between office cubicles.

culture, *worker culture*, *Japanese culture*, and *German culture*. Yet definitions of culture that are found in business management texts are often incomplete from the anthropologist's perspective (Morey and Morey 1994: 17; Harris and Moran 1996: 125; Jordan 2003: 84–88). Most such definitions center on ideas such as those found in the Box 2.1, namely lists of what constitutes culture, with a strong emphasis on traditional behaviors such as handshakes, bows, eye contact, attitudes toward time, appropriate dress, and so forth. In other words, manners and customs are the focus. Such behaviors, as you know, are a part of culture, but as you also know, the concept involves much more. An additional conceptual area associated with the term *culture* that businesspeople often fail to recognize is in the distinction between Culture (capital *C*, abstract culture or culture in general) and *c*ulture (lowercase *c*, a specific culture). When businesspeople use the term *corporate culture* (culture with a capital *C*, from the anthropologist's view), they typically discuss its features as if it were culture with a lowercase *c*, in other words, a specific culture or subculture (Jordan 1994b: 11). When the anthropological consultant helps to sort out these distinctions, those involved gain a better understanding of the problem's sources. This in turn leads to solutions.

Corporate culture is like other cultures and as such can be studied. Corporation members share cognitive processes (knowledge of product manufacture and sales, values such as profit motive, and beliefs about the job, the corporation, and its products), behaviors (appropriate dress, how to act at work, deference to managers, treatment of customers), and material items (artifacts used at work). This shared cultural system is transmitted to new members of the corporation. The members have differing degrees of power and authority; status is gained or lost according to understood values; there is a class system within the workplace; ideal and actual behaviors exist; the culture changes through time. Applied anthropologists examine corporate culture to find patterns of behavior just as do fieldworkers in any other cultural setting.

Some have challenged whether an organization such as a corporation should be called a culture, because one does not acquire this culture from childhood through the enculturation process. Although this is technically correct, if one carefully considers the issue, many parallels to enculturation can be seen.

TRY THIS
Analyze

Make a quick list of ways that learning about a job you have held is like being enculturated into your ethnic subculture. How did you learn to do the tasks required and to get along with coworkers and bosses? Compare and discuss your list with that of a classmate.

A Case Study of Anthropology in Business

This case study illustrates the usefulness of the anthropological perspective and is one of my favorites. I like it because the manager herself used anthropological tools to help solve a problem. David McCurdy (2000) reported on this case of applying anthropology, and I direct you to his excellent article for more details.

This situation occurred at a large multinational corporation that is diversified into manufacturing, research, and customer services, with customers in public, private, and government sectors. An educational division offers courses and programs to businesses and individuals who want special training or information—for example, special computer training for employees. One department within the education division produces learning materials such as books, pamphlets, and audiovisual materials that are used in the various courses and programs. Materials are shipped from a storage warehouse to customer outlets around the country. Difficulties with the shipment of course materials was the focus of the problem (McCurdy 2000).

A new manager was asked to take over the division responsible for the shipment of course materials. This manager had started as an employee and had just advanced to management. Her new assignment came with a provision. She was told to solve a serious problem with the warehouse inventory and improve customer service. Computer inventories often did not match actual numbers of books and pamphlets in the warehouse; customers received more or fewer books than they ordered and were disgruntled.

Other managers in the company believed that the problem in the warehouse resulted from workers' poor attitudes. They even referred to the warehouse workers as being without a good work ethic. They suggested to the new manager that she couldn't do anything with these workers. Others told her that the customers were the main problem because they were a bunch of complainers.

Traditional management techniques are often fueled by an *us versus them* attitude. New managers set up new procedures and work rules and rarely ask workers for their opinions, because the managers believe that to do so would show weakness and lack of control in leadership. Problem situations are often dealt with by offering retraining classes, developing employee work quota competitions (with rewards), or providing motivational pay incentives. Such solutions do not address the basic causes of problems, so they often fail in the long run.

The new manager took a different approach. She was not a professional anthropologist, but she knew some ethnographic field techniques, including how to conduct field interviews (informal and formal) and how to observe and analyze behavior. She spent six weeks discovering what workers did in the warehouse. She observed and talked at length to employees, customers, and sales people. She asked for advice on how to solve the problems. She listened. As she remarked, "And people were excited because I was asking and listening and, by God, intending to do something about it instead of just disappearing again" (McCurdy 2000: 393).

A number of specific problems were discovered: Orders took too long to get to the warehouse, quantities of materials shipped were often incorrect, customers were unhappy because they were billed for what they ordered regardless of what they received, and books arrived in poor condition with gouges and frayed edges.

The on-site ethnographic techniques used in the warehouse revealed the causes of the problems. Workers filled orders by going to the warehouse shelves, handpicking books, and placing them in boxes. Employees disclosed that they usually picked up what looked to be a stack of about the right number based on their experience. These estimates were, it turned out, usually incorrect. Yet they would then go to the computer and enter the number sent as the number ordered, which created errors in billing as well as errors in the computer inventory database. It was also revealed that shipments were often delivered to the ground floor lobbies of multistory buildings. Staff would open the boxes in the lobby and carry armloads of the books and pamphlets in the elevator up to the office. Observations revealed that people entering the building would help themselves to a copy of the book or pamphlet.

At the time the manager was searching for a solution to her warehouse problem, shrink-wrapping was a new packaging process. She decided that the few cents more that it would cost to have the books shrink-wrapped into packages of five and ten books before they arrived at the warehouse was a good investment. Most customers ordered books in units of five and ten, so counting was more accurate as orders were filled. She had these packages marked for *inside delivery* so that boxes would be delivered directly to the customers' offices upstairs.

Customers were happy with the results of these changes. Books arrived in good shape and in correct numbers. Morale improved in the warehouse as employees took pride in the service they provided. Customers responded positively and let people at the corporate headquarters know how they felt. Managers with previously negative attitudes about the warehouse workers were now asking questions about what was happening. The new manager attributed her success in problem solving to the use of ethnographic methods.

A Case Study in Design Anthropology

Design anthropologists are experts at using ethnographic methods to distinguish between ideal (what people say they do) and actual (what they really do) behaviors. They provide data with a *qualitative* dimension. This makes their input on product design, consumer product use, store policies (e.g., return or service policies), and workers' behaviors valuable to the business community. Quantitative data in these areas come primarily from sociological research methods such as questionnaires, interviews, and focus groups. The corporate world increasingly values input from the anthropological perspective and recognizes the richness it provides. In research on consumer preferences for a breakfast food company, anthropologist Susan Squires and her colleagues spent mornings with families observing, questioning, listening, and recording data (using pen, paper, tape recorders, and video cameras). They wanted to find out if what people *said they did* for breakfast matched what *they actually did*. They also followed family members to their jobs and schools to observe food-consumption patterns. They learned that many factors affected morning eating rituals. Mothers recognize the importance of a nutritional breakfast based on whole grains; kids were interested in fun; dads valued foods like those that they ate as children. The researchers discovered that children's metabolisms are such that they often don't want to eat a nutritious meal immediately upon arising at 6:30 or 7:00 A.M. but may be interested in a sugary cereal that turns milk blue—although they often don't eat it. One four-year-old child was videotaped eating his entire lunch at a 10:00 A.M. play break at his day care center—his hunger kicked in a couple of hours after leaving home. Everyone is busy in the morning, and few have time to eat much. Squires's team shared their insights with their client. The data were considered, and a product was developed—yogurt in a tube (Go-Gurt) (Squires and Byrne 2002; Jordan 2003; Squires 2006). This was a hit with mothers from a nutrition standpoint, and children liked the portability of the product. It earned $37,000,000 in first-year sales (Squires 2002; 2006).

ANTHROPOLOGY IN MEDICINE

medical anthropology The study of illness and health care from the perspective of anthropology.

Medical anthropology focuses on the application of anthropological methods and perspectives to issues of health and illness. It seeks solutions

ANTHROPOLOGY AROUND US

Folk Illness and Medical Anthropology

Folk medicine refers to the perceptions of ordinary people about health, illness, treatment, and cures. Stereotypes about folk medicine are that only poor and uneducated people use it. In fact, most people grow up learning ideas about sickness and health and use the remedies taught them by family members. We treat what we define as minor illness at home.

The work of ethnographers such as Juan Chavira (shown above left participating in a sweeping ceremony) has revealed the complexity of issues related to illness and health, including folk medicine. The use of multidisciplinary approaches and participant observation gives unique perspectives. Numerous studies of folk medicine among Hispanic populations in the United States, Latin America, and Mexico underscore this complexity.

A common folk illness found among Hispanics is *susto* (fright, magical fright, or fright sickness, where the soul is believed lost from the body). It develops when a person has had a sudden shock—for example,

to problems in areas such as maternal and child health, nutrition, public health, folk or ethnomedicine, epidemiology, and health care provider services. Medical anthropologists have backgrounds and degrees in both biological and cultural anthropology. They use a holistic perspective and eclectic and multidisciplinary approaches.

Several theoretical frameworks are the basis for work in medical anthropology. (1) A systems model approach. This model views medical care as a cultural system that should be considered within the context of other local cultural systems—practitioner culture (doctors, caseworkers, nurses) and patient culture (patient, patient's family and friends). The ethnocentrism of each can create barriers to effective treatment. (2) A biocultural approach with an ecological basis. This model approaches health by placing biological issues within a sociocultural environment and evaluates how these interact both within and across population groups (Wiley and Allen 2009: 5–8). This is a broad perspective, and a specific project may only focus, for example, on gender issues that affect health, or on genetic factors that place an ethnic group at risk for a specific disease.

a close relative's death, an accident, an intense argument, or watching a child nearly drown. Symptoms of *susto* include nervousness, daytime sleepiness, nighttime insomnia, depression, and diarrhea. Diagnosis includes the finding of a cluster of the above symptoms and the noting of a recent traumatic event in the person's life. Severe cases (often called *espanto*) are potentially fatal, and studies have shown higher death rates among long-term sufferers (cause of death is commonly attributed to diabetes mellitus, liver disease, or cancer). Folk healers treat *susto* with "sweeping" ceremonies, in which various herbs are passed over the body and the frightened soul is coaxed to return. Repeated ceremonies are required. Because such ceremonies are often effective in relieving symptoms, *susto* has been labeled a culture-bound psychological illness.

Medical anthropologist Arthur Rubel together with Carl O'Nell and Rolando Collado-Ardon designed a controlled multidisciplinary study to investigate *susto*. Three culturally distinct and historically independent communities in Mexico were subjects of the study. The project involved the use of participant observation, interviews, and questionnaires designed to test a series of hypotheses. Lifestyle, social stress, and levels of psychiatric impairment were variables under consideration as causes of *susto*. A sample of matched pairs of fifty individuals, one group with *susto* and the other consisting of individuals who did not have *susto*, were scrutinized, using medical examinations and other methods (Anderson 1996: 117).

The primary hypothesis was that *susto* is a unique culture-bound syndrome caused by social stress. The survey provided only weak evidence that this hypothesis was correct. The medical examinations showed people with *susto* actually had a measurably greater number of biological diseases than the control group. Both culture (social stresses) *and* biology (actual disease states) were responsible for the symptoms of *susto*. This project underscored the usefulness of medical anthropology to aid understanding of folk illness.

◎ What folk remedies did you learn from your family? Are there folk illnesses and remedies of others in your community about which you react ethnocentrically?

(3) A comparative framework that draws attention to the many attitudes about and treatments for health throughout the stages of life—birth, childhood, adulthood, old age, death. Cultures and subcultures worldwide often view and treat these biological experiences quite differently (Whiteford and Bennett 2005: 125). These theoretical approaches facilitate the application of research in medical anthropology to health care programs (Whiteford and Bennett 2005; Wiley and Allen 2009).

A Case Study of Anthropology in Medicine

This case illustrates how the consultant works as part of a team to investigate health issues and develop culturally sensitive solutions to problems. An investigation into an alternative cause of lead poisoning in children was launched as a result of a case in Los Angeles, California, that involved a child whose stomach was pumped in a hospital emergency room. A bright orange powder was found in the stomach contents, and a laboratory analysis established that the powder had an elemental lead content of over 90 percent. Health professionals interviewed the child's mother and were able to determine that she had given the child a folk remedy called *azarcon*. This remedy was used to treat a folk illness called *empacho*—a combination of constipation and indigestion. A public health alert was sent out based on this case. The health alert resulted in a nurse uncovering another case of *azarcon*-caused lead poisoning in Greeley, Colorado.

Lead poisoning most commonly affects children, and media messages often draw attention to the major causes of lead poisoning: lead-based paint chips eaten by babies and small children, and meals or drinks consumed from pottery decorated with improperly treated lead-based glazes. In these cases the usual sources of lead poisoning could not be established. The folk remedy called *azarcon* was a dangerous new source of lead poisoning, and health officials were concerned, especially when some initial research uncovered widespread knowledge of the remedy.

Robert Trotter, an anthropologist who had done research on Mexican American folk medicine, was brought in as a consultant on this case. He had not heard of *azarcon* in his previous research. Trotter's investigation began with research on *azarcon* in four Texas towns with large Mexican American populations. He searched herb shops (*yerberias*) and talked with folk healers (*curanderos*) but did not locate anyone who knew of *azarcon*. Meanwhile, the Los Angeles County Health Department discovered alternative names for the remedy. After receiving this information, Trotter returned to the towns and looked for *azarcon* under other names, such as *greta*. This remedy, which had the same amount of elemental lead content as *azarcon*, was sold in the herb shops as a remedy for *empacho*. Further investigation uncovered a wholesale distributor in Texas that was supplying more than 120 herb shops with *greta*. Most of the people buying and selling *greta* and *azarcon* believed them to be herbal compounds, probably because herbal remedies are common home remedies for Mexican Americans (Trotter 1987: 158).

Based on this initial research, Trotter began working on a health education project that ultimately served six clients, including the U.S. Food and Drug Administration and the regional office of the U.S. Department of Health and Human Services in Texas. Each of his clients wanted specific types of information about the use of *azarcon* and *greta*, or they contracted for Trotter to develop culturally sensitive materials on health awareness that would reduce the use of these remedies without attacking the local systems of folk medicine.

One of Trotter's projects was to help develop health education programs that focused on sources of lead poisoning. Media exposure included Spanish radio stations that broadcast public service announcements. Information packets about the hazards of *greta* and *azarcon* were sent to clinics that served immigrants. And a poster designed by Mexican American art students was placed in over 5,000 clinics and other public places in states

Folk herbalist shops like this one in Hong Kong, China, are sources for traditional herbal medicine in many parts of the world.

with concentrations of Mexican Americans (other Hispanic populations were not targeted because research revealed that *greta* and *azarcon* were not part of their folk remedies). Although no follow-up scientific research was carried out, two years after the education project the two dangerous compounds were hard to find (Trotter 1987: 154).

This case demonstrates the usefulness of anthropological research methods and knowledge in solving health care problems that are culturally related. Subsequent work showed that remedies similar to *greta* and *azarcon* were causing lead poisoning in Hmong, Saudi Arabian, and Chinese communities.

ANTHROPOLOGY IN AGRICULTURE

Agricultural anthropology is the study of agricultural activity from anthropology's holistic and comparative perspective. It focuses on "the human element in the total agrarian system, from production to preparation, distribution, consumption, and storage, along with cultural meanings and practices associated with these activities" (Rhoads 2005: 62–63). Anthropologists join with agricultural production experts, economists, botanists, entomologists, and ecologists, plus local farmers—with their unique knowledge and experience—to address agrarian issues. In preparation for this work,

agricultural anthropology
The study of agriculture using anthropological methods—holism, ethnographic fieldwork, and comparative method.

OLC
mhhe • com / lenkeit5e
See Web links.

agricultural anthropologists acquire strong backgrounds in biological and ecological sciences, economics, and GIS (geographic information systems). This foundation, together with employing our discipline's methodological emphasis on ethnography, fieldwork, holism, and the comparative method, positions them to act as effective team members in agricultural problem solving both locally and internationally. Applied anthropology's contribution to agriculture is demonstrated in the following case studies.

Case Studies of Anthropology in Agriculture

This classic case reported by Robert Rhoades (2005) illustrates how the anthropologist's ethnographic approach revealed numerous cultural issues that were overlooked by the original project planners. These issues were central to the lack of success of the original multimillion dollar project aimed at food security.

Rhoades was an anthropologist with the International Potato Center or CIP (Centro Internacional de la Papa) in Peru, where the CIP is headquartered. The CIP includes anthropological consultants on their research teams. The role of the CIP in this region focuses on its objectives of increasing crop production, maintaining biodiversity, protecting the environment, strengthening research, and improving policy.

The original project looked at the problem of food security in Peru—an area of concern to the United Nations Food and Agriculture Organization (FAO) and other agencies. Potatoes deteriorate rapidly after harvest, and city markets flooded with potatoes bring lower prices. A government-run national storage system would allow farmers to delay marketing part of their harvest until demand drove up prices. Engineers and agricultural experts designed and oversaw the building of large, technically perfect storage facilities, locating them in areas between cities and local farm communities. Millions of dollars were spent on the project (Rhoades 2005: 74). Farmers generally did not use the new facilities, however, and the storage experts didn't know why. At this point an anthropologist was brought in as part of a CIP postharvest team to explain the farmers' behavior—a project evaluation job.

The anthropologist began by observing and talking to farmers about potato storage and other farming problems and how they would like them solved. He discovered that farmers were not particularly concerned about market potato storage, i.e. consumer potato storage. They did not think of rotting potatoes as a loss because they used old shriveled potatoes to feed pigs, and they dehydrated them for later household consumption. Rather, the farmers were concerned about the storage of *seed* potatoes. Farmers stored seed potatoes in dark rooms. Darkness causes potatoes to grow long sprouts. It was time consuming to remove the sprouts, a job often done by women and children, and it was expensive to hire de-sprouters.

Additionally, the farmers wanted their seed potatoes kept safe. Theft was a major problem in the area, so they didn't store seeds or keep tools or animals in outbuildings. They also wanted to protect the seeds from the "evil eye" (the belief that a possessed person would pollute or damage the potatoes if they saw them) (Rhoades 2005: 74). The farmers didn't want centralized storage facilities, they wanted to keep the seed potatoes in their houses. This information provided the postharvest team with the perspective of the Andean farmers themselves.

The anthropologist, working as a "culture broker," communicated between the farmers and agricultural scientists, and information was shared. It was scientifically known that seed potatoes kept in diffused light sprout less and grow shorter sprouts. Light also causes the potato to turn green, making them inedible to people or animals (poisons form). Such potatoes could still be used for seed. The research team noticed that wide household roofs provided diffused light against houses and experimented with placing stacks of wooden trays full of seed potatoes in this location. Farmers joined in experiments and noted less sprouting and thus better seed potatoes, saving both labor and money. Farmers were concerned about the cost of wooden trays, but they found that by experimenting and improvising, trays constructed of local rustic wood worked as well. The diffused light storage technique for seed potatoes spread to over 20 countries worldwide (Rhoades et al., 1985). The input from the anthropologist on the CIP postharvest team brought focus to the importance of including the farmer in program development.

Another illustration of the contributions made by anthropologists working on agricultural issues comes from a comprehensive West African research project funded by USAID. Conducted by SANREM CRSP (Sustainable Agriculture and Natural Resource Management Collaborative Research Support Program), a Virginia Tech University–based research group, the project's focus is to support natural resource management by studying the interaction of ecosystems—physical, biological, and human (both institutions and communities that make management decisions) (SANREM CRSP 2010). Anthropologist Todd A. Crane was part of a multidisciplinary team in central Mali, working with Mali's Institut d'Economie Rurale and the rural Commune of Madiama. He conducted field research on farmers' knowledge and practices regarding local soils. Crane's research revealed that farmers had complex knowledge about local soil types, soil fertility, and topography. It also revealed local awareness of the physical landscape, including availability of water, and how all of this affected the management of crops and pastoral herds. Crane's findings fed back into the work of the project agronomists (Crane 2001; 2009). This was a participatory project, because local farmers and herders were involved in identifying resource management problems and addressing issues related to their making a living.

ANTHROPOLOGY IN ECONOMIC DEVELOPMENT

The United States has a long history of providing both financing and technical expertise in programs of economic development around the world. With the recognition that the anthropological approach enables the anticipation and avoidance of common barriers to culture change, anthropological consulting in economic development programs is on the increase.

A Case Study of Reforestation in Haiti

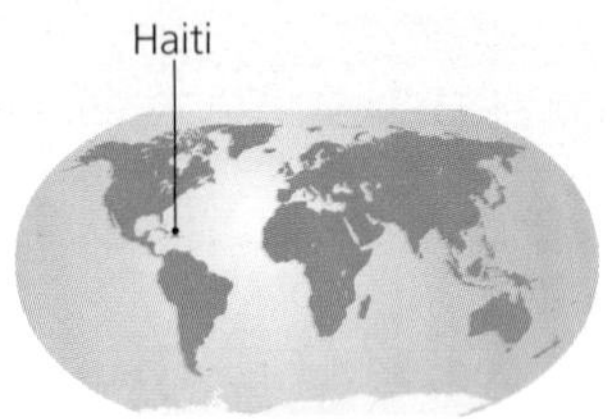

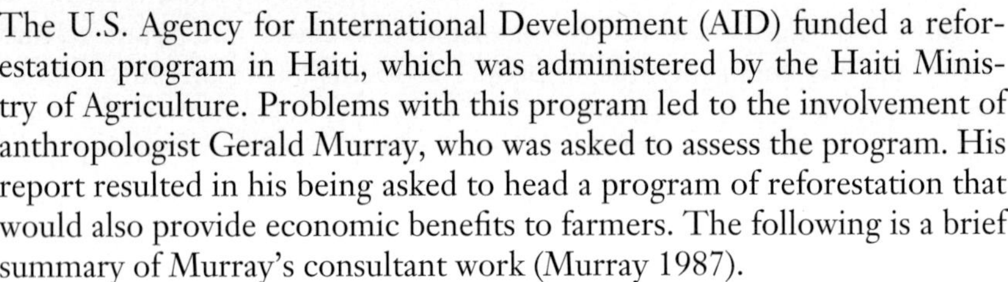

The U.S. Agency for International Development (AID) funded a reforestation program in Haiti, which was administered by the Haiti Ministry of Agriculture. Problems with this program led to the involvement of anthropologist Gerald Murray, who was asked to assess the program. His report resulted in his being asked to head a program of reforestation that would also provide economic benefits to farmers. The following is a brief summary of Murray's consultant work (Murray 1987).

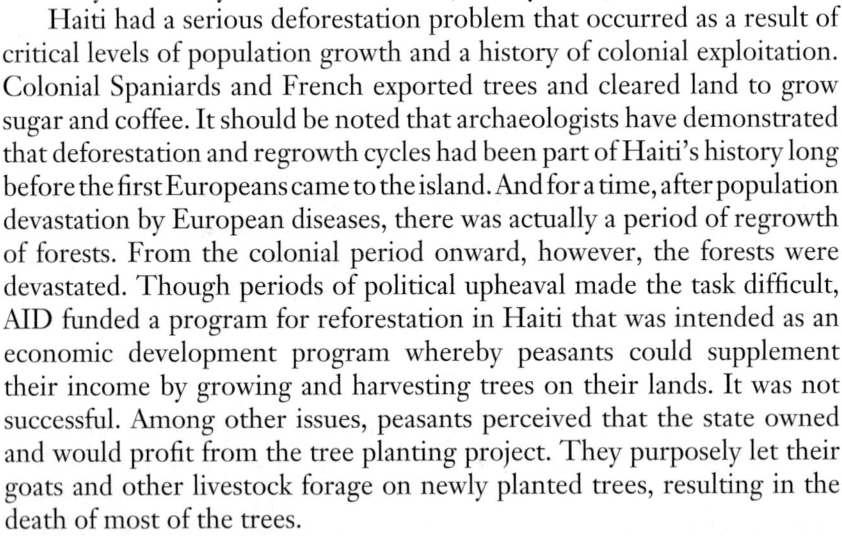

Haiti had a serious deforestation problem that occurred as a result of critical levels of population growth and a history of colonial exploitation. Colonial Spaniards and French exported trees and cleared land to grow sugar and coffee. It should be noted that archaeologists have demonstrated that deforestation and regrowth cycles had been part of Haiti's history long before the first Europeans came to the island. And for a time, after population devastation by European diseases, there was actually a period of regrowth of forests. From the colonial period onward, however, the forests were devastated. Though periods of political upheaval made the task difficult, AID funded a program for reforestation in Haiti that was intended as an economic development program whereby peasants could supplement their income by growing and harvesting trees on their lands. It was not successful. Among other issues, peasants perceived that the state owned and would profit from the tree planting project. They purposely let their goats and other livestock forage on newly planted trees, resulting in the death of most of the trees.

Evidence of the failure of the project and the political misdirection of project funds caught the attention of a U.S. congressman. He became interested in the problems of overpopulation and deforestation in Haiti and threatened a worldwide freeze on AID funding if results were not soon forthcoming in Haiti (Murray 1987).

Gerald Murray had conducted his doctoral research in Haiti. His focus was on how internal population growth had affected peasant land tenure. Because of his knowledge, Murray was able to look at the problem of why peasants were not embracing the reforestation project. He was asked to evaluate current and previous programs, and in his report he

Reforestation in Haiti.

noted that the existing system of land tenure, crop production, and livestock were compatible with the undertaking of reforestation efforts, plus he outlined a program to achieve this. He jokingly told people involved with the AID program that he could administer a successful program with fifty thousand dollars and a jeep (Murray 1987).

Murray was working in academia two years later when he was notified that a $4 million project for reforestation had been approved. The project was presented as he had outlined it in his earlier report. Murray was offered the job of administering the project, and he accepted the challenge. The technical issues and solutions associated with Murray's program (known as the Agroforestry Outreach Project, or AOP) were as follows:

First, Murray needed to identify fast-growing drought-resistant trees that produced wood suitable for construction and that produced good charcoal (a market existed for both products). Suitable tree species were found, and several had the added benefit of restoring nutrients to the soil. Some, such as *Eucalyptus camaldulensis*, would produce new growth from stumps, thus allowing multiple harvests from a single planting.

Next, the program had to produce microseedlings that were lightweight and could be produced in quantity and transported easily. The previously used seedlings were bulky and heavy. For example, only 250 traditional seedlings could be transported in an AOP project truck, whereas 15,000 of the new lighter microseedlings could be carried in the same truck.

Murray needed to develop ethnographic information on cropping patterns and solicit input from the peasants themselves. This helped to develop strategies in which planting trees, even on small holdings, was feasible. Trees were planted on perimeters and intercropped in ways that did not reduce the land occupied by other crops.

Meeting several potential barriers to the project head on was critical to project success. One barrier was the perception by peasants that trees took a long time to grow. This delay in receiving benefit from the plantings made the project undesirable to them. Fortunately, there were four-year-old stands of several of the project tree species already in Haiti. Taking groups of peasants to see what four-year-old stands of the trees looked like changed their perceptions.

Another barrier was the perception that too much space would be taken up by the trees. By creating a demonstration plot that showed the space needs of seedlings, farmers learned that they could plant other cash crops between the rows of tree seedlings for several years before the trees created too much shade.

AOP technicians also had to overcome the perception that somehow the project or the government would actually own the trees. Murray clearly communicated and presented the project in the form of a contract agreement. The project would furnish the trees. Each planter had to agree to plant five hundred seedlings and to allow AOP workers to make periodic survival counts on the trees. The AOP would not pay any wages for the work of planting, but they guaranteed that the planter owned the trees. No permissions would be needed to cut trees; there would not be penalties if trees died.

Finally, Murray's team actually calculated with peasants the income that they would derive from the sale of wood and charcoal. These profit figures clearly offset any loss from decreased production of other crops.

The AOP tree planting project was a huge success. By the time the four-year funded project ended, close to 20 million trees had been planted. By the end of the fourth year, trees were being harvested and money was being made (Murray 1987). Murray's application of anthropological methods when he conceived of and administered this program was at the core of its success.

TRY THIS
Analyze

Choose a problem at a place where you work or have worked. Think about things ***you*** complain about or listen to the complaints of coworkers to get ideas for a problem focus. Then list three specific ways that you could use the tools of anthropology to search for a solution to the problem.

ANTHROPOLOGY AND YOU—ON THE JOB AND IN THE COMMUNITY

It is my hope that you have learned enough about the basics of anthropology that you will use its perspectives and methods in your work and life. If you are going to be a teacher, you will deal with students of diverse subcultures. No place in North America is so isolated as to not have some cultural diversity, and such diversity can be the source of misunderstanding and conflict in a formal educational setting. Teachers, administrators,

OLC
mhhe • com / lenkeit5e
See Internet exercises.

and parents of students will benefit from viewing diversity through an anthropological lens. Those of you entering careers in the business world will be able to use these same concepts and perspectives as you deal with clients, competitors, employees, and managers domestically and internationally. Health care careers increasingly require awareness and sensitivity to diverse subcultural groups for the effective delivery of health care programs.

SUMMARY

Recently there has been a growing awareness of the application of anthropological perspectives and methods to the solution of practical problems. Corporations, both domestic and international, are calling on consulting anthropologists to study, analyze, and make recommendations for solving problems when traditional management techniques have failed. Private and government agencies are using anthropology to solve everyday problems. Participant observation and a focus on issues of culture can help in viewing situations through lenses that are unavailable with other approaches. Applying anthropology is not about standard lists of memorized approaches and facts; rather, it is about using the tools of anthropology to uncover the cultural issues unique to each situation.

Study Questions

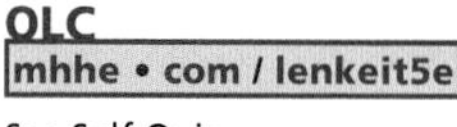

See Self Quiz.

1. What are some areas of practical application of anthropology?
2. How can an understanding of the culture concept be useful in solving problems in business, health care, and development programs? Cite and discuss a specific example.
3. Discuss the role of anthropology's holistic perspective in problem solving. Cite and discuss a specific example.

Suggested Readings

OLC mhhe • com / lenkeit5e

See Web links.

Fadiman, Anne. 1997. *The Spirit Catches You and You Fall Down: A Hmong Child, Her American Doctors, and the Collision of Two Cultures.* New York: Farrar, Straus and Giroux. Extraordinary account of Western medicine attempting to address epilepsy in an immigrant Hmong child. Both cultures learn a great deal about and from each other.

Kedia, Satish, and John Van Willigen, eds. 2005. *Applied Anthropology: Domains of Application*. New York: Praeger. Outstanding, readable coverage of major topical areas in applied work.

Sobo, Elisa J., and Martha O. Loustaunau. 2010. *The Cultural Context of Health, Illness, and Medicine*, 2nd ed. Santa Barbara, CA:ABC-CLIO, LLC. Packed with current examples, this title underscores the holistic perspective.

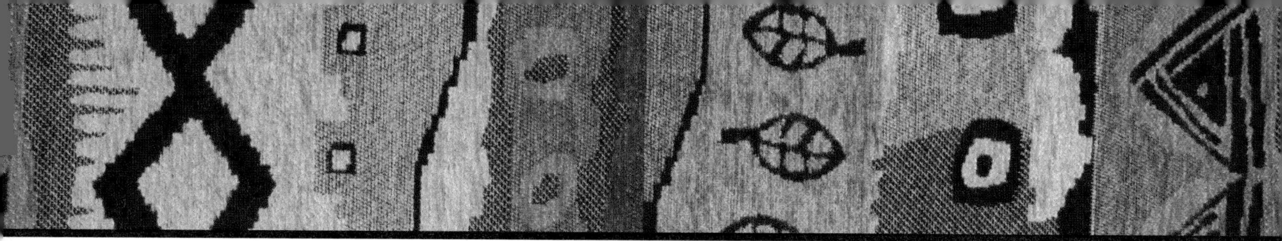

APPENDIX A
How Do You Read an Ethnography?

The following guide to reading ethnographies is intended to aid your reading and study of ethnographic material. It is directed at book-length ethnographies, but the approach may also be used to read, study, and assess shorter, topic-specific ethnographic accounts such as those often found in collections of readings.

WHAT TO DO AS YOU READ

I. Determine When the Fieldwork Was Conducted and When the Resulting Ethnography Was Published

When you first pick up an ethnography, check the dates. When was it first published? When was the fieldwork accomplished? The fieldwork may have occurred on more than one set of dates. Often the author of an ethnography has returned repeatedly to the same group and been with that group for varying lengths of time. Franz Boas emphasized that this was the only appropriate way to record the history of a culture, with revisits and restudies of the same group. One drawback to this approach is that one does not know from firsthand observation what happened between visits. The only sources for that information would be the recollections of the native members of the culture. Awareness of the dates is also important because the ethnography may be old. It is a snapshot of a group of people at the time of the study. You may want to do additional research to find out how the group has changed and adapted over time.

II. Identify the Perspective Guiding the Author

The approaches taken by the author should be clear. Identifying the author's perspective before your more careful reading of the text will be helpful as you analyze the data presented. The perspectives described here offer valuable information about other cultures, but it can be difficult to compare the data presented in accounts that use different perspectives.

Scientific Method Approach or Reflexive Approach? Look for a statement by the author of the perspective used or favored: the scientific method approach (see Chapter 1) or a reflexive approach (see Chapter 3). If the ethnography is based on the scientific method, it will include careful definition of terms and statements about the parameters of the research. It will often include one or more hypotheses being tested, plus the methods used in gathering data relevant to the testing of hypotheses. Finally, data will be presented quantitatively. In other words, every attempt is made to apply the scientific method (keeping in mind that it is difficult to control variables in a field setting the way one is able to control them in a laboratory setting).

If the ethnography is based on a reflexive approach, it will include discussions of how the ethnographer felt about what was observed and experienced. It may include material presented in the voice of the culture's native members. Dialogue between ethnographer and native members of the culture may be included. The ethnographer's personal reflections about not only the process of the fieldwork but also the ethics of the situation may be included. Data usually focus on an in-depth consideration of a few specific personal interactions rather than the presentation of quantified information.

Traditional Ethnography or Problem-Oriented Ethnography? Traditional ethnographies attempt to give a complete picture of an entire culture based on the ethnographer's experience living in that society for at least a year. In the past this was a major goal of ethnography, but recognition over time of the complexity of culture and society led anthropologists to reassess this approach. Today many ethnographers take problem- or issue-oriented approaches to fieldwork, concentrating on one aspect of the culture. Such work is often longitudinal, with repeat field stays and ongoing field research that may span decades. Teams of researchers are often involved.

III. Note the Table of Contents

Before you begin reading, compare the chapter headings in the ethnography's table of contents with the table of contents in this book. Also compare the topics with those in a second ethnography. You may learn quite a bit by doing this. Specifically you will see what topics are focal points of the ethnography. This may give you insight about the author's perspective.

Carefully consider how each major topic is defined or explained. Definitions sometimes differ (sometimes the differences are quite small). These differences affect the data and how they are interpreted. Consider this, for example: If two authors use different definitions of what constitutes a family, what difficulties will occur when you attempt to compare their data?

IV. Look for Notes on Fieldwork

Does the ethnography contain a "Fieldwork" section? This is usually one of the first parts of an ethnography. Inclusion of fieldwork sections in original ethnographies, and fieldwork editions (a republishing of an original ethnography with the addition of a section on the fieldwork experience), have been popular since the 1960s. Prior to 1960 many ethnographic accounts were published without any mention of the ethnographer's personal fieldwork experience.

When reading the fieldwork section, look for evidence of how the ethnographer (1) entered the community, (2) established rapport with the people, (3) coped with physical challenges of adapting to this environment, (4) experienced culture shock, (5) dealt with ethical issues, and (6) carried out research. How did this account illustrate the method of participant observation? Did the ethnographer use key informants, use formal or informal interviews, gather genealogical information, collect life histories, collect botanical samples, or collect myths and stories? Did the ethnographer discuss her or his personal interactions with the native members of the culture?

V. Write in the Margin

As you read, jot notes to yourself in the margin. Actively connect your readings in the ethnography with your text reading assignment in this book. Most ethnographic accounts give only cursory definitions of terms. It is expected that the reader of an ethnography understands common anthropological terms and concepts, the word *culture*, for example. If you are given reading assignments in this book and in an ethnography, always read the text first. This way you will be prepared with an overview of a topic before you read a specific illustration. By using this technique, you should also find yourself analyzing and comparing as you read. For example, if you read about a person preparing for a marriage celebration, the ethnography may not always identify this as part of a ritual known as a rite of passage. If you have just read the text section about different types of rituals found in cultures, you can identify this as a rite of passage and jot that in the margin.

ETHNOGRAPHIES WITHOUT INDEXES

Some ethnographies do not contain an index. These ethnographies are often written from a reflexive perspective. Because the author is telling of her or his experiences, what was seen and learned, the author does not expect that this information will be used in comparative scientific studies. Therefore, there is no index. This makes it difficult for the reader to quickly locate material. I strongly recommend notes in margins (for example, *marriage custom*). In addition I suggest that you "flag" pages with small colorful sticky notes (you can even use some form of color coding—green for food-procurement data, yellow for beliefs, red for rituals, blue for marriage and kinship).

YOU AND THE ETHNOGRAPHY

Reading an ethnography involves the examination of how people in a society live. It is also an exercise in reflection. You *read* about a custom rather than learn about it firsthand through participant observation. As you read, you will likely encounter customs or behaviors that will bring forth an inner voice that says, That is stupid, or, These people are ignorant. Or you may read of a custom that you consider wrong ethically and morally. You may be confused by these feelings. These are the same issues of ethnocentrism that the ethnographer must face while living in a cultural setting different from his or her own. You may find that you have similar reactions when you change jobs, or move to a new neighborhood, or travel to a different country—in other words, when you are in a new subculture. You must grapple with that inner voice. You must try to step back to a neutral place and examine both the ethnographic culture and your own culture. Remember that you are reading about a cultural and social system that works for these people. To appreciate it and respect it, you must push away your own provincialism and move, for a time, outside the walls of your familiar sociocultural environment.

Jot down notes regarding how you feel about what you read. This can be an uncomfortable process, even painful. But an education is about expanding horizons. In the end you will have a new recognition of your own way of life as well as a new respect for another way of life. This does not mean that you will or should change your own viewpoint. It simply means that you are exploring a different way of knowing and being. Keep in mind that had you been adopted as an infant and raised by parents in the other culture you would be of that culture, and all of its customs and behaviors would seem correct and morally right to you. If you follow these suggestions as you read, you will likely learn as much or more about your culture and yourself as about others.

HOW TO COMPARE TWO OR MORE ETHNOGRAPHIES

You will find it helpful to make a table when you need to process a lot of information. I recommend making a table as an excellent way to organize data and to prepare for comparison and contrast questions on exams. First, begin by making a table or grid for yourself. Second, choose major topics and concepts based on those in this book, your professor's lectures, and the table of contents of the ethnography. Place these topics along one axis of your table and the names of the ethnographies and ethnographers along the other axis. Finally, add information to this table each time you read. You can easily expand your table by taping 8½- by 11-inch pieces of paper together. These can then be folded and placed in a folder. Use this table as a quick source to study, to quiz yourself on the information, and to compare and contrast the ethnographies by topic. Note that this technique works well for materials in other courses too. Here is an example of such a table:

Topics	*[Ethnography—name of society]*	*[Ethnography—name of society]*
Dates of fieldwork		
Environment		
Subsistence strategy and technology		
Resource allocation		
Marriage pattern and residence		
Kinship and descent		
Political organization		
Belief systems		

GLOSSARY

acculturation The incorporation of knowledge, ideas, behaviors, and material creations from a different culture as a consequence of prolonged contact with that culture.

Acheulean hand axes Part of an African and European tool tradition associated with *Homo erectus* and *Homo ergaster*. The tradition also includes cleavers and some flake tools.

achieved status A status position that is earned through an individual's skills, actions, and accomplishments.

action anthropologist One who believes that he or she has a moral obligation to take the side of indigenous populations whenever such peoples' rights to self-determination are violated.

affinal kin Kin related by marriage.

agnates Members of a patrilineage.

agricultural anthropology The study of agriculture using anthropological methods—holism, ethnographic fieldwork, and comparative method.

agriculture A subsistence strategy based on intensive, continuous use of land for the production of plant foods. It typically includes one or more of the following: cultivation of soils, use of fertilizers, and irrigation.

ambilineal descent A unilineal descent system in which some members of the society acquire and pass on descent affiliation through females, whereas others do so through males.

ambilocal residence See *bilocal residence.*

anthropology The science or study of *Homo sapiens* using a holistic approach.

applied anthropology The branch of anthropology that focuses on the application of anthropological methods and approaches to the solution of problems, as distinct from academic anthropology.

applied archaeology The use of archaeological methods to study the material culture of contemporary societies. Data can be used to develop social programs.

archaeology The systematic study of the artifacts and ecofacts from past cultures as a means of reconstructing past lifeways.

artifacts Objects made by humans.

ascribed status The status a person is given at birth and over which that person has no control.

attribute A discrete characteristic of an artifact. Attributes include shape, size, design elements and their placement, and techniques of manufacture.

authority The exercise of legitimate power; the right to rule invested by members of the community in its leaders.

avunculocal residence A postmarriage residence rule that requires the bride and groom to reside with or near the groom's mother's brother.

balanced reciprocity Exchange and gift giving with the expectation of a return of equal value within a reasonable period of time.

band A type of society common in foraging groups and marked by egalitarian social structure and lack of specialization.

barter Exchange of products that does not involve currency.

behavioral archaeology An area of applied archaeology that focuses on the relationships between material culture and people's behavior.

bifurcate The distinction within kinship systems where father's side and mother's side of the family are labeled and treated differently, splitting mother's side of the family from father's side of the family.

Big Men Alternate term for *headmen* common in Melanesian societies. See *headmen*.

bilateral descent Descent that is traced equally through both mother and father.

bilocal residence The condition in which a newly married couple reside either with or near the groom's parents or the bride's parents.

biological anthropology A subfield of anthropology that studies humans as a biological species. Also called physical anthropology.

biped An animal that walks on two legs.

bridewealth A form of marriage finance in which valuable gifts are given by the groom's kin to the bride's kin.

carrying capacity The maximum population that a habitat can sustain.

caste A ranked group with membership determined at birth.

chiefdom A type of society with an office of chief, most commonly hereditary; social ranking; and a redistributive economy.

clan A descent group consisting of two or more lineages that trace their origin to a mythical ancestor.

class A group of people who have a similar relationship to wealth, power, and prestige.

cline The variation of a biological trait along a geographic continuum. Human skin pigments show distribution along a cline from the equator north and south.

colonialism Influence and dominance of one nation over another for the purpose of exploiting raw resources. The dominant nation-state establishes a physical presence and a colonial government. See *imperialism; hegemony*.

commodity money Currency in the form of valued objects such as shells or gold.

community An association of people who share a common identity, including geographic boundaries, common language, and culture.

comparative method The methodological approach of comparing data. Anthropologists use the comparative method.

consanguineal relatives Kin related by blood.

contagious magic A type of magic based on the idea that something that has contact with a person or animal contains some essence of that being and that magic performed on the item will have the same effect as if performed on the being.

contemporary human variation studies The study of the biological variation in living humans.

cross-cousin Ego's mother's brother's child and father's sister's child.

cultural anthropology A subfield of anthropology that focuses on human sociocultural adaptations.

cultural ecology The study of the processes by which a society adapts to its environment.

cultural evolution A model for the development of society that delineates a sequence of cultural change over time.

cultural relativism The perspective that any aspect of a culture must be viewed and evaluated within the context of that culture.

cultural resource management (CRM) The conservation and management of archaeological sites to protect them.

culture The sum total of the knowledge, ideas, behaviors, and material creations that are learned, shared, and transmitted primarily through the symbolic system of language. These components create a pattern (that changes over time) and serve as guides and standards of behavior for members of the society. The term *culture* is used in the abstract as well as to refer to a specific culture.

culture shock A label for the resultant feelings of homesickness, disorientation, helplessness, and frustration that occur after exposure to an unfamiliar culture.

descent group A group of people who share identity and come from a common ancestor.

descriptive linguistics The part of anthropological linguistics that focuses on the mechanics of language.

deviance The violation of an ideal pattern of behavior within a society.

diffusion The voluntary borrowing and exchange of items or ideas between cultures.

diffusionism Early theoretical school that explained the origin and spread of artifacts and ideas through borrowing between cultures.

displacement The ability of humans to communicate symbolically about distant time and place.

division of labor The manner of dividing work based on criteria such as age or gender.

double descent A descent system with two separate lines of descent that are both recognized at the same time.

dowry A form of marriage finance in which valuable gifts are given by the bride's kin to the groom's kin.

ecofacts The remains of plants, animals, or naturally occurring nonorganic substances.

ecological model A model that views a culture as part of a larger global ecological system with each aspect of the system interacting with all of the other parts.

egalitarian Refers to members of a society having equal access to status, power, and wealth within the same category such as age or gender.

egalitarian society A society in which individuals within the same category of age and gender have equal access to wealth, prestige, and power.

emic An insider's view of a culture. This perspective in ethnography uses the categories and ideas that are relevant and meaningful to the culture under study.

enculturation The process of learning one's culture while growing up in it.

endogamy A cultural rule that dictates that one must marry within a designated group.

ethnic group A type of subculture characterized by members sharing a culture of origin, often one originating in another country.

ethnoarchaeology The study of contemporary societies' behaviors and uses of material objects in order to better understand how human behavior translates into the archaeological record.

ethnocentrism Making value judgments based on one's own culture when describing aspects of another culture.

ethnography A written description of a culture based on data gathered from fieldwork.

ethnolinguistics A field of study in linguistics that analyzes the relationship between a language and culture.

ethnology The comparative study of cultures with the aim of presenting analytical generalizations about human culture.

ethnomusicology The study of the music of a contemporary society within the context of that society.

etic An outsider's view of a culture. This perspective in ethnography uses the categories of the anthropologist's culture to describe the culture under study.

evolutionary-ecological model A paradigm of human culture that combines both the neoevolutionary and ecological perspectives.

exogamy A cultural rule that dictates that one must marry outside of a designated group (e.g., outside of one's lineage, clan, or village).

experimental archaeology An aspect of archaeology in which experiments are performed to learn how prehistoric artifacts and features were made and used.

extended family Two or more nuclear families who are related by blood and who reside in the same household, village, or territory (e.g., a man and wife, their sons, and their sons' wives and children).

family band A type of band organization consisting of nuclear family units that move independently within an area. Joins others when resources are plentiful; travels alone at other times.

family of orientation A person's childhood family, where enculturation takes place.

family of procreation A kin group consisting of an individual and the individual's spouse and children.

features Nonportable evidence of technology at archaeological sites, such as roadways and fire hearths.

fiat money Paper currency backed by a nation-state's claim of its value.

fictive kin Unrelated family friends who are addressed by kin terms.

folate A metabolite essential for sperm and embryonic neural tube development that is destroyed by UVB.

foraging A food-procurement strategy that involves collecting wild plant and animal foods.

forensic anthropologist An applied biological anthropologist concerned with legal issues. Frequently focuses on the identification of skeletal material and the cause of death.

formal interviews An ethnographic research method in which planned, scripted questions are asked of informants.

gender The sociocultural construct of masculine and feminine roles and the qualities assigned to these roles.

gender role The tasks and behaviors assigned by a culture to each sex.

genealogical method The ethnographic method of recording information about kinship relationships using symbols and diagrams.

generalized reciprocity Institutionalized gift giving and exchange between close kin; accounts are not kept, and there is no expectation of immediate return.

globalization In anthropology, the rapid spread of economic, social, and cultural systems across continents.

half-marriage A custom among the Yurok of northwestern California and other patri-centered groups in which a man pays partial bridewealth and lives with the bride's family, and the couple's children belong to the wife and her family.

headmen Types of leaders found in tribal and chiefdom societies whose leadership is based on persuasive power. See *Big Men*.

hegemony The ideological domination by one cultural group over another through institutions, bureaucracy, education, and sometimes force. See *imperialism; colonialism*.

heliocentric diffusionism Diffusionist school that pointed to ancient Egypt as the center of cultural innovations and inventions that spread around the world.

heterogeneous culture Cultural group that shares only a few components. Typical of large societies such as states, where there are many subcultures such as ethnic groups.

heterosexuality Sexual attraction between members of the opposite sex.

historical archaeology A subfield of archaeology that studies the remains of cultures that existed during the time of written records but about which little was recorded.

historical linguistics The study of the history of languages, including their development and relationship to other languages.

historicalism Theoretical school, established by Franz Boas, who hypothesized that each culture had its own particular history that could be documented through repeated ethnographies. Comparisons of many such histories could uncover underlying principles of culture change. Also termed *historical particularism; American historicalism.*

holistic An integrated perspective that assumes interrelationships among the parts of a subject. Anthropology studies humans from a holistic perspective, including both biological and cultural aspects.

homogeneous culture Cultural group that shares most ideas, values, knowledge, behaviors, and artifacts. Typical of small cultural groups such as foragers.

Homo sapiens The taxonomic designation for humans.

homosexuality Sexual attraction between members of the same sex.

horticulture A food-procurement strategy based on crop production without soil preparation, fertilizers, irrigation, or use of draft animals.

household A common residence-based economic unit.

humanistic anthropology A label for research that focuses on individuals and their creative responses to cultural and historical forces.

ideal culture What people believe they should do.

imitative magic A type of magic based on the notion that working magic on an image of an animal or person will cause the same effect on the actual animal or person.

impact studies Ethnographic study of a situation to document effects of change. May take place during and/or after a program of cultural restructuring.

imperialism Influence and authority of one nation over another, often associated with exploitation of natural and human resources. See *colonialism; hegemony.*

informal interviews An ethnographic research method using open-ended questions that allow informants to talk about what they deem important.

informants Native members of a society who give information about their culture to an ethnographer.

innovation Something totally new.

invention Something new that is created based on items or ideas that already exist.

judgment sample A sample that is chosen based on the judgment of the ethnographer. Key informants are chosen using this method.

key informant An ethnographic interview subject who has been selected by judgment sample; a knowledgeable native who plays a major role in teaching the ethnographer about the informant's culture.

kindred A term associated with bilateral descent in which relatives calculate their degree of relationship to Ego. In a kindred, only siblings share the exact same set of relatives.

kinesics The use of the body to communicate—gestures, posture, and facial expression.

kinship system The complexity of a culture's rules governing the relationships between affinal and consanguineal kin.

kinship term A word that designates a social relationship between individuals who are related by blood or marriage.

law The cultural rule formulated by a society and backed up by sanctions.

levirate A marriage custom in which a widow marries her deceased husband's brother.

lexigrams Geometric figure symbols used to teach apes symbolic communication.

life history The ethnographic method of gathering data based on extensive interviews with individuals about their memories of their culture from childhood through adulthood.

life shock A sudden unexpected experience that causes one to faint, become hysterical, or vomit. More likely to occur when immersed in an unfamiliar setting.

lineage A unilineal descent group that traces its consanguineal relatives back to a common ancestor.

linguistics A subfield of anthropology that includes the study of the structure, history, and social aspects of human language.

low energy budget The expenditure of minimum energy to acquire the basic needs for survival.

magic The techniques used to manipulate supernatural forces and beings.

mana An impersonal supernatural force that flows in and out of people and objects.

market exchange The trading of goods and services through the use of currency.

matrifocal residence A residence group consisting of a woman and her children residing without co-residence of a husband.

matrilineage A unilineal descent group with membership passed on through females and traced to a common female ancestor.

matrilocal residence A postmarriage residence rule that requires the bride and groom to live in or near the residence of the bride's mother.

matri-patrilocal residence A temporary residence form in which the groom moves to live with the bride's family until bridewealth payments are complete and the couple take up permanent patrilocal residence.

medical anthropology The study of illness and health care from the perspective of anthropology.

melanin A pigment in the outer layer of the skin. It is responsible for skin color and blocks UVB from damaging lower layers of the skin.

microculture The smallest subgroup within a culture that shares specific cultural features such as values or behaviors.

midden Archaeological term to designate an area of discard; a trash heap.

mobile art Art forms that are not fixed to any place and can be moved or carried.

moiety An association that divides a society in half. Moiety affiliation is inherited unilineally and carries obligations to other members.

monogamy A form of marriage in which one woman is married to one man.

monotheistic A belief system that focuses on one all-powerful supernatural being.

morpheme The smallest combination of sounds in human speech that carry a meaning.

multilinear evolution An evolutionary model of culture emphasizing different development patterns for societies in different habitats.

narrative ethnography See *reflexive ethnography*.

nation-state A group that shares a common cultural heritage, territory, and legitimate political structure.

negative reciprocity An economic exchange aimed at receiving more than is given.

neoevolutionary model A model of cultural evolution based on types of food-procurement strategies and the sociocultural adaptations that resulted from them.

neolocal residence A postmarriage residence rule that requires the bride and groom to set up an independent household away from both sets of parents.

nomadic pastoralism A herding adaptation that makes the most of available forage for animals by frequent habitat moves.

nuclear family A group consisting of a married couple and their children.

Oldowan tools A very early African tool-making tradition associated with the first members of *Homo*.

optimal-foraging model A model that aims at understanding how foragers optimize the gathering of food.

paleoanthropology The study of human biological evolution.

pan-tribal sodality An association group that crosscuts a tribe and unites tribal members, not always voluntary. See *sodality*.

parallel-cousin Ego's mother's sister's child and father's brother's child.

parietal art Art executed on permanent features such as cave walls, rock shelters, and large blocks of rock.

participant observation The process of an anthropologist doing ethnographic fieldwork.

participant observer The role of an anthropologist doing ethnographic fieldwork.

pastoralism A food-producing strategy based on herding.

patrilineage A unilineal descent group passed on through males and traced to a common male ancestor.

patrilocal band A type of band consisting of related males and their wives and children who stay together and forage as a group.

patrilocal residence A postmarriage residence rule that requires the bride and groom to live in or near the residence of the groom's father.

phoneme The smallest unit of sound in speech that will indicate a difference in meaning.

phonology The general study of the sounds used in human speech.

phratry A group of two or more clans that have a tie to one another, often based on a historical relationship; obligations and rights are expected between clans in this relationship.

physical anthropology See *biological anthropology*.

plasticity The pliability or malleability of a biological feature. An individual's genetic growth potential is malleable depending on nutrition, maternal health, and exposure to sunlight.

polyandry Marriage of one woman to two or more men.

polygamy Multiple spouse marriage.

polygyny Marriage of one man to two or more women.

polytheistic A belief system consisting of many supernatural beings of approximately equal power.

postmodernism A complex theoretical perspective that applies a humanistic approach to ethnography with a focus on individuals and their voices.

postmodernist One who uses the paradigm of postmodernism.

power The ability to influence or cause people or groups to do certain things that they would not do otherwise.

prehistoric archaeology The analysis of the material remains of cultures that existed before the time of written records.

priest A full-time supernatural practitioner who is part of a bureaucracy.

primates Animals in the order Primates; includes humans, apes, monkeys, and prosimians.

primatology The study of nonhuman primates.

prophet A person, usually charismatic, who has had direct communication with a god. Often receives a message that articulates a plan of action for the group.

proxemics The study of the use of space in communication.

psychological anthropology The study of the relationship between culture and personality.

quadruped An animal that walks on four limbs.

race Biologically: a group within a species that shares a cluster of genetically determined traits. No such trait clusters occur among *Homo sapiens.* Culturally: a social construct based on physical differences interpreted through a cultural lens.

random sample A sample method in which all members of a population have a statistically equal chance of being chosen.

rank society A society in which the individual's access to prestige and wealth is limited by the number of positions available. A society may be stratified by rank, such as in a chiefdom.

rapport A harmonious relationship.

real culture What people can be observed to do.

reciprocity A form of exchange that involves the mutual giving and receiving of food and other items between people who are socially equal.

recursion A feature of language that allows for the generation of variation in sentences by using embedded or added clauses and phrases.

redistribution A system of exchange in which wealth is reallocated; found in chiefdom and state societies.

reflexive ethnography An approach to fieldwork that focuses on the personal experiences and perspectives of the ethnographer, as well as the voices of the native members of a culture. Also called narrative ethnography.

revitalization movement An organized movement, which occurs during times of change, that involves perceived loss of traditional cultural values. A prophet or charismatic leader predicts a revitalized society if a program is followed.

rites of intensification Rituals, often seasonal, that reinforce group solidarity, cultural values, and group social and political status relationships.

rites of passage Rituals associated with the social movement of an individual from one culturally defined role and status to another during the passage from birth to death.

ritual Behavior that is formalized, is regularly repeated, and has symbolic content.

role The culturally assigned behaviors and expectations for a person's social position.

Sapir-Whorf hypothesis A hypothesis about the relationship between language and culture that states that language constructs perceptions.

segmentary lineage A descent group consisting of sublineage sets.

sex The biological aspect of being female, male, or other, assigned at birth based on external genitalia.

sexual dimorphism The biological and behavioral differences between males and females.

shabano A Yąnomamö village.

shaman A part-time practitioner of the supernatural who has special powers to mediate between the supernatural world and the community.

silent language All of a culture's nonverbal symbolic systems of communication, including kinesics and proxemics.

sister exchange A common type of marriage consisting of the marriage of cross-cousins. Men exchange their sisters as marriage partners.

site The location of archaeological remains such as artifacts and features.

slash-and-burn The removal of plant materials by cutting and burning preparatory to planting. Also called swidden horticulture.

social control A process involving a structure and mechanisms to ensure that people do not violate the society's accepted forms of behavior.

social stratification Ascribed and achieved differences between two classes within a society.

sociolinguistics A subfield of linguistics that analyzes the relationship between language and culture with a focus on how people speak in social contexts.

sodality A group that crosscuts a society and whose membership is based on common interest rather than kinship or residence.

sororate A marriage custom in which a widower marries a sister of his deceased wife.

state A type of society characterized by a political structure with authority that is legally constituted.

status A person's position in society.

stratified random sample A random sample with divisions into categories such as age or socioeconomic level.

stratified society A society with unequal access to resources within the same gender and status group.

stratified state society A society in which institutions are based on coercive power and authority. Inequality exists within social groupings.

string figures A type of entertainment in which designs, or figures, are created by weaving string on the fingers. Patterns, tricks, and catches are performed and are often accompanied by stories.

structured interviews See *formal interviews.*

subculture Smaller group within a large cultural complex. Behaviors, values, attitudes, and artifacts are shared by group members.

supernatural beings Invisible beings that exhibit form, personality, attitudes, and powers.

supernatural belief A belief that transcends the observable, natural world.

supernatural forces Unseen powers that are not personified and may be manipulated to achieve good or evil.

syntax The manner in which minimum units of meaning (morphemes) are combined.

technology The knowledge, tools, and skills used by humans to manipulate their environments.

totem Mythical or symbolic ancestor of a clan.

traditions Cultural choices consistently made by a society and practiced generation to generation.

transhumance A variety of pastoralism in which herds are moved seasonally.

tribe A type of society marked by egalitarian social structure, based on horticultural and pastoral economies, and integrated by various types of kinship organizations and sodalities.

ultraviolet radiation A part of the electromagnetic energy from the sun that is not visible to the human eye.

unilineal evolution Early theoretical school that postulated that all cultures proceeded through a series of successive stages.

unstructured interviews See *informal interviews.*

urbanization studies Studies of the adaptations made by rural peoples as they move to cities.

uterine descent group See *matrilineage.*

UVB Ultraviolet radiation from the sun in the B wave length.

uxorilocal residence The custom of living with the wife's relatives after marriage.

virilocal residence The custom of living with the husband's relatives after marriage.

REFERENCES

Anderson, Robert. 1996. *Magic, Science, and Health: The Aims and Achievements of Medical Anthropology*. Fort Worth, Tex.: Harcourt Brace.

Angrosino, Michael V. 2000. The Culture Concept and Applied Anthropology. In *The Unity of Theory and Practice in Anthropology: Rebuilding a Fractured Synthesis*, eds. Carole E. Hill and Marietta L. Baba. *NAPA Bulletin* 18: 67–78.

Apodaca, Anacleto. 1952. Corn and Custom: The Introduction of Hybrid Corn to Spanish American Farmers in New Mexico. In *Human Problems in Technological Change*, ed. Edward H. Spicer, pp. 35–39. New York: John Wiley and Sons.

Archer, Dane. 1980. *How to Expand Your Social Intelligence Quotient*. New York: M. Evans.

Balikci, Asen. 1970. *The Netsilik Eskimo*. Prospect Heights, Ill.: Waveland Press.

Barley, Nigel. 2000. *The Innocent Anthropologist—Notes from a Mud Hut*. Prospect Heights, Ill.: Waveland Press.

Bartick, Melissa, and Arnold Reinhold. 2010. The Burden of Suboptimal Breastfeeding in the United States: A Pediatric Cost Analysis. *Pediatrics* 125 (May 2010): e1048-e1056. http://pediatrics.aappublications.org/cgi/content/abstract/125/5/e1048?maxtoshow=&hits=10&RESULTFORMAT=&fulltext=Bartick%2C+Melissa&searchid=1&FIRSTINDEX=0&sortspec=relevance&resourcetype=HWCIT (accessed on November 15, 2010).

Bates, Daniel G. 1998. *Human Adaptive Strategies: Ecology, Culture, and Politics*. Boston: Allyn and Bacon.

Bates, Daniel G., and Fred Plog. 1990. *Cultural Anthropology*, 3rd ed. New York: McGraw-Hill.

Bell, Kirsten. 2005. Genital Cutting and Western Discourse on Sexuality. *Medical Anthropology Quarterly* 19(2): 125–48.

Benedict, Ruth. 1929. *Patterns of Culture*. Boston: Houghton Mifflin.

Betzig, Laura, and Robert Knox Detan, Bruce M. Knauft, and Keith F. Otterbein. 1988. Discussion and Criticism on Reconsidering Violence in Simple Societies. *Current Anthropology:* 29 (4): 624–36.

Boas, Franz. 1938. *The Mind of Primitive Man*. New York: Macmillan.

———. 1964. *The Central Eskimo*. Lincoln: University of Nebraska Press (originally published 1888 as *The Sixth Annual Report of the Bureau of Ethnology*).

Bodley, John H. 2008. *Anthropology and Contemporary Human Problems*, 5th ed. New York: Altamira Press.

———. 2008. *Victims of Progress*, 5th ed. Lanham, MD. AltaMira Press.

Bogin, Barry. 1978. Seasonal Patterns in the Rate of Growth in Height of Children Living in Guatemala. *American Journal of Physical Anthropology* 49: 205–10.

———. 1988. *Patterns of Human Growth*. Cambridge, England: Cambridge University Press.

———. 1998. The Tall and Short of It. *Discover*, February, 40–44.

Bolter, D.R., and Zihlman A. L. 2010. Development and Growth. In *Primates in Perspective*, 2nd ed., eds. C. Campbell, A. Fuentes, K. MacKinnon, S. Bearder, R. Strumph. New York: Oxford University Press.

Bonvillain, Nancy. 2000. *Language, Culture, and Communication*, 3rd ed. Upper Saddle River, N.J.: Prentice-Hall.

Bower, B. 2005. The Pirahã Challenge: An Amazonian Tribe Takes Grammar to a Strange Place. *Science News* 168 (December 10, 2005): 376–77.

———. 2007. Shifty Talk—Probing the Process of Word Evolution. *Science News* 172 (October 13, 2007): 227–28.

Brace, C. Loring. 1995. *The Stages of Human Evolution*, 5th ed. Englewood Cliffs, NJ: Prentice-Hall.

———. 2000. A Four Letter Word Called "Race." In *Evolution in an Anthropological View*, ed. C. Loring Brace, pp. 283–321. New York: Altamira Press.

———. 2005. *"Race" Is a Four-Letter Word: The Genesis of the Concept*. New York: Oxford University Press.

Brace, C. Loring, Henneberg, M., and Relethford, J. H. 1999. Skin Color as an Index of Timing of Human Evolution. *American Journal of Physical Anthropology* 28 suppl.: 95–96.

Braun, D. P., and S. Plog. 1984. Evolution of "Tribal" Social Networks: Theory and Prehistoric North American Evidence. *American Antiquity* 47 (3): 504–25.

Brettell, Caroline B., and Carolyn F. Sargent, eds. 1997. *Gender in Cross-Cultural Perspective*, 2nd ed. Upper Saddle River, N.J.: Prentice-Hall.

Brown, Michael Forbes. 1989. Dark Side of the Shaman. *Natural History*, November, 8–10.

Brumann, Christoph. 1999. Writing for Culture. *Current Anthropology* 40 suppl.: S1–S27.

Bruner, Edward M. 2001. The Maasai and the Lion King: Authenticity, Nationalism, and Globalization in African Tourism. *American Ethnologist* 28 (4): 81-908.

______. 2005. Tourism Fieldwork. *Anthropology News* 46(5): 16-19.

Burton, Richard. 1991. *The Kasidah of Haji Abdu El-Yezdi.* London: Octagon (originally published private printing 1880).

Campbell, Bernard. 1983. *Human Ecology.* New York: Aldine.

Chagnon, Napoleon. 1974. *Studying the Yąnomamö.* New York: Holt, Rinehart and Winston.

______. 1997. *Yąnomamö*, 5th ed. Fort Worth, Tex.: Harcourt Brace.

Chomsky, N. 1988. *Language and Problems of Knowledge: The Managua Lectures.* Cambridge, Mass.: M.I.T. Press.

Cleveland, David A. 1993. Is Variety More Than the Spice of Life? Diversity, Stability and Sustainable Agriculture. *Culture and Agriculture* Winter/Spring 1993, no. 45–46: 2–7. (Posted online December 10, 2004)

Cleveland, David A., and Daniela Soleri. 2007. Farmer Knowledge and Scientist Knowledge in Sustainable Agricultural Development: Ontology, Epistemology and Praxis. In *Local Science vs Global Science—Approaches to Indigenous Knowledge in International Development*, ed. Paul Sillitoe. New York: Berghahan Books.

Cohen, Yehudi. 1968. *Man in Adaptation: The Biosocial Background.* Chicago: Aldine.

Colapinto, John. 2007. The Interpreter—A Reporter at Large: Has a Remote Amazonian Tribe Upended Our Understanding of Language? *The New Yorker*, April 16, 2007, 120–137.

Collier, John. 1967. *Visual Anthropology: Photography as a Research Method.* New York: Holt, Rinehart and Winston.

Comrie, Bernard. 1997. Historical Linguistics. In *The Dictionary of Anthropology*, ed. Thomas Barfield, pp. 235–37. Malden, Mass.: Blackwell.

Conkey, Margaret W. 1981. A Century of Paleolithic Cave Art. *Archaeology* 34 (4): 20–28.

Conkey, Margaret W., Olga Soffer, Deborah Stratmann, and Nina Jablonski, eds. 1997. *Beyond Art: Pleistocene Image and Symbol.* Memoirs of the California Academy of Sciences, number 23. San Francisco: California Academy of Sciences.

Crain, Cathleen, and Nathaniel Tashima. 2005. Anthropology and Evaluation: Lessons from the Field. *NAPA Bulletin* 24: 41–48.

Crane, Todd. 2001. *Ethnopedology in Central Mali.* Paper presented to the Sustainable Agriculture and Natural Resource Management Collaborative Research Support Program Research Scientific Conference, November 28-30, 2001, Athens, GA. http://www.oired.vt.edu/sanremcrsp/UGA/My%20Web%20Sites/SANREM%20UGA/www.sanrem.uga.edu/sanrem/conferences/nov2801/waf/Ethnopedology.htm (accessed on October 13, 2010).

Crane, Todd A. 2009. If Farmers Are First, Do Pastoralists Come Second? Political Ecology and Participation in Central Mali. In *Farmers First Revisited: Innovation for Agricultural Research and Development*, eds. Ian Scoones and John Thompson. Bourton on Dunsmore, UK: Practical Action Publishing.

Davidson, Iain. 1997. The Power of Pictures. In *Beyond Art: Pleistocene Image and Symbol*, eds. Margaret W. Conkey, Olga Soffer, Deborah Stratmann, and Nina Jablonski, pp. 125–59. Memoirs of the California Academy of Sciences, number 23. San Francisco: California Academy of Sciences.

D'Azevedo, Warren L., eds. 1986. *Washo.* Vol. 11 of *Handbook of North American Indians.* Washington, D.C.: Smithsonian Institution Press.

Deetz, James. 1967. *Invitation to Archaeology.* New York: Natural History Press.

DeFoliart, Gene. 1992. Insects as Human Food. *Crop Protection* 2: 395–399. http://www.food-insects.com/insects%20as%20Human%20Food.htm (accessed on January 23, 2008).

Dentan, Robert K. 1970. Living and Working with the Semai. In *Being an Anthropologist: Fieldwork in Eleven Cultures*, ed. George Spindler. New York: Holt, Rinehart and Winston.

Dettwyler, Katherine. 1994. *Dancing Skeletons: Life and Death in West Africa.* Prospect Heights, Ill.: Waveland Press.

———. 1995. A Time to Wean: The Hominid Blueprint for the Natural Age of Weaning in Modern Human Populations. In *Breastfeeding: Biocultural Perspectives*, eds. P. Stuart-Macadam and K. Dettwyler, pp. 39–73. New York: Aldine DeGruyter.

Diamond, Jared. 1987. The Worst Mistake of the Human Race. *Discover*, May, 64–66.

Dilly, Barbara J. 2005. Culture and Agriculture. *Anthropology News* 46 (5): 49–50.

Dissanayake, Ellen. 1988. *What Is Art For?* Seattle: University of Washington Press.

Douglass, William A., and Julie Lacy. 2005. Anthropological Angst and the Tourist Encounter. *NAPA Bulletin* 23: 119–34.

Downs, James F. 1966. *The Two Worlds of the Washo: An Indian Tribe of California and Nevada.* New York: Holt, Rinehart and Winston.

Duranti, Alessandro, ed. 2001. *Linguistic Anthropology.* Malden, Mass.: Blackwell.

Durkheim, Emil. 1961. *The Elementary Forms of the Religious Life.* New York: Collier (originally published 1912).

Elliston, Deborah A. 1999. Negotiating Transitional Sexual Economics: Female Mahu and Same-Sex Sexuality in Tahiti and Her Islands. In *Female Desires: Same-Sex Relations and Transgender Practices across Cultures*, eds. Evelyn Blackwood and Saskia E. Wieringa, pp. 230–52. New York: Columbia University Press.

Ersen, Mustafa Türker. 2002. Parallel Brides. *Natural History*, May, 72–79.

Eskridge, William N. 1993. A History of Same Sex Marriage. *Virginia Law Review* 79: 1419.

Evans-Pritchard, E. E. 1940. *The Nuer.* Oxford, England: Clarendon Press.

Everett, Daniel L., Brent Berlin, Maraco Antonie Goncalves, Paul Key, et. al. 2005. Cultural Constraints on Grammar and Cognition in Pirahã: Another Look at the Design Features of Human Language. Comments/Reply. *Current Anthropology* 46 (4): 621–647.

Farris, James. 1973. Pax Britannica and the Sudan: S. F. Nadel. In *Anthropology and the Colonial Encounter*, ed. Talal Asad, pp. 153–172. New York: Humanities Press.

Feder, Kenneth L. 1996. *The Past in Perspective.* Mountain View, Calif.: Mayfield.

Feder, Kenneth L., and Michael Allen Park. 1997. *Human Antiquity*, 3rd ed. Mountain View, Calif.: Mayfield.

Federal Bureau of Investigation. Uniform Crime Reports. http://www.fbi.gov/about-us/cjis/ucr/crime-in-the-u.s/2009/crime2009 (accessed on February 17, 2011).

Ferguson, R. Brian. 1995. *Yanomani Warfare.* Santa Fe, N.M.: School of American Research Press.

Ferraro, Gary P. 1994. *The Cultural Dimension of International Business*, 2nd ed. Englewood Cliffs, N.J.: Prentice-Hall.

———. 1998a. *Applying Cultural Anthropology Readings.* Belmont, Calif.: Wadsworth.

———. 1998b. *Cultural Anthropology: An Applied Perspective*, 3rd ed. Belmont, Calif.: Wadsworth.

Feuchtwang, Stephan. 1973. The Colonial Formation of British Social Anthropology. In *Anthropology and the Colonial Encounter*, ed. Talal Asad, pp. 71–102. New York: Humanities Press.

Fischer, Michael M. J. 1997. Postmodern, Postmodernism. In *The Dictionary of Anthropology*, ed. Thomas Barfield, pp. 368–72. Malden, Mass.: Blackwell.

Fluehr-Lobban, Carolyn. 2002. A Century of Ethics and Professional Anthropology. *Anthropology News* 43 (3): 20.

Fluehr-Lobban, Carolyn, and Monica Heuer. 2007. Ethical Challenges for Anthropological Engagement. *Anthropology News* 48 (1): 4.

Foley, William A. 1997. *Anthropological Linguistics: An Introduction.* Malden, Mass.: Blackwell.

Ford, Clellan S., and Frank A. Beach. 1951. *Patterns of Sexual Behavior.* New York: Ace Books.

Foster, George. 1962. *Traditional Cultures and the Impact of Technological Change.* New York: Harper and Row.

Fox, Richard G. 1977. *Urban Anthropology: Cities in Their Cultural Settings.* Englewood Cliffs, N.J.: Prentice-Hall.

Fox, Robin. 1983. *Kinship and Marriage: An Anthropological Perspective.* Cambridge, England: Cambridge University Press (originally published 1967).

Frazer, James. 1959. *The Golden Bough.* New York: Criterion Press (originally published 1911).

Fried, Morton. 1967. *The Evolution of Political Anthropology: An Essay in Political Anthropology.* New York: Random House.

Friedl, Ernestine. 1978. Society and Sex Roles. *Human Nature* 1 (4).

Frobenius, Leo, and Douglas C. Fox. 1937. *Prehistoric Rock Art Pictures in Europe and Africa.* New York: Museum of Modern Art.

Gadsby, Patricia. 2004. The Inuit Paradox. *Discover*: 25 (10): 48–55.

Galanti, Geri-Ann. 1991. *Caring for Patients from Different Cultures: Case Studies from American Hospitals.* Philadelphia: University of Pennsylvania Press.

Garza, Christina E. 1991. Studying the Natives on the Shop Floor. *Business Week*. September 30, 1991, 74-78.

Geertz, Clifford. 1973. *The Interpretation of Cultures: Selected Essays by Clifford Geertz.* New York: Basic Books.

Gibbs, James L., Jr. 1963. The Kpelle Moot: A Therapeutic Model for the Informal Settlement of Disputes. *Africa: Journal of the International African Institute* 33 (1): 1–11.

Goldstein, Melvyn C. 1987. When Brothers Take a Wife. *Natural History* 96 (3): 38–49.

Goodale, Jane C., and Joan D. Koss. 1966. The Cultural Context of Creativity among Tiwi. In *Anthropology and Art*, ed. C. M. Otten. New York: Natural History Press.

Goodenough, Ward H. 1963. *Cooperation in Change.* New York: Russell Sage Foundation.

______. 1981. *Culture, Language, and Society*, 2nd ed. Menlo Park, Calif.: Benjamin Cummings.

Gordon, Peter. 2004. Numerical Cognition Without Words: Evidence from Amazonia. *Science* 306 (5695): 496–499.

Graburn, Nelson H. H. 1976. *Ethnic and Tourist Arts: Cultural Expressions from the Fourth World.* Berkeley: University of California Press.

Gray, J. Patrick, and Linda D. Wolfe. 2002. What Accounts for Population Variation in Height? In *Physical Anthropology: Original Readings in Method and Practice*, eds. Peter N. Peregrine, C. R. Ember, and M. Ember, pp. 204–18. Upper Saddle River, N.J.: Prentice-Hall.

Greenberg, David F. 1988. *The Construction of Homosexuality.* Chicago: University of Chicago Press.

Gregor, Thomas. 1985. *Anxious Pleasures: The Sexual Lives of an Amazonian People.* Chicago: University of Chicago Press.

Gross, Daniel R. 2002. The Great Sisal Scheme. In *The Applied Anthropology Reader.* Boston: Allyn and Bacon. Originally published March 1971 in *Natural History* 80 (3): 49–55.

Hadingham, Evan. 1979. *Secrets of the Ice Age.* New York: Walker and Company.

Hall, Edward T. 1959. *The Silent Language.* New York: Doubleday.

Hameda, Tamoko. 2000. Anthropological Praxis: Theory of Business Organization. In *The Unity of Theory and Practice in Anthropology: Rebuilding a Fractured Synthesis*, eds. Carole E. Hill and Marietta L. Baba. *NAPA Bulletin* 18.

Harper, Ian, and Nayanika Mookherjee. 2009. Debates on Ethical Practice. *Anthropology News* 50 (6): 10-11.

Harris, Marvin. 1966. The Cultural Ecology of India's Sacred Cattle. *Current Anthropology* 7: 51–66.

______. 1968. *The Rise of Anthropological Theory.* New York: Thomas Y. Crowell.

______. 1998. *Good to Eat: Riddles of Food and Culture.* Prospect Heights, Ill.: Waveland Press.

Harris, Philip R., and Robert T. Moran. 1996. *Managing Cultural Differences*, 4th ed. Houston, Tex.: Gulf Publishing.

Hauser, Marc, Noam Chomsky, and W. Tecumseh Fitch. 2002. The Faculty of Language: What Is It, Who Has It, and How Did It Evolve. *Science* 298 (5598): 1569–1579.

Haviland, William A. 1999. *Cultural Anthropology*, 9th ed. Fort Worth, Tex.: Harcourt College Publishers.

Heider, Karl G. 1970. *The Dugum Dani.* Chicago: Aldine.

______. 1997. *Grand Valley Dani: Peaceful Warriors*, 3rd ed. Fort Worth, Tex.: Holt, Rinehart and Winston.

Herdt, Gilbert. 1981. *Guardians of the Flutes: Idioms of Masculinity.* New York: McGraw-Hill.

______. 1987. *The Sambia: Ritual and Gender in New Guinea.* Fort Worth, Tex.: Harcourt Brace Jovanovich.

Hickerson, Nancy Parrott. 1980. *Linguistic Anthropology.* New York: Holt, Rinehart and Winston.

Hitchcock, Robert K. 2003. *The San of Southern Africa: A Status Report*, 2003. http://www.aaanet.org/committees/cfhr/san.htm (accessed on September 4, 2007).

Hoke, Franklin. 1997. Mother's Milk: Nutrition and Nurture for Infants—and the Best Defense Against Disease. *News and Periodicals*, July 31. University of Pennsylvania Health System. http://www.uphs.upenn.edu/news/News_Releases/july97/milk.html (accessed on October 23, 2002).

Holmberg, A. R. 1946. The Siriono. Ph.D. diss., Yale University.

Holtzman, Jon D. 2000. *Nuer Journeys, Nuer Lives: Sudanese Refugees in Minnesota.* Boston: Allyn and Bacon.

______. 2007. *Nuer Journeys, Nuer Lives: Sudanese Refugees in Minnesota*, 2nd ed. Boston: Allyn and Bacon.

Horowitz, Irving Louis, ed. 1967. *The Rise and Fall of Project Camelot*. Cambridge: M.I.T. Press.

Hutchinson, Sharon E. 1996. *Nuer Dilemmas: Coping with Money, War, and the State*. Berkeley: University of California Press.

Hutter, Mark. 1981. *The Changing Family: Comparative Perspectives*. New York: John Wiley and Sons.

Igoe, Jim. 2011. Seeing Conservation through the Global Lens. In Angeloni, Elvio, ed. *Annual Editions Anthropology* 11/12, pp. 213-223. New York: McGraw-Hill.

______. 2004. *Conservation and Globalization: A Study of National Parks and Indigenous Communities from East Africa and South Dakota*. Belmont, CA: Wadsworth.

Inda, Jonathan Xavier, and Renato Rosaldo, eds. 2002. *The Anthropology of Globalization—A Reader*. Malden, Mass.: Blackwell.

Ingles, Palma. 2005. More Than Nature: Anthropologists as Interpreters of Culture for Nature-Based Tours. *NAPA Bulletin* 23: 219–33.

Jablonski, Nina G. 2006. *Skin: A Natural History*. Los Angeles: University of California Press.

Jablonski, Nina G., and G. Chaplin. 1999. The Evolution of Human Skin Pigmentation. *American Journal of Physical Anthropology* 28 suppl.: 159.

Jacknis, Ira. 1995. *Carving Traditions of Northwest California*. Berkeley, Calif.: Phoebe Hearst Museum of Anthropology.

Jayne, Caroline Furness. 1962. *String Figures and How to Make Them*. New York: Dover Publications (originally published 1906 as *String Figures*).

Jones, Del. 1999. Hot Asset: Anthropology Degree. *USA Today*, February 18.

Jordan, Ann T. 1994a. Organizational Culture: The Anthropological Approach. In *Practicing Anthropology in Corporate America: Consulting on Organizational Culture*, ed. Ann T. Jordon. *NAPA Bulletin* 14: 3–16.

Jordan, Ann T., ed. 1994b. *Practicing Anthropology in Corporate America: Consulting on Organizational Culture*. *NAPA Bulletin* 14.

______. 2003. *Business Anthropology*. Long Grove, Ill.: Waveland Press.

Keefe, Susan Emley. 1996. The Myth of the Declining Family. In *Urban Life*, eds. George Gmelch and Walter P. Zenner. Prospect Heights, Ill.: Waveland Press.

Keesing, Roger M. 1983. *'Elota's Story: The Life and Times of a Solomon Island Big Man*. New York: Holt, Rinehart and Winston.

Keesing, Roger M., and Andrew J. Strathern. 1998. *Cultural Anthropology*, 3rd ed. Fort Worth, Tex.: Harcourt Brace College Publishers.

Kehoe, Alice. 1989. *The Ghost Dance: Ethnohistory and Revitalization*. New York: Holt, Rinehart and Winston.

______. 2000. *Shamans and Religion: An Anthropological Exploration in Critical Thinking*. Prospect Heights, Ill.: Waveland Press.

Keiser, R. Lincoln. 1979. *The Vice Lords: Warriors of the Streets*, fieldwork edition. New York: Holt, Rinehart and Winston.

Kelly, Robert L. 1995. *The Foraging Spectrum: Diversity in Hunter-Gatherer Lifeways*. Washington, D.C.: Smithsonian Institution Press.

Kerby, S., M. Dowman, and T. L. Griffiths. 2007. Innateness and Culture in the Evolution of Language. *Proceedings of the National Academy of Sciences* 104 (12): 5241–5245.

Kingsolver, Barbara. 2007. *Animal, Vegetable, Miracle*. New York: Harper Collins.

Klass, Morton. 1995. *Ordered Universes: Approaches to the Anthropology of Religion*. Boulder, Colo.: Westview Press.

Kluckhohn, Clyde. 1951. *The Navajo*. Cambridge: Harvard University Press.

Kluckhohn, Clyde, and W. H. Kelly. 1945. The Concept of Culture. In *The Science of Man in the World Crisis*, ed. Ralph Linton, pp. 78–105. New York: Columbia University Press.

Knauft, Bruce M. 1987. Reconsidering Violence in Simple Human Societies: Homicide Among the Gebusi of Papua New Guinea. *Current Anthropology* 28 (4): 457–500.

______. 2010. *The Gebusi: Lives Transformed in a Rainforest World*, 2nd ed. New York: McGraw-Hill.

Köhler-Rollefson, Ilse. 1995. Camels in the Land of Kings. *Natural History*, March.

______. 2005. The Camel in Rajasthan: Agricultural Biodiversity under Threat 6–18. In *Saving the Camel and Peoples' Livelihoods: Building a Multi-Stakeholder Platform for the Conservation of the Camel in Rajasthan*. Proceedings of an International Conference held on 23–25 November 2004 in Sadri. Lokhit Pashu-Palak Sansthan, Sadri, Rajasthan, India. http://www.pastoralpeoples.org/docs/camelconfbrochurecolour.pdf (accessed on October 12, 2010).

Krader, Lawrence. 1968. *Formation of the State*. Englewood Cliffs, N.J.: Prentice-Hall.

Kreider, Rose M. 2010. Increase in Opposite-Sex Cohabiting Couples from 2009–2010 in the Annual Social and Economic Supplement (ASEC) to the Current Population Survey (CPS). *Housing and Household Economic Statistics Division Working Paper*. U.S. Bureau of the Census September 15, 2010. http://www.census.gov/population/www/socdemo/Inc-Opp-sex-2009-to-2010.pdf (accessed on December 14, 2010).

Kroeber, A. L. 1934. Yurok and Neighboring Kin Term Systems. *University of California Publications in American Archaeology and Ethnology* 35 (2): 15–22.

______. 1953. *Handbook of the Indians of California*. Berkeley: California Book Company (originally published in 1925 as Handbook of the Indians of California. *Bureau of American Ethnology Bulletin* 78).

Kroeber, A. L., and C. Kluckhohn. 1952. *Culture: A Critical Review of Concepts and Definitions*. New York: Vintage Books (originally published as *Papers of the Peabody Museum of American Archaeology and Ethnology* 47 [1]).

Kroeber, Theodora. 1959. *The Inland Whale*. Bloomington: Indiana University Press.

Kuper, Adam. 1999. *Culture: The Anthropologists' Account*. Cambridge: Harvard University Press.

Kutsche, Paul. 1998. *Field Ethnography: A Manual for Doing Cultural Anthropology*. Upper Saddle River, N.J.: Prentice-Hall.

Kuznar, Lawrence. 2008. *Reclaiming a Scientific Anthropology*, 2nd ed. Lanham, MD: Altamira Press.

Lassiter, Luke Eric. 2005. *The Chicago Guide to Collaborative Ethnography*. Chicago: University of Chicago Press.

Layton, Robert. 1999. *The Anthropology of Art*, 2nd ed. Cambridge: Cambridge University Press.

Leach, E. R. 1965. *Political Systems of Highland Burma*. Boston: Beacon Press.

Lederman, Rena. 2009. Comparing Ethics Codes and Conventions—Anthropological, Sociological, and Psychological Approaches. *Anthropology News* 50(6): 11–12.

Lee, Richard B. 1993. *The Dobe Ju/'hoansi*, 2nd ed. Fort Worth, Tex.: Harcourt Brace College Publishers (first edition published in 1984 as *The Dobe !Kung*).

______. 2002. *The Dobe Ju/'hoansi*, 3rd ed. Belmont, Calif.: Wadsworth.

Lee, Richard, and Ida Susser. 2003. AIDS and the San: How Badly Are They Affected? Appendix 1 to San of Southern Africa: A Status Report 2003. http://www.aaanet.org/committees/cfhr/san.htm (accessed on July 20, 2005).

Lehmann, Arthur C., and James E. Myers. 1997. *Magic, Witchcraft, and Religion*, 4th ed. Mountain View, Calif.: Mayfield.

Lehmann, Arthur C., James E. Myers, and Pamela A. Moro. 2005. *Magic, Witchcraft, and Religion*, 6th ed. New York: McGraw-Hill.

Leland, John, and Namo Abdulla. 2010. A Killing Set Honor Above Love. *The New York Times* (November 20, 2010). http://www.nytimes.com/2010/11/21/world/middleeast/21honor.html?_r=1 (accessed on November 22, 2010).

Leroi-Gourhan, Andre. 1967. *Treasures of Prehistoric Art*. New York: Harry N. Abrams.

______. 1982. *The Dawn of European Art: An Introduction to Paleolithic Cave Painting*. Cambridge, England: Cambridge University Press.

Lewis, David, and Werner Forman. 1985. *The Maori Heirs of Tane*. London: Orbis.

Linton, Ralph. 1936. *The Study of Man*. New York: Appleton Century Crofts.

______. 1937. One Hundred Percent American. *American Mercury* 40: 427–29.

Little, Michael A. 2002. Growth and Development of Turkana Pastoralists. In *Physical Anthropology: Original Readings in Method and Practice*, eds. Peter N. Peregrine, C. R. Ember, and M. Ember, pp. 219–38. Upper Saddle River, N.J.: Prentice-Hall.

Loustaunau, Martha O., and Elisa J. Sobo. 1997. *The Cultural Context of Health, Illness, and Medicine*. Westport, Conn.: Bergin and Garvey.

Malinowski, Bronislaw. 1922. *Argonauts of the Western Pacific*. New York: E. P. Dutton.

______. 1964. *A Scientific Theory of Culture and Other Essays*. New York: Oxford University Press (originally published 1944).

______. 1987. *The Sexual Life of Savages in North-Western Melanesia*. Boston: Beacon Press (originally published 1929).

Marcus, George, and Michael Fischer. 1986. *Anthropology as Cultural Critique: An Experimental Moment in the Human Sciences*. Chicago: University of Chicago Press.

Marshack, Alexander. 1997. Image Making and Symboling in Europe and the Middle East: A Comparative Review. In *Beyond Art: Pleistocene Magic and Symbol*, eds. Margaret W. Conkey, Olga Soffer, Deborah Stratmann, and Nina Jablonski. Memoirs of the California Academy of Sciences, number 23: 53–91. San Francisco: California Academy of Sciences.

Mascia-Lees, Frances E., and Nancy Johnson Black. 2000. *Gender and Anthropology*. Prospect Heights, Ill.: Waveland Press.

Matson, P. A., W. J. Parton, A. G. Power, and M. J. Swift. 1997. Agricultural Intensification and Ecosystem Properties. *Science* 277: 504–509.

Maybury-Lewis, David. 2002. *Indigenous Peoples, Ethnic Groups, and the State*, 2nd ed. Upper Saddle River, NJ: Pearson.

McCurdy, David W. 2000. Using Anthropology. In *Conformity and Conflict*, 10th ed., eds. James Spradley and David W. McCurdy, pp. 386–98. Boston: Allyn and Bacon.

McDowell, Margaret M., Chia-Yih Wang, and Jocelyn Kennedy-Stephenson. 2008. Breastfeeding in the United States: Findings from the National Health and Nutrition Examination Survey, 1999–2006. *Centers for Disease Control and Prevention* 5 (April 2008). http://www.cdc.gov/nchs/data/databriefs/db05.htm (accessed on November 15, 2010).

McFate, Montgomery. 2005. Anthropology and Counterinsurgency: The Strange Story of Their Curious Relationship. *Military Review*, March/April.

Mead, Margaret. 1937. *Cooperation and Competition Among Primitive Peoples*. New York: McGraw-Hill.

______. 1963. *Sex and Temperament in Three Primitive Societies*. New York: Dell (originally published 1935).

______. 1969. *Male and Female*. New York: Dell (originally published 1949).

Metcalf, Peter. 1978. Death Be Not Strange. *Natural History* 87 (6): 6–12.

Michaels, Eric. 1990. A Model of Teleported Texts. *Continuum: The Australian Journal of Media & Culture:* 3 (2). http://www.mcc.murdoch.edu.au/ReadingRoom/3.2/teleport.html (accessed on July 22, 2005).

______. 2002. Hollywood Iconography: A Warlpiri Reading. In *The Anthropology of Globalization*, eds. Jonathan Xavier Inda and Renato Rosaldo, pp. 311–24. Malden, Mass.: Blackwell.

Michener, James A. 1968. *Iberia*. New York: Fawcett Crest.

Miller, Jean-Chris. 2004. *The Body Art Book*. New York: Berkley Books.

Minderhout, David J., and Andrea T. Frantz. 2009. Native American Horticulture in the Northeast. *General Anthropology* 16 (1): 1–9. Malden, MA: Blackwell Publishing.

Molnar, Stephen. 2002. *Human Variation: Races, Types, and Ethnic Groups*, 5th ed. Upper Saddle River, N.J.: Prentice-Hall.

Montague, Ashley, ed. 1964. *The Concept of Race*. London: Collier Books.

Morales, Manuel R. 1997. When Beasts Go Marching Out! The End of Pleistocene Art in Cantabrian Spain. In *Beyond Art: Pleistocene Magic and Symbol*, eds. Margaret W. Conkey, Olga Soffer, Deborah Stratmann, and Nina Jablonski. Memoirs of the California Academy of Sciences, number 23: 189–99. San Francisco: California Academy of Sciences.

Morey, Nancy C., and Robert V. Morey. 1994. Organizational Culture: The Management Approach. In *Practicing Anthropology in Corporate America: Consulting on Organizational Culture*, ed. Ann T. Jordon. *NAPA Bulletin* 14: 17–26.

Morgan, Lewis Henry. 1963. *Ancient Society*. Cleveland: Meredian Books (originally published 1877).

Morgan, Marcyliena. 2001. The African-American Speech Community: Reality and Sociolinguistics. In *Linguistic Anthropology*, ed. Alessandro Duranti, pp. 74–94. Malden, Mass.: Blackwell.

Muir, Patricia S. 2008. *University of Oregon Extension Service. Erosion from Inappropriate Agricultural Practices on Crop Land*. http://oregonstate.edu/~muir/erosion.tm (accessed on July 19, 2010).

Murdock, George P. 1949. *Social Structure*. New York: Macmillan.

______. 1950. Family Stability in Non-European Cultures. *Annals of the American Academy of Political and Social Sciences* 272: 195–201.

______. 1967. The Ethnographic Atlas: A Summary. *Ethnology* 6 (2): 109–236.

Murray, Gerald. 1987. The Domestication of Wood in Haiti: A Case Study in Applied Evolution. In *Anthropological Praxis: Translating Knowledge into Action*, eds. Robert M. Wulff and Shirley J. Frisk. Boulder, Colo.: Westview Press.

NACSO. 1997. *Profile of Nyae Nyae Conservancy*. http://www.nacso.org.na/cons_profile/Nyae_Nyae.htm (accessed on September 4, 2007).

Nanda, Serena. 1999. *Neither Man Nor Woman*, 2nd ed. Belmont, Calif.: Wadsworth.

______. 2000. *Gender Diversity: Cross-Cultural Variations*. Prospect Heights, Ill.: Waveland Press.

Nash, Dennison. 1996. *Anthropology of Tourism*. New York: Elsevier Science.

______. 1999. *A Little Anthropology*, 3rd ed. Upper Saddle River, N.J.: Prentice-Hall.

Niehoff, Arthur H., ed. 1966. *A Casebook of Social Change*. Chicago: Aldine.

Nisbet, Robert A. 1967. Project Camelot and the Science of Man. In *The Rise and Fall of Project Camelot*, ed. Irving Louis Horowitz, pp. 313–338. Cambridge: M.I.T. Press.

Norbeck, Edward. 1961. *Religion in Primitive Society.* New York: Harper and Brothers.

Nordstrom, Carolyn, and Antonius C. G. M. Robben. 1995. *Fieldwork Under Fire.* Berkeley: University of California Press.

Oboler, Regina Smith. 1980. Is the Female Husband a Man? Woman/Woman Marriage Among the Nandi of Kenya. *Ethnology* 19 (1): 69–88.

Oliver, Douglas L. 1989. *Native Cultures of the Pacific Islands.* Honolulu: University of Hawaii Press.

O'Neale, Lila. 1932. Yurok-Karok Basket Weavers. *University of California Publications in American Archaeology and Ethnology* 32 (1): 1–182.

Orion, Loretta. 1995. *Never Again the Burning Times: Paganism Revived.* Prospect Heights, Ill.: Waveland Press.

Otten, Charlotte M., ed. 1971. *Anthropology and Art: Readings in Cross-Cultural Aesthetics.* Garden City, N.Y.: Natural History Press.

Pagel, Mark, Quentin D. Atkinson, and Andrew Meade. 2007. Frequency of Word-Use Predicts Rates of Lexical Evolution Throughout Indo-European History. *Nature* 449 (7163): 717–721.

Pasternak, Burton, Carol R. Ember, and Melvin Ember. 1997. *Sex, Gender, and Kinship: A Cross-Cultural Perspective.* Upper Saddle River, N.J.: Prentice-Hall.

Peters-Golden, Holly. 2002. *Culture Sketches: Case Studies in Anthropology*, 3rd ed. New York: McGraw-Hill.

Pew Research Center. 2010. *The Decline of Marriage and Rise of New Families.* Pew Research Center Publications. (November 18, 2010) http://pewresearch.org/pubs/1802/decline-marriage-rise-new-families?src+prc-latest&proj=peoplepress (accessed on November 22, 2010).

Pfeiffer, John E. 1982. *The Creative Explosion: An Inquiry into the Origins of Art and Religion.* New York: Harper and Row.

Powell, Mary F. 1988. *Status and Health in Prehistory: A Case Study of the Moundville Chiefdom.* Washington, D.C.: Smithsonian Institution Press.

Price, David H. 2007. Anthropology and the Wages of Secrecy. *Anthropology News* 48 (3): 6–7.

Puntenney, Pamela J., ed. 1995. Global Ecosystems: Creating Options through Anthropological Perspectives. *NAPA Bulletin* 15.

Raloff, Janet. 2008. Insects, the Original White Meat. *Science News* 173(18): 17–21.

Rappaport, Roy A. 1968. *Pigs for the Ancestors.* New Haven, Conn.: Yale University Press.

Rathje, William L., and Cullen Murphy. 2001. *Rubbish! The Archaeology of Garbage.* Tucson: University of Arizona Press.

Rhoades, Robert E. 2005. Agricultural Anthropology. In Kedia Satish and John Van Willigen, eds. *Applied Anthropology: Domains of Application*. pp 1–85.

Rhoads, R. E., R. Booth, R. Shaw, and R. Werge. 1985. The role of anthropologists in developing improved technologies. *Appropriate Technology* 11(4): 11–13.

Rice, Patricia, and Ann Peterson. 1985. Cave Art and Bones: Exploring the Interrelationships. *American Anthropologist* 87 (1): 94–99.

Richie, Donald, and Ian Buruma. 1996. *The Japanese Tattoo.* New York: Weatherhill.

Robbins, Richard H. 2005. *Global Problems and the Culture of Capitalism.* Boston: Pearson Education.

Rossbach, E. 1973. *Baskets as Textile Art.* New York: Van Nostrand Reinhold.

Sahlins, Marshall D. 1958. *Social Stratification in Polynesia.* Seattle: University of Washington Press.

______. 1968. *Tribesmen.* Englewood Cliffs, N.J.: Prentice-Hall.

______. 1972. *Stone Age Economics.* Chicago: University of Chicago Press.

Sahlins, Marshall, and Elman Service eds., 1960. *Evolution and Culture.* Ann Arbor: University of Michigan Press.

Salvador, Mari Lyn. 1976. The Clothing Arts of the Cuna of San Blas, Panama. In *Ethnic and Tourist Arts*, ed. N. H. Graburn, pp. 165–82. Berkeley: University of California Press.

SANREM CRSP West Africa. 2010. http://www.oired.vt.edu/sanremcrsp/ (accessed on August 2, 2011).

Sapir, Edward. 1921. *Language: An Introduction to the Study of Speech.* New York: Harcourt, Brace.

______. 1964. The Status of Linguistics as a Science. In *Edward Sapir: Culture, Language, and Personality*, ed. David G. Mandelbaum, pp. 65–77. Berkeley: University of California Press (Original 1929).

Saul, Mahir. 2004. Money in Colonial Transition: Cowries and Fancs in West Africa. *American Anthropologist* 106 (1): 71–84.

Schick, Kathy D., and Nicholas Toth. 1993. *Making Silent Stone Speak.* New York: Simon and Schuster.

Schneider, David, and Kathleen Gough, eds. 1962. *Matrilineal Kinship.* Berkeley: University of California Press.

Schneider, David, and G. Homans. 1955. Kinship Terminology and the American Kinship System. *American Anthropologist* 57: 1194–1208.

Schusky, Ernest L. 1972. *Manual for Kinship Analysis*, 2nd ed. New York: Holt, Rinehart and Winston.

———. 1974. *Variation in Kinship*. New York: Holt, Rinehart and Winston.

Schwimmer, Brian. 2003. Kinship Tutorial: University of Manitoba. http://www.umanitoba.ca/faculties/arts/anthropology/tutor/kinmenu.html (accessed on July 20, 2005).

Scott, Eugenie C. 1996. Science in Anthropology. *Anthropology Newsletter* 37 (3): 52.

Scupin, Raymond D., ed. 2000. *Religion and Culture: An Anthropological Focus*. Upper Saddle River, N.J.: Prentice-Hall.

Senft, Gunter. 1999. The Presentation of Self in Touristic Encounters: A Case Study from the Trobriand Islands. *Anthropos* 94: 21-33.

Service, Elman. 1962. *Primitive Social Organization: An Evolutionary Perspective*. New York: Random House.

———. 1978. *Profiles in Ethnology*, 3rd ed. New York: Harper and Row.

———. 1979. *The Hunters*, 2nd ed. Englewood Cliffs, N.J.: Prentice-Hall.

Shand, Hope. 1997. *Human Nature: Agricultural Biodiversity and Farm-Based Food Security*. Ottawa: Rural Advancement Fund International.

Shipman, Pat. 1984. Scavenger Hunt. *Natural History* 93 (4): 20–27.

Shostak, Marjorie. 1981. *Nisa: The Life and Words of a !Kung Woman*. Cambridge: Harvard University Press.

Slow Food http://www.slowfood.com (accessed on February 21, 2011).

Slow Food Foundation for Biodiversity. http://www.slowfoodfoundation.com (accessed on February 21, 2011).

Smith, Bruce. 1992. *Rivers of Change: Essays on Early Agriculture in Eastern North America*. Washington, D.C.: Smithsonian Institution Press.

Soleri, D., and D. Cleveland. 1993. Seeds of Strength for Hopis and Zunis. *Seedling* 10 (4): 13–18. http://www.ciesin.columbia.edu/docs/004-190/004-190.html (accessed on July 27, 2007).

Spicer, Edward H., ed. 1952. *Human Problems in Technological Change: A Casebook*. New York: John Wiley and Sons.

Spiro, Melford E. 1966. Religion: Problems of Definition and Explanation. In *Anthropological Approaches to the Study of Religion*, ed. Michael Banton. London: Tavistock.

Sponsel, Leslie. 1994. The Yanomami Holocaust Continues. In *Who Pays the Price? The Sociocultural Context of Environmental Crisis*, ed. B. R. Johnston, pp. 37–46. Washington, D.C.: Island Press.

———. 1998. Yanomami: An Arena of Conflict and Aggression in the Amazon. *Aggressive Behavior* 24: 97–122.

Spradley, James P. 1980. *Participant Observation*. New York: Holt, Rinehart and Winston.

Squires, Susan. 2002. Doing the Work: Customer Research in the Product Development and Design Industry. In *Creating Breakthrough Ideas: The Collaboration of Anthropologists and Designers in the Product Development Industry*, eds. S. Squires and B. Byrne, pp. 103–109. Westport, Conn.: Bergin and Garvey.

———. 2006. Solving Puzzles. In *Making History at the Frontier: Women Creating Careers as Practicing Anthropologists*, ed. Christina Wasson. *NAPA Bulletin* 26: 191–208.

Squires, Susan, and B. Byrne, eds. 2002. *Creating Breakthrough Ideas: The Collaboration of Anthropologists and Designers in the Product Development Industry*. Westport, Conn.: Bergin and Garvey.

Stanlaw, James. 2006. Dan Everett Cries Whorf. *Anthropology News* 47 (4): 17.

Stephens, William N. 1963. *The Family in Cross-Cultural Perspective*. New York: Holt, Rinehart and Winston.

Steward, Julian. 1968. Cultural Ecology. In *International Encyclopedia of the Social Sciences* 4, ed. D. Sills, pp. 337–44. New York: Macmillan.

Tannen, Deborah. 1990. *You Just Don't Understand: Women and Men in Conversation*. New York: William Morrow.

———. 1994. Why Don't You Say What You Mean? *The New York Times Magazine*, August 28, 1994, 46–49 (adapted from *Talking 9 to 5: How Women's and Men's Conversational Styles Affect Who Gets Heard, Who Gets Credit, and What Gets Done at Work*. 1994. New York: William Morrow).

———. 2005. *Conversational Style*. Oxford: Oxford University Press.

Textor, Robert B. 1967. *A Cross-Cultural Summary*. New Haven, Conn.: HRAF Press.

Thompson, David S. 1975. *Human Behavior: Language*. New York: Time-Life Books.

Tilman, David, Kenneth G. Cassman, Pamela A. Matson, Rosamond Naylar, and Stephan Polasky. 2002. Agricultural Sustainability and Intensive Production Practices. *Nature* 418: 671–677.

Trotter, Robert T., II. 1987. A Case of Lead Poisoning from Folk Remedies in Mexican American Communities. In *Anthropological Praxis: Translating Knowledge into Action*, eds. Robert M. Wulff and Shirley J. Frisk, pp. 139–50. Boulder, Colo.: Westview Press.

Trudgill, P. 1974. *The Social Differentiation of English in Norwich*. Cambridge, England: Cambridge University Press.

Turnbull, Colin M. 1983. *The Mbuti Pygmies: Change and Adaptation*. New York: Holt, Rinehart and Winston.

______. 1987. *The Forest People*. New York: Simon and Schuster (originally published 1961).

Tylor, E. B. 1958. *Primitive Culture*. New York: Harper and Row (originally published 1871).

Ucko, Peter, and Andree Rosenfeld. 1967. *Paleolithic Cave Art*. New York: McGraw-Hill.

______. 1971. Critical Analysis of Interpretations and Conclusions and Problems from Paleolithic Cave Art. In *Anthropology and Art*, ed. C. M. Otten. New York: Natural History Press.

University of Oregon Extension Service. 2008. *Erosion from Inappropriate Agricultural Practices on Crop Lands*. http://oregonstate.edu/~muirp/erosion.htm (accessed on July 19, 2010).

USAID. 2007. *Nyae Nyae Conservancy: First Million Namibian Dollar Concession*. http://africastories.usaid.gov/search_details.cfm?storyID=1034-countryID=16+sectorID=0+yearID=3 (accessed on September 4, 2007).

Van Gennep, Arnold. 1960. *The Rites of Passage*. Chicago: University of Chicago Press.

Wallace, Tim. 2005. Tourism, Tourists, and Anthropologists at Work. In *Tourism and Applied Anthropologists*; ed. T. H. Wallace. *NAPA Bulletin 23* (1): 1–26.

______, ed. 2005. Tourism and Applied Anthropologists: Linking Theory and Practice. *NAPA Bulletin* 23.

Ward, Martha C. 1996. *A World Full of Women*. Boston: Allyn and Bacon.

______. 2005. *Nest in the Wind*, 2nd ed. Long Grove, Ill: Waveland Press.

Waterman, T. T., and A. L. Kroeber. 1934. Yurok Marriages. *University of California Publications in American Archaeology and Ethnology* 35 (1): 1–14. Berkeley: University of California Press.

Weiner, Annette B. 1988. *The Trobrianders of Papua New Guinea*. New York: Holt, Rinehart and Winston.

Weinreich, Uriel, W. Labov, and M. Herzog. 1968. Empirical Foundations for a Theory of Language Change. In *Directions for Historical Linguistics*, ed. W. P. Lehmann and M. Yakov, pp. 95–188. Austin: University of Texas Press.

Werner, Dennis. 1990. *Amazon Journey: An Anthropologist's Year Among Brazil's Mekranoti Indians*. Englewood Cliffs, N.J.: Prentice-Hall.

Wheeler, Mortimer. 1956. *Archaeology from the Earth*. Baltimore: Pelican.

White, Leslie. 1959a. The Concept of Culture. *American Anthropologist* 61: 227–51.

______. 1959b. *The Evolution of Culture*. New York: McGraw-Hill.

White, Leslie, and Beth Dillingham. 1973. *The Concept of Culture*. Minneapolis, Minn.: Burgess Publishing.

Whiteford, Linda M., and L. A. Bennett. 2005. Applied Anthropology and Health and Medicine. In *Applied Anthropology: Domains of Application*, eds. Kedia Satish and John van Willigen. pp 119–147. Westport, Conn: Praeger.

Whiting, John W. M. 1993. The Effect of Polygyny on Sex Ratio at Birth. *American Anthropologist* 95: 435–42.

Wiley, Andrea S., and John S. Allen. 2009. *Medical Anthropology: A Biocultural Approach*. New York: Oxford University Press.

Williams, Jonathan, ed. 1997. *Money: A History*. New York: St. Martin's Press.

Wilson, Alexander. 1991. *The Culture of Nature: North American Landscape from Disney to the Exxon Valdez*. Toronto: Between the Lines.

Winterhalder, Bruce, and Eric Alden Smith. 1981. *Hunter-Gatherer Foraging Strategies: Ethnographic and Archaeological Analysis*. Chicago: University of Chicago Press.

Wolkowski, Richard, and Birl Lowery. 2008. *Soil Compaction: Causes, Concerns, and Cures*. pp 1-8. Madison, WI: Board of Regents University of Wisconsin System Cooperative Extension Publishing.

http://www.soils.WISC.edu/extension/pubs/A3367.pdf (accessed on July 19, 2010).

Womack, Mari. 2001. Emics, Etics, "Ethics" and Shamans. *Anthropology News* 42 (3): 7.

Yiridoe, Emmanuel. 1995. Economic and Sociocultural Aspects of Cowrie Currency of the Dagaaba of Northwestern Ghana. *Nordic Journal of African Studies* 4 (2): 17–32.

Zhang, Juzhong, Garman Harbottle, Chang-sui Wang, and Zhaochen Kong. 1999. Oldest Playable Musical Instrument Found at Jiahu Early Neolithic Site in China. *Nature* 401: 366–68.

Zihlman, Adrienne, Debra Bolter, and Christopher Boesch. 2004. Wild Chimpanzee Dentition and its Implications for Addressing Life History in Immature Hominin Fossils. *Proceedings of the National Academy of Sciences* 101 (29): 10541–43.

———. 2007. Skeletal and Dental Growth and Development in Chimpanzees of the Taï National Park, Côte D'Ivoire. *Journal of Zoology* 273 (1): 63–73.

PHOTO CREDITS

PART 1 p. 0, © Buena Vista Images/The Image Bank/Getty Images **Chapter 1** p. 2, © Frans Lemmens/Photographer's Choice/Getty Images; p. 4, © N. Keddie/Anthro-Photo; p. 9, Courtesy Don A. Lenkeit; p. 12, © John Reader/Science Photo Library/Photo Researchers, Inc.; p. 14, © STR/Reuters/Corbis; p. 15, © Peggy/Yoram Kahana/Peter Arnold Images/Photolibrary; p. 17, © Catherine Karnow/Corbis **Chapter 2** p. 24, Courtesy Roberta Lenkeit; p. 26TL, © Momatiuk/Eastcott/Woodfin Camp and Associates; p. 26BL, © M.P. Kahl/Photo Researchers, Inc.; p. 26R, © David Gillison/Peter Arnold, Inc./Photolibrary; p. 27, © Koichi Kamoshida/Getty Images; p. 30L, © Bruce Dale/National Geographic Society Image Collection; p. 30R, © Bildarchiv Preussischer Kulturbesitz/Art Resource, NY; pp. 34, 35, Courtesy Don A. Lenkeit; p. 36, © Joseph Van Os/Stone/Getty Images; p. 37, Ingram Publishing/SuperStock **Chapter 3** p. 48, © Ron Gilling/Lineair/Photolibrary; p. 53, © AP Photo; pp. 55, 59, Courtesy Don A. Lenkeit; p. 61, String figure of the butterfly by Ms. Finlayson (Ojibwa nation), © Canadian Museum of Civilization, photographer: Frederick W. Waugh, image no. 36650; p. 63, Courtesy Roberta Lenkeit; p. 65, British Library of Political & Economic Science, London School of Economics and Political Science; p. 68, © Konner/AnthroPhoto; p. 69, © Washburn/AnthroPhoto **Chapter 4** p. 72, © AP Photo/James A. Finley; p. 74, © Richard Lord/The Image Works; p. 78, © Betty Press/Woodfin Camp and Associates; p. 80, © Dan Budnik/Woodfin Camp and Associates; p. 84, © Michael Newman/PhotoEdit; p. 86, © H.S. Terrace/Anthro-Photo; p. 87, © Tim Shaffer/Reuters/Corbis; p. 91T, © Michael Mathers/Peter Arnold, Inc./Photolibrary; p. 91B, © J. Greenberg/The Image Works

PART 2 p. 94, © Xinhua/Chine Nouvelle/Eyedea **Chapter 5** p. 96, © Wolfgang Kaehler; p. 101, © Boltin Picture Library/Bridgeman Art Library; p. 104, © Ritchie Stirling/Hulton Archive/Getty Images; p. 105, © Karin Duthie/Alamy; p. 109, © Peter Johnson/Corbis; p. 110, Veronika Pataky Photo Collection. Special Collections Department. University of Nevada, Reno Library; p. 112, © Anthony Bannister/Gallo Images/Corbis; p. 115, Courtesy Robert Lenkeit **Chapter 6** p. 120, © Keren Su/The Image Bank/Getty Images; p. 125, © Bruce A. Dale/National Geographic Society Image Collection; p. 129, © Irven DeVore/Anthro-Photo; p. 131, © James P. Blair/National Geographic Society Image Collection; p. 133, © David Herbig/Danita Delimont.com; p. 136, © Keren Su/Getty Images/The Image Bank; p. 137, © Feng Li/Getty Images; p. 138, © A. Ramey/Woodfin Camp and Associates; p. 139, Courtesy Roberta Lenkeit; p. 140, © Ocean/Corbis **Chapter 7** p. 144, © Plush Studios/Blend Images/Getty Images; p. 150, © The McGraw-Hill Companies/Chris Kerrigan, photographer; p. 154, © Carol Beckwith & Angela M. Fisher/photokunst; p. 155, © 2009 Jupiterimages Corporation; p. 157, © Sebnem Evas/Atlas Geographic/Images & Stories; p. 161, © Picture Contact BV/Alamy; p. 166, © George Chan/Photo Researchers, Inc. **Chapter 8** p. 170, © Maureen MacKenzie, Courtesy Msquared Design; p. 175, © Brian Seed/Hulton Archive/Getty Images; p. 177, © David R. Frazier/The Image Works; p. 179, © Paula Lerner/Woodfin Camp and Associates, Inc.; p. 187, Blend Images/Getty Images **Chapter 9** p. 192, © Jacques Jangoux/Alamy; p. 195, Courtesy of the Institute for Intercultural Studies, Inc. New York; p. 198, © Nigel Pavitt/John Warburton-Lee Photography/Photolibrary; p. 199, © Kris Timken/Blend Images/ Getty Images; p. 200, National Museum of the American Indian. © 2008 Smithsonian Institution. (Neg. #N34256); p. 201, © Karan Kapoor/Corbis; p. 205, © Film Study Center, Harvard University—Gardens of War Plate #92; p. 210, © Miramax/Everett Collection; p. 212, © Thinkstock/Getty Images; p. 213, © AP Photo/Alexandra Zavis **Chapter 10** p. 216, © Jay Directo/AFP/Getty Images; p. 218, © Reuters New-Media, Inc./Corbis; p. 220, Imageshop/Punchstock; p. 222, © Megan Biesele/ AnthroPhoto; p. 224, © Irven DeVore/Anthro-Photo; p. 225, © Charles & Josette Lenars/Corbis; p. 229, © Peter Essick/Aurora; p. 233, © Wendy Stone/Corbis; p. 234, © Fran Caffrey/AFP/Getty Images; p. 236, © Film Study Center, Harvard University—Gardens of War Plate 145 **Chapter 11** p. 238, Photographer's Choice/Getty Images; p. 243, © Ray Ellis/Photo Researchers, Inc.; p. 244, Courtesy Roberta Lenkeit; p. 245, © A. Ramey/PhotoEdit; p. 246T, © Jack Fields/Photo Researchers, Inc.; p. 246B, © A. Ramey/PhotoEdit; p. 251, © David Alan Harvey/Woodfin Camp & Associates; p. 254, © Irven DeVore/AnthroPhoto; p. 258, Courtesy Don A. Lenkeit; p. 259, Ryan McVay/Getty Images; p. 261, © Kal Muller/Woodfin Camp & Associates; p. 262, Courtesy National Anthropological Archives. Smithsonian Institution. (Neg. #36-NAA) **Chapter 12** p. 264, © Lynn Seldon/DanitaDelimont.com; p. 266L, © Susan Kuklin/Photo Researchers, Inc.; p. 266R, © Robert Frerck/Woodfin Camp & Associates; p. 268, Courtesy Ministere de la Culture et de la Communication, Direction Régionale des Affaires Culturelles de Rhône-Alpes, Service Régional de Archéologie; p. 269, © Giraudon/Art Resource, NY; p. 271, © Naturhistorisches Museum, Wien. Photo: Alice Schumacher; p. 275T, Courtesy of the Phoebe Hearst Museum of Anthropology and the Regents of the University of California. 15-4846 #2; p. 275B, Courtesy of the Phoebe Hearst Museum of Anthropology and the Regents of the University of California. #2062; pp. 276, 277, Courtesy Roberta Lenkeit; p. 279L, © George Steinmetz/Corbis; p. 279R, © Charles & Josette Lenars/Corbis; p. 280, © AP Photo/Paul Warner

PART 3 p. 284, © Keren Su/DanitaDelimont.com **Chapter 13** p. 286, © Ding Haitao/XinHua/Xinhua Press/Corbis; p. 296, © Tina Manley/Alamy; p. 300, © Amit Dave/Reuters/Corbis; p. 303T, © Sean Sprague/The Image Works; p. 303B, © Macduff Everton/Corbis; p. 306, © Tatiana Markow/Sygma/Corbis; p. 307, © Wolfgang Kaehler/Corbis; p. 311, © Steve Starr/Index Stock Imagery/Jupiter Images/Getty Images **Chapter 14** p. 314, © Neil McAllister/Alamy; p. 318, © Monalyn Gracia/Corbis; p. 322, © Dr. Robert Trotter II; p. 325, © Bob Krist/Corbis; p. 329, Courtesy Operation Green Leaves **Appendix** Photos courtesy Roberta Lenkeit

INDEX

C

G

H

W

Y

Z

CHAPTER 1

The Azande

Witchcraft and Oracles in Africa

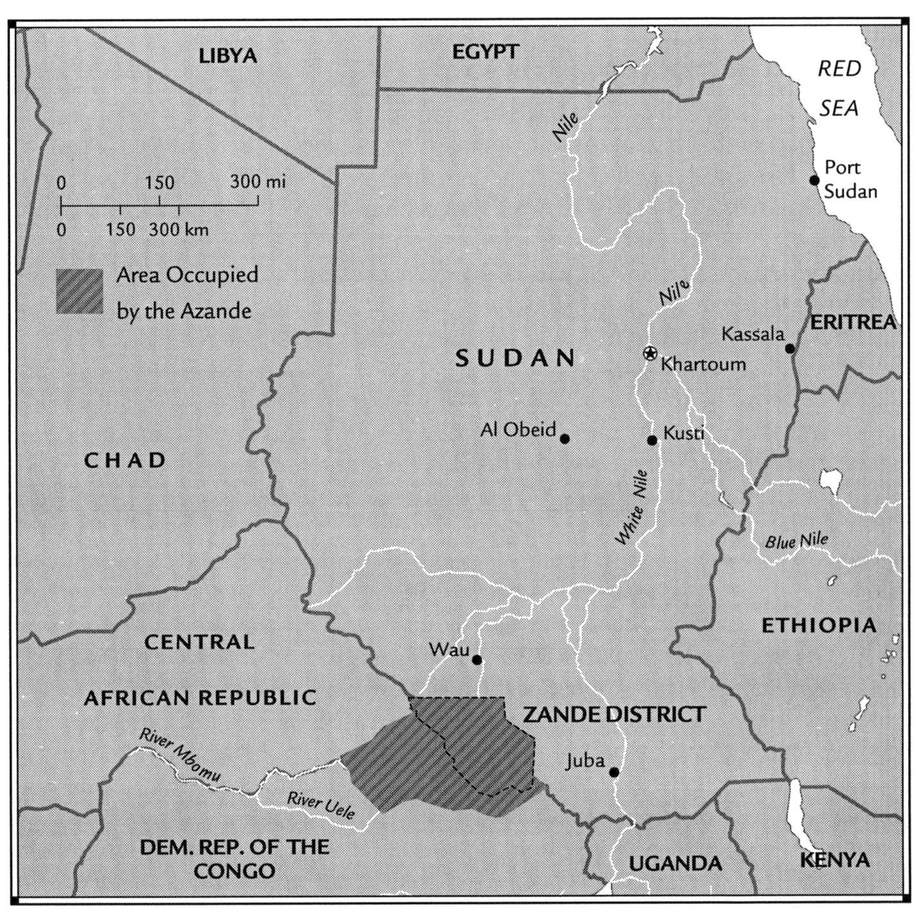

Location of the Azande in Africa.

✈ The Beginning

There are those who can set broken bones. Only they, and people healed by them, can do this. The first of them long ago fathered a child, and the child had no arms and no legs. He was round, like a cooking pot. People saw him and knew he was a child of Mbori, the supreme being. The ancestor had a dream. In the dream he was told to burn the child, and this he did. He was told to take the child's ashes and mix them with oil; this he could use to heal broken limbs. The ancestor did all he was told to do. He used the ashes of the child born with no limbs and created the clan of those who can heal the broken limbs of others.

✈ Introduction and History

The Azande people live in a large area in the center of Africa, overlapping the boundaries of three countries: southwestern Sudan, the eastern edge of the Central African Republic, and the northeastern portion of the Democratic Republic of Congo. Sudan is Africa's largest country, measuring roughly a quarter the size of the United States. Zande settlements occupy an area of rolling hills with abundant rivers and streams. On the banks of the waters grow tall trees, providing shade in which to build homesteads. Zande households were traditionally located at a distance from one another, with close families connected by footpaths winding through the grasslands. However, Azande fell victim to sleeping sickness spread by the tse-tse fly, breeding in their local waters. Colonial authorities forced them to relocate to concentrated settlements near roads, concerned about this exposure—and perhaps additionally motivated by the convenience of having their subjects in large settlements near easily accessible routes (Lyons 2002.) The closeness of the houses in these new settlements was especially problematic. As we will see, witchcraft figures prominently into Zande life. Structures along the riverbanks, which could be spread far apart, afforded protection from neighbors' potential witchcraft, which was only effective at close range.

The peoples known collectively as the Azande are a melding together of what were separate clans in the past. In earliest times, the clans who lived along the banks of the waters were autonomous local groups. Clan disputes were settled within the families of which they were composed. Disputes between clans were settled by elders from each. Zande history tells of a single individual who, through his wisdom and kindness, gained power within his own clan, the Avongara. Soon, under his able leadership, it became the dominant group. Moving eastward along the riverbanks, the Avongara conquered more than fifty other clans and eventually amalgamated into one Zande group. The history of the area is characterized by such invasions and warfare (Reining 1966). The name *Azande* means "the people who possess much land," in recognition of those conquests and the accrual of territory.

In the late nineteenth century, French and Belgian expeditions had set up military outposts in the Sudan; by the early twentieth century the Zande district was under British rule, which lasted until 1953. In that year, growing Sudanese nationalism led to Britain's granting of self-government. Sudan claimed independence in 1956, setting into motion a succession of unstable parliamentary governments and military regimes. Fundamentalist Islamic law was instituted in 1983 and was followed by a series of civil wars among Sudanese of varying religious, ethnic, and political allegiances.

Settlements

Traditionally, the individual homestead of each couple and their children is the focus of the economic system. The construction and maintenance of homes are constant occupations, especially owing to the toll taken on them by weather, insects, animals, and fast-growing vegetation.

Homes are built of mud and grass framed on wooden poles and thatched with grass. (One addition to traditional Zande homes is the European introduction of doors fitted with hinges and locks.) In addition to this living space, each household unit has a granary for storing millet. Houses are built around courtyards, which provide ideal places for gathering and conversation. These enclosed courtyards are seen as a window into the household life. Their upkeep is critical because they are seen as evidence of the responsibility or industriousness of their owners. Reining (1966:69) reports that his Zande informants would comment on the state of disrepair of their neighbor's homestead and "analyzed courtyards as reflections of the inhabitants." They did not exempt themselves from such scrutiny; he continues: "I received a number of apologies from the heads of households about the state of their courtyards, with full explanations for the deficiencies of which they were ashamed" (Reining 1966:69).

The traditional courtyard arrangement appears to have changed very little with European contact (Reining 1966), with the arrangement of each courtyard reflecting the composition of the household to which it is attached. Because each woman must have her own house and granary, a polygynous household will have numerous homes and granaries around its courtyard. In a monogamous household, the average courtyard space is about 65 feet in its largest dimension. Households with more adult women may have yards that are 100 feet square. Courtyards belonging to the households of chiefs are double this size.

"Kitchen gardens" are planted adjacent to the courtyards. These are used for plants that don't require large-scale harvesting or great attention. Pineapple, mango, papaya, and miscellaneous perennial plants used for meals immediately upon picking are found in these plots.

Subsistence and Manufacture

The Azande practice shifting cultivation (that is, no crop rotation, and incorporating a fallowing period), relying mostly on maize and millet, gourds and pumpkins, manioc and bananas, groundnuts, and beans. The tse-tse fly, problematic to animals as well as humans, makes cattle herding impossible. Whatever meat is consumed is secured through hunting. There is also a tradition of using forested areas to gather plants they do not cultivate. Dogs and chickens are the only domesticated animals.

The region has ample rainfall and many springs. These were a focus of Zande life, because they provided usable water nearly year-round. Water for daily use was carried from stream to homestead and the washing, among other activities, was done at the riverbanks. In fact, the stream was central to Zande life in conceptual as well as practical terms. For example, distance is expressed by the number of streams between the points in question; the length of a journey is the number of streams crossed during travel. When asked about an exact location (such as an individual's birthplace) the answer will be the stream nearest that location. Given the centrality of the stream to the Azande, their relocation by the European administration caused major disruption in their cultural beliefs and practices.

The year consists of two seasons, one rainy and one dry. During the rainy summer, Azande cultivate their land. Although they have a long growing season and no frosts, the soil is not rich and insects are troublesome. As the hot, dry weather begins, crops mature and are harvested.

Hunting was most feasible in the dry season, when tall grasses had died or were burned and when the harvest was over. During the rains, vegetation was too dense to allow necessary visibility.

Because rivers were low during this dry season, fish were more accessible. Men employed basket traps, which they set in the rapids of rivers; women dammed the streams into small shallow pools, drained them by bailing, and collected the fish, snakes, and crustaceans that remained. Termites were a favorite food, and their high fat and protein content made them a nutritious part of the diet.

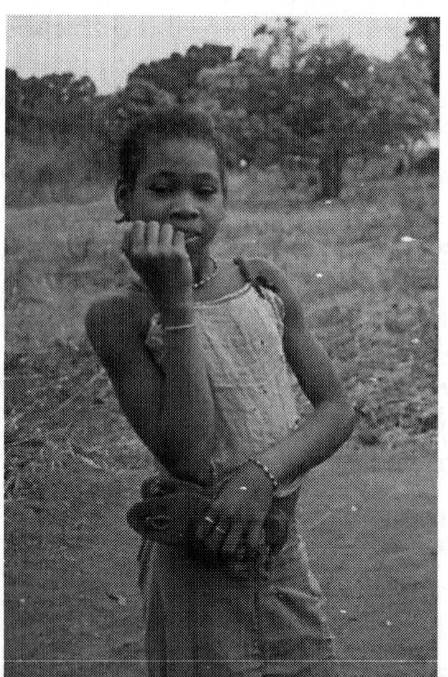

Zande girl.

In pre-European days, each family was an independent unit of production. Iron tools and spears were used as bridewealth items, but in general there was no tradition of exchange between households, which consisted of a wife or wives, husband, their children, and other dependents (such as widowed elderly). There was a sexual division of labor, and both women's and men's work were necessary to maintain an efficiently functioning household. Construction and repair of the house and granary were the responsibility of men. The arduous task of maintaining the courtyard and its gardens fell solely to women. Wealth, possessed mainly by chiefs, was primarily in the form of foodstuffs; the tradition of destroying a person's worldly goods upon death left little chance of inheritance of property.

Azande have no tradition of occupational specialization. All manufacturing and craftswork were considered largely avocations, done by most. Woodworking and pottery, making nets and baskets, and crafting clothing out of bark were the most important of these skills.

Social and Political Organization

Kinship

Among the Azande, clan affiliation was not stressed at the local level. E. E. Evans-Pritchard (1971), the ethnographer most responsible for knowledge about the Azande, found, as he endeavored to gather genealogies, that "except in the royal clan, genealogical relationships between clansmen were very seldom known and usually quite untraceable" (p. 14). Local groups, according to Evans-Pritchard, are, in essence, political units. He reports that his discovering members of the same clan living near one another is due as much to chance as anything else.

Chiefdoms

In pre-European times, the Azande were organized into a number of chiefdoms (sometimes called kingdoms), each of which was independent from the others. The Avongara were nobility; in the days of Zande chiefdoms, it was to Avongara lineages that chiefs belonged. Despite the fact that chiefs of differing groups all belonged to the same clan, there was ongoing hostility and warfare among them.

Chiefs ruled their lands and peoples by appointing emissaries (usually sons, but always Avongara) who were sent out to manage various sections of their territories. Within these communities, commoners were deputized to aid in administration.

Chiefs functioned as military leaders, economic leaders, and political leaders. Unmarried men were recruited into groups that functioned both as warriors and laborers on the king's lands. The governors of the territories had gardens that were also worked by these troops. Both governors and chiefs collected food from the peoples in their domain (provincial governors sending to the chief a portion of their tribute as well) to be redistributed. In addition to food, spears and other items (often payment for fines or bridewealth) were redistributed by the chiefs.

Warfare

Several miles of unsettled forest and bush were maintained between chiefdoms. Watch was kept on these borders by trusted sentinels who were designated to build their houses along these boundaries.

During the rainy season when grass grew tall and provided good cover, surprise attacks were made on these border sentries, usually ordered by the provincial leader. He undertook this action on his own, without permission granted from the chief. Counsel, however, was sought from a poison oracle, a process wherein poison is administered to an animal while questions are posed to the inhabiting spirit. The poisoned animal's behavior, as well as the point at which it succumbed to the poison, were interpreted by those with such skills. Information was obtained concerning the most propitious days and place for the raid, the expected level of casualties, and which companies of warriors should be entrusted with the most dangerous duties. If the oracle indicated that the time was not right for victory, the plans were abandoned.

The oracle also designated a suitable time and place for the attack, and the proper individual to act as a spy. This individual was sent to report on as many aspects of the homestead to be raided as he could determine. Often the spy went under the pretense of visiting a relative or wishing to trade. The best time for a raid was on a feast day when men would be involved in the festivities, not likely to be armed, and quite likely to be drunk. To determine the exact day of the feast, the spy would plan his visit during the preparations for the festivities. Because beer was always brewed for the celebration, the spy could determine the feast day based on the stage of the brewing process.

A successful raid yielded tools, arms, food, and chickens, some of which were sent to the chief for redistribution. Whatever could not be carried off was destroyed. Huts and granaries were burned.

In addition to raids, there were larger mobilizations of war campaigns on a grand scale. These were ordered by the chief, after having consulted his own poison oracle, and might continue over a period of weeks. While knives and spears were used exclusively in raids, the introduction of rifles into these larger confrontations resulted in a shift from hand-to-hand combat to shots being fired from a distance. Only when ammunition was exhausted would those warriors wielding spears converge on the enemy.

Marriage

The traditional Zande system of marriage was greatly disrupted by European involvement. Administrators legislated broad changes, especially regarding bride payment, divorce, and age at marriage. Although many of these were ostensibly designed to improve the status of women, ethnographer Reining (1966:61–62) regards them rather as "an experiment in altering some aspects of a culture without providing for changes in values. . . . [illustrating] the unpredictability of arbitrary cultural changes." Azande did not share the European view that marriage was especially disadvantageous to women, whom they never regarded as servile, despite administrative interpretation of their customs.

Traditionally, the instigation for marriage among the Azande came from the potential groom. When a man wanted to marry a woman, he asked an intermediary to approach her father with his offer. Unless the suitor was deemed undesirable immediately, her father would discuss the matter first with his brothers and sisters and next with the woman in question. If she was agreeable, the money sent with the intermediary was accepted.

Several days later, the suitor would visit his promised bride's parents, bringing gifts and demonstrating his respect. In turn, their daughter visited her suitor's home for a "trial period" of several weeks, after which she returned to her parents' home to make her final decision regarding the marriage.

During the time spent in reflection by the woman, the groom-to-be consulted oracles to determine whether the marriage, should it occur, would be a happy one. If both oracle and woman regarded the match favorably, the bride's family traveled to the home of the groom, where the ceremony took place. The marriage was sealed with the installation of the new bride's own cooking hearth.

Reining (1966) describes traditional Zande marriage as a process that continues indefinitely over time, with a protracted payment of bride-price. A small part of the price was paid at the time of the marriage ceremony, but in reality a husband was always indebted to his wife's family. It was always his responsibility to help in his in-laws' fields, and he had mortuary obligations in the event of a death in his wife's family.

The material payment of the agreed-upon bride-price was not, in fact, as important as the attitude and behavior of a husband to his wife and her parents (Reining 1966). If he was a gentle, loving husband and labored adequately for her parents, remuneration could be forestalled for years. This was often, in reality, the situation preferred by in-laws: it afforded them considerable influence over their daughter's husband. If the husband was not performing his duties adequately, the wife's parents might insist that their daughter move back to their home, forcing the husband to negotiate with her parents for her return. Thus, the relationship of primary emphasis in marriage was that of a son-in-law and his wife's parents. In polygynous situations, a man who had a good relationship with his in-laws often expressed the desire to marry his wife's sister because of the advantages of a good relationship with in-laws.

The topic of homosexuality in Azande culture has been regularly addressed, especially in the context of the unmarried warriors, who, during the several years spent living apart from women, had homosexual relations with the boys who were apprentice warriors. These practices, however, were not necessarily maintained as a lifelong pattern of sexual orientation. Generally, after their experiences with so-called boy-wives, the warriors entered into heterosexual marriages.

Less attention has been paid to Azande lesbianism, relationships that were often formed between co-wives. Although there is not a wealth of information concerning these practices, according to Evans-Pritchard (1970:1429), "All Azande I have known well enough to discuss this matter have asserted . . . that female homosexuality . . . was practiced in polygamous homes."

Zande husbands felt threatened by such activities, yet could not stop them; thus, women usually kept the sexual nature of their friendships secret (Blackwood in Suggs and Miracle 1993). Two Zande women who wished to formalize their relationship could do so in a ritual that created a permanent bond (Evans-Pritchard 1970). In addition to assuring both the emotional and economic support of the partner, it has been suggested that this formalization (a ritual akin to Zande "blood brotherhood") may have both widened a woman's trade network and enhanced her position in the community. Blackwood (in Suggs and Miracle 1993) interprets these relationships as indicating that Azande men's control over women did not extend into the realm of activities between women.

Religion, Beliefs, and Expressive Culture

Missionaries settled in the Sudan beginning in the early part of the twentieth century and attempted to draw on indigenous beliefs as a way to promote Christianity.

Mbori is defined by Evans-Pritchard (1937:11) as "a ghostly being to whom the creation of the world is attributed." Missionaries and government officials writing about the Azande attempted to create out of Mbori a deity that would fit their own tradition. Evans-Pritchard, however, warns against looking for religion, as organized elsewhere, in Azande culture. Mbori is not convincingly portrayed by the Azande as a god analogous to the supreme being as found elsewhere. They have no shrines to Mbori and no materials used in worship. There is only one ceremony in which his name is invoked, and that is performed infrequently at best. When he attempted to pursue the topic of theology, and Mbori in particular, Evans-Pritchard found the Azande "bored by the subject . . . and unable to express more than the vaguest ideas about him."

The Trickster Tales

One universal motif in folk literature appears to be that of the "trickster," and these tales are told among the Azande as well. To a large extent, the tales serve to assert and affirm social rules. They provide examples of the consequences one can expect if moral dictates are not observed. They are always told for the benefit of children, to supplement didactic social training. They are designed to appeal to a young audience (although they often contain very adult themes and are very much enjoyed by adults) by featuring a main character who possesses a child's curiosity and temptation to break the rules. Demonstrated in the behavior of the trickster are a child's propensity for imitation, the ramifications of overlooking part of a ritual, and the dangers inherent in exhibiting behaviors or assuming a role in society that are inappropriate.

Although there are many groups of trickster tales told among the Azande, the best known concern the adventures of a character named Ture. The stories focus on Ture's elaborate machinations as he attempts to secure what he is after, and end in describing his great success or dismal failure. His wants are generally basics; he is often in pursuit of food, such as meat, termites, porridge, mushrooms, and honey—the items most desirable in a Zande diet.

Ture's rashness often leads him to situations in which he must find a way to prevent his own death, often while in the form of a bird or animal. In many tales, he is intrigued by either fire or water, sometimes regarded as necessities, sometimes as playthings. Despite his need for everyday goods, he often pursues items of pure luxury: "salt to improve the taste of his food, a barkcloth which hums harmoniously as the wearer moves, and a means of opening termite mounds to provide him with a home instead of building huts" (Street 1972:83).

Ture often shows poor judgment and questionable values, striving for something only because it is novel or belongs to someone else, rather than because it is of any use to him. Thus, when he learns that someone possesses the ability to remove his own intestines and clean them, he wants only to be able to learn to do the same; when he obtains a secret formula for putting out fires, he sets his own house ablaze just so he can extinguish it. As the latter example suggests, oftentimes Ture will create ends just for the ability to use the means (Street 1972).

Once Ture has chosen a goal, he begins to set his strategy for its achievement. However, his strategies tend to ignore all social convention. He usually uses trickery or deception to get what he wants. However, his attempts to use others to satisfy his own needs usually end in failure.

Often Ture tries to use magical spells or rituals that are not his to use. Because he is not the rightful owner of the magic or ceremony, he is unable to obtain the results he seeks. (One is reminded of the troubles encountered by the "sorcerer's apprentice" who borrows his master's hat and attempts to perform his chores with magical assistance, only to be overwhelmed by the power he has unwittingly unleashed.)

For example, Ture overhears a discussion about how two sons found success in hunting after cutting off their dying father's toe. In his eagerness to try this formula for hunting success, Ture murders his father, buries the toe he has severed, and goes out to hunt. To his surprise, he catches very few animals, and most of his companions are killed during the effort. The formula, it turns out, is only effective when the toe is offered willingly.

In other instances, the formula backfires because it is in the wrong hands: Ture has obtained it under false pretenses, and he was not meant to have it. While Ture may overhear a strategy for success, or may be given the tool to implement a strategy, he often has to resort to trickery to get the desired secret or magic.

Although tales end with particular lessons—Don't attempt another's behavior without that person's skill; If you are greedy, your acquisitions will be too much to handle—the Zande tales are more than merely moral examples. They employ themes common to many peoples. Evans-Pritchard suggests that the tales "represent deeper psychological forces present in us all, those elements which we would like to give rein to but cannot because of the rules of society" (Street 1972:86).

The tales also endeavor to teach flexibility, because rules are not always functional in every situation. To instill the message that sometimes rules must be broken, Ture the trickster elaborates the middle ground between order and chaos, and moderation in the application of convention. Classically, trickster tales describe a society's boundaries and rules and assert its unique identity. If viewed from this perspective, the Zande tales help us to understand their society as well as some broader tenets of human nature.

Witchcraft and Sorcery

The Azande are perhaps better known for their pervasive belief in witchcraft than for any other aspect of their culture. However, in his classic description of witchcraft among the Azande, Evans-Pritchard asks the reader to be aware "that the Zande cannot analyze his doctrines as I have done for him. . . . It is no use saying to a Zande 'Now tell me what you Azande think about witchcraft' because the subject is too general and indeterminate . . . to be described concisely. But it is possible to extract the principles of their thought from dozens of situations in which witchcraft is called upon to explain happenings. . . . Their philosophy is explicit, but it is not formally stated as a doctrine" (1937:70). (In such situations, an anthropologist endeavors to construct such a "doctrine" through fieldwork. The resulting product may look quite dissimilar from the indigenous view [Barrett 1991].)

Witchcraft is thought to be an actual physical property residing inside some individuals, who may themselves be unaware of their power. The witchcraft substance, *mangu,* can be inherited, passed from father to son and mother to daughter. Azande believe that if the soul of the father is more powerful, the child conceived will be a boy; if the mother's soul substance is greater, their child will be a girl. Thus, although every child is a product of both parents, each also has more of one particular parent's soul. And if that parent is a witch, inheriting this inherent power to do harm is inevitable.

Because this property is organic, it grows as a person grows. Therefore an older witch is a more dangerous witch. Children, whose witchcraft substance is small, are never accused of major acts of harm (such as murder). They can, however, cause minor misfortunes for other children.

Sorcery differs from witchcraft in that it is an art that is learned and deliberately practiced. Unlike sorcery, which employs charms and spells, witchcraft is deployed by sheer willpower. Witches send the spirit of their own witchcraft entity to eat the flesh and organs of their intended victims. Thus, a witch may be at home asleep at the time illness or injury occurs. It is the "soul of the witchcraft" that travels through the night. This substance cannot travel great distances, however, and it is for this reason that the Azande feel more secure if they are able to live at a distance from their neighbors. The "short-range" nature of witchcraft allows the perpetrator to be more accurately identified; all those beyond the limits of a witch's capabilities, even with evil intent, may be eliminated. If a person is taken ill while traveling, it is that location where illness struck in which the witch must be found.

The Azande believe that witchcraft is at the base of all misfortune, great or small. If a potter opens his kiln only to discover his pottery cracked, he intimates witchcraft; if a child stubs her toe at play, she suspects witchcraft; if a hunter is gored by an elephant, he lays blame for the injury squarely on a witch.

Azande entertain no concept of "accidental" death. People die only as victims of murder, whether committed by witches or by the magic of revenge reserved for retaliation against suspected witches.

Despite these convictions, the Azande do not live in constant terror of witches (Nanda 1991). In fact, Douglas (1980) reminds us that Evans-Pritchard's assessment of the Azande was that they were the happiest and most carefree peoples of the Sudan. "The feelings of an Azande man, on finding that he has been bewitched, are not terror, but hearty indignation as one of us might feel on finding himself the victim of embezzlement" (Douglas 1980:1).

Because a witch's motivation is not random, but rather envy or hatred directed at a specific person, a victim searches for a suspect among those with whom he has argued, or in a person who may have cause to be jealous of him. Moreover, one cannot identify witches merely by sight; they look like everyone else. How then can he identify his aggressor? For this, and other purposes, the Azande consult a variety of oracles.

Oracles

The Azande consult oracles regarding a wide range of things about which they need information. They ask for guidance in planning a marriage, taking a journey, building a house, organizing a raid. In addition to whatever their current misfortune may be, they inquire about whether their health will be endangered in the future.

In pre-European times, Zande chiefs consulted oracles to confirm their military decisions, but chiefs were also charged with judicial duties. Every accusation was brought before the chief to adjudicate. To this end, he employed several people whose responsibility it was to assist in the consultation of oracles. It has been said that the Azande belief in witchcraft is the supporting framework of their entire judicial system (Mair 1974:221).

An oracle is a device for revelation. Among the Azande there are many from which to choose, with varying reputations for reliability. By far the most powerful is *benge,* the poison oracle, used by men alone. Its decisions are relied upon without question, and no undertaking of great import is attempted without its authorization. In attempting to convey its centrality, a Zande informant of Evans-Pritchard drew the analogy between the books of Europeans and the poison oracle of his own people. All the knowledge, guidance, memory, and truth that are derived from trusted Western writings reside for the Azande within the poison oracle. Evans-Pritchard came to view it as less a ritual than a necessity:

> For how can a Zande do without his poison oracle? His life would be of little worth. Witches would make his wife and children sick and would destroy his crops and render his hunting useless. Every endeavour would be frustrated, every labour and pain would be to no purpose. At any moment a witch might kill him and he could do nothing to protect himself and his family. Men would violate his wife and steal his goods, and how would he be able to identify and avenge himself on adulterer and thief? Without the aid of his poison oracle he knows that he is helpless and at the mercy of every evil person. It is his guide and counsellor. (1937:262–263)

Despite this seeming indispensability, later ethnographers have pointed out that *benge* poison, expensive and difficult to obtain, was most likely an oracle available regularly only to men of wealth. This limitation may have acted both to engender social obligations and to grant power and prestige. A man who cannot afford the costly poison, or who does not possess the proper chicken to which the poison must be administered, asks a wealthier kinsman, or deputy of the chief, to consult the oracle on his behalf. It is his duty to oblige. It is older men who are likely to have the means to seek counsel from the oracle: this access to information gives them power over younger men. They not only can ask the oracles about the intentions and behaviors of their juniors, but also are always supported in their decisions by the considerable weight of oracular authority, to which younger or poorer men have no direct access, and so cannot challenge (Evans-Pritchard 1937).

The *benge* poison ordeal is an elaborate procedure, requiring great skill and finesse in both the administration of the poison and the posing of the questions. Poison is administered, by an expert in the task, to a small chicken. The expert must know how much poison is necessary, how much time should elapse between doses, whether it should be shaken to distribute the poison, how long and firmly the chicken should be held, and in what position. Each barely perceptible movement made by the bird is significant to the trained eye.

Once the poison has been administered, the order in which questions are asked and whether they are phrased in a positive or negative frame must all be determined by the questioner. The oracle is addressed as if it were a person. Every detail of the situation in question is explained, and each individual question may be embedded in five or ten minutes of speech. The *benge* poison shows its answer by responding through the chicken to the directive, "If this is true, *benge* kill the fowl" or "If this is not the truth, *benge* spare the fowl." Each answer is then tested by repeating the interpretation of its reply, prefaced with the question, "Did the oracle speak the truth in saying . . ." (Mair 1974).

An oracle more readily available to all is the termite oracle. This is used as often by women as men, and even children may participate. Two branches are cut, each from a different tree. They are inserted together into a termite mound and left overnight. The answer is indicated by which branch has been eaten. Though certainly less elaborate and costly than the *benge* oracle, consulting termites is a time-consuming affair, because only one question may be posed at a time and one must wait all night long for the answer.

Least reliable but most convenient is the rubbing-board oracle, a device resembling a Ouija board, made of two small pieces of wood, easily carried to be consulted anywhere, at any time. One small piece of wood is carved with a handle and is rubbed across the top of a second piece, fashioned with legs to stand on. Questions are asked as the wood is moved; as it sticks or catches, so the answer is revealed.

Accusing a Witch

There are two distinct sorts of accusations of witchcraft: one in which illness or misfortune has occurred, the other after someone has died. These differ in both the function of accusing an individual and the ramifications of being found guilty.

The aim of accusing a person of witchcraft in the former situation is to bring about some resolution to the conflict that induced the attack and to return the relationship to equilibrium. Speaking ill of a person, or even wishing someone injury, is ineffectual without a social tie: the curse of a stranger cannot do harm. Thus, a relationship with the accused is a prerequisite for bewitchment. (An individual must be suspected, or else his or her name could not have been presented to the oracle for confirmation or denial of guilt.)

When the chicken dies during the *benge* poison ordeal, a wing is cut off, placed on a stick, and brought to the local deputy of the chief, telling him the name of the individual confirmed by the *benge*. A messenger, sent with the wing to the alleged witch, places it on the ground and announces that *benge* has been consulted regarding the illness of the accuser. Usually this charge is met with denial of any ill intent. At the very least, the accused pleads ignorance of harm derived from his or her own *mangu,* or witchcraft substance. As a demonstration of good faith, the alleged witch takes a mouthful of water and sprays it over the wing. So doing, she or he beseeches the *mangu* to become inactive, allowing the victim to recover. The messenger reports these events to the chief's deputy.

In the event of a "murder," the aim is not pacification but revenge. Restoring amicable relations is clearly not possible; a postmortem accusation is an indictment leading to heavy compensation, sometimes paid with the witch's own life. Exacting such a toll permanently alters the relationship between the kin group of the victim and that of the accused (McLeod 1972).

Witchcraft in Its Social Setting

The Azande chiefdom is formally structured in a clear-cut hierarchy, from the chiefs at the top through their deputies, armies, local governors, and ending with individual householders. Built into this structure is the elimination of most opportunities for unequal competition: that is, chiefly lineages did not compete with those lesser, nor did the rich with the poor, or parents with their children. As Douglas (1980) has observed, accusations of witchcraft arise only in those social situations that fall outside of the political structure. Thus, co-wives might accuse each other, as might rivals in other arenas. Because witches could be unintentionally dangerous, their *mangu* could be set into motion by understandable resentments and jealousies. The accusation and eventual demonstration of remorse will set these ill feelings to rights. Events that can be explained by an individual's lack of technical skill (such as the shoddy work of an inexperienced carpenter) or by personally motivated actions are not likely to be involved in the realm of witchcraft. As Parsons (1969:195) observes, one can imagine many motivations for people to claim that witchcraft was at the root of their adultery, but this would result in ridicule, "because everybody knows witches don't do that."

Witchcraft beliefs can function effectively as a way of managing the anxiety resulting from random misfortune. This is evidenced by the prominence given to illness and death as occasions for witchcraft accusations.

Witchcraft as Social Control and Leveling Mechanism

Witchcraft may serve as an effective agent of social control. The lengthy process involved in making an accusation acts to forestall hasty and emotional confrontations. Charges must have group support behind them and are not leveled carelessly.

An individual's behavior can be guided by the knowledge that wrongdoing might likely result in retaliatory witchcraft. Additionally, cognizance that jealous or hostile behavior might place one in a position of being suspect should misfortune occur might lead one to be quite circumspect. Wishing to be neither suspect nor victim, the Azande possess, in witchcraft, both an effective sanction against socially disruptive behavior and a vehicle for handling hostility.

Because an individual with great wealth is likely to engender the jealousy of others and the attendant bewitchment, Azande are not likely to attempt to outproduce one another. It is in this way that witchcraft acts as a leveling mechanism, indirectly keeping wealth balanced.

The "Logic" of Azande Witchcraft

The attribution of the cause of all misfortune to witchcraft may seem extreme. In fact, Evans-Pritchard himself engaged in lively debate with informants who described as witchcraft events that seemed to him the result of entirely "natural" phenomena. He eventually recognized that they did, in fact, have a very clear understanding about the contribution of the natural world to their misfortune. When Evans-Pritchard suggested to a boy, whose foot had been injured when he tripped over a tree stump, that a witch could not possibly have placed the tree stump in his way, the boy agreed. He recognized that nature had contributed the tree stump and, further, that the tree stump had cut his foot. His evidence of witchcraft was simply that despite his vigilance in watching out for tree stumps, as well as his safe passage on that same path hundreds of other times, *this time* he had been injured. This time, there was witchcraft.

Along these same lines, when a granary collapsed, injuring several people who had been sitting in its shade, Azande saw no contradiction in their dual assertions that termites had eaten at the legs of the building, resulting in its collapse, and that witchcraft was responsible. They further admitted that no witch had "sent" the people underneath the granary in order to trap them: it was afternoon, and they were merely seeking shade. While we would call this series of events coincidence, or perhaps "being in the wrong place at the wrong time," Azande are able to form an explanatory link between these events. That link is provided by witchcraft.

During his stay in the Sudan, Evans-Pritchard witnessed the suicide of a man who was angry with his brothers. Although his despair over his conflict was well known, and when his body was found hanging from a tree, all readily acknowledged that he had, in fact, hanged himself, the cause of death was considered witchcraft. At Evans-Pritchard's behest, a Zande friend explained:

> . . . only crazy people commit suicide; if everyone who was angry with his brothers committed suicide there would soon be no people left in the world; if this man had not been bewitched he would not have done what he did do (1937:71).

Once the supernatural premise that people have witchcraft substance in them and can harm others with it is granted, the Zande argument becomes logical.

As we will see later, these beliefs concerning witchcraft endure today, with some modifications. Resettlement has forced them to accept living in closer quarters, depending on screens to keep them out of their neighbors' view, if not their reach. When asked about fears concerning the proximity of witches, the Azande report that they feel able to relocate should misfortune occur. This would remove them from any nearby threat.

AZANDE TODAY: RESETTLED, UNSETTLED

The "Zande Scheme"

The decision by colonial authorities in the 1920s to move Azande out of the valleys to control sleeping sickness was only the first in a series of resettlement and development plans. Before midcentury, the Azande were subsistence cultivators. In the late 1940s and early 1950s, the British introduced the so-called Zande scheme, a program of cash cropping (chiefly of cotton) and industry (producing cotton cloth). Planners believed they could improve the lot of the Azande, who, it was thought, would be grateful for the introduction of more "modern" comforts and luxuries. The introduction of money and wage labor acted to weaken kinship ties by obviating the need for kin to work together outside the household. Young men and women could more easily leave their parents' homes and set up their own households with income from wages paid by Europeans. As part of the scheme, the Azande were once again resettled—more than 60,000 families by 1950—away from the roads, into farmland. The most detrimental feature of the resettlement plan was the arbitrary assignment of individuals to plots of land. This action was flawed in several ways: it disregarded family groupings, failed to take into account the Azande's desire for mobility and flexible living arrangements, and resulted in some farmers receiving land with good soil and others receiving land of poor quality. Tensions were engendered among resettled people that were counterproductive to the developers' wishes to create, through resettlement, a stable workforce. Anthropologist Conrad Reining (1966), in a study of the Zande scheme, concluded that while the project demonstrated the feasibility of establishing an industrial center among the Azande (provided cost was no object), and of convincing the Azande to produce copious amounts of cotton, it more convincingly showed how much could not be accomplished. Its primary weaknesses were in the realms of ecology, social organization, and communication—failures it shared with other such attempts. By the mid-1950s, cotton production slowed to a near halt. There was a move to restart the program in the 1970s, but civil war in Sudan, which would continue throughout the twentieth century and into the twenty-first, cut short the attempted revival.

Witchcraft and HIV

Anthropologist Tim Allen notes that the introduction to a recent republication of Evans-Pritchard's classic *Witchcraft, Oracles and Magic* asserted that the Azande life described therein represents "a world long vanished." (2007:359) This, he says, is not so. The Avongara have maintained their status: all chiefs in Ezo county, South Sudan, are Avongara, and they continue to preside over witchcraft disputes and adjudicate in such cases. Headmen wield enough power to exact fines for transgressions. Although many oracle readers have embraced Christianity, their practice continues largely unchanged, resembling that of nearly 100 years ago. In fact, the crisis engendered by HIV/AIDS has led to increased demand for their oracular gifts: local health centers may be without the resources to test for the disease, but the oracles are not (Allen 2007).

Certainly, factors such as public health programs, the spread of Christianity, and numerous sociopolitical and economic factors have contributed to the changing ways in which the Azande experience and explain illness. However, biomedical and Christian teachings have not supplanted older ideas so much as been included within the range of explanations. Allen (2007) finds that "[a]t one level, all deaths are still interpreted as a form of homicide" (p. 375), with the accused expected to undergo testing with *benge* poison.

Allen's ethnography elegantly demonstrates the ways in which witchcraft and sorcery wield powerful explanatory power regarding HIV/AIDS. He has found that the Azande in Ezo county Sudan identify HIV/AIDS as their worst health problem, despite relatively few cases locally. Increased migration from surrounding areas with higher prevalence rates have contributed to this growing fear, but there are more deep-seated reasons: Zande witchcraft beliefs inform their feelings of vulnerability to HIV.

Remember the qualities of *mangu,* and the properties of a witch: *mangu* is a powerful, dangerous substance residing deep within the body of a witch; witches cannot be outwardly identified with any certainty. Thus, HIV-positive individuals are much like witches: they look just like everyone else, yet they are secretly killing those around them.

Local belief systems are also at odds with public health policies. As Allen (2007) points out, while anonymity for those who test positive is accepted elsewhere as standard practice, it is, for the Azande, "the crux of the problem, one that resonates with local understandings of witchcraft" (p. 393). Individuals who are open about their positive status are seen as behaving responsibly. Those who keep their status hidden are seen not as maintaining their privacy, but as a threat. Without certainty of who is positive, anyone may be dangerous.

Witches may cause harm unintentionally; sorcerers do so deliberately. HIV-positive sorcerers may use their blood as poison, mixing it in food, or strategically placing a contaminated razor blade where it might be stepped on or grabbed. Allen (2007) has found that Ezo Azande greatly overestimate the danger of HIV infection from sharp objects.

The process of setting up screening and outreach programs in Ezo county is ongoing. Allen explains:

> No one knows what the actual rates of infection are, and very few people are able to find out their own status. The population has nevertheless been persuaded that healthy looking people living amongst them are killing them in large numbers. Everyone, from visiting traders and women selling mangoes at the market, to neighbours and loved ones in the home, are potentially like witches. (p. 393)

Civil War in Sudan

Strife in Sudan is as old as the independent country itself, with the first Sudanese civil war beginning in 1955. From the time Sudan gained independence in 1956, there was inequality between the Arab north and "black African" south. The British government concentrated power in the hands of the Arab north, and the Arab-led government in Khartoum held sway over peoples in the south, Africans who were either Christian or retained their indigenous beliefs. Shortly thereafter, the military seized power and attempted to impose Islam on the southern Sudanese, many of whom fled in response to increasing threats. In the early 1960s, southern refugees formed the Anya-Nya ("snake poison"), a liberation movement advocating an independent southern state. Throughout the 1960s, unrest continued as governmental and military rule changed hands. In the early 1970s, the Southern Sudan Liberation Movement (SSLM) was created, finally resulting in a cease-fire and the official end of civil war in 1972. This relative calm was short-lived. In 1983, the Sudanese government instituted Islamic law throughout the country, beginning a second civil war, which was in essence a continuation of the first. Numerous opposition groups were formed in the south, chief among them the Sudan People's Liberation Movement (SPLM), which has been accused of showing disregard for the rights of the civilians they champion (Kebbede 1999). There has been infighting among southern Sudanese peoples—Azande among them—as well as struggles with the powerful north.

The development of exportable oil resources in the south enriched the government, enabling it to purchase arms for the war against the south. Some scholars contend that while the ethnic and religious conflict in Sudan has long been central, the struggle to control resources has emerged as a powerful compelling force in the civil war (Kebbede 1999).

By the time peace talks between southern rebels and the government began in 2003, the civil war in Sudan had been among the longest-running in the world, devastating both the people and the land. Estimates of dead are as high as two million since 1983. In addition, Sudan also has one of the world's largest populations of internally displaced people—nearly 5 million. A Comprehensive Peace Agreement (CPA) was signed in 2005. Among its provisions was the eventual creation of an autonomous southern Sudan. The position of co-vice president (later president of South Sudan) was established, and John Garang, SPLM leader, was installed in the post. The valuable oil deposits were equally split between north and south. Three weeks after his appointment, Garang was killed in a helicopter crash. He was succeeded by Sudan People's Liberation Army (SPLA) founding member Salva Kiir, who was reelected president of South Sudan in 2010.

Despite the official agreement, armies in both the north and south remained in place, and fighting has not ceased. In 2007, the SPLM withdrew from the national unity government, leading many to fear a resurgence of violence. Central to the conflict is the oil-rich region on the north–south border.

"Home" to an Independent South Sudan: An "Uncertain Return"

One hope tied to the Comprehensive Peace Agreement was that it might provide an opportunity for the nearly 5 million displaced Sudanese to return home. John Garang envisioned what he thought of as a "New Sudan"—a unified, secular state. The final provision of the CPA, a referendum on the establishment of an independent South Sudan, was voted on in January 2011. The referendum passed with near unanimity: 99 percent voted in favor of independence, with official recognition of the new nation in July 2011.

More than 2 million southerners living in the North, as well as nearly 400,000 who fled to neighboring countries, have, in fact, returned to their homes since the signing of the CPA. Return is complex both for those who have been displaced and for those who have stayed behind. Those returning may be refugees, soldiers, or abductees; they may have been "internally displaced" in the north or may be in exile in neighboring African countries.

The Azande, like many other southern Sudanese displaced to the north, struggled under strict Islamic law. For example, women brewing traditional beer to earn money for their families faced jail for trafficking in alcohol, illegal in North Sudan. Some who fled will return with higher education or language expertise in English or Arabic. Some who have stayed behind express apprehension about returnees who will bring "foreign" ways home with them (Phelan and Wood 2006).

Many Azande were displaced from Sudan into the Democratic Republic of Congo. While they assert that their Zande identity is more central than their Sudanese nationality, once displaced from their country, being Sudanese offered another way to form community (Phelan and Wood 2006). Returning to Zande lands offers them the opportunity to once again place tribal ties above national ones. Although the land to which they may return has often been overgrown and depleted of nutrients, one Zande returnee to Ezo county explained, "One cannot hate his home, however poor it may be" (Phelan and Wood 2006:26). Many

Zande are content to move to a new piece of land, however, not only because it is more fertile, but also because, over time, old homestead boundaries are hard to discern. Another factor in resettlement is Zande unwillingness to settle on any land containing the burials of another family's ancestors.

An interim report on this process asks numerous questions, among them whether those born in exile can be thought of as returning "home" (Phelan and Wood 2006). Many who fled the south decades ago—changed people returning to changed villages—are doing so with children for whom their parents longed-for home is one they have never known.

Despite referring to the homecoming as "an uncertain return," a report on the impact of Sudanese returnees details the anticipation of those who await their family members: "Many people in southern Sudan are waiting for the return of the displaced as keenly as for the dividends of peace" (Phelan and Wood 2006:45)

Connecting the Azande Community

Throughout the decades of Sudanese civil war, thousands of Azande fled to other parts of Africa as well as Europe, Australia, and North America. Community organizations of Azande have been established throughout the world, with a London-based organization providing an umbrella under which these local groups can affiliate. The Azande Community World-wide Organization (ZACOWO) was established to "unite and bring all the Azande together so that the impact of scattering throughout the world is minimized" (www.azande.org.uk). Its Web site contains Sudanese news updates, job postings, and folk tales about Ture the Trickster. With the establishment of Internet services in Zandeland, the ZACOWO-run Zande net allows Azande diaspora to communicate with friends and family. Local groups, such as the Azande Organization of Portland, Maine, often began as refugee resettlement programs, providing both financial help and social guidance. Over time, and with a growing Azande population, groups have expanded their mission to address what they recognize as "the growing gap between the parents who immigrated and their children being raised here" (www.azandeorganization.org).

→ For Further Discussion

Witchcraft among the Azande traditionally served as an effective means of social control. What are the major institutions and beliefs in your own culture that function similarly? Think about the ways in which members of your society are compelled to behave in socially acceptable ways. How do these differ from one another? There is a "logic" to the Azande belief in witchcraft and the causality of misfortune. Do you employ logic that is similar or different when explaining negative events? Are there several different "systems of logic" that may be invoked, depending on the circumstances?

CHAPTER 2

THE AZTECS

Ancient Legacy, Modern Pride

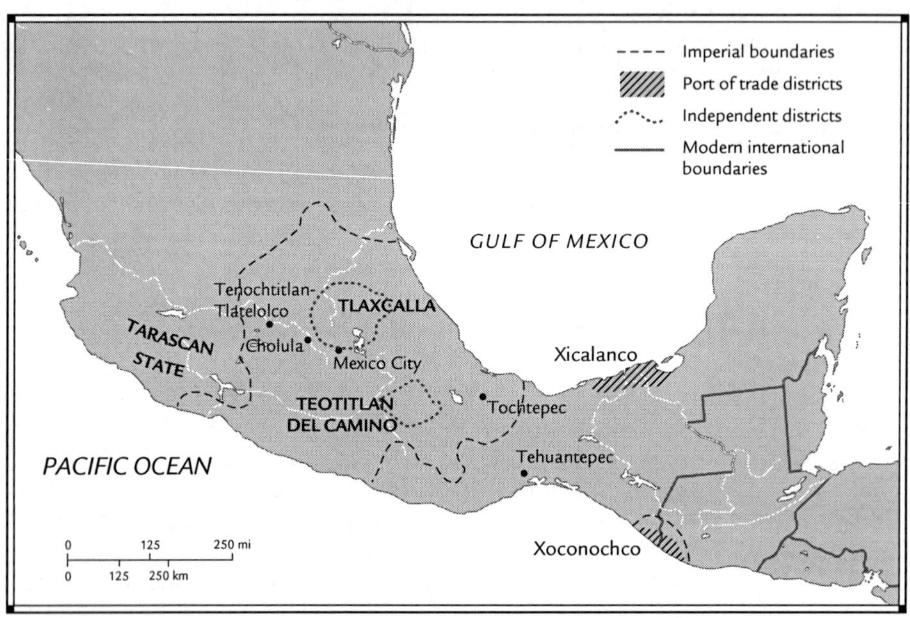

The Aztec Empire, 1519.

➢ The Beginning

The world before had existed not once, but four times, and these were the Ages of the Suns. Water, earth, fire, and wind each had their reign. Each ended in disaster.

The first people were formed of ashes, and when the water, came they were carried away and changed into fishes. In the next sun, there were giants, and tigers waited for dark to devour them. The giants were weak despite their size, and warned one another: do not fall. But they fell, and when they fell, they fell forever. During the third sun, the rain was made of fire, and all burned. The fourth sun was the wind, which swept everything away. The people became monkeys and fled to the mountains.

Now it is the fifth sun. New people are created from the remains of the old. Quetzalcoatl will restore them and feed them maize (León-Portilla 1992).

➢ Aztec History

Journey to the Valley of Mexico

The people referred to as Aztecs called themselves Mexica. Arriving in central Mexico as nomads in the thirteenth century, they had risen to a position of political and military power by the time the Spanish arrived in 1519. With Tenochtitlan as the capital of their empire, they had forged alliances with neighbors to the east and west.

Mexica migration into the Valley of Mexico began from Aztlan in the northwest some 200 years before their eventual arrival. As they marched south, they were met with great hardship, expelled from each place they attempted to settle. Throughout the Valley of Mexico, elaborate states were already flourishing. The peoples who had settled here had developed complex and specialized technologies, including a sophisticated system of irrigation, which afforded them a variety of crops in abundance. In addition, they possessed intricately organized social and economic systems. The nomadic Mexicas were not welcomed in their attempt to seek out unsettled land.

Their arduous trek was plagued with dissension from within (Berdan 1982) and treachery from without. Evidence for internal rebellion is found in numerous accounts of their journey. Along their route, whenever they stopped they constructed a temple for Huitzilopotchtli, the most revered of the deities, who provided guidance on their exodus. Among the ceremonies conducted at these sites were human sacrifices, for which the Aztecs have come to be known. Many explanations have been offered for the various sacrificial occasions in Aztec culture. Berdan (1982) suggests that those performed en route to their permanent home may have served the purpose of eliminating dissension by members of the group who were agitating to remain where they were and not continue on their journey as Huitzilopotchtli decreed.

The response of the ruler of Calhuacan to the Mexica request for asylum exemplified the rejection they experienced from others. Their petition to settle in his kingdom was met with the granting of territory he knew to be infested with poisonous snakes. He was sure this would put an end to these "undesirable Mexicas" (León-Portilla 1992:31). Instead, they roasted the snakes, ate them, and triumphed. Apparently surprised at the Mexica tenacity and impressed by their military skills, those living in the area engaged the Mexica as their mercenaries. Coupled with some of their more aggressive customs, these martial skills elicited both fear and hatred from surrounding peoples. When a ceremony to dedicate the king's daughter as a goddess resulted in her death and flaying, the Mexica were forced to flee once more.

Tenochtitlan

Camping by the marshy shores of Lake Texcoco, they were instructed by Huitzilopotchtli to look for the sign that would at long last indicate to them the site of their final destination. They saw this sign—an eagle resting atop a prickly pear cactus—and knew they had reached the end of their difficult journey. They named the place Tenochtitlan, "the place of the fruit of the prickly pear cactus" (Berdan 1982). The modern Mexican flag has at its center the eagle perched on the cactus, a snake in its talons.

The founding of Tenochtitlan in 1325 ended their wandering, but certainly not the struggle of the Mexica people. Both the physical and the sociopolitical environment presented enormous challenges. Tenochtitlan was built on an island on the western side of Lake Texcoco. Although the lake provided fish and aquatic birds, ease of canoe transportation, and *chinampas* cultivation (so-called floating gardens), the site was not without disadvantages. Chief among these were the lack of wood and stone for use in construction and the threat of floods.

Sociopolitically, the Mexica had established themselves on the boundaries of existing powerful states. Their history of overcoming adversity stood them in good stead. They attached themselves to the ruling Tepanec Empire and began to strengthen themselves by forging alliances through marriage.

Within the Tepanec Empire, it was the ancient Toltec line of nobility who were viewed as legitimate rulers. The first Mexica ruler in Tenochtitlan married a woman from a royal line, assuring the offspring of this union (and their descendants) legitimate claim to Toltec heritage. The ruler's son further cemented this bond by making a similarly politically astute marriage. Relations between the Mexica and the Tepanec ruler were cemented by these ties (especially after the birth of a son to the Mexica ruler and the Tepanec lord's granddaughter), and the Mexica became allies rather than subordinates.

As a result of these shifts in power relations, the Mexica population became increasingly socially stratified. Rulers headed a class of nobles who claimed private ownership of land and the prerogative to hold important public offices.

The largest portion of the Mexica population remained commoners who worked the land and fought the battles. Between these classes of commoners and nobility were occupational specialists: merchants and craftspeople (Berdan 1982).

While attending to war strategy and political power occupied the nobility, average Mexicas devoted themselves to the construction of temples and houses, and *chinampas* cultivation. The latter was of crucial importance, not only because fulfilling their own subsistence needs afforded the Mexica some degree of autonomy but also because it was a key to necessary expansion.

The Mexica population grew rapidly, in part because immigration supplemented natural growth. As conditions became crowded, people left Tenochtitlan to settle adjacent islands. Successful *chinampas* cultivation provided a consistent resource base, allowing the Mexicas to conquer other groups and exact tribute (Berdan 1982).

During this time, a powerful Mexica military force was being assembled. Joining with two neighboring allies, the Triple Alliance was formed, successfully dethroning the Tepanec Empire and beginning the most dramatic expansion in the history of Mesoamerica.

Economic Organization

Tenochtitlan was connected to the mainland by three raised, paved roadways. In the center of the city were eight or nine walled-off ceremonial sites, surrounded by the palaces and homes of the nobility.

Palaces were elaborate edifices with several buildings and courtyards. Housed in the palaces were artists, craftsworkers, servants, nobles, and government officials. Structures included a courthouse, warrior's council chamber, storage space for acquired tribute (and housing for those who looked after it), and chambers for singers, dancers, and instruction of various kinds. Occupants and daily visitors to the palace numbered more than a thousand.

Cities of this scope rely on material support. Central and southern Mexico was a place of environmental diversity, with intensive production and economic specialization resulting in a surplus of goods. The Valley of Mexico, heart of the Aztec Empire, was ideally suited to provide its inhabitants with resources for food, clothing, housing, and tools.

Subsistence

The Aztec Empire was built on agriculture, and at the core of this agriculture was maize. It formed the mainstay of the diet in various forms and could be successfully grown in both the high plateaus and the tropical lowlands. This success was largely climate dependent: maize thrives best where rains are concentrated in the summer, as they are throughout Mesoamerica. Summer rains allow early planting and harvest before early November frosts. The Valley of Mexico yielded one crop of maize per season; in the lower elevations, two crops were possible. It has been suggested (Berdan 1982) that Aztec conquest of the more temperate zones outside the valley may have been spurred by the desire for a reliable source of maize.

In the middle of the fifteenth century central Mexico experienced severe famine. Within fifty years the Triple Alliance had secured control of maize production in widespread ecological zones where maize could be harvested at different times. This system ensured that the effects of famine were less disastrous to the Mexica. Also helping to offset hunger were ritual feasts given by Aztec rulers in honor of the goddess of maize: prestations of food to people in need helped them through difficult seasons.

Its centrality in subsistence earned maize a glorified position in Aztec culture. Hardly a mere foodstuff, it was intimately involved in Mexica daily life. People personified maize and addressed it with reverence as it was planted. Poetry, hymns, sayings, and stories all deified the crop and linked people metaphorically to it. An individual speaking out of turn or imprudently was "like an ear of maize split open"; one who had gained great prestige was said to have "reached the season of maize."

Also widely cultivated throughout the Aztec Empire were beans, chiles, squash, maguey, and a host of other fruits and vegetables. From cactus were produced alcoholic beverages, fibers for clothing, medicinal remedies, and sewing needles. In the tropical lowlands, cotton and cacao (chocolate) were additionally cultivated.

In those areas of the highlands not conducive to irrigation, most employed systems of fallowing, supplemented by terracing and crop rotations. In shallow lakebeds or flatter stretches, floodwater irrigation was used. *Chinampas* agriculture was by far the most intensive irrigation agriculture strategy. Mud and vegetation were piled in shallow portions of a lake. Posts were attached to secure the plot until the roots of willows planted at the sides and corners could act as anchors. In the areas outside the densely populated urban centers, families cultivated *chinampas* plots that not only supported their own needs but also yielded enough surplus to be exchanged in the city for specialized goods and services. This funneling of surplus food into the urban area of Tenochtitlan most likely provided the subsistence to those specialists in service to the nobility who could not be provided for by the smaller, more crowded *chinampas* in urban areas.

Cultivation was usually combined with gathering wild foods, hunting, and fishing. Medicinal herbs were of great value, as were peyote and mushrooms. These, along with fruits available predominantly in the lowlands, were in great demand at the marketplaces.

Hunting held an esteemed place among the Mexicas, dating back to their nomadic past. In addition to providing food, fur, and skin, animals were hunted to supply the empire's zoos. Meat from land animals such as armadillo, deer, rabbits, boars, and opossum was all part of the regular diet, and the animals were hunted with snares or bows and arrows. The lakes provided plentiful fish, reptiles, and crustaceans. Duck, quail, pheasant, and partridge were hunted by the lakeshores and were valued as much for their feathers as for their flesh.

The Mesoamerican food-producing environment allowed both intensive and varied agriculture. This yielded two important consequences. First, it led to specialization in production. Those residing by the lakeshore could devote themselves entirely to fish and waterfowl; farmers in drier areas could specialize in products derived from cactus. Second, these specialized systems of food production resulted in enough of a surplus to allow many people to direct their talents to professional occupations other than agriculture.

Occupational Specialization

In the urban centers of Mexico, craft manufacture was highly elaborated, with entire residential sections of town home to painters, goldsmiths, silversmiths, featherworkers, and sculptors. Although their creations were held in high regard by the entire Aztec population, these products were available only to the nobility. Consequently, the artisans themselves enjoyed great prestige and organized into exclusive guilds that had privileged relationships to the state. They resided separately and had access to both temples and schools reserved especially for them. Featherworkers appear to have been especially esteemed, creating headdresses, fans, and costumes for nobility and the highest-ranking military personnel. Stoneworkers and metallurgists had similar exclusive residences and were granted political clout.

The craft practiced most widely was weaving, an endeavor reserved only for women and pursued by women of all classes. Although every girl and woman learned to spin and weave cloth, the materials with which they worked and the garments they produced varied greatly by the status of the weaver. Women of the lowest ranks produced simple goods for household use; noblewomen engaged in producing the elaborate ceremonial capes, using the finest cotton, rabbit fur, and feathers.

Clothing served the dual purpose of being both utilitarian and identifying the class of the wearer. Commoners were bound to wear garments made from only the coarsest fabrics. Nobility had no apparel forbidden to them but usually chose to exercise their privilege and wear the most elegant of vestments. Within the highest class, more decorative clothing signaled greater wealth.

Political, military, and religious specialists also emerged, as did "a host of miscellaneous occupations" (Berdan 1982:34), a situation to be expected in such a complex society. Astrologers, midwives, scribes, and prostitutes are counted among these.

Trade and Exchange

Markets were the economic link between different regions of production, the political focus for gossip and information, and the social setting for most neighborhood interaction.

The outdoor marketplace was the hub of every community, providing a meeting place for people of every age and social status to talk and share news as well as conduct business. Wares reflected the local environment in terms of items abundantly available; larger markets trafficked additionally in luxury items. Barter was typically the medium of exchange, but money in the form of cacao beans and cotton cloaks was common. Less usual were bells, beads, and quills filled with gold dust.

Textiles, which were bartered and sold in the marketplace, functioned as items of trade, religious offerings, marriage payments, decoration, and cremation cloths, among other uses. Trade was carried on by all members of the society, whether they were professional artisans or individual agriculturalists. Families routinely sold their surplus in public marketplaces. These small-scale producers were vendors in the marketplaces and traded their wares to all passersby. Professional merchants were important on an entirely different scale. Their status afforded them political importance and also economic sway: the luxury items they produced were of paramount importance for the nobility to display as symbols of their status.

Specialization required a fairly sophisticated system of exchange that began in the marketplace. Distribution of goods was also accomplished through tribute and trade routes, numerous enough for individuals to secure a wide range of goods. Trade, both foreign and domestic, forged political ties along with the economic.

The tribute collected from conquered regions provided revenue in exchange for the promise of protection. A wide variety of goods were given in tribute, with the majority typically being the most locally accessible items. Those provinces nearest the Triple Alliance capital cities most often provided surplus agricultural goods, textiles, and wood and paper products. Distant provinces located in different ecological zones provided more exotic goods, which might include rubber balls, chocolate, jade, quetzal feathers, and liquid amber.

Nahua ceremonial dress.

It was the commoners on whom the burden of tribute fell most heavily. Cultivators struggled to amass the tremendous amount of food demanded, and artisans turned over the most valuable items they wrought. For those living in provinces on the outskirts of the empire, little more than offers of future protection were given in return. Those closer to the capitals could hope to reap some of the subsistence goods and, as they more often paid tribute in labor than in goods, they were likely to be working on city-improvement tasks that ultimately were of benefit to them.

The enormous stores of tribute were used to sustain the large and complex bureaucracy of the empire, to finance the military, to support the royal palaces, to bestow gifts, and to promote foreign trade.

➔ Social Organization

Class Structure

The Aztec Empire was a complex, stratified society with social organization guided by the principles of hierarchy and heterogeneity (Berdan 1982). Although one's position at birth (ascribed status) circumscribed the positions to which one could aspire, there was room for upward social mobility through accomplishments (achieved status).

The most basic social distinction existed between the commoners and the nobility, and these statuses were conferred at birth. Initially, membership in the nobility demanded the ability to trace one's ancestry back to the first Mexica ruler. However, as Berdan (1982) points out, the practice of polygyny and the fact that noble status was passed through both males and females led to an exceedingly high number of people who could lay claim to noble birth. By the early sixteenth century, more stringent rules for reckoning legitimate noble descent were put into place.

Rigid dress codes made status differences readily apparent. Commoners wore simple clothes, and their cloaks had to end above the knee. The nobility alone could wear headbands, feathers, gold armbands, and jewels in their lips, ears, and noses. Only the ruler and his second-in-command could wear sandals.

Housing was also a status marker. Only those of noble rank could build two-story houses. When visiting the palace, commoners knew which rooms were open to them and which were reserved for nobility. Separate courthouses were maintained for passing judgment on individuals of different classes. In these courthouses, nobility were judged more severely than commoners. For example, a commoner charged with public drunkenness was punished by having his head shaved, while a nobleman would be put to death for this same offense. There are reports of rulers sentencing their own children to die for committing adultery.

Of course, the more far-reaching differences between classes were economic and political. Ownership of land, access to public and religious office, and control over important resources were tied to social class.

Along with the rights and privileges accruing (or denied) to each status, there were accompanying expectations of behavior and lifestyle.

The provincial rulers formed the top rank of the nobility. Their power was determined by the size of their territory. Those whose dominion was smaller or less central paid tribute to those who ruled the Triple Alliance capitals, Tenochtitlan, Texcoco, and Tlacopan. The responsibilities of all rulers included collecting tribute from commoners, organizing military expeditions, sponsoring religious feasts, and the ultimate adjudication of legal disputes that could not be settled by the courts. Despite the fact that this status was bestowed by birth, the personal qualities of an individual ruler often greatly influenced his ability to govern successfully. The ideal ruler was one who acted as a protector and unifier, assuming the burdens of leadership as well as its rewards. Although succession usually passed to brother or son, this was often contingent upon personal achievements.

Chiefs formed the rank below rulers, and this status was usually granted to those who had demonstrated superior military valor. Most chiefly duties involved military leadership, either advisory or on the battlefield, or service as a judge.

Sons of nobility were a recognized class, who accrued rights and privileges afforded nobility and who could expect to ascend to prestigious posts even if they did not themselves become rulers or chiefs.

The provincial nobility were largely concerned with agricultural and not urban issues, as might be expected. The administration of land and water rights was of greater import than the military, manufacturing, or trade.

The commoners made up the largest portion of the population. They worked the land, filled the lowest ranks of the military, and paid tribute. They were not, however, a homogeneous group. For example, commoners had varying access to land; some of the more well-off had tenant farmers.

Commoners were organized into *calpulli,* a territorial unit based on kinship, literally meaning "big household." Nuclear families, independent of one another, were strongly favored, but extended households were very common (León-Portilla 1992). Earlier, before the rise of large urban areas, assemblages of households who reckoned descent bilaterally from an apical ancestor constituted a *calpulli.* As these groups settled, *calpulli* came to be the designation for a ward, or barrio. Sometimes these were groups of occupational specialists. In every case, each *calpulli* had its own temple, in which the group recognized a particular *calpulli* deity, and through which they maintained a shared identity. In addition, *calpulli* had their own school, dedicated largely to martial training. *Calpulli* themselves were socially stratified, with a headman, council of elders, and members who worked the land.

There were also "serfs" (rural tenant farmers) and "slaves" in Mexica social structure. Each of these classes of individuals was drawn from the stratum of commoners. People who were homeless, through economic need or through warfare, made up the majority of these ranks. Individuals also sold themselves or their family members into slavery to meet subsistence needs. Those unable to pay debts, tribute, or fines also ran the risk of succumbing to this fate. This was, in almost all cases, an acquired status: children of serfs or slaves were born into freedom.

Kinship, Marriage, and Family

Early reports emphasize kinship as the single most important principle in Mexica society: the lineage was referred to as "the set of cords that unite humans" (León-Portilla 1992:127). The Mexica reckoned descent bilaterally, as did most indigenous central Mexican peoples. Both mother's and father's brothers were called "uncles," and both mother's and father's parents were called "grandparents." Relative age, more than lineality, was a factor in determining social relationships. Distinctions were made between one's older and younger siblings. Beyond one's own generation, however, distinctions continued to be made on the basis of sex in ascending generations (parents, grandparents) and the generation below (son, daughter) but not beyond (all grandchildren were referred to by the same term, regardless of sex). Kinship rules functioned as the guiding factors in marriage, residence, and patterns of inheritance.

Among the nobility, the primary aim of marriage was to strengthen or forge powerful political ties. Ruling houses of neighboring capitals often maintained their relationships through such marriages for hundreds of years. Typically, this pattern allowed for the manipulation of inheritance to the satisfaction of both ruling families. The nobility were polygynous, but the commoners were not. This practice produced many individuals who aspired to relatively few positions. Inheritance was not based solely on the dictates of kinship; achievement often tipped the scale in the awarding of titles to one of many "rightful" pretenders. Unlike titles or official positions, land and houses could be divided among several heirs.

Cross-cousin marriage was common, and class endogamy appears to have been the rule. The *calpulli,* too, tended to be endogamous, which acted to keep resources within a guild, in the case of *calpulli* organized by occupational specialty.

Marriages were arranged for youths by their parents. When they decided a child was of marriageable age, parents prepared a feast of tamales and chocolate to which all the youth's teachers were invited, and at which they ritually discharged the student from their care. There is little evidence that the youth's own wishes were taken into consideration in the search for a suitable mate. Older women of the community served as brokers for the match. Once married, it was the primary responsibility of the new couple to join or establish a household and have children.

One feature of kinship systems in which descent is reckoned bilaterally is the usual absence of strict postmarital residence rules, and this was the case in Mexica society. Actual residence patterns vary by location. In some areas, nuclear families predominated; in others, joint households were more common. Often the incentive to form either a nuclear or joint household would be provided by the demands of land tenancy and agricultural and subsistence needs. Flexibility in residence patterns ensured that family structure could be altered to adapt to available resources.

Aztec Life and Customs

The ideal attributes of a Mexica citizen were moderation and discretion in all pursuits. Men were expected to serve as providers and teachers, tending most assiduously to the world outside the household. Women operated in the domain of the household, weaving, educating small children, and overseeing the efficient conduct of the family. Children were expected to show parents respect and obedience.

Young children were expected to be dependent, and little was asked of them. By the age of 5 or 6, greater expectations were placed on all children. Instruction was aimed at instilling the virtues of honesty, obedience, and respect. Boys and girls were expected to be similar in their acquisition of these general characteristics. The practical skills to be developed and the chores assigned to each were different, however. Boys carried water and firewood, brought goods to market, learned to fish or produce feather crafts. Girls learned to spin and weave, to cook, and to be proficient at housework.

Formal education was compulsory for boys and girls, although girls generally attended for a shorter time. Beginning in early adolescence, formal teaching centered around songs, dances, and instrumental music. These were not only essential to ritual and religious participation, but their content also transmitted important historical lessons and cultural values. By age 15, boys attended schools whose curricula included history, calendrics, dream interpretation, and the skills necessary for various occupations, such as hunter or priest. Military instruction was the mainstay of commoner boys' formal education.

Law

The Aztec legal system incorporated both secular and supernatural sanctions in order to maintain social control. Behavior was expected to conform to established teachings. When it did not, threats of punishment were the items of first resort. Many religious traditions invoke banishment to "hell" or entry into "heaven" resulting as a consequence of an individual's conduct during life. Aztec belief, however, was that it was a person's death, and not his or her conduct in life, that determined events in the afterlife (Berdan 1982). Thus, no threat directed at an unpleasant afterlife could be issued. Secular law was exacting and punishment was swift. Drunkenness was invoked as the cause of the vast majority of unacceptable public behavior and criminal activity. Adultery resulted in stoning or hanging; homicide was usually punishable by death, although in some cases the murderer was turned over to the victim's family to serve them in slavery. Stealing was less severely punished than any of the foregoing.

Pretending toward a higher social status than one's rightful one, either in the form of dress and personal adornment or acquisition of property, was punishable by death.

Supernatural sanctions were inflicted by the god responsible for punishing that offense, and the consequences would be ones which reflected the affront. Thus, the god Macuilxochitl would inflict venereal diseases to punish those who did not practice sexual abstinence during ritual fasts. Other gods would retaliate if their shrines were not properly maintained, sending a variety of physical ailments that would identify the sufferer as one who had shirked some ritual responsibility.

→ Political Organization

The Aztec Empire boasted an intricately structured military and government. The type of political organization that predominated from the fourteenth through early sixteenth centuries was the city-state. Central Mexico was divided into some fifty or sixty of these units at this time, varying in size and political prowess.

Leadership and Government

The degree of autonomy enjoyed by rulers *(tlatoani)* of the city-states was variable. Some were not beholden to any other authority, while others were dominated by leadership of a higher order, most typically rulers of Triple Alliance cities (Berdan 1982).

The *tlatoani* functioned as a monarch. He was responsible for ritual, adjudication, waging war, and advocating for the rights of his citizens. In Tenochtitlan, the Mexica *tlatoani* was believed to be a descendent of the god Quetzalcoatl. Berdan (1982:100) reports: "The rulers were earthly counterparts of celestial deities; their rule was by divine right." While the position of *tlatoani* was an inherited one (often from brother to brother, and then to the firstborn son of the oldest brother), a ruler had to have been proven valorous in battle before ascending to leadership. In addition to his godlike status, he must possess great personal skills, especially in oratory. (*Tlatoani* means "one who is gifted with the facility of speech.") Possessing both exceptional understanding of the sacred and superior military prowess, the *tlatoani* embodied both "great priest and great military captain" (Carrasco and Matos Moctezuma 2003:22).

The Council of Four, close relatives of the ruling *tlatoani,* chose his successor. Once the new ruler was selected, a series of rituals were set into motion, culminating in the coronation. First, the new *tlatoani* appeared before the priests, who escorted him (along with the council) to a public ceremony, where citizens witnessed an offering of incense. The ruler and his council maintained a four-day fast, after which they returned to the temple and cut themselves, offering blood to Huitzilopotchtli.

The custom after this initial offering was for the newly chosen *tlatoani* to leave for the battlefield and return with prisoners. At the coronation, to which rulers from both allied and enemy lands were invited, a spectacular feast was given, expensive gifts exchanged, and war prisoners captured by the new ruler were sacrificed. This display served to strengthen alliances and warn enemies. It also served as fair warning to any who would contemplate rebellion.

The *tlatoani* was assisted by special counselors, relatives with whom he consulted on all important governmental matters. Advice was given by specialists in each realm of the political structure. For military matters, he had a war council drawn from those professional warriors who had proven themselves in battle. Judicial advice was rendered by high court judges in the complex system of courts.

Warfare

Warfare has been called "a cultural preoccupation" (Berdan 1982) of the Mexica, woven into the fabric of social, political, economic, and religious life. Militaristic themes abound. A boy was declared a soldier at birth, and if his mother died in childbirth she was glorified as a warrior and assured a blissful afterlife. Men were judged overwhelmingly by their militaristic skills and rewarded commensurate with their valor. Victory in battle brought privileges in dress and ornamentation as well as gifts. These returns were thought to inspire continued military success. Death in battle brought rewards in the afterlife.

If warfare was not quite itself a religion, it was at least bound up with religion. Patron gods not only sent soldiers into battle but also could only be appeased by human sacrifice gathered from enemy troops. There were even particular enemies whom the gods were thought to find especially pleasing (Berdan 1982). War, far from being only a means to expand territory, functioned as an end in itself. The conquest of new lands was a pursuit separate from the warfare engendered by the need to capture people to be offered as sacrifice, and to provide militaristic experience for young soldiers. In fact, Aztecs staged ritual wars—known as "flower wars" for the way in which men fell to the ground like so many colorful blossoms shaken from a bough—expressly for the purpose of gathering prisoners to be sacrificed (Townsend 1992).

Human Sacrifice and Cannibalism

While the topic of human sacrifice and cannibalism among the Aztec has generated much debate, there is no disagreement regarding the centrality of human sacrifice in their culture. The practice arose out of a debt owed to the gods: the consequence of not paying was no less than the end of the world.

Aztec myth describes the creation of the sun and the moon, and the inception of their movement. When the current sun—the fifth—was to be created, all the gods gathered at Teotihuacan to decide who would be willing to throw himself into a great fire and emerge as the sun. Two stepped forward, one wealthy and arrogant, the other poor and humble. As much as he wanted to be the sun, the arrogant god lacked the courage to throw himself into the flames. Instead, the humble god cremated himself and rose in the sky as the sun. Furious at being outdone, the first god followed, only to emerge as the moon, a pale reflection of the sun's great light. There they sat, together in the sky. The gods knew that they must be separated. One must shine brightly in the day and the other glow at night. One god threw a rabbit at the moon, some say to dim its light, others say to keep it distant from the sun. Even when this was done, the sun and moon still hung, unmoving, in the sky. It was then that the other gods sacrificed themselves, for only their blood could put the sun in motion. Life for humankind was only possible with a moving sun, and this the gods provided. It then became the responsibility of humanity to feed the sun thereafter, lest it stop and the universe cease with it. Although mythology states that sacrifice is to the sun, the wider notion is that there can be no human life without sacrificial human death (Berdan 1982).

The most common form of sacrifice was to open a man's chest with a sacred blade, tear out the still-beating heart, and offer it to the gods. Women occasionally had their heads severed before their hearts were removed. Children were most often drowned, securing good rainfall (Berdan 1982).

Special occasions and ceremonies dictated variations in the form of sacrifice, although the removal of the heart and display of the head were consistent. Priests upon occasion ceremonially wore the skin of a flayed victim. All forms of sacrifice were sacred, performed without vengeance and endured without regret. A captor honored and respected the person to be sacrificed. Those who died in this fashion were privileged to be the food of the gods. In dying to keep the world alive, they were assured a sublime afterlife.

Often, once the sacrifice was completed, the body was stewed and ritually consumed. Ritual cannibalism has been explained by some anthropologists as a religious phenomenon, while others propose an ecological explanation.

Those who see cannibalism as an extension of the religious motivation behind human sacrifice suggest that sacrifice made the victims divine. Eating the divine then made the consumer sacred. Thus, the belief that sacrifice is demanded by the gods and necessary for survival makes eating the flesh of the sacrificial victim an extension of the ritual process of maintaining the universe.

Those who argue against such a supernatural stance suggest that there were nutritional reasons for the practice of cannibalism, chief among them the deficiency of protein and fat in the Aztec diet. Formulated by anthropologist Michael Harner (1977), this theory proposes that cannibalism may have been couched in religious explanations but in fact alleviated a severe need for protein. If there was indeed a shortage of protein, feeding captives would only exacerbate the problem: sacrifice obviated the need to provision a prisoner, and cannibalism provided protein.

This assertion has been severely challenged on many grounds, including the fact that those who might be in greatest need of protein (commoners, children, and adolescents) were least likely to receive human flesh, accessible most typically to nobles. Moreover, there is debate as to whether protein deficiency existed in the first place (Berdan 1982).

Population control is another motivation proposed for cannibalism, although this aim could hardly be best served by the sacrifice of adult males (the most usual offerings) rather than women of childbearing age (Berdan 1982).

Religion and Expressive Culture

The Aztec worldview maintained that life was precarious, and it was the responsibility of humankind to attempt to control this uncertainty and assure their own continued existence.

Every half-century, a dramatic ritual was undertaken. All fires were extinguished, all houses swept clean, all hearthstones and cooking pots discarded. The entire population was awakened at night; babies, if they slept, would be turned into mice. They waited, poised, to hear of success in the ritual about to begin. Priests climbed to the top of a mountain in the dark, sacrificed a victim, and attempted to kindle a fire in his open chest cavity. If the spark caught, life would continue for another half-century. Citizens were notified of the new fire and, as they waited for messengers to bring them flames to start their own fires, they cut their ears and offered blood to the gods upon hearing the news. Should the fire not start, the sun would grow cold and the universe end. This ritual embodied the most salient tenets of Aztec culture: that the continuation of life is not ensured unless the people actively promote its survival through human sacrifice.

Aztec Gods

Aztec deities functioned in many ways like patron saints. Most were envisioned anthropomorphically, with human traits. Each *calpulli* had its own deity, and because, as we have seen, *calpulli* were often groups of occupational specialists, these deities came to be associated with the occupational group.

When the Mexica arrived in the Valley of Mexico, they found numerous cults that had grown up around gods of nature and which the Aztec made their own. Berdan (1982) describes theirs as an assimilative religion, rather than a proselytizing one. They embraced the deities of those they conquered, and soon had myriad gods. Townsend (1992) suggests that the conquest of each enemy town might be viewed as the "capture" of their deity.

Deities have been roughly divided into three categories: gods believed responsible for creation, those associated with the elements, and those affiliated with war—and thus with sacrifice.

The creation deities are ones that might best be described as supreme—they are the high gods, more abstract and omnipotent. Included among these are gods of fire, which is an important Aztec theme.

Priests devoted most of their rituals to the gods associated with rain, human fertility, and agricultural fecundity. These gods controlled the elements, on which the survival of the people depended. The majority of female gods, responsible for both subsistence and birth, are found in this pantheon of deities of the elements.

Huitzilopotchli, the patron deity of the Mexica who guided their journey into the valley, is a sun god categorized with the sacrificial war gods. The tie between warriors and the sun was direct and critical: it was only through the blood of sacrifice that the sun could be fed and kept alive. And it was largely through military capture that the staggering number of victims required could be supplied.

Aztec Priests

Because all the numerous gods claimed their own temples, were honored by their own rituals, and made their own particularistic demands, each needed a host of priests to serve its needs.

The structure of the priesthood closely resembled the structure of the rest of Aztec society in its hierarchical, "pyramidal" nature (Townsend 1992). It was from among the nobility that the most powerful priests were drawn, although even the lowest-ranking commoner had access to the priestly role.

Both women and men served in the priesthood, and infant girls and boys were often dedicated by their parents at birth. (Fewer women than men remained in the priesthood for the duration of their lifetimes, however.)

The majority of a priest's duties revolved around service to their deity. The idol must be cared for, its surroundings kept clean, temple fires lighted, and prayers and penance offered day and night. Priests were expected to regularly offer up their own blood, and the display of their penance smeared on their temple was an important sign of their dedication. A secondary duty of the priesthood was interpreting sacred texts and educating boys of the nobility. Priests used meditation, fasting, purifying baths, and occasionally hallucinogenic drugs as means to more effectively serve their deity.

Rites and Ceremonies

Aztec rituals and ceremonies were very much tied up with their reckoning of time. They kept an annual ceremonial calendar based on the 365-day solar year but also reckoned time by a 260-day ritual calendar. (This calendar contains the "movable feasts," which are any religious festivals unfixed to the solar calendar, such that they may fall on a different date each year [Berdan 1982].) The 260- and 365-day calendars have been conceptualized as two gears fitted side by side: when turning, the first days would align every fifty-two years. It is this alignment that gives rise to the half-century fire-lighting ceremony mentioned earlier (Townsend 1992).

Ceremonies occurred with great frequency: there were eighteen regularly scheduled rituals each month. The vast majority of these had to do with petitioning the gods associated with fertility, rain, and agriculture. Many of these included fasting, and offerings of some sort—from incense to human sacrifice—were always a part of every ceremony.

Magic and Omens

The formal religious system, with its elaborate rituals and supplication to powerful deities, existed alongside a more intimate and personal system of divination and magic. Shamans acted not on behalf of a deity worshipped by the masses, but for an individual petitioner who wished to manipulate the directives of the supernatural world.

Diviners played an important role in a belief system that saw an individual's fate as being predetermined. Although one's destiny was to a large extent fixed, it could be manipulated to some degree by following the recommendations of a diviner hired to "read" an infant's fate and suggest which days might afford the child the best its destiny could offer.

Divination was relied upon most heavily for prediction but could also be propitious in healing. To this end, shamans ingested hallucinogens to grant them access to divine information. They were able to read signs of illness by throwing grains of maize on a piece of cloth and interpreting their pattern, predict recovery by whether a knotted rope held fast or gave way, determine the severity of soul loss by the clarity of a child's reflection in a mirror.

Those illnesses with supernatural causes required supernatural intercession to effect a cure, and a shaman would be called upon to intervene.

Because they were ruled by fate and their destiny was already planned, it was only to be expected that Aztecs had to look around them for omens informing them of their destinies. Some omens were to be found in the behavior of birds and animals; others might be supernatural materializations. Each individual was believed to have an animal counterpart, a *nagual,* born at the same moment, sharing the same fate. Kept in the underworld in large corrals, these spiritual twins often revealed themselves in dreams. *Nagual* can serve as allies or prove deadly: any harm befalling the *nagual* is suffered by its "other self" as well (Knab 1995).

Aztec Arts and Sciences

The arts and sciences of the Aztecs were a blend of the scientific and the symbolic. This body of knowledge included calendars that were based on rigorous astronomical calculations but were used for ritual purposes. The practice of medicine employed a chemically active pharmacopoeia, but these agents were always used along with shamanistic divination. Complex technologies produced crafts that were used in religious ceremonies (Berdan 1982).

Aztec writing was hieroglyphic, demanding great skill in memorization, because the glyphs could only serve to jog the memory when looking through a text already known to the reader. Such skills were possessed solely by the nobility, who were the only literate members of Aztec society. The most common form of hieroglyphic was the pictograph, a stylized drawing of the object. Glyphs could also be ideographic, using one aspect of an object to represent the entire object itself—for example, a scroll to represent a speech to be given, footprints to represent a journey, or arrows and a shield to represent war. A third form of hieroglyphics was a phonetic system in which a word for which there was an easily drawn picture was used to represent a more abstract word that sounded the same. (This is a device commonly employed in "rebus" puzzles, where a sheep [ewe] might be drawn to stand for the word "you.")

Stone sculpture of human and animal figures was a skill that was formally taught and that led to a style of stoneworking that is readily recognizable. Craftwork in mosaics, gold, and feathers was also highly standardized; taught within the guilds, consistency of style is found within each medium.

Literature and music were highly valued, as were oratory skills. While speechmaking skills were generally only taught in noble schools, songs and dances were part of all mandatory education. Because a large number of people spanning all the social classes participated in the numerous religious rituals, it was imperative that all citizens be trained in these skills.

Conquest

For ten years prior to Spanish conquest, the Mexica had been visited by portentous omens. These were difficult to interpret specifically, but rulers were certain they foretold Aztec doom.

Finally, messengers reported sighting strangers off the coast. This was the final and most frightening omen. One year later, these strangers were back, led by Hernán Cortés. In 1519, Cortés and several hundred soldiers began to advance on Tenochtitlan. As they neared the Aztec city, they heard stories about the riches contained within, and pressed on, determined. When Cortés reached the city, he captured the Mexica ruler, and violent battles ensued. The siege on the Aztec city lasted more than seventy days, with tens of thousands killed. Despite their valiant defense, the Aztecs were overcome.

Although the Spaniards were smaller in number, their technology and strategies afforded them a great advantage. Their militaristic training taught them to fight to kill, not to capture. They had swords and muskets, horses and large dogs.

One of the first consequences of Spanish conquest was the decimation of the native population. By the early seventeenth century a population of 15 million had been reduced to just 1 million. Not only warfare, but also previously unknown diseases, famine, overwork under Spanish rule, and displacement all took their toll.

Within 10 years of the fall of Tenochtitlan, most of Mesoamerica was under Spanish rule. As more Spaniards arrived, the surrounding culture was changed. To the agricultural system were added Spanish technologies: the wheeled cart pulled by draft animals, machetes, plows. The introduction of both livestock and new crops contributed to the decline in the indigenous population by usurping much of the land formerly devoted to maize (Berdan 1982).

Aztec society became less stratified under Spanish rule. As is commonly the case under colonial rule, ascribed statuses gave way to achieved ones. Spaniards, not Aztecs, held the high political offices. Friars converted indigenous peoples to Christianity. Worship of Aztec deities was forbidden, along with its rituals of human sacrifice. Some indigenous peoples found ways to blend many of the similarities of the two systems of belief. Both Christianity and the Aztec religion contained rites of baptism and confession, along with a belief in virgin birth. The multitude of Aztec deities became linked with the many Catholic saints.

The Mexica had been conquered. However, Aztec and Spanish cultures were mutually influential, combining over the ensuing hundreds of years to produce an amalgam, a new way of life.

→ Mexican Nationalism: The Modern Aztec Legacy

With the Conquest 500 years ago, Reavis (1990) observes, "Mexico became a country in transition, from a Native American culture to the lifeways of the West" (p. 18). Aztec civilization can be found both within contemporary Nahua villages and throughout the broader culture of Mexico (Smith 1996). There is a wealth of recent scholarship exploring the national identity of modern Mexico, and Aztec history figures prominently into the discourse. Historians reexamining the event are searching for evidence of indigenous perspectives, "rereading the invasion" (Wood 2003), and asking how the native population viewed the conquest (Lockhart 1998, Schwartz 2000, Wood 2003). Mexico is a nation with a mestizo majority and nearly sixty indigenous ethnic groups. In the twentieth century, the state initiated policies aimed at unification of the multiethnic population, "a state project of cultural transformation" (Gutiérrez 1999). The identification of modern Nahua as "living tribute to Mexico's noble indigenous past" (Friedlander in Smith 1996:294) is not without its conflicts, because this status is lived within the reality of discrimination "for being Indian in a Mestizo-oriented society"(p. 294).

Alicja Iwanska (1977) examines two indigenous social movements, which she calls "realism" and "utopianism," each of which was a reaction to governmental plans for "integration of the Indian masses into Mexican society" (p. 2). The "realist" perspective proposed that this process be guided by people (like themselves) who were raised in Indian villages and who had maintained their ties with the families still there. (The slogan of the group was "Let's Mexicanize Indians and not Indianize Mexicans" [Gutiérrez 1999].) The "utopian" plan envisioned transforming Mexico into a modern-day Aztec Empire. This goal would be accomplished by cultural, economic, and political restructuring on every level: teaching Nahua culture and language in schools, returning to a *calpulli* system, taking Aztec names, and celebrating Aztec holidays.

Guillermo Bonfil Batalla (1996) writes of two Mexicos: the "imaginary Mexico," the modern nation that is an outgrowth of colonialism and aspires to subjugate Indian culture, and the "deep Mexico" (*Méexico profundo*), grounded in a collective Mesoamerican past. It is out of this deep and shared Indian culture that a true new nation must be formed. Bonfil's perspective has been taken up by others who also believe that there is a "transcendental Indian character that survives . . . beneath the asphalt" (Lomnitz-Adler 1992). In 1994, an Indian uprising in the Chiapas Highlands drew attention to the demands of indigenous peoples in Mexico. President Salinas had enacted policies that would have furthered the usurpation of Indian land and contributed to the continuing spiral of poverty in the Indian communities while further enriching the powerful local elite.

As Gutiérrez (1999) points out, access to technology, media, and advanced communication has resulted not only in upward mobility of formerly marginalized indigenous peoples. Such changes have also resulted in heightened ethnic awareness, rather than its rejection for more modern constructions of nationalism.

When presented with the culturally integrative plans of the nation-state, Gutiérrez (1999:206) observes that "ethnic peoples in modern times have not rejected their historical past; they remain attached to it because this is the claim that secures their survival." De La Peña (2006), in speaking of indigenous movements in Mexico and the self-empowerment and sociopolitical reform they embrace, points out that multiculturalism goes beyond mere tolerance for difference but in fact strives to create "new forms of public space, participation, representation and government" (p. 282).

→ For Further Discussion

Most people regard the Aztec as a civilization that was lost long ago. However, in Mexico today there are indigenous social movements that seek to link the present directly with an Aztec past. What might motivate contemporary Nahua peoples and others in Mexico to do so? What is the significance of the ways in which they have chosen to recognize the Aztec heritage? Is this phenomenon something that you recognize as happening among other groups, in other nations?

CHAPTER 4

Haiti

A Nation in Turmoil

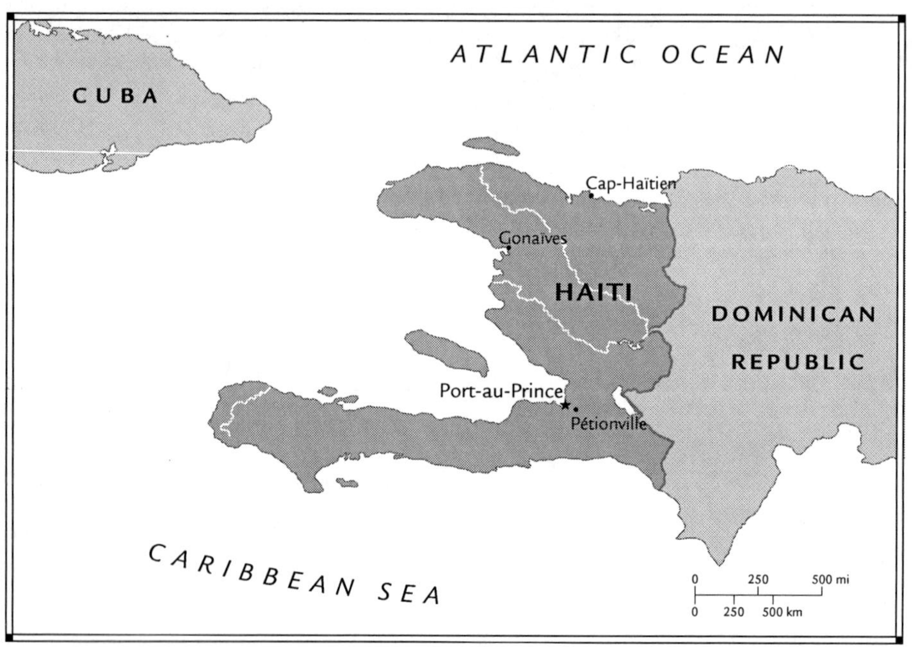

The Republic of Haiti on the island of Hispaniola.

✧ The Beginning

Kric? Krac!

In the beginning, there was only Damballah Wedo, the Great Serpent, whom the Creator asked to hold up the world, lest it topple into the sea. The creature lay underneath the earth, its 700 coils unmoving. One day, it began to stir, and the earth trembled. It reached up above the world and unleashed the stars and planets; it slithered along the earth, carving the valleys and rivers, rifting the mountains. It reared into the sky and brought forth thunder and lightning. From its body, Damballah Wedo filled the rivers, and the mist rose, and created Ayida Wedo, the Rainbow, who became the Great Serpent's wife. Together they gave birth to all the spirits in the world, all the blood, all the life, all the people.

✧ Introduction

The Republic of Haiti occupies the western third of the island of Hispaniola, which is the second largest island in the Caribbean. The remaining two-thirds, to the east, is the Dominican Republic. Situated about 600 miles southeast of Florida, Haiti spans about 11,000 square miles, approximately the size of Maryland. Its shape—two jutting peninsulas—is often described as resembling the head of a crocodile, jaws open and aimed menacingly toward Cuba, to the west (Brand 1965, Rotberg 1971).

Haiti was once an environment of tropical rainforest and lush Caribbean pine, but much of it has been cleared for timber and firewood. In fact, one source comments that there are few places in the world where "the destruction of the natural woodland cover [has] been so nearly complete" (Weil 1985:14). Adding to this, severe erosion has left very little commercial forest (Weil 1985). Rainfall is more plentiful on the northern peninsula (which juts into the Atlantic Ocean) than the southern (which is in the Caribbean Sea), and the extensive felling of trees has led to disastrous flooding during the heaviest rains (Rodman 1954).

The word *haiti* means "high land" in the Arawak language of the Taino, the island's original inhabitants. Although Haiti's elevations are lower than the Dominican Republic, nearly half of its land is above 1,500 feet. Two chains of mountains run the lengths of both peninsulas. It has been said that an early European visitor to the island, when asked to describe the terrain, crumpled up a large piece of paper and placed the tortuous shape on the table, as an accurate rendering of the precipitous slopes (Farmer 1994, Rodman 1954). In addition to cultivation of pine and mahogany forests and fruit trees, farming is practiced wherever possible. The hillsides are so steep that farmers often resemble mountain climbers, secured to the slopes by heavy ropes. One author reports hearing "jocular but vivid tales . . . of farmers falling to their deaths off their cornfields" (Weil 1985:7). Lowland regions have richer alluvial soil.

✧ HISTORY

Conquest and Slavery

The island that would later be named Hispaniola was originally populated in three separate migrations of nearby peoples, the first from the eastern part of Venezuela about 2600 B.C. Dugout canoes allowed travelers to move from island to island, fishing the coastal waters, gathering wild foods, and seeking shelter in caves or beneath large rock outcroppings by the riverbanks. Some 2,000 years later, the Taino (Arawak peoples) reached Hispaniola, displacing or absorbing the local population. Unlike their predecessors, the Taino were horticulturalists with a rich artistic tradition, mostly of ceramics (Anthony 1989, Doggett and Gordon 1999). Villages grew up around an economy of cassava and sweet potato cultivation, and individuals were skilled at fishing with nets and traps. A third wave of travelers, perhaps from the Peruvian Andes or Venezuela's Orinoco region, arrived just shortly before Christopher Columbus, who sailed to the island in 1492, naming it Hispaniola, or "little Spain."

In letters home, Columbus describes the warm greeting he received from the Taino. Writing of the nearly 400,000 inhabitants as "lovable, tractable, peaceable, gentle decorous Indians" (Farmer 1994:60), he assured his sovereigns that the people he encountered could be convinced to trade their gold and would not resist conquering.

Columbus set out from the island only to meet with disaster: offshore, the *Santa Maria* ran aground on a coral reef and was wrecked. Tainos saw the Spaniards' emergency and hastened to help the stranded sailors, whom they offered shelter. Columbus pressed onward in the *Nina* and *Pinta,* leaving the *Santa Maria* crew behind with orders to seek gold (Weil 1985). Later, other Spanish settlers joined them, enslaving the Taino population and forcing them to mine gold and turn it over to the settlers. For nearly a quarter of a century, the native population was subjected to cruelty and deprivation so harsh that many were driven to suicide (Doggett and Gordon 1999). Hunger and disease ravaged the population, and by early in the sixteenth century, the Taino population stood at less than 500.

Sugarcane had by this time been introduced into the island economy. Having decimated the Taino population, Spanish settlers were in need of replacement labor to continue mining gold and raising sugarcane, and they turned to the growing slave trade from Africa. By 1540 more than 30,000 Africans had been brought to Hispaniola (Farmer 1994).

As Spanish interests were piqued elsewhere, chiefly by the discovery of gold and silver in Mexico and Peru, they began to withdraw from Hispaniola. English and French pirates invaded from Tortuga, a small island to the north, and the French eventually gained a stronghold on the island. These "buccaneers," so named for their adoption of the Arawak practice of roasting meat over wooden spits, called boucans, settled in the western part of the island, with the French eventually driving out the English. Although they did not own the land, the French prospered there and resisted Spanish efforts to displace them. In 1697, the Spanish relented and signed a treaty ceding the western third of Hispaniola to the French colonists, who called it Saint-Domingue. The eastern land (Santo Domingo) remained under Spanish rule, with a border established between them.

Once the territory was officially theirs, French colonists flocked to the island, seeking their fortunes. Using slave labor, French colonists raised coffee, cacao, indigo, and sugarcane. By the end of the eighteenth century, large sugar plantations made Saint-Domingue the richest French colony in the new world, accounting for two-thirds of all of France's overseas investments (Anthony 1989). The need for workers was great, and Saint-Domingue became the main port for West African slave traders, bringing nearly 30,000 individuals annually. Farmer (1994) reports that by 1791, the island housed nearly half the slave population in all of the Caribbean. The brutality of Saint-Domingue plantation slavery was extreme, the death toll staggering (Anthony 1989). Disease, beatings, exhaustion, and starvation are estimated to have led planters to replace the entire slave population every twenty years (Anthony 1989), with one of every three slaves dying during his first three years of "intense exploitation" (Farmer 1994:63).

Small acts of revolt and resistance began to trouble plantation owners, who redoubled their efforts to keep the nearly half million slaves under control. Farmer writes:

> As the eighteenth century drew to a close, it became clear . . . that not even torture would permit such a tiny number of slave holders to control so many slaves. The cycle of repression, hysteria, and atrocities was spinning towards an inescapable finale: "This colony of slaves," observed the Marquis du Rouvray in 1783, "is like a city under the imminence of attack; we are treading on loaded barrels of gunpowder." (1994:66)

And so they were. The French Revolution was soon to spark a counterpart in Saint-Domingue.

Revolution and Independence

In the years leading up to the French Revolution of 1797, Saint-Domingue's population was made up of several distinct segments. These are most often described in terms of skin color: white (French slaveowners, who numbered about 35,000); black (500,000 West African slaves); and "mulatto," biracial individuals, originally the offspring of landowners and slaves, who numbered 28,000.

However, social distinctions, also of importance, did not map directly onto skin color. Not all the whites were wealthy plantation owners, and those who were poor artisans hated the planters (Farmer 1994). A group of individuals known as *affranchi* were free by law, but denied the social equality it promised. While the majority of *affranchi* were "mulatto" (also known as *gens de couleur,* people of color) there were some black *affranchi.* In addition, while the vast majority of slaves were black, there were a proportion who were mulatto (Nicholls 1985).

The French Revolution inspired strong sentiments in all quarters of the Saint-Domingue population. Wealthy plantation owners were alarmed at the burgeoning power of France's lower classes and did not want to see that situation replicated on the island (Anthony 1989). In addition, they saw an opportunity to declare independence from France. The brutalized slaves had more than ample reason to revolt. But it was the *affranchi,* who owned more than a third of Saint-Domingue property but were denied political or social equality with whites, who seized the opportunity to challenge this status quo (Farmer 1994).

In 1790, France issued a declaration guaranteeing equal rights to the *affranchi,* but the colonial administration of Saint-Domingue made it clear they had no intention of abiding by the law. *Affranchi* owned slaves, sent their children abroad to schools in France, and were determined that they should have rights equal to white landowners. (As Farmer points out, theirs was not the cause of emancipation. He writes "mulatto spokesmen made it abundantly clear that they wanted full civil rights in order to stand on equal terms with whites—as upholders of slavery" [1994:67].) The following year, an *affranchi,* Vincent Ogé, backed by an organization in France called *Les Amis des Noirs* (Friends of the Blacks) led a revolt against the colonial governor and was captured and executed. This action sparked a slave uprising of huge proportions. Tens of thousands of individuals set fire to 1,500 plantations; well over 10,000 lost their lives.

One of the leaders of the uprising was a freed slave, Toussaint Louverture, a man with uncommon military knowledge and charismatic leadership abilities. Over the next several years, war between France and Spain came to the island of Hispaniola. Toussaint led his armies for the Spanish. In 1793 France (some suggest, to gain black support against Spain [Anthony 1989]) abolished slavery in all its colonial holdings, and Toussaint, now a Spanish general, switched his allegiance and joined the French. Followed by his loyal troops, he helped defeat the Spanish armies, and in 1795 Spain ceded their two-thirds of Hispaniola to the French. The following year, Toussaint was installed as lieutenant governor of the island, determined to unite former slaves, whites, and *gens de couleur* in reestablishing the land's former prosperity, without the atrocities of slave labor.

Over the next several years, Toussaint's power increased, much to the dismay of Emperor Napoleon Bonaparte. In 1801, Toussaint wrote a constitution proclaiming Saint-Domingue self-governing, with himself at the helm. Napoleon sent in troops and captured Toussaint, who died in a French prison. Napoleon then announced his intention to reinstate slavery on the island. Two of Toussaint's former officers, Jean-Jacques Dessalines and Henri Christophe, regrouped the armies and drove back the French. In 1804 Dessalines proclaimed independence, renamed Saint-Domingue "Haiti," and began to rule the first black republic, the first independent nation in Latin America (and the second in the Western Hemisphere, after the United States), as Emperor Jacques I, a dictator of the first order.

A Nation in Turmoil

One of Dessalines's first acts was to refashion the tricolor French flag into the banner of Haiti. He removed the white stripe, declaring that with it went the white presence in Haiti. What would remain was the red and the blue, symbolizing the blacks and mulattos, though the latter were the object of his scorn. True to his word, he ordered that the whites who remained be killed and seized all the cultivated land in the country. His plan "was to have the state act as supreme landlord" (Trouillot 1990:45), and within months he had laid claim to all mulatto property. He imposed a military dictatorship, forcing the now-free slaves either back onto plantations or into the army. He refused to establish a system of education and ruled through fear. By 1806, however, his autocracy could no longer be tolerated, and he was ambushed and assassinated outside the capital, Port-au-Prince.

After his death, the country was riven in two, ruled in the north by Henri Christophe, a former slave who had served in Toussaint's army, and in the south by Alexandre Pétion, a mulatto educated in France and taken with the tenets of democracy.

It was Christophe's intention to model his reign after the British monarchy. He crowned himself King Henri I, established a court filled with titled nobles, and built several magnificent royal palaces, the most elaborate called *Sans Souci* (carefree). In the early years of his rule, he established a sound system of currency, instituted mandatory education patterned after the English system, printed books, created a judicial system, and kept a close eye on his tenant farmers. Before long, however, his leanings toward tyranny grew. Increasingly fearful that the French would return, Christophe poured much of the country's resources into building an enormous fortress, called the *Citadelle,* which took nearly fifteen years to complete, and which is seen, by some, to embody the last years of his rule: "Threatening, useless, inaccessible, conceived in needless fear and militarily absurd, it was constructed at untold cost of toil, tears and blood" (Rodman 1954:17). As his armies began to plot an overthrow, Christophe was struck down by a massive stroke. Able to move very little, and aware of the growing unrest, he committed suicide, shooting himself through the heart with a silver bullet, in *Sans Souci.* He was buried beneath the *Citadelle.* Meanwhile, Pétion's government in the south of Haiti was dramatically different. Embracing a democratic ideal, he parceled out the large plantations into smaller plots, which he gave to individuals for their own use. The forced-labor system of Toussaint, Dessalines, and Christophe had been harsh and unpopular, and Pétion's disinclination to replicate it changed the agricultural base of the southern economy. Christophe's citizenry were serfs, while Pétion's were free (Weil 1985), but this freedom resulted in the south becoming a subsistence-farming peasantry, with no export crops and a declining tax base. Foreign loans were obtained, but they carried exorbitant interest rates. Pétion died in 1818, "Haiti's best-loved ruler and the architect of her economic ruin" (Rodman 1954:18).

Jean Pierre Boyer, who had served in the Pétion government, succeeded Pétion in the south in 1818, and upon Christophe's 1820 suicide, reunited the two halves of Haiti. He continued Pétion's practice of dividing the land into small parcels, with disastrous results. Most of these aliquots were too small for sugar or indigo cultivation. Moreover, societal stratification had taken hold. Although democratic in their distribution of small plots of land to the populace, Pétion and Boyer both fostered a mulatto elite who held social and political dominance over the black majority (Weil 1985). Boyer attempted to shore up the economy by reinstituting forced labor, hearkening back to the strategies of Dessalines and Christophe. He also looked beyond Haiti's borders. Taking advantage of a revolt against the Spanish, in 1821 he annexed Santo Domingo, the eastern two-thirds of Hispaniola, which Haiti held until 1849 when its residents claimed independence and founded the Dominican Republic. His attempts to forge relations with France were costly, incurring long-lasting debt. In the face of accusations of corruption and treason, Boyer was ousted in 1843.

The years from Boyer's fall to 1915 saw twenty-two dictators come and go, each exacting a toll on the nation. Relations between the majority and the elites continued to be fraught with contention and violence. Of the twenty-two heads of state, most of them black military leaders, only one served a complete term in office. Fourteen were overthrown by civil revolution, the remainder assassinated or forced into exile.

The majority of the rural peasantry was apolitical (Doggett and Gordon 1999), but a substantial number figured quite significantly into Haitian politics in their function as mercenary guerrillas employed by the seemingly endless string of men who aspired to ruling the country. Known in the south as *piquets,* but more often as *cacos* in the north, they struck a bargain with those who hired them, overthrowing the existing regime in exchange for cash and the opportunity to loot towns en route to the capital with impunity (Anthony 1989, Weil 1985). With seven such presidential coups in as many years, the early years of the twentieth century were filled with bloodshed and civil unrest. They were also marked by increasing interest in Haiti by foreign powers, for economic reasons, but especially for its strategic position in the Caribbean. The United States was particularly interested in Haiti.

U.S. Military Occupation

The political situation in Haiti down-spiraled quickly between 1910 and 1915, culminating in the five-month rule of Vilbrun Guillame Sam. Sam, his own position secured by bribing the *caco* rebels, learned of a planned coup and summarily executed nearly 170 political prisoners, aligned with those who sought to unseat him. A riotous mob (many the family members of the murdered prisoners) stormed the embassy, seized Sam, tore his body to pieces, and "paraded through the streets with his remains" (Anthony 1989:66). The United States used this murderous incident as justification for invading and occupying Haiti in July 1915.

The waters between Haiti and Cuba are known as the Windward Passage and were a crucial shipping route between the United States and the Panama Canal. Germany, amassing World War I victories, sought a naval base in Haiti, and the United States feared this request would be granted because of the increasing number of Germans who were currying favor by financing *caco* rebellions (Weil 1985). While purportedly motivated solely by their intentions to stabilize Haitian unrest, the military occupation solidified U.S. economic aims. Taking full control of financial and military affairs, the United States rewrote the Haitian constitution to suit its own interests, disbanding the army and replacing it with an American police force. While the United States instituted many positive reforms—building hospitals and schools, repairing roads, engineering reservoirs and sewage systems—they did much of it by seizing peasant land and forming chain gangs of forced prison labor (Anthony 1989, Farmer 1994). Local resistance to the U.S. occupation grew, culminating in 1920 with the *Cacos* Rebellion, led by a "latter-day Toussaint Louverture" (Farmer 1994:96), Charlemagne

Péralte. The U.S. Marines reacted quickly and brutally, quashing the rebellion at the cost of 3,250 Haitian lives (Farmer 1994).

The U.S. presence remained in Haiti until 1934, after having shepherded the country through the election of a new president, Stenio Vincent, a mulatto, whose successor, Élie Lescot, was also a mulatto. The army successfully installed the next two presidents, representative of the black majority, Dumarsais Estimé (in 1946) and Paul Magloire (1950), but both were accused of corruption and unseated. For the nine months after Magloire's government was overthrown in 1956, seven unstable governments came and went. In 1957 a new and frightening era would begin in Haiti: the rule of the Duvaliers.

The Duvalier Years

In September 1957, Francois Duvalier, a seemingly unassuming country doctor (Farmer 1994), was elected president. Duvalier that been prominent in the *Noirisme* movement, a popular campaign that urged Haitians to embrace their African roots and reject European influence. Growing in popularity throughout American occupation, it galvanized blacks who were chafing under the favoritism shown mulattos. "Papa Doc" Duvalier wasted no time in assuring his absolute hold over all aspects of Haitian life. Acutely aware of the military's part in the scores of previous government overthrows, he greatly reduced both the size and power of the army. Instead, he relied on his own creation, a private force of terrorists dubbed the *Tontons Mocoutes* (Uncle Knapsack), named for an evil character in Haitian folklore who captures children and carries them away in his bag. The *Tontons Mocoutes* (officially the National Security Volunteers) reportedly killed tens of thousands of Haitians under Duvalier's orders (Farmer 1994). In response to this brutality, the Vatican excommunicated the Duvaliers from the Catholic Church. In 1964 Duvalier rewrote the constitution, naming himself president for life and providing for his eventual successor: when Francois Duvalier died in 1971, his 19-year-old son, Jean-Claude, stepped into his constitutional place. At first, "Baby Doc" seemed somewhat less dictatorial than his father, but this respite didn't last long. His economic policies alienated both the mulatto minority elite and the black middle class in turn, and with enemies on all sides, he reactivated the *Tontons Mocoutes*. By the early 1980s, Haiti's economic system was in utter chaos. Inflation, recession, and rapidly declining tourism all took their toll. Disease wiped out nearly 2 million pigs, leaving peasant farmers destitute. Antigovernment demonstrations were met with violence, and Duvalier had no choice but to flee to safety. In 1986, taking his family (and millions of dollars from the Haitian treasury), "Baby Doc" escaped to France. There was rejoicing in the streets of Haiti.

Aristide and Beyond

After being purged of the Duvalier regime, Haiti once again went through a string of leaders, four in three years. Jean-Claude Duvalier's successor was General Henri Namphy, who disappointed those hoping for radical change. He was replaced by General Prosper Avril, who was no less repressive. He fled the country, replaced by an interim president, Ertha Pascal-Trouillot, while elections were scheduled. The winner was a young priest, Jean-Bertrand Aristide, who had spent the few years since the end of the Duvalier regime preaching reform from his church at the edge of the Port-au-Prince slums. His campaign slogan, *Lavalas* (flood), resulted in just that: a flood of support from the oppressed Haitian populace, who elected him in a landslide victory. He took office in 1991 and began to implement change, retiring the majority of the army's high command, separating the military and the police force, lobbying to increase the minimum wage, instituting public-works projects to create jobs, and undertaking a battle against crime and corruption. Although his plans were ambitious, he had barely eight months in the attempt: an alliance of wealthy families and displaced army brass, led by General Raoul Cédras, staged a bloody coup. Aristide escaped, but more than 2,000 were killed in the first week alone.

Condemning the coup, the Organization of American States (OAS) issued a trade embargo, unsuccessfully attempting to unseat the military dictatorship. By the spring of 1992, however, tens of thousands of Haitians had taken to hastily constructed boats, sailing toward Miami. Of the 40,000 who set forth, the vast majority were intercepted by the U.S. Coast Guard, taken to a naval base, and eventually returned to Haiti on the grounds that they were fleeing poverty, not politics, and thus were not eligible for political asylum. It was a further embargo—on oil—the following year that resulted in negotiations and an accord, one provision of which was the safe return and reinstatement of President Aristide. Further violence demonstrated that this promise was not to be kept, and in 1994 U.S. troops arrived in Port-au-Prince, exiling Cédras to Panama and returning Aristide to a welcoming Haitian population.

The 1987 constitution provided for no reelections to a second consecutive five-year term. Thus, in 1995, elections were held to choose Aristide's successor. The candidate who prevailed was René Préval, the Lavalas candidate and Aristide's original prime minister. Other elections, however—for prime minister, legislators, and thousands of local officials to fill empty slots—had been stalled for years over political infighting and logistical stalemates. Elections were finally held in May 2000, with the presidential election following in November. Aristide, representing the Lavalas Party, emerged victorious, winning another five-year term. Aristide's presidency did not bring hoped-for reforms, and by early 2004 violent protests erupted. On the heels of an armed revolt, Aristide fled Haiti in February of 2004, replaced by a U.S.–backed interim government. In 2006, René Préval was reelected president.

→ Life in Haiti

Social and Economic Organization

Statistical data on the Haitian population describe unparalleled poverty. The annual income in 2009 was $450 per person (USAID 2009), with a life expectancy of fifty-three years. More than half the adult population is illiterate.

Haiti is the poorest country in the Western Hemisphere, with as much as 80 percent of its nearly 10 million people living under the poverty line in 2010. In the 1980s, Haiti's population was overwhelmingly rural, with only 25 percent living in urban areas. The vast majority practiced subsistence agriculture. Small plots of land, tilled with hoes and other simple gardening tools, typically yield beans, maize, bananas, coffee, or sweet potatoes. Along the coastline, there is some rice production and fishing. The land is not very productive, owing to the steepness of its mountains and the poor quality of the eroded soil. Half of the land slopes at a 40-degree angle; most of the population must rely on products grown on 30 percent of the arable land (Miller 1984).

Houses are generally wooden structures containing two rooms; some have thatched roofs in the style of ancestral West African dwellings. There is no electricity; cooking is done over charcoal fires outside of the house. Work is hard, and all family members are expected to contribute. Children are often called upon to help with any animals there may be, and women bring whatever surplus the gardens may yield to market. Under ordinary circumstances, men work their land individually. However, when there is a large task to be accomplished—clearing a field or building a house—they rely on informal local work associations called *combites.* Friends and neighbors come together to work for the day and are compensated with a festive meal at the end of the job, accompanied by singing, dancing, and games of riddles and storytelling.

Given the dependence of the majority of Haiti's population on subsistence agriculture, Haiti's crushing poverty is at least partly a result of the extreme

Haitian children waiting in line for food.

deforestation. There is barely a hillside that has not been stripped for firewood or housing: only 2 percent of the country's original forest remains (Catanese 1999). As a consequence, much of the soil has been eroded away, the topsoil running off into the ocean (where it takes its toll on marine life and fishing).

In his discussion of the environmental degradation of the Haitian landscape, Anthony Catanese (1999) points to several historical linkages between rural poverty and deforestation. The first is Haiti's long history of political instability. The succession of violent and chaotic regimes, sometimes lasting only months, made long-range planning for ongoing problems impossible and concerns about the environment and economy of the rural peasants singularly unimportant. Second, he points to a shift of power from rural areas to the capital, Port-au-Prince, resulting in "continuing avoidance of investment in rural human and physical capital in ways that would effectively improve agricultural productivity and rural income" (p. 22). Environmental degradation is only a problem in urban areas decades after it begins to take its toll on farmers. A third factor is the long-standing focus on individual needs to the detriment of the greater societal good. According to Catanese, serious attention to "public welfare . . . has been alien to most regimes" (p. 23).

In the 1980s Haiti's already devastated economy received two more blows. Creole pigs, a staple in the rural peasant economy, were struck by an outbreak of African swine fever. In an attempt to curb the spread of disease, the government (encouraged by the U.S. Agency for International Development, USAID) ordered every pig killed, without offering their owners any form of compensation. Recognizing the catastrophic results of this policy, a small number of an American breed of pigs were brought in, but they were unsuited to the Haitian environment and could not survive.

The second blow was leveled at the once-thriving tourism industry. The association of AIDS with Haiti, promulgated both by the media and by health experts, brought foreign travel nearly to a halt. In fact, it was American vacation travel that likely brought AIDS to Haiti in the first place, not the other way around (Farmer 1994). However, both political unrest and health concerns led to official warnings recommending that American citizens not travel to Haiti. The Haitian tourist market was unable to rebound.

The rural–urban balance has shifted tremendously over the past two decades. By 2003, 40 percent of Haitians lived in urban areas. Rising population and diminishing agricultural yield have led to an influx of rural peasants seeking jobs in the capital, Port-au-Prince. While designed to safely accommodate some 300,000, the city's population ballooned to 3 million. While agricultural work was sometimes available in earlier times, over the past twenty years it has become nearly impossible to find, resulting in urban centers of impoverished unemployed. In one such slum, nearly a quarter of a million people are packed into 5 square kilometers with neither running water nor a sewage system (Doggett and Gordon 1999).

While the law mandates compulsory, free education for all children between the ages of 7 and 13, less than 40 percent of Haitian children attend school, both in the rural areas and in the poor cities, resulting in a literacy rate that hovers somewhere under 50 percent.

There is, however, a different life in Haiti, though it is the privilege of the very few. In the hills above Port-au-Prince reside the Haitian elite, 1 percent of the population who control nearly half the country's wealth. By and large, these are the mulatto descendants of colonial times. The town of Pétionville consists of enclaves of mansions, owned by those who run the import/export businesses, manufacturing, and other lucrative businesses. Their children attend Port-au-Prince private schools. This is not a landholding aristocracy, as is found in other nations. The countryside belongs to the peasants. The elite of Haiti are an urban elite. While a middle class is emerging, it is very small. Just as the wealth and power are concentrated in Port-au-Prince and surrounding areas, so are nearly all the services. More than half of all the medical personnel in the nation are located in the capital city, and it boasts the only complete sewer system (Weil 1985). There are French restaurants, theaters, and elegant boutiques.

The distinction between Haiti's poor—90 percent of the population—and wealthy—the remaining 10 percent—is often drawn along the lines of religion, language, and skin color. The poor majority are of African descent, speak Creole, and practice *voudon* (voodoo). The wealthy are most often the descendants of African slaves and French landowners, lighter-skinned, French-speaking, and Roman Catholic. Michel-Rolph Trouillot, a Haitian anthropologist, describes the feeling most well-off urban Haitians have for "the common people of Haiti" as "contempt" (1990:229).

Language and Arts

French and Creole

Two languages are spoken in Haiti, but they are far from equal. The official language of Haiti is French, but it is spoken by only 10 percent of the population. Creole is the language of 90 percent of the Haitian people. This lopsided distribution is indicative of the chasm in Haitian society that disadvantages the masses by privileging the few. In colonial times, French was regarded as the "higher" language, spoken by the wealthy slaveowners. Creole was "the language of the subordinate and exploited masses constituted of African slaves" (Zéphir 1996). While very few slaves spoke French, most *affranchis* understood Creole. Anthony (1989) points out that the result was that "communication between a black and a mulatto was controlled by the mulatto" (p. 85). Today, most schools are taught in French, the government conducts official business in French, and the judicial system is entirely run in French.

Trouillot (1990) notes that most linguists no longer refer to Haiti as bilingual. Instead, they refer to a bilingual minority elevating one language as "the language of power" (p. 115) over another. He asserts, however, that this linguistic divide does not truly appear at the level of *communication.* All Haitians, even the few who speak French, speak Creole. (He notes, in fact, that "even the most francophile urbanites often prefer to use [Creole] in situations where everyone is competent in French" [p. 115].) Rather, the cleavage is in the *power* attached to French. Mastery of French provides access to power and prestige that Creole does not.

Culturally, it is Creole that expresses the richness of Haitian culture and through which oral traditions are preserved and passed along (Nicholls 1996). In tone, it has the lilt of French, from which it borrows vocabulary. Additionally, it incorporates some Spanish and English. Many words are derived from several West African languages, and it employs both African pronunciation and an African sentence structure that differs from French syntax. The use—or pointed avoidance—of speaking Creole figures prominently in the experience of Haitian immigrants in North America.

The Arts

Art, music, and literature in nineteenth-century Haiti were, for the most part, an extension of those art forms in France (Weil 1985). The intricate architecture and wide boulevards in Port-au-Prince and Cap-Haitien (Haiti's second-largest city) are distinctly French. The time of the American occupation, however, saw a rich blossoming of the arts, and some trace this to a renewed search for national identity while under foreign control (Weil 1985). Others point out that both the visual arts and music and dance have long-standing roots in *voudon* and, before being "discovered" and classified as artistic cultural products, were in the service of religious performance and ritual. In the 1940s, American art collectors visiting Haiti were greatly impressed by the vivid colors, bold lines, and lively movement in Haitian paintings they saw on doors and walls all over the countryside. Classified as "primitive" or "naïve" art, paintings depicting religious scenes or everyday market life were brought back to the United States by collectors, who generated tremendous enthusiasm for them in the art world.

Haitian music reflects all aspects of Haitian history, from slavery to revolution. The rhythms and sounds of West Africa and modern struggle and resistance are combined in traditional drumming and politicized lyrics. Both music and dance are central to *voudon* ritual and are also incorporated into rural daily life. Nearly everyone plays some sort of instrument, and music fills leisure time in the countryside where there is no electricity for radio or television. Bands of musicians often travel from village to village, performing for food and a night's shelter (Anthony 1989). The hard work of a *combite* is modulated by song. A modern jazz form, a fusion of *voudon* music and American jazz (itself of African origin) called *racines* (roots) music, emerged in the 1970s. It, too, combined musical tradition with political call to action in songs that encouraged peasant revolt and called for change. During the years of the military dictatorships in the 1980s and the coups of the 1990s, musicians endured harassment and threats from the army (Doggett and Gordon 1999). During *Carnivál,* before Lent, bands fill the city streets. After *Carnivál* is *Rara Carnivál,* highlighted by *Rara* bands, traveling the countryside until Easter. Bamboo trumpets *(vaskins)* and horns made of hammered tin *(kornets)* combine with maracas, drums, and pieces of metal struck together for percussion.

Storytelling holds a special place in Haitian culture, most likely influenced by the rich oral tradition of West Africa. Traditional fables were collected and published in Creole early in the twentieth century. Stories tell of the creation of the world, teach moral lessons, and feature tricksters and *voudon* spirits. Traditional storytelling sessions all begin the same way. The storyteller leans toward the audience and asks *kric?* The audience responds in unison, *krac!* and the tale begins.

Since the initial days of independence, Haitian literature, like music, has been a powerful vehicle for countering colonialism, racism, and imperialist constructions of Haitians as "primitive savages" (Doggett and Gordon 1999). American occupation further stirred Haitian writers to publish their own representations of their cultural identity. The Duvalier regime was a death knell to Haitian intellectual literary life: *Tontons Mocoutes* murdered at least one renowned writer. Others were exiled or fled in fear but continued to write abroad. During the Duvalier years, there were more Haitian authors working outside the country than within, writing—some in Creole—critiques of the terrorist regime at home (Anthony 1989, Doggett and Gordon 1999).

Catholicism and Voudon

The theme of dualism—French and Creole, African and European, black and mulatto, slave and *affranchi*—extends into Haiti's religious life. It is a well-worn truism that Haiti is 90 percent Catholic and 100 percent *voudon* (Heinl and Heinl 1978; Stepick 1998; Weil 1985). Roman Catholicism is the official religion in Haiti, and the Catholic Church serves as a powerful institution in urban areas. Between 10 and 20 percent of the population is Protestant.

Weil (1985) points out that French colonial Haiti was not nearly as influenced by Catholicism as were Spanish colonies, and he sees this as a result of the priorities of the colonials themselves. Plantation owners and buccaneers alike were not at all interested in converting slaves to their religion; their singular focus was on amassing riches. After independence, the Vatican was unhappy at the official separation of church and state set up in the new constitution and no longer sent priests to attempt conversion.

However, as the population of mulatto elite embraced French culture wholeheartedly, reinstituting Catholicism as the national religion became an important part of that alignment. They welcomed French and Belgian priests, who were of a similar social class, and used the Church as a symbol of their linkage to Europe and upward mobility and as a distancing mechanism between themselves and the *voudon* masses.

Voudon has been referred to as "perhaps the world's most misunderstood and maligned religion" (Stepick 1998:86). In fact, the word *voodoo* is commonly used as an adjective to denigrate whatever follows as unscientific, craven, or primitive. The word is derived from a Dahomean word meaning "god," and the rituals and pantheon draw heavily on West African animist tradition. Haitian *voudon* is heavily interlarded with Catholicism, with influences of the aboriginal Taino religion. One early important function of *voudon* was to provide a sense of unity and common ground among slaves brought from disparate tribal communities. In addition, its dances and songs could be used in the fields as a surreptitious means of revolutionary communication, even when slavemasters were present. It has been suggested that many of the similarities between *voudon* and Catholicism derive in part from a need to placate missionaries and plantation owners while still remaining true to the religion: icons of Catholic saints could be substituted for sacred *voudon* objects, generating a dual pantheon much like the differently named (but comparable) Greek and Roman gods. *Voudon* is, however, more than a syncretism of African and Catholic beliefs. Over time, elements for which there are no African or Catholic counterparts emerged (Bourgignon 1976), resulting in "a distinctly Haitian complex of philosophical tenets, religious beliefs, and ritual practices" (Trouillot 1990:115). While acknowledging African contributions, anthropologist Alfred Métraux (in Farmer 1994:65) describes *voudon* as "fundamentally the product of the plantation economy." *Voudon* centers around a single creator, the *Gran Mâit* (Great Master), served by a pantheon of deities, the *lwa*. *Voudon* rituals center around these spirits, who materialize through possession of the priest's body during trance. *Lwa* carefully select the people whom they will possess. Although possession is sometimes resisted, it is believed to be an honor to have been called to act as the "horse" which a *lwa* will "mount" during the ceremony (Bourgignon 1976). Each *lwa* is called by its own drum rhythm, which begins the ceremony. Priests—male *(houngon)* or female *(mambo)*—wield their sacred rattle *(asson)* to greet the Spirit of the Crossroads, the *lwa* who has the power to open the gate into the spirit world. Ritual attendants carry brightly colored flags to represent local *voudon* associations. Intricately patterned sacred symbols *(vevés)* are drawn on the ground in cornmeal (likely influenced by Taino tradition), which is then returned to the earth by the pounding feet of the dancers.

Damballah Wedo, the serpent *lwa,* often materializes next, causing the possessed individual to writhe on the ground, snakelike. The intensity and activity of the ceremony increase as more and more individuals are "mounted" by their *lwa,* each heralded by their drum rhythm and special song, playing together in a frenzy of excitement (Courlander 1960).

Perhaps *voudon*'s most sensational feature is what is seen as its darker side, exemplified by animal sacrifice and embodied in the *bocors* (sorcerers who visit illness and death upon their victims) and the legendary zombies, the "living dead" of Hollywood horror movies. In the 1980s attention was focused on the "science" of zombies, when Wade Davis (1985), a graduate student in ethnobotany, ventured to Haiti (financed by a Hollywood film director) in search of the substance that yields zombies. Davis felt he had found the secret: a poison, containing a nerve toxin like that found in the deadly Japanese puffer fish, which lowers the metabolic rate enough to replicate the appearance of death. (Students of Shakespeare will notice the resemblance to Juliet's feigned death, resulting from a potion that left her cold and still long enough to be presumed dead and placed in the Capulet monument.) A Haitian to whom the poison is administered seems to have died and is buried. Under cover of night, the perpetrator digs up the victim, allowing him to emerge from the ground when the effects of the toxin have begun to wear off. The zombie is groggy (and, owing to the power of the poison, perhaps brain damaged; surely traumatized [Stepick 1998]), and walks haltingly, back to the village, with the gait we have come to associate with this character. There is great controversy surrounding Davis's assertions (and the book and film resulting from his journey, both called *The Serpent and the Rainbow*), and Stepick (1998) reminds us that regardless of any pharmacologic "proof" of the existence of zombies, these elements are far from the essence of *voudon.* Like all religions, it seeks answers for the universal questions of life and death, describes a spiritual universe beyond our own, offers order and meaning to its adherents, and adds structure and legitimacy to life. He explains, in reference to the emphasis placed on gore and fright:

> Black magic's relationship to Voodoo is similar to that of Satanism to Christianity. Concentrating on the darker side of Voodoo is akin to writing a book on the satanic cults of southern California and saying that you have described Christianity. (p. 91)

As for the presumed conflict between Haiti's Catholicism and *voudon,* Haitian anthropologist Trouillot (1990) says that the cherished beliefs and practices of *voudon,* embraced by nearly all the population, have never seemed discordant with Christianity to the people who "live" *voudon.* While urban elites may be reticent to admit that they are comfortable holding both sets of beliefs, it is his contention that "they [share] religious beliefs rooted in the same African-dominated cosmology and [take] part in similar rituals" (p. 115). Despite a long history of attempted suppression, "anti-superstition" laws, and official government bans on its practice, *voudon* remains the living religion of Haiti, and, as Métraux asserted, "belongs to the modern world and is part of our civilization" (in Farmer 1994:65).

The Haitian Earthquake

In January 2010, a massive earthquake, located only fifteen miles outside of Port-au-Prince, devastated Haiti. More than 220,000 people were killed, 300,000 were injured, and 1.5 million were forced into makeshift camps. In the fifty or more aftershocks that followed in only two weeks, buildings left unstable in the original quake collapsed. Many Haitians whose homes were intact joined the homeless sleeping in the streets, fearing that standing buildings were at risk of toppling. From the Presidential Palace to the smallest wood-frame home, 70 percent of buildings in the area—including fully half of the nation's schools—were destroyed. The country's infrastructure was in ruins: hospitals were destroyed, communication systems severed, transportation by land, air, and sea impossible. The neighboring Dominican Republic immediately sent food, water, and emergency workers, who painstakingly made their way through mile after mile of rubble.

The outpouring of humanitarian aid—from governments, aid organizations, and citizens all over the world—was unprecedented. Still, six months after the quake there was still an estimated 25 million cubic yards of rubble and debris left uncleared, with hunger and disease a crushing reality. More than 1,300 tent cities pepper the landscape, and one in nine Haitians is homeless. Tens of thousands of survivors have escaped Port-au-Prince, doubling the size of some towns in the neighboring countryside.

As mentioned earlier, with only 2 percent of the land still verdant, deforestation has played a critical role in Haiti's poverty. The 2010 earthquake underscored the consequences of denuded land, unprotected by roots and trunks that prevent landslides. Without forest canopies to shield against wind and rain, tent dwellers and homeless Haitians are in great peril during the hurricane and rainy seasons, which together span six months of the year. More than 400 million Haitians have received food aid, and 1 million have been provided with a daily supply of safe drinking water. However, many environmental groups and agencies assert that attention to deforestation ought to be at the core of efforts to help Haiti rebuild. In addition to reforesting efforts, programs to provide alternatives to wood and charcoal as fuel—like those in place in the still-lush neighboring Dominican Republic—would serve to keep newly planted forests from overharvesting.

Haitian Migration and Diaspora: The Eleventh Department

Leaving Home

Haiti is divided into ten regions, called *departements.* The estimated 1.5 million Haitian emigrants worldwide are often referred to as the "Eleventh Department." Roughly one in four Haitians is part of the diaspora (Fagen 2009), with an estimated 900,000 in North America (Terrazas 2010). As many as 1 million Haitians live in the neighboring Dominican Republic.

Haitians have a history of temporary migration, with rural peasants having long worked as sugarcane harvesters in their neighboring Dominican Republic and wealthier urbanites sending children to attend school in France. Within the country, rural peasants have moved to the urban centers of Port-au-Prince and Cap-Haitien. In the late 1950s and early 1960s, Haitian intellectuals and professionals who voiced opposition to the Duvalier regime fled to the United States (Zéphir 1996). It was not until the late 1970s and early 1980s, however, that the United States became the destination of poorer Haitians in flight. Dubbed "boat people," tens of thousands of Haitians set sail for south Florida, only 800 miles from home. Their requests for political asylum were rejected by the Immigration and Naturalization Service (INS), which claimed they were economic, and not political, refugees—a distinction that is the difference between welcome and deportation. However, as Miller (1984) points out, the difference between these two categories is hardly more than academic and impossible to disarticulate. Economic conditions *are,* in fact, political situations. The fact that refugee status has been granted to Cubans while denied to Haitians has been a source of much debate in this regard (Miller 1984; Woldemikael 1989). Critics suggest that this discrimination results from two factors: that Cubans are fleeing a specifically communist regime and that Haitian refugees are overwhelmingly black (Catanese 1999; Miller 1984).

Coming to America

In part because many Haitians enter the United States without documentation, an accurate tally of their total numbers is elusive. Thus, the figures for the Haitian population in the United States, generally given as 900,000, is an estimate. (The

Haitian Diaspora Federation estimates more than 2.5 million, with 700,000 Haitians in New York alone. [2010.]) The World Bank predicts additional migrations of 20,000 per year (Orozco 2006). Geographic, economic, historical, sociological, and political factors as all weighing heavily in the choice of the United States as a destination: a reputation for championing liberty, the promise of economic opportunity, a pluralistic society, and its nearest shores only 800 miles away, accessible by boat. The great majority of Haitians who come to the United States settle in New York City and south Florida. These two locations alone account for nearly 75 percent of the Haitian population in the United States. When expanded to include two more areas of the urban northeast, Boston and New Jersey, fully 85 percent of the Haitian population is accounted for.

Several authors have provided rich ethnographic accounts of Haitians settled in the United States, in New York (Laguerre 1984), South Florida (Stepick 1998), and Chicago (Woldemikael 1989). Others provide insightful analyses of Haitian ethnic identity and struggle (Miller 1984; Zéphir 1996). Many general patterns inhere across enclaves of Haitians in the United States.

The family is the focus of the Haitian American community, beginning with gathering funds to emigrate, continuing with local associations of old and new friends and family members, and throughout the production of a new generation of Haitians born in the United States. In general, it is not the entire nuclear family that leaves Haiti. Laguerre (1984) posits that this is owing to the arduous process and expense of obtaining a visa and paying for transit. Most often, one family member emigrates, then sets to work to reimburse those who have paid for the transit: this is the primary obligation, once resettled. After the debt is repaid, other members of the family are brought over, and the first household will serve as what Laguerre (1984:86) terms "a stepping stone for newly arrived members of the family."

Stepick (1998) refers to this organized pattern as a migration chain, with each new individual another link. Newcomers, called *just-comes,* are introduced to the neighborhood, to new cultural norms, and are helped to find employment. Individual households are connected through neighborhood organizations and church groups, creating a web of support, both financial and social. Immigrants arrive without money, but not without "social capital" (Stepick 1998), networks of welcome and resource. Extra people are often included in households for days or weeks at a time if they have lost their job or need a place to stay. This "expansive hospitality" is passed along as just-comes get on their feet, move on, and become hosts to others, creating "a multiple-stranded, dense chain of transnational links between the United States and Haiti, all held together by extended family ties" (Stepick 1998:19).

Obligations to family are not limited to those who are brought over. It is of paramount importance that resettled Haitians send money to the family that remains in Haiti. This responsibility is not taken lightly, and this remittance of funds is substantial enough to have been the impetus for referring to those Haitians living outside the country as the "Eleventh Department." Haitians in diaspora send more than $1.6 billion annually to family members at home (Sheridan 2009); some estimates are as high as $2 billion. One in five Haitian households depends on such funds (Orozco 2006). Sent directly to individuals, it is sometimes literally the difference between life and death from starvation. Remittances in the form of goods are also crucial. Because the majority of available goods in Haiti are imported and thus very expensive, it is often less costly to send everyday food items, toiletries, and clothing. Live animals are also often sent for holiday meals; goats are especially popular sent at Christmastime (Fagen 2006). One consequence of the current economic downturn is a sharp decrease in monies sent back to Haiti, as family members in the United States and elsewhere lose jobs and cannot afford to continue sending remittances (Sheridan 2009). More than a decade ago, Stepick (1998) found that Haitians living in Miami feel less of an obligation to send funds as time goes by, but the practice continues as long as individuals are able because there is a compelling moral component to the economic imperative. In recent years, there has been increased evidence that younger Haitians, many of whom have never even visited Haiti, feel increasingly less compelled to continue sending remittances sent by an older generation, now approaching retirement (Haitian Diaspora Federation 2010).

Haitians in Canada

In addition to the northeastern United States and the southeastern Atlantic seaboard, more than 100,000 Haitians have settled in Canada, and the challenges faced by this population provide an interesting contrast. More than 90 percent of Canada's Haitians have settled in Quebec, and their experience is intertwined with the Quebecois struggle. The United States's reputation is that of a "melting pot," but according to Dejean (1980), this is most decidedly not the case in Canada. He points out that Canada's history is that of an uneasy federation of two cultures, English and French, resulting in "a two-pronged Canadian nationalism" (p. i) that has demanded that immigrants who are neither French nor English choose between the two upon their arrival. Haitians in Quebec find themselves in a peculiar position: arriving in Quebec during a time of intense French nationalism, they are the first immigrant group to be drawn to Canada specifically owing to this fervor. However, the overwhelming majority of the black population in Canada had been English-speaking, and Dejean notes that in public situations, black Canadians are automatically assumed to be anglophone and are persistently addressed in English, even if they respond in French. Thus, he concludes, "the Haitians in Quebec find themselves caught between the classic Canadian pattern of cultural-linguistic polarization, one where language operates as a dominant value," and which often sets the English-speaking black community at odds with Haitian Canadians. By contrast, it is not language but race that has been the focus of discourse about the complex Haitian experience in the United States.

"Becoming Black" in America

While the first wave of those seeking asylum were more financially secure, the overwhelming majority of Haitians arriving in the United States over the past thirty years have been poor. Although average Haitians working in the United

States earn twenty times the income of their counterparts at home (Catanese 1999), they are still struggling against numerous odds, not the least of which is racial discrimination. In his examination of Chicago's Haitian community, Woldemikael (1989) outlines the conflicts between racial and cultural identity faced by individuals unprepared for their status in American society. Laguerre (1984) describes similar findings among Haitians in New York. The fundamental conflict centers around the fact that Haitian immigrants define themselves based on their culture and language. However, not surprisingly, given the overwhelming focus on race in America, they are defined from without on the basis of their skin color. Haitians identify themselves as having a culture and history quite distinct from that of African Americans, but find that being black leads social institutions to gloss them with African Americans in a misguided (and racist) presumption of homogeneity. Their dilemma, according to Woldemikael (1989) was whether to "accept a new American identity based on race or try to maintain their distinct cultural and national identity" (p. 165). They chose the latter course, but there appears to be a discontinuity between generations in this regard.

Both Woldemikael (writing about Chicago) and Laguerre (whose work is in New York City) have found generational differences in Haitian identity. First-generation Haitians in Chicago find little motivation to become part of the African American community. They use other Haitians as their reference point (Woldemikael 1989), socialize with fellow immigrants, maintain strong ties with family back home, and resist ascription to the category of black American. Second-generation Haitians, however, often identify more as Americans, having been born in the United States. Children in school especially face pressure by peers to conform to African American norms, as both white students and school staff "fail to fully acknowledge a differentiated black [sic] student population" persisting in privileging phenotype over culture.

In Miami, Stepick (1998) finds that younger Haitians often attempt to "pass" as African American. Referred to as "coverups" by the Haitian community, they pretend not to understand the Creole spoken by the just-comes at school, pattern their dress and speech after their African American classmates, and will even lie about their Haitian heritage. They do this with some ambivalence, he notes; he has also observed some changes afoot.

Pride over Prejudice

In recent years, Stepick (1998) has noted a resurgence of pride in Haitian culture among younger Haitians. In high schools, numbers of students began to speak Creole and volunteered to bring traditional foods into class to demonstrate Haitian cuisine. Others began to dress in Haitian style and advocate for the recognition of Haitian culture in various school events. This was replicated in the wider culture of Little Haiti, as the enclave in Miami is known. Various local societies formally promote Haitian culture by organizing dance and music troupes and mounting Haitian drama in theaters. Storytellers travel to schools with folktales, and Haitian broadcasts can be heard on the radio 24 hours a day.

The vast majority of Haitians in the United States fled a dire political and economic situation in their homeland. Many found a racist and unwelcoming America and continued to live in poverty. However, in the wake of Aristide's reinstatement, myriad grassroots organizations sprung up, with connections to the popular movement in Haiti (Peters 1995). Their aim is to work for democratic reform. The situation in Haiti is a desperate one. International support has long focused on political issues (Catanese 1999), but in recent years, economic support has had an increasingly high profile. Countries and international organizations have pledged billions of dollars for rebuilding after the devastation of the 2010 earthquake. The World Bank estimates that 80 percent of Haiti's professionals—physicians, lawyers, engineers, and the like—currently live outside of the country. Participants in the 2010 Haitians Diaspora Unity Project have called for this population to consider a return to their native land.

Addressing the United Nations after the 2010 earthquake, President Preval said, "Let us dream of a new Haiti whose fate lies in a new project for a society without exclusion, which has overcome hunger, in which all have access to secure shelter . . . (and their) health needs provided." Many hoped that the presidential election held in late 2010 would pave the way for action, chipping away at the poverty faced by the citizens of the poorest nation in the Western Hemisphere. No candidate received the 50 percent of the vote needed to win, and plans for a run-off election scheduled for early 2011 spurred violent protests. Mirlande Manigat, a former first lady, garnered 31 percent of the vote, with the second-place candidate, Preval's protégé Jude Celestin winning 22 percent. Protest erupted at the elimination of musician Michel Martelly, the third place-candidate and a popular favorite. The election was widely criticized, with thousands unable to vote and charges of voter intimidation and ballot-box stuffing confirmed by U.N. observers. A run-off election between Manigat and Martelly resulted in victory for Martelly, who received nearly 70 percent of the vote. Headlines proclaimed his transition "from pop star to president."

Hundreds of thousands of earthquake survivors still have neither homes nor jobs. The rainy season that followed the quake resulted in a protracted cholera epidemic that sickened 300,000 and claimed at least 5,000 lives. In May 2011, standing in front of the ruins of the collapsed National Palace, Martelly was sworn in as president. Just beyond the fence stood a tent city of thousands of displaced citizens. His is a challenge of monumental proportions.

→ For Further Discussion

It is estimated that there are nearly 1 million Haitians now living in North America. In Canada, French-speaking Haitians find themselves at odds with English-speaking black Canadians. In the United States, Haitians find that they are classified on the basis of their skin color, assumed to identify with African American culture, while they define themselves on the basis of their Haitian history and culture. What do these conflicts and assumptions say about issues of race and ethnicity? Further differences are found between generations: while Haitian immigrants resist identification with mainstream African American culture, their children, born in the United States, feel differently. Why might this be so?

CHAPTER 5

The Hmong

Struggle and Perseverance

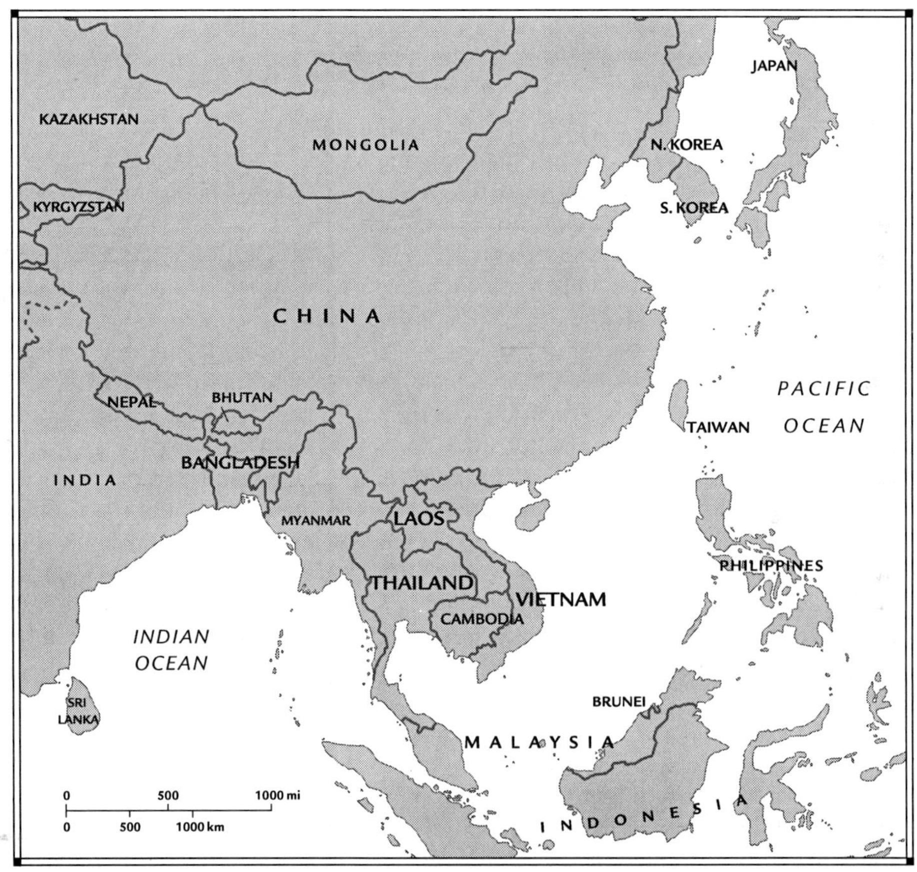

Hmong villages are located throughout China, Laos, Thailand, and Vietnam.

→ The Beginning

Four gods hold up the corners of the world and are responsible for creation. Long ago they sent a flood, and waters covered all the earth. Into a wooden barrel were placed a boy and a girl, who were sent by the Lord of the Sky to populate the earth. When the waters receded, they stepped out of their barrel and saw they were alone in the world. When their baby was born, it looked like an egg, smooth and oval. The boy and girl cut the egg into pieces, and scattered it over the land. Each piece grew into new people, until all the clans of the Hmong were born, and the earth was full of people.

→ Introduction and History

The Hmong are a tribal people who have traditionally lived in isolated mountain villages throughout China, Laos, Thailand, and Vietnam. Originating in southern China, the Hmong were historically referred to as Meo or Miao ("primitive" or "barbarian") by outsiders, a pejorative label they reject (Ovesen 1995). "Hmong" is their own word, meaning "free people." Hmong tales tell of an ancestral past in a land of ice and snow and perpetual darkness, leading some to posit European ancestry, assuming the stories are of Siberia (Fadiman 1997).

The story of the Hmong is a history of struggle, rebellion, and perseverance. Fadiman (1997:13) describes Hmong history as "a marathon series of bloody scrimmages, punctuated by occasional periods of peace, though hardly any of plenty." Chinese literature mentions the Hmong as early as the twenty-seventh century B.C., when they lived along the basins of the Yellow and Yangtse rivers for several centuries (Geddes 1976). Relations between the Hmong and the Chinese were never friendly. Hmong chose to retain their own way of life, preferring their own food, dress, language, and music over that of the Chinese, who attempted to incorporate (or at least influence) them. Emperors set up singularly punitive rules for the recalcitrant Hmong, who wanted nothing more than to be left alone (Fadiman 1997). Over hundreds of years, the Hmong skirmished with the Chinese, settling and resettling to avoid extermination. In the sixteenth century, the Ming dynasty constructed a wall one hundred miles long and ten feet high in an attempt to contain the Hmong in one area. In the eighteenth century, bloody battles were a regular occurrence. By the mid-nineteenth century, Chinese practices drove many Hmong out of the north from fertile lands to the rugged mountains southward, and from there to mountainous regions across Southeast Asia. Facing massacre and unwilling to give up their way of life, they chose poorer mountainous terrain because its inaccessibility afforded them greater safety (Yang 1993).

In the 1890s the French took control of Indochina, levying oppressive taxes on the population. The Hmong in Laos, no strangers to conflict with oppressive authorities, rebelled. In 1896, they refused to pay what they considered extortion. Armies were sent into the mountains to intimidate the Hmong, who organized a resistance force, leading to an eventual cease-fire, ordered by French authorities (Yang 1993). A second uprising, far more serious than the first, took place from 1919 to 1921. It was dubbed "The Madman's War," largely because the rebel leader, Pa Chay, was said to climb trees in order to "receive his military orders directly from heaven" (Fadiman 1997:17). Others bristle at this designation, claiming it makes light of a valiant attempt to resist colonial oppression (Yang 1993). The Hmong insurrection was successful enough to lead the French government to grant them special administrative status, which was essentially an official policy granting the Hmong their centuries-old wish: to be left undisturbed in the mountains with no forced participation in any world but their own. Peace prevailed only until the 1940s, when both World War II and the war in Southeast Asia would prove disastrous for the Hmong.

TRADITIONAL HMONG LIFE

Traditional Economy

The majority of Hmong (roughly 6 million) still live in southern China (Koltyk 1998). There are an estimated 350,000 in northern Vietnam, 250,000 in Laos, and 100,000 in northern Thailand (Ovesen 1995).

The Hmong practice slash-and-burn (swidden) agriculture, as part of their mobile way of life and migratory history. Fields are used until they are infertile, allowed to lie fallow, and then replanted when they have recovered. Land within two hours' walk of the village is planted. When this area is no longer usable, villagers move to another mountain and begin again, leaving a landscape dotted with patches of deforestation. The average time one settled area will yield crops is six or seven years, although some fields can be urged into production for as long as fourteen.

A field *(rai)* is selected based on its proximity to the village and its slope, since steep land that has been cleared loses much of its arable soil during monsoon season. Trees are cleared and the remaining brush is burned, with the ashes spread for fertilizer. Unless the plot is very close to the village, farmers construct several small shelters at the edge of each *rai* so they need not travel to and from the village during the peak of the season. In one, the farmer can sleep; in the others, animals can be housed and crops can be stored after harvesting (Yang 1993).

Rice and corn are the most important staple food crops, supplemented by a huge array of vegetables and fruits. Cucumbers, squash, soybeans, and cabbage are the most plentiful. Tropical fruits are cultivated, and the peach, carried to Laos from China over all the years of migration, is especially prized. Nonfood crops are also important, and none more so than the opium poppy.

Opium poppy growing has a long history among the Hmong, playing a central role in their traditional economy for well over a hundred years (Yang 1993). The flower originated in the Middle East, and during the eighteenth century use of the drug derived from its flower spread throughout India, where the trade was controlled by the East India Company, through which it reached China.

Profits there were tremendous, but Chinese authorities were alarmed at the consequences of the drug and mounted a campaign to discourage its use, leading to the Opium War between Britain and China in the mid-nineteenth century. It was at this time that the Hmong, driven out of their homes in southern China by the invaders who seized their land, began to cultivate opium in the limestone-rich mountain soil where it thrived. They soon became experts in the care of this difficult crop, and Hmong in China, Laos, and North Vietnam depended on the income (the majority of which they had no choice but to share with government and military officials) (Yang 1993). Opium was, in fact, their only cash crop, and one that was extraordinarily valuable. As Fadiman (1997:123) notes:

> One could hardly invent a more perfect commodity for mountain transport: easily portable, immune to spoilage, and possessing a stratospherically high value-to-weight ratio. One kilogram of opium was worth as much as half a ton of rice.

Lowland merchants (and Europeans) paid for opium with silver bars (or coins, called piasters), which constituted the Hmong definition of wealth. It was melted down for necklaces and used for bride-price. May Ying—Opium Poppy—is considered a name of unparalleled beauty and good fortune to bestow upon a daughter (Fadiman 1997). The Hmong use opium therapeutically, to relieve pain, as well as recreationally, but several studies point to its not being either a social or medical danger when used in traditional, local context (Ovesen 1995; Westermeyer 1968).

Livestock also figure importantly into the Hmong traditional economy. Roosters and hens are kept by every family, and their utility goes beyond their value as food. (In fact, eggs are rarely eaten: they are far more valuable for their part in shamanic curing rituals and other ceremonies [Yang 1993].) Poultry is used ritually to retrieve the lost soul of a sick child, to seal a marriage ceremony, and at funerals, to ease the transit of a soul from this world to the next.

Pigs are also owned by every family and are valued for both their flesh and their fat, which is used in cooking. Cattle are used not for agriculture but as objects of sacrifice when asking ancestors for help. Horses are of more help in the fields, carrying baskets of rice and corn to the village from the *rais*.

The Village

Hmong houses *(tsevs)* vary based on location and climate. In Thailand and Vietnam, where villages are at lower elevations (and are thus warmer), houses are often built on stilts above the damp ground to keep them dryer and breezier (Willcox 1986). Reached by wooden steps or bamboo ladders, raised houses also provide distance from snakes and insects, while adding covered storage space. The *tsev* is framed in bamboo, lashed together and covered with grasses, straw, or woven cut bamboo. Roofs are thatched shingles. Houses in Laos, by contrast, are built directly on the ground, often of wooden planks or split bamboo. The floor is packed earth, and the roof thatched with large leaves. Laotian *tsevs* are

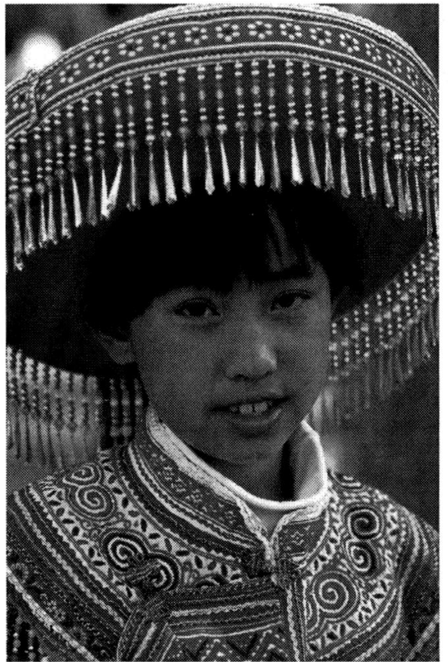
A Hmong girl in traditional dress.

constructed with heavy support beams, the most important of which is in the center (Ovesen 1995). It is home to a domestic spirit, which guards the house: it is honored by burying the placenta of a baby boy under the floor near its base (Fadiman 1997).

In the main room of the house is the cooking hearth with altars lining one wall. There is storage space under the eaves, and some *tsevs* house a granary inside. (Others have rice and corn storage in an adjacent building.) Married couples have rooms off the center room; visitors are accommodated by sleeping platforms that jut out from the walls. Mats of rice straw are coiled into seats, and large woven baskets serve as storage. Garden plots outside the houses are fenced off with bamboo sticks to prevent hungry pigs from eating the family's produce.

The arrangement of houses in a village is never random and often entails divination as well as practical considerations. When planning the construction of a new *tsev,* the first requirements are that it be near the *rais,* a source of water, and the houses of family members. After those features are in place, a ceremony is performed to ascertain the spiritual suitability of the location. One method is to place a small pile of uncooked rice in the proposed location of the central pillar. The rice is covered and left overnight. If it is there in the morning, unmoved, then the spirits have approved the site. Alternatively, a measured stick of wood can be positioned in the central pillar's hole. If it is longer by morning, the house may be built (Ovesen 1995). Construction is done communally and generally takes three or four men the better part of two weeks.

Language and Arts

For most of their history, Hmong tradition has been transmitted orally. It was not until the 1950s that the language was written, an activity undertaken by Western missionaries in order to promote literacy. There are several Hmong dialects, most of which are mutually intelligible. In Laos, speakers of the two main dialects are referred to as White Hmong and Blue (or sometimes Green) Hmong, a reference to the color of the women's traditional skirts. Most words in the tonal language are monosyllabic.

The fact that Hmong is a tonal language has been linked with the importance of music in everyday traditional life (Willcox 1986). Improvisational singing and sung poetry set the pace for working in the *rais,* begin ceremonies to honor ancestral spirits, and fill leisure time. Courtship is initiated with music, and at the end of life, the soul is sent to the spirit world with a song.

The most popular musical instruments are flutes made of bamboo reeds. The *qeej,* a mouth organ, is owned by most families and is often cited as the most beloved emblem of Hmong culture (Willcox 1986; Yang 1993). Its importance may be inferred from the fact that when faced with choosing only a few items to bring to the United States, the majority of refugee families were sure to include a *qeej* to accompany them on the "soul path from Laos, through Thailand, and finally to the United States" (Willcox 1986:31). Two-string violins and various percussive instruments are also important for celebrations and ceremonies. Several drums and rattles are the exclusive purview of shamans, played only during healing rituals or funerals.

Traditional Hmong dress is elaborate and colorful, and Hmong women are renowned textile artists. The traditional process of making clothing begins with cultivation of the plants (hemp and other woody plants). Fibers must then be spun and prepared and dyed before they can be transformed into the cloth that is embroidered into breathtaking garments. The most exquisite of these cloth pieces is the *paj ntaub* ("flower cloth"), on which geometric or organic designs are embroidered, appliquéed, or batiked. The stitching is painstaking, with the most prized sewing performed in stitches so tiny they resemble minuscule beads (Fadiman 1997). Dressing for special occasions involves donning several layers of skirts, vests, fabric belts more than twenty feet long, wound around the waist, and triangular cloth leggings. Over these are worn elaborate silver breastplates and a pagoda-shaped hat adorned in bright colors and tinkling coins. The central item is the skirt, which can take even the most skilled woman more than two years to make, but also demands up to three hours of labor simply to put it away after it is worn. The skirts may contain upwards of 500 tiny pleats. Because it is important that they hold their shape, after wearing, each pleat is stitched in place along its length, using a single thread from waist to hem. In order not to damage the embroidery, the stitching must be very tiny. When the skirt is to be worn, the storage threads are gently eased out of the pleats; the pleats are laboriously stitched back in place to preserve the pleating for the next wearing.

In addition to designs and scenes of nature, Hmong women have often used the skirts to tell stories, preserve traditions, and even communicate with one another. There are folktales about grandmothers finding long-lost grandsons by stitching clan signs onto the skirts and walking through the mountains, and clever women who avoided harm by elaborately embroidering snakes that looked so realistic it protected them from real snakes, who will not attack one another. During the time when Chinese authorities attempted to prevent the Hmong from speaking their own language, women were said to have devised a pictorial code that they appliquéed to the skirts, sending messages to one another and "poking fun at their oppressors" (Willcox 1986:42).

⯎ Social Organization

Patrilineal Clans

The meaning of individual households and village differs for Hmong, as compared with their countries' other ethnic groups. For most other groups, villages provide the most important organizing principle. The holding of ancestral land connects individual households and their members. For the Hmong, their migratory lifestyle and clan organization have resulted in a different set of priorities.

Ovesen (1995) describes Hmong villages as having a relative lack of cohesion as compared with those of other groups in Laos, with the focus directed more toward individual households. This is a result of two factors: the mobility demanded by a slash-and-burn economy and patrilineal clan organization.

Different sources cite different numbers of Hmong clan divisions: some say there are twelve (Willcox 1986), most list either eighteen (Ovesen 1995) or nineteen (Yang 1993). Children are members of their father's clan *(xeem),* and despite the fact that mobility means that clans are very widely dispersed over great distances, exogamy is very strictly practiced. Clan membership takes precedence over regional or village loyalties, and this solidarity is of great importance given Hmong migratory patterns. When the head of a household decides it is time to move on, he will contact clan members in the new village and obtain advice and sponsorship for the move. When Hmong are traveling through a village, even one in which they know no one, they may locate members of their own *xeem* and be assured of hospitality. (Ovesen [1995] points out that this practice is demonstrated in Hmong who resettle in the United States by the great importance of owning a telephone: listing one's clan name—used as a surname—in the phone book allows visitors to find their *xeem.*)

Patrilineal clans are further divided into lineages *(kwv tij),* and these ties are depended upon for economic help and daily assistance. In some ways, Ovesen (1995) points out, the lineage functions as a large extended family. While in other groups lineages may be traced back over many generations, Hmong lineages rarely are reckoned beyond three generations, meaning that the common "ancestor" may, in fact, be living in the household. Lineage members are those who help move a household, provide rice or even money during difficult times, or share land. But material assistance is often secondary to the social, emotional, and spiritual value of lineage connections. Hmong say that they are only happy when they are near their family. Ovesen (1995) notes that the spiritual importance of being close to lineage members is literal and has practical implications: the oldest lineage member possesses crucial knowledge and authority, as well as being in charge of the family's spiritual life. Thus, when he dies, the residence of his successor dictates the new home of the rest of the family, who will move to his village in order to be guided by him in their veneration of the spirits.

Each Hmong household is something of a self-contained unit. The oldest married man is generally considered the head and is the owner of all material goods, from livestock and land to the items in the house itself. As the individual who is responsible for the family's welfare, he decides when the land is exhausted and it is time to move on. Household size varies from a married couple and their young children to units that include married children and widowed elderly family members. All members must be of the same clan, however: *xeem* spirits do not allow members of different clans to reside together.

The fact that individual households are the focus of Hmong social and economic life, and that villages engender no particular attachments, is demonstrated in the fact that the Hmong do not care to name their villages. Their identity centers on clan and lineage membership, and their villages are named by local Lao authorities. Village organization is also subject to district rules, which mandate a village headman be elected by household heads and report in with district authorities. It is his responsibility to settle disputes over land and cattle, and minor domestic squabbles. He has no fixed term of office, remaining in his position as long as everyone is satisfied with his performance and he wishes to do so. Successful headmen rely on elders to advise them on matters ranging from maintaining peaceful interpersonal relations to judging the proper length of time the *rais* must lie fallow before replanting.

Marriage

Traditional Hmong marriages are arranged by the fathers of the bride and groom, with cross-cousin marriage the preferential form. Girls are generally married in their middle teens, boys from ages 18 to 20. Polygyny is permitted, though uncommon. Elopement is a permitted traditional alternative to an arranged match, regarded as performative declaration of the desire to marry. The boy and his friends would hide and "capture" the girl (with her happy participation), whose parents would come to her rescue and receive a silver piaster from the boy. The couple having thus announced their intentions, the fathers would initiate marital negotiations. There is no stigma attached to premarital sex among teenagers, and often pregnancy was a third route to marriage. Today, a boy will often send a friend with a silver coin to the girl's father as a request for negotiations to begin. Three days after the presentation of the coin, the couple spends a three-day period at the future groom's house. This visit begins the girl's entry into his clan, something to which the ancestral spirits must agree. During this time, ceremonies are performed to ensure the young couple's souls do not wander off; the girl in particular is at risk for this consequence, because her incorporation into her betrothed's group is "a spiritually delicate business" (Ovesen 1995).

Once this sojourn at the boy's house is complete, the families begin to negotiate in earnest, setting a bride-price and payment for the celebration. The amount spent on the wedding reflects the wealth of the families and the size of the affair. The bride-price is generally fixed by consultation between village elders and district authorities. Because bride-price reflects a woman's potential for reproduction and labor, compensation varies. A girl who has never been married demands the highest price. Women who have been widowed after less than six years of marriage demand a higher bride-price than those who have been widowed following a marriage of six to ten years. Women who had been married for more than ten years bring no bride-price at all. Various fines are levied around issues of pregnancy and refusal to marry (Ovesen 1995).

✧ Religion, Illness, and Healing

While between 10 and 20 percent of the Hmong have been converted to Christianity by missionaries, the vast majority are animists, who have a complex system of beliefs and practice revolving around the spirit world. Spirits *(dabs)* of various kinds are involved in every aspect of Hmong life (Nusit 1976; Vang 1984). The shaman *(txiv neeb)* is a crucial mediator between worlds.

The Spirits

The Hmong strive for equilibrium in all they do. Balance is the key to a fulfilling and valuable life. Harmony within oneself, between friends and family, between clans and lineages, and between humanity and nature is what one must strive for. It is with the spirits, whose presence is interwoven in all activities, that Hmong balance and well-being rests. As such, attention must be paid to their demands and requirements.

All spirits are caught up together in an intricate dance of life and afterlife. Ancestral spirits guide living clan members. Animal spirits are often thought of as kindred spirits who can exchange and share souls with human beings (Conquergood 1989). Every natural feature has an animated spirit, surrounding the Hmong with trees and rivers alive in multiple ways. Conquergood (1989) describes Hmong cosmology by saying:

> The Hmong celebrate their humanity, not as a discrete and impenetrable part of the natural order, but as part of the circle of life of all creation—caught up in the rotation of the seasons, and deeply connected with the configuration of the mountains, and the reincarnation of life from generation to generation, even from species to species. Life, in its myriad forms, is intimately articulated through souls and spirits. (pp. 45–46)

The most important categories of *dabs* are the household spirits, medicine spirits, nature spirits, and shamanic spirits (Ovesen 1995). The household spirits exert their influence before construction begins. Once their approval is obtained, they occupy several sites within the dwelling: there is a spirit of the house, a spirit of the door, a spirit of the center post, and spirits of the large and small hearth (Geddes 1976). It is the spirit of the house whose approval is sought for construction. Once the house is built, an altar to that spirit is constructed opposite the front door. At the beginning of each new year, a chicken or pig is sacrificed and its blood is applied to the altar constructed out of painted paper (Ovesen 1995). It is this spirit who is responsible for the general health and welfare of all who reside in the home. The ceremony for the spirit of the door is also one which must be performed annually, and always at night. Pork or chicken is cooked and arranged near the door. The head of the household closes the door, saying that it is his intent to feed the door spirit and keep good fortune in and ill fortune out. For the next three days, only residents of the house may enter through the door.

The ceremony for the center post of the house is performed every three years and is essential to secure the souls of the household that might wander, resulting in serious illness. As in the other ceremonies, a pig or chicken is sacrificed. These offerings to the spirits are the main impetus for raising chickens, pigs, and cattle, which are far more important as sacrificial animals than as food or draught animals (Geddes 1976). Herbalists, who are usually women, keep a second altar, dedicated to their medicine spirits, next to that of the main house spirit. When people fall ill, they (or their family members) bring money and incense to the herbalist's home. At her altar, she burns the incense and asks the healing spirits to guide her in gathering the correct herbs to effect a cure for that individual (Culhane-Pera et al. 2004).

Certain magical practitioners *(khawv koob)* have the ability to call forth the spirits of medicine to assist in warding off sickness, performing rituals employing metal, water, incense, and chanting. After an apprenticeship with an experienced magical healer, they forge a personal connection to the spirits, who bestow the ability to diagnose and treat a wide array of ailments (Culhane-Pera et al. 2004).

Outside of the household reside the spirits of nature, who prefer to live in out-of-the-way places, sometimes preparing to ambush an unsuspecting soul. While they are not evil spirits, they do not like to be disturbed and may take revenge if they are happened upon. When nature spirits are appeased, they bring protection against fires, floods, earthquakes, and drought. When displeased, the results can be disastrous.

The Natural and the Supernatural

The importance of equilibrium is especially salient in the natural world, where an imbalance of elements—heat and cold, wet and dry—can lead to illness. An individual's overall constitution may leave them susceptible to microorganisms, parasites, and a variety of pesticides and chemicals (many of which they feel they were exposed to in Laos, during the war) (Culhane-Pera et al. 2004). Those with weak immune systems, fragile bones, bad blood, and not enough fat are at risk for a wide range of diseases.

Soul loss is the most dangerous of all supernatural ailments, and consequently the Hmong's main site of vulnerability is the soul *(plig),* several of which inhabit each body and all of which have the tendency to wander, causing illness or death. A frightened soul may flee after an emotional shock; it may become entangled in a dream and be unable to return upon waking; it may be enticed away by a spirit and then left, unable to find its way home.

There are certain times of life when one is more vulnerable to soul loss, and special ceremonies are performed to prevent such an event or to call back the wandering soul once it has gone off. Calling back the soul *(hu plig)* is always performed for a newborn three days after birth, which is the time it takes for the body and soul to be bound up together, creating a full person (Ovesen 1995). It is performed for a bride on the third day of her married life to ensure that her souls will reside in her new home, that of her husband's clan. Calling back a soul is imperative when a person falls ill, and when both household members and *khawv koobs* are unsuccessful in this, a shaman must be summoned.

Shamans

It is in the person of the shaman through which the most deeply held beliefs of the Hmong are manifest. Through his or her healing trances, core tenets of the culture are performed and reinforced. The shamanic spirits, *dab neeb,* select their own representatives among the Hmong; it is not a matter of human choice. Most often, a person will fall ill, beset by fever and hallucinations. An experienced shaman called in to help is able to recognize that it is not merely soul loss that is causing the illness. Rather, the *dab neeb* of a deceased shaman have selected this individual to receive their gifts. After recovery, the chosen person must study with an established healer for several years, learning the identity and habits of the *dabs* and the chants and rituals to capture wandering souls, and perfecting his or her ability to go into trance and tremble. The shaking of the shaman, in trance, is an essential component of the healing process, and it is a dangerous and exhausting art that puts the shaman's own soul at risk.

The Social and the Personal

Clan ties and harmonious relationships among kin are of central importance to Hmong communities. Thus, social conflict can result in illness. Rancorous disputes can be overheard by spirits, who will visit sickness on the guilty party. Failing to show respect to her in-laws may cause a woman to have a difficult childbirth; teasing a disabled person may result in bearing a child with that same disability; unkind behavior toward a sick person may lead to suffering from that same illness (Culhane-Pera et al. 2004).

Personal behaviors such as smoking, drinking, or using drugs are recognized as risk factors for illness. However, disregarding taboos surrounding food, sex, and postpartum activities may result in a wide range of ailments.

War in Indochina

In the 1940s, the Japanese army attempted to occupy French Indochina. Because the French had paid little attention to the people of Laos except to extract punitive taxes, the Hmong began to organize themselves, and several clans emerged as the most political, competing for local administrative posts that the colonial authorities were willing to let them fill. When the Japanese invaded, some clans aligned themselves with the French colonialists, others with the Japanese troops. The French were loath to lose the revenue they reaped from opium, and officials were sent into the mountains to encourage Hmong loyalty (and to urge the Hmong to increase their opium poppy production) (Chan 1994).

In 1945, just before the Japanese defeat, Laos declared its independence. In 1946, the French retook Laos, and several anti-French movements arose, including the radical Pathet Lao, which became aligned with Communist forces in Vietnam.

The French were ousted in 1956, and a series of coalition governments ran Laos until the early 1960s, when the war in Vietnam began to take its toll on Laos.

The Hmong figured prominently in this conflict because they were recruited by the CIA to be part of a secret mercenary army, trained by the Green Berets. In 1960 a CIA agent was sent into the Laotian jungle to find Vang Pao, a Hmong military leader who had previously fought against North Vietnamese forces in northern Laos. Vang Pao agreed to help the American forces repel the Communist troops, and set up a meeting with Hmong clan leaders to enlist their support. American officials promised to support the Hmong in defeat or victory, and shipments of guns, ammunition, food, and medical supplies soon began. The Hmong helped to build air bases near their villages, trusting that the American army would keep its end of the bargain.

As the Pathet Lao advanced in Laos, Vang Pao evacuated some hundred thousand Hmong from their villages, resettling them in refugee camps where, unable to rely on their usual mode of subsistence, they became dependent upon CIA (U.S. Central Intelligence Agency) supplies in order to survive (Chan 1994). Meanwhile, the Hmong secret army continued to fight for the United States, by 1969 numbering more than 40,000 troops.

Although Laos had been guaranteed neutrality in the 1962 Geneva Protocol, neither the Americans nor the Communists abided by this agreement. Americans secretly began bombing in Laos, eventually dropping more than 2 million tons of bombs on the country in an attempt to stop the Pathet Lao. In the United States, this was referred to as the "Quiet War" (the war in Vietnam being the loud one), but it was hardly so for the Hmong, who endured one bombing raid every eight minutes for nine years (Fadiman 1997). Countless civilians were killed during these sorties, with entire Hmong villages wiped out. Estimates of the price paid by Hmong set the civilian death toll at 50,000 and the CIA-trained Hmong loss of life at 17,000 (Chan 1994). Surviving Hmong suffered as well. Parents, wives, and children of Hmong troops moved through the mountains, attempting to evade Communist forces while planting crops. It was often impossible to stay in one site long enough to harvest what they had grown, and so they were reduced to eating whatever they might find while fleeing through the jungle—leaves, bark, and when lucky, wild fruit.

In 1973 American military involvement in Southeast Asia ended with the Paris Peace Accords. Top-ranking Hmong officers were offered asylum in the United States, but the vast majority of the Hmong people were abandoned. Laos fell to the Pathet Lao, and Vang Pao asked the CIA to evacuate the rest of the Hmong, as promised, because they were seen by the new Laotian government as traitors and would surely be victims of reprisals. He was told that this was impossible; of the 10,000 Hmong who arrived at the Long Chen airbase hoping for help, only several hundred were evacuated. Confused and "stunned by the failure of the Americans to keep their promise" (Chan 1994:45) to provide aid and protection in return for their fighting, those left behind felt they had only two options: to flee into the jungles and attempt to hide from government-threatened "torment and death" (Trueba 1990: xxiii) or to attempt to leave the country on foot.

➔ Refugees and Resettlement

The Pathet Lao took over, and Hmong life was again altered beyond recognition. Those Hmong who were identified as having fought for the United States were captured and sent to "reeducation camps" where the majority died of malnutrition or cruelly hard labor (Chan 1994). Villagers found their world turned upside down by the new government regulations. Communism mandated that all farms be collective; thus, family land was consolidated and the yield was distributed by the state. Traditional slash-and-burn agriculture was outlawed, and anyone found practicing it was arrested (Fadiman 1997). Village leaders were displaced by government appointees. Clan membership, family structure, traditional social and economic relationships were all disrupted. Many Hmong were resettled in lowland areas to work in communist collectives where they were exposed to tropical diseases to which they had no immunities. Previously unencountered malaria—carried by mosquitoes that cannot live in the high altitudes of Hmong mountain villages—took a great toll.

The Pathet Lao troops that patrolled the villages brooked no disobedience. Hmong who seemed rebellious or slow to follow rules were told they needed to attend a "seminar" to learn the new ways. Those dissenters removed from the village by Pathet Lao patrols were sent to seminar camps and rarely returned. Hones (1999:70) reports being told "if you made a big mistake you'd go to a seminar and never come back." In response, some fled to higher, more inaccessible mountains in an attempt to hide from the troops.

Hundreds of thousands of Hmong chose a different path. Beginning in the spring of 1975, Hmong who expected reprisal, were starving, and were filled with terror set out for Thailand, most on foot. Some traveled in large groups, others as small families. The trip took most travelers a month or two, but there were many whose journey to the border took them years. They inched along, traveling only at night, attempting to avoid both capture and the land mines underfoot. Babies, the elderly, and those who fell ill were carried on the backs of those who were still able to manage. Silence was imperative for survival. Fadiman (1997) was told by one refugee that her son, 1 month old when the family left their village, knew not a single word when they finally reached Thailand two years later, because no one had dared to talk beyond an occasional whispered direction. To prevent a baby's cry, which could alert the Pathet Lao patrols, mothers would often mix opium in water to ensure a child would sleep. If the mixture was too strong, it was fatal. Such babies had to be left, without burial. Frail elders, the sick, and wounded also had to be abandoned, sometimes left with a little food or opium to ease their passing. These were excruciating sacrifices to a people who hold elders in reverence and who believe that without a proper funeral and burial, a person's soul will wander in eternal distress. Roots and insects were often the best food available. Fadiman (1997:162) was told that when "desperate to fill their stomachs, some people chopped up their sweat-soaked clothes, mixed them with water and salt, and ate them."

The destination of this arduous trek was the Mekong River, which marks the border between Laos and Thailand. It was heavily guarded by government troops, and once there, many who had managed to survive their journey were captured. Those who arrived during monsoon season were swept away in the rushing waters as they attempted to cross, in the dark, with their few possessions—and family members—on their backs. Most mountain-dwelling Hmong could not swim. Some were able to cross in boats; others fashioned makeshift rafts out of what little bamboo was left by the riverside. Some brought empty plastic jugs to use as flotation devices; still others attempted to float by blowing up plastic grocery bags. Stories of crossing the Mekong are told and retold by those who survived the passage. Women embroidered scenes of the exodus in the panels of story cloths *(pandau)* (Hones 1999). Nightmares of the crossing haunted refugees for decades (Fadiman 1997).

Some estimates place at half the number of Hmong who survived their attempt to escape Laos; others set the number lower than that. En route they encountered Pathet Lao and Vietnamese snipers, cluster bombs and land mines, "disease, starvation, exposure, snakebite, tiger maulings, poisoning by toxic plants, and drowning" (Fadiman 1997:165).

By the late 1970s there were more than twenty refugee camps on the Thai border, housing refugees from Vietnam, Cambodia, and Laos. The largest of these was Ban Vinai, which at its fullest held nearly 43,000, 90 percent of whom were Hmong. It became the largest Hmong settlement in the world, and its area was less than one square mile. Conditions at the camp were squalid; there was no electricity, no running water, no sewage system—and nothing to do. One former occupant explained:

> In Ban Vinai, you don't have the right to do anything except get a ration of rice and beans, and go to your tent, and you do that for five or ten years. People were born and grew up there. . . . The elderly person just sleep day and night, they just wait and see and wait and eat and wait and die and wait and die. (Fadiman 1997:166)

The Thai government was unwilling to absorb refugees into the local population. They wanted to repatriate the Hmong or have them resettled in another country. Hmong were terrified to return to Laos, but they also became terrified of the prospect of resettlement in the United States. The majority of Hmong who left Ban Vinai for other countries emigrated to America, both because of their previous association with the U.S. military and because General Vang Pao had settled in Montana (Fadiman 1997). Those still in Ban Vinai received horrifying letters from relatives in the United States describing urban violence, crumbling tenements, unemployment, and racial prejudice. Daily life in the inner cities—the most common resettlement sites—seemed a nightmare. Despite the egregious conditions at Ban Vinai, many Hmong began to see permanent residence there as preferable to the dangers that would await them back in Laos or in the United States. This was especially true because however crowded and filthy the camp was, unlike the alternatives, it was a place in which Hmong culture was alive and celebrated. Women produced traditional embroidery, families were able to raise vegetables and small livestock, and the sounds of the *qeej* and the chanting of shamans were everywhere (Conquergood 1989; Fadiman 1997). Older Hmong were especially unwilling to leave. Fadiman (1997) cites a Hmong refugee who left Ban Vinai for California as explaining:

> At the camp, the cultural tradition was still there. There was patrilineage. Children still listened to Grandpa. What is the good to come to America if all that change? And a lot of elderly people, though they never, never say it openly to strangers, what really haunt them is they are afraid in America they will not have a good funeral ceremony and a good grave, and that is more important than any other thing in the world. (p. 168)

Thailand declared Ban Vinai closed in 1992, and told the 11,500 Hmong who remained that they must choose between returning to Laos and resettling in another country. In preparation, many were periodically moved to other locations. According to Hones (1999:76), "these periodic shifts from camp to camp effectively terrorized the refugees because they could never be certain when they would be uprooted again or, worse yet, sent across the border" and back to Laos. About 7,000 did choose to return, although they were restricted to the lowlands, not permitted access to their home villages, and still prohibited from practicing slash-and burn agriculture. They were promised that at the very least they would be safe, and there would be no more collective farms and no more "seminars." However, Fadiman (1997:169) reports that although it has been denied by the Thai and Laotian governments (as well as U.S. sources), "some Hmong have been forced to return to Laos against their will, and, once there, have been persecuted or killed." As it turned out, more than 10,000 Hmong, most from Ban Vinai, fled the camps and neither returned to Laos nor chose to leave Thailand. Rather, they fled to an area north of Bangkok, on the land of a Buddhist monastery (Fadiman 1997). In December 2009, Thai government soldiers armed with riot shields and clubs descended on a refugee holding camp in a remote hilltop province 200 miles north of Bangkok. More than 4,500 asylum seekers were rounded up and forcibly repatriated to Laos. International agencies and officials from numerous governments have expressed concern over the health and safety of the repatriated Hmong, where they remain in two settlement camps, with little information available to outsiders.

HMONG IN THE UNITED STATES

The experience of Hmong resettlement in the United States is unlike that of many other groups who make up the fabric of the American population. Fadiman (1997) recounts one example of the "Americanization" of European immigrants, who worked at a Ford automotive plant in Dearborn, Michigan, in the early 1920s and who were given compulsory classes in becoming American, which consisted of instruction in table manners, hygiene, and work habits. (She reports that the first English sentence they were expected to memorize was "I am a good American."):

> During their graduation ceremony they gathered next to a gigantic wooden pot, which their teachers stirred with ten-foot ladles. The students walked through a door into the pot, wearing traditional costumes from their countries of origin

> and singing songs in their native languages. A few minutes later, a door in the pot opened, and the students walked out again, wearing suits and ties, waving American flags, and singing "The Star-Spangled Banner (pp. 182–183)".

The Hmong who fled Laos and Thailand were not searching for a new nationality. Their intent was not to climb into a giant melting pot and emerge transformed. Quite the reverse: their resolve was the same resolve they maintained in the face of Chinese attempts to force assimilation in the nineteenth century. They wanted nothing more than to resist attempts to change them; they wanted to remain Hmong. If they could have done so in Laos, they would surely have stayed in their own land. Fadiman (1997:183) quotes anthropologist Jacques Lemoine as observing that the Hmong "did not come to our countries only to save their lives, they rather came to save their selves, that is, their Hmong ethnicity." Because that is true, the Hmong faced great difficulties in their interactions with officials charged with their resettlement, as well as citizens of many of the communities in which they were placed. Their relocation has been described as "acutely involuntary, accompanied by painful losses of loved ones, of community, and of lifestyle" (Schein 2004:273).

General Vang Pao had advised the American government that all they needed to do to ensure successful resettlement was to allow the Hmong to be together in traditionally sized groups on a small amount of land—even inferior land—on which they could raise vegetables and chicken. Most Hmong brought only the few precious things they could carry, and many included a hoe. This suggestion ran counter to the goal of assimilation and was never considered. In retrospect, officials in charge of coordinating the "catastrophically mishandled" (Fadiman 1997:186) resettlement effort conceded that it had been a disaster, handled "shoddily." One said frankly, "It was a kind of hell they landed into. Really, it couldn't have been done much worse" (Fadiman 1997:186).

The overwhelming task of deciphering life in America led one Hmong man to a poignant observation: "In America, we are blind because even though we have eyes, we cannot see. We are deaf because even though we have ears, we cannot hear" (Fadiman 1997:187). In Philadelphia, Chicago, and other cities, Hmong were routinely victims of theft, assault, and racial violence. For some, the solution was what had often been so in the past: moving on. In keeping with the proverb "there is always another mountain," large numbers of Hmong who were without traditional group supports in colder climes migrated to California. According to the 2008 American Community Survey, the Hmong population in the United States is about 275,000. Of these, nearly 80,000 have settled in California, which has the largest population of Hmong residents. Minnesota has a Hmong population of more than 52,000; Wisconsin has nearly 35,000 Hmong residents.

In their so-called secondary migrations to warmer areas, Hmong families were financed by clan members in the United States. The original resettlement, however, had been contracted out by the federal government to private nonprofit groups, which then found local sponsors. Most of these voluntary resettlement agencies had religious affiliations, and the majority of Hmong found themselves being actively proselytized by church groups and pastors, who visited them at home and attempted to explain that an integral part of their new lives should be the embrace of Christianity. This has had serious consequences for both the Hmong who have been converted and those who have not. The mere fact that within families there is this divide has led to a breakdown of support. Christianity cannot support many of the most central tenets of Hmong culture, chief among them animism, animal sacrifice, and shamanism. Those who have become Christians refuse to participate in important family ceremonies (the soul calling of a newborn, for example) because of the traditional elements involved. Older Hmong whose children or grandchildren have converted fear that they will not have a traditional funeral, which will result in their souls never finding rest (Ovesen 1995). Within the converted community, clan and lineage solidarity is undermined by the message that the ideal is to consider all people to be your "brothers" and treated as such (Ovesen 1995).

Chan (1994) reports that Hmong elderly in particular have suffered, especially from the social marginalization of old people in American culture. Their status as revered providers of sage advice, respected and consulted on all matters, centrally involved in settling disputes and making decisions, seems lost to them. He observes:

> Unable to speak English, dependent on others to drive them places, fearful of taking public transportation in case they get lost, victimized by crime in the low-income neighborhoods where many of them live, many older Hmong may sit at home with nothing to do except watch television. (p. 57)

Marginalized and despondent, they say "We have become children in this country" and ask "Where is my dignity if I cannot do anything for myself?" (Chan 1994:57).

Secondary migration has many motivations beyond relocating to warmer climates. Seeking employment, education, job training programs, or a less hostile environment all figure prominently in families' choice to move on. In 2008, North Carolina was home to nearly 9,000 Hmong residents. In addition to milder seasons, it is seen as a safe place that offers the possibility of economic advancement, owing to a large manufacturing industry and the perceived welcome to new workers (Pinkel 2003). None of these factors is as important, however, as migrating to find relatives. In Laos, the extended family household lives under one roof, or in homes that are clustered together. In the United States, this family grouping *(tsev neeg)* is more scattered, with separate homes maintained, sometimes even miles apart, but functioning as a unit. Moving to facilitate this web of extended family is of crucial importance. Koltyk (1998), writing about the Hmong community in Wisconsin, reports that individual families from Kansas, Iowa, Colorado, Texas, Minnesota, and California all decided to come together in Wisconsin, to establish a series of homes near one another. Although the Hmong residences are separate houses, they are thought of as a collective *home,* such that children become accustomed to all of them, sleeping, playing, and eating in multiple residences, being cared for by many adults. Daily life centers around the activities of the sublineage. Women shop and cook together, work in one another's gardens, prepare communally for rituals and holidays, and provide childcare. Although men have dealings with Hmong men of other clans living locally, they spend most of their time with their brothers and their father's brothers' children.

When asked to name their friends, Hmong cite their relatives, often to the exclusion of other Hmong who live in neighboring apartments but who are not family. Koltyk (1998) was surprised to find that while unrelated Hmong do socialize for holidays or ritual events that involve the wider community, their overriding preference for depending only on kin is paramount: when a young mother's baby became desperately ill and needed hospitalization, she and her husband spent several hours attempting to locate a family member to care for their other children, despite the fact that their next-door neighbor was a Hmong woman with whom they attended English classes. Mutual aid organizations have been established in nearly every Hmong community, and they do provide a sense of larger community, organizing athletic leagues and providing counseling, housing information, language classes, and youth programs. While these services are used, and the language and culture classes are popular, they rarely result in extra-familial friendships outside of the classroom.

Hmong in many communities organize similarly. For example, households will almost always have freezers, but rarely washers and dryers (Koltyk 1998). A freezer, the first major appliance saved for, has come to represent a household's ability to provide for the extended kin group. It is stocked with enough food to share at a moment's notice, serving as a resource to other households in the network, and allowing many members to come together in one place and prepare a large meal. In the 1980s and 1990s, televisions, videocassette recorders, and videocameras became popular, both as ways to learn about American culture and to view videos in the Hmong language, as well as a vehicle to record and exchange family events and rituals with lineage members at a distance. Laundromats are often a popular place to socialize, and allow women to get out of the house and meet others, while still performing their domestic duties. Many laundromats with mostly Hmong clientele in California installed VCRs, encouraging groups to watch Hmong videos together while doing their laundry (Koltyk 1998). In addition to dramatic videos of love stories, martial arts adventures, and even music videos of Hmong bands, as many as twenty Hmong video companies in the United States produce documentaries of the Hmong homeland. Videos—and, in recent years, DVDs—present nostalgic scenes of mountain villages, terraced rice fields, and families in traditional clothing working together, narrated in Hmong and often marketed to the elderly, who cannot travel back home to visit as some younger, wealthier Hmong can (Schein 2004). Hmong scholar Gary Yia Lee (2006) describes the yearning of many Hmong for media about their homeland as "dreaming across the oceans." The growing industry includes CDs of traditional music, karaoke DVDs, music set in Laos, historical documentaries, original movies, and travelogues, all of which serve different purposes across generations. Older Hmong long to see their homeland and travel there vicariously while viewing DVDs of villages and farmland. Many younger Hmong eagerly consume music videos of Hmong artists who mix traditional instruments with electric guitars and record rap songs with both Hmong and English lyrics.

Health and illness are major concerns in the Hmong community, and shamans are kept busy caring for their clan members. Bowing to work and school schedules, healing ceremonies tend to be held on the weekends. Extended family members pool their resources to purchase the necessary ritual items, and convene at one home for what is usually an all-day ceremony. When a death occurs, however, a wider net is cast. The news spreads rapidly across the country and abroad, with relatives often traveling great distances to attend the funeral. Performing the requisite funeral rituals is of crucial importance, outpacing most other traditional ceremonies. The soul's passage to the afterworld is a dangerous journey and must be carefully guided. Accomplishing this in the United States is difficult, because at every step of the ritual process, Hmong face conflict with the law. Upon death, Hmong tradition mandates washing and preparing the corpse at home, which by law must instead be performed at a funeral parlor. Drums, *qeej* playing and chants, which are performed for long hours around the body to guide the soul on its way, must be tailored both to funeral home visitation hours and noise regulations. Just as Laotian houses are built only on a site that has been divined to be auspicious, so too must a burial place be assessed, which is often a problem for cemeteries. Perhaps the most onerous responsibility for family members, however—and the one that has the potential to cause the most trouble—is animal sacrifice, which is imperative. Several cows must be sacrificed, with the meat then used as the meal for mourners. The honor bestowed by performing this ritual obligation is sometimes the greatest consolation a dying person can receive; when death is imminent, family members will inform the ill individual of the number of cows they are planning to purchase, representing the person's great importance to the family (Koltyk 1998).

The rapidly growing Hmong population in the United States—which has doubled in the past twenty years—is a young population. Fifty-six percent of the Hmong are under 18 years of age; 26 percent of the entire U.S. population is under 18. The median age of U.S. Hmong is 16, as compared with a median age of 35 for the wider U.S. population (Pfeifer 2005). Hmong children in the United States are often described as caught between two cultures, expected to act as interpreters of customs they are learning in school and of a language their parents and grandparents may not know (Trueba 1990). The exclusive focus on socializing with family can lead to difficulties making friends in school. Yet they are also seen as the hope for the future, with higher education the key (Koltyk 1998). More and more, Hmong parents encourage their children to aim for college and beyond. It is clear, however, that this goal is framed neither as a way to become more American, nor as a route to individual success, but rather as a way to achieve economic security that will benefit the entire kin network. This leads to a dilemma: parents fear that their children's education will result in a loss of ethnic identity, and that rather than its being a vehicle to allow greater Hmong self-sufficiency and independence, it will instead lead them to reject the traditional way of life (Trueba 1990). In fact, while children's economic and professional successes are appreciated, "any earmarks of assimilation [are seen] as an insult and a threat" (Fadiman 1997:207). And, inevitably, children do reflect their American surroundings. Fadiman (1997:207) recalls a teenager explaining, "I know how to do *paj ntaub,* but I hate sewing. My mom says, why aren't you doing *paj ntaub?* I say, Mom, this is America."

Fadiman (1997:199) reports that the Hmong are often referred to as America's "least successful refugees," owing to the fact that rates of unemployment are high. She points out, however, that it is only by an economic yardstick that they are thus measured. By other indices—rates of child abuse, crime, domestic violence, responsibility for elderly family members—they can only be admired. That the Hmong community has held on so tenaciously to their ethnic identity runs counter to the American ideal of assimilation, and is likely also used as a measure of "failure." Fadiman (1997:208) cites anthropologist George Scott as observing that in the face of the hardships they have found in the United States, Hmong have responded "by becoming *more* Hmong, rather than less so."

Hmong in diaspora elsewhere have had different experiences, significantly shaped by settlement patterns, social policies, and governmental programs. The Mennonite Church played a central role in bringing Hmong, who now number 800, to Canada. Daphne Winland (1994) reports that Hmong felt particularly at home in the Mennonite church because they felt it embodied values that their own traditions emphasized, particularly large family size, community solidarity, and in-group mutual aid.

France, which once counted Vietnam among its colonial holdings, offered refuge to Hmong after the Vietnam War. In keeping with French official republican policy—which emphasizes individual citizenship and rejects the notion of subcultural identity—French officials visited Thai refugee camps to identify those Hmong who spoke or understood French, had served in the French military or civil service, or had family already in France (Xiong 2004). Once in France, Hmong spent six months in housing centers where they were tutored in French culture and attended daily classes in reading and writing French. Upon completion of the program, jobs were found for each male head of household, and nuclear families were settled throughout France. The estimated 15,000 Hmong in France—an estimate because France keeps no official statistics on ethnicity—were thus dispersed throughout the country. While secondary migrations allowed Hmong in the United States to resettle in extended family groups, fewer Hmong in France had those opportunities. Tied to the locations where employment had been found for them, isolated nuclear families sometimes found it difficult to maintain traditions, especially without elders, who are the repository of oral traditions, and ritual specialists, who are depended on for the knowledge and performative skills on which many ceremonies depend (Xiong 2004). However, the commitment to language training and job provision, coupled with social programs, has resulted in different economic realities for French Hmong. By the mid-1990s, 90 percent of Hmong families were employed. The French family allowance system provides monetary benefits to families with children, and subsidized child care and preschool programs allow women with young children to enter the workforce.

Hmong in the United States and France have settled largely in urban and suburban areas. French Guiana, an overseas region of France located in South America, offers yet another contrast. As mentioned earlier, Hmong in Thai refugee camps had heard distressing accounts of the struggles of those resettled in urban areas abroad.

In 1975, a French missionary suggested that French Guiana might provide a life that resembled their past in Laos. They could settle in rural farming communities, where they would be both self-sufficient economically and surrounded by family. This has proved to be an ideal situation for the now 2,100 Hmong in French Guiana. Village life revolves around farming, in which nearly all adults participate. Local school calendars reflect this centrality: they are closed on Wednesdays so children can help bring produce to the market and open on Saturday instead (Clarkin 2005). Despite their small number, the Hmong produce close to 90 percent of all the fruits and vegetables consumed in French Guiana (Géraud 1997). In comparing their experiences with those of relatives settled in other countries, French Guianian Hmong report great satisfaction in maintaining their tradition as farmers, rather than wage laborers, especially after experiencing the loss of freedom and self-determination in the Thai camps (Clarkin 2005). Because most villages are entirely Hmong, traditional practices, celebrations, and ceremonies form the center of daily life, providing what is likely "the greatest opportunity to retain cultural traditions within the Hmong refugee diaspora" (Clarkin 2005:11).

Hmong in France and the United States have been urged to assimilate; Hmong in French Guiana live in isolated rural enclaves. Those who have settled in Australia (roughly 2,200) have neither been urged to give up traditions nor settled in exclusively homogeneous regions. While most Hmong in the United States have been settled through church sponsorship and voluntary agencies with religious ties, Australian Hmong were admitted under government programs. That fact, coupled with official encouragement of multicultural activities, has resulted in far less conversion to Christianity and greater retention of traditional Hmong religious customs (Tapp 2005).

Balance and equilibrium are the key to a healthy Hmong life. Parents hope that by encouraging their children to pursue higher education, they will be creating strong new leaders to maintain Hmong collective identity in future generations (Koltyk 1998). Conquergood (1989:76) believes that "the capacity to hold different ways of knowing in productive tension is both possible and desirable." Perhaps the Hmong in the United States will prove him correct.

➔ For Further Discussion

History has shown both the empowerment and the violence that can ensue from ethnic pride and discrimination. As you have read, the story of the Hmong is a history of struggle, rebellion, and perseverance. Over hundreds of years, Hmong suffered persecution at the hands of many groups, while fiercely defending their ethnic heritage. Despite the ravages of war and resettlement, they continue to strive to maintain their traditions. How might their history influence their participation in American society? What factors contribute to being thought of as a "successful refugee"?

CHAPTER 7

THE KALULI

Story, Song, and Ceremony

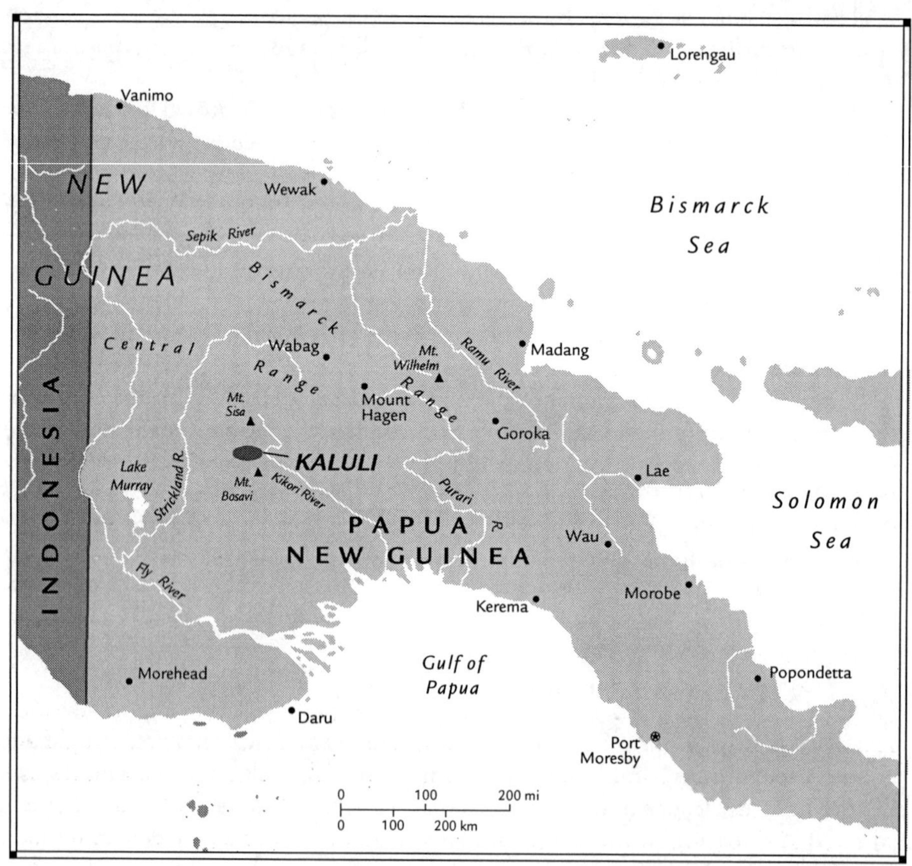

Location of the Kaluli in Papua New Guinea.

✈ The Beginning

"When the land came into form" there were no trees, there were no animals, there were no streams, there was no food. But there were people. People covered the earth. The people had no food, and so they were hungry. They had no homes, so they were cold. One stood up and gathered all the people together. He told one group to be trees, and they became trees. He told one group to be fish, and they became fish. He told one group to be banana, one sago and, finally all the plants and animals, rivers and hills, were there. The few who were left became the human beings (Schieffelin 2005).

✈ Introduction and History

The Kaluli live in the tropical rainforest in the Southern Highlands Province of Papua New Guinea on the Great Papuan Plateau at the northern base of Mt. Bosavi, the collapsed cone of an extinct volcano looming 8,000 feet above the land. They are the most numerous of four related horticultural groups who collectively call themselves Bosavi kalu, "people of Bosavi." The addition of the suffix *-li* (real) makes the meaning of Kaluli "real people."

The Bosavi people, whose number has been approximated from 1,200 to 2,000, live in about twenty longhouse communities built on ridges throughout the dense forest. Each community is about an hour's walk from the next, and the vegetation is nearly unbroken between them.

Although there are signs suggesting that the Kaluli are perhaps more closely related to lowland groups than to their closer neighbors in the New Guinea highlands, Bosavi tell no stories of their people coming to their present land from somewhere else. Their mythology tells that they have always lived on the plateau. Over the past several generations, they have been slowly moving eastward into unsettled, more heavily forested terrain. This movement may be a search for better gardening lands, an attempt to escape enemies, or flight from epidemics with which they have had to contend.

Kaluli traded extensively with friendly neighbors, but it was in the mid-1930s that the first Europeans visited the Great Papuan Plateau, bringing trade goods that had never been encountered. Chief among these were steel axes and knives, mirrors, beads, and pearl shells. World War II intervened, and European contact was broken until the 1950s. Between these two times, however, disaster struck the plateau in the form of measles and influenza epidemics. The populations of several groups were decimated, with the loss of lives ranging from 30 percent to, in some places, 70 percent of the population. The Kaluli lost fully one-quarter of their population. This threat is ongoing; despite public health programs, infant mortality is high and influenza epidemics still sweep the lowlands annually, resulting in a slowly declining population rate.

In the 1960s and 1970s the impact of evangelical Christianity could be seen in Kaluli communities. Schieffelin (2005) reports that earlier attempts by Seventh Day Adventist missionaries were unsuccessful. When it was learned that this religion forbade eating pork, it was concluded that the minister was crazy and he was forced to abandon his mission.

The Life of the Land

It is significant that longhouse identity is associated more with the land on which it sits than the clan affiliation of the people within. The name of a community's land becomes an integral part of their identity, and it is invoked in both friendly and hostile interactions. It is used much like a name in friendly socializing; in war these place names served other purposes. Enemies on the attack were on unfamiliar turf, with no knowledge of which ridges and trails might be well suited for defenders to hide behind in ambush. As they raced into battle, those defending their home territory hurled names of landmarks like weapons; these were met with the frantic cries of the enemies' own territorial names. Those that identified places of past victories were particularly powerful. Such a display was effective because it took advantage of the fright assumed to be felt by parties who were on strange land, who were someplace they didn't belong.

In both uses of place names—to identify themselves in friendly conversation and to verbally attack their enemies in battle—Kaluli are demonstrating how much their land is part of themselves. Edward Schieffelin, an anthropologist who has spent much time with the Kaluli, says it was explained to him this way: "When a man lives somewhere for a long time . . . his name is in the ground just like you put your name in that book" (2005:44). Often as he walked through the forest with informants, a Kaluli would point to a faintly discernible spot where the trees were thinner and remark that he had lived there as a small boy. A patch of weeds or remnant of a wooden post would be identified, with the individual remarking casually on whose garden or house it had been. Schieffelin came to understand that these places held for the Kaluli the content of their past; they call themselves by their places because they see themselves in their land.

The Kaluli traditionally marked time in a predominantly seasonal way. Their terms for seasonal change and the progression of time are not based on changes in weather, however, or phases of the moon, but rather are based on changes in forest vegetation. These changes are further demarcated by changes in the bird population. The appearance of a particular bird during the month of April hearkens the onset of a time that lasts through September and is often heralded by enthusiastic cries that the season is "really here: we heard *bili*," the bird that appears at this time, a comment sounding much like our "first robin of spring." Days, too, are apportioned by the birds—the morning calls of one awaken the children; the late-afternoon sounds of another alert people to come sit together for their meal. Not only time, but also space may be demarcated by birds. Their eating or nesting places may be used to describe portions of villages or trails, or to indicate direction.

→ SETTLEMENTS

The patrilocal village is made up of men belonging to the lineages of several patrilineal clans, along with their wives, children, and other female relatives. Relationships between villages are maintained by ties of marriage and matrilineal affiliation.

Each Kaluli community is structured with one longhouse and several smaller houses centered around a clearing. The longhouse is the main residence; smaller houses function more as temporary shelters for families from the longhouse who live nearer the gardens when it is time to harvest. A large longhouse may be sixty feet by thirty feet, with porches built onto either end. The entire structure is built up off the ground from five to twelve feet, and supported by poles. This elevation provides the best vantage point from which to see enemy raiders. Surrounding forests are cut down to enhance visibility, and the cavernous space left beneath the longhouse is inhabited by domesticated pigs, whose noise at the approach of strangers makes them effective "watchdogs."

The interior of the longhouse is divided in half by a hall running down its length. On either side are the men's sleeping platforms, made of bark and raised a foot or so off the floor. Near each is a firebox used for curing meat, and piles of firewood and smoked game are heaped near them. Other foods and possessions are hung by strings from the rafters, to keep them out of the reach of rats. Women, children, and piglets not yet consigned to the space beneath the longhouse sleep in closer quarters in passageways running down the sides of the house. Elderly men and unmarried youths occupy one corner of these, and older women of prestige, along with unmarried girls, share a section of the women's area.

Individual fireboxes are used for smaller, solitary meals or "snacks," but the longhouse functions as much as a town hall as it does a residence. When there are important matters to discuss, visitors to entertain, or important ceremonial occasions, the community fireboxes in the central hallway are the focal point. In all, about fifteen families, usually totaling about sixty people, reside in each longhouse. It is the longhouse community, more so than any other tie, that engenders feelings of loyalty in the Kaluli. People usually refer to themselves by the location of their longhouse rather than that of their clan. The residents build their house and plant their gardens together. They hunt and fish, sing and cook, in unison. When a youth is to be married, most longhouse residents contribute to the bride-price; when a gift of meat is received, it is shared with co-residents.

Although it may seem as if living in the longhouse would be cramped and might engender squabbling, this is usually not the case because families are often absent from the longhouse for weeks at a time. Small houses near garden sites, although certainly temporary shelters, are used often in two- and three-week blocks. At times when their own gardens are less demanding, families may travel to other longhouse communities to assist clan members with their own planting and gardening. In addition to local travel and gardening chores, hunting and trading expeditions take Kaluli away from the longhouses for extended periods of time. Old longhouses give way to new ones when gardens become exhausted. After two or three years of use, longhouses fall into disrepair and the residents plant new gardens and construct a new longhouse. Often the old structure is used less and less, as the garden fails, until finally it is abandoned and the new structure becomes permanent.

✧ Economic and Political Organization

In several ways, Kaluli society stands in great contrast to other groups in the New Guinea highlands.

Both politically and economically, Kaluli society is highly egalitarian. There are no formal positions of leadership and also no role of "big man," the wealthy individual who rises to an informal position of great influence, that is found so widely among other highland groups.

Absent, too, is the highland pattern of elaborate exchange for personal wealth. Whether exchange be formal and ceremonial or in the context of everyday activity, Kaluli do not use it as an occasion for enhancing status. Exchanges generally engaged in elsewhere in the region revolve primarily around life-cycle events and political activity. The most significant occasion of formal exchange in Kaluli society is marriage.

Subsistence Activities

The Kaluli are intimately familiar with the land they garden. Trees, hills, and streams are all referred to by their own names. Not only forest growth, but also inhabitants and travelers are recognizable; Kaluli can identify the footprints not only of one another, but also of individual pigs.

Kaluli practice swidden horticulture in extensive gardens and have a rich and varied diet. Their daily staple food is sago, a starch that they extract from wild sago palms that grow along streams a short walk from each village. Bananas, pandanus, breadfruit, sugarcane, sweet potatoes, and green vegetables from their gardens supplement the sago eaten at every meal. Most of the daily protein is gathered casually, by scooping up a small crayfish from underneath a rock or dipping a hand into a brook for a small fish. Small rodents or lizards darting across a Kaluli's path will be stabbed with a stick or summarily stamped underfoot.

There are fish in abundance in numerous rivers and streams throughout the area, and small game is easily come by in surrounding forests. The Kaluli may venture on several-day trips to unsettled forests where game is more abundant, but usually these treks are reserved for times when larger amounts of game are needed for an exchange. A small number of domestic pigs are kept. Forest foods are in dependable supply, particularly owing to the low population density.

Trade and Manufacture

Kaluli trade both with other groups and within their own community of Kaluli. While they have the most long-standing trade relationships with people to the north, trade has been more recently established with those living in the east. Each of several important trade routes was characterized by its own specific items. From the people in the west they secured hornbill beaks and strings of dogs' teeth; from the south came tree oil. To these items they added their own net bags, and traded all of these to the highland Huli. In return, the Huli provided salt, tobacco, and aprons woven from net.

Trade among longhouse groups was active, and relationships among the longhouses were forged by chains of marital alliances. These marriage ties and trading relations afforded the opportunity to travel between communities with hospitality assured, in addition to providing allies when needed for conflict resolution.

Kaluli manufacture tools for gardening, stone adzes, bows from palm trees, and net bags. The forest provides materials for constructing longhouses and fences. The most elaborate items of manufacture are the extravagant costumes created for important ceremonial occasions.

Division of Labor

Although the everyday activities of men and women are separate, and male and female gender roles are clearly differentiated, there is among the Kaluli none of the hostility between men and women often reported in the New Guinea highlands. Daily activities of labor and socialization are cooperative, and men and women are more complementary than competitive.

Women tend the gardens, look after the pigs, hunt small forest game, and gather other small protein sources. They are responsible for processing the staple starch, sago. It is to women that the important task of socializing the children is primarily entrusted.

Kaluli men.

Men often organize their labor as group activity, drawing on their networks of reciprocity and obligation to accomplish the strenuous tasks of cutting down and dividing trees, clearing large garden plots, building dams and fences, and planting.

Conflict and Control

Given that there is no formal system of control in the absence of a leader with the authority to enforce rules and exact punishment, such control is left to methods of informal sanction. Usually this is accomplished through gossip or ostracism. A person who has strayed outside the boundaries of personal or social parameters may be confronted by the injured parties and asked for compensation. Strong beliefs in the power of the supernatural to redress violations of taboos function as effective deterrents to misbehavior. In the past, the anticipation of enemy raids as retaliation was quite effective too, but in recent years this activity has been disallowed by the government. Schieffelin (2005) reports that rather than feeling resentment toward this official outside interference, most Kaluli are instead relieved that the danger inherent in the old days of retaliatory murder is gone.

The usual causes of conflict among the Kaluli are theft and death. It is the latter that, before government sanction, gave rise to intense violence. Deaths are believed to result from witchcraft; it was the offending witch who was the object of the counterattack. Witches are still held accountable for their actions but are not routed out of their longhouses and clubbed to death. Compensation of another sort is requested, although without formal sanctions in place such payment cannot be assured.

Social Organization

Kinship and Descent

Kaluli are organized into exogamous, patrilineal clans that are scattered throughout all the longhouse communities. In any single longhouse there reside the localized lineages of two or more clans. Even though clan membership is conferred through the male line, each Kaluli individual claims kinship to both mother's and father's groups. Paternal kin provide those ties within the residential longhouse; maternal ties connect an individual to relatives living in other longhouses. The group of individuals to whom one feels closest—those with whom one has grown up, or sees most often—take food from each other's gardens and share food in return. More distant kin (with distance in this case being two or more generations away) are lumped together with the same term ("grandparent" or "grandchild") used to refer to people who are no relation at all.

The most important tie in establishing relationships, however, is that of sibship. Siblings, among the Kaluli, are those who are one's actual siblings as well as parallel cousins (mother's sister's children and father's brother's children).

Marriage

The preferred Kaluli marriage is one in which the man and woman belong to different clans and refer to one another with the term reserved for distant kin and unrelated individuals.

Arrangements for marriage are instigated by the elders in the groom's longhouse, often quite without his knowledge. A woman is selected and the bridewealth collected, all unbeknownst to the couple. Schieffelin (2005) remarks that by the time arrangements are nearing completion, the groom is often the last to know, and his closest friends delight in being the ones to shock him with the news.

Marriage sets in motion a lifelong relationship of exchange. A formal relationship is begun with the collection and bestowal of bridewealth. Friends and relatives of the groom contribute goods, thereby solidifying their previous relationship with the groom and establishing a new one with the bride. This relationship involves the usual extension of food and hospitality that one might ordinarily expect from kin; but it further binds the contributors to the ongoing state of the couple's marriage. If the wife should die as a result of witchcraft, a bridewealth contributor seeks revenge. Should a woman commit adultery, he supports the husband in his dispute. In the event of the husband's death, contributors "officially" have the right to give their opinion on the fate of the children, but this option is rarely exercised. The relationship comes full circle when the friends and kin who contributed to the original bridewealth receive part of the bridewealth of the couple's daughters, commensurate to that which they contributed long ago.

The compensation inherent in bridewealth is both in recognition of the nurturance provided by her family as she grew, and also for loss: loss of the daughter they love, who will go away with her husband, and loss of her important contributions to the economy of their own longhouse. Especially affected are the girl's unmarried brothers, for whom she has labored domestically, much in the way a wife would. Although the ideal compensation is the groom's donation of a sister to the bride's family, such so-called sister exchange doesn't occur with great frequency. Another function of bridewealth payment is to describe the universe of in-laws as those who have received part of the payment.

SOCIALIZATION

The socialization of children in Kaluli society has been elegantly described by Bambi Schieffelin (1990), a linguistic anthropologist who weaves the general socialization of children together with the teaching of language.

Girls and Boys

One of the first social lessons children learn is the appropriate content of their gender roles. Because it is the mother who interacts most intensively with her children, the task of emphasizing the child's gender, taken up in the first days of life, falls to her. Whether she and the child are alone or surrounded by others, she calls attention to the child's gender by the way she structures the content of her conversation and interaction.

Sons are told how strong they will one day be. Mothers structure games and other activities that employ aggression and assertive behavior. Boys are expressly taught that they will get what they want if they are endlessly demanding and never give up their pursuit. They are taught to beg, to wheedle, and even to have vigorous tantrums until their needs are finally met. They are expected to perfect the talents to ensure both their behavior and their wishes will be attended to.

Daughters are taught something very different. Although all young children are recognized to be naturally "helpless," girls are not permitted to maintain this pose for very long. Unlike boys, who are endlessly needy and always on the receiving end, girls are assigned chores to do as soon as they are physically coordinated enough to begin to manage them. Their activities are those that are designed to serve others; daily they fetch firewood, carry water, weed gardens. In addition to this sort of labor, their nurturing skills are an important focus of girls' socialization. As soon as a new baby is born, a little girl becomes an older sister, which is a role of extreme importance in Kaluli life. She already knows that her own wants are secondary to those of others; when her mother presents her with a new sibling, this lesson is intensified. (In fact, so special is the relationship of an older sister to her younger brother that in order to facilitate his integration into the community, Steven Feld, an anthropologist studying Bosavi music, was introduced to the community by Schieffelin as her younger brother. The Kaluli welcomed him warmly as her sibling.)

As will be elaborated later, sharing plays a critical role in Bosavi social life. For any Kaluli to say, "I have none" is such a basic strategy that it is a named kind of talk (*gesema,* "make one feel sorrow or pity") and usually results in the receipt of whatever goods were lacking. Saying this conveys to the potential donor, "You have something I don't; I want it, and have rightful claim to it; you must give me some, while feeling sorry I have none." This basic mode of expression is elaborated in a boy's relationship with his older sister, as he is taught explicitly the proper whining and begging appeal with which to approach her.

"Hardening" Language and Behavior

It is recognized that all children—not just boys—are naturally dependent when they are small. Children, it seems, are always hungry; they beg and whine for food endlessly. Adults feel pity at such plaintive appeals and children are never denied.

But children cannot continue indefinitely in this vein. They are thought to beg and whine "naturally"; they must learn other important forms of communication socially. This they learn through lessons in language.

Reciprocity and sharing are the anchors of Kaluli life, and it is important that children learn to participate in a variety of important social exchanges. It is through learning appropriate language that children become participants in all varieties of social exchange. Although they may start out as helpless, by the time they are 3 years old, children are expected to be able to join in reciprocity—to be able to give as well as receive, and to ask and offer with the proper words.

Babies are thought of as "soft." They are unable to understand what is said around them, they have no control over their bodies' movements or functions; they are loose and "floppy." Children's early physical and mental development parallel one another; both are conceptualized as "firming up." They must not only become more physically sturdy and socially assertive, but must also "firm up" their language and be taught to be articulate members of their speech community. The process of a child's mind and body maturing together is called "hardening." When Schieffelin, raising her own small child among the Kaluli, asked for some indicators that such a process was in fact taking place, she was told that sometimes one can count a child's teeth as a marker of developmental stage; teeth allow for more exact speech.

"Hardening" of children puts them in control of themselves and others. Mothers actively guide their children in language use that will "harden" them. They tell their toddlers what to say and how to say it in "hard" language. Asking for something in the child's "natural" language of whining and cajoling must be supplanted by the hard way of asking for what one needs. This is important preparation for a life based on sharing and exchange. Once a child can use "hard" language to ask, then others may do the same and ask the child to share with them. Thus, a child can be drawn into the important activity of sharing with others in the household. The aim of socialization, therefore, is not only to "harden" them physically and mentally; once they have been "hardened" linguistically, they can be responsible members of the community.

The qualities of "hard" and "soft" are ones that go beyond the realm of childhood development. The world was once a "soft" place, until the mud was stamped on and made hard. A "hard" man is one who is strong and outspoken—who possesses the skill of using "hard" language.

In song and ceremony, key elements of Kaluli culture, a successful performance is one that brings the audience to tears. To have this facility in singing and composition is to "harden" the song, and only a "hardened" performance is a skillful one.

"Soft" things are likened to weakness and decay. Things that are "soft" can in fact be dangerous, in that they can impede the process of hardening. Children (thought to be themselves "soft") must never eat eggs, which are mushy, or any foods that are yellow, a color that symbolizes frailty and spoilage. They must also avoid the meat of birds whose high-pitched calls are "soft."

→ The Giving and Sharing of Food

The *Muni* Bird

A girl and her younger brother set off to a stream together to catch crayfish; while the girl was soon successful, her brother had made no catch. He whined to his sister, "I have no crayfish," but her reply was that he could not have hers, as it was for their mother. Soon she caught a second but her brother still had none and again whined for hers (and was again refused: it was for father). Upon her third catch her younger brother begged for the crayfish, only to be told it was for their older brother. Shortly after, the young boy caught a tiny shrimp, whose shell he placed on his nose, turning it bright red. As he looked at his hands, which held the meat of the shrimp, they became red wings. His older sister, frightened at her brother's transformation into a bird, begged him not to fly away. His reply was only the high, mournful cry of the *muni* bird he had become, as he flew off. Weeping, his sister called to him to take the crayfish she had caught, take them all, eat them all, but his song only continued; crying, he sang that he had no sister and he was hungry (Feld 1990).

The giving and sharing of food is perhaps the most fundamental theme in Kaluli interpersonal relations. It promotes friendship and familiarity; it is a vehicle for showing fondness.

Food is an avocation, an interest beyond mere survival. At times when he has no chores that need accomplishing, a man will stroll to his gardens to check the growth of his fruits, or make some other observation about the gathering of grubs or other food preparation.

Food is one of the primary ways of relating to children. They can be calmed, made unafraid of new faces, and shown affection all by the offer of food. Even as little as a day after their birth, Kaluli babies will be taken to the forest for several days' fishing and grub gathering. Newborns will be fed these gathered treats to make them strong, as well as to welcome them into this world and urge them not to return to the place from which they came. Such sharing of food with a baby allows a child's father and other family members to forge the crucial bond made by feeding which would otherwise be exclusive to the baby and breast-feeding mother.

This sets in motion the lifelong Kaluli pattern of sharing food as a form of sharing affection. A small piece of meat or portion of salt is an unequivocal declaration of feeling from one unmarried adolescent to another, and the exclamation, "He gave me pork!" is a heartfelt expression of the depth of loss felt after the death of a friend (Schieffelin 2005:47).

Sharing of food is the expected norm. When one family within the longhouse cooks, it is understood that all who are hungry will have some. Likewise, when one is in need of extra shoots to plant in a garden, or food at mealtime, it is expected that one will be provided for. This is especially true when the food in question is a delicacy, such as game meat.

At times when food is not, or cannot be, shared, Kaluli manners dictate that it should be consumed discreetly. Even if there is no greedy intent, excluded individuals are to be sheltered from any offense this might engender. For example, men eating fish of a kind taboo to their wives and children will be considerate enough to do so out of the sight of their families.

Anthropologist Edward Schieffelin, at the beginning of his years among the Kaluli, found that when he could enlist no aid from individuals for even double the expected wages, he could entice them to help for a cup of rice or a tin of meat. He reminds us that this interest in food does not derive from the lack of it.

The importance of food is found in its use as a focus of social relations. Schieffelin (2005) explains:

> I became aware of this as soon as I entered a longhouse on the plateau for the first time. I sat down wearily on the edge of the men's sleeping platform and was pulling leeches out of my socks when a man approached with a blackened, loaf-shaped packet in his hand. He broke off a piece and handed me a chalky-looking substance covered with grayish, rubbery skin. There was a pause while the people of the longhouse watched to see what I would do. Reluctantly, I took a bite. The flavor was strongly reminiscent of plaster of paris. "*Nafa?*" ("Good?") asked one of my hosts hopefully, using one of the few Kaluli words I knew at the time. "*Nafa,*" I answered when I could get some saliva back in my mouth. "Ah," said my host, looking around to the others. They relaxed. Having eaten sago, I was established as a fellow creature. (p. 46)

Kaluli do not share food because of the obligations of a relationship as much as to solidify and actualize the relationship through the giving of food. As Schieffelin (2005:63) explains, "it is through giving and sharing food that the relationship becomes socially real." In fact, the true definition of a mother, for the Kaluli, is less the woman who gives birth to a child as the one who feeds a child. By extension, if a woman feeds a child over some period of time her children "become" that child's siblings.

In the myth of the boy who became a *muni* bird, told on pages 131–132, we can identify several of what have now become familiar Kaluli themes—the sharing of food, the responsibility of a sister to her brother, the opposing postures of pleading boys and nurturing girls, and birds and their sad sounds.

A young boy, plaintive and whining in an appropriate manner, asks his older sister for what among the Kaluli should be his due; denying a child food is unthinkable. For an older sister to deny food, three times, to her younger brother runs counter to the most basic Kaluli social norms. As the younger brother is denied food by his older sister, he ceases to be her brother; even more—he is, in fact, no longer a person at all.

Birth and death, illness and health, mourning and joy all have mandates and taboos revolving around foodstuffs. The reason given for the Kaluli's appropriation of food as the ultimate vehicle for constructing social relationships and expressing affection is that food is the cornerstone of life. If food shows affection, then what does it mean to go hungry? It means more than an empty belly: it means loneliness.

Religion and Expressive Culture

The Unseen World

All that cannot be seen is a very real part of Kaluli life. The forest is thick and hides many things from the eyes, but is full of sound. The skittering flight and screech of a bird tells you of someone approaching as precisely as catching sight of the visitor does. Morning is not sunrise, but birdsong. Evening is not dusk, but cicadas. Schieffelin (2005) was unable to convey to a Kaluli friend the kind of bird whose name he wanted to know, however detailed his report of its appearance. But when he remembered the rattle of its wings and crumpled a piece of paper in description, the bird was immediately recognized.

These sounds are not merely sounds. When a Kaluli draws attention to the mournful call of a pigeon, saying that it is a little child calling for its mother, it may in fact be just that. It is not only that the bird's call sounds that way; there are spirits that live unseen, and indeed the soul of a child may call for its mother. (It is not unusual that birds and their sounds are prime examples of the importance to the Kaluli of what is heard. They hold a prominent place in Kaluli life, as we will see.)

There are people in the unseen world who are called with a term meaning "shadow" or "reflection." In this unseen world every person has a shadow. Shadows of men are wild pigs; shadows of women are cassowaries. These shadows lead their own lives in the unseen world, roaming the forests. Should the shadow be hurt, the person would suffer too. If the shadow is killed, it means death for its Kaluli counterpart.

Spirits of the dead also live in this unseen world, along with spirits who have never had a human life. These are not fearful sorts of spirits; on the contrary, they might once have been friends or relatives. Unlike other New Guinea peoples, the Kaluli think it impossible that the dead would bear the living any ill will.

There are large invisible longhouses on Mt. Bosavi that are home to another sort of spirit, quite different from the spirits of the dead. As humans have spirit reflections that are wild pigs and cassowaries, so these "people" have the reciprocal spirit; their shadows are the wild pigs and cassowaries that live in Bosavi. These shadows are not evil, but they are responsible for dangerous thunderstorms.

There is, however, a third kind of spirit, which lives in certain well-known areas of the land and whose anger can only be prevented by taking certain precautions. These shadows are dangerous, and may send foul weather, sickness, and even death.

Mediums and Witches

It is through mediums that Kaluli have knowledge of the unseen world. Men who have married spirit women in a dream gain access to this world when they have a child with their spirit wife. As the medium sleeps he leaves his body behind and wanders the unseen world. Once he has gone, spirits can enter his body and use his mouth to speak to the living.

Such seances are exciting occasions for Kaluli who wish to speak to departed loved ones. They are eager to learn what animal form friends and relatives have taken in the unseen world, inquire if they have enough to eat, and ask advice about curing the sick and locating lost property. They also petition their help to identify the *seis,* witches who live among them in the community.

Every Kaluli death, whatever the outward cause may appear to be (old age, illness, an accident), is caused by a *sei,* a term used to describe both an evil spirit and the person whom the spirit inhabits. *Seis* are usually men, but sometimes women, who have evil spirits lodged in their hearts about which they themselves may be unaware. While they sleep, the shadow creatures that dwell within them stalk the night for prey. *Seis* typically attack only strangers, but hunger or anger can cause them to turn on their own kin.

Although the *seis* are generally unseen, some people on their deathbed or with particular abilities have in fact seen them, and describe them as hideous. Their attacks leave sickness and disabilities that are often as invisible as they are: a painful, distended belly contains unseen stones; legs that cannot move have been amputated by the *sei,* but can still be seen. When the victim is fully compromised, the *sei* will pull out the victim's heart, killing him. Once the prey is dead, the *sei* will finish eating the rest of the body. This is evidenced by a corpse's ongoing decomposition and eventual disappearance.

Death and Afterlife

At death, a person's spirit is freed from the still body and retreats to the forest. There it begins a journey along a river, which to the spirit is a wide westward path, only to arrive at an enormous bonfire where it burns until finding deliverance in another spirit. This rescuer carries the burnt soul back to its own spirit longhouse, attending healing ceremonies along the way until the restoration is complete. Finally, the two are married. After this union, the newly departed will assume a new form and will resemble any other wild creature in the forest. Loved ones will not see it again but may look forward to conversation and advice through a medium.

Traditional mortuary practices have been outlawed by the government, which now requires that Kaluli bury bodies in a cemetery. Prior to this edict, issued in 1968, the body would be placed in a hammock outside the longhouse, with fires lit around it. Mourners would come for several days; afterward the body was removed to a small structure built near the longhouse, where it would decompose. Small possessions treasured by the deceased would be placed there with him or her, as sentimental reminders. These were not meant to travel to the afterlife with their former owner; what use would a wild pig in the forest, or a bird soon to live in a treetop, have for a necklace or bow and arrow? As soon as only bones remained, they would be gathered into a net bag and placed under the eaves of the longhouse front porch.

The children and spouse of the deceased were required to follow several taboos established for mourners; often others did so too, simply out of affection. If a woman has gathered food to eat with another before her own death, her intended companion might refuse to eat it, sad that they could not share it together as they had planned. One man gave up breadfruit upon his brother's death because it had been his brother's favorite food (Schieffelin 2005).

➔ Story, Song, and Ceremony

Songs of Birds, Sounds of Tears

Steven Feld was an anthropology student making a living as a jazz musician while he pondered the question of returning to school to complete his degree. At the home of his friends, anthropologists Edward and Bambi Schieffelin, he heard Kaluli music and was smitten. Deciding to merge his musical and anthropological interests, he went to Bosavi with the Schieffelins and studied sound—in the performance of poetry reading, song, and weeping—as a symbolic system.

Kaluli myth and music were the vehicles for his understanding of the way Kaluli relate to their world. Many Kaluli stories are about birds and their connection with sadness, often because of the sorrowful nature of their calls. As Feld listened to such stories, he began to reflect upon similar associations in his own musical culture, especially American blues and jazz. He recalled "literary and musical imagery, such as the common use of the mournful sounds of the whippoorwill in poetry and songs about sadness and love . . . associating a bird of the night with minor or descending pitches, sad sounds, blacks, the South, and the beginning of instrumental blues" (1990:23). Feld found a theme present in music and folklore in many diverse places. He began then to regard the themes woven through Kaluli myth and the sounds repeated in Kaluli music as "expressive embodiments of basic Kaluli concepts of sentiment and appeal" (p. 24).

Birds and their music are for the Kaluli, who are avid bird-watchers, metaphors for their own society. It is most often birds that become the "spirit reflections" of the dead. Skillful at identifying birds by their sounds, Kaluli analogize the particular pitches and melodies of different birds with different segments of their population (as when the whining and whimpering complaints of children are likened to that of the dove, whose call is said to be like that of "a hungry child calling for its mother").

Once Feld discovered the centrality of birds and their songs to Kaluli culture, he proceeded to collect and organize all the information he could about the birds in the Bosavi environment, and the ways in which the Kaluli regarded them. This endeavor inadvertently taught him more than he anticipated; he expected to discover Kaluli notions of bird classification, perception, and symbolism. What he learned instead grew out of the sheer frustration of his Kaluli informant who, after hours of imitating bird calls and nesting behaviors, blurted out, "Listen—to you they are birds, to me they are voices in the forest." Feld realized that he could not continue to impose his own system of classification on the Kaluli experience of these important "voices"; that the Kaluli understanding of birds and their songs is "based on certain fundamental premises about the world, such as the belief that things have a visible and invisible aspect; that sounds and behaviors have an outside, an inside, and an underneath; or that human relationships are reflected in the ecology and natural order of the forest" (1990:45).

Weeping conveys an emotional message from one person to another, which is very much connected to singing. In response to sorrow or loss, Kaluli may begin to cry. But feelings of disappointment, frustration, or self-pity may also lead Kaluli to burst into song.

Weeping and singing are very much bound up together. There are many "wept songs," usually about a lost loved one. Men and women have different socially dictated modes of weeping. Men begin with a high-pitched wail, which turns into an imitation of the short-burst call of the *muni* bird. They cry for a short period of time and stop abruptly. Weeping is a more common expressive form among women. Although both men and women cry similarly in response to a moving song, it is women who are likely to blend weeping and singing into the sung text of a "wept song." As Feld (1990:33) explains, "while sadness moves both men and women to weeping, it is weeping that moves women to song."

Out of the attempt to preserve the musical heritage of the Kaluli, Feld has joined with other musicians to produce a recording of Bosavi music, *Voices of the Rainforest.* Profits from its sale benefit the Bosavi People's Fund, set up to provide financial aid in the struggle to maintain Kaluli cultural survival in the face of threats to their rainforest environment.

The *Gisaro*

The usual occasions for Kaluli formal ceremonies are those they celebrate with neighboring longhouses, most often marriages or large gifts of meat. Pig feasts and similar large events take months to prepare.

Underlying these community events is the theme of reciprocity and exchange. After a particularly complex and moving ceremony, guests may be inspired to host a return event in their own longhouse community in great haste. Schieffelin (2005) reports witnessing a dance performed to ward off sickness. Guest dancers from another village came to the host community, singing throughout the night, and performing so poignantly that it moved many to tears. As soon as the dancers departed, elders called in kin from other longhouses and within two days had staged a ceremony at the dancers' village that (they were proud to note) caused all assembled to weep.

Of all the ceremonies performed in Kaluli life, none is as important as the *Gisaro*. It is presented as part of a larger ceremony (such as a wedding or pork prestation) and performed inside a host longhouse by guest dancers who begin at dusk and continue until dawn.

The cast is assembled by sending out requests to those who might like to participate, and it is rare that there are not enough men who respond to the call. For weeks before the event, *Gisaro* dancers compose songs and prepare elaborate costumes. The intended effect of the *Gisaro* performance is to overwhelm the listeners with powerful emotion. To this end, it is imperative to maintain the element of surprise, as to the identity of the dancers, pattern of makeup and costume, and content of the songs.

While the performers are rehearsing at least a dozen new songs and dances, the hosts are preparing food. On the day of the feast, dancers wait for dark and enter the longhouse, which is lit with the torches soon to be a central part of the *Gisaro*.

Gisaro dancers are painted and costumed alike, so as to be indistinguishable from one another. A rested dancer can thus replace an exhausted one, allowing the dancing and singing to continue unabated. The songs are heartbreaking—and purposely so. They tell of people and places loved and lost. The audience hangs on every word, their sorrow building until they can no longer contain themselves. Sobbing and wailing fills the longhouse, but the *Gisaro* performers continue, seemingly oblivious to the anguish they are causing, never showing any trace of emotion on their faces.

Amid their wailing and stamping, hosts angered by the pain inflicted on them by the wrenching *Gisaro* songs jump up and grab the huge resin torches. These they jam into the backs and necks of the dancers, searing their flesh. Still they continue, singing and dancing, as the enraged and grieving hosts continue to burn the dancers. The wailing and burning continues throughout the night. The visiting dancers inflict emotional pain on their hosts; the hosts, in turn, visit physical pain on the dancers (Houseman 1998).

Before the ceremony, dancers coat their bodies with sweet-smelling vegetable resin whose scent mingles with the burning flesh. It is thought to afford the skin some protection from the burns and diminish the pain somewhat, but most dancers suffer extensive second-degree burns across their backs, upper arms, and shoulders. The skin will sometimes blister and peel off during the dance; otherwise, it sloughs off in a day or two. Dancers generally spend the first ten days after their ordeal convalescing; after three or four weeks they have healed.

Edward Schieffelin (2005) details in his ethnography of the Kaluli the ways in which the *Gisaro* can be understood as the dramatic embodiment and crystallization of the major premises on which Kaluli culture is built. *Gisaro* is a way for them to understand and express their view of the world, the loss and sorrow contained within it, their link with those now invisible to them. He concludes, "the Kaluli [feel] that the forces of growth and life are generated in oppositions, and it is with this, as a life condition, with all its beauty, exuberance, tragedy, and violence, that they try to come to terms in *Gisaro*" (p. 223).

→ Kaluli Today

"Before" and "Now": Modernity and the Language of Missionization

Bambi Schieffelin (2002) reports that in 1961, a brochure printed by the Unevangelized Fields Mission (UFM; now the Asia Pacific Christian Mission, APCM) described the Kaluli as "stone age savages . . . primitive people [who] are half man, half animal" (p. S5). A fundamentalist group interpreting the Bible literally, they believed there was no time to waste in introducing Christianity to Mt. Bosavi. In the 1970s, missionaries built an airstrip, church, elementary school, clinic, and trade store. Missionized Papua New Guineans served as teachers, pastors, and nurses. Mission staff conducted daily church services and Bible study groups

(Schieffelin 2000). By the 1990s, dramatic change had been wrought, altering the ways in which Kaluli "interpret events, establish facts, convey opinions, and imagine themselves" (Schieffelin 2000:294).

As we have seen earlier in the chapter, a sense of place is central to traditional Kaluli life. Place-names were the mooring for ceremonies, significant events, and interpersonal experiences (Schieffelin 2005). Feld's (1990, 1996) investigation of Kaluli music describes the ways in which events and relationships are located in the places recalled in song. In her study of childhood socialization, Bambi Schieffelin (1990) notes the ways in which place-names link people to places, forging identity. Thus, it was place and not time that was used to invoke remembrance. Missionization demanded the adoption of European-based time. Bells, clocks, calendars, and schedules organized the mission's daily activities. But, as Schieffelin (2002) notes, "[t]he mission effort to control time was not just a practical strategy but a way of asserting hierarchic power and governance. By changing time the mission hoped to transform persons by changing their daily activities and the ways in which they thought and talked about them" (p. S7).

The introduction of European-based time allowed missionaries to construct the crucial opposition of "before" (the past) and "now" (the present). "Before" was the time prior to the arrival of missionaries, and the newly introduced word was used "to construct the past as amoral, chaotic, irrelevant" and a stumbling block to salvation, the fundamentalist goal for the Kaluli (Schieffelin 2002:S15). "Now" began with 1970s mission contact and continues through the present day. These new categories moved Kaluli from their traditional relationship to time and place to a fundamentalist orientation, "one with no need for a Bosavi past, a present charged with change, and a future that depended on choices made in the present" (Schieffelin 2002:S6). Kaluli Christians who embraced both the vocabulary of missionaries and the new temporal focus reshaped not only their language, but their identities as well. They were set apart from their non-Christian kin in such a way as to mark what Schieffelin (2002) identifies as the beginning of Bosavi social stratification. Traditional ways of constructing and marking relationships were discouraged by missionaries, who considered even *thoughts* about the times "before" to be a threat to conversion and belief. One aim of missionization was to align the Kaluli with the global anticipation of the Second Coming. In order to accomplish this, Bosavi peoples must share the same sense of time with other Christians, a change that would separate them from their unique Kaluli selves. As Schieffelin (2002:S16) explains, "[w]hat mattered was only whether they were saved; that would become their only meaningful identity."

Many indigenous peoples confront modernity in the form of Christianity and are challenged by its reliance more on speech than on ritual (Robbins 2001). In his work with a group in the New Guinea Highlands, anthropologist Joel Robbins (2001) reports the local population's frustration over just this aspect. On many occasions, he was told "God is nothing but talk" (p. 904). As a linguistic anthropologist, Schieffelin pays particular attention to the ways in which the introduction of new vocabularies and particular verbal expressions were used to accomplish missionary goals. She became aware of the pattern of language change while preparing a dictionary of English and two local languages.

The project began in the mid-1970s. In the mid-1990s, she and her collaborators were rechecking earlier entries with Kaluli assistants, who consistently claimed that many words were wrong, or not understandable, or no longer used. The team found it puzzling that they would have gotten so many words "wrong," and in an attempt to solve the mystery they presented their original texts—many of which had been provided by the fathers of those very Kaluli assistants. Their memories jogged, the assistants agreed that the translations were, in fact, correct. The most significant discovery, however, was *which* words had been dismissed by the Kaluli. Words that had been used in myths and traditional stories, employed in curing ceremonies, or associated with witchcraft were all reported to be no longer in use in the 1990s. Certain categories of emotions—for example, "anger"—were also diminished. When asked for an explanation, Schieffelin was told that "Christians no longer became angry, and therefore such words were no longer necessary" (2002:S9). The significance of this linguistic change went beyond the compilation of a dictionary. As Schieffelin points out, the loss of particular words in the Kaluli language "indicated the extent to which an alternative view of the Bosavi world . . . was being refashioned in its ways of speaking" (2002:S9).

Thus, these changes were representative of broader changes, especially the ways in which Kaluli had accepted the fundamentalist teachings of the primitive "before" and the enlightened "now" (which would prepare Kaluli for the inevitable Biblical future). Schieffelin (2002) notes that "in order to catch up, people who were 'behind the times' were required to detach themselves from their particular past. One way to do this was to make it impossible to speak about a past that increasingly had negative connotations; the erasure of words seemed like one way to do it." This, coupled with the introduction of new ideas about time, allowed the missionaries to accomplish their goal of Kaluli conversion, reorganizing both social and cosmological spheres. The Kaluli were told that the whole world awaited the Second Coming, and part of their preparation for salvation must be to join in keeping time on a world clock. As Schieffelin (2000) concludes, "under conditions of rapid social change, every language choice is a social choice that has critical links to the active construction of culture" (p. 323).

Logging, Land, and Loss

The Kaluli live in an area of extraordinary natural richness. The region surrounding Mt. Bosavi is an expanse of 2 million acres of pristine rainforest. It is no wonder that birds and their music are so central to Kaluli life: half of all New Guinea's bird species live in the Kikori river basin, and of the 800 species (including dozens of different birds of paradise), nearly 300 are found nowhere else in the world. More than 200 mammals, scores of brilliantly colored giant butterflies, and spectacular orchids, unique to the area, contribute to the remarkable diversity of the territory.

In 2009, a team of biologists from Great Britain, the United States, and Papua New Guinea were the first to explore the nearly two-mile-wide crater of Mt. Bosavi. In it they found a stunning array of new species: previously unknown frogs, fish, bats, and a giant rodent they named the Bosavi woolly rat. The size of a large housecat, it is believed to live nowhere but in the volcanic crater. Previous expeditions discovered fifty new spiders, striped geckos, tiny chirping tree frogs, and several new species of plants.

The Kaluli are among twenty or so groups—totaling some 60,000 people—who rely on the resources of the forests and waterways. Concern for the land is growing as commercial logging and mining industries threaten its flora and fauna and pollute water sources. Gold, copper, oil, and gas are among the most sought-after resources. Of particular concern are Malaysian logging corporations that, having exhausted timber stands in Indonesia, have set their sights eastward, toward New Guinea. As the largest of these companies moves steadily northward toward Mt. Bosavi's foothills, sacred sites are being destroyed. In an attempt to counter this encroachment, Kaluli and their Kasua neighbors, along with anthropologist Francois Brunois and the World Wildlife Fund, have established several wildlife management areas to protect and sustain the land while allowing depleted plants and animals to recover.

Anthropologist Michael Wood writes about Bosavi peoples' experience of loss as their land is transformed by industrial logging. Like the Kaluli, the Kamula, twenty miles to the south, have a profound relationship to place. They invest their land with personal identity and see the "appearance" of their ancestors there. In explaining the consequences of the logging industry's encroachment, one Kamula man described the loss of his family's presence in the land: "These will disappear. When they have disappeared I will look. Where is my father's appearance? Where is my mother's appearance? There is nothing" (Wood 2004:251).

Ethnographer Stuart Kirsch has written extensively about the consequences of pollution resulting from gold and copper mining in Papua New Guinea. He notes that "[t]he theme of loss has echoes throughout the indigenous world, often in association with damages to and/or displacement from their land" (2001:167).

Citing its dramatic landscape and unparalleled wildlife, UNESCO is working toward having the Bosavi territory designated as a World Heritage site, which will provide not only international protection, but also involve the local population—a partnership crucial to addressing the threats to their environment and ways of life. Anthropologist Deborah Rose (in Kirsch 2001) offers a poignant observation: land that is no longer tended to by its indigenous caretakers is land that has "a quality of deep loneliness" (p. 168).

→ For Further Discussion

The sharing of food is at the center of Kaluli social relations. Is this something you have seen as important in other societies as well? How is food used to create and solidify bonds in your own experience? What sorts of cultural messages can be transmitted through the giving and taking of food? Among the Kaluli, food shows affection; thus, to go hungry is to be lonely. What are some of the meanings of hunger in your society?

CHAPTER 9

The Nuer

Cattle and Kinship in Sudan

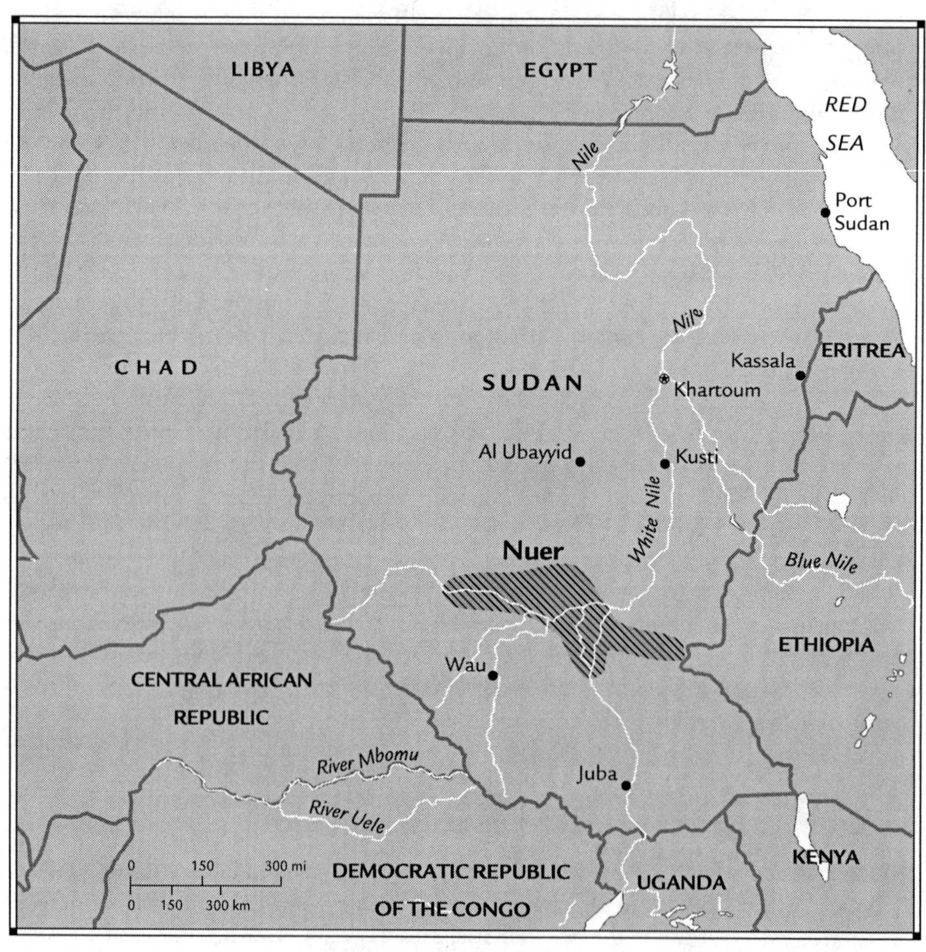

Location of the Nuer in southern Sudan.

⇢ The Beginning

Kwoth is everywhere. He is like wind; he is like air. He falls in the rain and roars in the thunder. The rainbow is his necklace. We are like little ants in his sight. *Ne walka*—in the beginning—there was a tamarind tree in the western land. Her name was Lic, and she was the mother. *Kwoth* created us to drop from her branches like ripened fruit. *Ne walka*—in the beginning—we were as the fruit of a tamarind tree.

⇢ Introduction and History

Sudan is the largest country in Africa, its area encompassing nearly 1 million square miles. It lies in the northeastern part of the continent and is a land of widely differing geography. In the north, it is covered with vast deserts; grassy palms fill the central region; and steamy jungles and swamps lie to the south. The Nile River is by far Sudan's most important geographic feature. Most of southern Sudan consists of a flood plain formed by its branches, with dense, junglelike vegetation covering much of the region. Mountain ranges rise along the borders shared with Uganda, Kenya, and Ethiopia. Rainfall averages from thirty-two to fifty-five inches annually. Wild animals, including gazelles, giraffes, lions, leopards, and elephants, roam the south. Along the Nile's branches live hippopotamuses and crocodiles.

The Nuer refer to themselves as *Naath*—"the people"—and are the second largest ethnic group in southern Sudan (Holtzman 2000), numbering more than a million (Hutchinson 1996) and living in the open savannah and swamps that line both sides of the Nile. The Nuer hold a unique place in the history of anthropology. Ethnographer E. E. Evans-Pritchard, conducting extensive fieldwork in the 1930s, provided several volumes of work that both examined Nuer life in rich detail and set the standard for subsequent inquiry. Perhaps second only to Malinowski's earlier work among the Trobriand Islanders (see Chapter 14), Evans-Pritchard's volumes about the Nuer have provided ethnographic data for analysis and reanalysis that have situated the Nuer at the heart of anthropological discourse (Hutchinson 1996). Anthropologists working among the Nuer today chronicle both the enormous sociopolitical changes that have occurred as well as those values, traditions, and local practices that endure.

Evans-Pritchard observed long ago that Nuer land, cycling seasonally as it does through a state of parched grass or soggy swamp, might appear to hold little value to an outsider. The Nuer themselves, however, held a very different view. "Nuer," Evans-Pritchard reports, "think that they live in the finest country on earth" (1940:51). As herders, they indeed assess their land correctly. Their soil is made of thick clay, which cracks in the sun during droughts. These deep grooves are soaked and filled in the rainy season, cradling enough water to allow certain species of grasses to thrive even during the driest of seasons, providing pasture for the cattle. During times of intense flooding, sandy areas in somewhat higher elevations offer refuge.

Rainfall and flooding from the rivers that cross their lands provide the Nuer with surface water and abundant grasses, which, at their peak, reach shoulder high. However, the seasonal changes from wet to dry and back again are sudden and often cataclysmic. Soggy swampland is rendered sere in a short time, as the blazing sun quickly evaporates the surface water from the clay soil. This, coupled with insufficient rainfall, may result in a shortage of pastureland.

This cycle of flooding and drought results in an environmental system that steers the direction of Nuer social and economic life, as we shall see.

ECOLOGY

Subsistence

Traditional Nuer economy is a mixture of pastoralism and horticulture. Such a mixed economy is dictated by their environment, because neither strategy alone would be sufficient to provide for their needs or those of their cattle. Of the two strategies, pastoralism is the one favored both by the environment and by the Nuer themselves. As Evans-Pritchard remarks, "the environmental bias coincides with the bias of their interest" (1940:57).

Although the Nuer might be able to rely solely on pastoralism were it not for the threat of certain cattle diseases, the balance in their economic strategy could never shift such that horticulture would predominate. Climate, flooding, and the flatness of the land result in an inability to cultivate most Central African food plants. Their staple crop is millet, consumed in the form of porridge and beer, and they supplement this with a small amount of maize and an even lesser quantity of beans. Some tobacco is encouraged to grow under the eaves of their huts, and gourds can send their vines up along the fences of cattle corrals. One of the richest agricultural areas is along the banks of the Baro River, which marks the border between Ethiopia and Sudan. Contemporary conflict across this border is exacerbated by the abundant crops of tobacco and maize that grow even during the dry season, watered by the river (Hutchinson 1996).

Millet's hardiness is such that the Nuer can reap two harvests per year, but even so it will not survive too much standing water, and thus gardens have to be established on higher ground. If the elevation is such that water from the gardens may be lost running down the slope, small dams are often constructed as a solution.

Although millet is able to weather the harsh climate once it has been established, the process of it taking hold initially can be undependable. Even a short drought can cause new shoots to wither; unexpected rains can beat small plants into the ground or wash them away. Weather is not the only environmental threat to crops. Evans-Pritchard (1940:78) reports having witnessed the toll taken by such events as swarms of locusts, unfettered grazing by ostriches and antelopes, and a parade of elephants stomping across the seedling beds.

The Nuer practice neither crop rotation nor fallowing, and neither fertilize nor irrigate. Instead, they move on to another site when the land is depleted.

Moving with the Seasons

The alternating floods and drought make it impossible for the Nuer to live in one location year-round. Floods send Nuer and their herds to higher ground; drought forces them out again. Those foodstuffs provided by their cattle—meat and milk products—must be supplemented by fish and grain. Millet is best sown inland; the rivers where fish are abundant are far away from these inland sites. During the rainy season, cattle must be moved to protected ground, because standing in sodden land quickly results in hoof disease. It is for this reason that villages are constructed on the highest ground available. However, once the rains cease, these elevated sites, selected precisely because they were the highest (and thus, driest) locations, soon must be abandoned for sites closer to pools and lakes in order to secure adequate water supplies. The vicissitudes of finding water are echoed in the search for vegetation. As they move seasonally, Nuer seek out both pastureland and drinking water, driving their cattle to locations where they know both will be available. Their movement across the vast plains is never haphazard in nature, but rather aimed directly toward the most succulent grasslands. It is in this way that changing water supplies and vegetational growth determine both the time and direction of Nuer movement. When the rains begin again, they can return to their villages.

SETTLEMENTS

Nuer are forced to build villages for protection against the flooding rains (and mosquitoes) and to practice horticulture. They are driven out of these villages into migratory camps to escape drought and to fish.

The aim in choosing a village site is to secure enough room for building homesteads, planting gardens, and grazing cattle. Most villages are built on elevated mounds, above the floodline and the mosquitoes breeding in the standing water, which stretch for a mile or two in length. In front of these sandy ridges there is land for grazing; gardens are cultivated in the back. Open ground is preferable to wooded areas, as it provides better protection to the cattle (from insect pests and predators in the woodlands) and because millet fares better in an open environment. Construction is of wood, and termites are generally better avoided in these open stretches of ground.

A typical Nuer homestead consists of a hut and a cattle barn. Families move from one section of the village to another, especially if there have been quarrels or pastures are exhausted. Huts and barns last about five years before they need to be rebuilt. After a decade or so, the gardens and pastures are no longer usable, and the entire village community may seek out a new site.

Camps, the Nuer settlements in the dry season, consist of flimsier structures, built close to the water source and oriented so that their backs are to the wind and their fronts face the cattle. These shelters can be erected in a few hours, using grassy material plastered with dung.

Throughout the dry season and in years when crops fail or herds fall victim to disease, it is fishing that sustains the Nuer. Opportunities to exploit the rivers, teeming with a variety of fish species, are as significant a factor as pasture and water when Nuer choose their campsites.

Nuer have no need of complex fishing techniques because the rise of the rivers during floods carries huge numbers of fish downstream, depositing them into streams and lagoons where they are easily speared. At nightfall, dams are constructed and fishers wait downstream by firelight. In a single night, as many as a hundred fish may be speared. As the dry season advances, fish are trapped in pools, the outlets of which have dried up and receded. It is a simple matter for the Nuer to stand along the pool's edge and spear all the fish within. Nuer can rarely see the fish they spear, but the sheer numbers of the prey yield adequate results even when spears are flung into the water at random.

Although Nuer territory is rich in game, hunting is not a strategy much relied upon. They rarely set out to hunt, pursuing only those gazelle and giraffe who present themselves at the camps. Their herds provide them with meat enough to suit them. Lions may be killed to protect cattle; leopards are valued for their skins, which figure prominently in Nuer social life.

CATTLE

"Their Social Idiom Is a Bovine Idiom"

Cattle are the focus of Nuer life. They depend on the herds for their very existence; they delight in caring for them; and their love for cattle and zeal for acquiring them are at the core of Nuer culture. Cattle are the thread that runs through Nuer institutions, language, rites of passage, politics, economy, and allegiances. Foreigners are classified in two ways: *Bar* (people with few cattle) and *Jur* (people with no cattle).

Nuer relations with their neighbors are directed in large part by their preoccupation with the herds. They have nothing but disdain for neighboring tribes who own few or no cattle; they have entered into warfare with others solely for the purpose of stealing cattle and pastures. Internecine disputes are most often about cattle, and political divisions follow tribal distribution of pastures and water. Disputes that *result* from cattle are often *settled* with cattle—such conflict often ends in grave injury or death, and cattle are the only acceptable compensation.

Cattle are cared for by groups of families because an individual household cannot protect or herd their cattle alone. In the dry season, when huts are hastily constructed around the cattle *kraal* (corral), one can identify which groups own and care for cattle together. Male household heads are identified as owning the herds, but wives and sons have some rights to their use. Sons marry in order of seniority and are given forty head of cattle when they do. It is not until the stock has been replaced that the next son may marry and take his share. The bond between brothers, forged by co-ownership of cattle, persists even after they have married and started families of their own. The bridewealth paid for a daughter of one's brother is shared among the brothers, and kinship becomes defined in large part by reference to cattle payments. It is as if the transfer of cattle from one individual to another is equivalent to the lines drawn on a genealogy chart (Evans-Pritchard 1940). When cattle are sacrificed, the meat is divided along kinship lines.

Personal names are frequently derived from features of the herd animals. Men are often called by names that refer to the color of a favorite ox; women take names from the cows they milk. When children play in the pastures, they call one another by cattle names; sometimes these names are proper names given at birth and handed down through the generations. Evans-Pritchard remarked that the genealogies he collected during his fieldwork often resembled the cattle inventory of a *kraal* more than a family tree (Evans-Pritchard 1940).

It is not surprising that the centrality of cattle would be reflected in Nuer ritual life. If one endeavors to contact the spirit world, this may be accomplished only through the cattle. Cows are dedicated to spirits—those spirits that are attached to the lineage of the owner, have possessed a living family member, or are the ghosts of ancestors. Thus, when asking about the history of any cow in the herd, one receives information not only about the ways in which that cow links one person to another—having been secured as bridewealth, for example, or as payment for a dispute—but also of the spirit world connections the animal represents. By rubbing ashes on the back of the cow, its owner may contact a spirit and seek its intervention or assistance.

As Evans-Pritchard soon learned, in order to understand the culture of the Nuer, one must first be thoroughly versed in the language of cattle. The complex negotiations surrounding marriage exchange, ritual, and the settlement of disputes were only intelligible once he could decipher the terminology of cattle colors, ages, size, sex, and other features. He laments, "I used sometimes to despair that I never discussed anything with young men but livestock and girls, and even the subject of girls led inevitably to that of cattle" (1940:19). Try though he might, every subject, approached in any way, soon yielded commentary on cows, heifers, oxen, steers, or kids. As he observed, "their social idiom is a bovine idiom"(1940:19).

Cattle are, of course, essential in a more mundane sense as well. Milk and millet are the mainstays of the Nuer diet, and whereas millet rarely lasts through the year, milk can be depended upon as a daily food. A single cow can sustain an entire family when milk is supplemented with fish. Even when the millet crop is abundant, Nuer depend on milk and cheese to make it palatable. Children especially need milk daily, and the Nuer say that children cannot be happy, much less healthy, without a dependable daily source of milk—of which elders will deprive themselves in order to ensure the children's share. When there is milk enough for the children, extra can be made into cheese. If a family cannot secure enough milk for their small children, relatives will unhesitatingly provide a cow, because kinship obligations include caring for the children of one's kin and neighbors. This is never thought to be the sole responsibility of the child's parents.

Because milk is so essential, cows are often judged by the amount of milk they produce, and one cow is never equivalent to another if its milk production is not commensurate. Any Nuer can immediately list, in rank order, the best and worst cows of the herd, paying no attention to those qualities he might cite in his oxen—fatness or color or horn shape—but only those features that promise a good milk cow. Nuer can scrutinize the back and haunches, veins, and bone structure of a cow and predict with great accuracy its lactating capacity.

Their dependence on dairy products directly influences other aspects of Nuer life and social structure. Cattle are not as numerous as they once were, owing largely to disease caused by cattle pests, and this relative shortage prevents the Nuer from leading an exclusively pastoral lifestyle, although this might be their preference. A mixed economy is essential to supplement their diet. As previously mentioned, one family unit often needs to depend on the larger kin group for dairy products, mandating that the basic economic unit for the Nuer must be a larger one than a single household. However, the importance of milk products not only introduces constraints, such as the foregoing, into Nuer daily life, but also provides flexibility. For example, while their need for horticulture prevents them from leading an exclusively nomadic life, their reliance on dairy products does allow them considerable mobility. Milk can be both stored and transported in the form of the dairy cows and is accessible wherever the herd may be. Moreover, since the production of milk depends on water and pastureland, this diet not only permits, but also *requires,* frequent movement.

Although herds are not raised for the purpose of slaughter, meat is important to the Nuer diet and economy as well. Honoring a ghost or spirit, mortuary rites, and marriage ceremonies are all occasions during which barren cows are sacrificed and consumed. (Such rituals are more commonplace in the rainy season, or early into the draught, because the festivities are never complete without beer, brewed from the millet available during these times of year.) Never do Nuer

A Nuer man.

slaughter animals solely because they desire to eat meat. There is the danger of the ox's spirit visiting a curse on any individual who would slaughter it without ritual intent, aiming only to use it for food. Any animal that dies of natural causes is eaten, although Evans-Pritchard notes that when a favorite animal has died, its owner often has to be persuaded to overcome his sorrow and share the meat. On an occasion such as this, the Nuer explain "The eyes and the heart are sad, but the teeth and the stomach are glad" (Evans-Pritchard 1940:26).

In addition to their value as foodstuff and ritual objects, oxen are also items of great prestige. Wealth is defined differently in different places; among the Nuer, it is only cattle that are truly valued in this way (Gross 1992:44). Prestige is derived from the shape, color, size, and form of the oxen, and Nuer will actively intervene in shaping the oxen, beginning at birth. They will manipulate the humps on a newborn ox's back, or train its horns to grow in a certain configuration. Cattle also provide raw materials for the manufacture of leather goods, drums, rugs, clothing, pipes, spears and shields, containers, ornaments, and cutlery. Their dung is used as plaster in construction and burned to provide ashes both for ritual use and also as "toothpaste" and mouthwash. Their urine is used not only for churning cheese, but to wash hands and face.

Sociopolitical Organization

The Nuer have no centralized political leadership. Theirs is a kin-based society, and it is only through an understanding of the kinship organization that one can apprehend the way in which their social system functions.

Evans-Pritchard found the Nuer to be a "deeply democratic" (1956:181) people, with an egalitarian approach to their communal life. It is the obligation of kin to help one another. When one household has a surplus, it is shared with neighbors. Amassing wealth is not an aim. Although a man who owns a large herd of cattle may be envied, his possession of numerous animals does not garner him any special privilege or treatment.

Segmentary Lineage Organization

The Nuer are perhaps best known as the most often cited example of the segmentary lineage organization. Marshall Sahlins (1961), in his classic study of this type of system, describes it as the inevitable result of tribal growth.

Among the Nuer, there are roughly twenty patrilineal clans. Each of these can be divided into maximal lineages, which can in turn be divided into major lineages. These are segmented into minor lineages, which are divided into minimal lineages. A minimal lineage group reckons its descent from one great-grandfather. It is these most minimal groups around which Nuer daily life revolves. There is neither leadership nor formal organization in the higher levels. They are potential connections waiting to be activated should the need arise. In a dispute between different minimal lineages, alliances can be formed by drawing from people related at a higher level. Each side of the conflict can mobilize more and more kin by reaching out to more and more distant kin. Mary Douglas (1966) comments, "[t]he Nuer afford a natural illustration of how people can create and maintain a social structure in the realm of ideas and not primarily, or at all, in the external, physical realm of ceremonial, palaces or courts of justice" (p. 143).

Warfare, Raiding, and Blood-Feuds

In the early nineteenth century, Nuer territory spanned about 8,700 square miles. Their neighbors, the Dinka, held nearly ten times that amount of land. By the end of that century, however, the Nuer had expanded their territory at the expense of the neighboring Dinka. The Nuer cut a wide swath through Dinka territory, in the end increasing their holdings to 35,000 square miles. Dinka culture resembled that of the Nuer in many respects, save the one that seems to have given the Nuer a significant military advantage—the segmentary lineage organization (Evans-Pritchard 1940:240).

The Dinka, who were the first to settle in the Sudan, had no neighbors to defend against, and thus had none of the mechanisms in place to mobilize distant tribal members. Sahlins (1961) suggests that the unique alliance-forming properties of the segmentary lineage system of organization allow its members to raid nearby territories held by groups without the ability to mobilize forces. Relatives are available for defense, too, but it especially allows groups to decide to make the first strike because lineage segments are assured that they can draw reinforcements from other lineages related to them at a higher level of the clan.

The Nuer are a people with a penchant for fighting (Evans-Pritchard 1956), and these disputes frequently end in death. One is unlikely to find an older tribe member without copious evidence of the visits of clubs and spears. An insult is justification for a fight, and the Nuer have been described as easily taking offense. Because there is no formal mechanism for redress if an insult has been hurled, an individual must take it upon himself to seek justice. He issues a challenge to a duel, and the challenge must be accepted. Children are instructed to settle any grievance by fighting, and skill in this endeavor is uniformly admired.

Whereas boys fight one another with spiked bracelets attached to their wrists, men fight those closest to them with clubs. Spears are reserved for use outside the local community, as there is a greater danger for more serious injury or death, and this has the potential to escalate into a blood-feud. After the battle is joined, no onlooker may intervene, and the combat rages until one of the parties is severely injured, at which point they will generally be pulled apart by those gathered around to watch the spectacle.

When the dispute involves men from different villages, however, it generally takes a different form. Spears are the weapons of choice, and every man in both villages is expected to participate. Because such a fight cannot end until there are several dead, Nuer are loath to enter into such a battle lightly. Instead, they will allow the conflict to be mediated by an informal adjudicator, the leopard-skin chief.

The Leopard-Skin Chief

Despite their reluctance to enter into a blood-feud, the Nuer fight often, and homicide is not uncommon as the battles escalate. When a life is taken, there must be compensation. Because the Nuer have no formal system of adjudication, it falls to the holder of an informal ritual office of mediation, the leopard-skin chief (so named for the skin he wears draped about his shoulders as the insignia of his office), to intervene and prevent further bloodshed. Although one advantage of the segmentary lineage organization is its effectiveness in mobilizing allied kin, the ease with which full-scale disruption can escalate is something that must be kept in check. Although the leopard-skin chief has no power to enforce his judgments, his intervention is generally successful.

Part of the leopard-skin chief's effectiveness derives from his status as an outsider to the lineage network. Such an individual is generally a man whose own lineage is not one of the local village. This affords him a more neutral stance, so neither his attempts at mediation nor his judgment about payment of compensation are seen as favoring one side or the other.

Sometimes a leopard-skin chief can step in and encourage de-escalation of a dispute before blood is shed. More often, however, he is sought out after there has already been a murder, and his role is to arrange settlement between the aggrieved lineages, allowing both sides to step back from the battle without admitting defeat and preventing any further bloodshed.

When one man has killed another, he retreats at once to the home of the leopard-skin chief. This is neutral ground for the murderer. While he is in residence there, no kinsmen of the deceased will seek revenge. The leopard-skin chief has the ability to ritually cleanse the slayer, and this begins immediately. A blood-feud resulting in death forges a mysterious bond between the murderer and victim. At the moment of death, blood of the slain passes into the body of the killer, propelled as a sort of dying vengeance (Hutchinson 1996). The murderer must neither eat nor drink until the leopard-skin chief has released the blood of the dead man out of his body, which is accomplished by making several incisions down the length of his arm with a fishing spear. Once this is accomplished, the murderer presents the leopard-skin chief with an animal to sacrifice, and the cleansing is complete.

A man may remain in the sanctuary of a leopard-skin chief's home for quite some time because negotiations cannot begin in earnest until the family of the deceased have completed their mortuary ceremonies and anger has begun to cool. His first attempts at negotiations may be met with some resistance. After ascertaining how many head of cattle the culprit's family are willing to offer as compensation, the chief approaches the victim's kin. It is a point of honor that they refuse this first overture. Negotiations proceed slowly, and generally the injured family begrudgingly accepts the payment—in theory, forty to fifty animals, paid out over the course of several years—when they determine that the chief has made his best offer and is becoming increasingly impatient with their refusals. When at least twenty head of cattle have been paid, the family of the murderer may begin to feel safe, no longer fearful of being ambushed by the enemy family as they walk abroad.

It is the leopard-skin chief who delivers the payment, with the murderer remaining in the asylum of the chief's home until completion of the initial transfer.

Even years after the debt has been paid, there is enmity between the two families. There is official prohibition against the families' eating or drinking together until the entire payment and all accompanying sacrifice are complete. However, in actuality they may choose not to share food for years, or even generations, out of injured feelings. Of this they say, "a bone lies between us." The healing is never really complete, as the murdered man's family is thought ever after "to have war in their hearts" (Evans-Pritchard 1956:154). Hutchinson (1996) confirms the continuing salience of this concept. The lasting enmity after homicide is still explained by saying "a bone exists between them," and Nuer often sum up the hostility of the civil war by referring to "our bone with the Arabs" (p. 110).

Contemporary Nuer, drawn into civil war, have added guns to their armamentarium and see a fundamental difference between the two. A spear is an extension of the person who throws it, gaining its power from the thrust of a strong arm. A gun's might is its own, owing nothing to the person who aims and shoots it. Over time, the Nuer asked whether these essential differences changed the relationship of the slayer to the slain. Killing someone with a spear left no doubt in the intention or identity of the perpetrator. Bullets—referred to as a "gun's calves"—could be fired accidentally. In a group battle, how might one be sure of the identity of either the victim or perpetrator, who, in a spear fight enter into a relationship of the "bone"? The numerous social and spiritual consequences that traditionally followed such an act—pollution, social obligations, and atonement expiated by the leopard-skin chief—were seriously challenged, raising troubling questions about the definition of homicide, the meaning of death itself, and moral responsibilities of the Nuer involved (Hutchinson 1996).

Religion and Expressive Culture

The Nuer speak of *kwoth* (spirit) as the creator, as a father and judge, as a guiding force and recipient of their prayers. Evans-Pritchard (1956) suggested that this overarching concept could be roughly analogized to a Western notion of "God." However, there are also two other categories of supernatural beings that figure prominently in Nuer religious thought. These are the "spirits of the above" and "spirits of the below." One of the ways in which these spirits differ from the rather larger concept of *kwoth* is that different individuals accord various spirits of the above and below varying interest and respect. A certain spirit may be significant for some individuals and families but not for others, whereas *kwoth* is recognized and revered similarly by all Nuer.

Spirits of the Above

Whether a person feels distinctly connected to any of the spirits ordinarily has to do with whether or not the individual or any family member has had direct contact with the spirit, usually in the form of possession. Sudden illness may be seen as possession and once recovered, the sufferer may come to regard the spirit that has sent the illness as one of his or her own *kuth* (the term applied to all spirits). Descendants of this individual may then continue to attend to this spirit. If they do not, the inherited spirit may send a reminder to alert the family to its need for attention. When the Nuer fall sick without an obvious cause, they may realize they have been neglecting a *kuth* who has visited an illness as a signal that it is not happy to have been forgotten.

Temporary spirit possession can be remedied by sacrifice. An animal is dedicated to the offending spirit, and recovery is expected to follow. There are instances, however, of spirit possession that are permanent. These may occur independent of an episode of illness or may follow it. Abnormal behavior may be manifest for some time, and it is then realized by others that this individual has been given, by the possessing spirit, powers of healing, prophecy, and divination. That person is then *gwan kwoth,* the owner of that spirit, hollowed out by the possession, and filled up with the gifts bestowed by the spirit. Such an individual's character is forever altered (Evans-Pritchard 1956).

In this new role, the prophet—usually male—is relied upon for certain ritual functions. He may perform sacrifices or aid in curing. But the most important function of one permanently possessed by a spirit of the above is in the realm of warfare. Orders to fight come through him, the possibility of victory is in his hands, and no large-scale military effort is ever undertaken without these prophets performing sacrifices and singing hymns. The main social function of such prophets is to direct cattle raids on neighboring tribes, most notably the Dinka.

One sort of spirit of the above is the *colwic,* who were once Nuer themselves. Individuals who have been struck by lightning, killed in windstorms, or found dead in the bush, unaccountably, are thought to have undergone a metamorphosis and emerged divine. Most lineages can cite at least one *colwic* patron spirit. Death by lightning is not uncommon, and violent electrical storms are cause for great anxiety. However, such a death is not thought to be retribution for any misconduct on the part of the deceased, as some deaths are regarded. Rather, the electrocuted person is seen as having been chosen by *kwoth* to be changed into a *colwic.* It is said that the individual has actually entered into a kinship relation with *kwoth,* as a result of this special selection (Evans-Pritchard 1956:54).

Spirits of the Below

Spirits of the above are also known as "spirits of the air." They are "great spirits" and much revered. Spirits of the below, however, are regarded quite differently. They are believed to have fallen from above, and as "spirits of the earth," they are "little spirits" and not held in the same reverence.

Spirits of the below can be classified into several categories, the most important of which is that of totemic spirits. These attach to specific clans and lineages, and are usually described in animal form—lion, lizard, crocodile, various birds, and snakes. Plants may be inspirited too, as may rivers and streams. Each of these aspects of nature is a material representation of a "spirit of the below." These spirits can act positively through the plant or animal, if the totem by which they are represented is shown the proper "respect" by the Nuer. This respect can be demonstrated by refraining from hurting or eating it; paying it the courtesy of acknowledgment, should it be met along one's way; or by some act meant to demonstrate regret, should it be encountered dead or hurt.

Spirits as Social Refraction

It is evident that the spiritual conceptualizations of the Nuer are intricately bound up with their social order. Spirits who "belong" to one lineage do not visit individuals of another lineage. Those that are represented by totems can act only for the clans whose totems they rightfully are. However, there are larger spiritual representations that do indeed belong to all Nuer, and in this way their religious structure resembles their social structure. The principle of segmentary lineage organization is that although lineages may be distinct and opposed to one another at one level, those same lineages may be affiliated with one another and opposed to another lineage at a different level of segmentation. It is in this same way that they can conceive of the spiritual realm as being specific to a smaller group at one level, yet "belong" to a larger segment higher up.

Kwoth and Nuer: Death, Soul, and Sin

Evans-Pritchard (1956) points out that to the Nuer, religion is a "reciprocal relation" between *kwoth* and humanity. Their religious tenets tell them not only about the nature of *kwoth* and various spirits, but also about their own nature.

The Nuer fear death, and it has been suggested that this is because they have no tradition of an afterlife. They profess neither knowledge nor interest in what happens to them after they die. Life comes from *kwoth,* and it returns to *kwoth,* in some sense, after death. They make a distinction between the mere "life" or "breath" of an individual (that which demonstrates being alive) and what might be thought of as the "soul" (that property that bestows unique personhood on an individual). Mere animation is not sufficient to demonstrate this latter property. This is demonstrated by the story of Gatbuogh, a man who returned to his village after years of wandering, having been given up for dead. He returned changed—he was distracted, disengaged, not communicative. It was said of him that he was alive but he no longer had his soul. Similarly, mortuary rites and mourning periods are not observed in the event of a small child's death. Although the Nuer describe conception as a result of male sperm entering the uterus, a child is also created by *kwoth* and is thus a product of both human and divine construction. Only when children are old enough to have begun to participate in the social life of the Nuer will they be deemed "real people." They are certainly alive, but not in possession of souls.

In the relationship of human to divine, sin is of paramount importance. The Nuer say that *kwoth* is both very near and very distant. This is what they want, because he can be of assistance if close but not dangerous in his powers of retribution if far away. The greatest "sinful" transgression regards a failure to show respect. This demonstration of respect is a broad concept, incorporating elements of avoidance, abstention, modesty, deference, and restraint. Such respectful relationships—*thek*—exist in a wide range of configurations. They are found between a man and his wife's parents, a woman and her bridewealth cattle, an individual and food belonging to strangers, the living and a corpse. Transgressions in these relationships bring dire consequences. Evans-Pritchard (1956) says of *thek* relationships that "[t]hey are intended to keep people apart from other people or from creatures or things, either altogether or in certain circumstances or with regard to certain matters, and this is what they achieve" (pp. 180–181). The result of sinning in these circumstances is the highest form of shame and despicability, in addition to the prospect of more corporeal punishment, such as illness, blindness, and death. Homicide, adultery, and incest are among the most serious infractions a Nuer can commit. These acts, however, pose particular dilemmas for the Nuer.

Evans-Pritchard reports that incest is something much talked about among the Nuer, and it is not difficult to see why. Two factors contribute to the frequency of incest outside close kin: the first is the lack of disapproval accorded to casual sexual relations before marriage, and the second is the nature of kinship relations in Nuer society. An individual may not be able to reckon with complete certainty whether a particular person in fact occupies a relational role that is prohibited or not. Homicide poses a dilemma as well, in that while the Nuer believe that killing a member of one's community is wrong, this disapproved behavior may occur as a result of following another *approved* behavioral code. Douglas (1966) points out that Nuer boys are instructed from an early age to use force in defending their rights. This may at times lead to homicidal behavior, however unintentional. Adultery, according to Evans-Pritchard (1951, in Douglas 1966) may be regarded "as a risky sport in which any man may normally be tempted to indulge." But it is dangerous behavior because it brings sickness to the wronged husband, who is at risk for severe pains in his lower back, caused by the pollution of his subsequent relations with his wife. Payment of an ox to the husband can avert this fate.

Mary Douglas, in her classic volume *Purity and Danger,* reflects on the utility of these threats of pollution, which she asserts can "serve to settle uncertain moral issues." Regarding incest, she writes:

> The Nuer cannot always tell whether they have committed incest or not. But they believe that incest brings misfortune in the form of skin disease, which can be averted by sacrifice. If they know they have incurred the risk they can have the sacrifice performed; if they reckon the degree of relationship was very distant, and the risk therefore slight, they can leave the matter to be settled *post hoc* by the appearance or non-appearance of the skin-disease. (1966)

As she goes on to point out, in a system such as the Nuer's, where the social structure is made up entirely of individuals whose relationships to one another are defined by marital categories and incest prohibitions, violations of the rules regarding incest and adultery strike at the heart of the local community's integrity. "To have produced such a society the Nuer have evidently needed to make complicated rules about incest and adultery, and to maintain it they have underpinned the rules by threats of the danger of forbidden contacts. These rules and sanctions express the public conscience." Moreover, because there is often no general outrage over adultery, Douglas suggests that the threat of pollution can act, in an impersonal way, to take up the moral slack when indignation is not engendered.

MODERN CHALLENGES: CIVIL WAR AND RESETTLEMENT

The Nuer figure prominently into the decades-long civil war in Sudan. As discussed in the Azande chapter, Sudanese independence from Britain in 1956 was established with inequities in place. The powerful north, home of the capital city Khartoum, seat of the Arab-led government, sought to impose Islam on the south, populated by Africans who adhered to Christianity or indigenous belief systems. Brutal violence inflicted by the military forced thousands to flee the south, and inspired formation of civilian-led independence movements. The most powerful of these, the Southern Sudan Liberation Movement (SSLM), effected a brief cease-fire in the 1970s, but violence soon erupted once more.

In addition to the enforced Islamization of southern Sudan, with policies in place to undermine the cultural identities of southern peoples, the northern elite set into motion a plan to gain control of land, oil, and water resources in the south (Kebbede 1999). A canal was planned, engineered to span the southern homelands of both the Nuer and the neighboring Dinka, among other groups. This canal, the Jonglei, was designed to channel water north from the Nile, to provide water for northern farmers whose agriculture produced cash crops, such as cotton, for export. This diversion of water would have resulted in the destruction of southern pasturelands crucial to pastoralists, such as the Nuer, who depend on their herds for their lives and livelihood. The expectation of Sudan's government was that nomadic groups would acquiesce to assuming a more "advanced" sedentary lifestyle, and southerners were neither included in the planning nor considered in the consequences (Kebbede 1999). The Nuer economy was deemed lesser, devalued because it provided mere subsistence, and not a marketable product (Kottak 1997). Faced with the loss of both grazing land and the inevitable change in their way of life, southerners in the SSLM succeeded in forcing a halt to the construction and focusing attention on environmental degradation and the struggle for resources as well as religion and cultural identity.

The civil war in Sudan was among the longest-running in the world, with an estimated loss of 2 million lives since 1983. The Nuer played a central role. Although at its inception in 1983 the dozen leaders of the Sudan People's Liberation Movement (SPLM) were drawn from all the area's ethnic groups, the majority of the rank and file were drawn from the Nuer and their southern neighbors (and traditional rivals) the Dinka. In 1991, a Nuer commander attempted to overthrow the SPLM founder, a Dinka, inciting warfare that claimed many thousands of lives. The coup resulted in the group's split into two factions: one Dinka-led and one Nuer. Violent battles continued between the two for several years, wreaking havoc on local civilians, their cattle holdings, and their lands. Anthropologist Sharon Hutchinson (2000) points out that traditional conflict between Dinka and Nuer specifically excluded violence against women, children, and the elderly. Such behavior was viewed not only as an act of cowardice but as an offense to God, leading inevitably to misery, illness, and even death, sent as divine retribution. Codes of warfare ethics also prohibited destruction of property. Homes and crops were protected. She cited the "gradual unraveling of these ethnic restraints" during the Sudanese civil war as "[representing] the gravest threat to the future viability of rural Nuer and Dinka communities in the South today" (2000:8). Hoping to find a resolution to the tribal fighting, a conference was held in 1998, resulting in an accord calling for future peace conferences. Several subsequent conferences were held, furthering reconciliation between the Dinka and Nuer. In 2002, an accord was reached. At the Dinka-Nuer Reconciliation Conference, held in Washington, DC, a declaration was issued, proclaiming that Dinka and Nuer were "now One People," reflecting the fact that their traditional names of *Jieng* (Dinka) and *Naath* (Nuer) both mean, simply, "The People" (Dinka-Nuer Washington Declaration, January 13, 2002).

As mentioned in the Azande chapter, a Comprehensive Peace Agreement between the SPLM and the government of Sudan was signed in 2005. Among its provisions was the eventual creation of an autonomous southern Sudan. This hope became a reality in January 2011, when the referendum passed with near unanimity: 99 percent voted in favor of independence, with official recognition of the new nation in July 2011.

Nuer in the United States

Sudan has the world's largest population of internally displaced people—nearly 5 million (Internal Displacement Monitoring Centre 2010). An additional half million, many of them Nuer, took refuge in camps in Ethiopia. The subsequent Ethiopian revolution forced many to move to settlements in Kenya, which provided not only a safe haven but the opportunity for an escape from refugee life. Programs designed to assist in finding permanent new homes allowed Nuer to emigrate, and by 1996 nearly 4,000 southern Sudanese were living in the United States (Holtzman 2000). In the Midwest, Nuer are challenged to forge a new community without the kinship ties and village links that are the underpinnings of traditional Nuer solidarity. Jon Holtzman, an anthropologist who has done fieldwork among Nuer both in Sudan and in Minnesota, has found that local church congregations have reached out to Nuer refugees. Because most of the resettled Nuer had been converted to Christianity by missionaries in Sudanese schools or Ethiopian camps, Holtzman observes that the church offers "perhaps the only continuity between Nuer life in Africa and Minnesota" (2000:123).

Church affiliation in Minnesota may derive from prior association in Sudan but may often be an extension of the resettlement effort. Individual church members, or the congregation at large, offered sponsorship to Nuer families, securing for them the ability to seek refuge in the United States. Thus, families often chose to join the sponsoring congregation. This was not necessarily part of the bargain; often Nuer sought out the denominations most familiar to their home community. Holtzman (2000) points out that Nuer often found joining any congregation a challenge, owing to their understandable desire to conduct services in their own language. One church accommodated their wishes, providing separate space for worship at the same time as regular services. Problems soon arose:

> [T]he Nuer service was a raucous, lively affair, with spirited singing to the pounding beat of African drums. This proved incompatible with the English service going on upstairs, and the minister was upset at having the tranquility of the chapel interrupted by persistent drumming—not to mention the effect this had on his sermon. (Holtzman 2000:126)

In addition to the sponsorship instrumental in helping Nuer gain resettlement permission, church groups often continued to raise money to provide material goods for resettled families. Thus, Holtzman found that "spiritual relationships have become deeply entangled in the negotiation of material ones" (2000:127), although the aid is provided out of a sincere dedication to humanitarianism and the promotion of Christianity.

The majority of Minnesotan Nuer are young families and single men in their late teens and 20s. Holtzman (2000) explains that parents were eager for their adult children to resettle, adventure being a prerogative of youth, while they remained to care for the family's traditional home. Close ties are maintained with relatives in Sudan or Ethiopia, to whom remittances are sent and who are often called upon to fulfill ritual requirements in their relatives' absence.

Traditionally, kinship is the paramount social bond in Nuer society, where everyone is related, however distantly, to everyone else. These various sorts of kinship bonds, activated at times when alliances need to be forged, are diffused in resettled Nuer, whose daily lives take on a more individualistic focus. Minnesotan Nuer find ways to reconstitute allegiances, often focusing more on the larger shared "Nuer identity" than on Sudanese concepts of kinship. Holtzman found that his questions about the tribal, clan, and subclan affiliations of a Minnesotan community were brushed aside dismissively with the comment, "Those things don't matter here. Here we are just all Nuer" (2000:44).

Some Minnesotan Nuer express the desire to return to their homeland, if peace can be found in Sudan. The high cost of living, long hours at work, and missing those who remained behind are all reasons that tug at those who wait for the opportunity to go home (Holtzman 2000). Not all who have resettled consider their move a temporary one, however. Those who have found educational opportunities and employment are committed to finding even greater success for themselves and their children. They look to the future, content to carve out a new life in a new land.

"The Lost Boys of Sudan"

One group of south Sudanese refugees has received particular attention: the so-called Lost Boys of Sudan, a group of more than 30,000 children, mostly Nuer and Dinka boys whose villages had been destroyed and families killed.

In 1987, government militia raided southern villages, killing the adults and capturing the girls. Terrified young boys, many outside of the village tending cattle, fled at the sight of the violence, meeting up with other children, mostly boys, as they trudged through desert and wilderness. Small groups found one another, and soon tens became hundreds and hundreds became thousands. Together, they walked hundreds of miles over several months toward Ethiopia. Many died of thirst and starvation; some fell prey to wild animals. When the survivors arrived at Ethiopian refugee camps, they had formed small cadres in which the older children—some only 9 or 10—looked after the younger ones. Relief workers named them the Lost Boys, after Peter Pan's band of orphans. In 1991, after three years in the camps, Ethiopian civil war forced them to flee again. Some perished as they attempted to ford the crocodile-infested rivers under gunfire. Survivors set off to seek shelter in Kenya, a thousand miles away, many walking for more than a year. Thousands were lost on the journey: more than 20,000 children set out from Ethiopia; 11,000 (3,000 of them girls) eventually arrived at Kenya's Kakuma Refugee Camp.

After surviving for nearly a decade in Kenyan camps on a single daily meal, in 2000 and 2001 nearly 4,000 Lost Boys—now teenagers—began to be resettled in the United States under international rules allowing for the resettlement of minor children. Younger children were placed in foster homes; older ones traveled in groups of three or four and were placed in group homes or apartments sponsored by local churches and refugee aid organizations. In 2004, a publisher in Dallas who was moved by the stories of several Lost Boys in his church congregation turned the tales of their harrowing experiences into a series of graphic novels, entitled *Echoes of the Lost Boys of Sudan.* Modeled after comic books depicting feats of superheroes, the series follows the lives of those four Lost Boys, now in their mid-20s, with part of the proceeds going to a national refugee education fund. A group of the Lost Boys has been working together to help the villages they fled decades ago. In 2007, the Duk Lost Boys Clinic opened in Southern Sudan—built by volunteers who gathered to assemble a 4,000-square-foot structure brought from the United States. The village has no electricity, so rooftop solar panels are used to provide power to refrigerators, stocked with vaccines. By 2010, the clinic had provided care for 28,000 people. Other projects include building schools and drilling wells for clean water.

Where Are the "Lost Girls"?

Of the 4,000 children resettled in the United States, fewer than ninety were girls. Whereas boys in the refugee camps were kept together in small groups, girls were generally placed with guardians. The boys formed a visible group, the target of outreach by aid workers. It was assumed that the girls were being cared for. Some lived with families, but not all had the girls' best interests at heart. They were valuable as unpaid domestic workers and would eventually bring in a dowry. Now young women, many married and with young children, they no longer meet the requirements for resettlement. Sudanese activists and refugee organizations have been urging humanitarian and government agencies to investigate their plight.

The first national conference and reunion for Lost Boys and Girls was held in Phoenix during 2004. Planned by elected leaders of fifteen communities of Lost

Boys across the United States in an attempt to unify those individuals scattered across the country, the conference was designed to forge a new solidarity among resettled Sudanese refugees. However, the girls were given only one session during the two-day event, and it was scheduled at 7:30 in the morning, a time that resulted in very few attendees to hear their stories (Harris 2009). In subsequent years, many local communities have sponsored reunions and conferences, in some cases reuniting young adults who as 6- and 7-year-olds had lived in the camps together and now have begun to work together toward rebuilding their home communities.

→ For Further Discussion

The Nuer traditionally employed a form of political organization called the segmentary lineage organization (SLO). It provided an effective way to resolve disputes and mobilize support. In the 1990s, however, civil war in Sudan brought a grave challenge to the Nuer and their neighbors. War cost millions of lives and resulted in widespread resettlement. Many Nuer took refuge in camps in Ethiopia. The subsequent Ethiopian revolution forced many to move on to settlements in Kenya. The search for permanent new homes brought many thousands of Nuer to the United States. Given the importance of political systems and the traditional Nuer way of life, what might be some of the challenges of forging a new community without the political ties and village links that are the underpinnings of traditional Nuer solidarity?

CHAPTER 10

THE OJIBWA

"The People" Endure

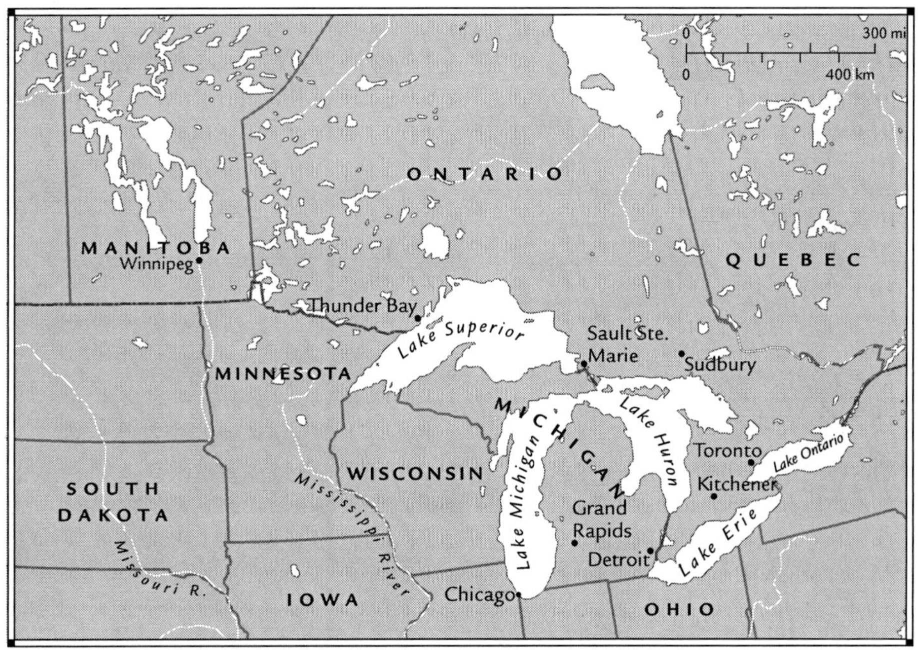

Ojibwa country in North America.

✧ The Beginning

Long before the world began, there was Gitchimanito, the Great Spirit. He made wind and water, fire and rock; he made the sun and stars and Earth. To the Earth he gave tall trees and green plants. He created animals that ran on four legs, animals that flew, animals that swam and, last, he created the people.

Gitchimanito arranged all he created by the four sacred directions—north, south, west, and east—and then two more: the sky above and the earth below.

Not long after, the seas flooded the earth, and the animals tried to find it again, to no avail. One after the other, they searched beneath the seas, until finally the muskrat scraped a pawful of soil from the submerged earth, and from that scrap the world was recreated. Gitchimanito envisioned a purpose for the spirit of all he created. Trees would grow large and give shade and protection. Plants would flourish and give food and medicine. Animals would be bountiful and their lives offered up as food and clothing for the people. But all this goodness would be recognized and appreciated by the people whose benefit it would serve. Nothing would be sacrificed without praise and thanks and a token of appreciation.

The people lived first by the great ocean in the east, but a vision carried them westward and, following it, they found the Great Lakes.

This is the beginning of the Ojibwa's tale, the explanation of their creation and of finding their home.

✧ Overview

The Ojibwa, a Native American group living in the northern midwest in the United States and south-central Canada, refer to themselves as *Anishinaabe,* which literally means "human being," a term by which many of the world's people are known to themselves. There is some speculation and disagreement about the origin of the name "Ojibwa." It has been said to refer to their style of moccasin ("*ojibwa*" meaning puckered up, and referring to the crimped stitching that edges the moccasins). Others (Tanner 1992) suggest that it is instead derived from "*ojibiweg,*" which means "those who make pictographs," and that their name refers instead to the paintings on birch bark that were traditionally used as a form of writing.

Originally, an area extending north of lakes Superior and Huron was home to the Ojibwa. Beginning in the seventeenth century, their geographic expansion resulted in a four-part division. These groups are the Salteaux (Northern Ojibwa); the Plains Ojibwa, or Bungee; the Southeastern Ojibwa; and the Southwestern Chippewa. By the end of the eighteenth century, the Salteaux occupied the Canadian Shield north of Lake Superior and south and west of Hudson and James bays. This is a flat area of poor soil and numerous lakes and swamps. Plains Ojibwa country, in southern Saskatchewan and Manitoba, is a region forested with oak and ash, with great rolling hills. The Southeastern Ojibwa in Michigan's lower peninsula, eastern upper peninsula, and adjacent areas of Ontario share an environment similar to that of the Southwestern Chippewa in northern Minnesota, extreme northern Wisconsin, Michigan's western upper peninsula, and Ontario between Lake Superior and the Manitoba border. Both live in countries of rolling hills; deciduous forests of maple, birch, poplar, and oak; and marshes, prairies, rivers, and lakes. They live with long, cold winters and short, hot summers.

The Ojibwa, one of the largest Native American groups north of Mexico, numbered at least 35,000 in the mid-seventeenth century. Today the Ojibwa have been given one hundred or more small reservations in Michigan, Wisconsin, Minnesota, North Dakota, Montana, and Oklahoma. The majority of the roughly 200,000 individuals live in the Canadian provinces of Ontario, Manitoba, and Saskatchewan.

HISTORY

In the mid-seventeenth century, the Ojibwa first encountered Europeans on their land. These explorers found an impressive natural bounty in rivers and forests. It wasn't long before the Gulf of St. Lawrence was crowded with fishing expeditions. The market for native furs—mink, bear, wolf, otter, and beaver—was tremendous, and by the end of the century, Ojibwa were heavily involved in the fur trade and eager to expand their trade for European goods.

The burgeoning desire for European trade goods led to escalating intertribal conflict centering on the rights to exclusive fur-trading privileges, especially fierce between the Iroquois and the Huron. In the mid-1600s, the combined effect of Dutch-issued firearms and the decimation by newly introduced diseases (smallpox chief among the epidemics) exacted a dramatic toll.

Earlier, the Ojibwa were closely allied to the Huron to their south. However, after the Huron were defeated by the Iroquois in their battle for control of the fur trade, the Ojibwa came under forceful Iroquois attack. In a successful attack that put an end to Iroquois power in their region, Ojibwa expanded both southward and westward.

Eventually, representatives from fifteen Indian nations negotiated peace in the trade wars, but not without great cost. By the beginning of the eighteenth century, Ojibwa culture had changed dramatically. Animals that had been hunted mainly for subsistence were now trapped primarily to be used in trade, and as dependence upon European trade goods increased, traditional patterns and activities diminished.

Also, with the development of the European fur trade, the exploitation of a particular hunting and trapping territory (which had been vaguely defined areas) evolved into discrete territories over which hunting and trapping groups had exclusive rights to fur resources. By the century's end, their major geographical expansion resulted in the four-part tribal fracturing.

With migration, too, came some significant modifications in traditional hunting, fishing, and gathering subsistence patterns. These modifications were most evident among the Northern Ojibwa, who adopted a subarctic cultural pattern borrowing extensively from the Cree, and the Plains Ojibwa, who incorporated numerous aspects of Plains Indian culture.

During the first half of the nineteenth century, Ojibwa began to experience the influence of the U.S. government. They became, once again, increasingly dependent on traders—this time Americans. Although fishing was plentiful in the summertime, winter found the Ojibwa without large game, which had been depleted, and left them in need of provisions owned by traders. Large parcels of land were ceded in return for the promise of continued blacksmith service (upon which they had come to rely for gun and trap repair, as well as fishing spears and ice cutters) and payments of salt and tobacco on an annual basis. Hunting and fishing rights on the land were given up. Demands for farmland forced Southeastern Ojibwa to cede their territory, and the movement toward reservations began in earnest.

Canadian officials attempted what they termed a "civilization" program, aimed at redirecting Ojibwa life to a reservation-based farming economy to replace traditional fishing, hunting, and gathering. Missionaries across North America embraced the "civilization" programs as a way to facilitate conversion to Christianity, which appeared easier to effect with a population that was less dispersed. With harsh winters and a short growing season, the copper-rich, forested land in Wisconsin and Minnesota was unsuitable for farming and thus not in jeopardy of being ceded to agriculturalists by government decree. But Ojibwa resistance was challenged by copper miners and the lumbering industry—eager to exploit the abundant resources on Ojibwa land and loath to allow the Ojibwa to remain living on land they had ceded, a right that had been granted them by the U.S. government.

In keeping with their plan for Ojibwa to adopt a farming economy, and under pressure from these burgeoning industries, the government attempted to resettle the Ojibwa west of the Mississippi where they could live in permanent shelters and farm the land. This initial attempt was unsuccessful, and an alternative program—to allot individual parcels of land within reservations to individual families—was introduced. A series of treaty conferences ensued, during which Native American leaders presented their complaints: promised payments had not materialized; settlers on Ojibwa land had gone through the woods and taken the game that had been left hanging on trees to cure; government-financed schools were not educating Ojibwa children, but only those of the traders. Perhaps the point of most contention was presented by Ojibwa from Sault Ste. Marie, whose land was destroyed by the construction of a shipping canal. Unsuspecting villagers were taken by surprise as 400 workers arrived in their village and began construction, which destroyed not only fishing sites but the village itself. Families were forced to flee their homes as the canal building proceeded.

Although treaties were signed promising permanent homes, farming acreage, equipment, and carpentry tools, this allotment process never came to fruition. By the time an official act was passed into law, nearly 90 percent of the land promised to the Ojibwa and others was already owned and settled.

Despite their desire to maintain their way of life, Ojibwa who had been resettled on reservations could neither fish nor gather wild rice on land unsuitable for these economies. Thus, consequences to Ojibwa culture, beginning with the earliest days of the fur trade, were cataclysmic. The technology introduced, the scattering and removal of the indigenous population, and the intertribal conflict engendered had dramatic effects on Ojibwa culture.

Before the middle of the nineteenth century, Ojibwa tools were fashioned of stone and bone. Bowls and spoons, canoe paddles and sleds, drums and snowshoes were all made of wood. Birch bark provided the material for canoes and containers. Spears and bows and arrows were the tools of the hunt, with animal skins providing the material for clothing, blankets, and tailoring. Hooks and nets were used for fishing.

With the advent of the fur trade, iron tools (scissors, needles, axes, knives), cooking utensils (kettles and pots), as well as guns and alcohol were introduced, with tremendous consequences. Iron tools transformed the approach to hunting. Pottery craft was reduced to obsolescence with the availability of sturdier and more efficient iron kettles. The European demand for fur, coincident with governmental plans to encourage a shift from the traditional economy to one based on farming, created an ironic dilemma, as Hallowell (Hallowell and Brown 1992:18) explains: "the continuing demand for furs, in the long run, entrenched most of these Indians more firmly in their occupation as hunters since so many of them were compelled to remain in a region where any transition to agriculture was impossible."

The European system of buying and selling introduced to the indigenous peoples a system of "debt" with which they were wholly unfamiliar. Goods were sold to hunters on credit, with payment in furs expected subsequently. European traders attempted to offset the risks inherent in giving goods on credit by establishing considerably higher prices for the goods they sold to the hunters. A host of factors, not the least of which was the unstable, seasonally changing availability of game, ensured that native peoples were rarely able to escape perpetual indebtedness. Although they were becoming more dependent upon trade goods, they were not able to incorporate the technology for producing or repairing such goods on their own, and thus were never able to benefit from the new technologies by employing them to become economically independent.

→ SETTLEMENTS

Ojibwa patterns of movement and settlement were guided largely by the seasons, and varied among groups as their environments varied. In general, bands dispersed in the winter, moving to hunting grounds where deer, moose, bear, and a variety of small game were available. In the spring, maple trees were tapped and the sap was gathered and boiled to produce maple syrup. Early Ojibwa established semipermanent villages in the summer and maintained temporary camps during the rest of the year, in keeping with their need to move in order to efficiently exploit fish, game, and wild plant resources.

Although the strategy of seasonal settlement and movement was found to some degree in all the Ojibwa groups, it was differently elaborated in each. Southeastern Ojibwa and Southwestern Chippewa returned to permanently established summer village bases to plant gardens. Plains Ojibwa were highly mobile and moved to the open plains in the summertime to hunt the bison herds upon which they focused their economy and whose skins were used to construct their familiar *tipis*.

The Northern Ojibwa spent the late fall, winter, and spring moving in dispersed winter hunting groups. As the ice melted, these small groups met up with other such bands, spending the summer months congregated in fishing settlements. In contrast to the isolation of winter hunting movement, the assembly of large groups at fishing sites afforded the opportunity to renew social ties and perform important communal ceremonies. In addition, many of these summer sites were near trading posts, where supplies could be secured for the coming year.

During the summer months spent in the villages, the gathering of wild nuts and berries, and planting of small gardens of maize, beans, squash, and pumpkins supplemented fishing. Wild rice, available most easily to the Southeastern Ojibwa and the Southwestern Chippewa, was harvested in the fall.

Kinship and Sociopolitical Organization

Despite the fact that there was seasonal movement, sometimes of small groups, these smaller units of Ojibwa belonged to a larger whole. In earliest times, the Ojibwa were organized into small autonomous bands of interrelated families. As is characteristic of band organization, these were flexible groups with an egalitarian structure. Band size and characteristics varied somewhat among different groups. Southeastern Ojibwa and Southwestern Chippewa bands were made up of several hundred people; Northern Ojibwa bands were smaller, each numbering from fifty to seventy-five individuals. Plains Ojibwa bands tended to be looser, more shifting units.

Kinship terms, used as both reference and address, functioned not only to identify the relationship of one person to another, but also as a vehicle to guide behavior and express the content of role relations and expectations. (For example, a child came to recognize that those men addressed by his father as "brother" all acted toward the child as his own father might.) Beginning with earliest childhood, kinship terms directed social interaction, allowing relations with both extended family and members of other groups as they moved among them.

Generally, Ojibwa society was organized into a number of exogamous totemic clans, with membership reckoned patrilineally. (Northern Ojibwa in the Berens River area of Manitoba were more likely to be endogamous within their bands.) Because these clans were not localized, most individuals could depend on finding some members of their own clan in any settlement to which their summer movement took them. Marriages, which involved little formal ceremony, were generally arranged by parents or guardians. Cross-cousin marriage, although practiced, was not preferred; most marriages were monogamous, even though polygyny was possible.

Ojibwa political organization was, like other aspects of their sociocultural system, dramatically influenced by contact with European fur traders. Traditionally, there were no powerful political "chiefs" among the Ojibwa. However, European traders sought to identify an individual within each band with whom they could negotiate. One individual was designated by a trader, and an official relationship was structured between the two men, a vitally important link for the trader whose livelihood depended on maintaining his access to pelts. As a result of the status granted and attention paid to the "chief," this individual gained status and prestige, which were reinforced by goods he was given to distribute as gifts. This newly defined position, "a convenient means of dealing with Indians whose native culture did not function through persons whose role it was to represent them in transactions with outsiders," was instituted among all the Ojibwan groups (Hallowell and Brown 1992:35).

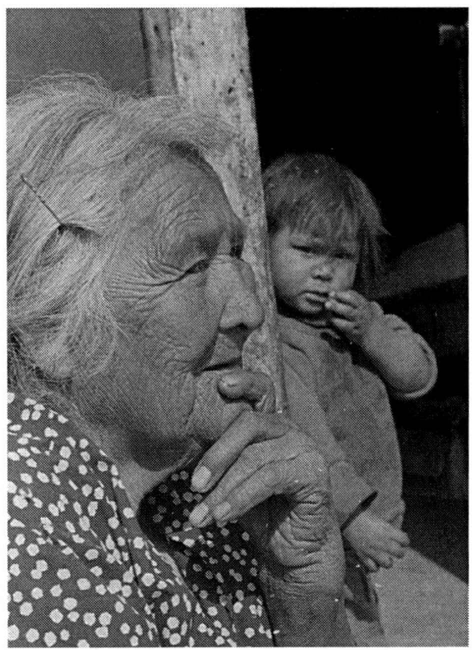

The Ojibwa across the generations.

Among the eighteenth-century Southeastern Ojibwa, bands were headed by less formal chiefs; as farming and more permanent settlement patterns were encouraged by the government, an elected chief, assistant chiefs, and a local council became the characteristic local political organization. Among the Northern Ojibwa, the individual selected for band leadership was usually a skilled trader whose kin group formed the basis of the band's membership. Plains Ojibwa bands had several chiefs, with one recognized as the head chief and secondary chiefs designated based on hunting skills, achievements in battle, generosity, and leadership ability. Elected councillors assisted the chiefs.

As Hallowell points out, the power held by these chiefs and councillors was derived primarily from their function as trade representatives, but this authority did not extend to matters arising within their "bands," which were also groups that were conceived largely by government agencies. Groups that were defined by the people themselves did not correspond to those conceptualized by traders and government officials. To the Ojibwa, the true seat of individual power was to be found in the indigenous healers, whose abilities acquired through dreams were truly matters of life and death.

OJIBWA CULTURE

The belief system of the Ojibwa centers on the important relationship between people and those who are other-than-people. Although skills and knowledge obtained from fellow Ojibwa are certainly important, there are crucial aspects of a successful life that can only be known and achieved through dependence upon those who are not human. Hallowell reports that he found "neither myth, tale, nor tradition [portraying] a human being as making any discovery, bringing about any change, or achieving any status or influence unaided by other than human persons" (Hallowell and Brown 1992:80).

To understand this, one must first understand that in the Ojibwa conceptualization there is no sharp division between the natural and the supernatural as defined by the Western scientific cultural model. There are animate and inanimate objects. The latter category is made up largely of manufactured items (although pipes are spoken of as animate); plants, fish, animals, and human beings are all classified as animate, as are the sun and wind and other elements. Also found among the category of animate beings are those animals that are known to exist but are rarely, if ever, seen. These include Large Snakes, Great Frogs, and Big Turtles. Of even greater importance are the Thunder Birds, whose wings make the sound of the thunder, and whose blinking eyes are the accompanying lightning. Thunder Birds are classified with other birds whose migratory patterns correspond to the stormy seasons during which thunder and lightning occur.

All plants and animals are controlled by their "owners," whose permission is an absolute prerequisite to securing them through hunting or gathering. This belief means that skillful techniques and an exhaustive knowledge of their environment are necessary but not sufficient talents for successful subsistence. To know the owners of each species, and to make certain that each plant and animal is correctly treated, is the only insurance against failure. The remains of an animal, which would be killed only for a useful purpose, must be disposed of and honored with proper ceremonial respect. Failure to accord plants and animals this right would inevitably result in retribution by the owner, generally the inability to secure that plant or animal again in the future. A hunter has a relationship with the owner of the species he hunts; the "use" of an animal results in a debt owed the species' owner, and such obligations must be fulfilled. Likewise, when plants are gathered, owners must be properly addressed and an offering (usually of tobacco) is left in the ground.

To the Ojibwa, the category of "persons" includes not only themselves—*Anishinaabe,* human beings—but also animate beings who are not human. These beings are more powerful than human beings and might be classified as "supernatural" beings in another cultural context. These persons are referred to as "our grandfathers" by the Ojibwa who, from childhood, have knowledge and experience with these beings. They have a real place in the lives of Ojibwa, through myth, ceremony, and dreams.

Myths told about "our grandfathers" were thought to be heard not only by the people assembled to listen, but also by the subjects of the stories themselves. It is believed that their delight in hearing them was so great that long ago one urged the others: "We'll try to make everything suit the Indians so long as any of them exist, so that they will never forget us and always talk about us" (Hallowell and Brown 1992:66).

Tales told about the "grandfathers" were generally told by elders—human grandparents—who were revered members of society. They educated adults and children alike, teaching through myths and dance and song those parts of wisdom deemed every bit as important as the practical skills of hunting, sewing, cooking, and fishing. Children, raised with little strictness and rarely reprimanded or punished, were in the care of women and elders for the first years of their lives. At age 7, boys began to be instructed by adult men in the ways of hunting and fishing; girls continued to be instructed about domestic life by their mothers. When an Ojibwa girl received the "gift . . . denied to men" (Tanner 1992:27)—her first menstruation—she became a woman, leaving the village for a time and returning with a new status. Special instruction was afforded to those young women and men who displayed the gift of healing powers, the gift to be among the *Midé*.

Religion and View of the World

Ojibwa religion is bound up with several distinctive features: dreaming, fasting, visions, and, above all else, the relationship with "the grandfathers," the other-than-human beings.

According to Hallowell, "faith in the power of the other than human persons, trust in the essential help they can offer human beings, and dependence upon them in order to achieve a good life define the . . . core of Ojibwa religion" (Hallowell and Brown 1992:81). Religious beliefs that emphasize this critical relationship direct behavior, and thus function as a primary way of maintaining the social order.

The primary contact between individuals and these other beings is achieved during dreaming, a state of primary importance in Ojibwa life. It is during dreams that power is given and received, and while contact can be made with "the grandfathers" outside of dreams, it is only in the dreaming state that the most intimate and powerful relationship is forged.

Just as a sharp dichotomy between the natural and the supernatural cannot be effectively drawn for the Ojibwa, neither can experience gained through waking and dreaming teachings be set in opposition. The world experienced while dreaming is not one of fantasy and unreality; it is another occasion for reflective thought. One difference between the experiences of sleep and waking, however, is the ability of the soul during sleep to break free of the body, allowing the most intense contact with other-than-human beings. During such contact, "blessings" of knowledge, and, thus, power, are bestowed; beginning in early childhood, one is encouraged to dream in order to receive these blessings.

To facilitate visionary dreams, boys especially were encouraged to fast, during which time they would be visited by "the grandfathers." During this state, the fasting boy would be approached by one who would take him under his wing and tutelage, whom he could see and hear. The fasting period might last a week before such "guardian spirits" would appear; the boy's father or grandfather might appeal to his own long-ago recognized teachers to help secure the boy's own blessing.

Once secured, the vision was not discussed. In fact, if a boy began to discuss his experience or ask for guidance in interpreting what he had dreamt, he was cautioned against it; seeking clarification through discussion of one's vision might be grounds to lose the blessing and the power it bestowed. A dreamer's family was made aware obliquely of the fast's fruition by a boy's change in behavior. He became somewhat withdrawn and introspective, observed new ritual obligations assumed to have been demanded of him in his dream. His proud family let his achievement be known to the rest of the community, but also only inferentially: they had found him in an altered state of consciousness, his manner had changed, they had seen differences in his behavior.

Dreams and visions vary greatly—in both content and intensity—from person to person. Some "dream visitors" impart only knowledge and access to trapping and fishing; others to warfare; still others impart the skills necessary for curing. One person may be visited by many guardian spirits; others may never fulfill their quest for a vision. Whether blessed by many or none, the dreamer is to remain equally silent, both because boasting is unacceptable and because it jeopardizes one's ability to hold onto the power received.

It has been suggested that one reason that Ojibwa feel a strong link between humans and the other-than-human spirits that are "the grandfathers" is that both classes of persons are bound by the same moral order. Primary among these shared values is the importance of mutual exchange. The guardian spirits give blessings and knowledge to their human grandchildren; they have an excess of power, more than they need, and thus they must share it.

The egalitarian focus that serves to distribute goods and services in a society without a market economy also guides the act of sharing across human and nonhuman boundaries. The accumulation of excess goods, indicative of greed, is as unbefitting to "the grandfathers" as it is to those who dream of them. Self-deprivation can be taken to excess as much as overacquisitiveness. One boy was reported to have been dissatisfied with the blessing he received during his initial fasting vision. His desire was to know everything in the world, to dream of every leaf on every tree so he could see beyond them to know all. He continued to fast. This desire, considered greedy, was granted, but with the proviso that as the leaves fell from the tree, so too would the boy fall ill. And when the trees were at last bare, his life too would end. As Hallowell explains, "Overfasting is considered as greedy as hoarding. It violates a basic moral value of the cosmic society of the Ojibwa" (Hallowell and Brown 1992:92).

In keeping with the rights and duties bound up in sharing and reciprocity, the blessings received during the dreams are not bestowed without obligation. If one is to utilize the knowledge and power obtained through vision to their fullest extent, both prohibitions and "debts" must be attended to. In some cases, food taboos are imposed by guardian spirits who are owners of that animal species. In others, items of clothing or adornment associated through myth with the bestower of one's blessings must be worn. Often contact is forbidden between the dreamer and certain other individuals. None of these observances may be explained; consequently, recipients of blessings often are forced to endure misunderstanding by others, requiring the exercise of great self-control. Infractions result not only in the withdrawal of the blessing; even unintentional violation of such taboos extracts a penalty, usually illness. Any breach of conduct between people or between humans and other-than-humans is punished eventually; there is no comfort to be taken in the passage of time. "Bad conduct . . . 'will keep following you.' Sooner or later you will suffer because of it" (Hallowell and Brown 1992:93). Moreover, it may be those closest to you who will pay the price for your own infraction; it may be your children who fall ill and die.

Thus, the fear of falling ill functions, in traditional Ojibwa society, as a powerful sanction against behavior that fails to conform to that which is expected. Ethnographers have pointed out that this set of beliefs—grounded in individual responsibility for behavior and a commitment to exercise self-control without explanation—acted against the acceptance of the government-introduced system of chiefdoms, which sought to impose sanctions by dictum from without.

In those settings where illness functions as a check on antisocial behavior, becoming ill has ramifications on two levels: not only as personal misfortune, but also as a clear indicator of some moral or behavioral transgression against wider cultural values. This is further reinforced by the public disclosure of the violation that has brought on the illness. A confession of sorts is a necessary element in the curative process; once the misconduct has been identified and made known, it functions as a warning to others.

In their elegant recounting of Ojibwa myths, Overholt and Callicott (1982) alert the reader of these tales to some of the important elements out of which they are spun. It is through the telling of the myths that central values are passed on from Ojibwa to Ojibwa; for people outside their tradition, examining the themes contained within the stories can be a window into the Ojibwa world.

Power is a recurrent theme in Ojibwa life, especially the power possessed and granted by the "grandfathers." One power possessed by humans and other-than-humans alike is that of metamorphosis, the changing of one's shape. Hallowell counts this as "one of the distinctive generic attributes of persons in Ojibwa thought" (Hallowell and Brown 1992:66–67). This thought is never more in evidence than when considering the bestowal of blessings, through dreams and visions. These are parts of life and awareness that are no less real than the more mundane pieces of one's day—and surely no less powerful. The Ojibwa view of themselves as not solely people who live with other people, but as human beings who live in a more broadly defined society, with other-than-human persons, is exemplified in two other features of Ojibwa culture: the shaking tent and the *Midéwiwin,* or Grand Medicine Society.

The Shaking Tent

The shaking tent (or shaking lodge) is a performance aimed at divining information not available through other means. Most often the questions asked have to do with the diagnosis and treatment of illness, the welfare of loved ones far away, or the location of game animals. The practice involves persons and powers from all the important realms of the Ojibwa world: the audience of Ojibwa, the "spirits" to be contacted, and the diviner.

In preparation for the event, a structure is erected. Poles are lashed together to form a barrel-shaped tent, or lodge, with skins, canvas, or birch bark draped over the framework. The diviner enters the tent after dark with the assembled audience outside. Songs and drumming are the vehicles by which the diviner calls his spirits to him. These are never a random assemblage of visitors whom he importunes: they are his own *pawaganak,* his own guardians.

The evidence of their arrival is the movement of the tent, which shakes from side to side with their appearance within. At times this movement is rendered even more impressive by the binding, hand and foot, of the diviner. Thus tied with rope, it could not be he creating the rhythmic motion. Hallowell (Hallowell and Brown 1992) tells of a diviner of such potency that he was said to have requested that four tents be constructed. He placed articles of his clothing in three, and himself entered the fourth. Once he had begun his songs, all four tents began to sway.

It is not only the movement of the tent that signals the arrival of the *pawaganak;* they can also be heard to respond to the diviner's song with singing of their own. In addition to guardian spirits, the souls of those living persons being inquired about can visit the tent to offer information and advice. These voices and songs are not believed to be "channeled" through the diviner; they speak for themselves. Although it is true that sometimes their voices could be heard by the audience outside the tent and sometimes not, they are always intelligible to the diviner who, though he may be interpreting them, is surely not creating them (Brown and Brightman 1988:153).

The *Midéwiwin*

One of the best known features of rich Ojibwa culture is the *Midéwiwin* (literally, "mystic doings") of the *Midé* (mystic) Society, sometimes referred to as the Grand Medicine Society.

The *Midéwiwin* is an organized society of men and women who possess the knowledge to cure by the use of plants and herbs. Initiates, who have experienced a vision in which curing powers have been imparted, must serve an extended apprenticeship, during which they are tutored, for a price, by an established *Midé* priest.

Much of the accumulated knowledge of the *Midéwiwin*—stories, songs, and dances—are inscribed as pictographs on birch bark scrolls. After sufficient time has passed, the aspiring *Midé* member participates in an initiation ceremony, during which he or she is "shot" with a white shell, ordinarily carried in the medicine bag of a member. Participants, in trance and falling unconscious after the magical shots, regain consciousness to spit the powerful shells from their mouths.

The earliest accounts of the *Midéwiwin* portray it as far more than a vehicle for curing illness. Beliefs about illness and curing in general reflect, as do other aspects of Ojibwa belief and practice, an individualism found at the core of Ojibwa culture. Ojibwa religion has been called "very much an individual affair," focused as it is on the personal experience through visions and dreams of an individual, which result in a unique relationship forged between one person and a guardian spirit (or, in some cases, spirits). So, too, illness is believed to be caused by sorcery or as retribution for misconduct toward the "grandfathers" or one's fellow humans. Although certainly important in the realm of solidarity among Ojibwa, it also has a strong flavor of singularity.

Contemporary Ojibwa medical practitioners feel linked to past generations of *Anishinaabe* healers, sometimes because they are direct descendants, but often because they recognize a spiritual connection between the medicine people of the present and those who have served the community in the past (Garro 2004). Women who are herbal healers have often learned their skills from other women in their family. While most herbalists are consulted for a variety of ills, some have special knowledge of a specific plant and are thus consulted for their efficacy in treating one condition. Unlike these herbalists, whose skills reside largely in their abilities to make medicines, another category of healers are those who have been blessed with the power to heal. Most often, these healing gifts have been bestowed by other-than-human beings with whom they have a special relationship. Through dreams and visions, they are able to determine both the cause and character of an illness as well as the best course of action for treatment—including advising the sufferer to seek out a physician instead of a medicine person. Healers who have received their gifts through visions and dreams may have developed their abilities to communicate with other-than-human beings early in life, but they come into the fullness of their powers in middle age (Garro 2004). Once learned, this medical knowledge is "private property, the visionary or dream inspiration of specific medicines and techniques exhibiting a high degree of individualism and variation" (Brown and Brightman 1988:174).

This individualism does not exclude the practitioners in the *Midéwiwin;* no standard curriculum is taught to all their members, no remedy known to all, leading to the interchangeability of practitioners so common to Western biomedicine. When asked about a cure, a *Midé* priest might reply, "I can tell you about my own medicines. I do not know about other people's medicines . . ." (Brown and Brightman 1988:174).

Thus, early writers (for example, Schoolcraft 1851), in describing the *Midéwiwin,* characterize it as transcending the limits of its curing responsibilities, having national participation, and engendering national pride. Others who observed the rites emphasized what they regarded as its unifying aspects: "Every person who had been initiated into the secrets of this mysterious society . . . [was] imperatively obliged to be present on every occasion when its grand ceremonies were solemnized. This created yearly a national gathering, and . . . bonds which united one member to another" (Hickerson 1988:56).

In recent years, there has been reexamination of the *Midéwiwin* and its origin and place in Ojibwa history. It had earlier been assumed to represent an aboriginal institution—that is, to have been part of Ojibwa culture arising from within its own tradition, present before contact with outside groups. This assumption has been challenged by more recent anthropological investigation.

Ojibwa culture and society, along with that of other native peoples, was forced to undergo major changes during European contact. One consequence of stressful contact, which challenges traditional patterns of both belief and behavior, is the appearance of "nativistic" or "revitalization" movements. The most well known of these include Melanesian cargo cults, the Ghost Dance of western Native peoples, and the Handsome Lake religion of the Iroquois.

It is the contention of anthropologist Harold Hickerson (1988) that the *Midéwiwin,* rather than originating in precontact times, is in fact another example of such a phenomenon. In a thoughtful and well-supported treatise, he details the evidence for his claim that the *Midéwiwin* among the Ojibwa and other groups emerged out of a reaction to the challenges of Christianity and European contact, and that its ceremonies "represented and reflected new modes of organization, not ancient ones" (p. 63).

→ Ojibwa Today

Historical descriptions of the Ojibwa detail the traditional life of the past. But in many ways, the current experiences of modern Ojibwa are portrayed in them too. The rich cultural heritage of the people who call themselves *Anishinaabe* survives through their continuing celebration of themselves in art, language, and ceremony.

Relocation: "This Hole in Our Heart"

Following the Great Depression in the United States, the economy of the Ojibwa suffered along with that of the rest of the nation, only to rebound during World War II. Ojibwa joined other native peoples in moving to urban areas and laboring variously in shipyards, factories, and aircraft plants for the war effort. As Tanner (1992) points out, however, diversion of funds to the military from domestic programs had an adverse effect on schools, roads, and hospitals on the reservation.

In the 1950s, a government relocation program attempted to reduce reservation living (thus government expenses) by urging Native Americans to migrate to urban areas and assimilate into mainstream American society. Nearly half the native population of Minnesota had been relocated to urban areas by the middle of the 1970s. The desire among some urban Native populations to blend into the non-Native mainstream was very much like that of a number of immigrant populations, eager to "become real Americans" by distancing themselves from other traditions. However, Deborah Davis Jackson, an ethnographer whose fieldwork was conducted among Michigan *Anishinaabe* communities, eloquently describes the experiences of individuals who were raised in urban environments with a veiled sense of their *Anishinaabe* heritage. The classic three-generation model of European immigrants to the United States describes the first immigrant generation as remaining distinctly "foreign," their American-born children as rejecting any vestiges of that ethnicity, and their own children rediscovering the cultural heritage of their immigrant grandparents. Jackson (2002) points out that this model is not entirely applicable to the situation of urban Native peoples. In the case of those who left reservations and rural communities for the city, two generations in the European immigrant model are compressed into one—these relocated individuals are both "leaving the Old Country" and "becoming mainstream Americans." Moreover, unlike "white ethnics," an invisible blending into the Caucasian population is not possible. Last, the collapse of the first two generations into one results in the loss of that "cushion" between an immigrant generation and a third generation raised by already assimilated parents. Jackson (2002:111) describes "an ambiguity, an ambivalence, a poignant tension" in the identity of those Ojibwa relocated to an urban environment. This results in their grown children's description of their unresolved position:

> The majority of us [city-raised Indian people] walk around with this hole in our heart. We know we're different, that there's a piece of our life that is missing. (Jackson 2002:100)

It was also during the 1970s, however, that government policy began to become more sensitive to the needs and desires of Native Americans, and both laws and funds began to be aimed at preserving traditional culture. Alternative schools offering instruction in Ojibwa language and beginning the day with traditional ceremonial observances came into existence. This was in direct contrast to the tradition of former "Indian boarding schools" run by the government from 1880 to 1930 and often explicitly aimed at assimilation (Northrup 1997; Pacquin and Doherty 1992). Ojibwa tribal councils provided scholarship money for students to attend universities, where they increasingly found programs allowing them to continue to learn about their own heritage and culture.

Tribal Casinos

In recent decades, gaming in tribal-owned casinos has garnered popular attention and is a source of debate both within Native communities and without (Northrup 1997; Vizenor 1990). Proponents believe it provides an opportunity for financial independence and the enhanced welfare of the tribe: gaming revenues, by law, must be used exclusively for tribal government operations, charitable contributions, and the economic development of the tribe and its members (Anders 1999). Such potential comes at a time when federal support of tribal operations is on the wane.

As we will see in further discussion, it was revenues from Native casinos that provided funds to effect a recent sweeping environmental victory.

Some non-Native critics claim that Native gaming privileges are an unfair government sanction. Within Native communities concerns are voiced about the negative social potential of gambling, as well as the erosion of traditional values. Perhaps the argument central to the Native position is one of sovereignty, the ability of individual tribal communities—sovereign nations—to make their own choices about the place of casinos on their reservations.

Environmental Degradation: Triumph over *Pijibowin*

Logging, mining, oil drilling, dam construction, and toxic waste storage and disposal are among the threats to habitats all over the world. The Ojibwa are among those indigenous peoples whose lands and economies are endangered by industrial development. Zoltan Grossman (1995) has remarked that "it is one of history's ironies that the 'wastelands' to which Native peoples were exiled are now coveted for their rich mineral resources."

In Northern Ontario, mercury seeped into the Grassy Narrows Band Ojibwa river systems from a paper mill upstream, contaminating fish consumed by those living on the reserve (Erikson 1994). In addition to toxic health effects, there were economic consequences as well: commercial fishing was halted once the river was declared unsafe, and Ojibwa could no longer earn income as guides for local sports fishing groups. As disastrous as it was to lose the only sources of outside employment and to fear the onset of mercury poisoning, Erikson (1994) observes that there was a third tragedy: the deeply spiritual blow of losing faith in the natural world. A Grassy Narrows elder told him:

> "We call it *pijibowin*. This is the Ojibwa word for poison. You can't see it or smell it, you can't taste it or feel it, but you know it's there. You know it can hurt you, make your limbs go numb, make your spirit sick. But I don't understand it. I don't understand how the land can turn against us." (1994:38)

Stuart Kirsch (1996), writing about ecopolitics in Papua New Guinea, notes that "indigenous peoples are becoming global activists in order to survive" (p. 15). In a struggle spanning nearly thirty years and eventually rallying support as far away as Australia, Wisconsin Ojibwa joined forces with local Potawatomi and Menominee to mount a battle against no less an opponent than Exxon, which in 1975 announced plans to build a zinc and copper mine just a mile from the Mole Lake Sokaogon Ojibwa's wild rice lake (Gedicks 1993; Grossman and McNutt 2003). This site is at the center of local Ojibwa culture, economy, and spiritual life. Wild rice is a dietary staple, an important cash crop, and a central aspect of sacred and ritual life (Gedicks and Grossman 2001). In surveying the site, an Exxon biologist referred to the wild rice as "a bunch of weeds" (Gedicks 1993:61).

The proposed site of the mine was at the headwaters of Wolf River, the state's largest whitewater trout stream and a popular tourist attraction. The estimated 58 million tons of acid waste that would be generated over the life of the mine, contaminating groundwater, was a potential disaster. Native groups protested with little community support throughout the late 1970s. In fact, the 1980s found Ojibwa and non-Native sport fishers embroiled in an acrimonious battle over fishing rights, a conflict that culminated in racist taunting, the assault of tribal elders, and vandalism to Ojibwa property (Grossman and McNutt 2003). However, within a few years these unlikely allies had come together to fight a larger mutual enemy. The environmental threat posed by the proposed mine provided common ground. An alliance of Ojibwa, Potawatomi, Menominee, and Oneida tribal governments—joined by environmental groups, local sport fishers, and grassroots organizations—worked tirelessly, mounting speaking tours and rallies, resulting in Exxon's withdrawal from the project in the mid-1980s. In 1993, Exxon returned with a new mining partner, intent on reviving their plan. In the intervening years, however, the four tribes had established casinos on their reservations, providing substantial resources. The Nii Win Intertribal Council (*Nii Win* is Ojibwa for "four") hired lawyers and technical experts, established Web sites, and forged international alliances. Their success was stunning: not only did they defeat both Exxon and BHP Billiton, the world's largest mining company, they achieved a far greater victory. In October 2003, the Mole Lake Sokaogon Ojibwa and Forest County Potawatomi communities pooled $16.5 million in gaming revenues and purchased the zinc and copper mine site along with the surrounding 6,000 acres of land. The tribes will share stewardship for the land, protecting wild rice lakes, Spirit Hill, an Ojibwa burial ground, and all the surrounding resources. In announcing their victory, the Mole Lake tribal secretary explained, "Protecting these lands has required a great personal sacrifice for tribal members. But it is a sacrifice that honors our ancestors and our children. Our ancestors lived here. They fought and died to protect these lands for future generations. It is our responsibility to continue that tradition" (Pommer 2003).

An ongoing struggle is taking place in Michigan's upper peninsula, where a multinational mining corporation has been granted permission to construct a nickel and copper mine. The Keewenaaw Bay Ojibwa community is concerned about pollution: the proposed mine is situated in a watershed, and acid runoff would drain through the several local rivers and into Lake Superior. Treaty rights allow Ojibwa to hunt, gather, and fish in the area, but to do so safely requires careful stewardship of the waterways. At the center of the resistance to the mine, however, is its location, which includes an outcropping of sacred and cultural importance known as Eagle Rock. Despite federal law that mandates protection for such sites—as well as a judge's recommendation that the plans be changed to preserve Eagle Rock—in 2010 the Department of Environmental Quality granted permission for the mine construction to proceed. They argued that "Eagle Rock is not a place of worship because it is not a constructed building, such as a Christian church or a mosque" (*Lake Superior Mining News,* Mar. 2, 2010).

Still *Anishinaabe*

Although the Ojibwa people are not a homogeneous group, there is still widespread adherence to traditional values and culture. Oral literature, art and craftwork, language and religion are still passed along to new generations. Hunting, gathering, and fishing continue. Tanner reminds us that "in ceremonies, dancing, and drumming, they are still *Anishinaabe*" (1992:111).

➔ For Further Discussion

How do the changes from traditional to modern Ojibwa life compare to those among the other groups about which you have read? What are some of the challenges faced by groups who comprise an ethnic minority within a nation? Are Native North Americans in a unique situation? Discuss the assertion made by Department of Environmental Quality lawyers that "Eagle Rock is not a place of worship because it is not a constructed building, such as a Christian church or a mosque."

CHAPTER 12

The Samoans

Matai *and Migration*

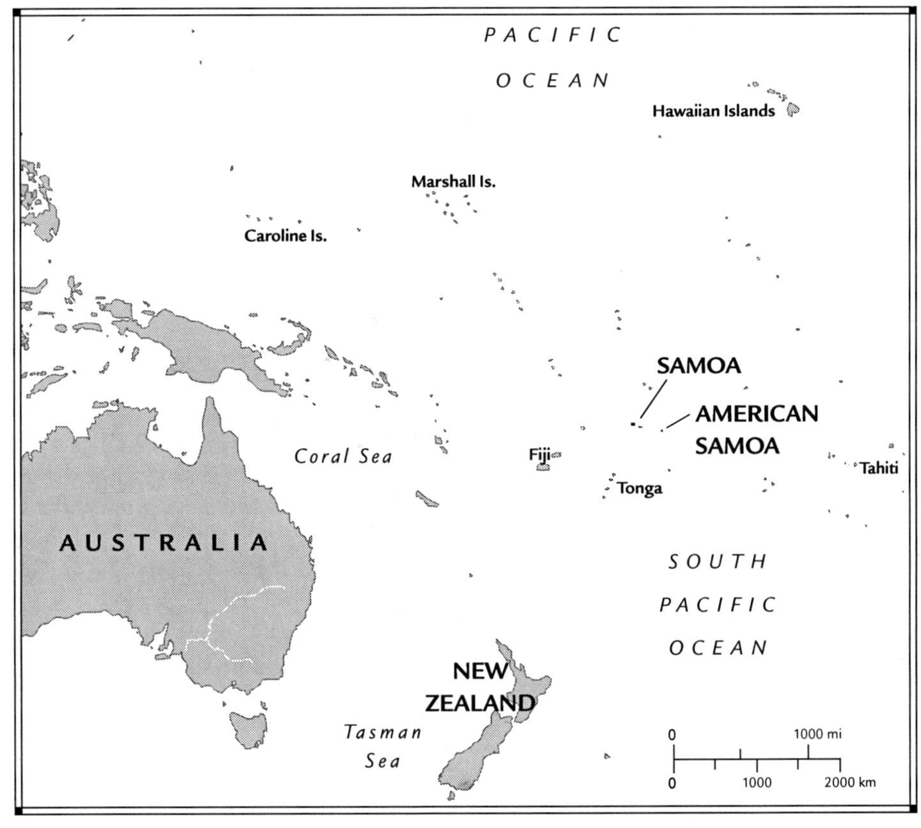

The Samoan Islands.

➔ The Beginning

There were heavens above and water below, and no place to stand. Tagaloa looked down from above and thought he would make such a standing place. This he did, and called the rock he had created Manu'atele. So pleased was he with his creation that he thought to make a second rock. He divided the first into little stepping stones—Tonga, Fiji, and other islands—and he tossed these into the sea. Tagaloa returned to Samoa and fashioned a vine to hug all the rocks in the sea. The vine spread and spread, and soon the leaves fell from the vine. Tagaloa saw that from the leaves emerged worms—worms that had no heads nor arms nor true life. Tagaloa gave them these things—arms and legs, heart and head—and thus made them people. He reached down and took pairs of these new people—one woman, one man—and set each pair upon an island. These islands needed a king, and so he created a king for each of his islands. But then he thought again: there must be a king of kings, one who would be greater than the others. He chose the son of Day *(Ao)* and Night *(Po)* to be this ruler. But when the boy was about to be born, Tagaloa saw that the baby was attached too strongly to his mother's womb. The boy was stuck by his abdomen, inside his mother's body. When he was born, his belly ripped away, and the wound was great. The scattering of islands that would be his home was thus named Samoa—"Sacred Abdomen."

➔ Introduction and History

Samoans are a western Polynesian people whose home is about 2,300 miles south of the Hawaiian Islands. The islands of Samoa all resemble one another topographically. They are of volcanic origin, with sandy beaches along a coral reef coast. Inland, there are ridges that rise to as much as 6,000 feet. Tropical climate and abundant rainfall yield lush vegetation, with dense green ferns and bushes covering the slopes. The temperature rarely drops below 70 degrees and does not peak much above 88 degrees. Tradewinds blow year-round, cooling the stickiest days. Although the nearly 200 inches of rain that falls annually might seem to result in a marsh underfoot, the volcanic soil quickly absorbs the water, which falls in short torrential bursts rather than as a slow, steady rain.

The Samoan Islands cover about 1,200 miles and have a population of about 193,000. The island chain is divided into two political units. The eastern islands have been a territory of the United States since 1925, and these seven islands—American Samoa—have a total area of seventy-six square miles and a population of about 37,000. Six of the islands form the Samoan chain; the seventh lies 200 miles north of the others. The islands of Western Samoa have been an independent nation since 1962.

The Dutch West India Company sent ships to the Samoan Islands in the early 1700s, but there is some evidence that Europeans had visited the islands even earlier (Holmes 1974). Toward the middle of the eighteenth century, French sailors traded cloth for yams, coconuts, and small implements. Most impressive to these visitors was the Samoans' prowess as boat builders, and it was this French expedition that called the chain "Navigator's Islands" in recognition of this talent. These visits all took place at sea, trading between ship and outrigger canoe. It was not until the late eighteenth century that Europeans disembarked on any of the islands.

In the early nineteenth century, missionaries arrived in Samoa, and their influence has been profound. Nearly 100 percent of Samoans have embraced Christianity.

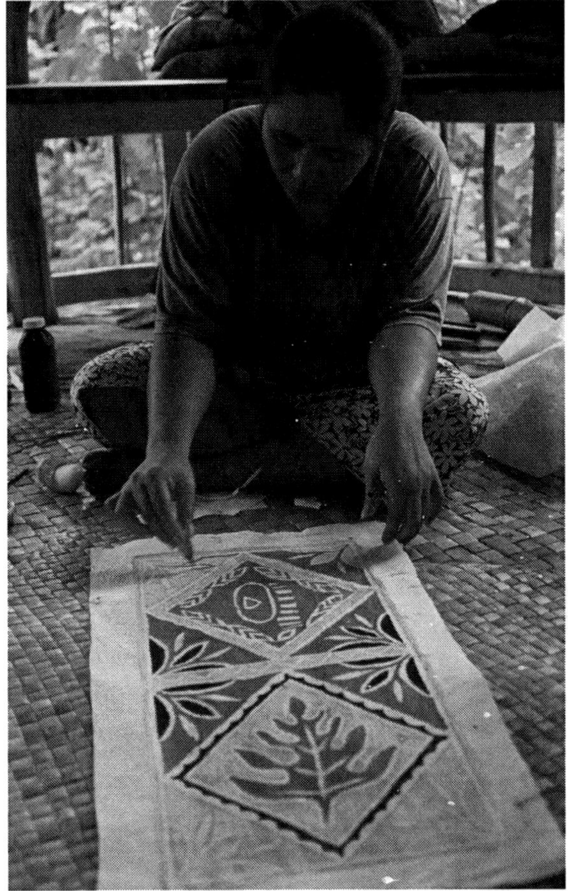

A Samoan woman makes traditional siapo cloth (bark or tapa cloth) in the village of Saláilva.

America, Germany, and Britain all had commercial interests in Samoa during the mid-nineteenth century. Coconut oil was the main commodity, but the United States was far more interested in Samoa as a location for a naval base. The first formal agreements to secure rights to build and maintain such a base in Pago Pago were secured by treaty in the late nineteenth century. The U.S. Navy originally administered the territory, but in the early 1970s this responsibility was transferred to the Department of the Interior. American Samoa has elected its own governor since 1977. In addition, the territory has a legislature with an eighteen-member Senate and a twenty-member House of Representatives. American Samoans send a delegate to the United States House of Representatives.

Sociopolitical Organization

The *Aiga*

Samoan villages are organized around the household and the extended family unit. Each household is headed by a man, the *matai,* who is responsible for those who live under his roof. The household is generally made up of a husband, wife, and their children, as well as elderly parents and other kin. One feature of Samoan household structure is mobility, with individuals having the ability to live with a wide variety of people, and often changing residence to do so. Within the village, each household owns a plot of land with separate houses for sleeping, cooking, guests, and an outhouse.

The household head is given a title by his extended family, the *aiga*. The *aiga* "owns" the title it confers—which will be either Chief or Talking Chief—although it is a title that is bestowed for life upon the *matai*. Each *aiga* has a home village where it owns land and where its elected *matai* resides. The portion of the *aiga* that resides with the *matai* must answer to the larger group for its maintenance of their property in the village.

Aiga are large because membership may be claimed not only through blood ties but also those of marriage and adoption. Individuals can therefore trace ties to as many as a dozen *aiga*, and it is a rare Samoan who cannot claim kinship ties to a king or "paramount chief" (Holmes 1974).

The *aiga* is an active group only on certain occasions. Chief among these are upon the death of a *matai*, when they must convene to elect his replacement, or those occasions when *aiga* members must supply the *matai* with goods for exchange purposes. More salient divisions are branches of the family, which are referred to as *faletama*, or "houses of the children." Each son and daughter of the *aiga*'s original *matai* would initiate a branch. There appears to be a special deference paid to the female branches, despite the fact that it is the male branches from which future *matais* will be elected. To ignore the preferences of female branch members is believed to result in misfortune at best, and sickness and death in the worst of cases. This special attention to the male and female branches of a family is reflected in a specific pattern of behavior between men and women. It is expected that those who stand in the classification of brother and sister to one another (which would include cousins as well as siblings) will not use sexual language in each other's presence, dance together, spend time alone together, or express affection openly.

The *Matai*

Electing a *matai* is a process of deliberation that may span weeks and is often hotly contested. Different branches of the family each have a candidate they wish to put forth, and they offer a variety of arguments to support him. These are generally based on the man's intelligence, wealth, ceremonial knowledge, previous service to family interests, and, in recent years, both his years of formal education and his ability to negotiate with Europeans in issues of politics and economics. Generally, if a son of the former *matai* meets all these criteria, he will have an advantage over other candidates. However, proven service to the greater good of the family may often take precedence over purely genealogical qualifications. It is also advantageous to have resided in the household of a *matai*, which affords the ability to begin participating in family service events at an early age. Men are rarely considered for election as *matai* before they are 40, and those young men who aspire to the position one day may begin to plan their strategy long in advance.

A man may choose to live in a household where he will be the only male of his age, thereby being the likely candidate put forth by the household when the time comes. Or he may move to his wife's household, if there are no male competitors, should he currently be residing in a household where he is one of several young men.

The process of electing a new *matai* is under the guidance of a *matai* who is related to the deliberating family. He will listen to all the arguments put forth in support of each candidate and preside over the vote. Once a new *matai* has been chosen, there is a feast for the family only, followed at a later date by an inauguration ceremony and feast that involves the entire village. It is at this time that the village council, with all the other *matais* in the village present, will observe the newly elected *matai*'s skill in delivering a traditional inauguration address. He is expected to display not only his wisdom but also his skill as an orator and recounter of Samoan myth.

Once he has pleased the other *matais* in this display, it is incumbent upon him to turn his attention to the community at large, providing food for a village-wide feast, at which occasion he will present the other *matais* with gifts. When this protocol has been accomplished, he is officially ensconced as the *matai* to his household, a position he will hold for the rest of his life. On rare occasions, a man who has been found to be either ineffective or cruel has been stripped of this title, but such events are rare. A more common occurrence is the election of a new *matai* before the death of the current man at the latter's request, when he is elderly and infirm and wants the family to have more active leadership than he can continue to provide.

The responsibilities of a *matai* are many. He is expected to provide leadership in all facets of family life. If there is a dispute, he is the arbiter. He encourages warm family relations, offers advice, directs religious participation. He oversees all family lands, and represents the family in village affairs. His demeanor must be different from his former posture as a man of lesser import. One *matai,* elected at a younger age than is the norm, observed:

> "I have been a chief only four years and look, my hair is grey, although in Samoa grey hair comes very slowly. . . . But always I must act as if I were old. I must walk gravely and with a measured step. I may not dance except upon most solemn occasions, neither may I play games with the young men. Old men of sixty are my companions and watch my every word, lest I make a mistake. Thirty-one people live in my household. For them I must plan, I must find them food and clothing, settle their disputes, arrange their marriages. There is no one in my whole family who dares to scold me or even to address me familiarly by my first name. It is hard to be so young and yet be a chief." (Mead in Holmes 1974:22)

Traditionally, families tend to the land communally, under the direction of the *matai.* The village as a whole may pool its labor for projects that have the entire community as a focus, but work is generally family-bound. The yield is also shared equally by family members, and it falls to the *matai* to see to it that every individual receives a fair share. It is also incumbent upon him to make certain that a reserve of wealth is accumulated to offset times of economic need or social obligation. This practice is changing somewhat in modern times, as individuals wish to add to their personal fortunes. However, such changes are occurring within the framework of the traditional system, as an addition more than a replacement of older values. Lowell Holmes, in his ethnography of the village Fitiuta, on the island of Ta'u, observes that despite increased financial opportunities for young people, their family and *matai* obligations remain unaltered. He writes:

> In spite of the greater emphasis now being placed on the individual in the economic and social interactions of the household, the average Samoan is still committed to the traditional system. Even among teachers and government office workers in Tutuila (the most acculturated of Samoans), it was found that better than three-fourths believed that the *matai* system is adequate for shaping the future of Samoan society. (1974:23)

Historically, there has been some misunderstanding of the *matai* system, in that his leadership has been reported to be dictatorial and oppressive. However, Holmes finds the Samoan household to be structured "very democratically." In fact, the freedom of movement between Samoan households works to effectively counter any excessive authoritarianism in *matais*. They must strike a balance between effective leadership, which ensures that tasks are efficiently accomplished, and a harsh and unreasonable style. If he is overly demanding, household members may simply move elsewhere. (One informant confided to Holmes that his strategy was to move to another household just before he knew he was to have a particularly dreaded set of tasks assigned to him.)

Chiefs and Talking Chiefs

The title *matai* is a chiefly one, but within this designation we can speak of Chief or Talking Chief. The former category has three ranked levels within it: High Chief, Chief, and Between the Posts Chief. Talking Chiefs also have three levels of status: Orator Chief, Legs of the Talking Chief, and Common Chief.

The roles of chiefs vary, to some extent, according to village structure. In some villages there is but one High Chief, and his singularity affords him more power. In larger villages there may be several "brother chiefs" who all hold this uppermost rank. In all cases, it is the role of the High Chief to oversee the village council, serve as host to visitors to the village, and mediate disputes. He receives the first servings (and most desirable portions) of food and drink at feasts. Chiefs of the secondary and tertiary rank participate less in village council decisions and are clothed in less grand costume.

High Talking Chiefs are the village orators and are famed for their exquisite ceremonial speech. In public ceremonies, the High Talking Chief bears the responsibility for all oratory portions of meetings, sports competitions, property and marriage exchanges, and other ceremonies. When exchange parties set out to another village, the High Talking Chief is always in attendance, and upon arriving in the host village, he must recite, from memory, a highly stylized recitation of salutations. In turn, the High Talking Chief of the host village must deliver an oratory to welcome the guests, entertain them for their stay, and bid them an elaborate ceremonial farewell. The art of oration is highly prized, and while there is ample opportunity for a High Talking Chief to improvise in spinning his speeches, peppering them with tales from mythology or phrases from the Bible, there is also protocol to be followed. Certain speeches are to be structured in a particular way and committed to memory. Talking Chiefs often employ poetics in their performances, usually in the form of *solo,* rhyming couplets with a prescribed meter, often concerned with mythological themes.

Holmes (1974) describes the oratory of Talking Chiefs in the ceremonial context as "[functioning] less as communication than as art" (p. 29). Talking Chiefs are superb performers, who are experts at commanding their audiences' riveted attention. Holmes describes a typical performance:

> Generally the voice volume rises from a whisper to nearly a shout as the speech proceeds. Now and again a special point will be emphasized with a gesture of the fly whisk or a sudden clipped phrase. A momentary pause or sudden reduction of voice volume highlights a thought of which the orator wants his audience to make special note. When interest appears to lag, a bit of sarcasm or humor or a proverbial cliché may be used to renew flagging attention spans. (p. 30)

In Samoa, as elsewhere in the Pacific, debates about the position and power of the traditional chief figure prominently in the modern national political agenda. Lindstrom and White (1997) call attention to this "renewed visibility of chiefs" (p. 2) in a number of modern nation-states, pointing out that chiefs occupy a strategic position today as they did in the colonial past. Occupying a powerfully strategic position between local groups and national authority, chiefs find themselves "mediating local realities and larger spheres of national and transnational interaction" (p. 3).

The *Aumaga* and the *Aualuma*

Chiefs, Talking Chiefs, and *matais* are the titled men of the village. Those who are untitled belong to a work cooperative called the *aumaga.* This group is sometimes called "the strength of the village" (Holmes 1974:31) because these men are truly the labor core of the entire community. The *aumaga* builds houses, repairs roads, plants and harvests the gardens, fishes from the coral reef, and cuts copra (coconut meat) for sale. There are ceremonial responsibilities that fall to the *aumaga* as well, largely concerning assisting the chief in ritual and cooking and serving food at ceremonies. They serve as informal keepers of the peace, and interact with one another as a large group of friends might, playing cards and cricket, or gathering for dances and parties. The *aumaga* is under the leadership of a relative of the chief, called the *manaia,* who convenes the group to plan their activities. Although the *manaia* need not be a true son of the chief, he is in a fictive kinship relationship such that he is referred to as "son" by the chief, whatever his actual kinship tie may be.

Unmarried women have a parallel group, called the *aualuma.* This association, like the *aumaga,* serves the needs of the village by undertaking all of the social, economic, and ceremonial tasks that chiefs' older wives can no longer accomplish. In the past, there was a woman who was in some ways analogous to the *manaia,* in that she was the "fictive daughter" of the chief much in the way the *manaia* was a "fictive son." However, hers was not a leadership position. The *taupou,* as she was known, was a ceremonial figure whose function was to publicly represent virginity. At the occasion of her marriage to a High Chief or *manaia* from another village, she was publicly "tested" by the village High Talking Chief, who wrapped his finger in white bark cloth and broke her hymen, displaying the blood as proof of her virginity. Although there is still an *aualuma* in every Samoan village, the position of *taupou* has changed. *Taupous* are women appointed by the chief—often married women with children—who function as official hosts to entertain visitors from other villages or assist with ceremonial duties. The ranks of the modern *aualuma* are made up of unmarried women and widows who are a subset of the Women's Committee. All these women work together on community projects such as fund-raising events for the church, staging dances for village celebrations, shellfish gathering at the water's edge, and helping out at the local clinic.

The *Fono*

The *fono,* or village council, is the central decision-making forum of the village. Informal gatherings of Talking Chiefs, which set the agenda for the council meetings, are important precursors of the formal *fono,* allowing all the *matai* to know what issues are to be debated and resolved. They can then prepare their thoughts about the matters and seek counsel and opinions from other family members. Such preliminary meetings also make evident the general sentiment about issues, so that all concerned will know which proposals are likely to have support and which are potentially more hotly contested.

The *fono* begins with a formal welcome provided by the Talking Chief. The *aumaga* sits outside the council house, and the Chiefs and Talking Chiefs convene within. In all Samoan villages, *fono* begin with the *kava* ceremony. *Kava* is a root that is cut and pounded into a pulp and then strained in water to make a drink. The preparation of the *kava* is a highly ritualized act, performed by the Talking Chief, who selects the root, and various members of the *aumaga.* One man cuts the root, another pounds it into a pulp, and it is then the job of the *manaia* to strain it over and over until it is the proper consistency. The *manaia* carefully observes the color of the *kava,* to judge its strength; as it splashes into the bowl from the strainer, he listens to the sound of the liquid falling and can determine when he has achieved the perfect concentration of pulp and water. At this, he pours the *kava* from a great height, so the assembled chiefs can see it. It is the Talking Chief who sings out that it is ready, and the chiefs applaud to signal their acceptance.

Serving the *kava* has a formal protocol as well. The order in which chiefs are served denotes their rank. Beginning at the top of the hierarchy, High Chief and then High Talking Chief are served; then the next level of these two categories of Chief, and so on. Prestige is accorded both the man who drinks first and the man who drinks last. The High Talking Chief serves the *kava,* sometimes calling out the names of the men; in the case of chiefs of very high rank, he calls out not their names, but the names of their cups. Only the most elite of chiefs have cup titles, which are usually phrases that allude to sacred myths, events, or places. Talking Chiefs are given their *kava* while being told "your *kava*"; chiefs without cup titles are given theirs with the directive, "drink."

Now the meeting can begin in earnest. Each item of the agenda is addressed in turn, with time allowed for discussion, differences of opinion, and evidence to support both sides of an argument should there be one. Each *matai* has the opportunity to speak, and it is the speech that is the official casting of a vote. No count is taken of raised hands or ballots cast or verbal "ayes" and "nays." Compromise and consensus are sought, but majority rules. This is not calculated in numbers of votes, because those of higher status hold greater sway in decision making. The vote of a High Chief counts more than that of a secondary one. Whatever the outcome of a decision, it is always assumed to be an issue that may be reopened at a future *fono*. Solidarity in the community is promoted by reaching solutions that satisfy all council members. If a decision leads to hard feelings, this will be counterproductive for the village as a whole, and thus no decision is seen as irrevocable.

Marriage and the Family

Gift giving holds an important place in Samoan social relations, and weddings are a primary venue for this sort of exchange. Because it is so central a feature, the planning of a marriage ceremony involves extensive preparation for the transfer of property: *toga* (female property) will be exchanged for *oloa* (male property).

The households of the bride and groom are equally involved in the planning and expense of the wedding. They provide the bulk of the enormous feast, with guests bringing smaller dishes to contribute. There are generally two ceremonies performed, one following the other. The bride and groom march through the village, wedding party attending them, to the district judge, who conducts a civil ceremony. From there, the newly married couple and their attendants walk to the church, where all the guests are gathered. A religious ceremony is performed, after which the feasting and gift-giving begin.

Newly married couples do not establish their own new household. However, they are free to choose which side of the family they will join. This is owing to the fact that Samoans have an ambilineal kinship system; individuals may choose to affiliate with any of a number of groups, through either their fathers or their mothers. There is a tendency to become most closely involved with the group where one resides, but membership in several groups is recognized.

Wherever a husband and wife reside, they are expected to work cooperatively with the rest of the household. Large families are economically advantageous, and older children are expected to care for their younger siblings when they themselves are hardly more than toddlers. For the first few years, children sleep with their mothers and their days are largely playful. By the time they are 3 or 4, they begin to shoulder some responsibilities. Girls are directed toward child care and housework; boys help with animals and water gathering, though their days are more leisurely than are those of their sisters. By the time children are 7 or 8, they have been fully indoctrinated into the usual tasks of Samoan life, having participated to some degree in agriculture, fishing, cooking, and child care. It is at this age that formal schooling begins, and the bulk of a child's day is spent at the village schoolhouse.

As Samoans age, status increases as responsibilities lighten. The elderly are valued by their fellow villagers and are shown special deference at public gatherings. Restrictions regarding food and social interaction become lax, and older people feel they are at the best time of life, visiting with family and friends, doing as much as they care to and no more.

When death occurs, funeral preparations begin immediately. The church choir is dispatched to the mourner's home, where the body has been bathed, dressed in white, and placed on a cushion of woven mats. During the twenty-four hours between death and burial, the family of the deceased stays with the body while the burial site is selected. The burial itself is a religious ceremony, followed by a meal for all those who assisted in the care and burial.

Economic Organization

Property

It is the *matai* who controls the land, in that he holds sway over allocation of plots and the ways in which those plots are used. He does not, however, have the authority to sell the land or will it to his own children upon his death. Family land essentially belongs to the corporate group. They vote on its disposition, and work it cooperatively.

Land in a Samoan village is divided into four categories. The first contains village house lots, not agricultural sites. There may be trees on the land from which fruits may be picked, or an occasional taro patch may be encouraged to grow. By and large, however, this land is where houses are built in clusters—main sleeping houses, a guest house, and latrines.

True plantation plots are situated outside the village, either on the hills overlooking the houses or along the coast. The former are best for breadfruit and bananas; the latter support coconut groves. Holmes (1974) describes these plots as deceptively overgrown; plants and trees grow in a seemingly haphazard placement, not in cultivated rows. Underbrush covers the land, and the uninitiated eye could easily survey a plantation plot and not recognize it as land under cultivation. Despite this appearance, however, these plots are owned by families, and their boundaries—rocks, streams, certain trees—are easily recognizable to all villagers.

A third category of land is the family reserve section, the plots where taro and yams are cultivated. These plots may be lent to other villagers, who may use them to grow crops for their own consumption. They are then regarded as owning the crops but not the land. Because the foodstuffs planted in these sections are those that mature and are harvested quickly, these sites are cultivated less intensively than the plantation plots.

The fourth type of land is village land, and it is both farther removed from the village sites and less often cultivated. Permission to plant here is granted by the village council because the land is community property and not family owned. An individual who is willing to expend the enormous effort required to clear the overgrown land may petition to do so. If he is given leave to undertake the project, he may continue to use it as long as he cares for it. Village land also provides a site for hunting wild pigs and birds. In addition to this land high up in the mountains, some coastal land is also village property. There, any individual who wishes to fish is free to do so.

Cultivation

Clearing the land for planting is hard work. Large trees and bushes are cut down with axes; knives slice down tall grass, ferns, and smaller scrubby bushes. Felled vegetation is left to dry and then is cut up further for burning. Small, well-controlled fires clear the land.

Digging sticks are then employed to dislodge rocks and loosen the soil for planting. Some crops—banana trees chief among them—never need to be reestablished in a formal way. Although new taro and yam patches are started from old plants, banana groves can be cut back, encouraging new suckers to grow from the base of trees and develop into another plant. Papaya trees are easier still: workers in the field eat papaya and toss the pits to the ground. Trees spring up regularly from discarded seeds. Oranges and mangoes grow wild but are sometimes planted from seed if additional trees are desired.

In this tropical climate, irrigation is unnecessary. Leaves from trees planted in the fields fall and decay into fertilizer, enriching the soil.

Coconut is the most important crop and the one with the widest variety of uses. Copra is produced for cash income, but the coconut meat is a dietary staple as well. The meat is eaten raw; it can be grated and pressed into "coconut cream." The nut of the mature plant is eaten as a snack. The wood of the tree is used for building a host of items, from houses to cricket bats. Leaves are woven into fans, hats, floor mats, baskets, toys, and shoes. The fibers in the outer husk provide rope for outrigger canoes. Coconut shells serve as bowls, water bottles, and utensils. Oil from the coconut kernel has cosmetic and medicinal uses.

Despite the value of coconut, taro is preferred as a food. Boiled or baked, it is eaten cold at nearly every meal. Breadfruit is eaten more often, but probably because it is so abundant.

There are many specialists in Samoan society, each with a distinctive talent. One may be an expert boat builder, or tattooer, or surgeon. There are, however, no agricultural specialists. Cultivation is the major part of everyone's day, whether it is organized by family, an *aualuma* or *aumaga,* or Women's Committee. Although everyone is expected to work, harvests are shared without regard to individual effort. Holmes (1974) observes, "[t]he industrious and lazy alike enjoy adequate food, clothing, and shelter" (p. 40).

Village councils generally set up a work schedule to organize the agricultural life of the community, day by day. These are hardly arbitrary lists of tasks; the schedule is planned with particular ends in mind. One of the most important of these is to regulate thievery. If copra is only to be cut on Tuesday, an individual sneaking into the bush to do so on a Thursday can be easily detected. Situating families in their banana groves on Mondays and Wednesdays ensures that no one else can be there, picking their bananas; for a thief to do so on another day would not go unnoticed: one is not to be carrying harvested bananas on any other days.

Fishing

Unlike cultivation, fishing does have its specialists. These are the *tautai,* who captain the thirty-foot-long outrigger canoes and sit in the stern of the boat, fishing for bonito, a breed of mackerel. Paddlers locate a school of bonito and keep the canoe in position. A fourteen-foot-long bamboo pole is secured on a shelf of blocks, which hold it steady at a 45-degree angle to the water. Line from the rod dangles a lure just at the surface of the water. The *tautai* keeps close watch on the bait, so he can jerk the catch out of the water quickly, sending it flying into the back of the canoe. The most skilled *tautai* have perfected the motion such that the fish is freed from the hook, eliminating the time it would take to manually remove the hook from the fish's mouth. The line can then be placed back into the school of bonito as quickly as possible. The paramount sign of a highly skilled *tautai* is the necessity of many of his crew to swim alongside the boat, on the return trip, owing to the quantity of bonito now occupying their place.

Much ritual is associated with bonito fishing, most of it after the catch has been brought back, and is centered around the division of the fruits of the day's labor. At the end of the day, all boats head to the outside of the reef to report the number of their catch to the fleet's chief. He offers a prayer of thanks for that day's yield and requires each *tautai* to state how many bonito are in his hold. Every boat must arrive home with an equal number of fish. Before heading for home, there is a ceremonial meal where the crews of each boat eat raw bonito, given to them by the chief as part of his allocation of the catch. *Tautai* eat first, the crew next, and then the boats return to shore. Families meet their canoes, pay the crew in more fish, and return home with the remainder of the catch. While the boats have been out, villagers have been at home, cultivation at a standstill, encouraging successful fishing with their prayers. Each time a fish slips off the hook is an occasion for the *tautai* to remark that the family at home is not offering adequate prayer.

Bonito fishing from large outrigger canoes is only one form of angling. Gathering along the coastline yields reef worms and turtles. Nets ensnare fish swimming close to the shore, and wooden traps capture lobsters, eels, and crabs. Pole and spear fishing for bass and snapper is popular. Entire schools of fish can be poisoned or dynamited inside the reefs, and men shoot spear guns armed with heavy wire, attacking from within the water and wearing the captured fish around their waists.

Those who enjoy the risk take to the water in rowboats in search of sharks. They entice them to the boat's edge by throwing meat into the water, and when the shark comes alongside to devour the bait, men slip heavy nooses of rope around the shark's head. Women are expert in reef gathering, and their efforts are sometimes rewarded with the discovery of an octopus, which they kill by biting it or by thrashing it against a rock.

Fishing took up more subsistence time in the past than it does in modern times. The Samoans' love for fish can be more easily satisfied by purchasing cans of sardines, tuna, and salmon at the local bush store.

Domestic Work

The traditionally strict division of labor between men and women is less pronounced in modern times. Traditionally, however, cooking was the exclusive domain of men. In Samoa today, men are still primarily responsible for food preparation, but they are especially involved in cooking traditional foods. When women prepare parts of the meal, their domain is "foreign" food—new items that are prepackaged, such as cake mixes or canned goods—which they often cook in modern vessels, among them pressure cookers and deep fryers. In the past, most dishes were prepared in an earth oven, and men still cook in them today. On the floor of a cooking house, stones are arranged to form the base, and kindling is lit on top to heat the stones. Another layer of stones is added once the blaze is at its peak, and in less than an hour the embers are removed, leaving hot rocks that can be spread out to accommodate the amount of food to be cooked. The food is placed on top of the rocks in the center and covered with leaves, and rocks from the edges are placed on top of the food. Layer upon layer is built, with the leaves acting to prevent the food from burning. The topmost layer is a canopy of broad leaves that serves as a lid, trapping the heat. This method is most commonly employed for cooking fish and vegetables. When pigs are roasted, their preparation is more complex. Pork is the focus of ceremonial meals, and both preparation and division of the meat once cooked are of the utmost importance. Holmes (1974) describes this process:

> Pigs are strangled by laying them on their back and standing on a stick placed across their throat. The carcass is then dragged across the heated stones of the earth oven in order to singe off the hair and bristles. The abdomen is then cut open, the internal organs removed and wrapped in leaves to be cooked separately, and the hollow abdominal cavity is filled with papaya leaves, which supposedly flavor the meat and act as a tenderizer. The whole pig is then placed on the circle of heated cooking stones with the feet tucked under the carcass. After receiving a cover of leaves, and sometimes a layer of damp burlap bags, the pig is allowed to cook for approximately one hour. (pp. 49–50)

Although the pork is not cooked thoroughly enough to eat in this amount of time, it is much easier to distribute in a partially raw state, when it can be cut accurately without falling apart. Meat is given based on rank, with certain parts designated for particular groups of individuals.

Barkcloth is an important commodity in Samoa, and its production is exclusively the domain of women. Cloth is made from mulberry bush bark. Branches are stripped and the inner bark soaked to soften. Sharpened clam shells scrape it smooth, and several strips are bundled together and beaten into strips of cloth about a foot long. They are then dried and decorated. Finished barkcloths have a variety of functions. They are worn as ceremonial garb, wrapped around as skirts; are used by women as shawls; serve as bedspreads; and are hung as room dividers. Women also weave pandanus leaf floormats and sleeping mats.

While young girls are introduced into the art of clothmaking and weaving by older women, young men are directed toward carpentry. Boat and house building are done without blueprints; young apprentices watch more skilled artisans and participate in more stages of the process as they become more skilled. House building is often a ceremonial affair, with feasts arranged to mark the beginning and end of construction.

→ Religious Life

The Supernatural Ones: *Atua* and *Aitu*

Samoan myth tells of the Tagaloa gods, the *atua,* who live as a family on the ten mountain tops that form heaven. These gods appear not to have been attended to in the ways in which many peoples worship their deities. There were no priests who attended them, although *matai* and Talking Chiefs might invoke their names at feasts and other ceremonies. At mealtime, spoken prayers of thanks might be offered. The *atua* were the higher level of deities. Beneath them were the *aitu,* the spirits of ancestors. Several *aitu* are known throughout Samoa and are something of "national figures," associated with particular activities (such as fishing) or sacred places. *Aitu* are a part of modern Samoan belief, often thought to be capable of wreaking havoc if displeased. They sometimes take human form again, dressing in white and appearing in the night. Certain spots are known to attract these ghosts, and it is the rare Samoan who does not have an experience to relate regarding a brush with an *aitu.*

If their families are behaving improperly, *aitu* send an illness, which is characterized by chills, fever, and bouts of delirious behavior. Cures may be effected by herbal remedies administered by local specialists. Families examine the recent past to see if any activities or decisions made could have incited an *aitu*'s wrath. Recovery can be hastened by remedying such mistakes.

Some *aitu* are significant only to a particular family or village. Taking the form of birds, fish, or game animals, these often become taboo food items for the group that recognizes them as spiritually important.

Tapu

The Polynesian word *tapu* is the source of "taboo." *Tapu* encompasses not only taboo's sense of the forbidden (a set of supernaturally dictated prohibitions), but also that of sanctity (a sacred bond). In asserting that the relationship between humanity and the land is *tapu,* Samoans underscore the sacred responsibility to care for the environment. Thus, *tapu* is both a set of restrictions and a set of responsibilities—all aimed at maintaining balance and harmony. In addition, certain categories of indigenous knowledge are considered *tapu* knowledge because such traditions are under the protection of *aitu* or *atua* spirits. This knowledge—genealogical information, rules for fishing and singing, the correct ways to build a house—are kept within the confines of the family, passed down through the generations. To share such information with outsiders would anger the custodial spirit. All relationships—between people, between humanity and the gods, between Samoans and the natural world—have boundaries, and these boundaries are defined and protected by *tapu.* Often these delineations demonstrate what is safe and what is dangerous. Breaches of *tapu* put an individual at risk, physically and spiritually.

Christianity

Christian missionaries came to Samoa in the early nineteenth century and were met with very little resistance. It has been suggested that the structure of indigenous beliefs was easily incorporated into the introduced religion. Tagaloa was identified as a central deity, and mealtime prayers were easily explained as saying grace. In fact, some *matai* argued that this new religion ought to be quickly accepted, as it brought with it the promise of acquiring valuable material goods such as those owned by the missionaries, and others agreed that wars might be prevented by embracing Christianity. For their part, missionaries recognized the power of the chiefs and realized that chiefly acceptance of Christianity was the means to successfully convert entire villages. The political influence of the chief meant that their acceptance of Christianity was, in essence, on behalf of their whole family, and thus the conversion of a village *matai* "[won] the souls of entire villages for the Lord" (MacPherson 1997:276). Samoan appreciation for verbal skills, institutionalized in the Talking Chief, resulted in their delight in "listening to the almost interminable sermons delivered by the mission pastors" (Holmes 1974:60).

Although some villages were slower in their acceptance, Christianity took hold in Samoa quite easily, aided by construction of church-run schools. Communion was accepted as being much like the *kava* ceremony, which it now accompanied; sermons were greeted with the same rapt attention Talking Chiefs inspired. The church became the focal point of community life. While Samoa is now almost entirely Christian, traditions and beliefs tied to *atua* and *aitu,* as well as the mandates of *tapu,* remain vibrant.

Margaret Mead in Samoa

One of the greatest debates in modern anthropology concerns the questions raised by Derek Freeman in 1983 about Margaret Mead's work in Samoa.

Mead, one of the discipline's most well-known and respected members, conducted ethnographic research among Samoan adolescents in the 1920s. At that time in the United States, the rebellion and turmoil that characterized the teenage years was regarded as a "natural" and universally human consequence of growing into adulthood. It was Mead's hypothesis that this turbulent time of life for American youth was not necessarily a biological dictate shared by adolescents everywhere. Rather, it was also greatly influenced by the culture in which children were raised. Mead found very little evidence among Samoan youth of the anguish and emotional upheaval so common to American teenagers. Her ethnographic studies were at the forefront of establishing the view that individuals are very much a product of the environments in which they live and are nurtured. Freeman, a sociobiologist, took issue with Mead's position, claiming that she painted a false picture of Samoa in order to promote her belief in the primacy of "nurture" over "nature." Mead's depiction was of a culture that had less repressive sexual mores than contemporary American society of the time and one in which there were fewer conflicts and tensions. Freeman asserted that Samoa was, in fact, a culture replete with tension and aggression. Moreover, he believed Mead was misled by her informants, who provided her with false reports. Serena Nanda (1994:147) writes:

> Freeman uses his criticisms of Mead's ethnographic work to put forth his own sociobiological view in which a large component of human behavior, particularly aggression, is seen as biologically determined. Many of Mead's former colleagues and students have defended her work, pointing out that her ethnography was done in 1925, when anthropology was still in its infancy as a science, and that she worked well within the tradition of ethnographic methodology as it was known at that time. They point out that although she may have been wrong about some of her facts and emphases, reinterpretation of ethnography is a standard practice in anthropology and is part of the growth and development of the field. Freeman's critics aptly point out that the attention given to his book in the media represents a current sympathy with politically conservative implications of his sociobiological stance. Both Mead's and Freeman's work must be seen in the context of the "nature/nurture" controversy. It was due in great part to Mead's work that the theory that we are products of our environment and that we can reshape that environment if we are willing took hold in American scientific and popular thinking in the decades between 1930 and 1960. Beginning with the publication of Edward Wilson's *Sociobiology: The New Synthesis* (1975), the stage was set for criticism of the kind of cultural emphases that Mead's work embodies.

In 1990, a lengthy volume was published, bringing together dozens of anthropologists commenting on the "Mead–Freeman debate." Many different viewpoints were represented. Some took issue with the manner in which Freeman's challenges were presented; some agreed that Mead's original fieldwork was flawed. Most offered insightful commentary on the fact that it was more than two people's contradictory interpretations that were at issue; the nature of truth, the meaning of science, the power of myth, and the politics of academics were all in play. As the editor of the collection, Hiram Caton (1990), observed, the controversy led to an entire discipline's taking stock of itself, past and present.

"The Great Migration" and Beyond

In 1950, the Navy turned its governance of American Samoa over to the Department of the Interior. Nearly 6,000 Samoans had been employed by the Navy, some acting as local police, called *Fitafita* guardsman, and their livelihoods were in jeopardy. In 1952, Samoan naval employees and their families were given the opportunity to move to Hawaii in search of employment. This began the so-called Great Migration of the 1950s; between 1952 and 1956, an estimated 7,500 Samoans resettled in Hawaii (Pouesi 1994). For those who remained, change came again in the 1960s, when the U.S. government escalated its interest in the islands. With budget appropriations for Samoa tripled, programs regarding industry, education, and tourism were vigorously mounted. Holmes (1974:97) observes that prosperity brought changes to Samoa:

> Because of employment in the new construction program and in a tuna cannery, Samoans had more money. Beer and soft drink consumption had soared. Bush stores sold a wide variety of European tinned food. Taxi-cabs and private cars were numerous and traffic was becoming a problem. Girls . . . had begun to wear makeup and European hairstyles . . . stereo[s] were not uncommon household products.

In the 1970s, Samoan emigration to Hawaii and the United States mainland increased dramatically. California is home to more than 90,000 Samoans, and Los Angeles alone has a Samoan community of more than 12,000—many of whom maintain ties with Samoan culture and continue to hold traditional Samoan values. Southern California has a number of Samoan community organizations designed to provide assistance to newly arrived individuals as well as social and financial aid to those already established. Chief among these are *Samoa Mo Samoa* ("Samoans for Samoans"), a nonprofit organization in San Francisco, and the National Office of Samoan Affairs (NOSA), based in Los Angeles.

Village *fonos* continue to wield considerable local power, with recent legislation securing the rights of local leaders to exercise authority in accordance with established village custom (MacPherson 1997). The traditional *matai* system also exerts a powerful influence on Samoan life in the United States. *Matai* leaders are local community leaders, called upon to settle disputes and organize activities. *Matai* leaders who emigrate retain their ties to their *aiga* and, as part of the obligation they incur to maintain their position, send money home to their families and villages. Some return to Samoa to vote in elections as another way to nurture their ties. Meleisea (1992) reports that it is not uncommon for representatives of political factions in Samoa to visit California and Hawaii to collect campaign donations. Janes (1990) refers to the ways in which Samoan migrants have responded to the urban, capitalist life they found stateside as "a creative kind of cultural consolidation" (p. 163). Within churches and local organizations, familiar forms of association and obligation have been altered to suit new demands. He points especially to the *fa'alavelave* (literally, "problem" or "difficulty"), events that constitute a life-crisis and demand communal effort. Funerals, weddings, and nonritual events that require economic assistance are the primary examples. In Samoa, *fa'alavelave* are characterized by the exchange of food and handmade goods. In the United States, these reciprocal exchanges are primarily made in cash. Local members pay dues and donations to help with the cost of weddings and funerals, housing and education, knowing that they will be guaranteed similar assistance if they should need it (Pouesi 1994). By tailoring traditional redistribution practices to local needs, Samoan migrant communities maintain solidarity (and prestige) and provide support. Janes, a medical anthropologist, has investigated the health effects of the social stressors involved in migration and adaptation of Samoans in California. He finds that the "monetization" of traditional Samoan institutions such as *fa'alavelave* can take its toll. The economic burdens involved, stress resulting from status shifts, and the exigencies of daily life in a new community have all resulted in ill health. However, those Samoans who are closely connected to church groups, who have kin groups that buoy them in times of economic crisis, and who are able to maintain traditional ties and values within their communities seem buffered from the health effects of stress.

Pouesi (1994) notes that in the late 1960s and early 1970s, Samoan-born adolescents were eager to define themselves as "Hawaiians" and "Californians" rather than as Samoans. However, young Samoans born in California and Hawaii, while perhaps less reliant on kin-based mutual support organizations, seem nonetheless to be part of a "revival of pride in Samoan heritage" (p. 86). Local Samoan organizations are experiencing a resurgence, with an infusion of young people attempting to maintain a "collective personality in the face of increasing individualism" (Pouesi 1994:86).

→ For Further Discussion

One of the greatest debates in modern anthropology surrounded the questions raised by Derek Freeman about Margaret Mead's work in Samoa. Mead hypothesized that the rebellion and turmoil that characterized American teenage years was not the "natural" and universally human consequence of growing into adulthood that it was believed to be. In Samoa, she found that adolescents experienced less repression, conflict, and tension and displayed none of the emotional turbulence of "typical" Western teenagers. This supported the view that individuals are very much a product of the environments in which they live and are nurtured. Freeman, a sociobiologist, took issue with Mead's position, claiming that she painted a false picture of Samoa in order to promote her belief in the primacy of "nurture" over "nature." He asserted that Samoa was, in fact, a culture replete with tension and aggression.

Using what you have learned about anthropology's holistic and comparative perspective, how might you address the Mead–Freeman debate? What might be the consequences, positive and negative, of such controversy for the discipline of anthropology? How might the potential for such challenges influence future fieldwork?

CHAPTER 14

THE TROBRIAND ISLANDERS

The Power of Exchange

Location of the Trobriand Islands.

✧ The Beginning

The world started underground. There, below, all the people were, and they were as they would be above. Underground, there were villages. Underground, there were clans. Underground, there were magic and land, gardens and canoes, there was art and there was craft.

Four clans, *kumila,* make all of humanity. Which of these is yours can never be changed. It is for more than one life; it is carried to the next world; it is brought back unchanged when the spirit returns. These have their names, and they are named Malasi, Lukuba, Lukwasisiga, and Lukulabuta.

The people wanted to start the world. They gathered their belongings, and they chose their earth. A brother and a sister came together, up through to the hole to their land, up through the hole to start their *dala* lineage above the ground.

Through each hole came only one *dala:* one brother and sister, one garden, one magic, one village.

✧ Introduction, History, and Geography

The Trobriand Islands are flat coral atolls off the coast of Eastern New Guinea. Four main islands form the group referred to as the Trobriands, but they are surrounded by more than a hundred smaller uninhabited islands. The island of Kiriwina is the most populous; it runs a length of twenty-five miles and is eight miles wide at its widest point. The 25,000 individuals who live on Kiriwina are settled in sixty villages, with the other atolls bringing the current population to nearly 30,000 (Lepani 2007).

The Trobriands are hot and humid year-round, with beaches of sand giving way to coral reefs that reach ten feet high off some shores. These extend some six miles out into the water and provide a vantage point for fine fishing.

The Trobriands were sighted by European sailors more than 200 years ago. American whalers visited in the mid-nineteenth century. In the late nineteenth century, Germans who had settled in parts of Melanesia traveled to the Trobriands to buy yams. For the better part of the twentieth century, the Trobriands were under Australian administration. Papua New Guinea gained independence in 1975.

✧ Settlements and Subsistence

Trobrianders live in thatched huts, some of which have metal roof coverings. Yam houses cluster in a central clearing, towering over the other buildings. Huts have a veranda in the front, where time can be spent carving, chewing betel, and visiting with neighbors.

Yams and pork are the most important foods, but lush Trobriand gardens also yield taro, squash, corn, bananas, tapioca, breadfruit, beans, and cassava. Pigs are only slaughtered on ritual occasions; it is fish that provide the major source of protein in the Trobriand diet. Open-sea fishing is not a year-round occupation, because two seasons of tradewinds churn up the waters and limit access. The lagoons, however, protected from the violent winds, provide good fishing year-round. Those who live in the coastal villages that line the lagoon sell fish to the inlanders. Thirty canoes set out to fish, and when they return to shore, their customers are waiting. Within a few minutes they have sold their entire catch. Found among many of the coral outcroppings are sheltered coves where fresh drinking water is abundant; these coves are favored places for swimming.

The production of yams is a central focus of daily life. Annette Weiner, the ethnographer who is most associated with Trobrianders in modern times, reports her informants as saying, "If a man has yams, he can find anything else he needs" (1987:137).

Yams are used both raw and cooked. Because raw yams can be stored for nearly half a year, they have a long potential exchange life. Once they have been cooked, they cannot function as investments. Thus, yams are both food and wealth, and there are different gardens for each. Food gardens are harvested as the yams are needed to eat. The yams are kept inside after harvesting, and great care is taken in planting to ensure there will be enough yams for food as well as exchange. Exchange gardens have a different character entirely. It is yams from these gardens that are displayed in the yam houses and that remain raw as long as possible.

Growing yams is primarily the domain of men. Some women have their own yam gardens, but these yams never enter into the formal cycle of exchange. A boy's first yam exchange garden is of great importance, and he cannot establish it independently. Boys prepare to enter the exchange system when they move out of their parents' houses in their early teenage years. Some boys will move into bachelor houses with their older brothers; others will live with other boys their age.

In order to make his first garden, a boy must work for an older male who has already established a garden. The younger will receive seed yams from the older, plant and reap the garden, and present the older man with the yield. Often a boy will plant a second garden, and these yams he will give to his father. This will enable him to claim rights to his father's land.

The planting of yam gardens is strenuous labor. Plots are cleared, and the soil is prepared. After planting, as the yams grow, their vines must be staked. Fences must be built around the garden plots to prevent pigs from destroying the new vines.

Taro gardens are planted by all Trobriand men and women, and food gardens, grown by women, yield all the rest of the Trobriand diet.

A Day in the Village

A village on Kiriwina today looks remarkably like it did when famed ethnographer Bronislaw Malinowski first conducted fieldwork there more than three-quarters of a century ago. Huts ring the yam houses, which circle a clearing in the village center. Though villagers at times wear Western clothes, they are most often dressed in fiber skirts and colorful cotton cloth.

The village rises early and, after breakfast, women gather water as men sit on the front porch, chewing betel, a nut that has roughly the same stimulant activity as

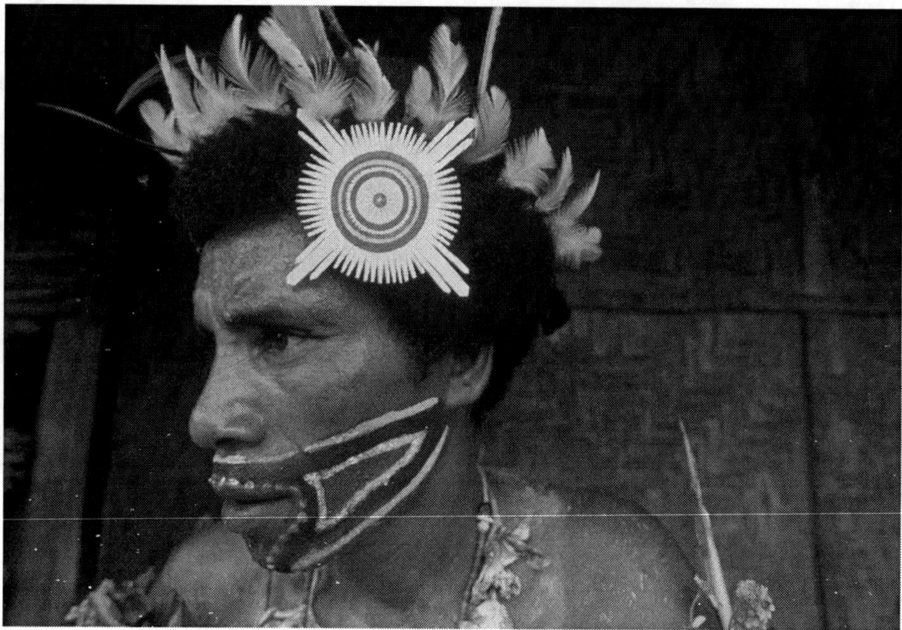

A Trobriand man in ceremonial dress.

coffee. Children play in the central clearing and, while it is still early, most of the adults leave the village to begin their day's gardening. Those who have a special task before them—men who are carving or women who are preparing for a mortuary ceremony—may stay behind, but, except for the few months in the summer when gardening is not a daily pursuit, it is the garden that sets the rhythm of a Trobriand day.

By mid-afternoon the village fills again, as preparation for the evening meal begins. As dusk arrives, teenagers begin their rituals of self-beautification, preparing to set off into the outskirts of the village, where they will dance and sing and court. Evening is a time to visit and gossip, work at crafts, chew betel, and relax. Nighttime is dangerous, as the threat of sorcery in the dark looms large. The village is quiet by midnight, with adults and young children sleeping until dawn takes them back to the gardens.

SOCIAL AND POLITICAL ORGANIZATION

The Substance of Personhood: *Kumila* and *Dala*

All Trobrianders belong to one of four matrilineal clans, called *kumila*. Clan identity is fixed at birth and is so literally a part of personhood that Weiner (1988) was assured that the lines on a person's palms can reveal their clan identity. (And, Weiner found, this was an important identifier when traveling between villages: the only villagers who may be asked to provide food are those who are members of the same clan.) *Kumila* membership dictates marriage rules: one must marry someone from another clan. As is true in many systems, preferred marital partners are those that strengthen ties. The best choice of partner is a member of one's father's *kumila,* a match that maintains a previous alliance.

In addition to belonging to a *kumila,* they also belong to their mother's matrilineage, a smaller unit called the *dala.* Trobrianders emerged from the earth with their *dala* membership in place, and it is an identity that is passed along through matrilineal ancestral spirits at conception. These original *dala* members also brought with them a host of belongings (land, wealth, decorations) and knowledge (dances, magic spells, stories, artistic techniques) that belong to the *dala* forever.

Taken together, *kumila* and *dala* are the "substance of personhood" (Lepina 2007:4), an identity that lasts beyond life. All *dala* and *kumila* members are classified as "brothers" and "sisters" to one another. Trobriand women, according to Weiner (1987), "control immortality" (p. 233), in that they alone can produce and reproduce *dala* identity.

Life's Beginnings

The island of Tuma, near the Trobriands, is a special place. It is there a spirit goes after death, and it is there that a new spirit child is created, returns to Kiriwina to enter a woman's body, and grows to be her child. This spirit seeks a woman who belongs to the same *dala* to which the spirit belonged when housed in a previous body. A baby is formed from the mixture of this spirit and the woman's own blood, and when the baby is born, its mother gives it a name that had belonged to a now-deceased member of her matrilineage. It is in this way that the matriline's identity continues through time. However, as the pregnancy progresses, a woman's husband contributes to the development of the baby through frequent intercourse. Additionally, though the child's "true" ancestral name is given by its mother, the baby's father asks his sister for a name from their own *dala.* It is generally by this name that the child will be called. As Weiner (1988) points out, a child's father thus "supplies the fetus with something more than its own inherited matrilineal substance, but his contribution does not in any way alter the basic physiological connection between a woman's blood and a spirit child" (p. 57).

Women nurse their children for the first 18 months of life, and Trobriand babies are the center of attention for all the villagers. Babies are cuddled and carried, affection bestowed upon them by all their neighbors. Villagers are often seen carrying babies who are not theirs, and elderly men who stay behind when others are off gardening delight in caring for their grandchildren.

In a practical sense, however, the responsibility to see to it that children are fed and clothed and have all they need rests squarely on the shoulders of their fathers. To fall short in these caretaking responsibilities has grave social and political consequences. Fathers are deeply involved in their children's care from the time they are quite small. While babies are still being nursed by their mothers, their fathers feed them bits of mashed food. Weaning is accomplished when babies are left with others for several days. As soon as this occurs, babies sleep with their fathers.

Fathers are charged with maintaining their children's beauty, which is part of every youngster's social persona. Weiner (1988) distinguishes between a child's "physical" beauty and "social" beauty. It is the latter for which a father is responsible. Infants are adorned with shell decorations, which demonstrate a father's wealth, power, and political connections to those with whom he has had to trade to secure highly prized shells. The adornments displayed on a child announce that there is wealth and power in the family.

Life's Endings

Death is never met with equanimity in the Trobriands. Its immediate effects are dramatic, but there are repercussions that last for the better part of a year.

When a person falls ill, a sense of danger is aroused in all the kin. A child who falls sick and dies is clearly the vehicle for someone's desire to strike at the power of the matrilineage. When a powerful adult is stricken, this threat is intensely magnified. All illness is seen as an enemy declaring the intent to do harm. As word of an illness spreads throughout and between villages, questions arise. Who wishes this person harm? And what of the victim's close kin? The sick individual may be asked "Who gave you betel to chew?" "With whom did you go fishing?" The culprit could be anyone. People do not simply die; people are killed. And once illness has resulted in death, the question becomes "Who has killed my kin?" (Weiner 1987).

As life ebbs, people surrounding the dying individual begin to perform tasks that differentiate them into two distinct categories. Some kin—members of the matrilineage—are "owners," and along with members of the village who are clan members, it is they who are responsible for organizing both the burial and the exchange rituals that follow. Owners are not permitted contact with the body and must not participate in the public display of grief. They do not shave their heads or wear the clothes of mourners. Theirs is a heavy burden nonetheless; it is incumbent upon them to perform crucial economic duties, distributing the deceased's valuables and repaying all those who were important during their relative's lifetime.

Other kin are designated as "workers." They are not members of the individual's matriline, but are clan members from other villages or those related patrilineally or by marriage. The first task for some of the women workers, as death draws nearer, is to bathe, dress, and decorate the sufferer. They paint the face of the victim, rub oils into the body, and carefully position shell body ornaments. The body is being prepared for its journey back to Tuma, where it will join the other spirits of Trobrianders who died before. On Tuma, the spirit will be renewed and have a different life. As they do this, they cry. Once death occurs, the process of mourning begins with dramatic wailing. Shrill cries fill the air, and the house where death has occurred is soon filled with sobbing relatives who embrace the corpse and give vent to their grief. The *dala* is diminished with every death. This is felt especially keenly at the death of young women, who hold within their bodies the power to renew the lineage.

From the time of death to the beginning of the mortuary ceremonies, crying becomes formalized. Four times a day, family members engage in ritualized crying. Male workers begin the process of binding the arms and legs of the deceased, and closing off all bodily orifices with coconut husks, so the body will remain straight and there will be no odor. Once the body is prepared, it is placed across the legs of those who have decorated it, with the spouse of the deceased cradling the head.

Men sing mourning songs, telling of the ancestors of the matriline. This unites the group in their grief and helps channel some of their fear, engendered by the sorcery that has caused the death. No workers sleep through the first night so as not to show disrespect to the owners. There is another function served by appropriate mourning: its lack casts suspicion of involvement in causing the death.

The death of an important man brings a multitude of mourners. When a chief fell ill and died during her fieldwork in Kiriwina, Weiner (1988) writes "[b]y early evening, several hundred men had congregated in the central plaza close to Uwelasi's resting place. The workers sat together in village groups, [and] in the dim light of the small fires I could see little except a sea of bodies" (p. 37).

Burial does not signal the end of these mourning obligations; in fact, it sets a whole chain of observances in motion. The spouse in particular must bear the brunt of these traditions, beginning with months of strict seclusion. The fear of sorcery in the Trobriands is great. Despite obvious care and affection displayed in their lives together, suspicion may nonetheless fall on the spouse, and lengthy seclusion is one demonstration of innocence regarding the cause of death.

For several days after the burial, widow or widower is prohibited from speaking to anyone. It is taboo to touch food, and so the spouse must be hand-fed by another. Work of any sort is forbidden, and for many months it is permissible to leave the house only for toileting purposes, which consist of running into the bush, wrapped from head to toe in a woven mat, and returning to the hut as quickly as possible.

As the months pass, members of the spouse's *dala* bring offerings of valuables to the owners, and one by one the bans are lifted. Such taboos extend to some other close relatives of the deceased. These prohibitions are of great seriousness, and one signifier of the way in which mourners are transformed during this period is that their names become taboo and are replaced, for a time, with terms that signify their mourning status. Weiner (1988) recalls, "When Dabweyowa's father died, I forgot that his name had become Tomilabova (the son of a dead man). One day, shortly after his father was buried and while we were working together, I called him Dabweyowa. Immediately, without saying a word, he got up and left my house. I did not see Tomilabova for two days, and when he did reappear we never discussed the incident. I never made that mistake again" (p. 43).

During the time the spouse and certain members of the deceased's matriline are in mourning, their ritualized weeping sets divisions of the day in the village. Four times a day, their wails can be heard, and this pattern is altered only when someone who has missed the funeral returns to the village. It is their obligation to go first to the mourning house and cry with the family.

For other workers, a host of mourning taboos are observed. Many pertain to foods and some to clothing and personal adornment. Many who are only distantly related wear black clothing or a black cloth armband; almost all shave their heads. These are undertaken once workers receive payment from owners for their part in the burial.

Such payments involve only small amounts of money; the bulk of the payments is made in yams. The size of the yams bestowed, as well as their number, is dependent upon the closeness of the relationship to the deceased. Making these payments is done publicly and often takes all day. Owners call up workers, one by one, and distribute the yams. The process is usually slowed by constant interruptions, as the amount of payment is challenged and negotiated before the next name can be called. For an important individual, who may have had hundreds of workers participating in the burial, the number of yams necessary to make adequate payments is staggering. Because this is so, the owners must depend on others to help with the payments. It is here that we can begin to see the importance of a strong matriline and to understand the power of exchange in Trobriand life.

The Politics of Yams: "Fathers and Brothers Give Yams; Husbands Receive Yams"

It is almost impossible to overstate the importance of yams in Trobriand culture. They are social signifiers of the highest order.

Men expend tremendous effort in their making of yam gardens. It is hard work and nearly constant work. Yet this work is not for themselves; it is all directed toward others. Men grow yams to give to women.

Once yams are harvested, they are displayed in the gardens for all to see, and then the gardener delivers them to their rightful owner, the woman for whom he has grown them. Young relatives of the gardener paint and adorn themselves and prepare to participate in the distribution. The yams are unstacked from their display, apportioned into baskets, and the youngsters set off to the home of the woman owner. Singing and shouting, they announce their arrival and pile the yams up again in front of the yam house of the owner's husband. It is the grower himself who will come, after they have been displayed for a few days, and stack them into the yam house. Once this has been accomplished, the owner's husband must repay the gardener and his young helpers. Yams and taro and pork are roasted and distributed. This entire exchange is a public presentation of the relationship between the two men, gardener and owner's husband. They are linked by the woman who owns the yams.

Yams and marriage are significantly linked. A couple declares that they are married by eating yams together, and after the first year of the marriage has passed, a woman's father begins a garden for her, which he will plant yearly. Her brother will eventually take over this obligation. This garden is small, but it is the hope of every man that his wife's brother will deem him worthy and grow more yams for his sister; enough so that in addition to growing yams for his sister, he will have to build a yam house to store them in. A yam house is a symbol of great accomplishment. It proclaims, "this is a man whose power has been recognized by his wife's brother." No man—not even a chief—can build a yam house for himself.

Not all men reach this position, and those who do will not achieve this status until a daughter is of marriageable age. At that time, he will begin a garden for her, as well as continuing the garden he makes for his sister. While he is doing this, his wife's father and brothers are making gardens for him. Thus, all men are linked together around women. It is only through his wife's family that a man can garner political strength and social power. (Later in life, men can develop other relationships through which they can amass yams.) In this way, marriage begins the yam exchanges that will cement relations throughout a person's life. When a man's life ends, his yam house is taken down. Although the yams may be distributed in mortuary payments, the structure itself cannot be passed on; it is an edifice that has grown directly out of a singular and unique relationship between the dead man, his wife, and her brother.

Hierarchy and Power

Chiefly Competitions: Yams and Dances

For two months of the year, the daily focus on the work of yam gardening is shifted. Although the growth of yams is so central that the months of the year are named for the growing cycle of the yams, the time from July to September is a time when yam work is finished and something on the order of a "vacation" ensues. Yams are harvested, the yam houses are filled, and the holiday begins. In years when harvests are large enough, this period is highlighted by yam competitions.

These events are meticulously planned festivals, designed to allow a chief or hamlet leader to enhance his status and become known in other villages. When new gardens are being prepared in September, the chief declares his intention to hold a *kayasa,* a yam competition, after harvest. This is an endeavor that demands the work of other men in the village, who must agree to grow additional gardens solely for the purpose of contributing to the competition. Members of his matriline are the first to join him in this, and his success will reflect directly upon them. But other community members will help too, because the chief will reward those who produce abundantly. Thus it is made a villagewide event, with gardeners competing to earn the valuables—money, ax blades, and other goods—with which the chief will compensate them. (And therefore even before declaring his intent to sponsor such a yam competition, the chief must amass the goods he will bestow upon the village gardeners.)

The year progresses, gardens are tended, and the harvest produces an abundance of yams. The chief rewards his gardeners, and they in turn carry yams, pigs, and betel nut to another chief or hamlet leader, who, in future years, will reciprocate in kind. It is in this way that yam competitions solidify alliances across clans.

During these holiday months, a chief also may choose, instead of a yam competition, to host dance competitions. Throughout these months, nightly dances are hosted by the chief. Unmarried Trobrianders from villages across the island are invited to come, dance, and find sexual partners in what the tourist trade now advertises as "the high point" of the summer months in the Trobriands. After two months of this "bacchanal of sorts" (Weiner 1988), the competition culminates in the display of traditional dances, taught by the founding ancestors hundreds of years ago. For this night, Trobrianders come from far and wide to watch the brightly costumed and painted dancers perform. Weiner (1988) describes one such night:

> To mark the end of the dancing and the competition, yam houses are metaphorically "overturned" and emptied of their harvest. Pigs are chased, tied up, and hung on poles; and wooden crates 10 or 15 feet tall, fastened against coconut palms, are filled with yams; one crate and one pig are divided among the residents of each hamlet who participated as guests and dancers. By the end of this event, by hosting nights of dancing and giving food to hundreds of people, a chief or hamlet leader demonstrates that he and his matrilineage are "best" (p. 113).

Trobriand Cricket

Missionaries were disturbed by the overt sexual activities associated with the yam competitions and dances. They introduced the British game of cricket expressly for the purpose of attempting to substitute it for these indigenous activities, as well as to supplant the fighting that always accompanied harvest time. In this replacement, they met no success. The cricket matches were accepted as a fine sport, but the Trobrianders made the game their own and used cricket competitions much in the same way yam competitions and dances had previously been employed. The element of sexuality is displayed in dress, chants, and dances. As Weiner tells us, "The words are sexual metaphors, used as one team taunts the other and exhibits their physical and sexual prowess to the appraising eyes of the young women on the sidelines" (1988:114). The cricket matches continue over the months, and the host village holds a feast when they are through. Pigs and yams and betel are distributed as they always were, and the chief's fame and wealth are known across the island.

Such fame and largesse are not without a dark side. Jealousy leading to sorcery and enmity is often an unwelcome outcome of these events. There is an unspoken assumption that the hosts of these lavish cricket matches must win. The guests, who must lose even if they have in "reality" won the game, return to their home village proclaiming that they had been treated unjustly by the umpire, and talking of revenge. In the 1980s, one such cricket match resulted in arson, with men on the losing team burning down houses in the host village.

Harvest-time fighting often springs from men asserting their gardens' superiority, which is generally done in abusive language, belittling the gardening abilities of others. Losers in these informal competitions are thought to be so humiliated by the process that they plot to destroy, through sorcery, the entire matrilineage of their taunters. Fear over sorcery invoked in this way can be passed down through several generations.

Trobriand Magic

Early in the twentieth century, anthropologist Bronislaw Malinowski contributed the first extensive ethnographies of the Trobriand Islanders. One feature to which he paid special attention was magic. In part to refute nineteenth-century notions that people such as the Trobrianders, whose belief system included magical practices, could not distinguish between the realms of "technology" and those of superstition, Malinowski detailed Trobriand technological knowledge in the practice of gardening, fishing, and sailing and contrasted this realm of knowledge with their use of magic. His best-known assertion explained the difference between fishing within the safety of calm lagoons and more dangerous travel on the open seas. According to Malinowski, calm lagoon fishing required no magic. Against the wind and rainstorms of the ocean, however, magic was relied upon to protect them from the dangerous elements. His point was that magic is employed in situations where Trobrianders lacked control and was unnecessary in those instances where their skills—technology—were sufficient, thereby demonstrating that they indeed understood and utilized logic.

Annette Weiner, whose work among the Trobrianders followed in the 1970s and 1980s, interprets Trobriand magic differently. She has recorded instances of Trobriand magic in situations other than those fraught with uncertainty—for example, when fishing in those calm lagoons. Rather than turning to magic in times of psychological stress owing to a natural world out of control, she interprets magic as a tool to bring about success that can lead to power, authority, and autonomy. Magic that results in a large catch of fish, essential for exchange, demonstrates an individual's efficacy and dominance (1988). She further asserts that it is incorrect to oppose (irrational) magic and (logical) technology: for the Trobrianders, magic *is* a powerful technology, rationally conceived and pointedly used to effect social and political advantage. While she agrees that magic may be employed as a means to seize control, she believes that "the hostile environment is one's social milieu" (1987:217), rather than solely the physical environment.

Many traditional spells are common knowledge, but others are bought or passed along through the *dala*. Men visiting other islands may give a spell to a woman as a token of his love, a gift in addition to betel or tobacco. Magical spells can be purchased on *kula* expeditions or travel to the city. A collection of spells is often written in a notebook and hidden away in the rafters of a house or a locked trunk, much like a diary. Beauty magic is chanted into coconut oil before it is rubbed onto skin; love spells are placed in tobacco. There is magic for wind, magic to induce pregnancy, magic to make the day dawn quickly. Magic for yam gardens is of great importance. Fathers teach their sons particular kinds of magic that they have learned from their own fathers. Mothers' brothers pass along *dala* magic, and these spells often depend on birth order. The oldest son of a man's oldest sister has access to more *dala* magic. Magic may be purchased with objects, and those who desire new magic and who have an axe or a pig to sell will wait patiently for someone who needs their goods but has only a spell to give in exchange.

Those who have possessed the most powerful magic in life can be dangerous even in death. They are often buried face down to prevent their spirits from escaping the grave and visiting illness or death on the living. The malevolent spirit will only stay nearby for a few days; during that time, the grave must be guarded by someone who possesses magic equal in power to that of the deceased (Weiner 1988).

Sorcery is a kind of magic—"poison magic." Some women are known to be "flying witches," who leave their bodies during sleep and cause illness or injury. These flights occur in darkness, and the darkest nights are especially dangerous. Weiner (1988) found that during a full moon, people strolled through the village unafraid. On moonless nights, they took care that their doors were pulled tightly shut, and they never ventured out.

Trobriand Exchange

Kula

The Trobriand *kula* ring is perhaps one of the best-known systems of exchange in the anthropological literature. In his classic ethnography, *Argonauts of the Western Pacific,* Malinowski described in exquisite detail the Trobriand practice of exchanging shell goods. His writing was a turning point in the understanding of non-Western economics; previous to his description, economies of other peoples were regarded as haphazard and "primitive." Malinowski's work influenced the theoretical perspectives of many of the most important anthropologists of the twentieth century.

Malinowski recognized the centrality of *kula,* referring to it as a "vast, complex, and deeply rooted" system for which Trobrianders have "a passion in their hearts" (1922:86). While *Argonauts of the Western Pacific* spanned more than 500 pages, Malinowski still referred to *kula* as "a very simple affair [which] only consists of an exchange, interminably repeated, of two articles intended for ornamentation, but not even used for that. . . ." (1922:86). In the years since, much more has been learned about the system of *kula* exchanges throughout New Guinea, and its importance has been underscored as its meaning has been illuminated.

Kula shells move through a series of islands on a particular path. Two types of shells are used in the exchange: white armshells *(mwali)* and red shell necklaces *(bagi)*. The *mwali* move in a counterclockwise path through the villages in which *kula* partners reside; the *bagi* pass through the same hands but circulate in the opposite, clockwise, direction. Men who do *kula* have partners on other islands. If we were to begin with any one man, draw a line tracing the path of the shells, as in a picture made by connecting the dots, we would have described a circle leading back to the origin point. A shell makes this circuit in anywhere from two to five years. Men generally know their *kula* partners whose islands are closest to them, because they sail to these islands to trade, and they host *kula* sailors who arrive. Those who are more distant are not known personally but are known by name.

A village chief will act as the leader in organizing a *kula* expedition. Generally, men from several local villages set off to the neighboring island to do *kula*. They set off ready to *receive* shells, not to bring them. When they return home, they will have the shells that other *kula* partners will come to receive. Six months to a year may pass between individual *kula* voyages. There are women who do *kula,* especially nowadays, but they are still in the minority. And those who do participate will often do so without leaving home to sail to other islands; men are designated to carry out the shell transactions on their behalf.

The *mwali* and *bagi* are assessed in value based on their size, color, and the beauty of their polish. In addition, shells increase in value with age, and both men and shells gain prestige in their association with one another. A man may gain fame and notoriety for having possessed a particularly fine armband; similarly, a necklace may be highly regarded for having been owned by a great man.

Such great men help younger ones enter into their *kula* career. A boy may be invited by his father or his mother's brother to come along on a *kula* expedition. There the young man will be able to observe the transactions, meet the *kula* partners, and begin to learn the ways of the *kula* ring. It is important to be well trained, because inexperience can cost dearly. A man's *kula* path and the partners therein are passed along to his heirs at death. But when the living *kula* partners are unsure about the younger man's expertise, they will not necessarily honor his "rightful position." Weiner (1988) reports:

> . . . although Peter's father was a chief and he left him three *kula* paths when he died, he lost two of them and his *kula* shells; his closest partner did not believe that Peter was "strong" enough, so he diverted Peter's shells onto a different path (p. 148).

Malinowski presented the *kula* exchanges as anchored in tradition in such a way that the shells appeared to move between men effortlessly, as if they were propelled by nothing more than the force of custom. Subsequent investigations into the workings of the system have uncovered aspects of the exchange that eluded Malinowski and that expand the foundation of *kula* beyond simple reciprocity. There are profits to be made. Weiner (1988) sums up the ultimate meaning of *kula* this way:

> The histories of shells written through *kula* participation are of individuals' talents and exploits, of partners long dead whose faces were never seen. Through the shells, a villager transcends the history of his or her own ancestral lineage and becomes a part of *kula* history. What is of consequence is that *kula* history legitimizes a person's right to win while others lose. In Kiriwina, *kula* participation enables players, if they are "strong," to create long-standing debts, to hold on to valuables for years, and to keep these shells free from kin-related obligations like marriages or deaths. In this way, *kula* allows individuals to protect their wealth from the exigencies of everyday social and political life. . . . [T]he ability to hold on to a *kula* shell allows a person to store wealth, even if only momentarily, in the face of continual kinship or affinal obligations (p. 156).

Traditionally, *kula* trading also provided an opportunity to accomplish more practical goals. In addition to the ceremonial aspects of trading shell ornaments, *kula* expeditions allowed islanders to trade their own surplus goods for items they needed. For example, Trobrianders with bountiful gardens could bring yams and taro to islands with unproductive soil, trading much-needed food for the local islanders' beautifully crafted canoes. Local economies produced what they could, and islanders traded these necessities for others.

Women's Wealth

The momentous position of yams and the fame of *kula* are two weighty aspects of Trobriand life. Another is the special wealth that is produced and controlled by Trobriand women.

Women manufacture skirts and "bundles" *(doba)* from banana leaves for the *sagali,* a mortuary exchange feast. These are crucial to the Trobriand economy and are intricately tied to other forces—chief among them yams and the matrilineages—in Trobriand culture.

As we have seen, the death of a villager sets in motion a huge amount of work. The loss of any group member disturbs the many social ties in which that individual was bound up. In a sense, exchanges at *sagali* are one step in the process of "mending the hole" left in social networks by that death.

One women's mortuary ceremony may consist of the distribution of as many as 5,000 banana leaf bundles and thirty intricately woven red fiber skirts. Women deal in skirts and bundles, as currency, throughout the year. But they are of central importance when kin die.

Women make skirts and bundles from the leaves of banana trees, which they own. They inherit trees from their mothers and sisters, and often men plant banana trees for their wives, expressly for the purpose of creating their wives' wealth. Men are dependent upon such wealth.

Women work for months producing the skirts and bundles they will distribute to those who participate in mourning. "Workers," both male and female, will receive bundles and skirts commensurate with their work. Men do not receive these directly; their mothers or sisters will collect these for them. Every individual who has had any association with the deceased will receive bundles. The chief distributor is the wealthiest woman, and she is distinguished by the long skirt of singular design she wears. She makes the first payment in every distribution.

Women's wealth is connected to yam production in several ways. When a death occurs in a woman's *dala,* it will be her responsibility, as an "owner," to distribute bundles. Because her brothers have made her a garden every year and put those yams in her husband's yam house, it is incumbent upon a husband to secure bundles for her to distribute, in addition to those she will make herself. In order to participate fully in mortuary distributions, a woman needs far more bundles than she can manufacture herself. One way in which a husband provides his wife with bundles is through his sisters, those women for whom he makes gardens. These women will present their "sister-in-law" with bundles in appreciation for the yams provided by their brother, her husband. It is not only for his "true" sisters, but also for other women who stand to him "like a sister." Thus, there may be a great number of these "sisters" who will contribute bundles. A man is also expected to exchange pigs, money, and other valuables for bundles to provision his wife. In fact, the debt that is set in motion by the giving of yams from a man to his sister and her husband can *only* be repaid in women's wealth. If a husband does not use his own wealth to buy the needed extra bundles for his wife's mortuary obligations, her brother will not produce as big a garden the following season. The husband will suffer, in yams. When a man's wife's brothers build him a yam house, they are contracting with him to provide her with bundles. In fact, the eventual accumulation of skirts and bundles is what underpins much of the work to produce large yam gardens. There are intricate layers of rights and obligations between matrilineages, all of which coalesce around women's wealth. Their economy spurs men's productivity.

Women's wealth, in *doba* bundles, is an economic force in modern Trobriand life. Weiner tells of meeting Joshua, a young single man from Kiriwina who had been away from the village for some time, attending medical school. They talked as they rode to the village together, and when they passed a village where a women's mortuary distribution was visible, Joshua remarked that he thought it was imperative that women put an end to this tradition. Weiner (1988) writes:

> [Joshua said] "If women stopped needing so many bundles, then men would have plenty of money for other things." In his shrewd comment, Joshua put his finger on the vulnerability of using such bundles as currency. From a capitalist perspective, he was right. Men take money, which can be used to purchase all sorts of things, and turn it into bundles. Yet despite the demanding need for money to pay school fees, government taxes, trade store goods, and even airfare to the capital, men continue to spend their money on bundles. Why women's wealth has not diminished in importance over the past one hundred years is a serious question, which Joshua, in his own way, was asking. But Joshua was not married and so his interest in the cost of bundles was limited. Had Joshua lived in a village where his wife's brother produced yams for him each year, he would not have framed his comments in Western economic terms (p. 120).

Malinowski in the Trobriands

Bronislaw Malinowski stands at the earliest edges of the science of anthropology. His first trip to New Guinea, in 1914, marked the beginning of a prodigious career. Few people before him had undertaken such intensive observation of a group of people over several years. Upon his return, he was tireless in his insistence that ethnography depended on rapport built up over time with local informants and had to be conducted in the local language, squarely situated in the center of a culture's own context. The detail with which he presented his own work set a standard in the early science.

Malinowski's theoretical views have given way in popularity to other perspectives, but his influence is undisputed. It was this legacy that Annette Weiner carried into the Trobriands with her, some sixty years after Malinowski's tenure there. Her work is a prime example of the ways in which the dynamic science of anthropology continues to grow, both relying on past studies and illuminating them.

The most serious points of divergence between Malinowski's work and Weiner's, so many decades later, grow out of Weiner's recognition of the importance of women's economic role in the Trobriands. Malinowski took note of women's importance, but his interpretation was one that rested on women's reproductive role. In a matrilineal society, where descent will be reckoned through women, they are surely of genealogical significance. In addition, Malinowski's explanation of Trobriand kinship centered around this same feature, that of matrilineality. In such a system, children are members of their mothers' matrilines and thus belong to the same group as their mothers' brothers, but not their fathers. Malinowski felt Trobriand fathers were both biologically and economically unimportant in their children's lives, and he pointed to the making of yam gardens by men for their sisters as evidence to support the tie between a mother's brother and his sister's son over that of a father. It is true that men make yam gardens for their sisters, but as Weiner has described, the motivation for this is not to ensure that a man's sister's children are adequately fed, as Malinowski assumed. Because he was unaware of the economic ties which grow out of women's wealth, he could not fully understand the complex exchange relationships that grew out of the production of skirts and bundles. Weiner (1988) summarizes:

> That Malinowski never gave equal time to the women's side of things, given the deep significance of their role in social and political life, is not surprising. Only recently have anthropologists begun to understand the importance of taking women's work seriously. In some cultures, such as the Middle East or among Australian aborigines, it is extremely difficult for ethnographers to cross the culturally bounded ritual worlds that separate women from men. In the past, however, both women and men ethnographers generally analyzed the societies they studied from a male perspective. The "women's point of view" was largely ignored in the study of gender roles, since anthropologists generally perceived women as living in the shadows of men—occupying the private rather than the public sectors of society, rearing children rather than engaging in economic or political pursuits (p. 7).

Modern Times

AIDS in the Trobriands: *Sovasova* and the Sickness of Sameness

Illnesses are experienced and explained in their local settings, using local frameworks. HIV/AIDS has a worldwide presence and presents local challenges.

The first documented case of AIDS in the Trobriands was on the island of Kiriwina in 2001 (Lepani 2007). The true incidence of HIV is difficult to ascertain throughout rural Papua New Guinea. Katherine Lepani (2007) has investigated the ways in which Trobriand Islanders fit the specter of HIV/AIDS into their traditional belief system and the consequences this has, especially for prevention programs.

As we have seen, Trobrianders belong to one of four exogamous matrilineal clans *(kumila)* as well as a *dala,* which, taken together, are the most important units of both identity and exchange. Identity given through matrilineal ancestral spirits creates two groups of people: "people like us"—(*veyola:* literally, "those with the same substance")—and "people different from us."

By following rules regarding both *kumila* and *dala* membership, marriage strengthens exchange ties and keeps *dala* resources within two linked lineages. Thus, sexual relations are, in one sense, a vehicle for bringing together "difference" in a socially productive way.

While sexuality is enjoyed and its expression encouraged in unmarried youth, its ultimate meaning as potential point of linkage between clans means that young people are expected to be secretive about their relationships until they have chosen a single partner and are ready to transform a sexual relationship into a formal alliance between two *kumilas.* The most important aspect of secrecy is the mandate for "brothers" and "sisters" to conceal their liaisons from one another. This prohibition extends even to conversation about sex. While individuals may be circumspect about discussing their relationships prematurely, they will never discuss them with their "brothers" or "sisters" at all. Weiner (1988) found that this was among the Trobriander's most serious rules concerning social relations. She once asked a woman about the romance of a neighbor, not remembering that the two were in the category of "brother" and "sister" to one another. Upon hearing the question, the woman stood up and walked out of the house without saying a word. Weiner was later told that the mistake had been so terrible that had she not been an outsider still new to the understanding of Trobriand rules, the offended woman would never have spoken to her again.

Given this anecdote, it is not surprising that sexual relations between classificatory "brothers" and "sister" has serious consequences. Both the incestuous transgression itself and the illness that results is called *sovasova.* It is, in essence, a sickness caused by "sameness of substance" (Lepani 2007:7), jeopardizing not only the health of the individuals but also the essential strengthening of the *dala* and *kumila* inherent in exogamy. The Trobrianders explain the pathology of *sovasova* by saying that "sameness" of the fluids that come together cause a stagnation or blockage that leads to the growth of worm-like parasites, causing debilitating chronic illness (Lepani 2007). She was told that *sovasova* "is not like a disease going from one person to another, no, but it is about exchange, the mixture when fluids come together. . . . Let's say it is an exchange of difference . . . With *sovasova,* there is nothing different to exchange" (p. 21).

Prevention of *sovasova* rests on the determination of clan identity. One young Trobriand woman, explaining that her mother told her about *sovasova* when she was in elementary school, told Lepani she has seen people suffering with the illness and knows it was a result of failing to take proper social precautions. "It is only through carelessness, that's how they get involved with this sickness, *sovasova.* We ask, '*Avaka kumila yokwa?* What clan are you?' 'Oh, sorry, my brother!,' if he is same clan. And we go our separate ways" (Lepani 2007:19–20).

The existence of *sovasova* in Trobriand culture has implications for their understanding of HIV/AIDS. The symptoms of *sovasova* resemble those of AIDS: weight loss, debilitating weakness, chronic malaise, and nausea. Trobrianders make the connection between the two. When a young Trobriand man was told that having multiple partners (common among young Trobrianders and acceptable social behavior) was a risk factor for contracting HIV, he replied:

> This kind of sexual behaviour [having multiple partners] is part of our custom so it is not really surprising to us about AIDS, because maybe we already know this disease through *sovasova.* [W]e have the clan system and we follow it in our sexual behaviour and if we don't follow it we get sick. So maybe people from other places don't understand about the clan system and they have too much mixing of same kind and that is how this virus has spread and made so many people sick.

Lepani (2007) reports that the Trobriands have been identified as a potentially important place for setting up prevention programs, in large part owing to factors that are identified as placing them at potential risk. These include early onset of sexual activity, frequency of multiple partners, high prevalence of sexually transmitted infections, and low level of condom use. Also noted is the contribution of their extensive trade networks: travel for *kula* exchange provides the opportunity to expand sexual networks as well.

Lepani (2007) points out that the beliefs and practices concerning *sovasova* may have important consequences for the way Trobrianders understand information about HIV and make decisions about treatment, should they need to do so. *Sovasova* is effectively treated with herbal preparations and with magic. Trobrianders openly wonder if these same preparations and strategies wouldn't be equally efficacious for HIV/AIDS, and Lipari suggests this confidence might both undermine efforts at prevention and engender a lack of concern about the potential seriousness of the spread of the disease. Attention to communication strategies is also at issue. As Lipari observes:

> The moralistic tropes of risk and promiscuity that dominate the language of HIV prevention are not easily accommodated by Trobriand ideations of sexuality, which celebrate premarital sexual activity as healthy and life-affirming, and which stress the productive values of reciprocity and relations of difference (2007:326).

Trobriand ideas about kinship and exchange, relations of difference and sameness, sexuality and illness provide a compelling example of the ways in which new information is always mediated through local understandings.

Tourism

Since 1975, the Trobriand Islands have been counted as part of Papua New Guinea, a nation-state that is one of the largest developing counties in the South Pacific. Trobrianders are not eager to give up their traditional culture, and they have consistently taken new ideas and made them their own, made them "Trobriand."

In the early 1970s, tourists were a constant presence on the islands, with charter flights arriving weekly. Villagers greeted visitors at the airstrip and at the local hotel, waiting to sell their carvings for cash. Traders and missionaries also bought indigenous arts and crafts to sell. As the tourist trade grew, some Trobrianders were unhappy; they were offended at their islands' portrayal, in travel brochures, as "The Isles of Love." Some believed the impetus to produce carvings to sell took its toll on gardening because some men were more eager to produce salable items than yams. However, most felt that the end result would be a positive one—economic security.

One Trobriander, John Kasaipwalova, studying nationalist movements as part of his university studies, left school to return to Kiriwina and urge fellow islanders to take control of their island's economic fate. It was his intention to build local industry—a hotel, stores, a shipping company—so that Trobrianders could truly be in charge of their economic future.

When a fire destroyed the island's hotel, the tourist industry came to an abrupt halt. This led to more villagers throwing their support to John Kasaipwalova, in opposition to local chiefs. Great debates ensued, and in the end Kasaipwalova was unsuccessful. Tourism never regained its foothold, and although there are still some carvings to sell to the occasional visitor, ebony forests have been ravaged and selling local arts and crafts can support no one.

Weiner (1988) points out that there is a long Trobriand tradition of resisting change: "tradition wins out despite people's willingness to try something new" (p. 25). The islands in the South Pacific were extensively involved in World War II, and despite the Trobrianders' contact with missionaries, soldiers, tourists, and a colonial government, they exhibit a fierce tenacity to traditional culture. Weiner sees the fundamental importance of women's wealth as playing a central role in this resolve. She explains:

> Throughout all the years of public disputes, fighting, competition between chiefs, and changes brought about by colonial law and traders' enterprises, women have gone about their business undisturbed by government officers and missionaries, who, like Malinowski, never thought they played any economic role. Men are the carvers, the gardeners, the fishing experts, the orators, and the chiefs. No one recognized the activity that is central to women's position and power in Trobriand society. Yet it is an activity that deeply interpenetrates the economics and the politics of men (p. 27).

Jutta Malnic (1998) undertook three expeditions, over four years, traveling the *kula* circuit. She notes that the Trobrianders are undergoing great change, with both tourism and a cash economy diverting the time and energy previously devoted to traditional social pursuits. Modern modes of transportation and communication hold the potential to alter the *kula* ring, but those with whom Malnic sailed are resolute that the essence of *kula* will endure. As one trader explained:

> Kula has lasted over time and will last into time. It will take on different dimensions and expressions; it may extend into new areas and change characteristics. But underneath it will always be an act of Giving and Receiving, which allows the receiver to grow and extend, materially and spiritually (p. 31).

In the course of his fieldwork on Kiriwina Island, anthropologist Gunter Senft (1999) has analyzed interactions between tourists who have been promised a chance to "'meet the friendly people' and 'observe their unique culture, dances, and art'" (p. 21) and the Trobriand Islanders who dance and sing for the European audiences. He describes the Islanders as creating, for these "customers," the performance they expect to see, retaining the upper hand through their control of the situation. Because it is staged, Trobrianders know that "neither they nor the core aspects of their culture will suffer any damage within a tourist encounter that is defined [by them]" (p. 21). Analyzing the texts of the songs, Senft describes humorous instances of the Trobrianders ridiculing their listeners, which he sees as evidence of indigenous pride and self-confidence, through which they protect their cultural identity while using it as a tourist commodity.

➔ For Further Discussion

Bronislaw Malinowski's first trip to New Guinea in 1914 marked the beginning of a long tradition of ethnography that depended on rapport built up over time with local informants, was conducted in the local language, and was squarely situated in the center of a culture's own context. Some sixty years later, anthropologist Annette Weiner undertook her own fieldwork in the Trobriands. Her findings both added to Malinowski's earlier work and challenged some of its assumptions.

How did Malinowski's and Weiner's approaches differ? What are some of the factors that might account for each of their perspectives? What are some of the challenges faced by ethnographers in the twenty-first century? How might modern technology change the way anthropologists conduct their fieldwork?

CHAPTER 15

The Yanomami

Challenges in the Rainforest

Location of the Yanomami in South America.

✧ The Beginning

One of the ancestors shot Moon in the belly. Moon's blood fell on the earth, and the drops of blood became men. These men were alone and went out collecting vines one day. There they saw the *wabu* fruit, and the fruit had eyes. The *wabu* began to fall to the ground and, where it fell, up sprang women. And the Moonblood men and the *wabu* women together made the Yanomami (Chagnon 1992b).

✧ Introduction: The Yanomami Environment

The Yanomami are a tribe of 26,000 who live in about 250 widely dispersed villages in Brazil and Venezuela. Although they are well known to students of anthropology owing largely to the lifelong study of Napoleon Chagnon, they have remained remarkably isolated and undisturbed until very recently. While some sources (Chagnon 1992a) claim theirs is a history of very little contact and retention of indigenous patterns, others (Ferguson in Salamone 1997) report that the Yanomami have been influenced by European contact since the early seventeenth century, when Spanish, Portuguese, and Dutch slave traders entered their territory. Moreover, contact continued after slave trading times, with missionaries being chief among those with whom the Yanomami have dealt closely. In any case, the most recent contact—with gold miners—has been dramatic and cause for international outcry.

The tropical forest in which the Yanomami live is dense and green, with varied growth. Its thick floor of vines and scrub makes it difficult to traverse; on cloudy days its impenetrable canopy keeps out most light.

Villages are at varying distances from one another and have differing degrees of social closeness as well. Those that harbor good relations host frequent visitors, and it is not unusual for individuals to travel several days to pay a visit (Smole 1976).

✧ Subsistence and Manufacture

Gardening and Foraging

The earliest reports about the Yanomami erroneously described them as solely hunters and gatherers, with no portion of their diet grown in gardens. Chagnon (1992a) postulates that this was based on the assumption that a tribe as isolated as the Yanomami could not possibly possess the sophistication to be cultivators. Currently, the vast majority of Yanomami (more than 95 percent) live within the Amazon forest and rely on both foraging and horticulture. The remainder have settled along the rivers, where fishing has replaced hunting (Salamone 1997).

For those Yanomami who are forest-dwellers, the abundant jungle supplements their diet. Ordinarily a tribal society settled in villages, the Yanomami exploit the wild foods found in their environment by trekking, mostly during the dry season. They break into small family groups to go off on collecting expeditions, traveling for several weeks when the jungle fruits and vegetables are ripe. Honey is the ultimate wild prize, and honeycombs are often consumed with the larvae still inside. Good (1991) estimates that roughly 40 percent of their time is spent on a *wayumi* (trek).

Game is plentiful, and during these expeditions they commonly hunt wild pigs, large and small birds, monkeys, deer, rodents, and anteaters. Armadillos, which live in underground burrows, cannot be hunted with bow and arrow. They are ingeniously smoked out. Once an entry to a burrow is located, a slow smoky fire is lit. Smoke escaping from other burrows indicate exits to be dammed up. Once all escape routes are blocked, hunters listen with an ear to the ground for the scurrying of the animal, and dig straight down to retrieve it. Insects and shellfish round out the protein portion of their diet.

Fish do not provide an extensive portion of the inland Yanomami diet, but when the rainy season is over and pools formed by overflowing rivers dry out, stranded fish can be opportunistically gathered by women. This practice includes the use of mild poisons, introduced into the water upstream. The drugged fish float to the surface where they are easily grabbed and tossed into baskets. Larger fish, which are less stunned by the poison, are bitten behind the head by the women and killed.

The bulk of Yanomami food (more than 80 percent) is grown in their village gardens. Garden sites are cleared by cutting down trees and brush and burning them, although not with the systematic precision of other slash-and-burn practitioners. Large tree trunks that have been felled but are too wet to burn are simply left where they fall, and either used as firewood once dry or allowed to serve as boundary markers between the gardens of different families.

The size of a garden plot is usually dictated by the size of the family it must feed. Because village headmen will have the responsibility of entertaining visitors and sponsoring feasts, they plant and care for larger plots.

Plantain is the most important domesticated crop. Manioc, taro, and sweet potato are also cultivated. Cane used in arrow manufacture is grown in village gardens, as is tobacco, a crop of central importance. All women, men, and children chew it daily and guard it jealously. Adults will often have wads of the soft leaves rolled into their lower lips all day long (Smole 1976). Chagnon (1992a) reports that it is the only crop that is fenced off to warn potential thieves. The value of tobacco (to which every Yanomami above the age of 10 is reportedly addicted) is evidenced by the fact that the local word for being "poor" is literally "without tobacco" (Chagnon 1992a).

Cotton grown in village gardens is used predominantly for the construction of hammocks, which are owned by everyone. It is also used to make what little clothing is worn. Men typically wear little more than a string around the waist, while more ornate belts are generally worn by the women. Single strands of cotton string are also tied around wrists and ankles.

Manufacture

The technology found among the Yanomami is not complex. Any necessary tool can be manufactured from materials readily available in any village. The knowledge of how to do so is widely held. The level of manufacture has been compared to that of typical foraging societies, despite the fact that they are horticulturalists (Chagnon 1992a).

Palm wood is used to make numerous items, among them bows and arrow points. A type of palm wood arrow point that is highly prized is the one used in hunting with curare, a poison extracted from a local vine. The point is dipped in curare and shaved to ensure that it will break off underneath the skin, preventing the victim from removing it. The curare, which induces muscle relaxation, is then sent into the bloodstream. Poison arrow tips are among the most popular items of trade between villages. Quivers that hold them are made from bamboo, and are worn hanging on the back. Arrows themselves are fashioned from cane and are quite long, resembling spears.

Other manufactured items include large shallow baskets used to collect fish and a rudimentary "razor," used to create the Yanomami's unique haircut, bowl-shaped with a circle shaved bald at the top center of the head, a style worn by both men and women. The exception is during a severe bout with head lice, when it is simply easier to completely shave the heads of affected men, women, and children.

Village Construction

Houses are constructed from readily available local materials, predominantly saplings for support posts, vines and leaves for thatching. These are not very durable, despite the substantial labor that goes into their construction. In addition to providing little protection against rains, after only a year or two the leafy roofs become so infested with insects that there is no other option but to burn them and start again. (Chagnon comments that roaches often grow to the size of small birds [1992a].)

Living space, called the *shabono,* is a series of individual homes, sheltered underneath a common roof. Men sink the four main posts into the ground, and women and children gather the vines and leaves used for thatching. Thousands of leaves are needed to cover the structure. Each family builds the section of the roof that covers their own compartment. When the structure is complete, there are numerous individual sections with a few feet between them, all underneath a long stretch of connected thatching, surrounding an open central plaza. The building site is chosen with an eye to the suitability of the surrounding land for gardening, access to potable water, and proximity of both allies and enemies.

If there is continual threat of enemy attack, a tall wooden fence is constructed behind the *shabono.* The fence is covered with dry brush at night, so that intruders will be heard by village dogs, who will in turn wake the residents.

Village size will, of course, reflect the size of the population, which may be as small as 40 or as large as 300. But another factor determining size is the number of neighboring villages with whom friendly relations are maintained. It is important to be able to accommodate any allies who will be visiting regularly.

Thus, a village size may reflect not the number of permanent residents, but the number of people it will have to house when visitors are expected.

To house visitors or to provide shelter on extended food gathering forays, less elaborate temporary shelters are constructed. These are usually made by lashing three poles together and covering them with broad banana leaves.

✈ Religion and Expressive Culture

The relatively simple technology and material culture of the Yanomami is not replicated in their systems of belief and expression. Although they have no tradition of writing, their use of language is elegant and verbal skills are highly prized.

The Yanomami envision the universe as being constructed of four layers hovering atop one another with a thin layer of space between them. The topmost stratum is empty and has least to do with current Yanomami life. Long ago, things may have come from here, but now it lies fallow. The layer below it is the sky. People can only see its underside, onto which stars are stuck, but the surface of the sky is believed to look much as the earth does, with trees and plants and animals. The most important residents of this layer are the souls of the dead, who carry on an existence there much like the one they had as living Yanomami. This layer—the sky—is believed to float quite close to the earth, as Chagnon (1992a) deduced from the repeated questioning about bumping into it when he flew in airplanes.

The third layer down, on which the Yanomami live, was created when a section of the "sky" layer cracked off and toppled down. The bottom most layer, which exists under the earth, was formed when sky fell to earth on top of a particular settlement, and pushed it down through the earth to the underside. There it has settled as the last layer, along with the people, their homes and garden. Unfortunately, their hunting grounds were left behind. Loss of the jungle in which to find game led them inevitably to cannibalism, and the unfortunate souls of Yanomami children are their usual prey. The belief that souls are regularly carried off to be eaten down below reflects the Yanomami's fear that natives of the earth can indeed fall into the practice of cannibalism. This possibility apparently both terrifies and disgusts them. Chagnon (1992a) elaborates:

> Whenever I hunted with them and we shot a tapir, I would always cut off a thick juicy slice of tenderloin and fry it lightly on both sides—a rare steak that dripped juicy delicious blood as I cut it and ate it. This so disgusted and alarmed them that they could not bear to watch me eat it, and invariably accused me of wanting to become a cannibal . . . a disgusting eater of raw flesh. For their part, they cook their meat so much that you could almost drive nails with it (pp. 101–102).

These dwellers of the bottom layer of the universe were in existence when the first people originated. Those original human beings were different from people today in that they were part human, part animal, and part spirit. When they died, they became all spirit—the *hekura* who figure prominently into Yanomami shamanism.

Myths

Many Yanomami myths are built around these original humans, called "those who are now dead." Although tales of their origin are spotty, they themselves are responsible for the creation of many plants and animals and are, in fact, the spirits of those living things that bear their names.

Men are generally the storytellers in Yanomami society, and they "perform" the recounting of a myth more than simply reciting it. Their histrionic style, often enhanced by drugs, leads to dramatic embellishments and provides enjoyable diversion for the audience.

Some stories incorporate a moral, designed to teach the ways of Yanomami. Others are told to explain why the world is as it is. Many are sheer entertainment.

The relationship of humankind to the jaguar is a theme that predominates in many stories. Chagnon (1992a) suggests that the jaguar may have been chosen because it effectively exemplifies a fundamental theme in Yanomami culture (and many others)—the distinction between "nature" and "culture." Jaguar is in some ways a figure in which nature and culture overlap. The Yanomami are proud that humans have culture and animals do not, yet the jaguar is a hunter as skilled as a Yanomami. Jaguar is an animal (a creature of nature) who shares traits with people (bearers of culture) and is both feared and respected. In many of their jaguar stories, the fierce and powerful jaguar is reduced to a clumsy, inefficient beast. In the creation of these stories, culture triumphs over nature.

The Yanomami Soul

The soul plays a central part in the "spiritual" world of the Yanomami. It is the soul that is consumed by the cannibals in the netherworld, and it is a rather sophisticated "organ."

The soul consists of several different portions, each of which has a function in both life and death. The part of the soul that is the "will" is the part that makes the journey to the afterlife. At death, it shimmies up the ropes of the deceased's hammock, entering the layer of the universe above the earth, and begins a journey down a road that divides into two separate paths. This fork is guarded by a spirit charged with assessing the generosity shown by the soul's mortal owner during life and then sending it down the appropriate path. Generous souls are directed down the path to the comfortable earthlike place; stingy ones are shepherded down the fork to a fiery place. (This latter fate is not one that causes them great worry; they are unimpressed by the intelligence of the guard and plan simply to lie and be sent down the preferred route.)

There is another part of the soul that is freed upon cremation of the body and lives, thereafter, in the jungle. This portion has the potential for evil, clubbing people who visit the jungle at night. Great caution is exercised to avoid them.

The most crucial portion of the Yanomami soul resides within the chest or flank (interestingly, that portion of the body attacked in stylized chest- and side-pounding duels) and is most vulnerable to attack. This component can be stolen, and then subject to supernatural attack. If this happens, the individual sickens and will likely die unless this portion of the soul is restored.

The last aspect of the soul lives both inside and outside the individual. Inside, it is a part of the individual spirit (the part captured by the camera when a person is photographed); outside it is a person's animal counterpart, which leads a parallel life. When the person eats, his or her animal self is doing the same. When the person is asleep, so too is the animal. Ordinarily one will never meet this animal alter ego, but if by some twist of fate one were to hunt and kill it, one's own death would follow (as it does when another hunter kills "your animal").

Illness, Healing, and Death

Illness is caused by the *hekura* spirits, which harm a person by consuming a portion of his or her soul, usually at the behest of someone from an enemy village. It is the charge of a shaman to call upon his own powerful *hekura* to counterattack, thus curing the sick villager.

Shamanism is a practice open only to Yanomami men; however, it is not a role restricted by birth or special characteristics or suitabilities. Anyone who wishes may undertake the training, if they are willing to undergo the rigors entailed. These include a fast that may last up to a year, during which the initiate becomes emaciated. Instructors, who are older shamans, guide the novices in the ways to call their own *hekura* spirits to them. One must learn the likes and dislikes of the *hekura* in order to lure them into one's chest. This is not an easy task—they are difficult to seduce and apt to be fickle and leave abruptly. An aspiring shaman must endeavor to make the interior of his body into attractive terrain in which the *hekura* may dwell in comfort. If they find verdant mountains and cool streams in the shaman's chest, they may stay. Older, more proficient shamans may have succeeded in attracting many *hekura* spirits to live within them, yet are always striving to keep them happy. Because *hekura* are repelled by sexual activities, younger novices have no hope of attracting and keeping the *hekura* unless they are celibate. This requirement alone often deters men from the pursuit of this status. Once a shaman has established a stable relationship with the *hekura,* he may engage in sex without fear of abandonment by his spiritual powers.

Hekura, which dwell among the Yanomami in the thousands, are both male and female, but all are exceedingly beautiful. Different sorts have different temperaments. The most fearsome are the "hot and meat hungry" *hekura,* for these are the ones who devour the souls of enemies.

Shamans have access to the *hekura* only while they are under the influence of hallucinogens. These drugs are used on a daily basis, and their preparation is ongoing. They are ingested in powder form, blown into the nose through a long hollow pipe placed in the mouth of another man. The initial effects are quite painful, leading to coughing, choking, watery eyes, and retching. Their power takes effect almost immediately. As the shamans begin to feel intoxicated, they begin their chanting, which calls their *hekura* to them. Because the *hekura* are themselves so beautiful, they require great attractiveness on the part of the shamans, who wear feathers and paint themselves elaborately. Once the *hekura* have danced down their trails and

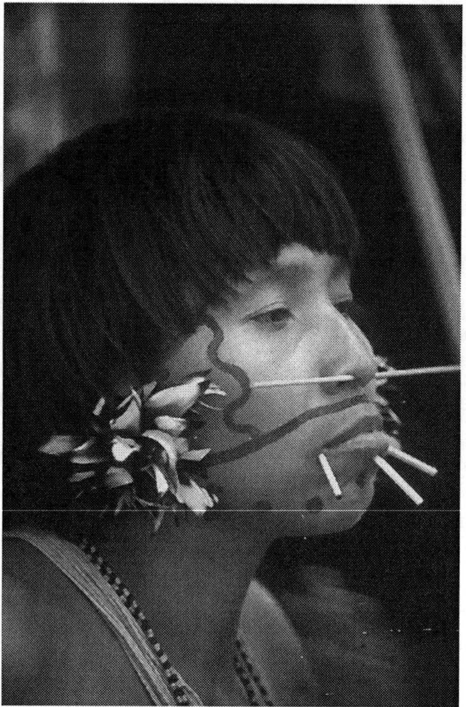

A Yanomami youth in ceremonial dress.

into the chests of their hosts, they can aid a shaman in curing. They can also be manipulated to go to enemy villages and avenge the sickness sent on local villagers.

When a Yanomami dies, the body is cremated. This is done by carrying the body to a prepared pile of firewood, where it is burned. One person is designated to watch the fire, making sure that the entire corpse is consumed, and nothing but ash and bone remains. A log is hollowed out to hold the teeth and bones, which are ground by a close kinsman and apportioned into several small gourds. Any ashes remaining in the log's hollow are consumed in soup, and then the log is burned. The gourds full of ashes are kept for a larger more elaborate ceremony during which they will be added to more soup and consumed by visiting kin from other villages. This practice, which continues today, is at the heart of an ongoing conflict between the Yanomami and several research institutions in the United States. In 1967, blood samples were taken from a number of Yanomami as part of a research project (see p. 283). Since learning in 2001 that the samples have been maintained in frozen storage for more than forty years, the Yanomami have been asking for their return. Accession to the world of spirits is impossible unless every trace of an individual has been removed. Thus, the existence of more than a thousand vials of Yanomami blood, much of it from individuals who are now deceased, is a source of grave concern and dismay. Moreover, *bore,* the spirits of the dead, have the power to cause illness. A *bore* is a piece of the Yanomami soul that can travel to a distant part of the forest after death, where it lays in wait to harm anyone who has wronged the individual during life. One major offense is an incomplete mortuary ceremony, one that does not completely destroy both property and corpse. As such, stored blood is an invitation to *bore* revenge. While the research centers in possession of the samples agreed in 2006 to return them, they have yet to do so. Yanomami spokesman Davi Kopenawa has expressed hope that this agreement will soon come to fruition, so the blood of their ancestors can be dissolved in local rivers (*Survival International News,* May 2010.)

If there are multiple deaths occurring at one time, all the bodies are taken into the jungle. Rather than being burned, they are wrapped with bark and positioned in trees until they decompose. Later the remaining bones are burned, and the same ash-drinking ceremony takes place.

Social Organization

Leadership

The Yanomami are generally egalitarian in that there is no ranked hierarchy. While women hold less status than men, among adult males prestige is achieved, and not ascribed, and "there are as many prestigious positions as there are people to fill them" (Salamone 1997:47). However, Yanomami villages generally have a headman, an individual who usually belongs to the largest kin group represented in the village. He serves more as a representative of his own village in dealings with other villages than as an authoritarian figure within his own. Chagnon (1992a), who in his visits to more than sixty Yanomami villages has seen the leadership styles of many headmen, reports that there is no one personality that typifies this status. Some headmen are quiet, introspective leaders; others are bombastic and dictatorial. What they have in common are the limitations inherent in the status afforded them. They act as hosts and negotiators. Their opinions carry somewhat more weight than those of other men. They lead by example and not by decree. If there is trouble within the village, it is the headman's responsibility to attempt to restore order. Because he must model the behavior he wishes others to exhibit, his life is often fraught with risks. He demonstrates the bravery, self-control, or industriousness that he expects others to display.

Male and Female

The realities of daily life differ greatly for Yanomami men and women. Chagnon (1992a) calls the culture "decidedly masculine," and this certainly seems borne out by other ethnographers as well (Good 1991; Lizot 1985; Salamone 1997).

Girls are aware at an early age that they have far less social room in which to maneuver than do their brothers. They begin to assume a productive role in their household very early on, and assume child care responsibilities while they are themselves small children.

Most girls are betrothed while they are still quite young, and they have no opportunity to voice any preference (or register any dissent) in this regard. The men to whom they are promised are usually much older. In some cases, a man identifies a girl and asks his relatives to make marriage inquiries. She may then be "raised" to some extent by the man who is to become her husband. Regardless of the age at which she is promised, a girl does not generally take up residence with her husband until reaching puberty.

Even when their marriage "officially" begins, life changes little for a Yanomami girl. She continues to spend her days as she has previously done: collecting firewood, cooking, and devoting herself to the needs of others around her. One aspect of her marital relationship, which does appear to be unique to the husband–wife dyad, is the physical cruelty to which Yanomami women are subjected by their husbands. According to Chagnon this is commonplace and expected behavior. Others, while agreeing that domestic violence occurs, refer to it as "occasional" (Good 1991:73). Women are physically disciplined by their husbands for a host of "infractions," ranging from being too slow to prepare a meal to suspected infidelity. Punishment runs the gamut from blows with firewood or axes, burns, and arrow wounds to murder. Women often depend on their brothers to protect them from an "unusually" cruel husband and despair of being promised to a man in another village where they will be separated from this potential source of protection.

Although women appear to gain no status from the transition from single girls to married women, they are afforded more respect and fear less for their safety as they age. Elderly women can travel even between warring villages without fearing harm, which, according to Chagnon (1992a), is more than they can be assured in their own homes when they are young wives.

Boys are socialized early into this behavior through the encouragement they receive to strike others, especially little girls, when they are angry. Boys as young as 4 or 5 are well aware of their license to "[inflict] blows . . . on the hapless girls in the village" (Chagnon 1992a:126) and are cheered on by their parents and others who often goad them into this behavior during play. (However, once he is grown, a woman's brother assumes the aforementioned expected responsibility to protect her from the mistreatment of others [Salamone 1997].)

"Play" lasts nearly twice as long for boys as it does for girls. While a girl of 10 spends the bulk of her day as a worker, boys in their late teens may still be enjoying childhood. This often causes difficulties, because boys of this age expend much effort attempting to seduce girls of their own age—who are generally married women, often with several children.

Children—both boys and girls—are particularly susceptible to malevolent spirits, often sent from enemy villages to attack their souls. They are vulnerable in this fashion because their souls are not yet moored securely within their bodies. Young souls, given to wandering, escape from the mouth when a child cries.

→ Political and Economic Organization

Forging Alliances

The focus of "political" life among the Yanomami centers on forging and maintaining ties between villages. There are several ways in which alliances may be formed.

Inherent in these ties is the obligation to offer asylum to residents of an allied village who are fleeing an enemy. Because leaving one's village means leaving one's garden—hence, one's economic base—it is sometimes necessary for this "visit" to be quite lengthy. Guests will stay in a village while they are establishing a new garden in a safer site. Chagnon (1992a) observed more than one occasion when an enemy's capture of a village led to the reliance of the displaced Yanomami on the hospitality of an allied village for a year or more. Such an imposition exacts a commensurate cost, and payment is usually demanded in women. The other options open to an invaded group are either standing ground and attempting to withstand the hostile onslaught or dispersing into small family units and joining other villages permanently. Neither of these is preferable to the pattern of "visiting" for only as long as it takes to establish a new garden elsewhere and then moving on.

With the threat of attack always looming, no village can afford to be without the alliances that ensure they will have somewhere to go after invasion. Chagnon (1992a) points out an inherent conflict in the need to forge alliances as protection against attack—warfare among the Yanomami is predicated on the belief that stronger villages should overpower weaker ones. This encourages villages to present as strong a face to outsiders as they possibly can. This posture is difficult to maintain while engaging in the development of dependent friendships. He summarizes, "Allies *need* but cannot really *trust* each other" (p. 160).

Trade relations and feasting are the usual channels for creating ties between villages, but the most secure alliances are formed by marriage. Cross-cousin marriage is the preferred form. Villages can cement relations with one another through betrothals between families living some distance apart (Salamone 1997). Chagnon (1992a) reports that not all relations between villages proceed to this final step because the mistrust always beneath the surface in intervillage relations leads Yanomami to suspect the promise of reciprocity. In fact, he observes that it is only the minority of villages that progress past the arguments and accusations about women that are produced in the course of trading and feasting, prerequisites for marital exchange. Salamone (1997), however, reports that Ramos found that 70 percent of the Yanomami villages she studied in Brazil forged marital alliances with one another, thus preventing conflict.

Trading

Trade between Yanomami villages follows a pattern that is self-propelling; that is, rules are established such that trade leads to more trade.

All items traded must be reciprocated with items that are different. Usually these are representative of the "specialty" of the village. The return gift must be presented in the proper time frame. It cannot be immediately exchanged. The former feature serves as an "excuse" to continue trading with a particular village.

One village doesn't usually possess a resource or skill that is unique. However, claiming that ties are being maintained with another village solely because it guarantees access to a needed item functions as a face-saving mechanism. It allows interdependence—in the form of repeated visiting to trade for the specialty item—without demonstrating weakness. The element of elapsed time results in an ongoing relationship of indebtedness; one village always owes payment to the other.

Chagnon (1992a) points out that these explanations for the "ulterior motives" of trading and feasting are not ones which the Yanomami themselves readily volunteer. Outwardly, they never say "we must maintain these ties so that we can call upon them during times of war." Feasts and trading expeditions are ends in and of themselves. Likewise, the hosts of such events seize the opportunity to demonstrate their power and wealth, without overtly expressing the fact that it places them in a position of strength.

Feasting

Feasts among the Yanomami are usually much anticipated occasions for both hosts and guests. They provide opportunities to eat, drink, and flirt; to display oneself proudly; and to affirm and deepen ties of mutuality. Given the constant undercurrent of defensiveness and opportunism, however, there is always the potential for something going awry and culminating in violence.

Men take the primary responsibility for preparing food for feasts. Because a hundred or more guests may be expected, hunting, gathering, and cooking is a large-scale task. Although a messenger is sent to the guest village with an invitation only on the day of the feast, preparation at the host village starts long before.

Game meat and plantain are the main foodstuffs that are served, and large quantities of plantain are harvested and hung to ripen in anticipation. Many of these will be used to make soup, cooked in large strips of bark that are cut and fashioned into troughs of sufficient size to hold up to one hundred gallons of soup.

A hunting party is organized to secure meat, and as the hunters set off, the excitement surrounding a feast begins to build. When they return, the meat is presented to the headman, smoked at his fire, and wrapped for later presentation.

Both village and villagers are groomed for the festivities. The central village clearing is weeded and swept to prepare it for dancing. Houses are neatened and scraps from the preparation of food and gifts are disposed of. Both men and women paint their faces and bodies and decorate themselves with bright feathers. Men further prepare by ingesting hallucinogenic drugs. Guests adorn themselves similarly, in anticipation of their formal parade into the center of the host village.

As the guest delegated to begin the processional enters the village, appreciative cheers erupt from the hosts. There is a formality in this presentation; he is elaborately painted and festooned with parrot feathers and monkey tails. Reaching the center of the clearing, he stops and strikes a predictable posture, standing still, haughty, weapons in the "visitor's pose" by his face. He maintains this stance for several minutes. He is there to be admired, but he is also there to express his peaceful intent. With his weapons held motionless and fully exposed, he declares himself to be without hostility and invites an easy shot if malice is contemplated.

This accomplished, he approaches the designated host (the village headman or his representative) and the two begin a chant that signifies the acceptance of the invitation by the guests, and officially initiates the feast. Spirited and at the top of their voices, the two dance and chant for five or ten minutes, and then the guest departs to arrange the formal entry of his village.

Guests assemble at the entryway, with the men in front and women and children holding gifts behind the front ranks. At their headman's signal, visiting dancers spring into the village in pairs, whirling and chanting along the edge of the central plaza and then returning to the rest of the group, still outside the village walls. Each man enters the village in this manner, displaying his own unique body painting, chant, and aggressive facial expression. When everyone has a chance to do this, attended all the while by the enthusiastic cheers and whoops of their hosts, the assembled group enters, one by one, dancing along the rim of the clearing, coming to a halt in the center of the plaza where they stand for silent inspection.

One by one, hosts approach the throng of guests and lead each family unit off to his own house. As the guests eat their first serving of plantain soup, the host men gather their village to make a formal entrance and display of their own decoration.

From dusk to dawn, all are engaged in chanting and trading. Visitors tell their headmen which items they want; these requests are relayed to the host headman, who entreats his villagers to provide them. Once presented, they are inspected by the recipient and his friends, who praise them even as the donors apologize for their obvious inadequacies. (Unless it is, in fact, truly inadequate, in which case the presenter calls attention to all its finer attributes, while the recipient points out each flaw.) In any case, the hosts always claim to have given more than they should; guests always assert they have been under compensated. Bickering accompanies every trade.

Should arguing escalate for any of a number of reasons—such as impoliteness, intimidation, or the exchange of insults—a chest-pounding duel may ensue. The entry into the host village to signify the acceptance of such a challenge bears little resemblance to that which begins a feast. Guests arrive waving their axes, clubs, bows, and arrows. They are received with the noises made by hosts clattering their arrows together and thumping clubs and arrows on the ground as they surround the guests, each host selecting the guest he will fight.

A chest-pounding duel is not a spontaneous brawl. The blows delivered are carefully calculated and stylized. One partner presents himself, daring the other to hit him. The recipient of the challenge assesses the position struck, realigns his victim's arms or chest so they can be most effectively pounded. He measures and remeasures the distance he wants his arm to be from the victim's chest, feinting several trial punches. Finally, "he . . . [winds] up like a baseball pitcher . . . and [delivers] a tremendous wallop with his fist to the man's [chest], putting all of his weight into the blow" (Chagnon 1992a:179). The victim, reeling from the punch, is urged on by his fellows not to back down, but to present himself for another blow. A maximum of four blows may be struck before victim and aggressor change places. Each aggressor is required to return the same number of poundings he receives. Only if severely injured in his receipt of the retaliatory blows may a victim withdraw from the fight after receiving fewer hits than he has inflicted. Fighting may continue in this vein for several hours, often with many agitating for its escalation to the use of axes. Although headmen often oppose this, knowing it will lead to bloodshed, there is a variation on the chest-slapping duel, "side" slapping, to which it sometimes escalates. This open-handed smacking of the opponent's side between rib cage and pelvis often incurs greater injury, especially when a fistful of stones replaces an open hand. While chest-pounding blows are directed to the muscular portion of the chest, there is no such protection of the organs beneath blows to the flank. In one fight witnessed by Chagnon (1992a), two young men died after a side-slapping fight, most likely because of ruptured kidneys. (Death occurs after chest-pounding, too, and it is not uncommon that participants cough up blood for several days after these confrontations.) As is evidenced by the outright choreography of the chest-pounding duel, many forms of fighting among the Yanomami are strictly regulated. The aggression so assiduously cultivated in males is released in these formalized duels, as an attempt to avoid warfare.

→ Yanomami Violence and Warfare

Within the anthropological community, there have been few more public disagreements in recent years than that which has arisen regarding the portrayal of the Yanomami as "the fierce people," as named by Napoleon Chagnon in his popular ethnography, first published in 1968. In it, Chagnon described the centrality of violence to the everyday life of the Yanomami. In addition to chest-pounding duels, Chagnon (1992a) describes attacks with clubs, often the result of arguments over women and food.

Chagnon observes that the tops of most male Yanomami heads boast a network of deep scars and asserts that some of the men who keep the top central portion of their heads shaved do so to proudly display the impressive thick knots they have received in club fights. Chagnon presents vivid accounts of villagewide club fights involving sides taken along kinship lines, beginning with accusations of adultery and escalating into full-scale "war."

During the course of a raid on an enemy village, women are often abducted. This, however, is not usually the objective around which the raid is organized, but rather a "side benefit" of a successful endeavor. In villages with acute shortages of women, wars have been initiated for the sole intent of capturing them. One such war is an example of *nomohori* ("dastardly trick"), the ultimate form of treachery and violence. Raiders arrive at a distant village, saying they acquired machetes and cooking pots through prayer to a previously unknown spirit. The raiders offer to teach the unsuspecting villagers this prayer so that they too might receive the goods. As the men kneel down and bow their heads, preparing to be instructed in prayer, the raiders kill them, capture the women of the village and flee (Chagnon 1992a).

Others have taken issue with Chagnon's presentation. Leslie Sponsel characterizes Yanomami duels as "public, institutionalized, conventionalized, and ritualized forms of interpersonal aggression that are governed by a set of rules" (1998:100). He suggests that they are analogous to combat sports found elsewhere, like boxing, albeit carried out with neither referee nor protective gear. Jacques Lizot, a French anthropologist whose work among the Yanomami began in the 1960s, wrote an ethnography in 1985, which he explicitly aimed at helping to "revise the exaggerated representation" of Yanomami violence (Lizot 1985:xiv). He maintains that while the Yanomami are indeed warriors and can be both brutal and cruel, such "violence is only sporadic; it never dominates social life for any length of time" (Lizot 1985:xiv). This assertion that Yanomami violence has been overemphasized is echoed by Kenneth Good, a former student of Chagnon's. While acknowledging, as Lizot did, that violence existed, he agreed with Lizot's position that this one aspect of Yanomami behavior had been sensationalized out of proportion. Raiding, killing, and domestic violence did occur, but it was not the defining feature of Yanomami life. Good offered an analogy: Chagnon's citing violence as the central cultural theme of Yanomami life, he maintained, was as misleading as asserting that all New Yorkers are muggers and knife-wielding criminals, and as such, anyone on a New York street may expect to be robbed at knifepoint.

> Of course these things do take place. But that doesn't mean it's an accurate or reasonable generalization to make about New Yorkers. It doesn't mean that

> someone would be justified in writing a book entitled *New Yorkers: The Mugging and Murdering People* (Good 1991:73).

Brazilian anthropologist Alcida Ramos concurs, having found the Yanomami to be an essentially peaceful group, despite acknowledged feuding. She characterizes Chagnon's ethnography as "sensationalistic," adding that the portrait of the Yanomami as "a bloodthirsty 'fierce' people who regularly kill each other is not supported by other anthropologists or anyone who has lived with the Yanomami for years" (in Rocha 1999:34).

Perhaps most significantly, the Yanomami themselves appear to have taken issue with their portrayal as "fierce people." Salamone (1996:10) reports that the Yanomami "argue that although there is violence in their society, they are not violent people." One Brazilian Yanomami man explained, "I have killed but I am not a killer" (Salamone 1996:10).

Some have suggested (Ferguson in Salamone 1997) that when Chagnon first visited the Yanomami in the 1960s, violence had reached an unusual height because this particular group had been subject to epidemics and disruption in trading and had experienced the loss of many aspects of their traditional way of life. The result was "violence [reaching] a level where it appears to be 'normal'" (Salamone 1997:49).

Brian Ferguson (1995), writing what he calls a "political history" of Yanomami warfare, presents an argument tying Yanomami violence specifically to unequal access to scarce and much-desired Western manufactured goods, especially steel and iron tools. He traces patterns of peace and violence through the presence and absence of Westerners (including anthropologists) and concludes that complex changes in Yanomami exchange relationships, often leading to intervillage violence, are largely the result of the Western presence.

Darkness in El Dorado

The controversy surrounding the veracity of claims regarding Yanomami violence escalated in 2000 when an investigative journalist, Patrick Tierney, published a book with accusations that generated heated debate within the anthropological community and beyond. In his book, *Darkness in El Dorado,* Tierney made allegations in two realms of Yanomami research. First, he claimed that Napoleon Chagnon and James Neel, a physician and geneticist, knowingly endangered the lives and health of the Yanomami communities they studied. Second, he asserted that Chagnon not only misrepresented the Yanomami as "fierce people," but in fact instigated and promoted violence and warfare.

Neel and Chagnon were among the Yanomami during a measles epidemic in 1968. Because the population had little immunity against such a disease, there was potential for disaster. Tierney claims that Neel caused thousands of deaths by deliberately using an outdated vaccine and by withholding medical treatment from sick individuals in order to test theories of eugenics. The scientific community (including the developer of the vaccine Neel used) and colleagues rallied to Neel's support, vigorously refuting all such claims (Baur 2001; Cantor 2001). They provided evidence that Neel had carefully chosen the proper vaccine, had administered it in a timely manner, and likely saved many lives by doing so. In addition, evidence points to the fact that Neel responsibly cared for sick Yanomami and in fact held none of the extreme eugenic beliefs attributed to him.

The second set of allegations assert that Chagnon breached ethnographic ethics in a number of ways, including inappropriate gift-giving that incited jealousy and enmity among villagers, using coercive methods to elicit information, instigating and staging the violence he wished to portray as central to Yanomami culture, and exploiting the Yanomami and their territory. Reactions to these charges were far more varied than to those against Neel, which were overwhelmingly refuted. Anthropologists were divided in their judgments: some came to Chagnon's defense against what they saw as Tierney's sensationalistic claims supported by flimsy and misrepresented sources; others pointed out the long history of controversy surrounding Chagnon's fieldwork practices and data. Numerous investigative bodies were assembled to investigate the charges, with the American Anthropological Association task force publishing a report several hundred pages long in 2002. The task force found that Tierney's book was, in fact, riddled with errors and unfounded accusations but also concluded that Chagnon did not, in fact, put the best interests of the Yanomami ahead of his own research agenda, a practice required by anthropology's ethical standards. They represent their charge as having been "not to find fault with or to defend the past actions of specific anthropologists, but to provide opportunities for all anthropologists to consider the ethics of several dimensions of the anthropological enterprise" (El Dorado Task Force Papers, Preface).

Yanomami: Changing Culture and Modern Tragedies

Life for the Yanomami is changing. Contact with missionaries began many years ago in some villages. In others, direct contact has yet to occur. Groups of Yanomami whose lives remain relatively unchanged from their traditional patterns are few and becoming fewer.

The introduction of disease to indigenous populations who have no immunity can have devastating effects. As we have seen, this was the case among the Yanomami, who were exposed to measles during an epidemic in 1968 that is believed to have started at several mission posts and then spread to surrounding villages (McElroy and Townsend 1989). Physician James Neel's team immunized as many unexposed individuals as they could in an attempt to curb decimation such as that wrought by previous measles epidemics among other indigenous peoples in Brazil. Their efforts, which included providing medical care to those already infected, greatly reduced the death rate as compared to that of the earlier epidemics (McElroy and Townsend 1989).

Encroachment on Yanomami land began in the 1970s as roads began to be built inside their territory (Ramos and Taylor 1979; Rocha 1999). However, the most dramatic—and horrific—changes to Yanomami life are the consequence of the 1987 gold rush in Brazil, which brought not only miners with guns and heavy machinery and a usurpation of land, but previously unencountered diseases that indigenous peoples could not withstand.

In the late 1970s, as the price of gold began to climb steadily, the Brazilian government opened up the Amazon to miners. Wildcat miners—*garimpeiros*—began to flood into the area over the next decade, with some estimating the invasion at anywhere between 250,000 and 1 million *garimpeiros*. In 1995, 300,000 were camped out throughout the Amazon (MacMillan 1995). Brazilian authorities were asked to expel the illegal miners, who were firmly entrenched in Yanomami territory, but their efforts met with little success. In fact, in response to this threat, *garimpeiros* claimed that if their presence was illegal, so was that of others working with the indigenous populations. The government acquiesced, expelling anthropologists, missionaries, and health workers. This evacuation brought an onslaught of *garimpeiros,* who, in a short time, had cleared more than a hundred airstrips in Yanomami territory (Chagnon 1992b). Brazilian president José Sarney's government refused to help, and, in fact, contributed to the devastation by reducing a proposed Yanomami reserve from 8 million to 2.4 million hectares, partitioned into nineteen little "islands" of communities (MacMillan 1995).

The Yanomami were devastated by the introduction of diseases such as malaria and tuberculosis, among others, to which they had little resistance. Hundreds died. It is estimated that in two short years, between 1988 and 1990, 15 percent of the Yanomami population was lost (MacMillan 1995). The destruction of the environment also took its toll. Hunting was compromised as game was either shot or scared off by miners. Vegetation was stripped from along streams, altering water courses. Drinking water was polluted, and the churning up of riverbottom sediments disrupted the life cycle of fish, endangering an important protein source (MacMillan 1995). More toxicity resulted from the use of mercury in the gold mining process, which enters the waterways and contaminates fish and reptiles, poisoning those who consume them. Hair-sample analysis from Yanomami living near mining centers revealed toxic levels of mercury (MacMillan 1995).

Further devastation has been wrought on both social organization and cosmology. Ramos (in Rocha 1999:31) describes the trails that connect Yanomami villages as "conveyor belts carrying the social impulses that keep alive the great chain of relationships between communities." It is these trails and streams that link the 300 Yanomami communities in Brazil and Venezuela, and it is these trails and streams that are being destroyed. The loss of territory also means that they are unable to resolve disputes in the traditional way, which involved feuding groups leaving a village to set up a new homestead elsewhere. Not only were new groups established in this way, but it also alleviated competition for resources in too concentrated an area.

In 1990 José Sarney was replaced by Fernando Collor de Melo, who revoked the privileges given to the *garimpeiros* and who, in 1991, made a dramatic and public trip to Yanomami territory in response to a growing international outcry for their protection. He ordered the illegal airstrips destroyed, and the numbers of *garimpeiros* began to wane. However, these efforts didn't last long; only a dozen airstrips were closed down, and these soon reopened (Chagnon 1992b). By 1992 Collor resigned under the specter of impeachment for corruption and was succeeded by his vice president, Itamar Franco, who held office until 1995, when he was replaced by Fernando Henrique Cardoso.

In 1993 the world was stunned by reports of a massacre among the Yanomami, perpetrated by *garimpeiros* in their territory. Eighteen Yanomami, including many children, were murdered in their village, their bodies desecrated. To a people for whom proper funerary preparations—cremation and the preservation of the ashes for the family—are so important, the state in which the bodies were left was particularly horrifying.

The destruction of the natural world has dire consequences for the spiritual world (MacMillan 1995). Davi Kopenawa, a Brazilian Yanomami who has emerged as a spokesman for the tribe, explains that during mining, a vaporous spirit is released from the soil and causes sickness. Moreover, this spirit has the power to destroy the *hekura* spirits, who hold up the sky, preserve the forests, and cure through the actions of shamans. Thus, continued mining will result in the eradication of the *hekura,* which, for the Yanomami, "heralds the end of the world" (MacMillan 1995:51).

In 1995, after eight years of requesting permission from the Brazilian government to be allowed to investigate human rights violations in Yanomami territory, an international Human Rights commission was allowed entry. Their report was scathing, and the following year, nearly 300 Yanomami leaders representing thirty villages came together to address their dire situation and make a formal plea to national leaders and international agencies, to no avail. In December 1997, President Cardoso instituted a human rights program, promising that indigenous peoples and their organizations would have a voice. In March 1998, disaster struck again in the form of raging fires resulting from a drought. With the Yanomami rainforest threatened, international attention was once more focused on the area (Rocha 1999).

In 1969 Survival International was founded in direct response to the endangerment of indigenous peoples in the Amazon (Rocha 1999). For the past twenty years, various nongovernmental organizations (NGOs) have worked with the Yanomami to defend their land and culture. The Pro Yanomami Commission (CCPY) administers health and education projects. Anthropologist Napoleon Chagnon, after a career invested so heavily in the Yanomami people, has devoted extensive efforts to their protection and the task of safeguarding the rights and cultures of other indigenous groups. The Yanomami, in many ways, have come to represent indigenous peoples worldwide, though their role as such has been played "unwittingly and often reluctantly" (Rocha 1999). The structure of traditional Yanomami society is such that no one "leader" may speak for the group as a whole. Thus, there are those who are skeptical about any spokesman who may claim to do so (Sanford 1997). However, Davi Kopenawa has eloquently expressed views that appear to be representative of the wishes and beliefs of other Yanamami (Salamone 1997). His 1992 plea to the General Assembly of the UN was to

> stop the destruction, stop taking minerals from under the ground and stop building roads through forests. Our word is to protect nature, the wind, the mountains, the forest, the animals, and this is what we want to teach you (Rocha 1999:40).

The Yanomami live in two nation-states, Venezuela and Brazil, and national policies and programs affect their communities. Venezuelan President Hugo Chavez has long declared his support for indigenous peoples, pointing to social welfare programs for the Yanomami (*New York Times,* Oct. 7, 2008). In January 2003, Worker's Party candidate Luis Inacio Lula da Silva took office as the president elected by the largest popular margin in Brazil's history. Leaders in Brazil's Indigenous Movement were hopeful that as a representative of the political party identified with social justice, change, and the struggle of the oppressed, President Lula would work to overcome the threats to their land, health, and culture. In a document following a national indigenous congress in April 2004, after a year of escalating violence, they petitioned President Lula with a simple declaration: "Fear should not overcome hope" (Indigenous Leaders' Document to President Lula Brasilia-DC, May 10, 2004). His actions in 2010 to approve construction of a dam over the opposition of indigenous peoples has been cause for disappointment; the creation that same year of a Secretariat for Indigenous Health was deemed a victory. In November 2010, Dilma Rousseff was elected Brazilian president. Stongly supported by outgoing President Luiz Inacio Lula da Silva, Rouseff has pointed to the eradication of poverty as one of her primary aims. She has vowed to follow in Lula's footsteps as a champion of indigenous rights.

The Yanomami are engaged in efforts to help themselves, but Chagnon has urged the international community to join forces with them. He writes, "The Yanomami [sic] are now a symbol for all tribesman everywhere, perhaps the ultimate test case of whether ordinary concerned, educated and determined people can stay a destructive process that will [otherwise] be inevitable" (1992a:246).

→ For Further Discussion

Recently there has been great controversy surrounding ethnographic work among the Yanomami, including questions about the introduction of disease, the accuracy of reported violence, and the role of social scientists who witness political and economic victimization of indigenous peoples. These issues bring to the fore many important questions about ethnographic fieldwork and the role of the anthropologist. Napoleon Chagnon has said that the Yanomami stand as a symbol for tribal peoples everywhere. What are some of the ethical issues involved in fieldwork among peoples who have had very little previous contact with outsiders? Does this differ from ethnographic work carried out in an industrialized setting? What is the role of the anthropologist in conflicts between indigenous peoples and the governments of the countries in which they reside? Should an anthropologist be an objective observer, an advocate, or neither of these? What are some of the difficulties involved in choosing a position?